Property, Trusts and Succession

This edition is dedicated to Archie and Esme Gretton

Property, Trusts and Succession

Third Edition

George L Gretton

Lord President Reid Professor of Law Emeritus,
University of Edinburgh

and

Andrew J M Steven

Senior Lecturer in Law, University of Edinburgh

with a chapter on human rights by

Alison E C Struthers

Assistant Professor of Law, University of Warwick

Bloomsbury Professional

Bloomsbury Professional

An imprint of Bloomsbury Publishing Plc

Bloomsbury Professional Ltd	Bloomsbury Publishing Plc
41–43 Boltro Road	50 Bedford Square
Haywards Heath	London
RH16 1BJ	WC1B 3DP
UK	UK

www.bloomsbury.com

**BLOOMSBURY and the Diana logo are trademarks of
Bloomsbury Publishing Plc**

British Library Cataloguing-in-Publication Data

A catalogue record for this book is available from the British Library.

ISBN:	PB	978 1 52650 056 4
	Epub	978 1 52650 057 1
	Epdf	978 1 52650 058 8

Typeset by Phoenix Photosetting, Chatham, Kent

Printed and bound by CPI Group (UK) Ltd, Croydon, CR0 4YY

To find out more about our authors and books visit
www.bloomsburyprofessional.com.
Here you will find extracts, author information, details of forthcoming events and the option to sign up for our newsletters

Preface

Like its previous editions, this book is aimed at LLB students in Scotland studying property, trusts and succession. We attempt to explain, often by use of examples, the rules of statute and common law which apply in these areas. While the book is about Scots law, we both believe firmly in the value of comparative study. We have therefore made reference in a number of places to the position in other legal systems.

The most significant development in the law covered since the publication of the second edition has been the enactment of the Succession (Scotland) Act 2016. But there have been numerous other new statutes and cases. We have also concluded that the subject of prescription merits its own chapter.

In preparing the book we benefited greatly from the course materials used at the University of Edinburgh and in this regard we owe a particular debt to our fellow teachers, Professor Kenneth Reid and Professor Martin Hogg. The influence of Professor Reid's great contribution to Scots property law will be apparent in much of this book. We are also grateful to Professor Roderick Paisley, Lorna MacFarlane, and Susan Sutherland for their assistance. Thanks are due to Martin Corbett and others of the Department of the Registers of Scotland for providing the sample title sheet reproduced in Chapter 7. Once again we are very grateful to Alison Struthers for contributing the chapter on human rights.

George L Gretton

Andrew J M Steven

30 April 2017

Contents

8   Acquisition by involuntary transfer

9 Original acquisition

10 Co-ownership

15   Landownership

16   Tenements and developments

21   Rights in security

Contents

22 Liferent

Contents

Contents

Contents

Table of Statutes

References are to paragraph number.

Table of Statutory Instruments and Codes

References are to paragraph number.

Table of EC, International and other Material

References are to paragraph number.

Table of Cases

References are to paragraph number.

I

C

G

H

List of Abbreviations

STATUTES

AB(S)A 2004	Antisocial Behaviour etc. (Scotland) Act 2004
AFT(S)A 2000	Abolition of Feudal Tenure etc. (Scotland) Act 2000
AH(S)A 1991	Agricultural Holdings (Scotland) Act 1991
AH(S)A 2003	Agricultural Holdings (Scotland) Act 2003
ALC(S)A 1991	Age of Legal Capacity (Scotland) Act 1991
A(S)A 1987	Animals (Scotland) Act 1987
B(S)A 2003	Building (Scotland) Act 2003
CFR(S)A 1970	Conveyancing and Feudal Reform (Scotland) Act 1970
CIA 1994	Coal Industry Act 1994
CPA 2004	Civil Partnership Act 2004
C(S)A 1993	Crofters (Scotland) Act 1993
CTI(S)A 2005	Charities and Trustee Investment (Scotland) Act 2005
CE(S)A 2015	Community Empowerment (Scotland) Act 2016
FL(S)A 1985	Family Law (Scotland) Act 1985
FL(S)A 2006	Family Law (Scotland) Act 2006
HRA 1998	Human Rights Act 1998
H(S)A 1987	Housing (Scotland) Act 1987
H(S)A 1988	Housing (Scotland) Act 1988
H(S)A 2001	Housing (Scotland) Act 2001
H(S)A 2006	Housing (Scotland) Act 2006
LR(MP)(S)A 1985	Law Reform (Miscellaneous Provisions) (Scotland) Act 1985
LR(MP)(S)A 1990	Law Reform (Miscellaneous Provisions) (Scotland) Act 1990
LR(S)A 1979	Land Registration (Scotland) Act 1979
LR(S)A 2003	Land Reform (Scotland) Act 2003
LR(S)A 2012	Land Registration etc. (Scotland) Act 2012

LR(S)A 2016	Land Reform (Scotland) Act 2016
LW(CD)(S)(A) 2015	Legal Writings (Counterparts and Delivery) (Scotland) Act 2015
MH(FP)(S)A 1981	Matrimonial Homes (Family Protection) (Scotland) Act 1981
PL(S)A 1973	Prescription and Limitation (Scotland) Act 1973
PH(T)(S)A 2016	Private Housing (Tenancies) (Scotland) Act 2016
RoW(S)A 1995	Requirements of Writing (Scotland) Act 1995
SOGA 1979	Sale of Goods Act 1979
S(S)A 1964	Succession (Scotland) Act 1964
S(S)A 2016	Succession (Scotland) Act 2016
TC(S)A 2003	Title Conditions (Scotland) Act 2003
T(S)A 1921	Trusts (Scotland) Act 1921
T(S)A 1961	Trusts (Scotland) Act 1961
T(S)A 2004	Tenements (Scotland) Act 2004

BOOKS

Bell *Commentaries*	G J Bell *Commentaries on the Law of Scotland and the Principles of Mercantile Jurisprudence* (7th edn by J McLaren, 1870; reprinted 1990)
Bell *Principles*	G J Bell *Principles of the Law of Scotland* (4th edn 1839, reprinted 2010)
Carey Miller with Irvine *Corporeal Moveables*	D L Carey Miller with D Irvine *Corporeal Moveables in Scots Law* (2nd edn, 2005)
Chalmers *Trusts*	J Chalmers *Trusts: Cases and Materials* (2002)
Cusine and Paisley *Servitudes*	D J Cusine and R R M Paisley *Servitudes and Rights of Way* (1998)
Erskine	J Erskine of Carnock *An Institute of the Law of Scotland* (8th edn by J B Nicholson, 1871, reprinted 1989)
Gloag and Henderson *The Law of Scotland*	W M Gloag and R C Henderson *The Law of Scotland* (14th edn by Lord Eassie and H L MacQueen, 2017)
Gloag and Irvine *Rights in Security*	W M Gloag and J M Irvine *Law of Rights in Security, Heritable and Moveable including Cautionary Obligations* (1897, reprinted 1987)
Gordon *Scottish Land Law*	W M Gordon *Scottish Land Law* (2nd edn, 1999)
Gordon and Wortley *Scottish Land Law*	W M Gordon and S Wortley *Scottish Land Law* (3rd edn, 2009) vol 1
Gretton and Reid *Conveyancing*	G L Gretton and K G C Reid *Conveyancing* (4th edn, 2011)
Halliday *Conveyancing*	J M Halliday *Conveyancing Law and Practice in Scotland* (2nd edn by I J S Talman) vols I (1996) and II (1997)

Hiram *Succession*	H Hiram *The Scots Law of Succession* (2nd edn, 2007)
Hume *Lectures*	Baron David *Hume Lectures 1786–1822* (ed by G C H Paton, Stair Society vols. 5, 13, 15, 17–19, 1939–58)
Johnston *Prescription*	D Johnston *Prescription and Limitation* (2nd edn, 2012)
Macdonald *Succession*	D R Macdonald *An Introduction to the Scots Law of Succession* (3rd edn, 2001)
MacQueen and Thomson *Contract*	H L MacQueen and J Thomson *Contract Law in Scotland* (4th edn, 2016)
McAllister *Leases*	A McAllister *Scottish Law of Leases* (4th edn, 2013)
McBryde *Contract*	W W McBryde *The Law of Contract in Scotland* (3rd edn, 2007)
McDonald *Conveyancing Manual*	D A Brand, A J M Steven and S Wortley *Professor McDonald's Conveyancing Manual* (7th edn, 2004)
Paisley *Land Law*	R Paisley *Land Law* (2000)
Paisley and Cusine *Unreported Cases*	R R M Paisley and D J Cusine *Unreported Property Cases from the Sheriff Court* (2000)
Rankine *Landownership*	J Rankine *The Law of Landownership in Scotland* (4th edn, 1909)
Reid *Feudal Abolition*	K G C Reid, *The Abolition of Feudal Tenure in Scotland* (2003)
Reid *Property*	K G C Reid (with G L Gretton, A G M Duncan, W M Gordon and A J Gamble) *The Law of Property in Scotland* (1996), being a revised reprint of *The Laws of Scotland: Stair Memorial Encyclopaedia* vol 18
Reid and Gretton *Land Registration*	K G C Reid and G L Gretton, *Land Registration* (2017)
Reid and Zimmermann *History*	K Reid and R Zimmermann (eds) *A History of Private Law in Scotland*, vols 1 (Introduction and Property) and 2 (Obligations) (2000)
Stair	J Dalrymple, 1st Viscount Stair *Institutions of the Law of Scotland* (6th edn, by D M Walker, 1981)
SME	Sir Thomas Smith et al (eds) *The Laws of Scotland: Stair Memorial Encyclopaedia* (25 vols, 1987–96) with cumulative supplements and reissues
Van Erp and Akkermans *Property Law*	S van Erp and B Akkermans (eds), *Cases, Materials and Text on National, Supranational and International Property Law* (2012)
Wilson and Duncan *Trusts*	W A Wilson and A G M Duncan *Trusts, Trustees and Executors* (2nd edn, 1995)
Zimmermann, Visser and Reid *Mixed Legal Systems*	R Zimmermann, D Visser and K Reid *Mixed Legal Systems in Comparative Perspective: Property and Obligations in Scotland and South Africa* (2004)

OTHER

A1P1	Article 1 of Protocol 1 to the European Convention on Human Rights
BGB	Bürgerliches Gesetzbuch (German Civil Code)
Cc	Code civil (French Civil Code)
DCFR	Draft Common Frame of Reference (C von Bar and E Clive (eds), *Principles, Definitions and Model Rules of European Private Law: Draft Common Frame of Reference* (2010))
ECHR	European Convention on Human Rights
ECtHR	European Court of Human Rights
OSCR	Office of the Scottish Charity Regulator
TMS	Tenement Management Scheme

Glossary

Necessarily, we have been selective. In many cases what is given is a general, imperfect definition. For the Latin terms we have sometimes preferred an explanation to a literal translation. Where a word or phrase is in bold it is explained elsewhere in the Glossary.

Accession (*accessio*)	The attachment of one thing to another so as to become part of it, such as paint to a wall.
A non domino	From a non-owner. An *a non domino* transfer is normally invalid.
Advance notice	A notice that can be registered in the Land Register in advance of the settlement of a transaction, protecting the grantee from adverse entries.
Aemulatio vicini	Spiteful acts against a neighbour.
Animus acquirendi	The intention to acquire.
Animus domini	The intention to hold as owner.
Animus sibi habendi	The intention to hold for one's own use.
Animus transferendi	The intention to transfer.
Animus revocandi	The intention to revoke.
Application record	One of the four parts of the **Land Register**. Consists of pending registration applications.
Archive record	One of the four parts of the **Land Register**. Composed of the documentation (dispositions etc) on which the entries on the title sheets are based.
Assignation	Transfer of **incorporeal property**.
Assignatus utitur jure auctoris	An assignee takes the same right as the **cedent** had.
Benefited property	The land benefited by **a real burden** or **servitude**. The more traditional term is '**dominant tenement**'.
Bona fides – in bona fide	Good faith – in good faith.
Bona vacantia	Ownerless property.
Burdened property	The land burdened by a **real burden** or **servitude**. The more traditional term is '**servient tenement**'.

Glossary

Cadastral map	A map of Scotland which identifies properties by their registered boundaries. One of the four parts of the **Land Register**.
Cedent	Assignor.
Completion of title	The step whereby a grantee receives a real right, eg registration.
Conditio si institutus sine liberis decesserit	Literally, the condition that the institute dies childless. For the real meaning, see ch 28.
Conditio si testator sine liberis decesserit	Literally, the condition that the testator dies childless. For the real meaning, see ch 28.
Corporeal property	Tangible property.
Crown	The monarch, ie the state.
De cujus	The deceased person whose estate is being wound up.
Deed	A **juridical act** that has been formally executed in paper or electronic form.
Derivative acquisition	Transfer of property where the transferee acquires the transferor's title. See also **original acquisition**.
Disposition – dispone	Deed transferring ownership of land – to grant a disposition.
Dominant tenement	The more traditional term for **benefited property**.
Dominium	**Ownership**.
Electronic document	Document which is in electronic form and is signed digitally.
Encumbrance	A right to which a property is subject, such as a **subordinate real right**.
Erga omnes	With effect as against everyone; against 'the world'.
Ex lege	By force of law.
Ex voluntate	By force of will, ie intentional.
Feudal system	The system of tenure which existed in Scotland until 28 November 2004, under which land was not held absolutely but of **superiors** and ultimately of the **Crown**.
Floating charge	**Right in security** that can be granted only by business organisations.
Goods	Generally used in the narrow sense of corporeal moveable property.
Heritable property	Generally speaking, land or rights in land.
Heritable security	**Right in security** over **heritable property**.
Hypothec	**Right in security** in which the debtor retains **possession**.
Improper liferent	**Liferent** under which the thing is held by trustees and the holder of the liferent is a beneficiary under the **trust**.

Incorporeal property	Intangible property.
Intestate	Opposite of **testate**.
Intimation	Formal notification of **assignation**.
Involuntary transfer	**Derivative acquisition** which does not require the consent of the transferor.
Inter vivos	Between living persons, as opposed to *mortis causa*.
Juridical act	A voluntary and lawful act that makes a change in the legal universe, such as making a contract, granting a **disposition**, paying a debt. Also called a juristic act.
Jus in re aliena	Right in another person's property – ie subordinate **real right**.
Jus relictae (jus relicti)	Indefeasible succession right of widow (widower).
Keeper	The Keeper of the Registers of Scotland, who administers numerous registers including the **Land Register**.
Land Register	Established by LR(S)A 1979 and now regulated by LR(S)A 2012. Consists of four parts: (i) the **title sheet record**, (ii) the **cadastral map**, (iii) the **archive record** and (iv) the **application record**.
Lex domicilii	The law of the place where the person in question is domiciled.
Lex situs	The law of the place where the property is situated.
Lease	Contract under which one person, the lessor, grants to another, the lessee, the right to use the property for a fixed time in return for a periodical payment known as rent. It is capable of becoming a **real right**, by **possession** or registration depending on the type of lease. A long lease (over 20 years) can be registered.
Legacy	Right to money or property given in a **testament**. Also called bequest.
Legatee	Beneficiary of a **legacy**.
Legal rights	In succession law, the indefeasible rights of spouse (*jus relictae/i*) and issue (**legitim**) to apart of the estate.
Legitim	The indefeasible succession rights of issue.
Lien	A possessory **right in security** arising by implication of law.
Liferent	The right to use a thing for life.
Mala fides – in male fide	Bad faith – in bad faith.
Missives	Letters collectively forming a contract. When the contract is formed the missives are said to be 'concluded'.
Mortis causa	On account of death.
Moveable property	All property which is not **heritable**.

Glossary

Nemo dat quod non habet	Nobody transfers what he or she does not have.
Nemo plus juris ad alium transferre potest quam ipse haberet	Nobody can transfer to another more right than he or she has.
Numerus clausus	Closed list. There is a *numerus clausus* of **real rights**.
Occupancy (*occupatio*)	The appropriation of something ownerless.
Original acquisition	Where an acquirer of property obtains a brand new title. See also **derivative acquisition**.
Ownership	The principal and most extensive **real right**, defined classically as the right to use, consume and destroy.
Patrimonial rights	Rights with economic value, such as **real rights** and **personal rights**.
Patrimony	The totality of a person's (a) **patrimonial rights** and (b) liabilities.
Personal right	Right enforceable only against a specific person or limited class of persons. Example: contractual right.
Pledge	**Right in security** over corporeal moveable property requiring delivery to the creditor.
Possession	The control of a thing with the intention to hold it for one's own use.
Prescription	Negative prescription is the extinction of **personal** or **real rights** by the running of time. Positive prescription is the acquisition of **real rights** by the running of time.
Prior tempore, potior jure	Earlier by time, stronger by right.
Pro indiviso	Shared (title). Example: a couple buy a house together. Each has a *pro indiviso* share of the property.
Proper liferent	**Liferent** where the holder has a real right in the thing.
Real burden	An obligation affecting land, normally of a positive or negative character.
Real right	Right directly in a thing, enforceable against the world. Two types: (i) **ownership** and (ii) **subordinate real rights**.
Right in security	A right held by a creditor against a debtor in addition to the personal right to recover the debt, which improves the chances of payment. Where it is a right in a piece of property it is known as a real security.
Sasine Register	The older register of land, established by the Registration Act 1617. Full name is the General Register of Sasines. Gradually being replaced by the **Land Register**.
Separate tenement	**Heritable property** owned separately from ownership of the ground.
Servient tenement	The more traditional term for **burdened property**.

Servitude	**Real right** which allows a landowner to make limited use of neighbouring land.
Specification (*specificatio*)	Creation of new thing, eg barley into ale.
Standard security	**Heritable security** regulated by the CFR(S)A 1970.
Subjects	Oddly, not the subject but the object. A conveyancer might say 'my client bought the subjects last year', meaning the house or farm etc.
Subordinate real right	**Real right** other than **ownership**. Some examples: **servitude, right in security, liferent.**
Superior	Under the now abolished **feudal system**, a person of whom land was held.
Tantum praescriptum quantum possessum	**Prescription** is measured by **possession**.
Tenement	Building in which different parts belong to different persons.
Testament	A testament is a direction as to what is to happen after death. Also called a will.
Testate	An estate is testate if there is an operative **testament**, in which case the law of testate succession applies.
Testing clause	Clause of attestation at end of deed.
Title sheet	The **Land Register** has a title sheet for each registered property. The title sheet has four sections: (A) the Property Section; (B) the Proprietorship Section; (C) the Securities Section; (D) the Burdens Section.
Title sheet record	The totality of **title sheets**. One of the four parts of the **Land Register**.
Traditional document	Document written on paper or similar tangible surface.
Traditionibus, non nudis pactis, dominia rerum, transferuntur	**Ownership** is transferred by an external act, not by mere contract.
Trust	Where property is held by one person (trustee/s for the benefit of others (beneficiary or beneficiaries).
Ultimus haeres	Ultimate heir. (Failing any nearer heir, the **Crown** is the ultimate heir.)
Unregistered holder	A person who at any time is able to complete title to land.
Vassal	Under the now abolished **feudal system**, a person who held land of a **superior**.
Vigilantibus non dormientibus jura subveniunt	If you snooze you lose.
Warrandice	Guarantee.

Chapter 1

Introduction

WHAT IS PROPERTY LAW?

1.1 In its narrow sense, property law is the law of physical things, such as land and buildings, apples and bicycles. When people speak of 'property' they often mean just land or buildings, that is to say 'immoveable' property. Nevertheless, things such as apples and bicycles are also property – moveable property. Whilst there are important legal differences between moveables and immoveables,[1] both lie in the

---

[1] Eg as to the rules on transfer.

field of property law. Moveables are not necessarily less valuable than immoveables: a painting by Raphael is worth much more than an average house. Property law in the narrow sense deals with the *rights* that people can have in *things*. The most important of these rights is ownership, but there are other types of property right as well, such as servitudes[2] and leases.[3] Property law deals with (i) the nature, (ii) the creation, (iii) the transfer and (iv) the extinction of such rights.

1.2   Property law also has a broader sense. Suppose that Jack borrows £1,000 from Jill, and she transfers her right to repayment to Mary. What is transferred is a contractual right, and so not a property right in the narrow sense. A contractual right is a right as between two persons. But when we look outside that person-to-person relationship, a contractual right can behave rather like a property right (narrow sense). For example, much of the general law about the transfer of rights is the same regardless of whether the right is a personal right (such as a contractual right) or a right of (for example) ownership of land.[4] A contractual right is an asset, as a right in physical property is an asset, or, in technical terms, both are *patrimonial rights*. So, in its broader sense, property law includes not only rights in physical things but also other types of right – provided that they are patrimonial rights, as contractual rights are.[5]

1.3   Succession law is sometimes seen as part of property law: roughly speaking, it deals with what happens to property on death. Sometimes it is seen as part of family law or, to take the larger category, the law of persons. And sometimes it is seen as a separate branch of private law. Much the same can be said of trust law, for, however one likes to classify the law, succession and trusts are closely linked. The rest of this chapter for the most part deals with property law in its narrower sense: trusts and succession are treated later.[6]

HISTORICAL AND COMPARATIVE

1.4   The relationship between Scots law and English law varies according to the area. Property law (other than intellectual property law) differs sharply north and south of the border. So the Scottish student must be wary of English sources. Though there has been some English influence, Scots property law is based ultimately on Roman law and thus has much in common with continental systems.[7] As a result, Scots property lawyers tend to be less interested in English property law than in

---

[2]   A servitude is a right in favour of one property over a neighbouring property, such as a private right of way. See **CHAPTER 13** below.
[3]   See **CHAPTER 20** below.
[4]   See **CHAPTER 4** below.
[5]   For patrimonial rights, see **PARA 1.9** below.
[6]   See **CHAPTERS 23** and **26** below.
[7]   We reproduce without comment the amazing remarks of the English judge Lord Hobhouse of Woodborough in the Scottish case of *Burnett's Tr v Grainger* 2004 SC (HL) 19 at para 53: 'What does surprise me is that Scotland, now a highly developed economy, should have a land law which is still based on the judicial development, albeit sophisticated, of the laws of Rome … .'

civilian systems,[8] and mixed systems[9] such as those of Louisiana, South Africa and Sri Lanka. Although the detailed rules vary among such systems, the basic ideas and principles tend to be similar, because of the common origins.

> 'A lawyer trained in Scotland can without difficulty (other than linguistic difficulty) read and understand a book about the law of property in Germany … But he is likely to be perplexed and bewildered by a book on the law of property in England.'[10]

1.5 Most property law systems in Europe, including Scotland, adopted feudal law. This affected land but not moveables. Scotland was slow in removing it. It was reduced in importance by a long series of enactments starting in the fifteenth century, and by the end of the twentieth century little remained. That little disappeared following the Abolition of Feudal Tenure etc. (Scotland) Act 2000. Feudalism played a major role not only in the history of Scots property law, but indeed in the entire history of Scots law, and accordingly even now the student needs to know something about it.[11] Finally, a word about udal law. Scots law applies in Orkney and Shetland, but there are certain local rules applicable there, collectively known as 'udal law', deriving from the Norwegian law that applied in Orkney and Shetland before their annexation by Scotland in the fifteenth century. Udal law is non-feudal, so one effect of feudalism's abolition has been to lessen the distinctiveness of udal law.

THE SOURCES OF PROPERTY LAW: STATUTE LAW AND COMMON LAW

1.6 Property law is a mixture of statute law and common law. The former is, unfortunately for the student, not dealt with in a single core statute. In countries where there is a civil code the main principles of property law are in the code,[12] with other statutes dealing with supplementary matters, such as land registration rules. There is nothing like that in Scotland. For example, many of the basic topics mentioned in this chapter, such as the real/personal,[13] heritable/moveable[14] and corporeal/incorporeal[15] distinctions, are almost wholly non-statutory. Sometimes the mixture is odd. Thus the rules about the passing of ownership of, say, a bicycle, are statutory where the reason for the transfer is a contract of sale, but they are common law in other cases, and the rules are different. If Pete gives (donates) his bicycle to Rosie, ownership cannot pass without delivery[16] while if he sells it to her, ownership can

---

[8] 'Civilian' systems are those in whose history the influence of Roman law has been particularly strong. Roman law has influenced English law, and the many systems rooted in English law, but only to a limited extent.

[9] 'Mixed' systems are those in which there is a mixture of civilian and English influence.

[10] Reid *Property* para 2.

[11] See the **APPENDIX** at the end of the book.

[12] Eg Book 3 of the BGB, *Sachenrecht* (property law, literally 'law of things').

[13] See **PARAS 1.15–1.18** below.

[14] See **PARAS 1.21–1.22** below.

[15] See **PARA 1.20** below.

[16] See **PARA 5.17** below.

pass without delivery.[17] The statutory material is scattered over numerous separate enactments, some rather old. In this book the student will encounter such still-in-force legislation as the Royal Mines Act 1424[18] and the Leases Act 1449.[19] This mixture of common law and statute, and the fact that the statute law is scattered, make it harder to get a feel for the sources. It may be added that one or two areas have been quasi-codified, such as the law of real burdens.[20]

REFORM

1.7   Law is a ship that is being constantly reconstructed while it is afloat. That is as true of property law as it is of other topics. Law reform is not some modern enthusiasm. Anyone who reads through the statute book of the fifteenth century will see a good deal of property law reform, and the process has been going on ever since. For example, on 28 November 2004, there was major reform when three statutes came into force: the Abolition of Feudal Tenure etc. (Scotland) Act 2000 mentioned already; the Title Conditions (Scotland) Act 2003; and the Tenements (Scotland) Act 2004. More recently there have been the Land Registration etc. (Scotland) Act 2012[21] and the Long Leases (Scotland) Act 2012.[22]

EUROPE

1.8   Constitutions around the world commonly have property protection clauses. In Scots law this role is played by the European Convention on Human Rights, especially Article 1 of Protocol 1, though other provisions can be relevant, such as Article 8.[23] As for the European Union, Article 345 of the Treaty on the Functioning of the European Union (TFEU) provides that 'the Treaties shall in no way prejudice the rules in Member States governing the system of property ownership.' There is room for debate as to what 'property ownership'[24] covers. It does not cover *contracts* about property.[25] But in general terms EU law has no bearing on property law as such. Nevertheless there has long been, and continues to be, discussion of ways of harmonising or even unifying property law across the EU,[26] though for that to

---

17   SOGA 1979. See **PARA 5.22** below.
18   See **PARA 15.17** below.
19   See **PARA 20.11** below.
20   See **CHAPTER 14**.
21   See **CHAPTER 7** below.
22   See **CHAPTER 20** below.
23   See **CHAPTER 32** below.
24   The French text says 'le régime de la propriété' and the German text says 'Eigentumsordnung.'
25   For instance Directive 93/13/EEC, implemented in the UK by the Unfair Terms in Consumer Contracts Regulations 1999 (SI 1999/2083). This is relevant not only to contracts for the sale of goods but also contracts for the sale of immoveable property.
26   The literature is large. See eg U Drobnig, H Snijders and E-J Zippro (eds), *Divergences of Property Law, An Obstacle to the Internal Market?* (2006), and S van Erp, A Salomons and B Akkermans (eds), *The Future of European Property Law* (2012). The DCFR has provisions on moveable property law and on trusts.

happen Article 345 would first have to be amended. Moveable property has tended to be the focus. For land, the main discussion has concerned the possibility of a 'Euromortgage.'[27] But the relevance of EU law will change as and when Brexit takes place.

PATRIMONY AND THE PATRIMONIAL RIGHTS

1.9   A patrimonial right is a right with an economic value. An obvious example is ownership of land: it is a patrimonial right. The ownership of moveable property, such as a bicycle, is equally a patrimonial right. If Alan owns land and grants to Beth the right to use it for her life (this is called a liferent[28]), that too is a patrimonial right. Contractual rights are patrimonial too. If Beth lends Alan £1,000, her right to be paid is a patrimonial right. If she writes a bestseller, her copyright is a patrimonial right. In short, a patrimonial right means an asset. It would be shown as such on a company's balance sheet. Such rights are sometimes called property rights, using 'property' in a broad sense.

1.10   Some rights are non-patrimonial. Examples are the right to vote, the right to marry, the right to make a will, the right to have a passport and the right not to be defamed. If such rights are violated, that may give rise to a right to be paid damages, and a right to damages *is* a patrimonial right. But the underlying right, the right that was violated, was non-patrimonial.[29] That is not to say that the law of delict protects only non-patrimonial rights. It equally protects patrimonial rights.

1.11   *Patrimony* is the totality of a person's assets (patrimonial rights) and liabilities. Thus a company's balance sheet sets out its patrimony. The term 'estate' is sometimes used instead.[30] A patrimony is like a suitcase with two compartments: one for assets and the other for liabilities. Patrimony is the container, not the contained. Every person (whether a natural person or a juristic person such as a company) has a patrimony: *personality implies patrimony*. But the patrimony may have little in it: a newborn baby is a person, and so has a patrimony, but to begin with the suitcase is empty.

1.12   Although every person has a patrimony, not every person has just one patrimony. 'One person, one patrimony' is indeed the norm, but in certain special cases a person may have more than one patrimony. That happens when there is a trust.[31]

---

27   See **PARA 21.68** below.
28   See **CHAPTER 22** below.
29   The law of delict distinguishes between (i) damages for patrimonial harm; and (ii) damages for non-patrimonial harm. For example, if a careless driver runs down a cyclist, the damages for the destruction of the bicycle are for patrimonial harm, but the damages for the cyclist's suffering are for non-patrimonial harm. But in each case the damages themselves constitute a patrimonial right: thus the cyclist might be entitled to £500 for each. The £1,000 claim is an asset.
30   But 'estate' has several meanings.
31   See **CHAPTER 23** below.

PRIVATE LAW AND PUBLIC LAW

General

1.13   Property law is part of private law. There are, however, public law aspects to property. For example, planning law[32] and licensing law[33] belong to public law but relate to property. Another example is capital gains tax.[34] This book does not deal with the public law aspects of property, except occasionally.[35] That is not to say that those aspects are not important. They are. For example, the lawyers acting for a company that wishes to buy land and develop it for commercial purposes will have as much concern with the public law aspects as with the private law ones.[36]

Location within private law

1.14   The Romans divided private law into (i) the law of persons; (ii) the law of 'things'; and (iii) the law of actions[37] – *who* has rights, *what* rights there are and *how* rights are enforced. By 'things' they included the whole of the law of obligations and the law of property. The Scotland Act 1998 defines 'Scots private law' as meaning:

'(a) the general principles of private law (including private international law),

(b) the law of persons (including natural persons, legal persons and unincorporated bodies),

(c) the law of obligations (including obligations arising from contract, unilateral promise, delict, unjustified enrichment and *negotiorum gestio*),

(d) the law of property (including heritable and moveable property, trusts and succession), and

(e) the law of actions (including jurisdiction, remedies, evidence, procedure, diligence, recognition and enforcement of court orders, limitation of actions and arbitration)'.[38]

This is the Roman classification, modified. A preliminary category (general principles) has been added, while the 'things' category has been split into two – the law of obligations and the law of property. This book is about paragraph (d). Although obligations and property fall into separate categories, it has been seen[39] that rights arising out of the law of obligations are, in relation to third parties, part of property law in its broad sense.

---

[32]   See, eg, N A Collar *Planning* (4th edn, 2016).

[33]   See, eg, J C Cummins *Licensing (Scotland) Act 2005* (2nd edn, 2009).

[34]   See, eg, N Lee et al *Revenue Law – Principles and Practice* (34th edn, 2016) chs 19–27.

[35]   Our main departure from the general rule is public access rights. See **CHAPTER 19** below.

[36]   For a general overview, see *McDonald's Conveyancing Manual* ch 20.

[37]   '*Omne autem jus ... vel ad personas pertinet, vel ad res, vel ad actiones*' (Justinian *Institutes* 1, 3, 12).

[38]   Scotland Act 1998, s 126. It adds: ' ... and include references to judicial review of administrative action'. Many would regard that topic as belonging to public law.

[39]   See **PARA 1.9** above.

REAL RIGHTS AND PERSONAL RIGHTS

Personal rights

1.15   A personal right[40] is a right against a person. Contracts result in reciprocal personal rights. For example, if Fiona owns a house and enters into a contract of sale with Hamish, the result is that she has a personal right against him (to be paid the price) and he has a personal right against her (to be given possession and also a deed of transfer, called a disposition).[41] Likewise, if John is liable to Kate in the law of delict, in the sense that he must pay her damages, that is a personal right for Kate. Unlike a contract, there is no reciprocity; against her he has no right.

Real rights

1.16   A real right is a right directly in a thing.[42] The principal real right is ownership. When Fiona performs the contract of sale by transferring ownership to Hamish, he will have acquired the real right of ownership. Previously, at the contract stage, he had a personal right against Fiona, but no right in the house itself, the personal right being a right against Fiona to acquire ownership of the house.[43] Now he has the right of ownership. There are different kinds of real right. In **CHAPTER 2** these will be considered, but the right of ownership is the primary one.

Comparison

1.17   The holder of a personal right has a power – over the other person. The holder of a real right has a power – over the thing. *A personal right is as good as the person against whom it is held.* If Jack borrows £1,000 from Jill, and she is able and willing to repay, his claim is as good as gold. But if she becomes insolvent, it is of limited value. For example, if she is sequestrated[44] and her trustee pays creditors at 5%, that claim is worth only £50. *A real right is as good as the thing in which it is held.* If Jack owns a rare book worth £1,000, and it is destroyed in a fire, Jack has nothing but ashes. So the question of whether real rights or personal rights are 'better' is absurd: everything depends on context. If Jill is insolvent, Jack would prefer 1,000 £1 coins rather than the claim against her. But coins can be stolen, which is one reason why people commonly prefer to have personal rights against banks rather than keeping much cash. (To have money in the bank is to be owed money by the bank: the bank is a debtor just as much as Fiona is.)

---

[40]   *Jus personale* (personal right) or *jus in personam* (right 'in' (against) a person).
[41]   See **PARA 4.1** below.
[42]   *Jus reale* (real right), or *jus in rem*, or *jus in re* (right in a thing). *Res* means 'thing' and the adjective formed from it is *realis* (or *reale* in the neuter), whence the word 'real'.
[43]   *Jus in personam ad rem acquirendam* (a personal right to acquire a thing).
[44]   Sequestration is what non-lawyers call bankruptcy. The insolvent debtor's assets pass to the trustee in sequestration, who realises them for the benefit of the creditors. The current statute is the Bankruptcy (Scotland) Act 2016.

1.18   Personal rights are sometimes called 'relative rights', and real rights are sometimes called 'absolute rights', or rights 'against the world' or *erga omnes*.[45] That is because a real right can be regarded as being a set of personal rights against everyone in the world. Hamish's right of ownership is good not just against one person (as his contractual right against Fiona was) but against everybody. Everybody has the duty not to interfere with the house. This idea that real rights are, so to speak, multiple personal rights, rights against each of the planet's 7 billion inhabitants, is the 'personalist theory', whilst the theory that real rights are rights in things is the 'classical theory'. There are difficulties with both views. At this level it is not necessary to discuss the issue.[46]

Intellectual property

1.19   Intellectual property rights, such as copyright and patents, are sometimes regarded as real rights, because they are clearly not personal rights (there is nobody against whom they are held) and they are absolute. Others disagree, arguing that real rights can exist only in physical things, and that therefore the class of absolute rights is broader than the class of real rights. The issue will not be discussed further here, because intellectual property rights are not covered by the present work.

CORPOREAL AND INCORPOREAL

1.20   'Corporeal' property means physical things such as bicycles and houses; 'incorporeal' property means everything else. If the distinction is framed in terms of rights rather than things, then real rights of ownership are corporeal property while everything else (notably personal rights, and subordinate real rights) is incorporeal property. If Jack owes Jill £1,000, that is, from her standpoint, an asset just as much as a bicycle is an asset. It is her incorporeal moveable property. If Jill writes a book, she has copyright in it, which is incorporeal moveable property. If she buys shares in a company, those shares are incorporeal moveable property. And so on.

HERITABLE AND MOVEABLE

1.21   A second distinction is between 'heritable' and 'moveable' property. 'Heritable' is perhaps a misleading term: moveable property can be inherited just as much as heritable property. Heritable property means land and rights connected with land. It means the same as immoveable property. A field is heritable property.

---

[45]   *Erga omnes* – as against everyone.
[46]   See, eg, Paisley *Land Law* para 2.1. It may be added that some thinkers argue for the polar opposite of the personalist theory, ie that all personal rights are in the final analysis real rights because personal rights are enforced against the debtor's assets.

So is a house. Any subordinate real right[47] in heritable property is itself heritable, with the partial exception of security rights.[48] Contractual rights about real rights in land are heritable.[49] Thus if Donna owns land and Ewan contracts to buy it, his contractual right is itself heritable. Property other than heritable/immoveable property is moveable property. That includes not only corporeals such as apples and bicycles but also most contract rights, and all rights under the law of delict and the law of unjustified enrichment. Intellectual property rights and company shares are other examples of incorporeal moveable property. The latter are personal rights, but of a special kind.

1.22 Although, in general, heritable property is connected with land, there are two exceptions. Peerages, such as the earldom of Govan, are heritable property. So is the rather obscure category of rights that 'have a tract of future time' of which the accepted definition is Erskine's: 'rights of such a nature that they cannot be at once paid or fulfilled by the debtor, but continue for a number of years ... without any relation to any capital sum or stock'.[50] This includes annuities and pensions. These rights are moveable property for some purposes but heritable property for others.

COMBINING THE CATEGORIES

1.23 If the corporeal/incorporeal distinction and the heritable/moveable distinction are combined, four categories emerge. The first is corporeal moveable property, such as a bicycle. The second is corporeal heritable property, such as a house. The third is incorporeal moveable property, such as most contractual rights,[51] and all rights arising in delict and in unjustified enrichment. Company shares are another example, as are intellectual property rights. Finally, there is incorporeal heritable property, the main examples being subordinate real rights in land. One misconception is that all personal rights are moveable. That is not so. Most are, but not all. For example, a contractual right to acquire land is personal and heritable.

THREE TERMS: 'PROPERTY', 'LAND' and 'GOODS'

1.24 'She bought property in France.' We understand the speaker to mean immoveable property: in ordinary speech, as mentioned already,[52] that is how the word 'property' is often used. Sometimes it is used in a broader sense: 'That's my property!' might be said of property other than land, and we all know that what is

---

[47] A subordinate real right is a real right other than ownership. See **CHAPTER 2** below.
[48] The security in itself is heritable. The debt it secures is moveable, except for some purposes: Titles to Land Consolidation (Scotland) Act 1868, s 117.
[49] So not all heritable rights are real rights, although most are.
[50] Erskine III, 2, 6.
[51] The exception has already been mentioned: contractual rights about real rights in land.
[52] See **PARA 1.1** above.

at a lost property office is moveable property. The legal sense of 'property' is broad: thus 'property law' is not limited to immoveable property.

1.25   There are some statutory definitions of 'property' in particular contexts, but they are mostly of little value, even for those contexts. For instance the Proceeds of Crime Act 2002, says: '(1) Property is all property wherever situated and includes (a) money; (b) all forms of property.'[53] That is largely circular, and it continues in this rather pointless vein: '(a) property is held by a person if he holds an interest in it; (b) property is obtained by a person if he obtains an interest in it…'[54] Equally useless (and circular) is the definition in the Insolvency Act 1986: '"Property" includes money, goods, things in action, land and every description of property wherever situated and also obligations and every description of interest, whether present or future or vested or contingent, arising out of, or incidental to, property.'[55]

1.26   'Land' means immoveable property. Thus, houses and flats are 'land', and 'land registration' includes the registration of a small top-floor flat just as much as a large estate in Argyll. Ordinary legal usage is, for instance, followed by the LR(S) A 2012 reflects when it says that '"land" includes buildings and other structures' and 'land covered with water'.[56]

1.27   The word 'goods' – always in the plural – is generally used (as in the Sale of Goods Act 1979[57]) in legal language[58] to mean corporeal moveables. In other languages (eg *les biens* in French, *die Güter* in German, *bona* in Latin), the equivalent word means property in general.

TRANSFER OF RIGHTS, CONSTITUTION OF RIGHTS, EXTINCTION OF RIGHTS

1.28   Much of property law is about the transfer of rights from one person to another, in other words, from one person's patrimony to another's. Different rights are transferred in different ways. The real right of ownership of land is transferred by registration in the Land Register: the outgoing owner's name is deleted and that of the incoming owner is substituted.[59] A right to money is transferred by an 'assignation' that is completed by notice to the debtor.[60] And so on.

---

[53]   Section 150(1).
[54]   Section 150(2). The whole section is remarkable. Our favourite is perhaps s 150(2)(e): 'references to an interest held by a person beneficially in property include references to an interest which would be held by him beneficially if the property were not so vested.' Eh?
[55]   Section 436(1). 'Things in action' (or, more usually, 'choses in action') is an English term meaning incorporeal moveables.
[56]   LR(S)A 2012, s 113.
[57]   See s 61.
[58]   Economists use the term in a much broader sense, and, unlike lawyers, are happy to use the singular.
[59]   See **PARA 7.45** below.
[60]   See **PARAS 5.39–5.52** below.

1.29 But transfer is not the only thing that can happen to a right. There are also birth and death or, to use legal language, constitution (also called creation) and extinction. Taken in order of time, the three events are therefore (i) constitution, (ii) transfer and (iii) extinction.[61] An example of creation would be where Oliver, owner of Blackmains, grants to his neighbour Nigella, owner of Whitemains, a servitude of way across his land.[62] That is a new right. If, a century later, Nigella's successor as owner of Whitemains grants a 'discharge' of the servitude, then the servitude is extinguished. Another example: Kate owns Greenmains, and grants to Linda a 100-year lease.[63] That creates a new right. A few years later, Linda assigns[64] the lease to Mandy. That is a transfer: a right passes from one person to another. What has changed is not the right but its holder. Later still, Mandy agrees with the current owner (who may or may not still be Kate) that the lease will come to an end: extinction. Extinction is not transfer. Kate does not become tenant to herself. The lease simply ceases to exist, like a bursting soap bubble. Often the same or similar steps are required to constitute, transfer or extinguish a right. For example, with a standard security all three events require registration.[65] There is also (iv) variation, but in fact variation is not a truly independent category. For instance, suppose that there is a servitude of way, which is available for all purposes. The owners of the two properties agree to vary it by limiting it to pedestrian use and also partly changing its route. Here there is a partial extinction (as to the type of use) a further partial extinction (part of the route cannot now be used) and a partial grant (the right now exists over new ground).

1.30 A given right may not experience all three events. A right might never be transferred. Most personal rights are never transferred.[66] If Jack, a decorator, contracts with Jill to redecorate her flat, it is unlikely that he will transfer his right to be paid to anyone else,[67] and it is very unlikely that she will transfer her right to have the flat redecorated. In theory it could happen: for example, before the work is done she sells the flat to someone else and also transfers the right against Jack. Again, extinction may never happen. Although contract rights tend to be short-lived, real rights are often long-lived and some, such as servitudes, are potentially everlasting. Ownership is often transferred but is seldom created or extinguished.

A CHART OF PATRIMONIAL RIGHTS

1.31 This shows the basic chart. One issue is where intellectual property rights should be placed. In Scotland they are usually regarded as real rights. An alternative

[61] See also **PARA 31.4** below.
[62] On servitudes, see **CHAPTER 13** below.
[63] On leases, see **CHAPTER 20** below.
[64] See **PARAS 5.38–5.52** below.
[65] See below, **PARAS 21.43–21.56**.
[66] If it is transferred, this is done by assignation. See below, **PARAS 5.38–5.51**.
[67] But larger businesses often do so.

approach is to divide patrimonial rights into (i) absolute and (ii) relative (personal) rights. Absolute rights are then divided into (i) real rights and (ii) intellectual property rights.

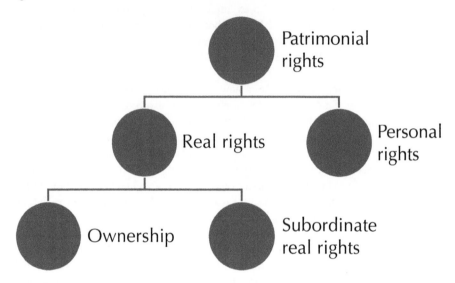

LITERATURE

1.32   Useful introductions to Scots property law can be found in Reid *Property* paras 1–16, K Reid, 'Property Law: Sources and Doctrine' in Reid and Zimmermann *History* vol 1 at 185–210, in Paisley *Land Law* Ch 1 and in C Anderson, *Property: A Guide to Scots Law* (2016). See also D N MacCormick, *Institutions of Law: An Essay in Legal Theory* (2007), which locates property law within law in general, as does his shorter 'General Legal Concepts' (SME Reissue 2008).

1.33   To a large extent the basics of property law are common to the civilian and mixed systems. Reading about such other systems can be enlightening. Excellent texts available in English include the following. (i) M F Planiol, *Treatise on the Civil Law* (three vols, 1959, a translation of *Traité élémentaire de droit civil*), about French law, (ii) E J Cohn, *Manual of German Law* (2nd edn, 1968), (iii) A N Yiannopoulos, *Property* (4th edn, 2001), about Louisiana and (iv) P J Badenhorst, J M Pienaar and H Mostert, (eds) *Silberberg and Schoeman's The Law of Property* (5th edn, 2006) about South Africa.

1.34   For broader comparative views, see Van Erp and Akkermans, *Property Law*, and M Graziadei and L Smith, *Comparative Property Law: Global Perspectives* (2017). A journal devoted to comparative property law is the *European Property Law Journal*.

Chapter 2

Real rights

THE PRINCIPAL REAL RIGHT AND THE SUBORDINATE REAL RIGHTS

Ownership: the principal real right

2.1   The principal real right is *ownership*.[1] The person who has that right is called the 'owner' or 'proprietor'. The terms mean the same. Often ownership is the only real right in an item of property, and indeed that is almost always true for corporeal moveables. But, as well as ownership, there can be 'subordinate' real rights in something, and this is common for immoveable property.

---

[1]   The Latin term, *dominium*, is often encountered, as is *dominus* (owner).

Subordinate real rights

2.2   A subordinate real right is a real right in something, held by someone other than the owner. It can also be called a 'secondary real right', 'subsidiary real right', 'limited real right',[2] 'encumbrance' or, in Latin, a *jus*[3] *in re aliena*. The Latin expression neatly stresses that a subordinate real right exists in something that is owned by *someone else*. In other words, if there is a subordinate real right in something, there must be at least two real rights in it: the real right of ownership of X and the subordinate right of Y. In the last chapter,[4] we met Oliver, the owner of Blackmains, and Nigella, the owner of neighbouring Whitemains. Oliver granted to Nigella a 'servitude' allowing her to use a track across his land, including the right to drive vehicles. (From the standpoint of property law, the reason why he did this does not matter. It may be because money changed hands – i.e. she bought a servitude from him.) The servitude is registered in the Land Register, appearing in both the 'title sheet' for Blackmains and in that for Whitemains.[5] There are now two real rights in Blackmains: Oliver's real right of ownership and Nigella's real right of servitude.

2.3   Is this servitude any different, in practical terms, from a contract between Oliver and Nigella allowing her to cross his land? In the short term, 'no'. In the long term, 'yes'. Suppose that after a couple of years Oliver sells Blackmains to Tara. Can Nigella carry on? If her right is contractual, the answer is 'no'. A contractual right is a personal right, a right against a person. That person is Oliver. Nigella has no contract with Tara. Tara can refuse to let Nigella cross her land. That may leave Nigella with a claim against Oliver for damages for breach of contract, but even if such a claim can be enforced it still does not mean that she can use the track. By contrast, a servitude is a real right – a right *in the land itself*, not a right against Oliver. So it matters not whether Blackmains is still owned by Oliver. A subordinate real right is like superglue. Nothing – or almost nothing – can detach it, regardless of who owns the thing itself.[6]

ENCUMBERED OWNERSHIP IS STILL OWNERSHIP

2.4   A plot of land might be encumbered by a dozen servitudes, a liferent, a long lease, three standard securities and a public right of way. These might dramatically lessen the value of the right of ownership.[7] For example, in 1960 the owner of Greymains grants a 150-year lease for a fixed rent of £250 per annum. Most of the economic value of the land is now held by the current tenant. If the landlord (owner)

---

[2]   'Limited' is the commonest term internationally; eg German law calls subordinate real rights *beschränkte dingliche Rechte*.

[3]   The plural of *jus* (right) is *jura*.

[4]   See **PARA 1.29** above.

[5]   See **PARA 7.35** below.

[6]   Though some subordinate rights are time-limited, such as lease and liferent. See **CHAPTERS 20 AND 22** below.

[7]   They do not lessen the value of the land.

sells, the price will be low, while if the tenant sells (ie sells the lease[8]) the price will be almost as high as it would have been if the tenant had been outright owner. Yet the landlord's right remains the right of ownership, no matter how encumbered it may have become. The tenant is not the owner.

2.5 Sometimes real rights are thought of as fragments of ownership that are split off to be held by somebody else. The expression 'dismemberments of ownership' is used in some legal systems,[9] though not in Scots law. Some people find the 'dismemberment' idea a useful one, but it must not be allowed to give the false impression that what remains is anything other than the right of ownership. Ownership is a well that remains a well, no matter how many bucketfuls are drawn.

REAL RIGHTS AND INSOLVENCY

2.6 The difference between (i) a contractual right of way; and (ii) a real right of way was illustrated above by the case where the owner, after granting the right, transfers ownership.[10] The incoming owner is bound by a real right but will not normally be bound by a contractual right. The same point could have been illustrated by the use of insolvency law. Suppose that Nigella has a contractual right, and Oliver then becomes insolvent. His creditors use diligence to attach the land.[11] Alternatively, he is sequestrated, which works as a collective diligence in favour of all creditors.[12] Nigella will find that she cannot enforce her right.

2.7 Nigella will have a claim for damages against Oliver but since Oliver is insolvent, the full amount will not be recoverable.[13] And here we see why insolvency is so interesting as a test of real right. In the example above, if Oliver is solvent, though Nigella loses her contractual access right she can recover its monetary equivalent – damages. But if the right is lost because of Oliver's insolvency, then damages, though claimable, cannot be recovered in full, and perhaps not at all. The theory of real rights would be important even if nobody ever became insolvent, but the danger of insolvency gives to that theory a special significance. A full understanding of property law requires an understanding of insolvency.

WHICH ARE THE SUBORDINATE REAL RIGHTS? THE *NUMERUS CLAUSUS*

2.8 The law recognises only certain types of real right. A choice can be made from a short menu: people cannot create their own. There is a contrast here with

---

8   Such a sale is implemented by assignation. See **PARA 20.33** below.
9   Eg France, Louisiana, Quebec and the Netherlands.
10   See **PARA 2.3** above.
11   On diligence, see Gloag and Henderson *The Law of Scotland* ch 48.
12   See Gloag and Henderson *The Law of Scotland* ch 49.
13   It may be that nothing can be recovered: in many insolvencies ordinary creditors are paid at 0%.

contract law. The law does, it is true, recognise certain specific types of contract – the nominate contracts – but people are free to modify those standard types as they see fit[14] and, indeed, to fashion wholly new types of contract – the innominate contracts. Property law is less flexible: it offers a fixed list of nominate real rights. This is sometimes called the *numerus clausus* ('closed number').[15] Whereas innominate contracts are competent, innominate real rights are not. 'Real rights' not on the list are not available. What are these recognised types of subordinate right? They are:

(i)   servitude;
(ii)   negative real burden;[16]
(ii)   proper liferent;[17]
(iv)   right in security;[18] and
(v)   lease of immoveable property.

Some of these in turn have subdivisions: for example, there are particular types of security right, such as pledge, lien and standard security.

2.9   Sometimes other rights are added to the list. One is the set of rights over land held by the public, such as public rights of way and public rights in the foreshore.[19] Such rights certainly resemble real rights but it can be argued that since they belong to public law rather than private law they should not, strictly speaking, be classified as real rights. A second is 'exclusive privilege' which in effect means intellectual property rights.[20] Such rights are certainly like real rights: they are absolute rights, not relative (personal) rights. The counter-argument is that they do not relate to physical property. Some legal systems therefore divide absolute rights into two: real rights and intellectual property rights. A third possibility is possession. It is a complex subject and one must distinguish possession as a fact (eg the thief is in possession), the right to possess (which the true owner has in relation to the goods both before and after they were stolen) and rights generated by the fact of possession. To some degree the latter have a real quality and accordingly possession is sometimes classified as a real right.[21]

2.10   Legislation can create new types of right and is not bound to fit such rights into traditional categories. An example can be found in 'occupancy rights'. If Pat and

---

14   There are some qualifications to this statement, especially where the contract is between (i) a business party, and (ii) a consumer. See, eg, MacQueen and Thomson *Contract* paras 7.55–7.85.
15   For a comprehensive comparative study, see B Akkermans *The Principle of Numerus Clausus in European Property Law* (2008).
16   There is also the affirmative real burden. This is not a real right, but a 'real obligation', for which see **PARA 2.19** below. Real burdens have much in common with servitudes, and indeed they form the two main branches of the category of 'title conditions'. See **PARA 14.3** below.
17   There is also something called an 'improper liferent' or 'trust liferent'. This is not a real right. See **PARA 22.14** below.
18   Rights in security are rights to a creditor to enforce payment of a debt by selling the property. See **CHAPTER 21** below.
19   See **PARAS 19.25–19.28** below.
20   The term is slightly wider than 'intellectual property rights', because it includes non-intellectual monopoly trading rights.
21   See **PARA 12.18** below.

Kim are married, or are civil partners, and the home is owned by Pat, then Kim has 'occupancy rights' in it.[22] These rights seem to be personal rights with real aspects.

MULTIPLE REAL RIGHTS IN THE SAME THING

2.11   The very concept of a subordinate real right means that there is more than one real right in the same thing:

    (i)   the principal real right, ownership; and

    (ii) a subordinate real right held by somebody other than the owner of the thing.

There can also be more than one subordinate real right in something – i.e. a total of three or more real rights. Suppose that Oliver grants a servitude to Nigella, and later grants a proper liferent to Tess, and this too is registered in the Land Register. A proper liferent is a subordinate real right that gives the holder the right to possess the thing for the holder's lifetime. There are now three real rights:

    (i)   Oliver's real right of ownership;

    (ii) Nigella's real right of servitude; and

    (iii) Tess's real right of liferent.

Each is a direct and absolute right in the land. There could easily be more than three. For example, servitudes might exist in favour of several neighbours, and there are other possible subordinate real rights, such as lease and standard security. Most land is subject to subordinate real rights and most moveable property is not. That is partly because three types of subordinate real right (servitude, negative real burden and lease) can exist only in land but not in moveables, and partly because of practicalities.

2.12   If something is subject to multiple real rights, these generally lead an independent existence. For example, suppose that Iona owns Whitemains. She grants a servitude to her neighbour, Nick, and this is registered in the Land Register. Later, she grants a ten-year lease to Larry.[23] Later still, she borrows £125,000 from Bank A and in security of the loan grants to the bank a security over the house, and this is registered in the Land Register. There are now four real rights in the house: Iona's right of ownership, Nick's right of servitude, Larry's right of lease and the bank's right of security. Suppose that Iona now transfers ownership to Steve. The transfer is registered in the Land Register. Steve is owner. The three subordinate real rights are unaffected. (Larry has a new landlord but that does not affect his rights as tenant.)

2.13   Steve is not liable to Bank A. After all, he has no contract with the bank. Iona remains liable. If she fails to pay, the bank can enforce its right by selling the house.[24] That may sound harsh on Steve but he would know about these subordinate

---

22   See **CHAPTER 11** below.

23   This is not registered because only leases over 20 years can be registered. See **PARAS 20.11–20.12** below. But it will nevertheless be a real right.

24   Suppose it sells it for £200,000. The bank pockets £125,000. The balance goes to the ex-owner, Steve. As a result of the sale the security is extinguished. The number of subordinate real rights falls from three to two.

real rights when he bought the property, because they are publicised either by registration or possession.[25] (In practice a buyer will usually insist that any secured loans are paid off by the seller.) The sale will not affect the rights of Larry or Nick.

2.14   In this example, the various real rights co-habited reasonably happily. It can, however, be otherwise. For instance, suppose that Iona had borrowed another £125,000, this time from Bank B, granting a security for this new loan. This second security would be valid but postponed to the first. Suppose that Iona became insolvent and Bank A sold the property for £200,000. Bank A would have taken the full £125,000 it was owed, and Bank B would have received the balance of £75,000. The reason is that the priority of real rights is determined by the date they become real, a principle summed up in the maxim *prior tempore potior jure* – earlier by time, stronger by right.[26]

2.15   In general, the only person who can grant a subordinate real right is the owner. But there are some exceptions. The holder of a registered lease can (in some cases) grant a security over the lease,[27] and can also (in some cases) grant a sub-lease. These are subordinate real rights, and they are over subordinate real rights. One can call subordinate real rights 'daughter rights' and these lower-level rights 'granddaughter rights'. They are sometimes described as 'real rights in real rights'. These granddaughter rights can arise only in certain types of case, of which the main ones (sub-lease, and security over a lease) have just been mentioned. For example, nobody except an owner can grant a servitude or a real burden[28] or a liferent.

SEPARATE TENEMENTS

2.16   A 'separate tenement' is a right of ownership that is held by someone other than the owner of the land itself.[29] Examples include flats,[30] mineral rights and salmon fishing rights. Thus, Kenneth owns a Perthshire estate, but the salmon fishing rights on one of his rivers belong to Donald, unworked gold and silver to the Crown, unworked coal to the Coal Authority, and other unworked minerals to Constance. All these real rights co-exist. Functionally, such rights, except Kenneth's, can be compared to subordinate real rights, encumbering Kenneth's ownership, but in law separate tenements are not subordinate real rights but ownership rights. Separate tenements are considered further in **CHAPTER 15**.

---

[25]   For the publicity principle see **PARA 4.19** below.
[26]   See **PARA 4.45** below.
[27]   If there is default on the secured loan, what the creditor sells is the lease, so that the owner will have a new tenant.
[28]   A partial exception to the statement is to be found in the Registration of Leases (Scotland) Act 1857, s 3, but just what that provision means is controversial.
[29]   For separate tenements in general, see **PARAS 15.13–15.18** below.
[30]   See **CHAPTER 16** below.

PRIVATE PROPERTY, PUBLIC PROPERTY, COMMON GOOD, *REGALIA*

2.17 Some property belongs to public bodies such as local authorities or the Crown. Such property is, as far as property law is concerned, no different from private property: it is just property whose owner happens to be a public-sector body. The powers and duties of public authorities are subject to public law, and that may affect what they can and cannot do with property they own, but these rules belong to public law, not to property law. To this general picture there are one or two footnotes to be added. Some land (eg parks) owned by local authorities is 'common good' property and as such subject to certain special rules as to use, and power of sale. These restrictions sit near the border between public and private law.[31] Crown property is divided into Crown Public Estate and Crown Private Estate. The former is property held by the Crown as head of state and is thus state property. Most of it has hitherto been administered by the Crown Estate Commissioners, but it is being devolved.[32] Crown private estate belongs to the sovereign as private property. Her Majesty could sell it, or on her death bequeath it, as she saw fit. Some property is owned by the Secretary of State. Some (e.g. Edinburgh Castle) is owned by the Scottish Ministers. To return to the Crown Public Estate: Crown property rights, corporeal and incorporeal, are called the *regalia*, but the concept is nowadays of little significance. The *regalia minora* are simply property rights that happen to belong to the Crown. For example, most of the foreshore belongs to the Crown, as does all the sea bed. The *regalia majora* are rights that cannot be sold and which are held by the Crown for the public benefit. For instance the Crown can sell the foreshore, but when it does so, the public rights to use the foreshore are unaffected. Really these are simply public rights that have no particular link with the Crown. For example, if enforcement action is needed, the action can be raised by anyone, not just by the Crown.

THE 'UNBRIDGEABLE DIVISION'? REAL OBLIGATIONS, 'OFFSIDE GOALS' ETC.

2.18 Whether the division between personal and real rights is truly 'unbridgeable'[33] can be debated. Occupancy rights[34] are statutory rights enforceable by one spouse, or civil partner, against the other, and are thus essentially personal. But in some situations, though not others, they can also be enforced against third parties. Such rights may not bridge the division, but they perhaps could be said to straddle it awkwardly.

---

[31] A Ferguson, *Common Good Law* (2006). The leading modern case is *Portobello Park Action Group Association v The City of Edinburgh Council* 2012 SLT 1137. See further M M Combe 'Lessons in Scots law: the common good school' (2013) 17 *Edin LR* 63. Some of the law on common-good property is in s 75 of the Local Government (Scotland) Act 1973 as amended by s 77 of the Land Reform (Scotland) Act 2016, and in Pt 8 of the Community Empowerment (Scotland) Act 2015.

[32] Crown Estate Act 1961; Scotland Act 2016, s 37.

[33] *Burnett's Tr v Grainger* 2004 SC (HL) 19 at para 87 *per* Lord Rodger of Earlsferry.

[34] See **CHAPTER 11** below.

2.19   More important is the class of rights usually called 'real obligations', or *obligationes propter rem*.[35] Here, a personal right is valid against whoever is the owner of given property for the time being. Positive real burdens are examples. (By contrast, negative real burdens are true real rights.[36]) A security right is not a real obligation. Suppose that Selina owns Redmains and grants a standard security over it to Bank X, in security of a loan of £500,000. She then transfers ownership to Aeneas. If she fails to repay the loan, the land will be sold, and so Aeneas will lose it, but he has no personal liability for the debt. For example, if the bank sells Redmains for £400,000, he is not liable for the balance of the debt.

2.20   As for leases, at common law they are contracts and nothing more. If Candice owns land and lets it to Diana for five years, and during that period Candice dispones to Katy, Katy can require Diana to flit, leaving Diana with merely a breach of contract claim against Candice. But for most leases of heritable property the common law is disapplied by statute[37] and the contract changes from being a Diana/Candice contract into being a Diana/Katy contract, with Katy having Candice's rights and duties. Whether such leases – leases not subject to the common-law rule – should be regarded as true real rights, or as real obligations, or indeed as a mixture of the two, is an unsettled point. In practice they are always called real rights. The statutes that confer real effect on leases apply only to leases of immoveable property. Leases of moveable property – such as a one-year lease of a motor vehicle – remain subject to common law, and so have contractual effect only.[38]

2.21   Then there is the so-called 'offside goals' rule. This is discussed later,[39] but in brief a buyer can occasionally be subjected to the contractual obligations of the seller. There is some resemblance here to real obligations but, unlike a true real obligation, the 'offside goals' rule results in an essentially passive liability.

2.22   There are other possible cases where rights may have a real as well as a personal quality. Only one will be mentioned: trusts.[40] The rights of a beneficiary under a trust are personal rights – rights against the trustees – but they also have characteristics which make them sometimes behave like real rights. But the law is settled that such rights are personal, not real, and their seemingly semi-real effects can be explained without resorting to the theory that they are mixed in their nature.

---

[35]   Obligations on account of property.
[36]   See **PARA 14.41** below.
[37]   Leases Act 1449; Registration of Leases (Scotland) Act 1857. Almost all leases of land fall under one of these. See **CHAPTER 20** below.
[38]   See **CHAPTER 20** below.
[39]   See **PARAS 4.48–4.51** below.
[40]   See **CHAPTER 23** below.

'INTEREST'

2.23   The word 'interest' can be used to mean a right in relation to property. A broad and slightly fuzzy term, its use does not commit the writer to saying what sort of right is in question. Often it is used to mean a real right.

'BENEFICIAL INTEREST', AND 'BENEFICIAL OWNERSHIP'

2.24   The term 'beneficial interest' means the right that a trust beneficiary has in trust property. A beneficial interest is a special type of personal right: a particular type of personal right that a trust beneficiary has against the trustee, in relation to what is to happen to property held by the trustee. The term 'beneficial ownership' (or 'beneficial owner') has the same meaning, but is less commonly used in Scotland, because ownership is held by the trustees, not by the beneficiaries.[41] The term comes from English law, where ownership can be divided between (i) 'legal ownership' and (ii) 'equitable' or 'beneficial' ownership.

2.25   These terms ('beneficial interest', 'beneficially interested', 'beneficial owner' etc) are in UK-wide legislation, such as tax legislation and companies' legislation, and it is not always clear whether the term is being used in the sense of trust law, or bears some broader meaning, for the professional drafters of such provisions generally have English law in mind. An unimportant but illustrative example:

> 'The Director of Savings may accept as conclusive proof of the death of the holder of a bond, stock, a certificate or children's certificate any evidence which establishes to the Director of Savings' satisfaction that the holder has not been heard of for a period of seven years or more (and, for the purposes of this paragraph, "holder of a bond, stock, a certificate or children's certificate" includes any person beneficially interested at any time, whether absolutely or contingently, in the personal estate of the deceased).'[42]

Does this, in relation to Scotland, go beyond trust beneficiaries? It is impossible to say. (We use this example because of the neatly tell-tale use of the word 'personal' in its English sense to mean not personal but moveable.)

2.26   Whilst it was said above that 'beneficial ownership' etc is a concept used in general Scots law only in connection with trusts, there are some reported cases in which the existence of some broader concept is asserted or presupposed, a notable example being the decision of the House of Lords in *Sharp v Thomson*.[43] This

---

[41]   See **CHAPTER 24**.
[42]   National Savings (No. 2) Regulations 2015, reg 78(2).
[43]   1997 SC (HL) 66.

broader concept is somewhat hard to pin down, the reason being, in our view, that it has the same existential status as the tooth fairy.[44]

SOME ENGLISH TERMS: 'FREEHOLD', ETC

2.27   English property law is rather different from Scottish property law, and has its own terminology; some of these terms are on occasion encountered north of the border. One or two may be noted here. 'Real' and 'personal' mean not what we mean by them: they mean, roughly, immoveable/heritable, and moveable, respectively. Hence 'real estate' means immoveable/heritable property. 'Freehold' means ownership of land.[45] (The term is not used for ownership of goods.) English law does not have our idea of subordinate real rights, though for goods (not land) it comes near with 'general property' and 'special property', meaning, roughly, ownership and the subordinate real rights. This usage can be found in UK-wide legislation, without (as one would expect) any 'kilt' provision.[46] Lastly, a term of English law that has become widely used is 'mortgage', which in Scots terminology means heritable security, ie a security over heritable/immoveable property.

LITERATURE

2.28   The texts mentioned at the end of the previous chapter are also relevant here. See also Paisley *Land Law* Ch 2.

---

[44]   This book should be kept out of the reach of children.
[45]   This statement is approximate only. Actually freehold is a genus with four species, namely the estate of fee simple, the estate of fee tail, the estate for life and the estate pur autre vie. When estate agents describe a property a 'freehold' they mean the first, or, more narrowly, what is called the estate of fee simple absolute in possession, which is the nearest English law comes to ownership of land.
[46]   For example the, Sale of Goods Act 1979, s 61 and the Consumer Rights Act 2015, s 4(1).

Chapter 3

Ownership

WHAT IS THE RIGHT OF OWNERSHIP?

3.1   Whether the right of ownership can be defined is doubtful. It can at least be described. Ownership is the most comprehensive right that can be had in an object. It is, as Stair says, 'the main real right'.[1] Erskine calls it 'the right of using and disposing of a subject as our own, except in so far as we are restrained by law or paction'.[2] Ownership must be distinguished in particular from: (a) the other types of real right, ie the subordinate real rights, such as servitude;[3] and (b) possession.[4] For example, if Keith owns land and grants a 100-year lease to Louise, she thereby acquires a real right, but not ownership. Keith is still the owner.

---

[1]   Stair II, 1, 28.
[2]   Erskine II, 1, 1.
[3]   See **CHAPTER 13** below.
[4]   See **CHAPTER 12** below.

Bundle of rights?

3.2   In legal systems based on the French tradition, ownership is thought of as composed of three elements, namely the right to use (*usus, jus utendi*), the right to transfer or to destroy (*abusus, jus abutendi*) and the right to take the 'fruits' (*fructus, jus fruendi*). In the US a similar conception exists, called the 'bundle of rights' theory, whereby ownership is thought of as composed of elements (there is some disagreement about which ones) such as the right to possess, the right to control, the right to exclude, the right to transfer etc. Sometimes it is said that each of these elements itself is 'owned.' (The 'bundle of rights' theory is often associated with the 'personalist' theory whereby all real rights are in the final analysis personal rights.[5]) But in many systems, such as legal systems based on the German tradition, ownership is a unitary conception, and whilst rights can be broken off, these are conceptualised as subordinate real rights rather than as chunks of ownership. Scots law belongs to this third group. The issues are more of theoretical than practical importance.

UNLIMITED?

3.3   Ownership is absolute, in the sense that it is not a relative (personal) right. But it is seldom – perhaps never – absolute in the sense of being unlimited. If there is a subordinate real right, that restricts the scope of the right of ownership and may even take away most of its economic value.[6] Most heritable property is subject to subordinate real rights. Where there are no such rights, ownership is perhaps unlimited from a private law standpoint. But often there are public law limitations.[7] Land is subject to planning law (Town and Country Planning (Scotland) Act 1997) and building control law (Building (Scotland) Act 2003), and may be subject to other public law regimes, such as the Planning (Listed Buildings and Conservation Areas) (Scotland) Act 1997 or the Ancient Monuments and Archaeological Areas Act 1979. Most land is subject to public access rights under the Land Reform (Scotland) Act 2003.[8] Public law can affect moveables too. For example, motor vehicles, aircraft, locomotives and ships are subject to a good deal of public law. If you want to sell something to a foreign buyer, the Export Control Act 2002 will not stop the sale but may prevent it from being implemented.[9] And so on.

---

[5]   See **PARA 1.18**.
[6]   See **PARA 2.4** above.
[7]   See **PARA 1.13** above.
[8]   See **PARAS 19.2–19.12** below.
[9]   'The Secretary of State may by order make provision for or in connection with the imposition of export controls in relation to goods of any description.' (s 1).

OWNERSHIP OF WHAT?

3.4   Most would agree that one owns 'things' but there is disagreement as to what this means. Ownership is possible of physical things, such as fields and bicycles. (And indeed gas.[10] Electricity is less clear.[11]) But can rights be owned as well? A tenant does not own the land, but might he or she be regarded as owning the tenancy? Is a money claim owned by the creditor? Is a company share owned by the shareholder? Is a patent owned by the patent holder? In ordinary speech we commonly say that a person owns shares in a company, or owns a patent, though we would perhaps feel less comfortable saying that a bank lending money to a customer owns the right to be repaid, or that a tenant owns the tenancy.

3.5   On one view, patrimonial rights can be owned, as well as things. (Indeed, on this view 'things' include both physical things and rights.) This is the predominant view. Some who hold this view make an exception for the right of ownership: that is, they say, the only right that cannot be owned.[12] The other view is that only physical things are the objects of ownership. The relationship between a person and a right is, on this view, not a right of ownership. A person *has* rights, but does not *own* them: the right of ownership is one type of right a person may have. The issues involved in this debate are complex but their practical implications are limited.[13]

UNOWNED THINGS AND ANIMALS

3.6   Most physical objects are owned, but not all. The air is not owned, nor is sea water or fresh running water, though all these can be taken into ownership by occupancy.[14] The same is true of wild animals. As far as private law is concerned, the ownership of animals is the same as ownership of inert objects. Legislation protects them from abuse,[15] but as far as private law is concerned they are simply moveable property. German law provides that 'animals are not things'.[16] This is a statement of values but has limited legal effect: a horse can be owned and bought and sold in German law.

---

[10]   Paisley *Land Law* para 1.15.
[11]   The criminal law classifies the unlawful abstraction of electricity as theft: G H Gordon *The Criminal Law of Scotland* (4th edn, 2017, ed by J Chalmers and F Leverick) para 21-15 and 21.16. The implications for private law are uncertain.
[12]   This is the position taken in Reid *Property* para 16.
[13]   The minority view, held by one of the authors but not the other, is set out in an unreadable article: 'Ownership and its Objects' (2007) 71 *Rabels Zeitschrift* 802.
[14]   See **PARA 9.2** below.
[15]   Notably the Animal Health and Welfare (Scotland) Act 2006.
[16]   'Tiere sind keine Sachen.' BGB § 90a.

BONA VACANTIA – ULTIMUS HAERES – 'TREASURE TROVE'

3.7   Subject to those qualifications, physical objects cannot be ownerless. If the owner dies intestate and without traceable family, the property passes to the Crown, who is everybody's *ultimus haeres* (ultimate heir).[17] If a juristic person[18] is dissolved still holding its assets, those assets are called *bona vacantia* and likewise fall to the Crown.[19] Abandoned things are also *bona vacantia* and also pass to the Crown. 'As a result of the discarding of litter, every day Her Majesty becomes the owner of countless items such as cigarette ends, crisp packets and chewing gum.'[20] In *Mackenzie v Maclean*[21] hundreds of damaged cans of McEwen's Export and McEwen's Pale Ale were dumped in a skip, from which locals helped themselves. The case was a theft prosecution. The sheriff noted that the cans, on being abandoned in the skip, became Crown property. Whereas property that never has been owned, such as a wild animal, can be appropriated by anyone,[22] property that has been owned is not so available. Such property cannot become ownerless, and if there is no other owner it belongs to the Crown.

3.8   Lost property is not the same as abandoned property. An absent-minded professor who leaves a book on a bus does not abandon it. Loss does not terminate ownership. However, the standard view is that after 20 years of being out of possession, the right of ownership is cut off by the long negative prescription whereupon ownership passes to the Crown.[23]

3.9   The English expression 'treasure trove', though commonly used, has no technical meaning in Scotland. If, say, an ancient coin hoard is discovered, it belongs to the Crown, not by virtue of any special rule, but because of one of the doctrines already mentioned.[24] Thus it does not belong to the finder, nor to the owner of the land where it is found. In practice the Crown usually rewards the finder. The term 'treasure' is misleading. Items dug up from a prehistoric burial site belong to the Crown just as much if they are earthenware as if they are gold or silver.

3.10   Procedure for handling lost and abandoned property is contained in Pt VI of the Civic Government (Scotland) Act 1982.[25] Where property falls to the Crown, whether under the *bona vacantia* rule or the *ultimus haeres* rule, the Crown is represented by the Queen's and Lord Treasurer's Remembrancer.[26] (But there is an

---

[17] See **PARA 29.27** below.
[18] Only persons can have rights and duties. Persons are divided into natural persons (human beings) and juristic persons (such as companies).
[19] This is a common-law rule. For companies, it is also statutory: Companies Act 2006, s 1012.
[20] Scottish Law Commission, Report on Prescription and Title to Moveable Property (Scot Law Com No 228, 2012) para 5.2. In most countries, by contrast, abandoned moveable property becomes ownerless. The SLC report recommends that this should likewise be the rule in Scotland.
[21] 1981 SLT (Sh Ct) 40.
[22] By occupancy. See **PARA 9.2** below.
[23] See **PARA 6.21** below.
[24] *Lord Advocate v University of Aberdeen & Budge* 1963 SC 533.
[25] See Carey Miller with Irvine *Corporeal Moveables* para 2.08.
[26] See www.treasuretrovescotland.co.uk/ and also **PARA 29.27** below.

exception: wrecked ships and their cargo fall under the jurisdiction of the Receiver of Wrecks.[27])

ACQUISITION: ORIGINAL/DERIVATIVE

3.11   If Natalia owns land and transfers it to Oliver, he *acquires* ownership and she *loses* it. Loss and acquisition thus almost always go to together. There is an overarching distinction between: (a) derivative acquisition; and the less common (b) original acquisition. In the former the right is acquired from the previous owner by the voluntary act of the owner (or of someone authorised by law to act on behalf of the owner). For example, if Becca goes to a baker and buys a loaf, the right of ownership of the loaf passes from the baker to Becca: derivative acquisition. This is easy to understand: the right is handed over. Original acquisition is where the right of ownership is acquired by some legal process that gives the right of ownership to the beneficiary of that process, regardless of anyone's consent, other than that of the acquirer. There are some problems about where to draw the line between original and derivative acquisition, but a standard list of cases of original acquisition would be:

(i)   occupancy: when an ownerless object is taken into possession;[28]

(ii)   accession: when one object becomes part of another, as, for instance, when a car is painted, the paint becomes part of the car and so owned by the owner of the car;[29]

(iii)   specification: when an object is so altered that it loses its identity (e.g. barley into ale), the result being that ownership vests in the person who carries out the transformation;[30]

(iv)   positive prescription: whereby ownership is acquired by long possession.[31]

ACQUISITION: VOLUNTARY/INVOLUNTARY

3.12   In original acquisition, it is irrelevant whether the previous owner, if any,[32] consents: the acquisition happens anyway. In derivative acquisition, the consent of the previous owner is normally necessary: Becca's acquisition of the ownership of the loaf presupposes the baker's consent. In general, a person cannot lose ownership involuntarily. But nevertheless it can happen that derivative acquisition is involuntary – involuntary, that is, on the part of the person losing ownership. This is discussed in **CHAPTER 8** below.

---

[27]   Merchant Shipping Act 1995 Part IX.
[28]   See **PARA 9.2** below.
[29]   See **PARAS 9.4–9.18** below.
[30]   See **PARAS 9.20–9.22** below.
[31]   See **CHAPTER 6** below.
[32]   In the case of occupancy there is normally no previous owner.

EVIDENCE OF OWNERSHIP

3.13   This book is generally about the substantive rules of property law, not evidential issues. But in practice these can be important. How does a person who claims to be the owner of something establish that fact? There is no short answer. But, for corporeal moveables, an important evidential rule is that possession gives rise to a presumption of ownership.[33] Of course, it is not conclusive: if it were, every thief would be happy. But the burden of proof is thrown on to the person who, not being in possession, claims to be the owner. Thus, if goods are bought, whether from a shop or elsewhere, the fact that the seller possesses the thing raises a presumption of ownership. That is not wholly satisfactory, because the presumption is rebuttable, but it is all there is. Thus, actual proof of ownership is hardly possible. Even if it could be established that a person has possessed something for, say, 40 years, that is, strictly speaking, not enough because our law may not admit prescriptive acquisition of moveables.[34]

3.14   For land, the starting point is what the Land Register says. That is presumptive evidence of good title. Only in exceptional cases is it inaccurate, eg by saying that James is owner when in fact Ian is owner. Even if it is inaccurate, a third party can rely on it. For example, if James dispones to Kate, or grants some other right to her, she will normally be protected, assuming that she is in good faith.[35]

'The title deeds'

3.15   Non-lawyers often speak of 'having the title deeds' as being evidence of ownership, or even as being constitutive of ownership of land. To say that Donna owns land they might say that 'she has the title deeds'. This is not right: subject to certain minor ifs and buts, the physical title deeds matter little. If Donna owns the farm of Blackmains, she could burn her title deeds to keep warm, or as a protest against Capitalism, or could turn them into an avant-garde papier mâché statue of her favourite Beatle (Ringo), and the consequences would be slight. She would still own the farm, and if, for instance, she wished to sell it, she could still satisfy the buyer that she could do so. What matters is what is in the Land Register. To become the owner she will need to have received a deed – a disposition – from the previous owner, but after there has been registration the original physical deeds matter little.

LITERATURE

3.16   See generally Reid *Property* paras 530–535 and 547–553. See also Carey Miller with Irvine *Corporeal Moveables* paras 1.12–1.17.

---

[33]   See further **PARA 12.19** below.
[34]   See **PARA 6.21** below.
[35]   See **PARAS 7.73–7.74** below.

Chapter 4

Acquisition by voluntary transfer: the general principles

INTRODUCTION

4.1 Jill owns something. She contracts with Kate to sell it to her. Contractual obligations are created by agreement but, having been created, they still need to be performed. Kate's obligation is to pay. Jill's is to transfer. The right of ownership is in Jill's patrimony. The question is how to get it to Kate's. Although the mechanisms vary according to the type of property, there are certain basic ideas of general application which are covered in this chapter. **CHAPTER 5** considers each of the four categories: corporeal moveable property; incorporeal moveable property; corporeal heritable property; and incorporeal heritable property. This chapter is about transfer *inter vivos* (between living persons).[1] Transfer *mortis causa* (on account of death) is dealt with elsewhere.[2]

4.2 The distinction between the constitution, transfer and extinction of rights has been discussed already.[3] This chapter and the next focus on transfer, but also cover the constitution of new rights: on the whole, the rules for constitution are the same as for transfer. For example, the transfer of ownership of land happens by registration. The same is true (with minor exceptions) for the constitution of subordinate real rights in land.

SOME TERMINOLOGY

4.3 The words 'grant', 'granter' and 'grantee' are useful terms with a broad sense. For instance, the transferor of land is a 'disponer' and the transferee a 'disponee', and the transferor of incorporeal moveable property is a 'cedent' and the transferee the 'assignee' but the broad terms 'granter' and 'grantee' can also be used. They can also be used for cases where there is not a transfer at all but the creation of a subordinate right. For example, if an owner of land creates a standard security or a servitude over the land, the words 'granter' and 'grantee' are used.

4.4 A 'successor', or 'successor in title', is anyone who subsequently acquires a given right. So if Mary transfers her bicycle to Nigel and thereafter Nigel transfers it to Olivia, Nigel is Mary's successor, and Olivia is Nigel's, and both Nigel and

---

[1] The term *inter vivos* is used even where a juristic person such as a company is involved, even though a juristic person is not a living human.
[2] See **CHAPTER 26**.
[3] See **PARAS 1.28–1.30** above.

Olivia are Mary's successors. Successors are traditionally divided into 'singular' and 'universal'.[4] Nigel and Olivia are singular successors to Mary: they have simply acquired one particular right that she had – the right of ownership of the bicycle. Most successors are singular. A universal successor is someone who takes over the whole patrimony of someone else. An example would be an executor.[5] If X is the universal successor of Y, that means that X is bound by Y's obligations. But a singular successor is normally not so bound. Suppose that Mary was liable in delict to Larry for having knocked him down while riding too fast: that liability does not transmit to Nigel or Olivia. They are Mary's singular successors, not universal successors.

4.5   'Transfer' is self-explanatory: a right is transferred when it passes from one person's patrimony to another's. 'Alienate' and 'convey' also mean 'transfer'. Thus if Lorraine buys a cake from a baker, the baker could be said to transfer or convey or alienate the cake to her.[6]

4.6   In English law a distinction is sometimes drawn between 'transfer' and 'transmission', and this distinction can sometimes be found in legislation that applies to Scotland as well as elsewhere in the UK.[7] A 'transfer' happens by voluntary juridical act of the holder, eg by way of sale. The term 'transmission' covers involuntary cases such as the passing of property on death, or on insolvency.

CAPACITY AND CONSENT

4.7   Both sides must have capacity. Capacity belongs to the law of persons and so will not be discussed here,[8] except briefly. Everyone has *rights capacity* – the capacity to hold rights, including real rights. Thus, a baby could own land. But not all human beings have *transactional capacity*, such as the capacity to transfer or acquire ownership. This may sound a paradox, for if a baby cannot acquire land, how could he or she own it? The answer is given by the law of persons: human beings who lack transactional capacity can have another person act for them. A baby's parents have the power to enter into juridical acts on the infant's behalf. If an adult suffers from mental disorder, a guardian can act. So when a person is described as being an *incapax*, that refers to transactional incapacity, not to rights incapacity.

4.8   Organisations have capacity if they are juristic persons, such as registered companies. Otherwise they do not. Suppose that a university debating society buys a silver cup to be its annual prize. Unless the society is incorporated, which is most unlikely, it cannot buy the cup and cannot own it, for it lacks both transactional

---

4   See, further, Reid *Property* para 598.
5   See **PARAS 26.44–26.45** below.
6   Usually 'convey' is used in connection with heritable property.
7   A random example: the Merchant Shipping (Registration of Ships) Regulations 1993 reg 1 speaks of 'the registration of a transfer *or transmission* of a ship'.
8   See, further, Gloag and Henderson *The Law of Scotland* ch 43.

capacity and rights capacity. What happens in the eyes of the law is that the members buy the cup, and own it, jointly.[9]

4.9   A juristic person's capacity may be limited: this depends on the applicable legislation and on the organisation's own constitution. Most, but not all, juristic persons have the capacity to own property. When lawyers deal with organisations, they check capacity.

4.10   As well as capacity, there must be mutual consent. The principle is the same here as for the formation of contract. No consent, no contract and, in the same way, no consent, no transfer. The transferor must have the *animus transferendi dominii* (the intention of transferring ownership) and the transferee must have the *animus acquirendi*[10] *dominii* (the intention of acquiring ownership). The consent can be through a representative, such as an agent appointed by the person in question, or through anyone else empowered to act for that person, such as, say, the guardian of an *incapax*, or a judicial factor, and so on.

TRANSFERABILITY

4.11   Private law rights are generally transferable. There are some exceptions. Whether a liferent is transferable has been debated but the better view is that it is not.[11] A servitude cannot be transferred by itself, though it can be transferred as a pertinent of the land that it benefits, and the same is true of real burdens, other than personal real burdens.[12] Some leases are transferable without the landlord's consent, but others are not.[13] Contractual rights are usually transferable.[14]

4.12   Non-transferability is not the same as a duty not to transfer. Jack owns the Old Manse and contracts to sell it to Jill. The day after the contract, Jess makes him a better offer and he transfers the property to her. The transfer to Jess was valid, and it was valid because the Jack/Jill agreement had not made the property non-transferable. Jill can claim damages from Jack. If Jess knew of the prior contract, her title may be voidable.[15] But the fact remains: the property was *capable* of being transferred by Jack to Jess – however wrongfully. Likewise, if an owner is interdicted from transfer, that does not make the property in question non-transferable. Nor does an inhibition.[16]

4.13   The fact that something is encumbered by a subordinate real right does not affect transferability. The transfer leaves the subordinate real right intact and

---

9   See **PARAS 10.17–10.18** below.
10   This word can also be spelled '*adquirendi*'.
11   See **PARA 22.12** below.
12   See **PARA 15.12** below.
13   See **PARAS 20.33–20.34** below.
14   See **PARA 5.38** below.
15   See **PARAS 4.48–4.50** below.
16   See **PARA 5.6** below.

unaffected. If Bashful owns land and grants a lease to Doc, and later transfers the land to Dopey, the transfer is valid and the lease is unaffected. The same would be true if one substituted 'standard security' for 'lease'.

THE SPECIFICITY PRINCIPLE

4.14   Only what can be identified can be transferred. It is a common law principle, though there is also a statutory statement of it for the sale of goods.[17] The principle does not apply to contractual obligations. Jack can contract to sell 1,000 tonnes of mild steel to Jill. That is a valid contract even if it is not possible to point to any particular steel to which the contract relates. Indeed, the contract would be valid even if at the moment of the contract Jack does not have any steel at all. But Jill cannot acquire a real right unless it is possible to point to the steel in question. The principle is called the *specificity principle*. (It would be tempting to rename it the pointability principle, but that would make sense only for corporeals. The principle also applies to incorporeals.)

4.15   As far as land is concerned, the common law interpretation of the principle was fairly relaxed. Thus, a disposition of 'all and whole[18] the farm of Nether Auchnashuggle, Fife' was valid, assuming that one could go there and, with the assistance of local knowledge, walk the boundaries. In the modern system of land registration, the specificity principle is applied more strictly: it requires, subject only to minor exceptions, that the land's boundaries be laid out in the cadastral map.[19]

4.16   Certain qualifications to the specificity principle exist. (Whether these qualifications are true exceptions is arguable.) One is the landlord's hypothec.[20] Another may be the floating charge,[21] though there the charge becomes a real right only at the time when specification is possible, at the time of attachment. Another is the Sale of Goods Act 1979 (SOGA 1979), s 20A which says that if Edward purports to transfer to Jane 5,000 tonnes of oil he has in a tanker containing 50,000 tonnes, then that operates as a transfer of a 10% *pro indiviso* share of the whole 50,000 tonnes.[22]

CONTRACT AND CONVEYANCE

4.17   An obligation to transfer is not the same as a transfer, any more than an obligation to pay is the same as a payment. Oliver owns a house. He sells it to Betty.

---

[17]   SOGA 1979, s 16.
[18]   The time-honoured words used to start a description of land.
[19]   See **CHAPTER 7**. This issue was clarified in *PMP Plus v Keeper of the Registers of Scotland* 2009 SLT (Lands Tr) 2 and *Lundin Homes Ltd v Keeper of the Registers of Scotland* 2013 SLT (Lands Tr) 73.
[20]   See **PARA 21.65** below.
[21]   See **PARAS 21.37–21.40** below.
[22]   Payment by Jill is needed. See **PARAS 5.28–5.30** below.

The sale is a contract. A contract results in mutual obligations. Those obligations have to be performed. The contract binds Betty to pay. It binds Oliver to transfer possession and ownership. Thus, the sale contract creates obligations to perform: it is not itself the performance of those obligations. Betty's obligation to pay is performed by payment. Oliver's obligation to give possession is performed by moving out and handing over the keys. His obligation to transfer ownership is performed by delivering to her a paper (or digital) deed of transfer, known as a disposition, which she then registers in the Land Register.[23] The contract of sale is thus the reason for, or 'cause', of the transfer. There can be other reasons for transfer, such as gift (donation) but, regardless of the reason, the transfer takes the same form. Thus, if Betty later decides to give the house to her daughter Deirdre, a disposition will again be used. The verb 'sell' and the noun 'sale' are often used to mean the whole process of contract and transfer. If someone says 'I have bought a bicycle' both the contract and the transfer can be inferred. But when the transaction is analysed, it is seen that sale is not a transfer.[24] Sale is a contract,[25] and thus a reason for a transfer, not itself a transfer. Contract and conveyance are separate juridical acts. This separation of contract and conveyance is an important aspect of property law.

4.18   Not only is conveyance *separate* from contract, but its validity does not *depend* on the contract either. As Stair wrote (II.3.14):

> 'We [in Scotland] follow not that subtility of annulling deeds, because they are *sine causa* … and therefore narratives expressing the cause of the disposition, are never inquired into, because, though there were no cause, the disposition is good.'

The word cause (*causa*) means the reason for the deed, such as a contract of sale. Stair is saying that the validity of the act of transfer (or constitution, or extinction) does not depend on its having a valid (or, indeed, any) cause. The contract could be void, or voidable and then avoided, and the grantee's title will still be valid. (Though there may then be an obligation on the grantee to undo the transaction, eg by reconveyance. But 'transfer should not have been made, and so should be reversed' is not the same as 'transfer should not have been made, and so is deemed never to have happened.' This contract/conveyance independence is called the principle of 'abstraction'.[26] There are, however, some situations in which both contract and conveyance are void for the same reason, such as where someone who is incapax because of dementia, enters a contract and then grants a disposition. Both are void.

---

[23]   This has long been the law. It is currently stated in LR(S)A 2012, s 50.
[24]   An odd usage is to be found in the Sale of Goods Act 1979 with its three terms, 'contract of sale', 'sale' and 'agreement to sell'. The middle term means simultaneous contract and transfer.
[25]   SOGA 1979, eg in its definition of 'sale', departs somewhat from general property law. See **PARA 5.16** below.
[26]   In some countries, such as France and the Netherlands, the conveyance is dependent on the validity of the contract. This is the 'causal' system of transfer. See, eg, L P W van Vliet, *Transfer of movables in German, French, English and Dutch law* (2000) ch 7.

THE PUBLICITY PRINCIPLE: THE NEED FOR AN EXTERNAL ACT

4.19   The act of transfer is not only separate from the obligation to transfer but is carried out differently. Contract requires only mutual consent. For transfer, mutual consent is necessary, but is not sufficient.[27] An external or overt act is needed. For example, for land, the external act is a registered deed, and for corporeal moveables it is delivery. In this context the following passage from the *Codex* is often quoted: *traditionibus, non nudis pactis, dominia rerum, transferuntur* – ownership is transferred not by mere agreement but by delivery.[28] In modern law registration is sometimes an alternative to delivery, but the underlying idea – that there must be an external act – remains generally valid. Moreover, it applies not only to acts of *transfer* but also to acts of *constitution*, such as, say, the grant of a standard security.

4.20   The underlying justification for the requirement of an external act is the *publicity principle*: acts that can affect third parties should be made public, so that third parties can know of them. It is not limited to property law but is particularly important in that area.[29] It is only a broad principle, and not a firm rule. It applies especially to real rights in land – hence the Land Register. It is rather weaker for real rights in moveables[30] and for intellectual property rights. An illustration of the principle: a formal agreement said: 'The home is a property purchased in the sole name of the first party for convenience. The parties agree that the home shall be owned by the parties in equal shares.'[31] Since the property was 'in the sole name' of one party, that meant that he was the sole owner, and so it was impossible for the property to be owned by both, unless and until there was a disposition registered in the Land Register. The agreement created valid personal rights (relative rights, between the parties), but not real rights (absolute rights, good against 'the world' – *erga omnes*). In another case Ms Spence owned a property, and she signed an agreement with Mr Wheeldon, saying that he 'now assumes full legal title to Powfoot Hall on 20/12/1993 and becomes owner of said property.' But there was no disposition. Result? Ms Spence remained sole owner. His rights under the document were personal not real.[32]

4.21   Some terminology: when the external act happens (registration, or intimation, or delivery) it is said that the transferee 'completes title', and that immediately before doing so has an 'uncompleted title'. The phrase is a standard one, but potentially misleading, for it suggests that the transferee has a sort of half-real right before title is completed.

---

[27]   Except under SOGA 1979. See **para 5.22** below.
[28]   This is the standard form of the maxim, though in fact the wording in the *Codex* is slightly different: *traditionibus ... dominia rerum non nudis pactis transferuntur*. (C. 2, 3, 20.)
[29]   See also **para 23.64** below.
[30]   The transfer of corporeal moveables does not need delivery if the *causa* is sale, but still needs it in other cases such as donation. See **paras 5.16–5.29** below.
[31]   *Johnston's Tr v Baird* [2012] CSOH 117.
[32]   *Wheeldon's Exr v Spence's Exr* [2014] CSOH 69.

TRANSFER IS INSTANTANEOUS

4.22   If Julie sells her house to Christopher, various things will happen, notably the making of the contract of sale, the handing over of the keys to Christopher, the handing over of the disposition to him, its registration in the Land Register, and the payment of the price to Julie. Before all these have happened, she is the owner, and after they have all happened, he is the owner. While they are happening, what is the position? Are they both owners, one being the owner for certain purposes or in certain respects, and the other the owner for other purposes or respects? Some legal systems – that in England, for example – answer that question in the affirmative. Scots law answers it in the negative. Ownership passes not like honey oozing from a spoon on to a slice of bread, but like a bullet fired from a gun. Actually, even that image is insufficient, for a measurable interval elapses between the moment of leaving the barrel and the moment of reaching the target. Transfer of a right is instantaneous. One instant the right is in Julie's patrimony and the next it is in Christopher's. One moment the right is wholly and solely hers and the next it is wholly and solely his. Scots property law is *unititular.*[33] It is not possible for a grant or transfer of a right to occur 'as between the parties' only. 'A completed real right, good in a question between granter and grantee, and bad against all the rest of the world, is an absolute legal contradiction in terms.'[34]

THE *SHARP v THOMSON* SAGA

Facts

4.23   In 1989, the Thomsons (brother and sister) contracted to buy a new flat in Aberdeen from Albyn Construction Ltd. Thus began the saga of *Sharp v Thomson.*[35] No case in Scots property law has ever generated such a volume of academic debate.[36] Inevitably, the account given here can only scratch the surface.

4.24   The Thomsons paid the price on 12 June 1989 and were given the keys. Normal conveyancing practice is for the disposition to be handed over at the same time and registered immediately. That did not happen. The disposition was not handed over until 9 August 1990. It was registered[37] on 21 August 1990. But on 10 August Albyn Construction Ltd went into receivership. A receivership is a means

---

[33]   Reid *Property* para 603; *Sharp v Thomson* 1995 SC 455 at 469 per Lord President Hope, citing with approval Professor Reid's analysis.

[34]   *Young v Leith* (1847) 9 D 932 at 945, *per* Lord Fullerton, giving the opinion of the majority of the court.)

[35]   1994 SC 503, aff'd 1995 SC 455, rev'd 1997 SC (HL) 66.

[36]   Especially if one takes it, as one must, with its successor case, *Burnett's Tr v Grainger* 2004 SC (HL) 19. The literature is listed in Appendix B of Scottish Law Commission, Report on *Sharp v Thomson* (Scot Law Com No 208, 2007).

[37]   In the Sasine Register, because at that time the Land Register had not yet been extended to Aberdeenshire. But this point is of no significance for the dispute.

of enforcing a floating charge, a security right that extends over the whole property of the debtor company.[38] So long as the company in question remains solvent, the floating charge is not a real right. But when the charge *attaches,* for example by receivership, it becomes a real right. So the holder of the floating charge (Bank of Scotland) obtained a real right (security) before the Thomsons acquired their real right (ownership). That did not mean that the Thomsons did not become owners. The bank's real right was only a subordinate real right. But the Thomsons apparently acquired ownership subject to that right, so that their ownership was effectively worthless, because the receiver could sell the property from under their feet, applying the proceeds of sale for the benefit of the Bank of Scotland.

The approach of the courts

4.25   The matter was interpreted in the above way by both the Outer House[39] and the Inner House.[40] This was not as disastrous for the Thomsons as might at first appear. A conveyancer who hands over the price except in exchange for a deed is *prima facie* liable in negligence if loss results. But on a further appeal to the House of Lords the decision of the Court of Session was reversed. The grounds are unclear. One theory is that the House of Lords considered that at some stage in a transfer (perhaps the delivery of the disposition) the transferee acquires something called a 'beneficial interest'. This term is commonly used to describe the right of a beneficiary in a trust:[41] what, if anything, it could mean outside the context of trust law was unclear. Perhaps it meant that half way through the transaction ownership is somehow split, with one sort of ownership still held by the seller and another by the buyer – in short, Scots property law was not unititular. Another interpretation was that the House of Lords was not in fact saying anything much about property law, but was merely interpreting the legislation about floating charges.

Burnett's Tr v Grainger

4.26   The transaction in *Sharp v Thomson* took place in 1989–90. In 1990–91 another unhappy transaction was taking place, in Peterculter: *Burnett's Tr v Grainger.*[42] Mr and Mrs Grainger entered into a contract to buy a house from Ms Burnett. In November 1990 the buyers paid the price and were given the keys and the disposition. But their solicitors did not register the disposition. On 29 May 1991 Ms Burnett was sequestrated. Sequestration is, among other things, a conveyance to the trustee of the bankrupt's heritable property. On 10 December 1991 Ms Burnett's

---

[38]   For floating charges, see **PARAS 21.37–21.40** below.
[39]   1994 SC 503.
[40]   1995 SC 455.
[41]   See **PARAS 2.24–2.26** above.
[42]   2002 SC 580, aff'd 2004 SC (HL) 19.

trustee was registered as owner of the house. When, the following month, the Graingers' solicitors finally sought registration, it was too late. Though Ms Burnett had been the owner when she delivered the disposition to the Graingers, by the time they sought registration Ms Burnett was no longer the owner and so the deed was now *a non domino*. The Graingers had lost the 'race to the register' – though, of course, they had a damages claim against their solicitors.

4.27 But the decision of the House of Lords in *Sharp v Thomson* might, on a broad interpretation, mean that the settled authorities were no longer applicable. The Graingers argued that on delivery of the disposition they had acquired the 'beneficial interest' in the property, so that a sort of ownership had already passed to them. This argument succeeded before the Sheriff Principal. On appeal the Inner House disagreed, arguing that *Sharp v Thomson* lacked a clear *ratio* and that it should be narrowly construed so as to make it fit in, as far as possible, with property law.[43] The case was appealed to the House of Lords, which upheld the decision. The trustee had won.[44]

4.28 The House of Lords did not overrule *Sharp v Thomson*, but that case must now be understood as having a narrow *ratio*, limited to the law of floating charges. The *ratio* is that property can be freed from the ambit of a floating charge even before it ceases to belong to the debtor company. When and how that happens is unclear, but as far as heritable property is concerned it is probably the time when the disposition is delivered. The 'unititularity' of property law is thus confirmed. In addition, there is no such thing as 'beneficial interest', except in the context of trust law.[45] As Lord Hodge has said:

> 'The disponee who has not registered his title enjoys no real right in the subjects. Scots law does not recognise a right which lies between a real right and a personal right ... There is no such thing as a "quasi-real right".'[46]

---

[43] 2002 SC 580. At this point Mr Grainger gave an interview to *The Scotsman* (17 May 2002):

> 'We are totally exasperated by the whole thing. The law is very strange. We paid the money in 1990, we have cleared the mortgage, we have spent another £13,000 over the years to maintain the property – yet we have nothing. Apparently, this is quite an unusual case and it is being used for teaching in law faculties. But that is little consolation.'

[44] The Graingers received damages from their solicitors.
[45] And tax law. Tax law tends to be conceptualised in English terms.
[46] *3052775 Nova Scotia Ltd v Henderson* [2006] CSOH 147 at para 11.

PAYMENT AND TRANSFER: THE STRUCTURE OF INSOLVENCY RISK

4.29   In sale, a buyer who pays before acquiring title runs the risk of the seller's insolvency – as in *Sharp v Thomson* and *Burnett's Tr*.[47] Conversely, a seller who transfers title before receiving the price runs the risk of the buyer's insolvency. Three possibilities exist.

(1) Ownership passes before payment. Here, the seller is at risk. This is often the position in the sale of goods, and accordingly an important theme in the property side of sale of goods has been buyer insolvency.

(2) Payment is made before ownership passes. Here, the buyer is at risk. This is the normal position in the sale of heritable property. Hence such cases as *Sharp v Thomson* and *Burnett's Tr*. If proper conveyancing practice is adopted, the buyer does not pay except in exchange for a disposition, but even so there may be a short period of risk, because ownership does not pass when the disposition is delivered but when it is registered.[48] (This type of case can also happen in the sale of goods.) Until LR(S)A 2012, this 'gap risk' was covered by a 'letter of obligation' granted by the seller's law firm. This, however, did not help in *Sharp v Thomson* or *Burnett's Tr v Grainger*, because such a letter is conditional on the buyer completing title within fourteen days, which did not happen in those cases.[49] Now gap risk is covered by advance notices.[50]

(3) Simultaneity: ownership passes to the buyer and payment is made by the seller at the same time. Here, neither party is at risk. That would be the ideal, but in practice it is hard to achieve.

4.30   Where there is no simultaneity, the party at risk can sometimes be protected by some sort of priority right. For example, in the sale of goods an unpaid seller may be protected by a lien or by retention of title.[51] One interpretation of *Sharp v Thomson* was that the House of Lords was creating a priority right for a buyer who has paid. Though that view of *Sharp v Thomson* cannot now be adhered to, conveyancers have developed a mechanism which, if it works, has much the same effect: the trust clause. This is a provision where the seller, after delivery of the disposition, is deemed to hold the property in trust for the buyer.[52] A new type of priority right has been introduced by LR(S)A 2012, namely the advance notice.[53]

4.31   From the seller's point of view, the greatest security is to be had by retaining ownership until payment: a 'suspensive condition'. In the sale of goods it is

---

[47]   The rule is the same for diligence against the seller. The classic illustration is *Mitchells v Fergusson* (1781) Mor 10296 on which see G L Gretton 'Equitable Ownership in Scots Law?' (2001) 5 *Edin LR* 73.

[48]   With the advent of electronic deeds, this can sometimes be done the same day.

[49]   For letters of obligation, see **PARA 5.14** below.

[50]   See **CHAPTER 7** below.

[51]   See **PARAS 5.25–5.27** below.

[52]   See **PARA 22.14** below.

[53]   See **PARAS 7.55–7.64** below.

common to do that.[54] It may be wondered whether the same effect can be achieved by a 'resolutive condition': that if the buyer fails to pay, the transfer will be rescinded so that ownership reverts to the seller. The parties can indeed so agree. But the agreement works only contractually. As Bell says, 'an express paction, made by the seller when delivering property, that the property shall be reinstated in him if the price be not paid … is … ineffectual against the buyer's creditors'.[55] The seller cannot become owner again without a re-transfer of ownership. Unless and until the buyer does that, the property still belongs to the buyer, and so attachable by the buyer's creditors. Subject to certain qualifications, ownership cannot be subject to a resolutive condition having real effect.

WARRANDICE

4.32   'Warrandice'[56] means warranty or guarantee. In a sale, warrandice by the seller is presumed. It is also often expressly stated. There can be warrandice of the physical quality of what is sold, but from a property law standpoint the main concern is with warrandice as a guarantee of good title. In the sale of goods, warrandice is implied by SOGA 1979, s 12. In other sales it is a matter of common law.[57]

VOID, VOIDABLE AND ABSOLUTELY GOOD

General

4.33   Most titles are absolutely good. (The acquisition of an absolutely good title has already been explained in general terms, and further details are given in **CHAPTER 5**.[58]) Sometimes a title may be void. A third possibility is that it is voidable. A voidable title is one that exists but is precarious because it may be made void. These possibilities can be set out in a chart:

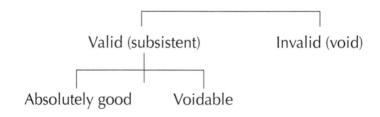

---

54   See **PARAS 5.26–5.27** below.
55   Bell *Commentaries* I, 260.
56   Some pronounce the last syllable to rhyme with 'miss', others to rhyme with 'mice'. Dictionaries prefer the former.
57   See **PARAS 5.9–5.13, 5.33** and **5.49** below.
58   See **CHAPTER 5** below.

Void titles: why?

4.34   A void title happens either

  (a) because the granter did not have the right in the first place, so that the granter's title was itself void, or

  (b) though the granter did have the right, there has been some fatal defect in the process of grant, making the juridical act of transfer void, and, as a result, the grantee's title is void[59]

An example of (b) would be if Chris owns a bicycle and Danielle forces him to hand it over at gunpoint. The transfer has been brought about by 'force and fear' and so is void. It would be the same if Chris gives it to her when he is insane. What is lacking is Chris's consent, the *animus transferendi dominii*. Or there might be consent, but some other fatal defect in the transfer process, such as, in the case of land, a failure to register. For examples of (a), one just has to think of examples of (b) and then add a second transfer. Thus, if Danielle transfers to Elle, Elle's title will be void.

Voidable titles: why?

4.35   A voidable title arises when someone validly acquires property, but in a way that is somehow contrary to the rights of another person. That other person then has the option of avoiding the title. For example, Oliver owns land. Fay fraudulently induces him to dispone to her. The effect of fraud is less radical than the effect of, say, force and fear: Oliver's consent is considered as being (unlike Chris's) a true consent, albeit a revocable one.[60] So Fay is now owner. But her title is voidable. That is to say, Oliver has the option to avoid it, thereby re-acquiring the property. It is only an option, and for one reason or another voidable titles are often never avoided. There are numerous grounds of voidability: the following are some examples. The first is fraud. The second is inhibition. This is discussed later,[61] but the basic idea is this: Martin is owner and Norah his creditor. She inhibits him, with the result that if he dispones any heritable property thereafter, the grantee's title will be voidable, unless she is paid what she is owed. Third, there are grants that prejudice the interests of the granter's creditors. This area of law (the *actio pauliana*) is divided into the law of gratuitous alienations[62] and the law of unfair preferences.[63] A fourth case is transfers in breach of a contractual obligation. This is called the 'offside goals' rule.[64] Finally,

---

[59]   Underlying the theory of absolutely good, void and voidable titles is the theory of absolutely good, void and voidable juridical acts.

[60]   A distinction is sometimes drawn between 'vices of consent' which make the consent (and hence the transfer) voidable, and 'real vices' which make the consent (and hence the transfer) void.

[61]   See **PARAS 5.6–5.7** below.

[62]   It is partly common law and partly statutory: Bankruptcy (Scotland) Act 2016, s 98; Insolvency Act 1986, s 242.

[63]   Also partly common law and partly statutory: Bankruptcy (Scotland) Act 2016, s 99; Insolvency Act 1986, s 242.

[64]   See **PARAS 4.48–4.50** below.

there is transfer by a person whose title is already voidable, i.e. X transfers to Y, and Y obtains a voidable title for some reason (e.g. fraud), and Y then transfers to Z. Z *may* get a voidable title.[65]

Voidable titles and voidable contracts

4.36   Voidable titles should not be confused with voidable contracts. For example, suppose that Carla, creditor of Doris, inhibits her. Doris thereafter contracts to sell her land to Egbert. The contract is then carried out by a disposition, which Egbert registers. Egbert is now owner. His title is voidable. But the Doris/Egbert contract is not voidable. Take another case. Fraser owns land. Gordon persuades him to swap it for shares in a non-existent South American mining company. The swap is embodied in a contract, and the contract is then implemented by a disposition to Gordon. Gordon is now owner. Both the contract and the title are voidable. But avoiding the contract will of itself not return the property to Fraser. This distinction between avoidance of contract and avoidance of title is often misunderstood.[66] The validity of a title does not depend on the validity of the contract on which that title is based.[67] The Carla/Doris case was one where the conveyance was voidable but not the contract. The Fraser/Gordon case was one where both contract and conveyance were voidable. Just to complete the picture, a contract can be voidable but not the conveyance, though that seldom happens. Harry, elderly and unworldly, owns some land worth £300,000. Ian, a con-man, produces a fake valuation saying it is worth £200,000. Ian offers Harry £250,000 and Harry accepts, on 30 April. During May an economic crisis develops, and property values plunge. At the end of May, when the land is worth £200,000, Harry discovers the fraud. Obviously, he will not exercise his option to avoid the contract. On settlement day, say 15 June, he is delighted to receive £250,000. The disposition he hands over in exchange is not voidable.

Reduction and other remedies

4.37   If a title is voidable, what remedies are available? In the first place, if there has been a voidable transfer from X to Y, X can demand that Y re-transfer ownership.[68] In the second place, given that a voidable contract can be avoided by notice, is notice enough to avoid a voidable title? The general answer is 'no', but a possible exception exists in the case of corporeal moveables. Alfred fraudulently induces Bronwen to sell him her car. She delivers the car to him. She can rescind the

---

[65]   See **PARA 4.41** below.
[66]   Eg *MacLeod v Kerr* 1965 SC 253. The case turned on the avoidance of the contract, when in fact the only relevant issue was avoidance of title. See further Reid *Property* paras 609 and 610.
[67]   This is the principle of abstraction: see **PARA 4.18** above.
[68]   As in *Short's Tr v Chung (No 2)* 1999 SC 471. However, this remedy is not available to an inhibitor. Inhibition is enforced by reduction.

contract simply by notification. But does ownership automatically pass back to her? The law is uncertain and cannot be discussed in detail here. The predominant view, with which we would agree, seems to be that it does not.[69] This follows from the fact that transfer is abstract. What Bronwen can do, having rescinded the contract, is demand a re-transfer. That needs re-delivery.[70] In the third place, there is reduction. This is available only if there is a deed of transfer to be reduced, so it is not available in sale of goods. In the case of a Land Register title, the decree must be registered, for the defender loses ownership (or other right in question) only when the decree of reduction is registered.[71]

4.38   Reduction of a voidable title is of two types.[72] The first is 'catholic' reduction, in which the title is simply avoided. For example, if there is a transfer of ownership from X to Y and Y's title is avoided, X becomes owner again. Or if X grants a servitude to Z and the servitude is avoided, it disappears and X's ownership is now unencumbered. The other is reduction *ad hunc effectum* which means that the title is avoided only in relation to the person who has avoided it but remains valid in relation to everyone else. That is to say, it is not absolutely invalid but only relatively invalid – void relative to the avoider. Reduction based on an inhibition is an example. Whether there are other examples is unclear. One theory[73] is that if avoidance is by one of the parties then its effect is catholic, while if it is by a third party it is *ad hunc effectum*.

TRANSFER: NATURE OF GRANTER'S TITLE

4.39   In the following paragraphs, the effect on the transferee will be considered of the three types of title the transferor may have: absolutely good, or voidable, or void. In each case it is assumed that the act of transfer itself has been validly done. Thus it is assumed, for example, that the parties are sane, that neither has acted under compulsion, and so on.

[69]   In *MacLeod v Kerr* 1965 SC 253 it seems to have been assumed that rescission of the contract would suffice to transfer ownership back to the seller. But the case is weak authority for that view, since it was about rescission of the contract.

[70]   As will be seen in **CHAPTER 5**, ownership of corporeal moveables can pass without delivery only in a sale. But the transfer back to Bronwen is not a sale.

[71]   LR(S)A 2012 s 54, inserting new s 46A into the Conveyancing (Scotland) Act 1924. The rules about giving effect to a decree of reduction under LR(S)A 1979 were complex and obscure.

[72]   Confusingly, 'reduction' is also used for actions to declare void titles to be void. Such reductions are really declarators. They do not affect or change anyone's rights, but merely prove what is already the legal position. By contrast, the reduction of a voidable title goes beyond being declaratory: it leads to a change in the actual property rights of those concerned. The two types may be called declaratory reduction and operative reduction.

[73]   Professor Gretton's.

Transfer where granter's title absolutely good

4.40   If the granter's title is absolutely good then the grantee's right will likewise be absolutely good, at least in the normal case. The main exception is where the transfer breaches the right of a third party, such as where there is an inhibition[74] or where the offside goals rule applies.[75]

Transfer where granter's title voidable

4.41   First of all, if a title is voidable and has in fact been avoided, then it has become a void title.[76] Here we are considering a voidable title that has not, or not yet, been avoided, and perhaps never will be. The effect of voidability on the grantee's title depends on various factors.

(1) If the grantee knew that the granter's title was voidable (unusual in practice) then the grantee's title is also voidable.

(2) If the grant was gratuitous, then the grantee's title is also voidable, regardless of whether the grantee knew of the voidability of the granter's title. For example: Darius owns a Mercedes. When insolvent he gives it to Edwina. Under the Bankruptcy (Scotland) Act 2016, s 98 the transfer is voidable. Soon afterwards, Edwina gives the car to her daughter, Florence. Florence is now owner. Her title is voidable even though she had not known that her mother's title was voidable.

(3) In other cases, in practice the majority, the grantee's title is absolutely good.[77] For sales of corporeal moveables there is a statutory statement of the rule: 'When the seller of goods has a voidable title to them, but his title has not been avoided at the time of the sale, the buyer acquires a good title to the goods, provided he buys them in good faith and without notice of the seller's defect of title.'[78]

Timing is important: if there is a voidable transfer by X to Y, and Y later transfers to Z, a good-faith buyer, then Z is safe if but only if Y's title had not been avoided before the Y/Z transfer. By contrast, if the X/Y transfer had been void, Z's title would be void, regardless of timing.[79]

---

[74]   See **PARA 5.6** below.
[75]   See **PARAS 4.48–4.50** below.
[76]   See **PARA 4.38** above.
[77]   Assuming, of course, that no other grounds exist for challenging the transaction, e.g. lack of capacity etc.
[78]   SOGA 1979, s 23. See **PARA 5.37** below.
[79]   This explains the difference of result between *Morrisson v Robertson* 1908 SC 332, where the X/Y transfer was void, and *MacLeod v Kerr* 1965 SC 253, where it was only voidable, and not yet avoided.

Transfer where granter's title void: the *nemo plus* principle

4.42   If the granter's title is void, the grantee's title is normally void: *nemo plus juris ad alium transferre potest quam ipse haberet*: nobody can transfer a better right than they have in the first place.[80] (There is a shorter maxim with the same substance: *nemo dat quod non habet*.) It is among the most important principles of property law. If Xerxes steals something from Yvonne, and then sells it to Zelda, ownership stays with Yvonne, even if Zelda acted in good faith. Xerxes cannot transfer a right he does not have. The principle applies to all types of right, not just ownership. Suppose that Fraser owes £10,000 to Gregory Ltd, a company wholly owned by Gregory. The right to be paid money is transferable.[81] Gregory transfers it to Henrietta. The transfer is void. The right was not Gregory's, so he could not transfer it. The *nemo plus* principle is a common law one, but there are also a couple of statutory restatements of it.[82]

4.43   The next example is perhaps less obvious. Charles owns some land. On Monday he delivers to Doris a deed granting her a liferent of the land. On Tuesday he delivers to Euan a disposition of the land. On Wednesday Euan registers in the Land Register. On Thursday Doris applies for registration. Her application will be rejected. Why? When the deed was delivered to her, the granter, Charles, was the owner. But, real rights in land arise not when the deed is delivered but on registration.[83] At that moment Charles was not the owner: Euan was. The deed to Doris was thus *a non domino* – from a non-owner. *Nemo plus* again. Euan's title is, from Doris's point of view, a 'mid-impediment', ie an intervening event which prevents something from having its anticipated effect. (This example, like many in property law, raises questions about contract, delict, fraud and so on. Those questions are important, but they are not property law questions.) The result is as stated regardless of whether Euan was in good or bad faith, though if he was in bad faith his title, while not void, might be voidable, under the offside goals rule.[84]

4.44   There are exceptions to the *nemo plus* principle: most of them are mentioned in the relevant places in this book.[85] But *nemo plus* is the default rule.

---

[80]   D 50, 17, 54. The words are Ulpian's, and it is not wholly impossible that he wrote them here. For his visit to Scotland, see T Honoré *Ulpian* (2nd edn, 2002) 21–22. Professor Paisley has pointed out to us that Ulpian was not the only Roman jurist to visit: Papinian did so too (Cassius Dio, *Historia Romana* 77:14). Why are there no Ulpian and Papinian tartans?
[81]   By assignation. See **PARAS 5.38–5.51** below.
[82]   SOGA 1979, s 29(1); LR(S)A 2012 s 49(4).
[83]   The main exception is for leases of 20 years or less.
[84]   See the offside goals rule, below **PARAS 4.48–4.51**.
[85]   For the exceptions in SOGA 1979, see **PARAS 5.34–5.36** below. The modern land registration system does not fully adhere to the *nemo plus* principle: see **PARA 7.74** below. For deeds by unregistered holders, see **PARAS 4.53–4.54** below.

PRIOR TEMPORE, POTIOR JURE

4.45   *Prior tempore, potior jure*[86] means 'earlier by time, stronger by right'. The principle is closely allied with the *nemo plus* principle,[87] and indeed they may be viewed as two expressions of a single idea. Euan was earlier than Doris in obtaining his real right, and so his real right trumped hers. The expression *prior tempore, potior jure* is mainly applied to security rights. Suppose that Julius borrows £1m from Keira and £500,000 from Loretta. He owns Bluemains and he grants to each of his two creditors a standard security. He becomes bankrupt and the land is sold by his trustee in sequestration for £1,100,000. What happens to this money? The first question is whether an owner can grant two security rights, or whether the second would simply be void – as the second right was void in the case involving Doris and Euan above. The answer is that two or more securities can co-exist. That being so, one must ascertain which of the two became a real right first. That in turn depends on the order of registration. Suppose that Loretta's was registered first. In that case she would be paid £500,000 and Keira would take the balance of £600,000. Had it been the other way round, Keira would have been paid £1m and Loretta £100,000. *Prior tempore, potior jure.* Keira's security 'ranks' before Loretta's.[88]

TO WHAT IS THE GRANTEE'S RIGHT SUBJECT?

4.46   When a grantee acquires a real right, it is subject to the existing real rights of third parties. That is the principle discussed above, under the headings of *nemo plus* and *prior tempore*. So someone who acquires ownership does so subject to all existing subordinate real rights, whether he or she knows of their existence or not. (Because of the publicity principle, their existence should normally be readily discoverable. That is the point of the publicity principle.) The personal rights of third parties against the granter do not normally affect the grantee. This fact is one of the key facts of property law. Personal rights are enforceable against a given person. They are not normally enforceable against other persons.

4.47   This principle – that the acquirer of a real right is unaffected by personal rights held against the granter – has certain exceptions. One is that if the granter's title is voidable (and voidability is a manifestation of a personal right held by the person entitled to avoid) then the grantee's title is also voidable, unless (as is usually the case) the grantee was unaware of the third party's right and also acted onerously.[89] Another exception comes from trust law. The common law rule was that if (i) trustees transfer trust property in breach of trust; and (ii) the transferee knows of the breach of trust or acquires gratuitously, then the transferee takes subject to the rights of the beneficiaries. The rule was modified by the Trusts (Scotland) Act 1961,

---

[86]   Or, more fully, *qui prior est tempore potior est jure*.
[87]   See **PARA 4.42** above.
[88]   See **PARAS 21.22–21.23** below.
[89]   See **PARA 4.41** above.

s 2, which provided that when trustees sell, the buyer's title cannot be challenged; however, this modification leaves the common law intact in relation to gratuitous transferees.[90] A third exception is the 'offside goals' rule.

'OFFSIDE GOALS'

4.48

> 'The appellants assumed that their title would be safe once the goal of the Register House was reached. But in this area of the law, as in football, offside goals are disallowed.'

These were the words of Lord Justice-Clerk Thomson in *Rodger (Builders) Ltd v Fawdry*,[91] thereby giving a new name to an old rule. The owner of land (Mark Fawdry) concluded missives to sell to Rodger (Builders) Ltd.[92] When the company failed to pay the price, he sold to Marjorie Bell. A disposition was granted to her and recorded in the Sasine Register. She was now owner. But the company raised an action of reduction against her. The first argument in the case was that the first set of missives had never been validly rescinded. The court agreed. The second was that since she knew of the first set of missives, the company was entitled to reduce the disposition to her. The court agreed and the disposition was reduced. The idea behind the rule is that Marjorie Bell was considered to have acquired in bad faith – because she knew that the acquisition was in breach of the company's contractual right. This is a case of a personal right prevailing over a real right. (The term 'offside goal', though now well established, is slightly misleading. In football, offside goals are void, not voidable.) The rule is controversial.[93] There are those who think that it should be abolished, because it introduces complexity and uncertainty to the law, without counterbalancing benefits. (After all, in cases of this sort, somebody or other – in this case, either the company or Ms Bell – is going to have to rely on damages as a remedy.)

4.49 For the rule to apply, certain conditions must be satisfied. In the first place, it can apply only if B2 (the second buyer) actually or constructively knew of the prior personal right of B1 (the first buyer).[94] Thus in *Rodger (Builders) v Fawdry* B2's title would have been absolutely good if she had been unaware of B1's contract. It is unclear whether B2 is affected only if she knows of B1's right *before* she (B2) acquires the personal right, or if the information is received at any time before she

---

90   See **PARA 24.32** below.
91   1950 SC 483. The exposition of the law in Reid *Property* para 695 ff has had great influence. The subsequent literature has been extensive. See eg McDonald *Conveyancing Manual* ch 32.
92   For the transfer of heritable property, see **PARAS 5.1–5.15** below.
93   See eg R Rennie 'Marching towards equity – blindfolded' 2009 *SLT (News)* 187.
94   'Prior' is important. Take the following. On 1 May X contracts to sell to Y. On 2 May X contracts to sell to Z. On 3 May X delivers a disposition to Z. On 4 May Y learns about Z. On 5 May X delivers a disposition to Y. On 6 May Y registers the disposition. There has been no offside goal, because Y's personal right predates Z's.

acquires a real right – the latter being the more severe form of the rule.[95] In the second place, B2's title is not voidable unless there was a *breach* of the seller's obligation to B1. The classic case is – as in *Rodger (Builders) Ltd v Fawdry* – where the seller transfers to someone else,[96] but the breach can be the grant of some other right, such as a standard security.[97]

4.50   In the third place, the 'offside goals' rule applies only to *voluntary* grantees. Therefore it does not apply to creditors doing diligence or to trustees in sequestration. So in *Burnett's Tr v Grainger*,[98] Mrs Burnett was contractually bound to give a good title to Mr and Mrs Grainger. She was sequestrated. Her trustee knew of the contract, but nevertheless transferred title to his own name (for the benefit of the creditors). The 'offside goals' rule could not be pled against him by Mr and Mrs Grainger. In the fourth place, the rule applies only if B1's right was capable of becoming a real right. The leading case here is *Wallace v Simmers*.[99] William Simmers agreed with his daughter, Margaret Simmers, that she could occupy a cottage on his farm indefinitely and rent-free. Later, he conveyed the farm to his son, William Simmers the younger. The latter knew of the agreement with his sister and was happy with it. Years later, he sold the farm to Robert Wallace and Douglas Wallace. They asked Margaret Simmers to leave. When she refused they sued to have her removed. She pled that they knew of her right before buying. Whether they did or not know was never established, because the court held that even if they did know, they were not bound thereby. Margaret's right was not a lease. It was a personal right incapable of becoming a real right and so was outwith the scope of the 'offside goals' rule.[100]

4.51   Finally, something must be said of *Trade Development Bank v Warriner & Mason (Scotland) Ltd*.[101] Here, Lyon Group Ltd granted a standard security to Trade Development Bank. In doing so it agreed not to let out the property. In breach of that agreement it let the property to Warriner & Mason (Scotland) Ltd, which had actual, or at least constructive, knowledge of the agreement. When Lyon Group Ltd became insolvent, the bank sought to reduce the lease as being an 'offside goal'. It was successful. Here, the bank did not have a personal right capable of being made real, but a real right itself. That real right was earlier in time than the lease. It could be argued that the 'offside goals' rule was inapplicable, and that the bank had power to sell the property free of the lease, regardless of whether the lease was in breach of a contractual term and regardless of whether the lessees knew of that term. The issues involved are, however, too complex for discussion here.

---

95   In *Alex Brewster & Sons v Caughey* 2002 GWD-10-318, the court upheld the more severe form of the rule but the soundness of the decision is doubtful: S Wortley, 'Double Sales and the Offside Trap' 2002 *JR* 291.

96   But this is not necessarily a breach: *Advice Centre for Mortgages v McNicoll* 2006 SLT 591.

97   *Trade Development Bank v Crittall Windows Ltd* 1983 SLT 510.

98   2002 SC 580, aff'd 2004 SC (HL) 19. See **PARAS 4.26–4.28** above.

99   1960 SC 255.

100 For another example of the application of the 'capable of being made real' requirement, see the complex case of *Advice Centre for Mortgages Ltd v McNicoll* 2006 SLT 591. See also *Gibson v Royal Bank of Scotland Plc* 2009 SLT 444.

101 1980 SC 74.

ACCRETION OF TITLE

4.52   Suppose that the title of the granter (X) is void, with the result that the title of the grantee (Y) is also void. And then suppose that at a later date X acquires title from the true owner, Z. Then, as soon as Z's title passes to X, Y's title is validated, without the need for any new deed. The doctrine in practice has been largely confined to heritable property, where it is called 'accretion of infeftment',[102] but it can apply to any type of property.[103] The doctrine applies not only where the X/Y transaction is a transfer, but also where it is the grant of subordinate right. Accretion presupposes that the X/Y transaction contains absolute warrandice. If it does not, it seems to be the law that accretion will not operate. (Though even in the absence of warrandice it will operate if the X/Y transaction contains a clause conveying the granter's 'whole right, title and interest present and future'.)

DEEDS BY UNREGISTERED HOLDERS

4.53   An 'unregistered holder', also called an 'uninfeft proprietor',[104] is someone who has the power to complete title but who has not yet done so. Suppose that Bill is owner and delivers a disposition to Ben. At this stage Ben is not yet owner, for he has not yet registered. But he can register whenever he likes. Someone in this position – with *power* to complete title – is an unregistered holder. If Ben had completed missives with Bill, but had not yet received a disposition, he would not have been an unregistered holder, for, without the disposition in his hands he cannot complete title. Another example of an unregistered holder is an executor who has obtained confirmation to heritable property but who has not completed title.[105]

4.54   The state of being an unregistered holder is usually short-lived. Ben is likely to register within a few days of the delivery to him of the disposition. But occasionally the state is, for one reason or another, lengthier. And the law allows an unregistered holder to grant certain types of deed *as if* owner. For example, Ben, instead of registering his disposition, could dispone to Betty. Betty, on registering her disposition, would become owner: in that case ownership would have passed from Bill to Betty without ever having vested in Ben. This rule can be regarded as an exception to the *nemo plus* principle: Ben, though not owner, can make Betty owner. The deeds that link the currently registered owner (Bill) with the applicant (Betty) are called 'midcouples' or 'links in title'. This example has been chosen because of its simplicity. In practice the important cases of unregistered holders occur in trust and executry conveyancing. For example, X owns land and dies. Y is confirmed

---

102   Strictly speaking, 'infeftment', being a feudal term, should not now be used.
103   R G Anderson *Assignation* (2008) ch 11. On the doctrine in general see Reid *Property* para 677.
104   'Uninfeft proprietor' is an unhappy term, in both its parts. 'Uninfeft' is a feudal term and so, strictly speaking, should not be used since feudal abolition. 'Proprietor' is wrong because an uninfeft proprietor is not a proprietor. But the term is better known than 'unregistered holder'.
105   See **PARAS 26.46–26.47** below.

as executor. Y will usually convey the land to the beneficiary, or to a purchaser, without having first completed title. There can be other examples too. For example, an Act of Parliament is passed with a section saying that the property of a given state corporation now 'vests' in another state corporation. The section operates as a conveyance. So the second corporation is now an unregistered holder.[106]

RISK

4.55   The issue of risk (*periculum*) is one that applies to sales (or other onerous transfers) of corporeal property. The question is: who bears the loss if the property is damaged without the fault of either party? At a certain point the risk is said to 'pass' but that is just a turn of phrase: risk is not an entity that can pass from one person to another. The contract often has a clause about risk, especially in heritable transactions. In the absence of such agreement, there are default rules. The common-law rule is that risk passes when the contract of sale is made.[107] But where SOGA 1979 applies, the default rule is that risk passes with ownership,[108] except in a business-to-consumer sale, in which case risk passes on delivery.[109]

JUDICIAL RECTIFICATION

4.56   Suppose that a conveyancing deed is bungled: it fails to reflect what the parties intended. There are numerous different possibilities but in practice the two common cases are that (a) less land or (b) more land is conveyed than provided for in the sale contract. In the first case the buyer can normally solve the problem by insisting that the contract be fully implemented. This will be done by a supplementary disposition from the seller. In the second case, the buyer is obliged to re-convey the excess land, because it was transferred without legal basis (*sine causa*). In other words, the obligation to re-convey arises out of the law of unjustified enrichment. But in 1985 an additional remedy was introduced: 'judicial rectification of defectively expressed documents'.[110] The court is empowered to 'rectify' the deed, ie to rewrite it so that the new text reflects what the parties intended. Moreover, this rewriting works not as from now (*ex nunc*) but as from the original date (*ex tunc*). The deed is altered retrospectively. Suppose that Alex owns 20,000 square metres and in 2013 he sells 5,000 square metres to Beth, but the disposition in fact conveys only 4,000. In 2015

---

[106]   Eg Coal Industry Act 1994, s 7. The same happens when new local authorities are created, eg Local Government etc. (Scotland) Act 1994, s 15.

[107]   *Sloan's Dairies v Glasgow Corporation* 1977 SC 223.

[108]   SOGA 1979, s 20(1).

[109]   Consumer Rights Act 2015, s 29.

[110]   LR(MP)(S)A 1985, ss 8 and 9. These provisions were based on English law. They are not limited to conveyancing deeds. They apply generally, though notably not to testamentary deeds: s 8(6). For an account of the provisions from a conveyancing standpoint, see Gretton and Reid, *Conveyancing* ch 17.

the mistake comes to light and Beth successfully applies for judicial rectification. The result is that the deed is deemed *always* to have been for the full 5,000. But what about the Land Register? That is not changed retrospectively: the decree must be registered, and the change takes effect from that date.[111]

DONATION

4.57 Scots property law has nothing to say about donation (gift): donation is not a property law issue. The rules of transfer are the same regardless of the reason for transfer. For land, transfer is by registered deed, for corporeal moveables it is by delivery, for ordinary incorporeal moveables it is by intimated assignation, and so on. Donation is simply one reason among others why a transfer may be made. There is a semi-exception for corporeal moveables. If Jack sells a bicycle to Jill, delivery is not necessary for ownership to pass. But if he donates it to her, delivery is needed. At first sight this looks like a special rule for donation. But in fact it is not: it is a special rule for sale. Until the Sale of Goods Act 1893 (now replaced by the Sale of Goods Act 1979) the rule was that delivery is necessary to transfer corporeal moveables, regardless of the reason for the transfer. That Act dispensed with the need for delivery, but only in cases of sale. Where the reason for the transfer is other than a contract of sale, the general rule continues to apply. That includes donations and also other cases, such as exchange.

LITERATURE

4.58 Reid *Property* paras 597–718 is a comprehensive study, covering also the subject matter of our next chapter.

---

[111]   LR(S)A 2012 s 55, amending LR(MP)(S)A 1985, ss 8 and 9.

Chapter 5

Acquisition by voluntary transfer: the rules for the various types of property

HERITABLE PROPERTY

Introduction

5.1   The main topic here is transfer of *ownership of heritable property.* (At the end of the section, subordinate heritable rights will be discussed.) For purposes of discussion we assume that the property is being sold. But the actual transfer is by registered disposition, and that is equally true regardless of the reason for transfer: for instance, if land is being donated (transferred gratuitously) the method is the same – registered disposition – and what is different is a matter of subtraction: one subtracts the bits about the sale contract. The sale of land usually has three stages: the contract, settlement and registration. Ownership passes on registration of the deed of transfer, ie the disposition.[1]

Contract

5.2   The first stage is the contract of sale. The subject belongs to contract law and to conveyancing practice, so little will be said here.[2] Such a contract has to be in writing, signed by the parties or (typically) their agents.[3] It usually takes the form of *missives*. A missive is a letter, so 'missives' means an exchange of letters. The first is an offer to buy or, less commonly, an offer to sell. The reply may be a straightforward acceptance[4] or it may be what conveyancers call a 'qualified acceptance', which is, in the eyes of the law, a rejection coupled with a counter-offer. Once consensus has been reached the missives are said to be 'concluded'. The buyer does not yet have a real right. The next stage is 'settlement', or, to use the English term that is now normal where the sale is of commercial property, 'completion'. How long this happens after conclusion of missives varies: between one and two months would be fairly usual.

5.3   Contracts for the sale of land were once short. Now they typically run for several pages, covering not only the core issues of 'parties', 'property' and 'price' (the three Ps) but also other matters such as the physical condition of the property.

---

[1]   LR(S)A 2012, s 50. (This is merely a modern restatement of an old rule.)
[2]   E Sinclair and A Stewart, *Conveyancing Practice in Scotland* (7th edn, 2016) gives a good practical account of the conveyancing process.
[3]   Requirements of Writing (Scotland) Act 1995 (RoW(S)A 1995) s 1(2)(a)(i): 'a contract ... for the ... transfer ... of a real right in land'. See **PARA 31.3** below.
[4]   Known as a *de plano* acceptance.

A standardised style is now normally used, though obviously it can be adjusted for the particular transaction.[5]

5.4   The core of the contract is that the seller will give to the buyer (i) possession and (ii) ownership and the buyer will give to the seller the price. In theory, this contractual stage could be omitted. The parties could go straight from a non-binding handshake to settlement. But that would usually be inconvenient. Each side wishes to prepare for settlement in the comforting knowledge that the other party is bound. Moreover, as mentioned, the contract usually contains provisions beyond the core.

5.5   In the interval between contract and settlement, the buyer's solicitor will check the title. This is usually fairly straightforward. The seller's solicitor sends a copy of the title sheet.[6] This sets out the boundaries of the property, who owns it and what the encumbrances are. Then a report needs to be obtained from the Land Register to see if there have been any changes since the copy was issued. There seldom are such changes. If, however, the title to the property is still in the Sasine Register, checking the title is more complicated.[7] The buyer's solicitor also checks in the Register of Inhibitions that the seller has not been inhibited or sequestrated. If the seller is a company, the Companies Register must also be checked. One of the risks is that what appears to be a company has never in fact been registered or, conversely, that it was validly registered but has since been struck off the Register. A search in the Companies Register will also reveal whether the company is in liquidation, and list the current directors (which enables the buyer to verify that the disposition is signed by the right people).

Inhibition, sequestration and the Register of Inhibitions

5.6   An inhibition is an order from a court that affects the inhibitee's power to grant deeds affecting title to heritable property, in particular dispositions and standard securities.[8] It can be obtained by a creditor who holds decree for payment, and also by a pursuer during an action, as a protective measure. The latter, called inhibition on the dependence, becomes void if the action fails. An inhibition is discharged, obviously enough, if the debtor pays the debt. The inhibition is registered in the Register of Inhibitions. This, like the Sasine Register and the Land Register, is administered by the Keeper.[9] As well as inhibitions, this register has other entries, such as sequestrations. The register is name-based, not property-based. When there is a transaction affecting heritable property, the Register of Inhibitions is normally checked. Obviously, if a seller turns out to be inhibited, or sequestrated, a buyer will

---

[5]   The standard style for residential cases can be found on the Law Society of Scotland website (https://www.lawscot.org.uk/ – search for 'Scottish Standard Clauses'.) For commercial cases see the Property Standardisation Group website (www.psglegal.co.uk/).

[6]   See **PARAS 7.32–7.35** below.

[7]   See **PARAS 7.8–7.13** below.

[8]   See further G L Gretton *The Law of Inhibition and Adjudication* (2nd edn, 1996).

[9]   See **PARA 7.4** below.

refuse to settle, unless the disposition has the consent of the inhibitor or the trustee in sequestration. It is an implied term of the contract of sale of heritable property that the seller has an unrestricted power to dispone.

5.7   If a deed is granted notwithstanding an inhibition, it is not void, but is voidable at the inhibitor's option. Avoidance is carried out by an action of reduction *ex capite inhibitionis*. The effect of such a reduction is not to annul the grantee's title, except in a question with the inhibitor. Rather, the inhibitor, can now take further steps to enforce his or her rights *as if* the offending deed had never been granted. Suppose that Romulus owns land, and Ophelia, his creditor, inhibits him, and thereafter he dispones to Nestor. Nestor, on registering his disposition, becomes owner. Ophelia decides to reduce the disposition, and obtains decree. Even now, Nestor remains owner. But Ophelia can now take further steps of diligence against the property *as if* Romulus were still the owner. (Whereas the general principle of the law of diligence is that only assets within the debtor's patrimony are available as target assets.)

Settlement and registration

5.8   At the 'date of entry' what is called 'settlement'[10] takes place. The buyer pays the price. The seller gives possession and delivers the disposition, i.e. the deed of transfer, duly executed. Here is an example of a disposition:[11]

> 'WE, JOHN POLLOCK (born the first day of May in the year 1979) and JANE CHRISTINE LORCA or POLLOCK (born the sixth day of June in the year 1977), residing together formerly at Seven Mitchell Gardens, Thurso and now at Forty Four Portsoy Avenue there, heritable proprietors of the subjects hereinafter disponed, IN CONSIDERATION of the sum of TWO HUNDRED AND TEN THOUSAND FIVE HUNDRED POUNDS (£210,500) paid to us by CHARLOTTE DARCY ROXBURGH, residing at Fifty Ellis Road, Thurso, of which sum we do hereby acknowledge receipt, DO HEREBY DISPONE to the said Charlotte Darcy Roxburgh ALL and WHOLE Forty Four Portsoy Avenue, Thurso, Caithness, being the subjects registered in the Land Register of Scotland under Title Number CTH 1234567; WITH ENTRY AND ACTUAL OCCUPATION as at Third July Two Thousand and Seventeen; And we grant warrandice: IN WITNESS WHEREOF we have subscribed these presents at Thurso on First July Two thousand and Seventeen in the presence of Fiona Cairns of Thirty Two Meadow Street Thurso.
>
> *Fiona Cairns, witness*   John Pollock
>
>   Jane C Pollock'

---

[10]   The English term 'completion' is also used.

[11]   At the time of writing the possibility is being discussed of making all dispositions electronic, in which case they would look rather different, though the essentials would be the same.

On delivery of the disposition, the buyer does not acquire ownership, but rather the power to become owner, without any further co-operation by the granter, simply by registering the disposition in the Land Register. A person in this position is called an 'unregistered holder' of land, or a person with an 'uncompleted title', or an 'uninfeft proprietor'.[12] To 'complete a title' is to acquire a real right. A grantee who registers a disposition 'completes title'. The subject of land registration is dealt with in **CHAPTER 7**.

Warrandice

5.9   'Warrandice' means the guarantee given by the granter to the grantee that the title is good. In practice a deed contains an express 'grant' of warrandice but if the deed is silent, warrandice is implied by law. There are three levels of warrandice.[13]

(1)   The lowest is 'simple' warrandice. (This is what the law implies for gratuitous deeds.) The granter guarantees only that he or she will not grant any subsequent deed that could prejudice the deed now being granted. Actually, that could almost never happen anyway. Suppose that Jane owns a flat and, besotted by love, dispones it to her boyfriend, Dirk, gratuitously, and he promptly registers. Nothing she could do thereafter could prejudice his title anyway. So it is hard to breach simple warrandice. But it could happen. For example, suppose that he delays to register the disposition. They have a row. She gives her new boyfriend, Doug, a disposition of the flat. He registers. Doug is now the owner. Jane is liable to Dirk for breach of warrandice.

(2)   The middle level is 'fact and deed' warrandice. Here, the granter guarantees the grantee's title against any future *or past* act by the granter. For example, suppose that Ruth dispones to Simon and grants fact and deed warrandice. She is indeed the owner but there is a standard security over the property held by Tamsin. If that security was granted by Ruth, then she is in breach of her warrandice to Simon.

(3)   The highest level is 'absolute' warrandice.[14] Deeds often say simply 'I grant warrandice' without specifying the type: in that case the meaning is absolute warrandice.[15] Absolute warrandice is the implied level in both the contract of sale (or other onerous contract) and a disposition in implement of such a contract.

5.10   Absolute warrandice is a guarantee by the granter to the grantee that:

(i)   the grantee will acquire ownership (or other right being granted) and

(ii) the title will be unaffected by any encumbrances (notably subordinate real rights).

Title conditions[16] are a partial exception: a title condition is a breach of warrandice only if it was unknown to the grantee, was of an unusual type and materially

---

[12]   See **PARA 4.53** above.

[13]   There is a fourth type, for the transfer of personal rights, warrandice *debitum subesse*, on which see **PARA 5.49** below.

[14]   See **PARA 5.10** below.

[15]   Titles to Land Consolidation (Scotland) Act 1868, s 8.

[16]   See **PARA 14.3** below.

lessens the property's value.[17] The special status of title conditions in relation to warrandice is because they are so common – most properties have them – and are the sort of things that buyers in general can be expected to tolerate. (By contrast, though heritable securities are common, a buyer cannot be expected to accept a property encumbered by an undischarged security. Such acceptance would require special agreement.) Another possible exception, but a controversial one, is *Lothian & Border Farmers Ltd v McCutcheon*,[18] holding that the existence of a lease does not mean breach of warrandice. The logic behind this decision is that the existence of a lease should not, in the normal case at least, mean a diminution of the value of the property, because the value of the rental stream should equate to the value of possession. The issue seldom arises, because in practice if the buyer expects vacant possession (also known as actual occupation) both the missives and the disposition will have a guarantee of that.

5.11   Warrandice exists in both the missives and the deed. The remedy for breach of warrandice *in a deed* is damages.[19] No claim based on the first leg of the guarantee (that the grantee will acquire ownership) can be made unless the grantee is faced with 'eviction' or 'threatened eviction'.[20] Thus, in one case, Harold and Pamela Beck disponed to Sheila Palmer an area of land. It then turned out that the title to part of it was bad. Mrs Palmer sued them for breach of warrandice. But since no attempt had been made by the true owner to assert title to the area in question, there was no eviction and so the action failed.[21] 'Eviction', as the word is used here, does not have its ordinary meaning of physical removal. It means a successful assertion of the right of the true owner. For example, if the true owner obtains a declarator that his or her title is good, that is 'eviction'. Eviction is not a pre-requisite for a claim made under the second leg of the guarantee (no encumbrances).

5.12   As to warrandice *in the contract*, the buyer is in a stronger position, and indeed contractual warrandice is more important than deed warrandice. Eviction is irrelevant: the buyer can simply refuse to settle until given what has been bargained for. If the defect amounts to a material breach, rescission is possible. Thus Mrs Palmer would have been in a stronger position if her solicitor had identified the title problem before settlement.

5.13   The benefit of warrandice can be, and usually is, assigned. Thus X dispones to Y, and later Y dispones to Z. The warrandice that X granted to Y is assigned by Y to Z. This will give Z the benefit of two warrandices, for Y will also (in the typical case) be granting warrandice to Z.[22] Of course, there are limits to this. Suppose that the title problem is that the property is encumbered by a standard security granted by

---

[17]   Reid *Property* para 705.
[18]   1952 SLT 450.
[19]   *Welsh v Russell* (1894) 21 R 769.
[20]   *Clark v Lindale Homes Ltd* 1994 SC 210.
[21]   *Palmer v Beck* 1993 SLT 485. For a case with strange facts, that arguably changes the meaning of 'eviction', see *Morris v Rae* 2013 SLT 88.
[22]   See, eg, *Cobham v Minter* 1986 SLT 336.

Y: clearly, X is not responsible for that. No separate process of assignation is needed: the benefit of warrandice is automatically included in what is called the 'assignation of writs' that is implied in every disposition.[23]

Gap risk: letters of obligation and advance notices

5.14 The reports from the registers may be a day or two old at the day of settlement, and moreover the buyer may not be able to register the disposition instantly. So the buyer is at risk, for the seller has the money and is still owner of the property. In particular, what if, in the gap period, the seller were to become insolvent, with the sorts of problems discussed in the previous chapter in connection with *Burnett's Tr v Grainger*?[24] To cover this risk, the practice used to be for the seller's solicitors to give the buyer a 'letter of obligation'. This guaranteed that, provided that the buyer registered within a defined period (such as 14 days), any unexpected entry in the registers would be cleared at the expense of the seller's solicitors. But practice has now changed following the introduction, by the LR(S)A 2012, of advance notices. Such a notice can be placed in the Land Register in advance of settlement. It creates a 'protected period' of 35 days, and provided that the disposition is registered within the protected period, it will trump adverse entries made in either the Land Register or the Inhibitions Register.[25]

Subordinate real rights in land

5.15 The real right of ownership of land is transferred by disposition. Subordinate real rights in land are incorporeal property and so are transferred (assuming that they are transferable[26]) by assignation. The assignation of a registered lease is registered in the Land Register. An unregistered lease is assigned by taking possession and intimating the assignation to the landlord.[27] A standard security is transferred by registration in the Land Register, unless the property itself is still in the Sasine Register, in which case the assignation is registered in that register.[28]

CORPOREAL MOVEABLE PROPERTY

Introduction

5.16 Confusingly, two sets of rules exist for the transfer of corporeal moveable property. The Sale of Goods Act 1979 (SOGA 1979) applies to all cases where the

---

[23] LR(S)A 1979, s 16.
[24] 2002 SC 580, aff'd 2004 SC (HL) 19.
[25] See **PARAS 7.55–7.65** below.
[26] Servitudes and praedial real burdens cannot be transferred separately. They are pertinents of the benefited property. See **PARA 15.12** below. Proper liferents cannot be transferred. See **PARA 22.12** below. Some leases are non-transferable. See **PARA 20.33** below.
[27] For the assignation of leases, see **PARAS 20.33–20.34** below.
[28] For the assignation of standard securities, see **PARA 21.49** below.

transfer is in implement of a contract of sale. Otherwise, the common law rules apply. For example, those rules apply to transfers by reason of barter, otherwise known as exchange or, to use the strictly accurate term for Scots law, 'excambion'. They also apply to transfers by way of donation (gift). If you buy a book at a bookshop, the transfer of ownership is governed by SOGA 1979 but if you then give the book to a friend as a Christmas present, that transfer is governed by common law. Of course, in practice, most transfers are because of sale.

5.17 At common law, transfer of ownership requires delivery, i.e. the transfer of possession. This external act thus corresponds to registration in the case of heritable property. If your friend merely *tells* you that the present is yours, that is not enough:[29] no delivery, no transfer.[30] Although ownership cannot pass *before* delivery, it can *pass* after it, if the parties so agree. That follows from the fact that mutual consent is necessary for ownership to pass. So if your friend delivers the book to you subject to the condition that ownership will pass when you accept him as a friend on Facebook, ownership will pass only when you do this.

5.18 The common law rules originally applied to sales too. This was changed by the Sale of Goods Act 1893, later replaced by SOGA 1979. In contrast to the common law, the statutory rules, covered in the rest of this chapter, are complex.[31]

Goods

5.19 'Goods' under SOGA 1979 essentially means corporeal moveable property,[32] though it includes heritable property that the parties agree will be 'severed', for example a contract to sell standing timber.[33] (This is odd because it leads to conflicts between the law of heritable property on the one hand and the statute on the other.) 'Existing' goods are those that the seller already has, while 'future' goods are those 'to be manufactured or acquired by him after the making of the contract of sale'.[34] 'Specific' goods are existing goods that are identifiable at the time of the contract.[35] For example, a contract for the sale of a bicycle, physically seen and touched by the parties, is a contract for specific goods. The contrast is with 'unascertained' goods: a contract for the sale of 1,000 tonnes of wheat would be an example. It may be that the seller has 3,000 tonnes but no particular grains of wheat can be identified as being those sold. Assuming that the contract goes ahead, the time must come when unascertained goods become ascertained. Logically, one might think that they then become 'specific' but SOGA 1979 reserves that word for goods identifiable when the

---

[29] Delivery – by Santa Claus or otherwise – is required.
[30] For the different methods of delivery, see **PARAS 12.13–12.17** below. For discussion of the common law rules of transfer, see Reid *Property* paras 619–623.
[31] It is not possible to go into all the difficulties here.
[32] See **PARA 1.23** above.
[33] SOGA 1979, s 61(1).
[34] SOGA 1979, s 5(1).
[35] SOGA 1979, s 61(1).

contract is made.[36] Unascertained goods, on becoming separately identifiable, are said to become 'ascertained'. The same process happens to future goods, though here SOGA 1979's terminology seems to become wobbly. Unless and until goods are specific or ascertained, ownership cannot pass:[37] this is simply the specificity principle.[38]

Registered moveables: cars, aircraft, ships

5.20   Corporeal moveable property is unregistered, with three qualifications: motor vehicles, ships and aircraft. As for motor vehicles, there is a registration system, handled by the DVLA at Swansea,[39] but its role is administrative. It has no private law function. (In many countries vehicle registration does have a private law function.) So when a motor vehicle is sold, registration with the DVLA is not necessary for transfer as a matter of property law.[40] The register for aircraft[41] is comparable: its function is one of public rather than private law. But there is an odd twist. There exists a separate register for mortgages over aircraft[42] and this does have a property law role. So whilst the transfer of ownership of an aircraft does not have to be registered (as far as private law is concerned) a mortgage does. Aircraft, like cars, are subject to SOGA 1979.

5.21   The position for ships is complex, and in some respects obscure, and can only be touched on lightly here.[43] The Ship Register[44] is in some respects comparable to the Land Register. Although ships have a port name (such as Aberdeen or Southampton) painted on their hulls, there is a single UK register. Both transfers and mortgages are registrable. Transfer is a three-stage process, beginning with what is often called a 'sale form' (like missives), followed by delivery of a 'bill of sale' (cf delivery of a disposition) and finally registration. Unlike the Land Register, it seems that the right is established by delivery of the bill of sale, but that failure to register will mean that the right is defeasible, eg by a sale to someone else.[45] But two classes of ships, 'small' ships and fishing vessels that have only 'simple' registration, are subject to the property law rules of SOGA 1979.

---

[36]   SOGA 1979, s 61(1).
[37]   SOGA 1979, s 16.
[38]   See **PARAS 4.14–4.16** above. There is, however, a qualification: the sale of quasi-specific goods. See **PARAS 5.28–5.30** below.
[39]   Road Vehicles (Registration and Licensing) Regulations 2002 (SI 2002/2742).
[40]   Cf *Central Newbury Car Auctions Ltd v Unity Finance Ltd* [1957] 1 QB 371 at 397.
[41]   Air Navigation Order 2009 (SI 2009/3015).
[42]   Mortgaging of Aircraft Order 1972 (SI 1972/1268).
[43]   See further G Gretton, 'Ships as a Branch of Property Law' in A R C Simpson, S C Styles, E West and A L M Wilson (eds), *Continuity, Change and Pragmatism in the Law: Essays in Memory of Professor Angelo Forte* (2016) 367-397.
[44]   Merchant Shipping Act 1995, especially sch 1; Merchant Shipping (Registration of Ships) Regulations 1993 (SI 1993/3138).
[45]   Merchant Shipping Act 1995, sch 1 para 1(1).

Transfer: SOGA 1979, s 17

5.22   The basic rule of transfer is given by SOGA 1979, s 17: assuming that the goods are specific, or have become ascertained, 'the property in them is transferred to the buyer at such time as the parties … intend it to be transferred'.[46] No external act, such as delivery, is needed. Hence the parties are free to agree that ownership ('property') passes before delivery, which is impossible at common law. They are equally free to agree that it passes at delivery, or after delivery. Agreement that it is to pass after delivery is common. It happens when goods are sold and delivered on credit. In such a case the seller is at risk because the buyer might become insolvent, in which case the seller is merely an ordinary unsecured creditor. Hence it is common for sellers to insist that the sale contract should contain a clause providing that ownership passes on payment.[47]

Transfer: the default rules

5.23   In written contracts for the sale of goods, it is usual to have a provision saying when ownership is to pass. But sometimes – and usually in oral contracts – there is nothing. SOGA 1979, s 18 therefore provides five default rules, ie rules that apply 'unless a different intention appears'.[48] Rule 1 is the most important: 'where there is an unconditional contract for the sale of specific goods in a deliverable state, ownership passes when the contract is made and it is immaterial whether the time of payment or the time of delivery, or both, be postponed'. So if Alice agrees to sell her bicycle to Boris, to be delivered next week, cash on delivery, ownership passes immediately, unless otherwise agreed. Rules 2 and 3 are about goods which, though specific, need something to be done to them by the seller. In such a case the parties are presumed to intend that ownership passes when the work has been done and the buyer informed of that fact. Rule 4 relates to goods delivered to the buyer on approval or on sale or return: here, the rule is the ownership passes when it becomes clear that the buyer means to keep the goods.[49]

5.24   Rule 5 is about contracts for the sale of unascertained or future goods by description. The rule is[50] that the parties are presumed to intend ownership to pass when goods meeting the contract requirements are 'unconditionally appropriated to the contract', made identifiable. SOGA 1979, s 19 is a sixth rule: if the contract contains a 'reservation of a right of disposal' unless certain conditions are satisfied, then the parties are presumed to intend ownership not to pass until those conditions have been satisfied. For example, the contract says 'if the buyer fails to pay the price by 2 May, the seller can resell the goods'. In that case the parties are presumed to

---

[46]   SOGA 1979, s 17(1).
[47]   See **PARAS 5.26–5.27** below.
[48]   All of them are subject to SOGA 1979, s 16 – the specificity principle.
[49]   Rule 4 is puzzling because such contracts are probably not contracts of sale. This is one of the many puzzles in this Act.
[50]   This is an approximate statement. The details are difficult.

intend that ownership is not to pass before payment of the price. The same result can be obtained more directly under SOGA 1979, s 17.[51]

The seller's lien

5.25   Rule 1 of SOGA 1979, s 18 often applies in practice. It creates a risk for the seller: ownership passes immediately the parties shake hands on the deal, without payment. What if the buyer becomes insolvent? To meet this difficulty, SOGA 1979, s 41 says that the seller, on losing the real right of ownership, acquires a subordinate real right, called the seller's lien.[52] But this lien is lost as and when the goods are delivered. Hence sellers who wish to be protected even after delivery will opt for retention of title.

Retention of title

5.26   As has been seen, SOGA 1979, s 17 says that ownership passes when the parties intend it to pass. So a sale contract can say that it passes when the buyer pays. In practice most written contracts for the sale of goods have such a provision – a clause of retention of title, or reservation of title.[53] ('Title' is a word with more than one meaning, but often – as here – it means ownership.) If the buyer fails to pay, the seller can rescind the contract on the ground of material breach and then demand re-delivery of the goods (assuming that they have already been delivered) on the basis that the seller is still the owner. A clause of retention of title can validly say that ownership is not to pass unless *all* sums owed by the buyer to the seller (not just the price due under this contract) have been paid.[54] Most retention of title clauses take this form.

5.27   A retention of title clause looks like a perfect protection against the risk of the buyer's insolvency. And such clauses do often work. But often they do not.[55] One reason is that accession or specification may occur.[56] Goods such as, say, bricks or paint are destined to accession. Goods that are processed by the buyer may undergo specification. In all such cases the seller's retained ownership will be defeated. Another reason is that the buyer may resell the goods to a second buyer, in which case SOGA 1979, s 25 may, depending on the circumstances, award ownership to the second buyer.[57]

SOGA 1979, ss 20A and 20B: sale of quasi-specific goods

5.28   In commercial practice it sometimes happens that a quantity is sold out of a particular and identifiable bulk, such as 200 tonnes out of 1,000 tonnes. The rules

---

[51]   See **PARAS 5.26–5.27** below.
[52]   For liens, see **PARAS 21.58–21.64** below.
[53]   If the Consumer Credit Act 1974 applies, a sale with retention of title is called a 'conditional sale'.
[54]   *Armour v Thyssen Edelstahlwerke AG* 1990 SLT 891.
[55]   For what happens in practice, see S Wheeler, *Reservation of Title Clauses* (1991).
[56]   See **PARAS 9.8–9.12** and **9.20–9.22** below.
[57]   See **PARA 5.36** below.

discussed so far would mean that ownership of the 200 tonnes ('quasi-specific goods', as they are sometimes called) could not pass until they had been 'appropriated to the contract'. This would involve separating them from the other 800 tonnes. Of course, this would happen on or before delivery. But in the meantime ownership would not have passed.[58]

5.29   A pre-paying buyer runs the risk of the seller's insolvency.[59] In the sale of goods the concern is usually the other way round: the concern is for the seller if ownership passes before payment. Nevertheless, pre-paying buyers are far from unknown in the sale of goods. Eventually it was decided to change the law so that a pre-paying buyer is protected from the seller's insolvency. To achieve this objective the complex set of rules in SOGA 1979, ss 20A and 20B was enacted.[60] The idea was that the pre-paying buyer would take a *pro indiviso* share[61] of the bulk. This legislative generosity applies only to quasi-specific goods. Rather than go through the rules as such, here is an example of how they work. An aspirin should be swallowed first.

STORY	ANALYSIS
1. Pete has 120,000 tonnes of oil in a ship.	Pete owns 100%.
2. He sells 40,000 tonnes to Rachel. She pays 75% of the price.	Rachel becomes owner of 75% of 40,000 tonnes = 30,000 tonnes = 25% of the whole bulk. Pete owns the other 75%.
3. Pete sells 60,000 tonnes to Sarah. The sale is on credit.	Sarah has paid nothing yet, so no property consequences.
4. The 60,000 tonnes are delivered to Sarah.	60,000 tonnes remain. Rachel's ownership shares increase from 25% to 50%. Pete's falls from 75% to 50%.
5. Rachel pays the balance of the price.	Rachel's ownership share increases from 50% to 66.667%. Pete's falls from 50% to 33.333%.
6. Pete sells 20,000 tonnes to Tom. Tom pays.	Tom becomes owner of 33.333%. Pete now owns nothing.
7. The 40,000 tonnes are delivered to Rachel.	Rachel becomes sole owner of what is delivered, and Tom sole owner of the rest.

---

[58]   SOGA 1979, s 16.
[59]   See **PARA 4.27** above.
[60]   By the Sale of Goods (Amendment) Act 1995.
[61]   See **PARA 10.2** below.

5.30   In this story Pete does not become insolvent, and so the buyers had nothing to fear anyway. Had he become insolvent, then any buyer with co-ownership is protected. For example, had Pete been sequestrated after Stage 2, Rachel could still have insisted, as against his trustee in sequestration, on taking 25%.

The *nemo plus* principle

5.31   SOGA 1979, s 21 states the *nemo plus* principle:[62]

> 'Where goods are sold by a person who is not their owner, and who does not sell them under the authority or with the consent of the owner, the buyer acquires no better title to the goods than the seller had, unless the owner of the goods is by his conduct precluded from denying the seller's authority to sell.'

The last part of the provision is about personal bar. Whether its effect is to confer ownership is uncertain, but the balance of opinion is that it is.[63]

Example

5.32

Fiona owns a grandfather clock. It is stolen. Years later, she notices it for sale in an antique shop. She speaks to the dealer, Donald, and after extensive correspondence Donald finally agrees that the clock in his shop is the same one that was stolen from Fiona. But Donald points out that he bought the clock in good faith from the Earl of St Monans, who himself bought in good faith from a Dundee dealer, who is now dead. Further than that, the provenance of the clock cannot be traced. It is likely, however, that the thief sold direct to the Dundee dealer. The antiques dealer says he would be happy to give the clock to Fiona, but only if she pays him what he paid to the Earl of St Monans, namely £14,550. The answer? *Nemo plus.* The thief's title was void. Hence, the Earl's title was void. Hence, Donald's title is void. The clock is Fiona's and she can insist on resuming possession of it without paying anyone anything.

5.33   This is unfair to Donald. But the opposite rule would be unfair to Fiona. Both parties are innocent, yet one must suffer. Donald is entitled to damages from the Earl for breach of warrandice,[64] which transfers the loss to another innocent party. Ultimately, the thief should make the loss good but the chances that the thief can be traced, and, if traced, made to pay, are poor. The result is that anyone who buys corporeal moveable property – as most of us do every day – takes a risk.

---

[62]   See **PARA 4.42** above.
[63]   See E C Reid and J W G Blackie *Personal Bar* (2006) paras 11.16–11.25.
[64]   SOGA 1979, s 12.

Should good faith buyers be protected?

5.34   Most European countries tend to protect the good-faith buyer more than we do. Some, for example German law,[65] say that if the owner gives up possession *voluntarily* (eg Fiona had lent the clock to someone who turned out to be untrustworthy) then a good-faith buyer will obtain a good title. Others (e.g. Italian law[66]) go further and say that a good-faith buyer *always* gets good title. Our law has no general rule protecting good faith buyers, but there are two exceptions.

The exceptions to *nemo plus*

5.35   SOGA 1979 has two exceptions to the *nemo plus* principle: ss 24 and 25.[67] Section 24[68] can be illustrated by this example.

Example

Leontes has an antique shop. Maria calls and buys a grandfather clock. She pays, and it is agreed that she will collect it the next day. Leontes forgets to mark it as sold. The same afternoon, while Leontes is out of the shop, his assistant, unaware of the prior sale, sells the clock to Nigel, who pays for it and takes it away. Nigel is of course unaware of the events of the day before. Here there is a seller (Leontes) who has possession but not ownership (which passed to Maria), and who resells to a second, good faith buyer, who takes delivery. Ownership would have passed from Leontes to Maria on the first day, but then (s 24) to Nigel on the second day. The result would have been the same if the second sale had not been, as here, by reason of inadvertence, but deliberate – but in either case Nigel must be in good faith, and it should be stressed that for s 24 to be engaged there has to have been *delivery* to the second buyer.

5.36   The other exception is SOGA 1979, s 25. This is textually difficult and moreover has complex exceptions. The core idea can be illustrated by an example.

Example

Beth sells and delivers a car to Clara. The contract has a clause saying that ownership passes when Clara pays. Before Clara pays, she sells and delivers the car to Dugald. He is in good faith. Dugald acquires ownership: thus ownership passes from Beth to Dugald. In keeping with its difficult wording, SOGA 1979, s 25 does not actually say this: it says that the transfer 'has the same effect as if the person making the delivery or transfer were a mercantile agent in possession of the goods or documents of title

---

[65]   BGB §§ 932 and 935.
[66]   Codice civile, art 1153.
[67]   Or three exceptions if personal bar is included: see **PARA 5.31** above.
[68]   Inexplicably, the provision contained in SOGA 1979, s 24 is also contained in s 8 of the Factors Act 1889, extended to Scotland by the Factors (Scotland) Act 1890.

with the consent of the owner'[69] which is an oblique reference to the Factors Act 1889, s 2, as applied to Scotland by the Factors (Scotland) Act 1890. SOGA 1979, s 25 is an exception to s 21. SOGA 1979, s 25 itself has a sub-exception, stated in s 25(2), which is that if the Beth/Clara sale is a business-to-consumer credit sale (i.e. what the Consumer Credit Act 1974 calls a 'conditional sale') then Dugald is not protected. This sub-exception itself has a sub-sub-exception, which is that if the thing sold is a motor vehicle then Dugald is protected. This sub-sub-exception has a sub-sub-sub-exception, which is that if Dugald is a business buyer then he is not protected. These rules are located in the Hire Purchase Act 1964, s 27. (Despite that Act's title, s 27 applies to sales, not just to HP.) The law is a mess.

5.37   Finally, SOGA 1979, s 23. This is not an actual exception to *nemo plus* but can conveniently be dealt with here. It says that 'when the seller of goods has a voidable title to them, but his title has not been avoided at the time of the sale, the buyer acquires a good title to the goods, provided he buys them in good faith and without notice of the seller's defect of title'. For example, Robert owns a car. Sara, by fraud, induces him to sell. Sara becomes owner but her title is voidable. Sara sells to Tim, who is in good faith. Tim is now owner and his title is not voidable. SOGA 1979, s 23 thus restates the common law about voidable titles. It is not an exception to *nemo plus* because when Sara transferred to Tim she held the right of ownership: her title was not void but merely voidable.

INCORPOREAL MOVEABLE PROPERTY: PERSONAL RIGHTS

Introduction

5.38   Personal rights are transferred by assignation completed by intimation.[70] Such rights can be of various types, but in practice it is usually personal rights to be paid money which are transferred. Three parties are involved. Suppose that Leonard owes £10,000 to Maria. From Maria's point of view, that is an asset. She can transfer it to Nick. The result will be that Nick will be substituted for Maria as Leonard's creditor. Maria is the 'assignor' or (more usually) the 'cedent', and Nick is called the 'cessionary' or (more usually) the 'assignee'. The transfer is called 'assignation' (or, rarely, 'cession').[71] Though it is unusual for a non-contractual personal right to be assigned, it is possible. For example, Imogen negligently harms Anton. He has a damages claim against her. This delictual claim could be assigned by him to Penelope.

---

[69]   What if something belongs to W, is sold by X to Y under retention of title, and is then sold by Y to Z? SOGA 1979, s 25 says that Z gets a good title. In *National Employers Mutual General Insurance Association Ltd v Jones* [1990] 1 AC 24 the House of Lords held that notwithstanding the wording of the statute, Z does not get good title.

[70]   The possibility of registration as an optional alternative to intimation is under consideration: Scottish Law Commission, Discussion Paper on Moveable Transactions (Scot Law Com DP No 151, 2011).

[71]   In English law, the term is 'assignment'.

Transferability

5.39   Personal rights are presumptively transferable. The consent of the debtor is not required. However, occasionally a claim (using that term in the sense of a personal right) is non-transferable. Some are unassignable by statute.[72] Where a debt arises from a contract, this may forbid assignation, and such a clause is effective.[73] This is called *delectus personae creditoris* ('choice of the person of the creditor', ie choice of that particular creditor) and may be an express or an implied term. There exists a power to ban anti-assignation clauses, but thus far the Scottish Ministers have not exercised that power.[74] The issue is a controversial one.

5.40   The expression 'assignation of contract' is sometimes encountered. That is a muddle. Contractual rights can be assigned; contracts cannot be assigned. (Borrow £1,000,000 from a bank and then try to assign the loan contract to a down-and-out. It would be fun if it were possible!) The object of an assignation is a right. The transfer of a contract can be achieved, but only by a combination of assignation of the rights and delegation of the duties.[75] There are one or two qualifications, one in the context of heritable property being that a contract of lease is often, though not always, assignable, and when it is assigned the incoming tenant replaces the outgoing tenant in the whole contract, both rights and obligations.[76]

Transfer by debtor?

5.41   A debtor cannot assign the obligation to pay. That would be absurd: it would mean that you could borrow money, spend it and then happily assign the debt to an undischarged bankrupt living in Outer Mongolia. However, to this general principle there exist some qualifications. The first is that such a transfer can, of course, take place if the creditor consents. So if X owes money to Y, X's obligation to pay can be transferred to Z if all three parties so agree. This is called 'delegation'. The second is that a debtor is normally[77] free to *subcontract* performance of the obligation. That, however, does not let the debtor off the hook. So if Bob contracts to build a house for Jane, he might subcontract the electrical work, but if that proves defective, he is liable to Jane for breach of contract. In the third place, the contract itself may expressly or implicitly permit transfer by the debtor. Finally, it might be wondered why anyone would ever wish to take on someone else's obligation or why the creditor would ever be prepared to consent. The short answer is: commercial deals.

---

72   Eg Social Security Administration Act 1992, s 187.
73   *James Scott Ltd v Apollo Engineering Ltd* 2000 SLT 1262.
74   Small Business, Enterprise and Employment Act 2015, s 1.
75   See **PARA 5.41** below.
76   See **PARA 20.33** below.
77   But the contract may provide, expressly or by implication, that this is not permitted. This is *delectus personae debitoris*. The two types of *delectus personae* are quite different, a fact that has not prevented them from being confused: see, eg, *Cole v Handasyde & Co* 1910 SC 68 and *Scottish Homes v Inverclyde District Council* 1997 SLT 829.

Assignation: how

5.42   As with other transfers, there is a distinction between contract and conveyance.[78] (i) The contract to assign does not have to be in writing. (ii) Before the RoW(S)A 1995, the assignation itself had to be in writing, but that requirement was abolished by that Act.[79] The Transmission of Moveable Property (Scotland) Act 1862 sets out a simple style of assignation, but it is not compulsory, and the courts have been prepared to recognise all sorts of documents as being assignations.[80]

5.43   Just as the transfer of land occurs not on delivery of the disposition but on registration, so transfer of a claim takes place not on delivery of the deed of assignation but on 'intimation' (formal notice) to the debtor – Leonard, in the example above.[81] Suppose that Maria agrees to transfer to Nick, and then delivers to him a deed of assignation, but she is sequestrated before Nick intimates to Leonard. Nick is too late.

5.44   Intimation can in theory be done by the common law method, which involves a notary, but this seldom happens in modern practice. The Transmission of Moveable Property (Scotland) Act 1862 introduced the alternative of 'transmitting a copy [of the assignation] certified as correct by post' to the debtor. This method is often adopted, but often all that happens is a notice, without a copy of the assignation. Is this valid? Seemingly it is,[82] but the law is perhaps less than clear. The law recognises certain alternatives to formal intimation. One is the raising of an action by the assignee against the debtor, for the action in itself is regarded as intimation.

Effect

5.45   Upon intimation the personal right passes from the cedent's patrimony to the assignee's. The assignee (Nick) replaces the cedent (Maria) as creditor of the debtor (Leonard).

5.46   'All exceptions[83] competent against the cedent before the assignation or intimation are relevant against the assignee, as payment, compensation etc.'[84] For example, suppose that Leonard had paid off £2,000 of the debt, so that the debt was reduced to £8,000. At this stage Maria assigns the claim to Nick, but purports to assign the whole original claim of £10,000. Assume that Nick was in good faith. Leonard is liable to Nick for £8,000, not for £10,000. This principle has a cumbersome Latin tag: *assignatus utitur jure auctoris*. The classic illustration is *Scottish Widows Fund*

---

[78]   See **PARAS 4.17–4.18** above.
[79]   RoW(S)A 1995, s 11(3)(a). (The change does not make sense because a copy of the assignation has to be sent to the debtor.)
[80]   See, notably, *Carter v McIntosh* (1862) 24 D 925 and *Brownlee v Robb* 1907 SC 1302.
[81]   See **PARA 5.38** above.
[82]   *Christie Owen & Davies plc v Campbell* 2009 SC 436, on which see R G Anderson at (2009) 13 *Edin LR* 484.
[83]   An 'exception' is a defence.
[84]   Stair II, 1, 20.

v Buist,[85] where Mr Moir took out a life assurance policy, assuring the company that he was in good health and of sober habits. In fact, he suffered from syphilis and alcoholism. He assigned the benefit of the policy to Mr Buist. When Mr Moir died, Mr Buist, who had acted in good faith, sought payment of the policy proceeds. The company refused to pay, citing the *assignatus utitur* principle. The defence was upheld. Suppose that Mr Moir had not assigned the policy. Then, on his death, the company could have refused to pay his executor. The assignee could not be in any better position.

5.47   The *assignatus utitur* rule applies to matters as they are at the date of intimation. A good illustration is *Macpherson's JF v Mackay*.[86] Hugh Macpherson was one of the beneficiaries of a large trust set up by his late father, Archie Macpherson. A beneficial right in a trust is incorporeal moveable property (a type of personal right against the trustees) and can, in most cases at least, be assigned. Hugh married Alice. A separate family trust, a marriage trust, was established. (We will call this new trust 'Trust 2', to distinguish it from his father's trust, 'Trust 1'.) Hugh assigned his share in Trust 1 to the extent of £1,000 to the trustees of Trust 2.[87] The assignation was intimated to the trustees of Trust 1. As it happened, Hugh was a trustee of Trust 1 and indeed latterly the sole trustee. Over time, Trust 1 paid out to Hugh the whole amount allocated to him under the trust. After Hugh's death, the trustees of Trust 2 claimed £1,000 from Trust 1. The trustees of Trust 1 pled *assignatus utitur*, arguing that Hugh could not have claimed that money, and so his assignees could not either. This defence failed. At the time when the assignation was intimated, the money was there.

5.48   The *assignatus utitur* principle is a shield, not a sword. A good illustration is *Binstock Miller & Co Ltd v E Coya & Co Ltd*.[88] There was a sale of orange juice. The buyers paid part of the price and the sellers then assigned their right to the balance. When the assignee sought payment, the buyers refused to pay, saying that the orange juice was disconform to contract and had been rejected by them. The buyers not only refused to pay the balance, but sought to claim back from the assignees the part of the price that they had already paid to the sellers. It was held that, although the buyers were entitled to refuse to pay the balance (assuming, of course, that what they said about the juice was correct), they could not recover their money from the assignees. They would have to claim that from the sellers.

Warrandice

5.49   The cedent is presumed to grant warrandice *debitum subesse* – 'that the debt subsists'. This is a guarantee that the claim being assigned does indeed exist in

---

[85]   (1876) 3 R 1078.
[86]   1915 SC 1011.
[87]   Partial assignation, though uncommon in practice, is competent.
[88]   1957 SLT (Sh Ct) 47. And see *Alex Lawrie Factors Ltd v Mitchell Engineering Ltd* 2001 SLT (Sh Ct) 93.

the form that it appears to have. Thus, if Maria assigns to Nick a claim for £10,000 and in fact £2,000 has already been paid off, she is in breach of her warrandice to him. This default type of warrandice is only that the claim is *payable* to the cedent, not that it *will actually* be paid. For example, Oliver owes money to Percy and Percy assigns the claim to Rosi. When Rosi seeks to collect from Oliver she finds that he has become bankrupt. Rosi has no remedy against Percy in terms of the warrandice *debitum subesse*. (By contrast, in the law of negotiable instruments, a transferor warrants not only that the debt is payable but that it will be paid.[89])

Example

5.50   The first document is the assignation and the second is the intimation.

'I, FERGUS DUGALD STEWART of 43 Maitland Street Airdrie in consideration of the sum of Fifty-five Thousand Pounds (£55,000) paid to me by HOLSTEBRO CALEDON LIMITED, a company incorporated under the Companies Acts under number 987654321 having its registered office at 1 Vierzon Way Fraserburgh, DO HEREBY ASSIGN to the said Holstebro Caledon Limited all sums due or to become due to me by Airdrie Meteorological Consultancies Ltd, a company incorporated under the Companies Acts under number 123456789 having its registered office at 23 Calafell Road Glasgow, in terms of a contract between me and the said Airdrie Meteorological Consultancies Ltd dated 1 April 2017 and registered in the Books of Council and Session on 27 April 2017.

IN WITNESS WHEREOF these presents are signed at Glasgow on Twenty seventh October Two thousand and seventeen in the presence of Elizabeth van Groenewegen Cowper, Five Dryden Street, Glasgow.

Elizabeth Cowper (witness)   *Fergus Stewart*

'To:
Airdrie Meteorological Consultancies Ltd,
23 Calafell Road,
Glasgow

28 October 2017

Recorded Delivery

NOTICE is hereby given that by assignation dated 27 October 2017 Fergus Dugald Stewart of 43 Maitland Street Airdrie assigned to Holstebro

---

[89]   Bills of Exchange Act 1882, s 55(2). This is on the assumption that the transferor endorses. A non-endorsing transferor warrants only that the debt is payable: s 58(3).

Caledon Ltd 1 Vierzon Way Fraserburgh all sums due or to become due to him in terms of a contract between him and yourselves dated 1 April 2017 and registered in the Books of Council and Session on 27 April 2017.

Dated at Glasgow the 28th day of October 2017.

Lorraine Woods

Member

Valeria Victrix LLP

Solicitors, 1 Meadow Lane, Glasgow.
Agents for Holstebro Caledon Ltd.'

5.51   Attached to this will be a photocopy of the assignation with 'Certified a true copy' written on it and signed on behalf of Valeria Victrix LLP. Alternatively, of course, the notice and the certification could be signed by a director of Holstebro Caledon Ltd. There will also be a covering letter, which will ask Airdrie Meteorological Consultancies Ltd to confirm receipt.

Non-standard cases

5.52   What has been described so far is the ordinary law of assignation. There are also some non-standard cases.

(1) If the debt has been embodied in a fully negotiable instrument, special rules apply. In particular intimation is not required and the *assignatus utitur* rule does not apply. The rules are in the Bills of Exchange Act 1882, which covers almost all types of negotiable instrument. (One or two types are subject to common law, but the common law rules are essentially the same as the 1882 Act rules.)[90]

(2) Rights under life assurance contracts are assignable, but there exists special legislation: Policies of Assurance Act 1867, s 5. Whether this actually applies to Scotland is doubtful, but in practice it is assumed that it does.

(3) For certificated company shares and bonds the Stock Transfer Act 1963 applies. The transferor signs a stock transfer form and delivers it, with the share certificate, to the transferee, who then sends them both to the company, and is issued with a new certificate in his or her name. For 'dematerialised' shares there is a dematerialised form of transfer.[91]

---

[90]   The standard work is N Elliott (ed), *Byles on Bills of Exchange and Cheques* (29th edn, 2013). See also E McKendrick, (ed), *Goode on Commercial Law* (5th edn, 2016) ch 19.

[91]   Companies Act 2006, s 783 ff.

INCORPOREAL MOVEABLE PROPERTY: INTELLECTUAL PROPERTY RIGHTS

5.53   Intellectual property (IP) rights, such as copyright and patents, are patrimonial rights and can be sold, donated, bequeathed and so on.[92] They are transferred by assignation. Unlike ordinary incorporeal moveable property, they are not personal rights: there is no person against whom such a right is held. Thus there is no third party to whom intimation should be, or could be, made. Some IP rights, notably copyright, exist without registration, and these are assigned by simple consent, provided that it is in writing.[93] The requirement of writing applies to the transfer of all types of IP right. Most types of IP rights are registered, and in that case so must the assignation.[94] There are uncertainties as to whether the right passes to the grantee at the time of registration (as in the case of heritable property) or whether registration has merely the effect of delivery in the sale of goods. It may be that the IP right passes on delivery of the deed of assignation, but that until it is registered a good faith buyer from the seller might obtain a good title in much the same way as is contemplated by SOGA 1979, s 24.[95]

LITERATURE

5.54   As for the previous chapter, Reid *Property* paras 597–718 is valuable. For detailed accounts of conveyancing see E Sinclair and A Stewart, *Conveyancing Practice in Scotland* (7th edn, 2016) and Gretton and Reid, *Conveyancing*. (Other works on conveyancing are now rather dated.) For corporeal movable property the standard work is Carey Miller with Irvine *Corporeal Moveables*. On the sale of goods two excellent works are P S Atiyah, J Adams, and H MacQueen, *The Sale of Goods* (13th edn, 2016) and R M Goode and E McKendrick *Goode on Commercial Law* (5th edn, 2016). For a detailed study of the transfer of incorporeals see R G Anderson, *Assignation* (2008). (Information about other systems of transfer of corporeal moveable property can be found in such works as J M Rainer and J Filip-Fröschl (eds) *Transfer of Title Concerning Movables Part I* (2006), L P W van Vliet *Transfer of Movables in German, French, English and Dutch law* (2000), and Van Erp and Akkermans, *Property Law*.)

---

[92]   See **PARA 1.19** above.
[93]   Copyright, Designs and Patents Act 1988, s 90.
[94]   Eg Patents Act 1977, s 33.
[95]   See **PARA 5.35** above.

Chapter 6

Prescription

GENERAL

6.1   Time changes many things: acorns to oaks; oaks to firewood or sawdust. Rights too can grow or die by the running of time. There is a name for this: prescription. Prescription is of two types: the creation of rights by time (prescriptive acquisition, or acquisitive prescription), and the loss of rights by time (prescriptive extinction, or extinctive prescription). The terms 'acquisitive prescription' and 'extinctive prescription' are used in some countries,[1] but in Scots law the terms used are 'positive' and 'negative' prescription. The subject is regulated by the Prescription and Limitation (Scotland) Act 1973 (PL(S)A 1973).[2] Whether prescription is fair is a matter on which opinions differ.[3] The argument for prescription is that if there is a split, or discrepancy, between (i) the *de facto* position, the position in social reality, and (ii) the legal position, then that split or discrepancy should not last indefinitely: a time should come when the law adapts itself to the social reality. It can result in unfairness in individual cases, but the argument is that it is fairer overall than a rule that allows an indefinitely long divergence between the law and the social reality, and that allows long-forgotten rights to be resurrected at any time. In the words of the old maxim, *vigilantibus non dormientibus jura subveniunt.*[4] The law should not protect *for ever* those who do nothing to enforce their rights. Most legal systems allow for prescription to take place.

6.2   This chapter deals with prescription in general, and particularly in relation to ownership. But prescription is also important in relation to subordinate real rights, and indeed in practice perhaps affects them more often than it affects ownership, and that aspect of the subject is discussed in more detail elsewhere.[5] As far as ownership is concerned, the replacement of the old Register of Sasines with the modern Land Register has led to the reduction, but not the complete elimination, of the role of prescription in relation to the ownership of land.

NEGATIVE PRESCRIPTION

Negative prescription: personal rights

6.3   Negative prescription applies mainly to personal rights. For example, a right to be repaid a debt normally prescribes after five years.[6] Thus, in 2012 Abigail borrows money from Brendan, the loan contract saying that repayment is to be on 15 May 2014. She does not repay. If between 15 May 2014 (when the loan matures) and 15 May 2019 she pays nothing and does not acknowledge the debt's existence and he does not raise an action, the debt will be extinguished.

6.4   Negative prescription should be distinguished from limitation, which is also covered by PL(S)A 1973. Whereas negative prescription extinguishes an obligation, limitation does not, but it bars the raising of an action except with the permission

---

[1]   Eg *la prescription acquisitive* and *la prescription extinctive* in French law, or acquisitive and extinctive prescription in South African law.

[2]   This statute has been amended many times. Further amendments are in contemplation: see The Scottish Law Commission, Report on Prescription (Scot Law Com No 247, 2017).

[3]   For the views of the European Court of Human Rights see *J A Pye (Oxford) Ltd v UK* (2006) 43 EHRR 3.

[4]   The law protects those who are awake, not those who sleep. More pithily: 'if you snooze, you lose'.

[5]   See **PARAS 19.19, 19.26, 13.27 13.45** and **14.66**.

[6]   PL(S)A 1973, s 6. This is called the short negative prescription, or the quinquennial prescription.

of the court. The limitation period is three years. It applies only to certain defined obligations, notably the obligation to pay damages for causing personal injury.[7]

Negative prescription: subordinate real rights

6.5   Subordinate real rights can also be extinguished by negative prescription, through non-exercise for 20 years.[8] For example, if there is a servitude, but it is not exercised for 20 years, then, at the end of that period, it is extinguished.[9] In practice, negative prescription is more significant for title conditions, such as servitudes, than it is for other subordinate real rights.

Negative prescription: the real right of ownership

6.6   The real right of ownership of land is excluded from negative prescription:[10] as the legislation says, it is 'imprescriptible'.[11] Heather inherits a house in 2000. She neither uses it nor lets it out and in fact never visits it. It is taken over by squatters. In 2025, has her ownership been cut down by non-possession for 20 years? No. But whilst ownership of land is imprescriptible in the sense that it cannot be lost by *negative* prescription, it is still capable of being lost by prescription, for it can be lost if someone else acquires it by positive prescription.[12] (Possibly by the squatters, but as will be seen below acquiring prescriptive ownership of land is not just a question of taking possession.) As to whether the real right of ownership of *corporeal moveables* can be lost by negative prescription, there is some difficulty, but it seems that the answer is that it can, by loss of possession for 20 years. This is discussed below.

POSITIVE PRESCRIPTION

Positive prescription: introduction

6.7   Positive prescription applies to real rights in land.[13] It probably does not apply to real rights in moveables,[14] and it does not apply to any other types of right, such as personal rights or intellectual property rights or public law rights. In practice, the main cases in which a prescriptive title can be obtained to a real

---

[7]   PL(S)A 1973, s 17.
[8]   PL(S)A 1973, s 8.
[9]   See **PARA 13.45** below.
[10]   So too is a registered lease: PL(S)A 1973, Sch 3.
[11]   PL(S)A 1973, Sch 3 para (a).
[12]   See **PARAS 6.7 ff** below.
[13]   The governing legislation is PL(S)A 1973 ss 1, 2 and 3.
[14]   See **PARA 6.22** below.

right in land are ownership, servitudes and public rights of way.[15] Of course, positive prescription is relevant only in a minority of cases, for rights in land are usually validly granted from the outset, and so the question of validation by the running of time is irrelevant. Still, positive prescription is a significant aspect of property law. As already mentioned, in this chapter we deal only with positive prescription as a means of acquiring ownership.

Prescriptive acquisition of ownership of land: the basic Idea

6.8   To acquire ownership of land by prescription, there are two requirements. The first is possession for ten years. The second is that the person has an *ostensible* registered title. So, if Annabelle possesses land for 15 years, that on its own is not enough, but if she possesses for 15 years, **and** there was also a registered disposition in her favour, that works. The ten-year period is calculated from either (i) the beginning of the possession or (ii) the registration of the deed, whichever is later. So, if a disposition (latently invalid) in favour of Annabelle is registered in 2016, and she possesses as from 2017, her title is validated as from 2027 (not 2016) and, conversely, if she possesses from 2015 her title is validated as from 2026 (not 2025).

Effect of positive prescription

6.9   What is the effect of positive prescription? That depends on whether the title in question was voidable or void. (If it was neither, the assistance of prescription is not needed.) (i) If it was voidable, the effect of positive prescription is to remove the voidability, so that the title becomes absolutely good. Ownership is not transferred, because ownership has already been transferred. Suppose that Adam owns land and in 2015 dispones it to Hannah. There was misrepresentation by Hannah, the result of which is that the transfer is voidable. But Adam does nothing. In 2025, the title ceases to be voidable. But ownership does not pass: ownership passed to Hannah in 2015, when the Adam/Hannah disposition was registered. (There is perhaps a lack of logic in the law here, for in this case positive prescription is actually operating as negative prescription – to extinguish a right.) (ii) If, however, the problem is that the disposition was void, the effect of prescription is to transfer ownership.[16] Take the previous example, and suppose that the disposition was void, because, unknown to Hannah, Adam was incapax. The registration of the disposition could not transfer ownership. But in 2025 there will be a flash of lightning and roll of thunder, and ownership will pass to Hannah. That fact will not involve any change in the Land Register. The Land Register will look the same the day after the tenth anniversary as it did the day before.

---

[15]   Actually, it may be that a public right of way is not a real right. The argument is that real rights can exist only in private law, and that public rights of way exist in public law. But the point is of theoretical rather than practical significance.

[16]   PL(S)A 1973, s 5(1A) as inserted by LR(S)A 2012.

Nor, in all probability, will Hannah even know what has happened, because she has no doubt assumed that she had good title all along. (The examples in this paragraph presuppose that she has been in possession for the ten years.)

The foundation deed

6.10   The deed that creates the ostensible title is known, for the purposes of prescription, as the 'foundation' deed (or 'writ', for 'writ' is sometimes used in the sense of 'deed'). If the deed is absolutely good, prescription is irrelevant anyway. Prescription becomes relevant if the foundation deed is void or voidable. The foundation deed must *appear* to be valid. Nothing within the four corners of the deed must suggest otherwise.[17]

The Keeper's role

6.11   In general, if the Keeper knows that a deed is void when it is submitted to her, it will not be accepted for registration, and so prescription can never run. But there are occasions where the Keeper does not know the position, or, by human error, makes a mistake. For example, if a deed is void because the granter was incapax, the Keeper is unlikely to know that fact. Following registration, prescription can run in favour of the grantee. A disposition might include a border area that the granter possesses but has no title. The Keeper for one reason or another might not realise that there is a problem and might simply register the disposition as it stands. Prescription could then run in favour of the grantee.

6.12   In some cases, however, the Keeper does know that a disposition is wholly or partly void, because the granter has no title, and nevertheless accepts it. Such a deed is known as an *a non domino* disposition. That means 'from a non-owner'. Actually, *any* disposition from a person with a bad title is an *a non domino* disposition, but the term tends to be used in practice to refer to dispositions that are known to all parties to be *a non domino*. Under what circumstances will the Keeper accept such a deed? The first condition is that the property must already have been possessed by the granter (or by both granter and grantee) for at least one year. (So that overall there would have to be 1 + 10 = 11 years of possession before ownership could be obtained.) The second is that the person who appears to be the true owner must be notified. If no one else can be identified, the Queen's and Lord Treasurer's Remembrancer must be notified, because the Crown takes property that is otherwise ownerless. If the Keeper does accept such a deed, the entry in the Register is marked 'provisional' and the Keeper's warranty of title does not apply.[18] Registration does

---

[17]   This point was explored in *Watson v Shields* 1996 SCLR 81 and *Aberdeen College Board of Management v Youngson* 2005 SLT 371.
[18]   LR(S)A 2012, ss 43–45.

not transfer ownership, but it does make it possible for prescription to run, so that ownership may be acquired ten years later.

6.13   In practice these rules mean that a deed that is known to be *a non domino* is seldom accepted for registration. Whether that is a good thing is controversial. Traditionally, the *a non domino* disposition was used to settle title to property that was in someone's unchallenged possession but where no valid title could be discovered, such as a farm that had been in the same family for generations, but with the current 'owner' unable to prove any title. Ten years after registration the title would be good. But today any such attempt is likely to lead to the farm being claimed by someone else. Some think that it should be made easier to obtain prescriptive title.

Good faith?

6.14   Does the grantee have to be in good faith for prescription to run? The general answer is no. But there is an exception, concerning forgery. Contrast two cases. (i) Cornelius owns land and Darius impersonates him and forges his signature on a disposition to Elfrieda. Elfrieda is in good faith and the disposition is registered. The disposition is void and she does not acquire ownership. But prescription will run, and after ten years she will become owner. (ii) But if she knew that the deed was forged, prescription does not run in her favour.[19]

Possession must be without 'interruption'

6.15   The possessor has to possess 'openly, peaceably and without any judicial interruption'.[20] So possession obtained and maintained by force does not count. 'Judicial interruption' means a court action.[21] On 1 June 2018 a disposition to Maxine is registered and she takes possession. On 31 May 2028 Petronella, claiming to be the true owner, raises an action to recover the property. Maxine's possession has been judicially interrupted, and, assuming that Petronella's claim is sound in law, Maxine is not protected by prescription – even if the action takes another two years to be concluded.

Possession must be 'founded on' the foundation deed

6.16   The possession must be 'founded on' the foundation deed.[22] Take this case. Julius grants a 25-year lease to Indira. She sneakily manages, somehow, to get an

---

[19]   PL(S)A 1973, s 1(2).
[20]   PL(S)A 1973, s 1.
[21]   PL(S)A 1973, s 4.
[22]   PL(S)A 1973 s 1; *Houstoun v Barr* 1911 SC 134.

ostensible title on to the Land Register. After ten years, does ownership pass to her? No. She has possessed the land as lessee, not as owner. The point is sometimes expressed as being that the possession must be 'adverse' ie incompatible with the rights of the owner.

What sort of possession?

6.17   Possession is of two types, direct (natural) or indirect (civil),[23] and either type can be invoked for the purposes of prescription. Thus, suppose that there is a latently invalid disposition to Polonius, registered in the Land Register. He immediately grants a 25-year lease of the property to Queenie, who possesses the property as tenant. Here we have civil possession (Polonius) and natural possession (Queenie). Prescription runs in his favour and after ten years his title will be good.

6.18   Often the facts of possession are clear. But with some types of property they may not be, such as derelict land, and moreover neighbours in dispute over a boundary area will commonly come up with wholly different stories as to who has been in possession. All such disputes will if necessary have to be decided by the courts.[24]

Positive prescription: Sasine Register and Land Register compared

6.19   The law applies to both registers, with only minor differences.[25] The main difference concerns the importance of prescription: in the Sasine Register it played a more significant role than it does in the Land Register. In the latter, if Benedict buys property in good faith from Caspar, he is protected from any invisible invalidity in Caspar's title. This is for two reasons. The first is that the *nemo plus* principle is disapplied in some types of case involving the Land Register, so that Benedict will probably become owner immediately.[26] In the second place, even if, on the facts of the case, the *nemo plus* principle is not disapplied, so that his title is invalid, nevertheless he will in most cases enjoy the protection of the Keeper's title warranty, so that if the worst comes to the worst and he loses the property, he can be sure of receiving compensation. But in the Sasine Register, a buyer was less well protected. The *nemo plus* principle always applied, and there was no Keeper's warranty of title. So, prescription played a vital role in Sasine Register conveyancing.

---

[23]   See **CHAPTER 12**.
[24]   See, ie, *Hamilton v McIntosh Donald Ltd* 1994 SLT 793 and *Stevenson-Hamilton's Executors v McStay* 2001 SLT 694.
[25]   Under LR(S)A 1979 there was a large difference, in that prescription could not run on indemnified titles. This irrational rule has disappeared under the new legislation.
[26]   See **CHAPTER 7** below.

Positive prescription: subordinate real rights

6.20   Positive prescription is also possible as a means of acquiring certain subordinate real rights, in particular servitudes and public rights of way. The period is 20 years.[27]

Corporeal Moveables

6.21   It is unfortunate that the PL(S)A 1973 does not mention corporeal moveables, either for positive or for negative prescription. For negative prescription, s 8 probably applies. Vera owns a painting. Wendy steals it and hangs it in her own house. After 20 years of non-possession, it seems to be that Vera loses ownership. But that does not mean that the wicked Wendy acquires it: the Crown does. This is, at any rate, the best guess as to what the law is, the logic being that when Vera's ownership is cut off by negative prescription, the painting becomes ownerless, and property that becomes ownerless passes to the Crown.[28]

6.22   As for positive prescription, the law is again unclear. Perhaps it does not apply at all to corporeal moveables, or perhaps there is a common-law rule whereby ownership is acquired after 40 years.[29] Most corporeal moveables are of limited value and of limited lifespan, so prescription is not usually a significant issue. But some are long-lived and of high value, as everyone in the world of antiquities and art knows. The lack of a clear rule to settle title after long possession is surprising. Most other legal systems have such a rule. In 2012, the Scottish Law Commission recommended that a 20-year period for positive prescription should be introduced.[30] Unfortunately this recommendation has not been implemented.

COMPENSATION

6.23   If prescription takes place, whether positive or negative, no compensation can be claimed. The reason is that those who suffer have no one to blame but themselves. Those who dislike prescription will dislike this logic.

---

[27]   PL(S)A 1973, ss 2 and 3. See below, **PARAS 13.27** and **19.19–19.20**.
[28]   Reid, *Property* para 675.
[29]   The key case is *Parishioners of Aberscherder v Parish of Gemrie* (1633) Mor 10972 but there is uncertainty as to the ratio, and a paucity of later authority. See generally Carey Miller with Irvine, *Corporeal Moveables* ch 7 and A R C Simpson, 'Positive Prescription of Moveables in Scots Law' (2009) 13 EdinLR 445.
[30]   Scottish Law Commission, Report on Prescription and Title to Moveable Property (Scot Law Com No 228, 2012).

LITERATURE

6.24   The standard work is Johnston *Prescription*. The subject is covered in all texts on property law and conveyancing, but the older ones do not take account of the changes made by the Land Registration etc (Scotland) Act 2012. Detailed coverage of the latter can be found in CHAPTER 17 of Reid and Gretton *Land Registration*.

Chapter 7

Land registration

INTRODUCTION

Medical overview of the chapter

7.1   This chapter has four parts. First, there is the introduction. Next there is the anatomy of the Land Register. Thirdly, there is physiology: the normal healthy functioning of the register in day-to-day registrations. Lastly, there is pathology (with therapeutics): what happens when things go wrong. The divisions are only approximate: for example, the Keeper's warranty is discussed in the last part, because it is relevant only when things go wrong, but it could equally be allocated to the third part, because it is a normal part of the registration process.

Registration: an introduction

7.2   Registration is a good way – perhaps the best – of satisfying the publicity principle.[1] The idea is so obvious that the question to ask is not why property rights in land are registered but why *all* property rights are not registered.

   (1) It is not only land rights that are registered. Most intellectual property rights are too – the main exception being copyright. So too are ships, and aircraft mortgages.

---

[1]   See **PARA 4.19** above.

(2) A registration system costs money, and so is justifiable only if the average values are high enough. Thus, registration is justifiable for rights in land but not for rights in bicycles.

(3) Land has some features that make registration easier than for some types of property: in particular, it is permanent and does not move, and so in principle is easily re-identifiable over time.

(4) More types of right can exist in land than in moveable property. Thus, title tends to be more complex and the more complex the title, the more convenient it is for the rights to be recorded publicly.

7.3   Immoveable property registration was introduced in Scotland by the Registration Act 1617.[2] This established the Sasine Register which still exists today. A replacement system was introduced by the Land Registration (Scotland) Act 1979 (LR(S)A 1979), the new register being the Land Register of Scotland, usually called just the 'Land Register'. Properties are being gradually transferred from the old register into the new. Some terminological points: although the Sasine Register is, obviously, a register, deeds are commonly said to be 'recorded' there, rather than 'registered', with the latter term being used for the Land Register. The expression 'first registration' means the transfer of a property out of the old register into the new, and 'unregistered property' means property that is not yet in the new register. (It will therefore still be in the Sasine Register.)

7.4   In many countries land registration is decentralised; for instance with a separate register for each local area. Scotland has a unitary system, based in Edinburgh. That is so, both for the old register and for the new. However, each register has 33 divisions, one for each county. (The old counties, not the modern local authority areas. Thus, for land registration purposes Edinburgh is in Midlothian. An exception is that Glasgow has always formed a separate division under the picturesque name of 'the Barony and Regality of Glasgow'.) Both the Sasine Register and the Land Register are administered by the Keeper of the Registers of Scotland – in practice called simply 'the Keeper'. Everything is done in the Keeper's name, though in reality the Keeper is simply the manager of a department – the Registers of Scotland (RoS).[3] This department runs many registers, including the Register of Inhibitions and the Books of Council and Session. (By contrast, in other countries the department that handles land registration generally does nothing else. An example is HM Land Registry in England.) It employs more than a thousand staff. RoS pays its own way, mainly by charging registration fees. Thus it is not a burden on the taxpayer. Despite its name, several important registers are outwith the remit of RoS, for example the Companies Register and the Register of Births, Deaths and Marriages.

---

[2]   For the history of property registration in Scotland, see (i) L Ockrent *Land Rights: An Enquiry into the History of Registration for Publication in Scotland* (1942) – happily, war does not always suspend scholarship: cf T Cooper *Select Scottish Cases of the Thirteenth Century* (1944) – and (ii) Reid and Gretton, *Land Registration* chapters 1 and 2.

[3]   www.ros.gov.uk/.

The incentive to register

7.5   A register sounds a good idea, but how does one persuade people to co-operate? The answer is simple. The law makes registration a necessary part of the process of conveyancing: no registration, no real right. While the Land Register and the Sasine Register differ in many respects, both adopt that principle. Registration is 'compulsory' only in the sense that those who do not register do not acquire a right that has real effect. No *compulsion* exists. Property law always and necessarily has the task of laying down *how and when* a real right is created, transferred or extinguished.[4] If it did not say 'registration' then it would have to say something else instead. The Sasine Register system could be summarised in one sentence: a deed creating, transferring or extinguishing a right in land takes real effect (if at all) when it is recorded. To that sentence there are some additions and qualifications to be made, of course. But that is the essence. Thus the Sasine Register system does not really *modify* property law. The Land Register, as will be seen, goes rather further in modifying property law, but even there the basic idea is similar.[5]

7.6   To state the obvious, the 'no registration, no real right' principle applies only to *real* rights, not to personal rights. Adam owns land and enters a contract of sale with Eve. She thereby acquires a personal right – to require Adam to grant her a disposition, in exchange for payment of the price. The contract creates personal rights only, and is thus valid without registration. (Indeed, generally speaking personal rights cannot be registered in the Land Register.)

Public access and the title glasshouse

7.7   The Sasine Register and the Land Register are, like other registers, public. But for the Sasine Register, it was unusual for non-lawyers to look at it, because getting information out of it was difficult and needed legal expertise. The transition to the Land Register has not been a change in the *theory* of public access, but it has made a difference to the *practice*, for information is easy to get, and is fairly easy for non-lawyers to understand. If Fergus transfers his house to Ingrid, that fact can readily be discovered by his creditors, by the local council, by his snooping neighbours, by HM Revenue & Customs, by his friends and relatives, by his enemies, by the police, by scandal-sniffing journalists, or indeed by anyone else, by payment to the Keeper of a modest fee. Properties may have opaque walls; property titles do not. Not everyone is happy to live in a title glasshouse. Some public figures such as politicians and media celebrities prefer to have ownership vested in a nominee.

---

[4]   Thus property law has to define the event by which ownership of moveables passes, etc.
[5]   LR(S)A 1979 made fairly deep inroads into property law; LR(S)A 2012 reversed much of that.

The Sasine Register: 1617 and all that

7.8   The full name of the old register is the General Register of Sasines. In practice it is called the 'Sasine Register', the 'Sasines Register', the 'Register of Sasines' or the 'GRS'. It was established by the Registration Act 1617, which remains in force, though amended and supplemented over the centuries by piecemeal legislation. The Sasine Register is a collection of copies of deeds. Suppose that in 1800 David disponed to Esther.[6] She presented the deed[7] to the Keeper. A member of staff copied it, using a quill pen, into a large leather-bound volume. (As from 1934 deeds were photocopied. Later still digital scanning was adopted.) After recording, the deed was returned to Esther, marked with the recording date. This was the date when she became the owner. If someone lost a recorded deed, that did not matter much because an official copy (an extract[8]) could be obtained from the Keeper, i.e. a copy of the recorded copy. A deed did not have to be plan-based, and if there was a plan there was no assurance of its accuracy. Many deeds in the Sasine Register identified the property with a description which, though long-winded, was in reality not much more than a postal address.

7.9   The Sasine Register is *a public warehouse of private deeds*, and the warehouse keeper is the Keeper. The warehouse used to be physical, and for the most part still is, though nowadays scanned deeds can occupy virtual shelves, not actual ones. Like a warehouse keeper, the Keeper keeps a stock inventory. Everything is indexed, by (i) names of parties and (ii) property. Without this system, which is run efficiently, the register would be unworkable, because the warehouse contains many millions of copy deeds, accumulated since 1617. Each deed, as it comes in, is assigned to whichever registration area the property is in. But apart from that there is no sorting. So, for the Perthshire division, a disposition of a flat in central Perth might be followed on the next page of the volume by a standard security over a farm near Dunkeld, and so on. If Janet wishes to buy 57 Harry Potter Loan, Auchterarder, the title to which is still in the Sasine Register, and wishes (as she will) to see what the recorded deeds are that relate to that property, before she hands over the money to the seller, finding those deeds in the register would be like finding a needle in a haystack, were it not for the indexing system.

7.10   The indexing system made it possible for all the relevant recorded deeds to be identified quickly and reliably (albeit subject to the occasional glitch). To speak of the Sasine Register in the past tense, is in fact misleading, for many properties are still in that register. If today, in 2017, Janet is buying 57 Harry Potter Loan, and if that property is still in the old register, she will need to check the Sasine Register just as she would have done before the Land Register was introduced, though this will

---

[6]   It is sometimes said that at common law women could not own immoveable property. Not so.

[7]   A complication that need not be gone into here is that in 1800 it was not the disposition itself but a further deed, based on the disposition, called the instrument of sasine, that was recorded. (Recording of the disposition itself arrived with the Titles to Land (Scotland) Act 1858, s 1.)

[8]   An extract is a full and officially certified copy from an entry in a register. The term is not limited to the Sasine Register or Land Register.

be the last time such a check would be needed, because her title will be registered in the Land Register, and when, in, say, 2027, she comes to sell, the eventual buyer will need to check only the Land Register.

7.11 A search of the register can be done for as many years as is desired, even all the way back to 1617. Unlike a real warehouse nothing that goes in through the gates ever goes out again. And subject to one or two qualifications, one does not have to worry about unrecorded deeds because these cannot normally affect the title. (That is the incentive to register.) This 'no registration, no real right' principle (which applies equally in the Land Register) constitutes the central value of a property registration system.[9] It brings with it a radical simplification when it comes to finding out who has what rights in land.

7.12 Since the system is simply a collection of indexed copy deeds, there is nothing that officially says 'Jack is the owner of Redmains' or that 'Bank of Airdrie Plc has a standard security over Greenmains'. Nor is there anything that officially sets out the boundaries of properties. If Janet wishes to be satisfied, before she hands over the purchase price, that the seller, Jack, is indeed the owner, and moreover that the property is free from subordinate real rights, she has to work this out for herself or, in practice, hire a solicitor to do so. The Sasine Register is a register of deeds,[10] not of rights. Therefore *the rights have to be inferred from the deeds.* This is far from simple. If Janet locates a disposition by Alan to Tara and another from Tara to Jack, she may infer that Tara was owner and that as a result Jack is now owner. That inference is probably right, but not certainly. Perhaps the deed is invalid for some non-obvious reason. What Janet is interested in ascertaining is Jack's right. The Sasine Register does not set out that information. It offers, without comment, a set of juridical acts. In practice, a skilled conveyancer can check Jack's title with a high degree of accuracy. But it takes time (and hence money), and there is always a slight element of uncertainty.

7.13 Suppose that it is the year 1980[11] and Janet paid her money, obtained a disposition and recorded it in the Sasine Register. It then turned out that Jack's title was defective as to part or even all of what Janet thought she was buying. Janet would have been unprotected by the system. It never promised her anything more than a set of deeds to examine. This is not quite as bad as it sounds. She would have had a damages claim against Jack,[12] and she might (depending on what exactly has gone wrong) have had a negligence claim against her own solicitor. Nevertheless,

---

[9] In many deeds recording systems round the world, ownership passes without recording, but is precarious until recording happens. (Here, it was not until *Young v Leith* (1847) 9 D 932 that it was settled that in the Sasine Register system there is no real right before recording.) Whichever approach is adopted, third parties are, broadly speaking, unaffected by unrecorded deeds.
[10] What is a 'deed'? It is a juridical act that has been formally executed in paper or electronic form.
[11] Today a Jack/Janet sale would result in her title being registered in the Land Register, not the Sasine Register.
[12] In warrandice. See **PARAS 5.9–5.13** above.

as will be seen, the Land Register offers her more. It offers what people are mainly interested in: the rights themselves.

THE LAND REGISTER

Introduction

7.14   From about 1900, pressure began to replace the Sasine Register with a title register,[13] but events moved slowly. The Land Register was finally set up by the Land Registration (Scotland) Act 1979 (LR(S)A 1979), and the first registration took place on 6 April 1981. Over time it became apparent that the 1979 Act had faults, and it was replaced by the Land Registration etc (Scotland) Act 2012 (LR(S)A 2012), which came into force on 8 December 2014. The change from LR(S)A 1979 to LR(S)A 2012 is a story of evolution rather than revolution. The revolution happened with LR(S)A 1979.

7.15   Is the Land Register system more or less complicated than the Sasine Register system? The answer is: both. The *law* is more complicated, but the *practice* is less complicated. The Sasine Register simplified the process of finding out who has what rights in property, and the Land Register has made that process even simpler. As noted earlier, an intelligent non-lawyer can use the Land Register, whereas the Sasine Register is usable only by experts. But the achievement of that simplicity of use has required some complication of the legislative framework, rather as a machine may become easier to use by a higher degree of sophistication in its inner workings. Students of property law need to know the inner workings.

Switching properties from the old register to the new: (i) the system until 2014

7.16   LR(S)A 1979 provided for the 33 registration divisions to become 'operational' one by one. The first was Renfrewshire in 1981 and the final batch were made operational in 2003. (The 1979 Act did not provide for registration in the territorial seabed – that is, within 12 nautical miles of the coast – but that was changed by LR(S)A 2012, and a new registration area was set up, covering the whole of Scotland's territorial seabed, so that today the traditional 33 registration areas have become 34.)

---

[13]   Title registration originated in Germany and now exists in a substantial minority of states round the world. A common system is the 'Torrens' system, developed in Australia. Each state that has adopted it has made its own variations, so it is not so much a single system as a family of systems. The modern system as it exists under the LR(S)A 2012, has been influenced by the Torrens system, the English system and the German system.

Renfrew[14]	6 April 1981	Berwick	1 October 1999
Dunbarton	4 October 1982	East Lothian	1 October 1999
Lanark	3 January 1984	Peebles	1 October 1999
Glasgow	30 September 1985	Roxburgh	1 October 1999
Clackmannan	1 October 1992	Selkirk	1 October 1999
Stirling	1 April 1993	Argyll	1 April 2000
West Lothian	1 October 1993	Bute	1 April 2000
Fife	1 April 1995	Midlothian	1 April 2001
Aberdeen	1 April 1996	Inverness	1 April 2002
Dumfries	1 April 1997	Nairn	1 April 2002
Ayr	1 April 1997	Banff	1 April 2003
Dumfries	1 April 1997	Caithness	1 April 2003
Kirkcudbright	1 April 1997	Moray	1 April 2003
Wigtown	1 April 1997	Orkney & Shetland	1 April 2003
Angus	1 April 1999	Ross & Cromarty	1 April 2003
Kinross	1 April 1999	Sutherland	1 April 2003
Perth	1 April 1999	Seabed	8 December 2014

7.17   When a county became operational, that did not mean that all properties immediately switched to the new register. The rule was (in broad terms) that a property would switch when it was first sold after the county became operational. Thus if a property in Renfrewshire was sold in 1982, it would switch to the new register. But if a property in Argyll was sold on the same date, there would be no switch. The trigger was *sale*. So if in, say, 1985 Henrietta bought a house in Fife and in, say, 2010 donated it to her son Donald, the 2010 disposition would be recorded in the Sasine Register, not the Land Register. Or if, instead of a donation to her son, the transaction was a standard security, again the standard security would be recorded in the Sasine Register. But if the property had been in Lanarkshire, the story would be different. For when she bought the house in 1985 the disposition would have gone into the Land Register, and every deed since then would also have gone into that register, for the movement of properties between the registers is one way only. Once a property is in the Land Register, no deed affecting that property can be recorded in the Sasine Register.

7.18   In 2014 about 26% of Scotland was in the Land Register, calculated by area, and about 58%, calculated by title units,[15] the reason for the difference being that smaller properties tend to change hands at shorter intervals than larger properties.

---

14   By an odd convention, where a county name ends in 'shire' that element is dropped. So 'Renfrew' means not Renfrew but Renfrewshire.
15   Registers of Scotland's website: www.ros.gov.uk/property-data/land-register-coverage.

(A title unit, or plot of land to use the expression in LR(S)A 2012,[16] might be a large estate in Perthshire, a small farm in Moray, a house in Glasgow, etc. There are about 2.3 million title units.) The Cadastral Map is still an uncompleted jigsaw.

7.19   Although the Land Register has gradually expanded at the expense of the Sasine Register, the process has been slow and under the provisions of the 1979 Act would have taken centuries to complete. One of the major changes made by LR(S)A 2012 was that the extension of the new register has been speeded up.[17]

Switching properties from the old register to the new: (ii) the new system

7.20   In 2014 it was announced that the target was completion of the Land Register by 2024.[18] Whilst it is unlikely that that target (which is not legally binding) will be met, clearly by that date not many properties will still be in the Register of Sasines. How is this rapid extension of Land Register coverage being achieved? The subject is complex, but LR(S)A 2012 introduced four main changes.[19]

7.21   In the first place, no disposition can be recorded in the Sasine Register.[20] So for instance if today Myfanwy donates her house to her son Nestor, and title is still in the Sasine Register, the disposition will be registered in the Land Register. Or suppose that instead of donating it to him inter vivos, she dies, and bequeaths it to him. Her executor dispones it to him, and the disposition will be registered in the Land Register. (By contrast, under LR(S)A 1979 dispositions not by reason of sale did not trigger first registration in the Land Register.)

7.22   In the second place, anyone who still has a Sasine Register title has the right to transfer it into the Land Registration – so-called voluntary registration.[21] (Under the previous legislation this could only happen at the Keeper's discretion.)

7.23   In the third place, no standard security can be recorded in the Sasine Register.[22] Professor and Mrs Gretton co-own the house that they live in. Their title is still in the Sasine Register, and if they wished to grant a standard security, they would first have to carry out a voluntary registration.

[16]   LR(S)A 2012, s 3(4).
[17]   'Completion of the Land Register is considered to be the most important policy aim of the Bill.' (Scottish Government, Land Registration etc. (Scotland) Bill: Policy Memorandum (2011) para 14).
[18]   Registers of Scotland, *Completion of the Land Register: Public Consultation* (2014); Reid and Gretton, *Land Registration* para 7.4. See further John King, 'Completion of the Land Register' in F McCarthy, J Chalmers and S Bogle (eds), *Essays in Conveyancing and Property Law in Honour of Professor Robert Rennie* (2015).
[19]   We cover the chief points, omitting some of the fine detail, especially about long leases.
[20]   LR(S)A 2012, s 48(1). This closes the Register of Sasines to any disposition, so that the Land Register is the only way of bringing about transfer of ownership.
[21]   LR(S)A 2012, s 27(1).
[22]   LR(S)A 2012, s 48(1). This came into effect in April 2016.

7.24   In the fourth place, there is 'Keeper-induced registration' (KIR), which is to say that the Keeper can complete the jigsaw by switching any property into the new register, without there being either (i) a registrable transaction or (ii) an application by the owner for voluntary registration.[23] The owner's consent is not needed. Without KIR the completion of Land Register coverage would have taken many decades or even longer: for instance, for many public-sector properties there may be no registrable transaction for centuries. (Some properties have even been in the same hands – the Crown, a local authority, one of the older universities) since even before the Registration Act 1617 – so have never even made an appearance in the Sasine Register.) Even in the private-sector there may be no registrable deed for very long periods, such as property owned by some companies.

7.25   It had at one stage been thought that KIR would be an endgame strategy, not to be activated to any significant degree until the 2012 Act had been in force for perhaps 20 or 30 years. But the announcement of the target of 2024 for completion of the Land Register meant that KIR would have to be used early and aggressively. One or two trials were done in 2015 (St Kilda[24] being joint first, together with the Georgian House in Edinburgh's Charlotte Square). KIR began in earnest in late 2016, and RoS were hoping to have registered about 100,000 properties through KIR by the end of 2017. In its 400th anniversary year the Sasine Register is approaching its end.

THE ANATOMY OF THE LAND REGISTER

The four parts of the Land Register

7.26   The Land Register is divided into four parts:[25] (i) the Cadastral Map, (ii) the Title Sheet Record, (iii) the Archive record and (iv) the Application Record. This structure was not mentioned in LR(S)A 1979 but it developed *de facto*, and is now set out in part 1 of LR(S)A 2012.

First part of the Land Register: the Cadastral Map

7.27   Everyone is familiar with maps. The Ordnance Survey (OS) produces accurate maps at a variety of scales. The largest scale, 1:1250, shows such detail as garden walls and the individual shapes of houses. OS maps are 'topographic' maps, which is to say that they show the physical features on the ground, whether natural or man-made. They are a formalised version of what one would see from a balloon on a typical Scottish cloudless day. Topographic maps sometimes show

---

23   LR(S)A 2012, s 29.
24   Hence the cover picture for this edition.
25   LR(S)A 2012, s 2.

public law boundaries, such as international boundaries, and some internal public law boundaries, such as county boundaries or constituency boundaries. But they do not show private law boundaries, ie title boundaries, any more than one could see such boundaries from a balloon. Of course, they often show them *indirectly*. The title boundary between 'Dunroamin' and 'Nia Roo'[26] is a garden wall, and the largest-scale OS map will show that wall. But it does not say that the wall stands on the line of the title boundary. Indeed, many walls do not stand on title boundaries, and some title boundaries have no physical feature marking them – no wall, no hedge, no fence, no burn. The OS contains no information about title boundaries, nor, indeed, do the OS surveyors even enquire into such matters. A map of a country or territory that shows title boundaries is called a 'cadastre' or 'cadastral map'. Until recently there was no such map for Scotland.[27]

7.28 Under LR(S)A 1979 its creation began, though at first unconsciously. LR(S)A 1979 contemplated that each property unit would have its own title sheet[28] and each title sheet would have its own plan, so that the completed register would consist of more than two million separate plans. But that did not happen. In reality only one plan was created, an electronic megaplan of the whole of Scotland, showing registered properties and their boundaries. Each title sheet was linked to the single map, so that when the Keeper issued a copy of the title sheet, the plan attached was just a piece of data lifted from that megaplan, and then inserted into the copy issued. LR(S)A 2012 recognised the reality, and named the megaplan the Cadastral Map.[29] As already explained, it is not yet complete, because not all title units have yet been registered, and so not yet plotted on to the Cadastral Map. The map is a half-completed jigsaw.

7.29 The Cadastral Map makes use of the Ordnance Survey; it is a layer over the latter. It can be pictured[30] as a transparent plastic sheet spread over the OS map, with the title boundaries being marked on the plastic sheet. For the purposes of land registration, the OS map is called the 'base map'.[31] The 'layer' picture is subject to some qualifications. Land registration has a 3-D element, because of separate tenements, notably flats in a tenement building, and underground mineral rights. Another qualification arises because the Cadastral Map also has to show certain property units that exist concurrently in the same land in a non-3-D manner, notably salmon fishing rights (which are separate tenements)[32] and long leases (which are not separate tenements but which behave very like separate tenements).

---

[26] A name sometimes chosen by homeowners with a combined taste for Lallans and anagrams.
[27] Cadastres first developed for land tax purposes. Actually, a primitive sort of tax-orientated cadastre was done in Scotland in the reign of Alexander III. The classic work on the subject is T Thomson, *Memorial on Old Extent* (ed J D Mackie, Stair Society Vol 10, 1946). The modern cadastral map has no tax functions, though H M Revenue & Customs can use it.
[28] See **PARA 7.26** below.
[29] To see what it looks like, view Appendix F to SLC Report on Land Registration.
[30] Merely a picture: the Land Register exists in electronic form.
[31] LR(S)A 2012, s 11(5) and (6).
[32] See **PARA 15.17** below.

7.30   In the case of leases or separate tenements, their boundaries may or may not match the boundaries of ordinary cadastral units. For example, Alex might own two hectares, which are subject to 20 separate registered leases, their boundaries all being included within the single cadastral unit for Alex's property. Or underground mineral rights might extend to many hectares, with hundreds of separate properties at the surface.

Second part of the Land Register: the Title Sheet Record

7.31   The second part of the Land Register is the Title Sheet Record. Each registered title unit has its own title sheet. 'The title sheet record is the totality of all … title sheets'.[33] Each has a unique number, beginning with the relevant county code. Example: 'MID 1' is Edinburgh Castle. At the end of this chapter there is a sample title sheet. A title sheet has four sections,[34] which are interchangeably referred to either by their names or by their letters: (A) the Property Section, (B) the Proprietorship Section, (C) the Securities Section and (D) the Burdens Section. Sometimes the C Section has nothing in it, and this is also possible, though rare, for the D Section.

Title sheets: the A Section

7.32   The Property Section[35] (A Section) defines the property. It does so by reference to the relevant unit in the Cadastral Map, and indeed the numbers of title sheets match up with the numbers of the cadastral units. As well as the reference to the Cadastral Map there may also be a verbal description. This can be useful to add detail that is not apparent from the Cadastral Map. Where the property is the benefited property in relation to any servitudes or real burdens, that should be stated in this section, including the identity of the burdened property, in so far as known to the Keeper.[36] These rights are 'pertinents' of the property, ie rights over neighbouring property. Every pertinent is also an encumbrance – a pertinent for one, and an encumbrance for another.[37]

---

[33]   LR(S)A 2012, s 3(3).
[34]   LR(S)A 2012, s 5.
[35]   LR(S)A 2012, s 6.
[36]   LR(S)A 2012, s 6(1)(b).
[37]   But the converse is not true. For example, if a property is subject to a standard security, that is an encumbrance. But there is no other property that has a matching pertinent.

Title sheets: the B Section

7.33   The Proprietorship Section[38] (B Section) identifies the owner/s. If there is a special destination[39] it will state that too. In cases of co-ownership it will state the title shares: for instance, that Jack and Jill own the property equally, or that Felix, Gertrude and Horatia own the property 20%, 25% and 55% respectively. If the owner holds as a trustee, that will be noted, if known to the Keeper,[40] but a trust is still effective even if the B Section is silent on the point. So, if Lord Voldemort buys land and arranges that it will be registered in the name of ZYXW Ltd, the fact that the B Section gives only the name of that company does not affect the fact that it owns the property in trust for He Who Must Not Be Named.

Title sheets: the C Section

7.34   The Securities Section[41] (C Section) sets out any standard securities that encumber the property.

Title sheets: the D Section

7.35   The Burdens Section[42] (D Section) sets out any other rights that encumber the property, such as (i) real burdens, (ii) servitudes and (iii) long leases. (A long lease is a lease for more than 20 years.[43]) In the case of the first two, the title sheet should identify the benefited property, so far as known to the Keeper. Note that servitudes and real burdens go into the D Section if they are *encumbrances*, but into the A Section if they are *pertinents*. Say Blackmains and Redmains are neighbouring properties, and the former has the benefit of a servitude of way across the latter; the servitude should (at least in the normal case) appear in the Land Register twice, in the A Section of the Blackmains title sheet and in the D Section of the Redmains title sheet.

Shared plot title sheets

7.36   Ordinary title sheets have just been described. There can also be 'shared plot' title sheets.[44] Suppose that there is amenity ground that belongs to a group

---

[38]   LR(S)A 2012, s 7.
[39]   For special destinations, see **CHAPTER 30** below.
[40]   LR(S)A 2012, s 7(1)(a) read with the definition of 'designation' in s 113.
[41]   Formerly called the 'charges' section.
[42]   LR(S)A 2012, s 9.
[43]   See **PARA 20.12** below.
[44]   LR(S)A 2012, s 17 and s 18.

of 30 houses. For the amenity ground the Keeper can set up a shared plot title sheet. Instead of naming 30 sets of owners, as would an ordinary title sheet, the shared plot title sheet simply identifies the 30 properties, doing this in its B Section. Having been set up, it will seldom or never have to be changed. Each of the 30 'sharing' title sheets has, in its A Section, a reference to the shared plot title sheet. Thus, if Moira dispones her house to Norbert, the disposition will automatically carry with it a share in the shared plot. It is a matter for the discretion of the Keeper whether to set up a shared plot title sheet, or whether to have an ordinary title sheet. (Before LR(S)A 2012 the Keeper's practice was not to have a separate title sheet for the amenity ground, but to include it in all 30 title sheets. This problem of land being included in more than one title sheet, which could also arise in other types of case, is tackled by LR(S)A 2012, whose general principle is: *one plot of land, one cadastral unit, one title sheet.*)

Title sheets: some further details

7.37   Cadastral units and title sheets can be split or combined.[45] Thus, if Tom owns land and conveys part of it to Ursula, a new cadastral unit and new title sheet (with a new number) will be created for Ursula's area, and that area will be removed from Tom's. Likewise, cadastral units and title sheets may be merged. For instance, Vera owns Greenside. Her neighbour is Wilma. Vera dispones to Wilma. The two properties could now be merged. Divisions are commoner than mergers. For example, every time a developer buys land, builds houses and sells them off, the original cadastral unit and title sheet will be divided.

7.38   If there is a long lease, that can be entered in the Land Register in two ways, at the Keeper's option. One is simply to note the lease in the D Section of the property's title sheet. The other is, as an extra step, to create a separate title sheet for the lease.[46] Under LR(S)A 1979 registered leases *had* to have their own separate title sheets, and that has continued to be the Keeper's practice. As for separate tenements, they have their own title sheets (and their own cadastral units).

2012 Act gives only the framework

7.39   Part 1 of LR(S)A 2012 provides a general framework for what is to appear in the register: title boundaries, pertinents, property owners, security rights and other encumbrances. But to a large extent it leaves it to *other* legislation to determine the details. This approach is spelt out in s 49(1), and can also be seen elsewhere,

---

[45]   LR(S)A 2012, s 13. This is framed in terms of the combination or division of cadastral units.
[46]   LR(S)A 2012, s 3(2). (Note the word 'may'.)

such as s 9(1)(f), which says that the D Section is to contain, as well as certain items specifically mentioned, 'any other encumbrance the inclusion of which in the register is permitted or required, expressly or impliedly, by an enactment.'

Public law entries?

7.40   The Land Register is primarily for the registration of private law rights – ownership and the subordinate real rights. But to a limited extent encumbrances under public law do appear, in the D Section. Two such cases are specified by LR(S) A 2012 itself: these are that (a) public rights of way (in so far as known to the Keeper) and (b) path orders under the Land Reform (Scotland) Act 2003 should be entered into the D Section.[47] Moreover, certain other statutes provide for registration of miscellaneous public law rights and obligations. 'Here are some random examples: tree preservation orders, suspension orders in relation to mineral workings, orders applying the code for the management of houses let as lodgings or occupied by members of more than one family, and control orders (and notices of revocation of such control orders) in relation to such houses, and suspended forfeiture orders and forfeiture certificates in respect of the proceeds of crime. One single section of the Housing (Scotland) Act 2006 specifies no fewer than six types of document that must be registered in the Land Register.'[48] These public law entries are very miscellaneous, and it is often unclear why registration is required for some things and not others. Whilst these public law entries need to be mentioned, their importance in the land registration system is minor.

'Overriding interests?'

7.41   Under LR(S)A 1979 the starting point was that *all* rights (whether in private or in public law) affecting a property should appear in the title sheet, and, if they did not, they would not affect the property. Since that was obviously a hopeless aspiration, the Act then went on to try to enumerate all the types of right to which that principle would *not* apply, ie whose validity would be unaffected by non-appearance. (Such rights were given a name: overriding interests.) This was a task as difficult as any confronted by princes in fairy tales. LR(S)A 2012 dropped the hopeless aspiration. As will be seen later, a buyer is (as under LR(S)A 1979, at least in broad terms) protected against 'omitted encumbrances', ie third party rights that are not disclosed in the title sheet, but this applies only to such encumbrances as should, by specific legislative provision, have been entered in the title sheet. All *other* third party rights are unaffected by non-registration, but that is obvious,

---

[47]   LR(S)A 2012, s 9(1).
[48]   Scottish Law Commission, *Report on Land Registration* (2010) para 13.32 (footnotes omitted).

because they are *non-registrable*, and so there is no need for a special category of 'overriding interests' with its complex and unworkable engineering. Take an example: the planning law status of a particular property – for example, that it can be used only for residential purposes. That will not appear in the title sheet. Why? Because the planning legislation has no such requirement. There is no need for planning law to be listed, in the land registration legislation, as an 'overriding interest'.

The title sheet's limitations

7.42   In broad terms, a title sheet can be expected to give an accurate and complete picture of the title, and to do so in a way that makes sense to the intelligent non-expert. But to this statement there are significant qualifications, some of which may be mentioned here. (i) As explained in the previous paragraph, only registrable rights can be expected to be found in the register. Thus, for example, merely contractual rights will generally not be found there. As to whether the owner holds in trust, the position is half-and-half: the title sheet will disclose that fact if known to the Keeper, but the validity of the trust is unaffected if the title sheet is silent. (ii) Although the A Section should show all title conditions that benefit the property, there may be omissions because of the Keeper's lack of knowledge. For instance, there might be the benefit of a servitude that came into being by prescription. (iii) The D Section will show all servitudes that encumber the property, but only if the Keeper knows of them, which is not always the case. (iv) Short leases (i.e. for 20 years or less) do not appear. (v) The B Section may still show someone who has died since the latest registration, or may show a company that has subsequently been dissolved. Such events will eventually lead to further conveyancing, but there may be a delay, sometimes quite long. (vi) Though the C Section reveals any security rights, it does not reveal how much is owed. The original loan may have subsequently increased or (more commonly) decreased over time, or even have been paid off completely.[49] (vii) Floating charges do not appear.[50] (viii) Whereas the A, B and C sections are usually fairly easy to understand, the D Section is made up, on the 'scissors and paste' method, from deeds, some of them old. Even if the deeds were expertly drafted, the result can be hard to make sense of, and often they were not expertly drafted. Many purported real burdens that appear in title sheets are void.[51] The D Section, often long and usually obscure, is the section of the title sheet that is most likely to be incomprehensible for non-conveyancers, and often causes problems even for conveyancers.

[49]   In such a case a discharge will usually be registered fairly promptly, but this does not always happen.
[50]   Floating charges must nevertheless be registered. Under current law they are registered in the Companies Register: Companies Act 2006, Pt 25. Part 2 of the Bankruptcy and Diligence etc. (Scotland) Act 2007 provided for registration in a new register (the Register of Floating Charges) but it now seems that this is never to be brought into force – most unfortunately.
[51]   In which case their presence constitutes an inaccuracy in the register.

Third part of the Land Register: the archive record

7.43   The third part of the Land Register is the Archive Record. This is repository in which the Keeper puts (i) copies of all documents submitted when registration applications are made, or in relation to rectifications, and (ii) superseded data, i.e. data about previous states of the register.[52] (i) The former are important because they are the basis of what title sheets say. Say Tanya applies, in 2018, to be registered as owner of Greenmains, on the basis of a disposition to her from Victoria, the existing registered owner. The Keeper deletes Victoria's name from the title sheet, and substitutes Tanya's. The correctness of that registration – the accuracy of the register – depends on the validity of the Victoria/Tanya deed. So, a copy needs to be kept. (ii) Assume that the Victoria/Tanya deed is valid. In 2020, a legal problem arises in which it becomes important to know who owned Greenmains in 2017. So a copy of the title sheet, as it stood in 2017, is needed. The Archive Record will contain a copy of that.[53]

7.44   The Archive Record backs up what appears on the title sheet. But it also, in some cases, backs up what does *not* appear. For example, suppose that a property is subject to a standard security. That fact appears in the C Section, and the Archive Record will contain a copy of the deed itself. Later the owner pays off the secured loan. The creditor will now grant a deed of discharge, and this will be submitted to the Keeper. The Keeper then deletes the entry from the C Section, and places a copy of the deed of discharge in the Archive Record. This copy deed thus backs up the current blankness of the C Section.

Fourth part of the Land Register: the application record

7.45   Section 15 of LR(S)A 2012 provides: 'The application record is to consist of all (a) applications for registration as are for the time being pending, and (b) advance notices as are for the time being extant.' There are two elements here. (a) Suppose that Sheenagh owns Yellowmains. She is selling to Arthur. On 1 May she delivers a disposition to him, and on 3 May he submits the disposition to the Keeper for registration. Now, it may be that Arthur's application can be dealt with instantly. But that is not always possible, and sometimes applications can take weeks or even months to deal with. Let us suppose that the process is completed on 20 August, the day when her name is deleted from the B Section and his name is inserted. During all the period from 3 May to 20 August the Yellowmains title sheet still shows Sheenagh as owner. Is that a problem? If ownership passes to a disponee

---

[52]   LR(S)A 2012, s 14.
[53]   The Archive Record is not of interest just for legal problems. It enables local historians, family historians etc to trace land ownership, as can be done with the Sasine Register, back to the seventeenth century.

when the act of registration is finally carried out (here 20 August), the answer is no, there is no problem. So, if a third party checked the title sheet on 1 July and saw that Sheenagh was owner, that would be fine, because on that date she *was* the owner. However, the law is (for good reasons) that if a registration application is accepted, it is deemed to take effect on the day of the application, here 3 May.[54] Put another way, as from 3 May there is a 'wait and see' period, in that until the Keeper makes the final decision as to whether to accept or reject Arthur's application,[55] it cannot be known who is the owner. For this reason, it essential that third parties can find out about pending applications – about what is in the Keeper's in-tray. This is what the Application Record is for. (b) The Application Record is also the home of advance notices. The reason that they appear here, not in the title sheet, is that they are like mayflies: charming but short-lived. These are considered below.[56]

THE PHYSIOLOGY OF THE LAND REGISTER

Registrable deeds

7.46   'A person may apply to the Keeper for registration of a registrable deed' says R(S)A 2012, s 21(1). 'Registrable deed' means a deed of a *type* that is registrable, for obviously any individual deed might be invalid and if so should be rejected. So what types of deed are registrable? The answer is given by s 49: 'A deed is registrable only if and in so far as its registration is authorised (whether expressly or not) by (a) this Act, (b) an enactment mentioned in subsection (3),[57] or (c) any other enactment.'[58] So if a deed is not of a type that is said by some statute to be registrable, it follows that it is not registrable. Take, for example, leases. The Registration of Leases (Scotland) Act 1857 provides that leases of over 20 years can be registered. What of a lease for 15 years? Can that be registered? No. No statute permits its registration, so it is non-registrable.[59] Or, to take another example, missives could not be registered, because there is no enactment that says that missives can be registered.

---

[54]   LR(S)A 2012, s 37(1).
[55]   Of course, in the vast majority of cases, applications are accepted.
[56]   See **PARAS 7.55–7.65** below.
[57]   This mentions four statutes that are of particular importance for listing registrable deeds: (a) the Registration of Leases (Scotland) Act 1857, (b) the Conveyancing (Scotland) Act 1924, (c) the Conveyancing and Feudal Reform (Scotland) Act 1970, and (d) the Law Reform (Miscellaneous Provisions) (Scotland) Act 1985.
[58]   There are very many statutes that provide for the registration of something. Most are of very limited significance. Some of them are private or local statutes.
[59]   But such a lease can still have real effect, under the Leases Act 1449. See **CHAPTER 20** below.

7.47   If the Keeper by mistake does register something that is not registrable,[60] the register is inaccurate to that extent,[61] and must be rectified by the deletion of the offending entry. This prevents the system becoming clogged up.[62]

7.48   In practice the deeds most commonly registered are dispositions, standard securities, and discharges of standard securities. Also important, though less common, are long leases, servitudes and real burdens. There are also many other deed types that are registrable, some so obscure that a conveyancer might never come across one in a lifetime of professional experience.

Registration: further requirements

7.49   There are various other requirements, as well as the requirement that the deed be of a registrable type.[63] One obvious one is that the deed be valid.[64] Another is that the property can be identified on the cadastral map. That simply involves giving the title number.[65] But in split-off deeds (eg where a builder has bought a large area and is selling off individual houses) the deed must not only state the existing title number but also contain an appropriate deed plan from which the Keeper can establish a new title sheet. Another requirement is that the deed should be probative.[66] Registration of 'souvenir plots' is not allowed.[67] Souvenir plots are a long-established business.[68] A company buys some land in a remote area and 'sells' small plots, eg of one square metre. Even if the company offers a disposition, this cannot be registered, so ownership cannot pass. Hence the company takes the money but remains owner. 'Buyers' receive a bit of paper, usually drawn up in English or American style. 'Buyers' are told that they are now 'legally entitled' to call themselves 'lairds' and so on. This is all nonsense, of course, but do buyers realise that? Do they realise that they will not acquire the plot that they are 'buying'?[69]

---

60   Which happens. The main example is where a deed contains a burden whose effect is contractual only, ie it is not a valid real burden. Such non-real burdens should not appear in the Land Register, but nevertheless often do so.
61   LR(S)A 2012, s 65(1)(c).
62   Those who wish to register written contracts, and other documents that are not registrable in the Land Register, can (and do) use the Books of Council and Session.
63   See in particular LR(S)A 2012, s 22 and s 26. The former sets out the 'general application conditions.'
64   This requirement is mentioned at various places in LR(S)A 2012, most notably in s 26(1)(a). Validity is defined in LR(S)A 2012, s 113(2).
65   In a first registration there is no existing title number. The deed must either contain a suitable plan, or refer to another, Sasine-registered, deed that contains such a plan.
66   RoW(S)A 1995, s 6 and s 9G (as inserted by LR(S)A 2012).
67   LR(S)A 2012, s 22(1)(b). The term is defined in s 22(2). See J Robbie and M Combe, 'A square foot of old Scotland: ownership of souvenir plots' (2015) 19 EdinLR 393.
68   An internet search will yield interesting results.
69   Some websites claim that buyers receive 'personal ownership.' There is no such thing. Some websites falsely claim that the non-registrability of souvenir plots means that ownership can pass without registration.

7.50   The burden lies on the applicant to satisfy the Keeper.[70] If the applicant does not satisfy the Keeper, the application must be rejected,[71] and, conversely, if the applicant does satisfy the Keeper, the application must be accepted.[72] The Keeper has no discretion, though in the occasional case of difficulty a judgment must be made one way or the other. An unsuccessful applicant can appeal.[73] Unlike the pre-LR(S)A 2012 system, there is no possibility for a problematic application to be kept in the application record while the applicant amends it.[74] An unsuccessful applicant can always reapply, with better paperwork.

Date when an application takes effect

7.51   'Where the Keeper accepts an application for registration, the date of registration is the date of the application', provides LR(S)A 2012, s 37(1). As explained above there is a 'wait-and-see' period between the application being submitted to the Keeper and the Keeper deciding whether or not to accept it.[75] This 'wait-and-see' period is the reason why the application record is so important.

The queue, and the 'as at the date of application' principle

7.52   The Keeper's decision is to be made on the basis of the position 'as at the date of application'.[76] Here are three examples. Example (i). Lucia dispones to Michael. He submits his application on 1 May. He dies on 2 May, and the Keeper is informed. The Keeper at that time has not yet decided whether to accept or reject the application. That decision is made on 15 May. Assuming that the application was valid, the Keeper should enter Michael's name in the register as owner. Example (ii). Dugald owns land. On 1 April he delivers a standard security to Prospero. On 2 April he delivers a disposition to Imogen. On 3 April Imogen applies for registration. On 4 April Prospero applies for registration. The Keeper will accept the disposition and reject the standard security. Why? In the first place, 'the Keeper must deal with two or more applications for registration in relation to the same land in order of receipt.'[77] There is an orderly queue.[78] So the Keeper deals first with Imogen's application. Assuming the application to be in order, it will be accepted, and the registration takes effect as from 3 April (see above).

---

[70]   See in particular LR(S)A 2012, s 21(2).
[71]   LR(S)A 2012, s 21(3).
[72]   LR(S)A 2012, s 21(2).
[73]   LR(S)A 2012, s 103.
[74]   This represents one of the many changes from the previous system.
[75]   See PARA **7.45** above.
[76]   LR(S)A 2012, s 21(2). See Report on Land Registration paras 12.61 ff.
[77]   LR(S)A 2012, s 39(1).
[78]   For what happens if two applications arrive on the same day, see LR(S)A 2012, s 39(4).

The Keeper then considers Prospero's application. As at 4 April, the owner of the property is not Dugald but Imogen. Therefore the security deed is invalid and will be rejected: *nemo plus*. It is true that Dugald was the owner when he signed and delivered the security deed, and it is true that if Prospero had jumped into a taxi and arrived at RoS the same day, clutching the deed, the application form and the registration fee, he would have won the race to the register. But that is not what happened. Imogen won that race.[79] Example (iii). This example is the same as the last, but with the queue inverted. Prospero applies for registration on 3 April, and Imogen on 4 April. Prospero has won the race to register. But that does *not* mean that Imogen's application will be rejected. On 4 April who is the owner? It is still Dugald. So the disposition by him to Imogen is valid. Hence Imogen will be registered as owner in place of Dugald. But – and this is the point – her title will be subject to Prospero's standard security.

Electronic conveyancing

7.53   The Land Register can be, and in fact is, kept in electronic form.[80] But deeds continue to be paper deeds. A limited exception was introduced with 'automated registration of title to land' (ARTL).[81] But only certain types of registrable deed were allowed, under ARTL, to be electronic, and in any case the system proved unpopular with conveyancers. Its significance has thus been marginal. No general provision for electronic deeds existed until LR(S)A 2012 amended the Requirements of Writing (Scotland) Act 1995. But even now electronic deeds cannot be registered (unless within the ARTL system) because the necessary statutory order has yet to be made.[82]

7.54   At the time of writing it is likely that all this will soon change. On the one hand, the ARTL system will probably be discontinued, and, on the other hand, not only will it become possible for registrable deeds in general to be in electronic form, but it is likely that in most cases it will actually be compulsory that they be so. Details of the new system – assuming that it in fact introduced – have yet to be firmed up.[83]

---

[79]   It is possible – depending on the precise facts of the case – that he could invoke against her the offside goals rule, on which see **PARAS 4.48–4.51** above. But a voidable title is not the same as a void title.

[80]   LR(S)A 2012, s 1(4).

[81]   The main legislative provision was the Automated Title to Land (Electronic Communications) (Scotland) Order 2006.

[82]   Requirements of Writing (Scotland) Act 1995, s 9G(3).

[83]   A fairly complete account of all that is known at the time of writing can be found in K G C Reid and G L Gretton, *Conveyancing 2016* (2017) p 152 ff.

Advance notices

7.55   One of the most important changes introduced by LR(S)A 2012[84] is the system of advance notices.[85] These replace letters of obligation.[86] Ideally, when Lisa buys property from Claudius, it would be possible for her (i) to know the exact state of the registers at the time she pays the price, so that she can be sure that there are no 'adverse entries' whether against the property (Land Register) or against Claudius personally (Inhibitions Register) and (ii) instantly to register her disposition, so that there is no risk of any adverse entries appearing between paying the price and acquiring ownership. (There is a risk here since ownership does not pass until registration.) In practice this is not usually possible. There may be a short gap between (a) the last moment that she checked the registers and (b) the time she pays the price. And there may also be a short gap between (a) the time she pays the price and (b) the time when the disposition is registered, and she becomes the owner. (Of course, any adverse entries relating to *Claudius* after ownership has passed will not matter to her.) So there may be a period of several days when she is at risk. Usually there is nothing to fear. But the risk is not so small that it can be ignored.

7.56   What sort of risks are there? A full account would involve a long excursus into conveyancing technicalities, so just a couple of illustrations must suffice. Suppose that Claudius is a fraudster and is selling the property simultaneously to two different people, each of whom is of course unaware of the other. Lisa finds herself pipped at the post: the other buyer registers first.[87] Another risk is that a creditor of Claudius uses diligence against the property.[88] In this case there is a race to the register: whichever of (i) the adjudication by the creditor or (ii) the disposition to Lisa is registered first will prevail.[89]

7.57   An advance notice can be registered, creating a 'protected period' of 35 days.[90] So long as Lisa registers her disposition at some time during that protected period, she has priority over any adverse entries that relate to Claudius and that appear in that period.[91] So take this sequence. On 1 April Lisa and Claudius conclude missives. On 1 May an advance notice is registered. On 8 May Flora, a separate buyer from Claudius, registers a disposition. Also on 8 May Lisa pays the price and

---

[84]   Part 4.
[85]   See Report on Land Registration part 14. In developing the system, the SLC paid particular attention to the English system (search with priority) and the German system (*Vormerkung*).
[86]   See **PARA 5.14** above.
[87]   This fraud is difficult to pull off, because the timing has to be perfectly done. But, nevertheless, it does occasionally happen.
[88]   The oddly-named diligence of adjudication. The provisions of the Bankruptcy and Diligence etc. (Scotland) Act 2007, which would have replaced it with 'land attachment', have not been brought into force.
[89]   See **PARAS 4.29–4.31** above for the risk of the seller's insolvency.
[90]   LR(S)A 2012, s 58.
[91]   LR(S)A 2012, s 59.

receives a disposition. On 15 May Lisa submits the disposition for registration. What happens? On 8 May ownership passes from Claudius to Flora. On 15 May ownership passes from Flora to Lisa, on the basis of the Claudius/Flora disposition. This may seem hard on Flora. But she too could have protected her position by an advance notice[92] and moreover Lisa's advance notice was in the register, for all eyes to see, including Flora's.

7.58   Now, vary the example, so that all the facts are the same except that Lisa is slow to submit her disposition to the Keeper, not doing so until 3 July. That is outwith the 35-day protected period. The result is that Flora's title remains. When Lisa makes her application on 3 July the Keeper will reject it, because the Claudius/Lisa deed will, by then, be from a person (Claudius) who is not the owner, so that the *nemo plus* principle applies, and Lisa no longer enjoys the benefit of the advance notice.

7.59   Two points should be noted. The first is that the protected period does not work as a *freeze* on the title sheet, which is why the Claudius/Flora disposition could be registered. The title sheet remains open for new entries. But such entries, if made within the protected period, are subject to the effect of the subsequent registration of the protected deed – if, but only if, that takes place within the protected period. The other point is that the advance notice system works more or less automatically, without – at least in ordinary cases – the need for judicial intervention. Thus in the first example, the Keeper, on receiving Flora's application, will simply check that there is an advance notice and that the application is within the protected period, and will proceed accordingly.

7.60   There could be a competition between advance notices. In such a case the earlier advance notice wins – assuming of course that the relevant protected deed is registered within the protected period.[93]

7.61   In the examples above, the competition was between two dispositions. Advance notices can also work as between a disposition and a deed creating a subordinate real right, and, indeed, as between two subordinate real rights. Example (i). On 1 March an advance notice is granted in respect of a prospective disposition by X to Y. On 15 March X grants a servitude to Z, which is registered on 17 March. On 1 April X delivers the disposition to Y and it is registered on 5 April. The servitude is thereby extinguished. It existed only from 17 March to 5 April. Example (ii). On 1 March an advance notice is granted in respect of a prospective servitude by X to Y. On 15 March X grants a disposition to Z, registered on 17 March. On 1 April X delivers the deed of servitude to Y and it is registered on 5 April. Even though

---

92   For the case of two competing advance notices, see **PARA 7.60** below.
93   LR(S)A 2012, s 59(1)(b).

X was no longer owner on 1 April, the Keeper will accept the deed of servitude, and so the property (now owned by Z) is encumbered by the servitude as from that date.

7.62   The advance notice system also offers protection against adverse entries in the Register of Inhibitions.[94] Say John owns Redmains. An advance notice is registered in favour of Susan in respect of a prospective disposition. The notice is registered on 1 May. On 2 May John is inhibited by Archimedes. On 3 May, he and Susan conclude missives. Later he delivers to her a disposition, and this is registered on 25 May. Susan's title is unaffected by the inhibition against John.

7.63   An advance notice must be agreed to by both parties. It can be done at any time, even before conclusion of missives. There can be a further advance notice. For example, suppose that (as quite often happens, not least in commercial transactions) there is 'delay in settlement', which is to say that the settlement date that the parties intended has to be postponed. That may mean that the eventual settlement date will fall outwith the protected period. The solution is simply to register a second advance notice. A new advance notice is not the same as extending the first notice. Take this case. Björn owns land and concludes missives to sell it to Solveig. He grants to her an advance notice, registered on 1 June. On 25 June he grants a standard security to Harald, this being registered the same day. He grants to Solveig a second advance notice, registered on 1 July. He later grants to her a disposition and this is registered on 20 July. The disposition is not protected against the standard security, because the first advance notice is now dead, and whilst there is a second advance notice, it cannot give her protection against adverse entries prior to its date, i.e. before 1 July. Hence Solveig acquires ownership, but encumbered by the standard security. Thus a new notice is not the same as renewing an existing notice: the latter is not possible.

7.64   An advance notice has to identify the protected deed, ie the prospective deed. For that it needs to specify four things: (i) the type of deed (eg 'disposition'[95]), (ii) the granter, (iii) the grantee and (iv) the property. The property is normally identified simply by title number. But if the property is not an existing one, for instance where a developer is selling off new houses, the advance notice must have a proper plan.

7.65   Going back to the earlier example, it is likely that Lisa will be granting a standard security to a bank, for the funding needed to buy the property. If so, the advance notice that protects the Claudius/Lisa disposition will also protect the Lisa/bank security. One final point is that an advance notice will be seen by anyone checking the register. So Flora and Lisa in the example given above[96] are likely to be

---

[94]   LR(S)A 2012, s 61.
[95]   An advance notice can be granted to protect any type of registrable deed, but in practice dispositions are the main example.
[96]   At **PARA 7.57**.

aware of each other before either has paid the price to Claudius, a fact which in itself tends to prevent problems from arising.

THE PATHOLOGY (AND THERAPEUTICS) OF THE LAND REGISTER

Inaccuracy and rectification

7.66   Usually the register is accurate, but not always. 'A title sheet is inaccurate in so far as it (a) misstates what the position is in law or in fact, (b) omits anything required, by or under an enactment, to be included in it, or (c) includes anything the inclusion of which is not expressly or impliedly permitted by or under an enactment.'[97] If the register says that X has a certain right (e.g. ownership), that is not conclusive that X does have that right. The register might be inaccurate. Suppose that Tigran owns a house and that Henry, an identity thief, impersonates him and sells the house to Martin, who is in good faith.[98] Martin is registered as owner. The disposition, being a forgery, is void, and accordingly Martin's title is void, Tigran still being owner.[99] As LR(S)A 2012, s 49(4) says, 'registration of an invalid deed confers real effect only to the extent that an enactment so provides.' There is no enactment that confers real effect in favour of Martin. Of course, Martin believes himself to be the owner, and he appears to the world at large to be the owner. But he is not. Suppose that the problem comes to light. Assuming that Martin has not, in the meanwhile, sold on (as to which, see below), the register will be rectified, by the deletion of Martin's name from the B Section, and the re-instatement of Tigran's. That change in the register does not alter ownership. Just as the original registration in favour of Martin did not transfer ownership to him from Tigran, so the rectification does not transfer ownership back to Tigran, for Tigran had never ceased to be owner. What is happening, by rectification, is that the register is being brought into line with the actual legal position. For the question of what happens if, before the problem comes to light, Martin sells on, see below.)

---

[97]   LR(S)A 2012, s 65(1).
[98]   ID theft does happen in practice. If Henry is not in possession how can he make the sale work, given that he cannot show prospective purchasers round, and so on? One way is to do the fraud for a property that he is tenanting. As well as the forged disposition (which is the example here) there is the forged standard security. Here Henry borrows a large sum on the strength of a forged security that he grants. He then vanishes with the money. See e.g. *Cheshire Mortgage Corp Ltd v Grandison* [2012] CSIH 66. In such cases the fraudster needs good quality fake ID, but that can be bought. The fraudster also looks for properties that are free of a standard security, so as to maximise the take. This requires an ability to check the Land Register or Sasine Register. So Henry needs to have legal knowledge. For a case involving astonishing facts, one of which was that the fraudster did *not* disappear, see *Frank Houlgate Investment Co Ltd v Biggart Baillie LLP* 2012 SLT 256.
[99]   Under LR(S)A 1979, the Keeper's Midas touch (see **PARA** 7.77 below) would have operated, making Martin the owner.

Rectification: evidence and procedure

7.67   If an inaccuracy comes to light, the Keeper is under a positive obligation to rectify it.[100] This might seem obvious, but under the previous system the Keeper could leave inaccuracies unrectified, and indeed in some cases *had* to leave them unrectified, i.e. the legislation positively promoted an inaccurate register.[101] Under LR(S)A 2012 there is no need for an application, let alone a court order. But whilst there exist no procedural hurdles, there is an evidential hurdle. For rectification to happen the inaccuracy must be 'manifest.'[102] That means that the fact of inaccuracy must be not merely probable but too plain for argument. The 'manifest' requirement means that often there will be no rectification unless the problem has been before a court. For example, Jules and Jim are neighbours. They are in dispute about a boundary area, which the register says is part of Jim's property. (Disputes about the accuracy of the Land Register need not be neighbour disputes, but often are.) Jules lobbies the Keeper, and though the Keeper thinks, on balance, that he is right, 'on balance' is not enough, and so the Keeper must not rectify. So if Jules wishes to take matters further he will have to litigate with Jim, by raising an action of declarator. (Of course, it may be that an amicable settlement is possible between Jules and Jim.) In that action, the court will apply a balance of probabilities test. But the effect of a court decree, once obtained, is to create certainty. If the court sides with Jules, it is *now* manifest that the register is inaccurate.[103] The action is between Jules and Jim and does not involve the Keeper, and should not include any order against the Keeper. Any such order is unnecessary, for as soon as the Keeper sees the decree, rectification goes ahead.

Keeper's warranty

7.68   'The Keeper, in accepting an application for registration, warrants to the applicant that, as at the time of registration, the title sheet to which the application relates is accurate ...'[104] So if it turns out to be inaccurate, the Keeper is liable to pay compensation. Take the case of Tigran, Henry the fraudster, and Martin the innocent buyer.[105] Suppose that the problem comes to light. Assuming that Martin has not, in the meanwhile, sold on (as to which, see below), the register will be rectified, by the deletion of Martin's name from the B Section, and the reinstatement of Tigran's. The Keeper is liable for the loss that Martin suffers. (The person primarily liable is of course Henry, but in practice he may be untraceable, and, if traceable, it may not be possible to get money out of him. Moreover,

---

[100]   LR(S)A 2012, s 80(2).
[101]   LR(S)A 1979, s 9. This may seem hardly credible, but it was so.
[102]   LR(S)A 2012, s 80(1).
[103]   Decree in absence would suffice.
[104]   LR(S)A 2012, s 73(1).
[105]   See **PARA 7.66** above.

Martin can claim immediately from the Keeper.[106] In that event the Keeper can chase Henry.[107]) There is a default level of warranty, which can in special cases be altered: for example, if the Keeper thinks, on balance, but only on balance, that an application should be accepted, the right course for the Keeper is to accept it but limit or exclude warranty.[108] Default warranty is granted where the title seems good, so in a sense the warranty is granted when it is least needed, and not when it is most needed. But it must be borne in mind that warranty is free. If warranty is refused, the person registered can always seek title insurance from a commercial provider. (Such cover must of course be paid for.[109])

7.69   The Keeper's warranty, while it does protect against voidness, does not protect against the possibility of voidability. At first sight this may seem odd: voidness is worse than voidability, so why should there be protection against the former but not the latter? In fact the rule makes sense. It can be explained in two ways, one technical and the other policy-based, though at a deeper level the two are linked. The technical explanation is this. If X dispones to Y, and the disposition is voidable, and the Keeper registers Y, the register is perfectly accurate. It says that Y is the owner, and Y *is* the owner. The policy-based explanation is this: the general law imposes voidability only on those it regards as undeserving, such as those who have acted in bad faith.[110] There is no reason why the Keeper should protect such persons.

7.70   The Keeper warrants that the register is, in respect of that title sheet, accurate at the time of registration. The property may be subject to all sorts of encumbrances that are not mentioned in the title sheet, but that fact will not amount to a breach of warranty unless their omission amounts to an 'inaccuracy'. That term is defined at some length in LR(S)A 2012, s 65. An example may help. Suppose that Bertie buys a plot of land, where he plans to build a shop, and then discovers that under planning law the plot is restricted to residential use. He is upset, asks why the title sheet did not mention it, and claims against the Keeper. The claim fails. The title sheet's silence about the planning law situation did not amount to an inaccuracy, because planning status is not registrable in the Land Register. Alongside this basic link with the idea of accuracy/inaccuracy, there are various specific types of case which the Act says that default warranty does not extend to, such as the possibility that the property is encumbered by a servitude created by prescription.[111]

---

[106]   LR(S)A 2012, s 77(3).
[107]   LR(S)A 2012, s 77(5). Henry would also be liable to the Keeper under s 111.
[108]   LR(S)A 2012, s 75(1).
[109]   Title insurance is bought for a one-off premium, the amount of which is based on the value of the property and the degree of risk. More than one company offers this service. There is no point in it if the title is, as most titles are, Keeper-warranted.
[110]   See **PARA 4.35** above.
[111]   LR(S)A 2012, s 73(2).

7.71   LR(S)A 2012, s 73(2) lists certain specific things that the default warranty does not cover. For instance, in relation to the D Section, there is no default warranty that the property is free of servitudes created by prescription, which is something that the Keeper is unlikely to have reliable knowledge about. Another is that there is no default warranty that the mineral rights have been validly acquired. The reason for this is that mineral titles are notoriously problematic. The Keeper's liability is subject to certain specific exclusions even in cases where warranty ostensibly exists, e.g. where the title sheet is indeed inaccurate but the inaccuracy was caused by the claimant's own fault.[112]

Duty of care owed to the Keeper

7.72   Everyone involved in a registration (both the parties themselves and their law firms) owes a duty of care to the Keeper not to cause the latter to make the register inaccurate.[113] Take the case mentioned above about Henry impersonating Tigran. Suppose that the law firm that acted for the fake 'Tigran' failed to carry out ordinary ID checks. In that case it would be presumptively liable to the Keeper, who, as we have seen, will be out of pocket because of the requirement to pay compensation to Martin. This duty of care does not increase the burden on law firms, because such firms are bound to exercise reasonable diligence *anyway* as a matter of professional practice. The duty is only one of ordinary care. As to the parties themselves there will seldom be liability, because they will ordinarily leave the conveyancing to be carried out by their law firms. As well as this civil law duty of care to the Keeper, LR(S) A 2012 also imposes a criminal law duty of care,[114] though most of the situations covered by this provision would in any event be covered by the common law offence of fraud.

Protection of good faith grantees: the money or the mud

7.73   Grantees do not normally need protection, for the vast majority of transactions are perfectly regular: for instance, A sells to B, and B is then registered, and no problem exists, because A had a good title and the A/B deed was valid. But on occasion protection is needed – assuming of course that the grantee has acted in good faith. The general protection works through the Keeper's warranty, as already explained. But there is another, parallel system, which applies in certain types of case. Under the Keeper's warranty, Tigran remains owner and Martin is compensated: the former takes the mud and the latter takes the money, as it is sometimes expressed. That is the default system. But in some important types of case

---

[112]   LR(S)A 2012, s 78.
[113]   LR(S)A 2012, s 111.
[114]   LR(S)A 2012, s 112.

it works the other way round: it is the good faith grantee who takes the mud, and it is the other party who takes the money. To explain which system applies when, it is necessary to introduce a distinction between (i) transactional error and (ii) register error. In the former, something goes wrong with the transaction. The Tigran case is an example. Martin's problem, in other words, was not that the register incorrectly showed Tigran as owner. It showed Tigran as owner and was right in doing so. The error lay in the fact that the disposition was a forgery: Tigran did not sign it. But now suppose that, before the problem has come to light, Martin sells to Norma. The Keeper, being unaware of any problem, will register her as owner. Here we see register error at work. There is no transactional error (the Martin/Norma deed is not forged), but the register, in showing Martin as owner, was wrong. A transactional error is where an invalid deed leads to an incorrect registration. A register error is where an incorrect registration is relied on by a third-party grantee. It will be noted that register errors stem from transactional errors.

7.74   In *all* cases of merely transactional error, the protection is a money protection only. Tigran keeps the mud, and Martin receives compensation. When it comes to register error, in *some* cases the same is true, but in other cases it is not. The main case where the good faith third party grantee is protected by mud, not money, is where there is a disposition from a seller in possession.[115] The possession must have lasted at least a year. Suppose that Martin, by the time that he sold to Norma, had been in possession for over a year. Then Norma, assuming of course that she was in good faith, will have mud protection. What that means is that she acquires ownership. ('Mud' protection can be regarded as an exception to the *nemo plus* principle.[116]) That being the case, she suffers no loss and so neither needs nor gets monetary compensation. What about Tigran? When Norma acquires ownership, he loses it: he has been non-consensually expropriated. So he is the person who is compensated by the Keeper.[117]

7.75   What has just been described is the first and most important case of 'mud protection'. There are also some others. The second is where a registered lease is assigned to a good faith assignee.[118] The rules here are much the same as for dispositions. The provision applies only to cases where there is a valid lease, but the problem is that the register says it is held by Matthew when in fact it is held by Jamie. (Jamie is entitled to compensation from the Keeper.) The provision cannot validate an invalid lease. The third concerns servitudes. Suppose that Martin, before rectification, grants a servitude to his neighbour, Rebecca. Again, and subject to the same general conditions, the servitude is valid (and Tigran is entitled to compensation from the

---

[115]   LR(S)A 2012, s 86. Note that this section applies only to transfers of ownership, not to subordinate real rights.
[116]   See **PARA 4.42** above.
[117]   LR(S)A 2012, s 94. His delictual claim against the fraudster will then pass to the Keeper: s 94(5).
[118]   LR(S)A 2012, s 88.

Keeper).[119] As an aside, it may be noted that the legislation does not resurrect dead servitudes. For example, suppose that in 1990 a valid servitude of way is created in favour of Bluemains, and is entered as a pertinent in the Bluemains title sheet, Section A. The servitude is used for some years, but in 2002 it permanently stops being used. That means that in 2022 it is extinguished by negative prescription.[120] The servitude is, however, not deleted from the A Section. In 2025 the owner of Bluemains, X, dispones to Y. The servitude does not revive.

7.76   The fourth and last case of 'mud' protection concerns the 'extinction of omitted encumbrances.'[121] Blackmains is worth £700,000 and is encumbered by a standard security, for a loan of £450,000. The security has been duly registered and thus appears in the C Section. The owner of Blackmains, Theodora, is a fraudster. She forges a discharge of the standard security, gets it registered, and then sells the property to Farrah (who is in good faith). Theodora pockets the money and disappears. (Had the security not been fraudulently got rid of, she would have received the free proceeds only, £250,000.) Immediately after the registration of the forged discharge, what is the position? The position is that, because the discharge is void, the security is still fully valid, even though the register says the property is unencumbered. If the bank at this stage had discovered what had happened, it could have insisted on the rectification of the register by the reinstatement of the security in the C Section. But that did not happen. When the Theodora/Farrah disposition is registered, the standard security ceases to exist as a real right, assuming Farrah to have been in good faith.[122] She acquires unencumbered ownership. The bank is entitled to compensation from the Keeper.[123] This is just one example: the principle is a general one and can operate even where there is no fraud, and can apply to encumbrances other than securities.

Effect of registration and the Midas touch

7.77   LR(S)A 1979 had a provision about the effect of registration: 'registration shall have the effect of vesting in the person registered as entitled to the registered interest in land a real right in and to the interest...'[124] This seemingly reasonable provision was the cause of endless difficulty. There was no problem if the person registered was entitled to be registered, as was of course usually the position. But in other cases the provision meant that the person registered *had* the right in question, however wrongfully. This was the Keeper's Midas touch: everything the Keeper

---

[119]   LR(S)A 2012, s 90.
[120]   PL(S)A 1973, s 8. See **PARA 13.45** below.
[121]   LR(S)A 2012, s 91 ff.
[122]   It remains valid as a contract.
[123]   This type of fraud happens in practice.
[124]   LR(S)A 1979, s 3(1).

touched turned to valid.[125] Take the case where Tigran owned property, and Henry impersonated him, and sold to Martin, forging Tigran's signature. Under LR(S) A 1979, Martin, on being registered, acquired ownership. A key feature of a title registration system is that third parties should normally be able to rely on what it says. If it says that Martin owns the house, then someone buying from Martin[126] should be able to rely on that. But this 'reliance on the register' principle can be achieved, and achieved more simply, without the Midas touch.[127] It can be achieved through a combination of the Keeper's warranty and the fact that in many types of case a good faith buyer will obtain an absolutely good title (mud protection).

7.78   If the 'registration results in a valid right' approach of LR(S)A 1979 was wrong, what is right? What should land registration say as to the effect of registration? The answer is simple: nothing. It is *other* statutes, dealing with such matters as transfer of ownership, creation of security rights, creation of servitudes, the noting of certain public law encumbrances,[128] and so on, that say 'this is to be registered' and go on, either expressly or by implication, to say what the effect of registration is, or what the effect may be if registration does not happen. Hence LR(S)A 2012 simply says that the effect of registration is the effect provided for in the enactment that authorises the registration, combined with the common law.[129] As a matter of fact, LR(S)A 2012 does itself in one or two types of case set out the effect of registration,[130] but that is merely as it happens. The effect of most registrations is *not* governed by LR(S)A 2012. The Act does, however, have a negative provision: 'registration of an invalid deed confers real effect only to the extent that an enactment so provides.'[131] Strictly speaking this provision was not necessary, for it is implied by the framework of the Act as a whole, but given that the Midas touch had existed under LR(S)A 1979 it made sense to set the point out expressly.

Caveats

7.79   A caveat[132] can be entered in the register on the order of a court, where there is pending litigation about a registered title. Its effect is not to prevent the person who is currently registered as owner from transferring the property, or

---

[125]   For details see the first edition of this book at **PARA 6.30 ff**.

[126]   Or taking some other real right from him, such as a standard security.

[127]   The issues are fully discussed in the SLC's first Discussion Paper on Land Registration (Scot Law Com DP 125, 2004).

[128]   Rather randomly, some such encumbrances have to be registered, and others not. See **PARA 7.40** above.

[129]   LR(S)A 2012, s 49(2). For the common law, see s 49(2)(d). A good deal of property law is non-statutory, and is relevant and often crucial background when interpreting and applying any statutory provision.

[130]   Such as prescriptive claimants and good faith purchasers from sellers in possession.

[131]   LR(S)A 2012, s 49(4).

[132]   Part 6 of LR(S)A 2012 covers the procedural side of caveats, but not their substantive effects, for which see s 75(2), s 76(4), s 86(3)(e), s 88(3)(f), s 90(3)(d), s 91(2)(b), and s 92(2)(b).

otherwise dealing with it (eg granting a security). But if that person does deal with the property, the caveat (i) has implications for the warranty that the grantee receives and (ii) excludes from operation the rules protecting good faith grantees. So, for example, Jules and Jim are neighbours and in dispute about the ownership of a boundary area that the Land Register includes in Jim's title sheet. Jules raises an action of declarator that Jim's title to the boundary area is void and that he, Jules, owns it. He persuades the court to grant a caveat and this is duly registered. Jim now sells to Ruth. Suppose that Jules is right. If it were not for the caveat, Ruth would be protected and would become owner of the whole of the area in Jim's title sheet, including the disputed area.[133] (Assuming that the various conditions are satisfied, notably as to possession and good faith.) But the caveat prevents that from happening. Of course, it might be that Jules is wrong, and that Jim's title to the boundary area is perfectly valid. In that case Ruth will have become owner of the whole property, including the boundary area, notwithstanding the caveat. The caveat will have proved irrelevant. Or suppose that instead of granting a disposition to Ruth, Jim granted a standard security to Titania. Absent a caveat, Titania would have the protection of the Keeper's warranty. But if there is a caveat at the time when the security is granted, the Keeper's warranty is to that extent limited, so that if Jules prevails in the court action, Titania will lose the security in respect of the boundary area without compensation from the Keeper.

7.80 A caveat is also relevant if the issue with the title is not that it is void but that it is (allegedly) voidable. The common-law rule about voidability is that a grantee who is aware of the issue at the time of grant is unprotected. A caveat on the title sheet will alert any prospective grantee, and thus mean that the voidability (if such there is) would affect the grantee too. So Alan dispones to Beatrice, but later claims that the disposition was induced by fraud and is therefore voidable. He raises an action of reduction, and the title sheet is caveated. A few weeks later she grants a disposition to Carl. He cannot claim to be in good faith, so if Alan's action succeeds, Carl will lose the property.

Challengeable deeds: (A) reduction

7.81 The way reductions worked in the land registration system was one of the many difficulties with LR(S)A 1979.[134] LR(S)A 2012 made matters much more straightforward. As explained elsewhere,[135] 'reduction' is ambiguous. It may refer to a declaratory action, asking the court to rule that the defender's title is already void, eg because of forgery. A decree of reduction in this sense is declaratory: it does not alter the substantive property rights of the parties, but merely declares what those

---

[133] LR(S)A 2012, s 86.
[134] See Report on Land Registration part 28.
[135] See **PARA 4.38** above.

rights already were before the raising of the action. Or an action of reduction may be an action to set aside a voidable title. This is entirely different, for if the pursuer is successful, the decree will result in an actual *change* in the substantive rights of the parties: it is an operative reduction. For instance, if Zara fraudulently induces Alan to convey to her, her title is voidable. (Fraud of this type results in voidability, not nullity.) Suppose that he then decides to reduce the disposition, and succeeds, the effect will be that ownership will pass back to him.

7.82 As explained above, the effect of the first type of reduction will be to make it manifest that the register is inaccurate, and the Keeper will promptly rectify it. As for the second type of reduction, the position is different. Ownership has to pass from Zara to Alan, and for this to happen Alan must submit the decree of reduction to the Keeper for it to be registered.[136] He re-acquires ownership on the day of registration. This is a matter of registration, not of rectification. In short: (i) declaratory reduction is given effect to in the Land Register by rectification, and (ii) operative reduction is given effect to in the Land Register by registration. In both types of reduction it is a wise precaution for the pursuer to seek a caveat as soon as the action is raised.

Challengeable deeds: (B) rectification

7.83 A topic closely connected with reduction is the judicial rectification of documents under s 8 of LR(MP)(S)A 1985. Under that provision, if it can be proved that a deed fails to express the common intention of the parties, the court can 'rectify' it, i.e. rewrite it so that it conforms to the common intention. There are difficulties with the provision, not least with its interaction with land registration.[137] Under LR(S)A 2012[138] the rule is essentially the same as for reductions of voidable deeds: the decree (assuming that a registered title is in question) must be registered and takes real effect only on such registration. This is a matter of registration, not of rectification.

Postscript: actual and bijural inaccuracies and the transition from LR(S)A 1979

7.84 Under LR(S)A 1979, inaccuracies could be either (i) actual or (ii) bijural.[139] An actual inaccuracy was one where the statement in the title sheet was contrary to the

---

[136] LR(S)A 2012, s 54, inserting a new s 46A into the Conveyancing (Scotland) Act 1924.
[137] See Report on Land Registration part 29.
[138] LR(S)A 2012, s 55, amending LR(MP)(S)A 1985.
[139] See Scottish Law Commission, Discussion Paper on Land Registration: Void and Voidable Titles (Scot Law Com DP No 125, 2004). LR(S)A 1979 itself does not use these terms, and indeed does not distinguish the concepts. The concepts and terminology are however to be found in LR(S)A 2012 Sch 4.

actual legal situation. For example, if the title sheet said that Blackmains was owned by ZYXW (Largs) Ltd, and there never was such a company, then the title sheet was actually inaccurate. A bijural inaccuracy was one where the entry in the title sheet was one that should not have been made, but which, by virtue of the Keeper's Midas touch, meant that the rights in the property were (albeit wrongfully) as stated in the title sheet. For example, suppose that Constantine owned Greenmains, and there was a standard security over it in favour of Bank of Troon Plc. Constantine forged a deed of discharge and had it registered. Because of the Keeper's Midas touch the outcome was that the property was no longer encumbered by the security. The title sheet was thus bijurally inaccurate, because the entry (deletion of the security from the title sheet's C Section) should not have taken place, so that there was a tension between what the legal position *was* and what it *should* have been. Inaccuracies were sometimes rectifiable, but sometimes not.[140] Under the new legislation the concept of bijural inaccuracy disappears, as does the concept of an unrectifiable inaccuracy. Under the new legislation, any inaccuracy is an actual inaccuracy, and any inaccuracy can and must be rectified. But that rational reform does not say what is to happen to existing inaccuracies, i.e. inaccuracies that arose under the previous legislation and that are still there, unrectified, when the new legislation comes into force. So LR(S)A 2012 has transitional provisions.

7.85   The rules are as follows. (i) 'If there is … an inaccuracy which the Keeper has power to rectify under s 9 of [LR(S)A 1979] then, … (a) any person whose rights in land would have been affected by such rectification has such rights (if any) in the land as that person would have if the power had been exercised, and (b) the register is inaccurate in so far as it does not show those rights as so affected..'[141] And (ii): 'If there is in the register …. an inaccuracy which the Keeper does not have power to rectify under s 9 of [LR(S)A 1979], then on that day it ceases to be an inaccuracy.'[142] Here are one or two illustrations. (i) The case mentioned in the previous paragraph. When the new legislation comes into force, the standard security will come back into existence (because under the old legislation it would have been a rectifiable bijural inaccuracy). The title sheet will not yet show it again, though it will do so as soon as the Keeper learns the true facts. But if Constantine were to dispone to a good faith disponee before the security reappears on the title sheet, the disponee would take free of the security, because of the rules about omitted encumbrances, discussed above. At that point the security would be extinguished. (ii) Bluemains was owned by Janice. Jasmine was the tenant. Jasmine impersonated Janice and sold the property to Jessica, who was in good faith. Jessica was registered as owner and moved in. Under LR(S)A 1979 this was an unrectifiable bijural inaccuracy. Under the new legislation, the title sheet becomes accurate.

---

[140]   LR(S)A 1979, s 9, a notoriously difficult provision.
[141]   LR(S)A 2012, Sch 4, para 17.
[142]   LR(S)A 2012, Sch 4, para 22.

LITERATURE

7.86   The main text is Reid and Gretton *Land Registration*. LR(S)A 2012 was based on the Scottish Law Commission project on land registration, and the SLC publications are a useful resource for understanding the new law:

(a) Scottish Law Commission, Discussion Paper on Land Registration: Void and Voidable Titles (Scot Law Com DP No 125, 2004);

(b) Scottish Law Commission, Discussion Paper on Land Registration: Registration, Rectification and Indemnity (Scot Law Com DP No 128, 2005);

(c) Scottish Law Commission, Discussion Paper on Land Registration: Miscellaneous Issues (Scot Law Com DP No 130, 2005);

(d) Scottish Law Commission, Report on Land Registration (Scot Law Com No 222, 2010). The website of the Registers of Scotland (www.ros.gov.uk/) has huge amounts of valuable information.

LAND REGISTER OF SCOTLAND	Officer's ID / Date 1234 22/8/2016	TITLE NUMBER ANG999999
N	ORDNANCE SURVEY NATIONAL GRID REFERENCE	70m
		Survey Scale
	NO8241SE NO8341SW	1/1250

CROWN COPYRIGHT © - Produced from on 22/08/2016 at 11:32 with the authority of Ordnance Survey pursuant to section 47 of the Copyright, Designs and Patents Act 1988. Unless that act provides a relevant exception to copyright, the copy must not be copied without the prior permission of the copyright owner. This copy has no evidential status. OS Licence No. 100041182.

LAND REGISTER OF SCOTLAND

TITLE NUMBER ANG999999   **A 1**

A. PROPERTY SECTION

DATE OF FIRST REGISTRATION
18 JAN 2016

DATE TITLE SHEET UPDATED TO
18 JAN 2016

REAL RIGHT
OWNERSHIP

DESCRIPTION
Subjects cadastral unit ANG999999 79 ACACIA AVENUE, ARBROATH DD18 9EX
edged red on the cadastral map.

LAND REGISTER OF SCOTLAND

TITLE NUMBER ANG999999   **B 1**

B. PROPRIETORSHIP SECTION

ENTRY NO	PROPRIETOR		
1	JERMAINE BRADFORD and JOCELYN ASHWORTH BRADFORD spouses 14 Paper Street, Dundee, DD12 5ZY equally between them and the survivor of them.	**DATE OF REGISTRATION** 18 JAN 2016	**CONSIDERATION** £143,711 **DATE OF ENTRY** 15 JAN 2016

LAND REGISTER OF SCOTLAND

C. SECURITIES SECTION

ENTRY NO	SPECIFICATION	DATE OF REGISTRATION
1	Standard Security by said JERMAINE BRADFORD and JOCELYN ASHWORTH BRADFORD to BANK OF SCOTLAND PLC, incorporated under the Companies Acts (Company Number SC3270007), Halifax Division, 1 Lovell Park Road, Leeds, West Yorkshire LS1 1NS.	18 JAN 2016

LAND REGISTER OF SCOTLAND

D. BURDENS SECTION

ENTRY NO	SPECIFICATION
1	Feu Charter by William Hall and Son (Dundee) Limited to Catherine Alibar Stone and her heirs and assignees (hereinafter referred to as "the Feuars"), recorded G.R.S. (Angus) 2 Jun. 1961, of the subjects in this Title, contains the following burdens:

(First) The Feuars shall be bound to erect and thereafter to uphold and maintain and when necessary to renew or rebuild on the feu to the satisfaction of the Superiors no more than one good and substantial self-contained dwellinghouse of the villa or bungalow type with necessary and suitable offices (which dwellinghouse shall be no more than two storeys in height and which offices may include a garage which shall be used for private purposes only) built of stone or artificial stone and lime or brick and lime harled and with roof covered with slates or good quality clay tiles or erected of such other materials as may be approved by the Superiors in writing all conform to ground, elevation and block plans to be approved by the Superiors in writing before work is commenced, the said dwellinghouse and offices connected therewith (excluding said garage) being of a capital value of not less than Two Thousand Pounds; There shall be no buildings other than those above specified and the ground not occupied by such dwellinghouse and offices shall remain unbuilt on and shall be used exclusively for garden or for planting or as ornamental ground and shall be maintained in good order in all time coming;

(Second) The Feuars shall not have power to use and are hereby prohibited from using the feu or buildings or erections thereon or any part thereof for any commercial or industrial purpose nor shall the feu be used for any purpose which may be deemed by the Superiors as offensive or injurious to the amenity of the neighbourhood or a nuisance;

(Third) Whereas the feu is or is to be bounded on the north west and north east by a mutual wall or fence and on the south east partly by a mutual wall or fence and partly by the mutual gable separating the garage erected or to be erected on the feu from the garage erected or to be erected on the plot or area of ground on the south east, it is hereby declared that the Feuars shall be bound to maintain at their own expense the said mutual walls, or fences and mutual gable until such time as the ground adjoining on the north west, north east

LAND REGISTER OF SCOTLAND

D. BURDENS SECTION

and south east is feued whereupon the adjoining feuars on the north west, north east and south east shall be bound to relieve the Feuars of one half of the cost of maintenance and renewal of said mutual walls, fences and gables if and when that should become necessary; And Whereas the feu is bounded on the south west is formed by a wall or fence erected wholly on the feu said wall or fence shall be maintained solely by the Feuars in all time coming; declaring that no claim whatever shall lie against the Superiors in connection with any such boundary walls or fences or the maintenance thereof and declaring further that the Feuars shall have no claim against the proprietors of the feus adjoining on the north west, north east and south east for the cost of erection of any such walls or fences or gable walls;

(FOURTH) Whereas the main drain serving the buildings erected or to be erected on the feu serves also the several buildings erected or to be erected on ground adjoining on the north west and south east, it is hereby declared that said main drain is mutual and the expense of maintenance and renewal thereof shall be borne equally by the Feuars and the proprietors of the said adjoining subjects having an interest therein in all time coming; declaring also that the subjects hereby disponed are so disponed with and under the burden of a right of wayleave through the subjects hereby disponed for said main drain serving the feu and said adjoining subjects and of a right of access thereto for all necessary inspections, renewals and repairs of said main drain subject to payment to the Feuars for all surface damage caused in making said inspections, renewals or repairs and the cost of restoring the ground.

Chapter 8

Acquisition by involuntary transfer

INTRODUCTION

8.1   In derivative acquisition the consent of both transferor and transferee is essential.[1] Therefore, if Alice is the transferor she must intend to transfer ownership and if Ben is the transferee he must intend to acquire it. If Alice does not intend a transfer to take place, there can be no transfer. She cannot be deprived of her property unless she agrees.

---

[1]   See **PARA 3.11** above.

8.2   That is the general principle. But sometimes the consent of the *transferor* is not needed. This is known as 'involuntary transfer'. It is still derivative, not original, acquisition.[2] Alice's right of ownership passes to Ben, albeit without her consent. In contrast, in original acquisition Alice's right of ownership is extinguished and a new title is created in Ben. The difference is important, because, as in other cases of derivative acquisition, the transfer is subject to the *nemo plus* rule.[3]

8.3   The main cases of involuntary transfer are:
(a)   compulsory purchase;[4]
(b)   sale by a secured creditor;[5]
(c)   diligence;[6]
(d)   insolvency;[7]
(e)   death;[8]
(f)   forfeiture as a criminal penalty;[9] and
(g)   special statutory rules.[10]

COMPULSORY PURCHASE

General

8.4   Statutory powers authorising compulsory acquisition of land are held by certain public bodies. These include local authorities and the Scottish Government. Land might be compulsorily acquired, for example, to construct a motorway or a development such as the Glasgow 2014 Commonwealth Games site. Where the powers are exercised, the owner's consent is unnecessary. However, that party must be compensated. This is necessary as a matter of fairness and not least to conform to Article 1 of Protocol 1 to the ECHR.[11] Where agreement cannot be reached on compensation, the matter is determined by the Lands Tribunal.[12]

8.5   The first part of a compulsory purchase is the service of a 'compulsory purchase order' (CPO). Second, there is the actual transfer of ownership, effected either by a 'schedule conveyance' or by a 'general vesting declaration' (GVD).

---

2   See **CHAPTER 9** below.
3   See **PARA 4.42** above.
4   See **PARAS 8.4–8.10** below.
5   See **PARA 8.11** below.
6   See **PARAS 8.12–8.14** below.
7   See **PARAS 8.15–8.16** below.
8   See **PARAS 8.17–8.18** below.
9   See **PARA 8.19** below.
10   See **PARA 8.20** below.
11   See **CHAPTER 32** below.
12   Land Compensation (Scotland) Act 1973, s 8. The whole area of compulsory purchase is the subject of a Discussion Paper by the Scottish Law Commission. See Scot Law Com DP No 159, 2014. The Commission published the responses to the consultation on its website in 2016. The Scottish Government is to decide how to take reform forward.

Compulsory purchase order

8.6   The CPO is drawn up in the prescribed form.[13] It is then served on the parties affected, and also publicly advertised. There is a period for objections of at least 21 days. After that the CPO may be 'confirmed' by the 'confirming authority'. This is usually the Scottish Ministers. If objections are made, the confirming authority must either allow the objector a hearing or hold a public local inquiry. If the CPO is confirmed, this must be intimated to the affected parties.

Conveyancing procedures

8.7   There are two types of conveyancing procedure following the confirmation of the CPO. The transferor (the current owner) can be asked to execute a special form of disposition, known as a 'schedule conveyance', or the acquiring authority can proceed without the transferor and execute a GVD. If the transferor is unwilling to co-operate, a GVD must be used. A single GVD can also be used for several properties. A schedule conveyance is, however, quicker in practice than a GVD.

Schedule conveyances

8.8   The Lands Clauses Consolidation (Scotland) Act 1845 regulates schedule conveyances. There is a statutory form of disposition in a schedule to the Act – hence 'schedule conveyance'. The transfer process begins with a statutory 'notice to treat'.[14] Despite this name, the notice, when served on the transferor, may be regarded as a binding contract of sale.[15] The procedure which follows is similar to that in an ordinary transfer. The transferor executes and delivers the conveyance. On registration in the Land Register, ownership passes to the acquiring authority.

General vesting declarations

8.9   A transfer by schedule conveyance is not, strictly speaking, *involuntary*. The transferor does actually consent to the transfer by executing the disposition, although the reason for doing so is the CPO. A GVD is different. Here, the transferor is not involved. A GVD is drawn up in the prescribed form and executed by the acquiring authority.[16] On registration of the GVD in the Land Register, ownership is transferred to the acquiring authority.

---

[13]   See the Acquisition of Land (Authorisation Procedure) (Scotland) Act 1947, Sch 1.
[14]   See the Acquisition of Land (Authorisation Procedure) (Scotland) Act 1947, Sch 2, para 3.
[15]   For discussion, see J Rowan Robinson with E Farquharson-Black, *Compulsory Purchase and Compensation* (3rd edn, 2009) paras 3-08–3-09.
[16]   Town and Country Planning (Scotland) Act 1997, Sch 15.

Miscellaneous compulsory purchase rights

8.10 Sometimes a right of compulsory purchase is conferred by statute, exercisable by requiring an ordinary conveyance from the owner. Examples are crofters,[17] other tenant farmers,[18] crofting community bodies[19] and community bodies.[20] In some of these cases the right is only a pre-emption right – a right to buy in preference to other bidders if the owner wishes to sell. In others, the right to buy does not depend on the owner's willingness to sell.

SALE BY A SECURED CREDITOR

8.11 Often rights in security give the creditor a power of sale.[21] This means that if the debtor defaults on the loan the creditor can sell the security subjects and recover the debt out of the proceeds. The balance, after deduction of expenses, then goes to the debtor. On a sale by a secured creditor the transfer following thereon is involuntary, i.e. there is no role for the owner (the defaulting debtor). Although the debtor owns the property and the creditor does not, the act of transfer is effected by the creditor and not by the debtor. The transfer itself is carried out in the normal way for the type of property in question.[22]

DILIGENCE

General

8.12 Diligence is the process by which a creditor, typically an unsecured creditor, attaches the debtor's property to enforce payment.[23] A distinction can be drawn between 'seize diligences' and 'freeze diligences'. In a 'seize' diligence the creditor seizes property belonging to the debtor; in a 'freeze' diligence the debtor is prevented from disposing of the property.

Seize diligences

8.13 It is seize diligences which are relevant to involuntary transfer. The main cases are attachment, adjudication, and arrestment and furthcoming. Attachment seizes corporeal moveables. Adjudication seizes land.[24] Arrestment and furthcoming

---

[17] Crofters (Scotland) Act 1993, ss 12–19. On crofters, see **PARA 19.50** below.
[18] Agricultural Holdings (Scotland) Act 2003, Pt 2. See also **PARA 19.49** below.
[19] LR(S)A 2003, Pt 3. See **PARA 15.20** below.
[20] LR(S)A 2003, Pt 2. See **PARA 15.20** below.
[21] See **PARA 21.24** below.
[22] See **CHAPTER 5** above.
[23] See Gloag and Henderson *The Law of Scotland* ch 48.
[24] See *Hull v Campbell* 2011 SLT 881. It will be replaced by a new procedure called land attachment when and if the relevant provisions of the Bankruptcy and Diligence etc. (Scotland) Act 2007 are brought into force. See Gloag and Henderson *The Law of Scotland* paras 48.34–48.41.

seize moveable property (both corporeal and incorporeal) which is in the hands of a third party, for example a bank account.

8.14   In seize diligences the creditor probably acquires, not ownership, but a right in security over the property seized. The next step is to realise the property and thereby recover the debt: this is broadly similar to enforcement by any other secured creditor.

INSOLVENCY

Sequestration

8.15   A natural person who becomes insolvent may be sequestrated. A *trustee in sequestration* is appointed to realise the assets and distribute the proceeds rateably amongst the various creditors, who are the beneficiaries of the trust that the sequestration sets up. Sequestration is governed by the Bankruptcy (Scotland) Act 2016. The debtor's assets 'vest in', ie are transferred to the trustee, in trust for the creditors. The transfer is an involuntary one.[25] The trustee obtains an immediate right of possession and administration. For some types of property, such as corporeal moveable property and most incorporeal moveable property the trustee acquires title by virtue of the fact of sequestration. But for property, such as land, where title depends on registration, the sequestration functions as a delivered deed of conveyance to the trustee, conferring the power to complete title by registration. For example, Val is sequestrated, and owns a house and a bicycle. Ownership of the bicycle passes to the trustee at once, without the need for delivery. But ownership of the house does not pass until the trustee registers in the Land Register or Sasine Register. The trustee is thus an unregistered holder.[26] Registration is required before ownership is acquired.[27] But in practice this may not happen, for, like any other unregistered holder, the trustee can convey to a purchaser without having first completed title in his or her own name.

Corporate insolvency

8.16   When a company goes into liquidation the position is different from sequestration. There is no vesting in the liquidator.[28] A liquidator has power of administration, and can dispose of the company's assets as its representative. However, a liquidator can apply to the court for the assets to be transferred to him or her, and if that happens the position becomes the same, from the standpoint of

---

[25]   Though the sequestration can be initiated by the debtor.
[26]   See **PARA 4.53** above.
[27]   *Burnett's Tr v Grainger* 2004 SC (HL) 19. Immediate registration is not possible: see the Bankruptcy (Scotland) Act 2016, s 78.
[28]   Subject to the Titles to Land Consolidation (Scotland) Act 1868, s 25.

property law, as a sequestration. Such applications are almost unknown in practice.[29] Whether liquidation is really involuntary transfer is arguable. A juristic person acts through representatives: their consent is its consent. The liquidator is the company representative. A similar point can be made about the other forms of corporate insolvency, administration and receivership.

DEATH

8.17   The property of a person who dies is administered by an executor, whose function is to gather in and then distribute the deceased's estate in accordance with the will or, where there is no will, the rules of intestate succession.[30] The executor must obtain decree of *confirmation* from the sheriff court. This operates as a judicial conveyance to the executor of the deceased's estate.[31]

8.18   Like the act and warrant of a trustee in sequestration, the confirmation alone does not transfer heritable property. There must also be registration in the Land Register. In practice, executors do not usually register. Their interest in the property is temporary and as holders of an unregistered judicial conveyance (the confirmation) they are already unregistered holders, enabling them to transfer the property on by a disposition in which title is deduced through the confirmation.[32]

FORFEITURE AS A CRIMINAL PENALTY

8.19   The criminal courts have statutory powers to order forfeiture of property belonging to offenders. Some of these relate to specific offences, for example the poaching of fish.[33] In addition, the Proceeds of Crime Act 2002 has detailed general provisions allowing prosecutors to move for the confiscation of assets and, if necessary, their subsequent sale by enforcement administrators.[34]

SPECIAL STATUTORY RULES

8.20   In several situations statute enables a non-owning seller of corporeal moveable property to transfer ownership to the purchaser.[35] For example, if Stephanie has agreed to buy a car from Robert and has taken delivery of it but not yet become owner, because they have agreed that this will be dependent on her paying for it next

---

29   Insolvency Act 1986, s 145(1).
30   See **CHAPTERS 28 and 29** below.
31   S(S)A 1964, s 14(1).
32   See **PARA 4.53–4.54** above.
33   Salmon and Freshwater Fisheries Consolidation (Scotland) Act 2003, s 60.
34   Proceeds of Crime Act 2002, ss 92–155.
35   These provisions are discussed in more detail at **PARA 5.35–5.36** above.

week, she has power as a 'buyer in possession' to transfer Robert's title to Tiffany.[36] If it turns out that Robert has a void title, then it is that same bad title that Tiffany, the purchaser, will receive.[37] The effect of these special statutory rules is an involuntary transfer from the third party, in our example Robert, to the purchaser (Tiffany). In relation to the transfer of land, s 86 of the Land Registration etc. (Scotland) Act 2012, which is discussed elsewhere,[38] is another important example of where statute effects an involuntary transfer.

LITERATURE

8.21 For further detail on involuntary transfer, see Reid *Property* paras 663–668. On the subject of statutory titles to land, see McDonald *Conveyancing Manual* ch 29. On death and transfer, see Gretton and Reid *Conveyancing* ch 25 and McDonald, *Conveyancing Manual* ch 30. On compulsory purchase, see Gordon *Scottish Land Law* ch 29 and Rowan Robinson, J, with Farquharson-Black, E *Compulsory Purchase and Compensation* (3rd edn, 2009).

---

[36] SOGA 1979, s 25. See also SOGA 1979, ss 21 and 24; the Factors Act 1889, ss 8 and 9; and the Hire Purchase Act 1964, s 27.
[37] *National Employers Mutual General Insurance Association Ltd v Jones* [1990] 1 AC 24.
[38] See PARAS **7.67–7.68** above.

Chapter 9

Original acquisition

INTRODUCTION

9.1   In 'original acquisition', the acquirer gains a brand new title to the property. This contrasts with 'derivative acquisition', where the title is only as good as that of the previous owner.[1] Instances of original acquisition can be divided into two broad categories. The first is where the property has never been owned. This category is confined to moveables, for, in the normal case at least, land cannot be ownerless. (Land, unless owned by someone else, belongs to the Crown.[2]) The second category

---

[1]   See **PARA 3.11** above.
[2]   Erskine II, 1, 11; Reid *Feudal Abolition* para 1.14. For positive prescription, see **CHAPTER 6**.

is where the property has been owned. Here, the law extinguishes the existing title at the same time as it confers the new title on the acquirer. Naturally, such a serious consequence means that the operation of original acquisition is strictly limited. It is also restricted by the rule that property, if abandoned, passes to the Crown, rather than becoming ownerless.[3] For example, if a married couple separate acrimoniously and the wife throws her wedding ring away, it becomes the Crown's. Similarly, where title to moveables is lost by negative prescription, it falls to the Crown.[4] For these reasons, derivative acquisition is far more common. Several of the original acquisition doctrines come from Roman law and do not always meet the needs of the modern age.[5]

PREVIOUSLY UNOWNED CORPOREAL MOVEABLES: OCCUPANCY

9.2   Where something moveable is not already owned it can be acquired by occupancy (*occupatio*). This is achieved by taking possession of the property with the intention to become owner.[6] For the reasons explained above, there is little ownerless property. The main examples are shells, pearls, gems and pebbles on the seashore, running water and wild animals. With an exception, occupancy can take place only once. For example, once collected a pearl becomes owned. It can never be ownerless again.

9.3   The exception concerns wild animals. If they regain liberty, they become unowned once more.[7] Thus the mouse which escapes from its pursuer, Debbie, who managed to get hold of it temporarily under the cupboard in the kitchen, is no longer Debbie's property. The rule does not apply to farmed fish, on the basis that they are not truly wild.[8] Animals which have freedom of movement but return to a particular place, such as bees and pigeons, remain owned provided that they continue to come back. Where game is seized illegitimately by poachers on someone else's land they will acquire a title by occupancy, but this can be subsequently forfeited by a court.[9]

---

[3]   Erskine II, 1, 12; *Lord Advocate v University of Aberdeen & Budge* 1963 SC 533; *Mackenzie v Maclean* 1981 SLT (Sh Ct) 40. A Latin maxim found in older authorities is *quod nullius est fit domini regis*: what belongs to no one becomes the property of the lord king. See also **PARAS 3.7–3.9** above. But the Scottish Law Commission, Report on Prescription and Title to Moveable Property (Scot Law Com No 228, 2012) proposes that abandoned property becomes ownerless.

[4]   PL(S)A 1973, s 8. But the Scottish Law Commission, Report on Prescription and Title to Moveable Property (Scot Law Com No 228, 2012) proposes that negative prescription for corporeal moveables is abolished and a new positive prescription rule introduced in its place.

[5]   See, eg, N R Whitty, 'Rights of Personality, Property Rights and the Human Body in Scots Law' (2005) 9 *Edin LR* 194.

[6]   In the words of the Latin maxim, *quod nullius est fit occupantis* (what belongs to no one becomes the property of the taker).

[7]   Erskine II, 1, 10.

[8]   *Valentine v Kennedy* 1985 SCCR 89. See C G van der Merwe and D Bain 'The Fish that Got Away: Some Reflections on *Valentine v Kennedy*' (2008) 12 *Edin LR* 418.

[9]   See **PARA 8.19** above.

PROPERTY WHICH HAS ALREADY BEEN OWNED

Accession

General

9.4   Accession (accessio) takes place when two pieces of corporeal property become joined in such a way that one is considered to have become subsumed into the other.[10] The property which is subsumed is known as the 'accessory'. The property into which it is subsumed is known as the 'principal'. For example, a house accedes to the land on which it is built. A window frame accedes to the house and so to the land. The paint accedes to the frame and so to the land. An engine accedes to the car into which it is installed. Accession is a mechanical doctrine dependent on objective factors. It follows that parties cannot contract so as to exclude its operation.[11]

Elements

9.5   Three elements of accession have been identified.[12] The first and most important is physical union. The pieces of property must be attached to each other. The greater the level of attachment, the more likely it is that accession has operated. The panelling built into a wall is a strong candidate for accession. The picture hung from a nail is not. The second element is functional subordination. The accessory must be subordinate to the principal. The entryphone system in a tenement is attached for the improvement of that building. The third element is permanency. The more permanent the attachment, the greater the likelihood there is of accession. Buildings accede: marquees do not. Similarly, cinema seats can be compared with seats fixed to the floor of a hall for one night of boxing.[13]

Effects

9.6   Accession has three effects.[14]
   (1)   The accessory becomes part of the principal. This means that rights created in respect of the principal automatically affect the accessory. For example, if Penelope has a contractual right to acquire ownership of a house, she is entitled to everything that has acceded to it. The seller in such circumstances should make express provision for any accessory which is not to be included. For instance, it could be stipulated that the ornamental bird bath in the back garden is excluded from the sale and will be removed by the seller.

---

[10]   The term used by the DCFR Book VIII. – 5:203 is 'combination'.
[11]   *Shetland Islands Council v BP Petroleum Development Ltd* 1990 SLT 82 at 94 per Lord Cullen.
[12]   Reid *Property* para 571.
[13]   T B Smith, *A Short Commentary on the Law of Scotland* (1962) 504.
[14]   Reid *Property* para 574.

(2) The second effect is known as 'conversion'. This occurs when the accessory is moveable and the principal is heritable. The result of accession is to make the accessory heritable. Thus, bricks are 'born' moveable but become heritable on being used to build a house. Occasionally, moveable property which has a purpose devoted to land, for example, a house key, is deemed heritable and is known as a 'constructive fixture'.

(3) The third effect is that the existing title to the accessory is extinguished. Where it and the principal have different owners, the result is to give the owner of the principal an original title to the accessory. For example, if Bob takes Carol's slates and attaches them to his roof, he becomes their owner. Carol, if she did not consent, is left with a compensation claim.[15]

9.7   If the accessory is subsequently separated ('severed') from the principal, effects (1) and (2) are reversed, but not effect (3). If Carol removes the slates from Bob's roof, the slates no longer form part of that roof and become moveable property again. They still belong to Bob because accession operated. Effect (3) can be seen to have serious consequences. It has been suggested therefore that whether it operates depends on the parties involved (for example that it should not operate in the case of tenants). The better view, however, is that there is a unitary law and distinctions based on the circumstances are not admitted.[16]

Moveables to land

9.8   Moveable property which has acceded to land is a 'fixture'. Fixtures can be contrasted with 'fittings'. These are items found in a building, such as furniture, which do not satisfy the requirements for accession. Whether accession takes place depends on the application of the three elements discussed above. First, there must be physical union. Things which are irrevocably attached, such as buildings, are always fixtures. A heavy object may accede because of its weight alone.[17] If the accessory cannot be removed without seriously damaging it or the principal, then it will have acceded.[18] Unless the 'physical union' test provides a decisive result, the other two elements must be considered.

9.9   As to the second element – functional subordination – the question to ask is: does the item appear to be attached for the improvement of the land or for the better enjoyment of the item? Sometimes the answer is clear. A heating system is clearly installed to improve a house and therefore accedes.[19] In other cases, the attachment

---

[15]   See **PARA 9.18** below.
[16]   Reid *Property* para 575; *Brand's Trs v Brand's Trs* (1876) 3 R (HL) 16.
[17]   *Christie v Smith's Exr* 1949 SC 572 (a summer house).
[18]   *Elitestone Ltd v Morris* [1997] 2 All ER 513. This is an English case but the law here north and south of the border is similar, following *Brand's Trs v Brand's Trs* (1876) 3 R (HL) 16. For a comparative account, see L P W van Vliet 'Accession of Movables to Land' (2002) 6 *Edin LR* 67 and 199.
[19]   *Assessor for Fife v Hodgson* 1966 SC 30.

may enhance both the moveable and the land. A picture is better viewed if hung, but it also enhances the wall. Much depends on the circumstances.[20]

9.10   Only quasi-permanency is required to satisfy the third element. In the leading case of *Brand's Trs v Brand's Trs*[21] machinery was installed by a tenant under a mining lease, with the intention of removing it at the expiry. It was held, nonetheless, to have acceded. Various factors should be considered when assessing permanency.[22] If the physical attachment used is greater than is necessary to secure the item then that points to accession.[23] So too does mutual special adaptation, as where lace looms were installed into a shed which had been adjusted to take them.[24] Also relevant is whether the item is something normally left or removed when a building changes hands. For example, industrial machinery may well be left in a factory for the new owner taking over the business. Domestic items such as dishwashers are commonly removed. There are many borderline cases, such as fitted carpets, though perhaps these are nowadays regarded as fixtures. Finally, the length of time which the item takes to install or remove should be considered. For example, industrial machinery which needs several weeks to be fitted or removed will be regarded as an accessory.

9.11   The deemed intention of the person who installed the item (who might be a hirer) has been said to be relevant when assessing whether there has been accession.[25] This seems to be contrary to House of Lords authority.[26] The better view is that accession should be decided solely by objective factors. As one writer has put it, '[a] fixture should be a fixture if it is patent for all the world to see'.[27]

9.12   In limited circumstances, tenants have a right to sever something even if it has acceded. This is recognised for trade fixtures.[28] There is also a statutory right of tenants to remove agricultural fixtures.[29] In English law, tenants may also remove domestic and ornamental fixtures but there is no authority on the point in Scotland.[30]

Moveables to moveables

9.13   Moveable property can accede to other moveable property, for example a button to a coat or paint to a car. In broad terms, the same rules for deciding whether

20   *Cochrane v Stevenson* (1891) 18 R 1208.
21   (1876) 3 R (HL) 16.
22   Reid *Property* para 582.
23   *Leigh v Taylor* [1902] AC 157.
24   *Howie's Trs v McLay* (1902) 5 F 214.
25   *Scottish Discount Co v Blin* 1985 SC 216.
26   *Brand's Trs v Brand's Trs* (1876) 3 R (HL) 16.
27   C G van der Merwe 'Accession by Building' in Reid and Zimmermann *History* vol 1, 245 at 268.
28   *Brand's Trs v Brand's Trs* (1876) 3 R (HL) 16.
29   Agricultural Holdings (Scotland) Act 1991, s 18. The strict effect of this provision rather bizarrely is that such fixtures are to be treated as not having acceded in the first place.
30   Reid *Property* para 586.

accession has taken place apply as for moveables-to-land accession. Here too there can be borderline cases. It has been held in South Africa that tyres do not accede to a car because removing them is relatively straightforward.[31] In the aviation industry there is a consensus that an aero-engine does not accede to the airframe.

9.14   In the case of fixtures, there is no difficulty in identifying the principal. It is always the land. Here, it is more complicated and the law is not settled. Bell's analysis[32] is as follows. First, if, with two substances, one can exist separately and the other cannot, then the first is the principal. An example is paint used on a car, which no longer has an independent existence.[33] Second, where both things can exist separately, the principal is the one 'which the other is taken to adorn or complete'.[34] For example, the button accedes to the coat. This might be expressed alternatively that the principal is the item which gives its name to the finished product. Bell's final rule is that if the two foregoing rules are not relevant then 'bulk prevails; next value'. In the absence of case law it is not certain that this is correct. Bulk was given some importance in the South African case of *Khan v Minister of Law and Order*.[35] There, a BMW car turned out to be the front of one car and the back of another.[36] The rear part had been stolen. It included the bodywork up to the windscreen and was held to be the principal. Hence the front acceded to it, and so belonged to the owner of the principal.

Land to land

9.15   The extent to which land is covered by water is subject to change. Any new dry land created will accede to that which exists already. This is called 'alluvion' (*alluvio*).[37] Alluvion also operates where the extent of the land under an area of water increases. In that case there is accession to the land already covered. There are two main conditions.

(1) The addition must be permanent. Temporary change is insufficient, for example an inland loch that shrinks somewhat in summer.

(2) Sudden additions do not count. Such changes, for example those caused by a storm, are known as 'avulsion'.

Whilst alluvion normally happens naturally, it can happen by human intervention, such as by the building of a wall. In *Stirling v Bartlett*[38] some debris had come

---

[31]   *J L Cohen Motors v Alberts* 1985 (2) SA 427. See also Carey Miller with Irvine *Corporeal Moveables* para 3.20.

[32]   Bell *Principles* § 1298.

[33]   See Carey Miller with Irvine *Corporeal Moveables* para 3.19.

[34]   Bell *Principles* § 1298.

[35]   1991 (3) SA 439.

[36]   In slang terms, a 'cut and shut'.

[37]   See further J Robbie, *Private Water Rights* (2015) paras 4.59–4.63 and Reid and Gretton, *Land Registration* para 5.17.

[38]   1993 SLT 763.

floating down a river, breaking it up into different channels during the 1960s. By agreement with his counterpart on the other side, one of the proprietors of land beside the river constructed a new channel. This altered the route of the river slightly. In the 1990s a successor proprietor objected. It was held that the change was permanent and the objection came too late.[39] In other circumstances, deliberate human act may be classed as avulsion.[40]

Fruits

9.16   Where the accessory is produced by the principal, this is known as 'accession by fruits'. There are three principal examples. The first is crops, trees and plants. On taking root and receiving nourishment from the ground, they accede to it. But 'industrial growing crops', such as barley, wheat and potatoes, which require 'annual seed and labour', are moveable.[41] Where a tree is on the boundary of two pieces of land, ownership will be determined by the situation of its trunk. If the trunk straddles the boundary, the tree will be common property.[42] This contrasts with the rule in Roman law, where the situation of the roots was the determining factor.[43]

9.17   The second case is the young of animals, not yet born. They accede to the mother.[44] The third is natural products of animals or plants, such as milk or raspberries. These accede to the animal or plant in question, until such time as they become separate. This is an example of the more general rule that accession ends by separation. Therefore, the tree uprooted by the storm or the baby foal now born is no longer an accessory. Separation, however, in principle does not change ownership. A lamb belongs to the ewe's owner. Apples stolen from a tree still belong to the tree's owner. (Though in the case of a lease, the tenant normally acquires the fruits.)

Compensation

9.18   The erstwhile owner of the accessory may be entitled to compensation for loss of title on the basis of unjustified enrichment. This depends on who brought about the accession, and why. If it was the owner of the principal, then there is an enrichment claim. (Unless, of course, the accession was consensual, in which case compensation, if any, depends on the agreement.[45]) The quantum is the value of the

---

[39]   For discussion, see Gordon and Wortley *Scottish Land Law* para 3.23 and D L Carey Miller, 'Alluvio, Avulsio and Fluvial Boundaries' 1994 *SLT (News)* 75.

[40]   See Scottish Law Commission, Report on the Law of the Foreshore and Sea Bed (Scot Law Com No 190, 2003) paras 6.1–6.5.

[41]   Erskine II, 2, 4; *Boskabelle Ltd v Laird* 2006 SLT 1079.

[42]   *Hetherington v Galt* (1905) 7 F 706.

[43]   Reid *Property* para 179.

[44]   *Lamb v Grant* (1874) 11 SLR 672.

[45]   Stair II, 1, 38–39; Bankton I, 9, 43; A J M Steven, 'Recompense for Interference in Scots Law' 1996 *JR* 51 at 61.

materials but if there has been bad faith, a higher level is payable.[46] If the act was that of the accessory's owner then there is generally no enrichment claim.[47] There is an exception, however, where that person had a reasonable belief that he or she owned the principal.

Commixtion and confusion

9.19   The mixing of solids so that it is impossible to distinguish them is 'commixtion' (*commixtio*). For example, Janet's sheep may become mixed with John's. If the sheep have identifying marks upon them and can be separated, commixtion does not operate. The equivalent doctrine for liquids is known as 'confusion' (*confusio*) – for instance, different whiskies being blended together.[48] The essential criterion here is mixing or fusion rather than joining. The result is common property in proportion to the value of the constituent materials. Assuming that Janet and John had an equal number of sheep and that these had the same value, they would both now own a one-half *pro indiviso* share of each sheep. The materials must, however, be of substantially the same kind, otherwise specification (discussed below), or perhaps accession will operate. Professor Carey Miller suggests, for example, that soda water added to whisky will accede to it.[49]

Specification

9.20   Where a new kind of thing is manufactured from materials belonging wholly or partly to others, this is 'specification' (*specificatio*).[50] For example, Jill bakes a cake using Kirsten's butter, eggs and flour. The case always cited by the institutional writers,[51] following Roman law, is making grapes into wine. This is more apposite to the temperate climate of Italy than Scotland. Stair's example of wood being used to build a boat seems more appropriate.[52] It is essential that a new type of thing is created, i.e. a new species (*nova species*). In one case it was held that joining two halves of a car together met this requirement.[53] This, however, is accession, as it is merely joining and there is no *nova species*.[54] Conversely, where a vehicle is built from scratch out of raw materials such as metal, this is truly a new species.[55] It was argued unsuccessfully in one case that where baby salmon (smolts)

---

46   Steven 'Recompense for Interference in Scots Law' at 61.
47   See, eg, *Jones v Muir* 2015 GWD 11–183.
48   J Thomson *Scottish Private Law* (2006) para 3.07. The term used in the DCFR for commixtion and confusion is 'commingling': see DCFR Book VIII. – 5:202.
49   Carey Miller with Irvine *Corporeal Moveables* para 5.05.
50   The term used by the DCFR Book VIII. – 5:201 is 'production'.
51   For example, Erskine II, 1, 25.
52   Stair II, 1, 41.
53   *McDonald v Provan (of Scotland Street) Ltd* 1960 SLT 231.
54   This analysis was accepted in *Khan v Minister of Law and Order* 1991 (3) SA 439.
55   *Wylie & Lochhead v Mitchell* (1870) 8 M 552.

are industrially reared in a fish farm so as they grow to become adults, specification takes place.[56] A Dutch court in a similar case involving eggs being specially hatched to produce chickens reached the opposite result.[57] As there is no actual change of species, this seems questionable.

9.21 The issue of who owns the new species was controversial in Roman law.[58] Some jurists favoured the owner of the materials; others, the manufacturer. A middle view developed that the manufacturer acquired ownership if the work carried out was, in a practical sense, irreversible. If it was not, title was given to the owner of the materials. An example of practical irreversibility would be a boat, which in theory could be returned to planks of wood, but not in a way in which it appears that the boat was never built in the first place. This middle view has been accepted in Scotland. Of course, the manufacturer may be carrying out the process as the agent of the owner of the materials. In that case the latter will naturally acquire ownership. Likewise, the matter in general can be governed by an agreement between the parties.[59]

9.22 A difficult question is whether the manufacturer needs to be in good faith in order to acquire ownership. The better view is that state of mind should be relevant only to the issue of compensation. The rules on recompensing the party who does not acquire title are similar to those for accession. Where ownership has been acquired by the manufacturer, that person must repay the value of the materials to their erstwhile owner. In *International Banking Corporation v Ferguson Shaw & Sons*[60] oil had been used in good faith to make margarine. The value of the oil had then to be paid to the former owner. Where ownership remains with the owner of the materials the manufacturer has no claim, unless that person reasonably believed that he or she owned them.

Money and bills of exchange

9.23 For reasons of commerce, special rules enable the acquirers of money (legal tender) and negotiable instruments to acquire an original rather than a derivative title.[61] As regards money, say that Charlie finds a £1 coin in the street and goes into a shop to buy chocolate with it. The shopkeeper acquires an original title to the coin. The fact that it does not belong to Charlie does not matter. However, good faith on the part of the shopkeeper is required.[62] Similarly, a 'holder in due course' of a bill

---

[56]   *Kinloch Damph Ltd v Nordvik Salmon Farms Ltd,* Outer House, 30 June 1999 (unreported, available at http://www.scotcourts.gov.uk/opinions/ca291499.html).
[57]   HR 24 Mar 1994, NJ 158. See Van Erp and Akkermans, *Property Law* 697–699.
[58]   Reid *Property* para 560.
[59]   *Wylie & Lochhead v Mitchell* (1870) 8 M 552.
[60]   1910 SC 182.
[61]   See, for example, the discussion of money in Stair II, 1, 43 and Carey Miller with Irvine *Corporeal Moveables* para 1.19.
[62]   *Crawfurd v Royal Bank* (1749) Mor 875. See K G C Reid, 'Banknotes and their Vindication in Eighteenth Century Scotland' in D Fox and W Ernst (eds), *Money in the Western Legal Tradition: Middle Ages to Bretton Woods* (2016) 556–572.

of exchange, i.e. someone who takes it in good faith and for value, gains an original title. Therefore, if the person from whom the bill was obtained had a bad title, this does not matter.[63]

Positive prescription

9.24   Where someone has possessed land openly, peaceably and continuously without being challenged in court for a period of ten years, on the basis of a conveyance which has been registered in the Land Register or the Sasine Register, the title will be exempt from challenge.[64]

Registration in the Land Register under LR(S)A 1979

9.25   The effect of the Keeper entering a person as proprietor of property in the Land Register under the Land Registration (Scotland) Act 1979 was to cure any defects in that person's title.[65] Therefore if Beth disponed land to Carol and the Keeper registered Carol as owner, Carol was owner, even if Beth was not owner or that the disposition was invalid for other reasons. This is not the position under the Land Registration etc. (Scotland) Act 2012, which in general follows the ordinary rules of property law.[66]

LITERATURE

9.26   For an alternative overview, see Thomson, J *Scots Private Law* (2006) ch 3. More detailed accounts can be found in Carey Miller with Irvine *Corporeal Moveables* chs 2–5, Gordon and Wortley *Scottish Land Law* ch 5 and Reid *Property* paras 539–596 and 673–676. For a comparative account see Van Erp and Akkermans *Property Law* ch 7. For detailed treatments of accession of moveables to land, see C G van der Merwe, 'Accession by Building' in Reid and Zimmermann *History* vol 1, 245–268 and L P W van Vliet, 'Accession of Movables to Land' (2002) 6 *Edin LR* 67 and 199.

---

[63] Bills of Exchange Act 1882, s 38(2). See I G MacNeil (ed), *Scots Commercial Law* (2014) para 9.33 (M Solinas).
[64] PL(S)A 1973, s 1. Positive prescription is discussed in more detail in **CHAPTER 6** above.
[65] See **PARA 7.72** above.
[66] See **PARA 7.73** above.

Chapter 10

Co-ownership

INTRODUCTION

10.1   Two persons can own the same thing at the same time: for example, Jack and Jill buy a house together. On the Land Register, both names will appear on the proprietorship section of the title sheet. Each owns everything. Each room is owned by both. Each wall in each room is owned by both. Each brick in each wall is owned by both. Each atom in each brick is owned by both. The same can be true of moveable property. Jack and Jill may co-own some or all of the contents of the house – each chair, each rug, each plate. Co-ownership is not just limited to two people. Bashful, Doc, Dopey, Grumpy, Happy, Sleepy and Sneezy could be the co-owners of a fairy-tale cottage.

10.2   Co-ownership, also called undivided ownership, or ownership *pro indiviso*, is of two very different kinds: common ownership and joint ownership.[1] 'Common

---

[1]   Formerly, landownership was divided between superior and vassal, but no longer: see **APPENDIX**. There is – or was – also something called 'commonty' but the Division of Commonties Act 1695 provided a mechanism for the termination of commonties on a case-by-case basis, and it is doubtful whether any now survive.

ownership' is the standard case. 'Joint ownership' is the special case, the main example being in the law of trusts. The property is called 'common property' or 'joint property' respectively,[2] though in practice those who are not specialists in property law often use the word 'joint' for both. The two terms are not ideal. Roman–Dutch law, which has the same distinction, uses the terms 'free' co-ownership for common ownership and 'bound' co-ownership for joint ownership.[3] Perhaps Scots law should follow suit.

10.3   It is not only ownership that can be held by two or more persons. So can other patrimonial rights. For example, two or more persons might be co-tenants. However, the law has been developed in connection with ownership, which is in practice the most important case. This is what is discussed in this chapter. For other types of right, the principles are applied by analogy, but the law is rather undeveloped.

COMMON OWNERSHIP

General

10.4   Common ownership arises in many situations, but three represent the great majority. The first is where two people buy a house together and take the title 'in joint names' as common property (and not, as the expression suggests, joint ownership). The second is where two people live together as spouses, civil partners or cohabitants, for then the moveable contents of the house are in practice usually co-owned, and indeed are presumed to be co-owned, regardless of who owns the house itself.[4] The third is where there is a building development and certain parts are co-owned by the owners of the various units. An example is where a developer builds, say, 30 houses and each house has a share of the planted areas, the children's play park, shared parking areas etc. The best-known illustration is in tenements, where certain parts of the building will be co-owned by the various flat owners.[5]

10.5   The first two situations are functionally different from the third, for in the third the co-ownership is usually a permanent arrangement, and unaffected as and when individual units are sold. The common parts are shared corporeal pertinents of each unit.[6] The share in the common parts thus attaches to each flat. As a result, the law treats such cases slightly differently. Usually there are real burdens that regulate

---

[2]   The terminology was settled by the leading case of *Magistrates of Banff v Ruthin Castle Ltd* 1944 SC 36.
[3]   D Kleyn and S Wortley 'Co-ownership' in Zimmermann, Visser and Reid *Mixed Legal Systems* 703–734.
[4]   See **CHAPTER 11** below.
[5]   See **PARAS 16.10–16.11** below.
[6]   On pertinents, see **PARAS 15.9–15.12** below.

such matters as repairs, and in that case the general law of common property is to that extent displaced.[7] For tenements, there is a statutory regime and, here again, the general law of common property is to that extent displaced.[8]

10.6   Each co-owner has a *pro indiviso* share of the property. The law presumes that the shares are equal, so that if there are two co-owners, each has a half share; if there are five, each has a fifth; and so on. This is only a presumption. The shares can be unequal. For example, two brothers buy a flat for £180,000. One contributes £120,000 and the other £60,000, and so they decide that their shares should reflect their contributions, ie two-thirds and one-third. That will be stated in the disposition and on the title sheet. There is, however, no legal requirement that the size of the share and the size of the contribution match. The brothers would have been free to agree an equal share of the title or, indeed, that title would be vested in just one of them. However, if title share does not match contribution, the parties should have an agreement as to whether the amount of the mismatch is to be treated as a gift or as a loan.

Possession and use

10.7   Possession is shared. Each co-owner has a right to make use of 'every inch'[9] of the property. Jack may dislike it if Jill is in the kitchen when he is cooking but as co-owner she has the right to be there. The parties are free to agree otherwise: Jack and Jill can agree that he is to have the exclusive right to use the ground-floor bathroom and she alone may use the first-floor bathroom. Here, the right of exclusive use is based in contract law (or perhaps just a non-binding understanding), not in property law. Each is still co-owner of the whole house. This 'every inch' principle is the first of three principles (all variable by agreement) about possession and use of common property.[10] The second is that only 'ordinary' use is permitted. In one case it was held that the owner of a flat was not entitled to use the passage of a tenement for keeping a wheelchair.[11] The third is that one co-owner cannot take 'excessive benefit' at the expense of the others.[12] An example is where one co-owner assumes exclusive possession of part, or indeed all, of the property without the consent of the other co-owners. Whether a person who has a larger share is entitled to a greater degree of use than someone with a smaller share is uncertain.

---

[7]   See **CHAPTER 14** below.
[8]   See **CHAPTER 16** below.
[9]   Erskine II, 6, 53.
[10]   Reid *Property* para 24.
[11]   *Carmichael v Simpson* 1932 SLT (Sh Ct) 16. See also *Rafique v Amin* 1997 SLT 1385.
[12]   See, eg, *Bailey's Exrs v Upper Crathes Fishing Ltd* 1987 SLT 405 where interdict was granted. But financial compensation may not be a competent remedy: see *Denholm's Trs v Denholm* 1984 SLT 319. But see further Reid *Property* para 24, fn 24.

Repairs and alterations

10.8 Repairs and alterations require unanimous agreement.[13] There is an exception for 'necessary' repairs, where any co-owner can go ahead.[14] The boundary between necessary repairs on the one hand, and unnecessary repairs and alterations on the other, is in practice often difficult to draw. Minimal alterations may be lawful without consent, for example affixing a brass name plate.[15] As mentioned above, there are special rules for common property in tenements.[16] Moreover, the unanimity requirement is subject to any real burdens.

Death and insolvency

10.9 Each share forms part of the co-owner's patrimony. If a co-owner dies, the share simply forms part of the estate and is dealt with according to succession law. For example, if Fred and Gillian are co-owners of a car, he is free to bequeath his share to Heidi, so that after his death Gillian will find that her co-owner is Heidi. Even if Fred dies intestate, that does not mean that his share passes to Gillian.[17] Likewise, if Fred, instead of dying, becomes insolvent, his share is available to his creditors. So if Jack and Jill own a house in common and he is sequestrated, his share passes to his trustee in sequestration. (In practice the trustee will offer to sell the share to Jill. If she declines, there will be an action of division and sale.[18])

Juridical acts

10.10 Can one co-owner, without the consent of the others, transfer his or her share, or grant a subordinate real right? The answer is 'yes' if the share can be dealt with separately from the other shares. Otherwise the answer is 'no'. A co-owner can dispone the share without the consent of the others. For example, if Jack and Jill are co-owners of a house, she can dispone her share to Julius without Jack's consent – and indeed without telling him.[19] She can even dispone her half-share to 50 different disponees, each taking a 1% share of the whole property.[20] This sort of thing could make co-ownership unworkable, but a solution always exists: the action of division

---

[13] For an example of this rule, see *Rafique v Amin* 1997 SLT 1385.
[14] Bell *Principles* § 1075; *Deans v Woolfson* 1922 SC 221.
[15] *Barkley v Scott* (1893) 10 Sh Ct Rep 23.
[16] See **CHAPTER 16** below.
[17] But if their shares are subject to a special destination, the position may be different. See **CHAPTER 30** below.
[18] See further **PARAS 10.12–10.14** below.
[19] But if Jack and Jill are spouses or civil partners, Julius, though acquiring Jill's share, would not be entitled to move in. See **PARA 11.8** below.
[20] *Menzies v Macdonald* (1854) 16 D 827, affd (1856) 2 Macq 463. Despite this decision, the issue is problematic: see Reid *Property* para 28.

and sale.[21] Jill can also grant a standard security over her share.[22] In practice, of course, a lender will not usually be interested in taking security over less than 100% of the title because if the security has to be enforced, it would be difficult to find a buyer for a mere share. It can, however, happen that a single share is disponed, or granted in security, without the grantee so intending. This can happen if one co-owner forges the signature of another. Suppose that Jack and Jill own a house and Jill grants a standard security to a bank, signing her own name and forging Jack's. The deed is valid for her share but void for his.[23]

10.11 A servitude could not exist over just a share of the property, and so has to be granted by all the owners. If Jill, acting on her own, purported to grant to Jessica a servitude it would be void.[24] The same is true of real burdens[25] and leases.[26] An issue that sometimes arises is whether co-owners, acting unanimously, can validly grant a lease to one of their own number. While the co-owners are free to agree, as a matter of contract, that one of them will have sole possession and will pay the others rent, that is not classifiable as a contract of a lease.[27]

Ending it all

10.12 'The successful operation of a *pro indiviso* ownership of property will depend upon mutual compatibility, goodwill and understanding.'[28] So long as that sort of co-operation exists, all will be well. If one party wishes to exit, an arrangement can be come to whereby the share is bought at a fair value by the others, or the whole property is put on the market. When couples who co-own a house or flat split up, one or other of these is usually what happens because, despite the split, they can still co-operate about the property. But not always. The law is that any common owner can demand to be let out whether the others like it or not: *in communionem ... nemo compellitur invitus detineri.*[29] This is particularly important because, whether the common owners are in a personal relationship or not, *communio est mater rixarum.*[30] If an action is raised the court (subject to certain exceptions[31]) cannot refuse it.[32]

---

21   See **PARA 10.13** below.
22   *Schaw v Black* (1889) 16 R 326. The case involved a predecessor to the standard security.
23   *McLeod v Cedar Holdings Ltd* 1989 SLT 620. Such cases happen quite often.
24   See, eg, *Grant v Heriot's Trust* (1906) 8 F 647 and *Fearnan Partnership v Grindlay* 1990 SLT 704. *Unus ex dominis communium aedium servitutem imponere non potest.* ('One out of a group of owners of a property cannot grant a servitude'). Ulpian D 8, 1, 2.
25   TC(S)A 2003, s 6(3).
26   *Bell's Exrs v Inland Revenue* 1987 SLT 625.
27   *Clydesdale Bank plc v Davidson* 1998 SC (HL) 51.
28   *Bailey's Exrs v Upper Crathes Fishing Ltd* 1987 SLT 405 at 406 per Lord Weir.
29   No one can be forced to remain in co-ownership: C 3, 37, 5.
30   Common property is the mother of quarrels.
31   See **PARA 10.14** below.
32   *Upper Crathes Fishings Ltd v Bailey's Exrs* 1991 SLT 747.

10.13   The action is called an action of division or sale (also called an action of division and sale). The court will either:

(a)   physically divide the property, so that each of the common owners becomes 100% owner of a part, the division being done by the extent of the shares, so that, for example, a 25% owner would get less than a 50% owner; or

(b)   order that the property be sold as a unit, with the proceeds being divided among the various (former) co-owners according to their shares.

The decision between (a) and (b) is for the court. The presumption is in favour of (a); (b) will happen only if division is not reasonably practicable.[33] But in fact such actions almost always end in sale, not in division.

10.14   The right is sometimes called 'absolute' but in fact there are some qualifications. (i) It is excluded where the property is, to quote Bell, 'a thing of common and indispensable use as a staircase or vestibule'.[34] There is little other authority. His meaning is no doubt not merely that the thing is so used, but that it is so used as a pertinent of other properties, the owners of those other properties being the co-owners. (ii) Where the co-owners are spouses or civil partners, there are special rules.[35] (iii) Where one co-owner is sequestrated, the trustee in sequestration can insist on division and sale, but, to protect members of the bankrupt's family, the court can delay the sale for up to three years.[36] (iv) Finally, if a co-owner has contracted out of the right to raise an action, that is effective[37] but would not bind a singular successor.[38]

10.15   Can the pursuer ask the court to order, not the sale of the property on the open market, but that the defender should sell his or her share to the pursuer at market value? (Say the market value is £250,000: Jill asks the court to order Jack to transfer his share to her for £125,000.) Authority is conflicting.[39] An obvious difficulty with the 'right to buy-out' is: what should happen if both co-owners make the same demand? The answer appears to be that there would then be an auction in which only the co-owners could bid.[40]

---

[33]   *Thom v Macbeth* (1875) 3 R 161.
[34]   Bell *Principles* § 1082.
[35]   See **CHAPTER 11** below.
[36]   Bankruptcy (Scotland) Act 2016, s 113.
[37]   *Upper Crathes Fishings Ltd v Bailey's Exrs* 1991 SLT 747. *Fraser v Fraser* 2014 Hous LR 66.
[38]   *Grant v Heriot's Trust* (1906) 8 F 647.
[39]   Bankton I, 8, 40; Bell *Commentaries* I, 62; Reid *Property* para 33; C Anderson *Property: A Guide to Scots Law* (2016) paras 9-32 – 9-40; *Milligan v Barnhill* (1782) Mor 2486; *Scrimgeour v Scrimgeour* 1988 SLT 590; *Berry v Berry (No 2)* 1989 SLT 292; *Gray v Kerner* 1996 SCLR 331; *Ploetner v Ploetner* 1997 SCLR 998; *Wilson v Hervey* 2004 SCLR 313; *Collins v Sweeney* 2014 GWD 12-214.
[40]   As was observed in *Scrimgeour* 1988 SLT 590 at 593 by Lord McCluskey, referring to the decision of AD 214 (C 3, 37, 1) that developed this solution.

Timeshares

10.16   In a 'timeshare' the right to use something is divided between different people by time. For instance, one might buy the third week in April. Holiday properties are sometimes timeshared. So are salmon fishing rights. Timesharing is sometimes done by having the various parties as owners in common, coupled with a contract between them about time of use, maintenance and so on. But such contracts do not bind singular successors.[41] Moreover, a successor can end the scheme by insisting on division or sale. Co-ownership timeshare schemes also have problems about management and collection of upkeep payments. Accordingly, timeshares are usually done either by vesting the property in a trustee, with the timesharers having beneficial interests in the trust, or by vesting the property in a company in which the timesharers have shares.

JOINT OWNERSHIP

10.17   The two accepted cases of joint ownership are trusts[42] and, less importantly, unincorporated associations. Joint ownership arises in a trust if there is more than one trustee. Suppose that there are three: 'There is no such thing as a separate but *pro indiviso* right to a third in each trustee. Each has the full title along with the other two; and if they die, his title carries the whole right, to the exclusion of any others. If one dies, the title in him as trustee becomes extinct – it is absorbed by the title subsisting in the other two. He is blotted out of the title, and the infeftment of the other two is as good and perfect as if he never had been in the title.'[43] The property can be dealt with only as a unit. For example, if Julia and Tom own land as trustees, and Julia purports to transfer 'her share' to Janette, this is a nullity. If a trustee resigns, no conveyance to the ongoing trustees is needed of the resigning party's non-existent 'share'.[44] If a joint owner dies, nothing passes to the estate: the remaining joint owners have 100% of the title. Likewise, there can be no action of division or sale.

10.18   In the case of an unincorporated association, such as, say, a chess club, any assets (the chess sets, the silver championship cup etc.) are the joint property of the members. A member who leaves (or dies) automatically ceases to be a joint owner of the club's assets. Conversely, a person joining automatically becomes a joint owner. In trusts, any kind of property can be joint property. But for unincorporated associations, joint property is possible only for moveables. Some clubs make the office-bearers trustees for the members, in which case the law of trusts applies, with

---

[41]   Nor can this be circumvented by use of real burdens: TC(S)A 2003, s 6(3).
[42]   See **CHAPTERS 23–25** below.
[43]   *Gordon's Trustees v Eglinton* (1851) 13 D 1381 at 1385 *per* Lord Justice Clerk Hope. (Infeftment equates to ownership.)
[44]   This is confirmed by statute: T(S)A 1921, s 20.

the office-bearers owning the chess sets (etc.) jointly as trustees, the members for the time being the beneficiaries.

LITERATURE

10.19   Reid *Property* paras 17–36 is the leading account. Another valuable account can be found in Gordon and Wortley *Scottish Land Law* ch 15. G MacCormack, 'The *Actio Communi Dividundo* in Roman and Scots Law' in A D E Lewis and D J Ibbetson (eds) *The Roman Law Tradition* (1993) presents the subject from a historical standpoint. A most interesting study Is D Kleyn and S Wortley, 'Co-ownership' in Zimmermann, Visser and Reid *Mixed Legal Systems* 703–734.

Chapter 11

Sexual property law

INTRODUCTION

11.1   Once upon a time this subject was called 'matrimonial property law'.[1] Now marriages can be either other-sex or same-sex,[2] and same-sex couples (but not other-sex couples) can enter into civil partnerships which are almost the same as marriage. At the same time, cohabitation without marriage has grown.[3] An umbrella

---

[1]   See, eg, E M Clive *The Law of Husband and Wife in Scotland* (4th edn, 1997) para 14.001.
[2]   Same-sex marriage was introduced by the Marriage and Civil Partnership (Scotland) Act 2014.
[3]   The number of weddings in Scotland in 2015 was 29,691. (Of which 1,671 were same-sex.) In the 1970s the average number was 40,000. The number of civil partnerships in 2015 was 64, sharply down from the previous year (when the number was 436), this presumably being due to the introduction of same-sex marriage. Source: National Records of Scotland.

term is needed for the legal area dealing with the patrimonial consequences of such relationships. We offer, tastelessly, 'sexual property law'.

11.2 Families tend to operate as economic units. If Jack and Jill are married and she has money problems, the family has money problems. If she inherits £100,000 from Uncle Albert, then the family benefits. Whether she owns the house or he does or it is co-owned, it is the family's home. A family is usually a communist unit in which assets and obligations are pooled and in which each takes and gives according to what is fair. Of course, families vary. Those embarked on second marriages are often less communistic than young lovestruck newlyweds. The overall picture, however, is usually that the patrimonies[4] of the couple, and also of any non-adult offspring, are treated, *de facto*, more or less as a unity. And so long as the family remains reasonably happy, all works reasonably well. Most legal systems in history have recognised that family members behave not as strangers but as a unit. Many jurisdictions have a 'community' system in which the assets, and often the liabilities too, of husband and wife are held in common, or indeed that there is only one patrimony and not two.[5] Some systems, such as the older Roman law, included the children – even adult children – in this single patrimonial unit. Other systems have gone less far. Ours has varied over the centuries.

MARRIAGE

The basic principle: separation of patrimonies

11.3 'Marriage shall not of itself affect the respective rights of the parties … in relation to their property.'[6] But this modern principle of patrimonial separation is subject to extensive qualifications. Indeed, it might perhaps be argued that *functionally* speaking our law in fact comes close to community of property. The subject may be divided into (i) the position while the marriage exists, where we deal with (a) sections 25 and 26 of the Family Law (Scotland) Act 1985 (FL(S)A 1985) (b) the Matrimonial Homes (Family Protection) (Scotland) Act 1981 (MH(FP)(S) A 1981), and (ii) the position where the marriage ends, the latter subdividing into (a) death and (b) divorce.

Family Law (Scotland) Act 1985, ss 25 and 26

11.4 Section 25 of FL(S)A 1985 says that a married couple's household goods are presumed to be co-owned. Household goods are 'any goods … kept or used at any

---

4   The words 'matrimony' and 'patrimony' carry much baggage. That baggage will not be unpacked here. But, for more on 'patrimony', see **CHAPTER 23** below.

5   Eg South Africa.

6   FL(S)A 1985, s 24. 'Property' here means all patrimonial rights, not just real rights.

time during the marriage in any matrimonial ... home for the joint domestic purposes of the parties to the marriage' but excluding money, 'securities',[7] vehicles, caravans and pets.[8] A puzzle is that whilst s 25(1) is expressed merely as a presumption, not as a rule imposing co-ownership, s 25(2) says that the presumption cannot be rebutted even by proof that 'the goods ... were purchased ... by either party alone or by both in unequal shares'. This seems to make the presumption irrebuttable, i.e. not a presumption. Furthermore, the supposed presumption applies only where the 'household goods [are] obtained ... other than by gift or succession from a third party'. This is not easy to follow. A presumption applies only where actual evidence is lacking. If it is *known* that the grandfather clock was a legacy to Jill from Uncle Walter then the presumption could not apply *anyway*. This is further support for the argument that s 25 is not a presumption but a rule of law, imposing community property for (most) household goods. It is difficult to arrive at a confident conclusion as to the section's meaning. Turning to s 26, it says that 'money derived from any allowance made by either party for their joint household expenses or for similar purposes' and 'any property acquired out of such money' is co-owned. This is a substantive rule, not an evidential presumption. It too has problems. Suppose that Jill bets the money on the Lottery and wins.[9] With the winnings she buys a house, in her own name. Section 26 says that the house is co-owned. But the seller conveyed it to her alone, and the Land Register says it is hers alone. As with s 25, it is difficult to ascertain the section's meaning.

Matrimonial Homes (Family Protection) (Scotland) Act 1981

Introduction

11.5   The main aims of this Act were (i) to ensure that each spouse would have equal rights to occupy the matrimonial home, regardless of whether it is owned by one, or the other, or both, and (ii) to allow the court to exclude violent spouses, again regardless of ownership (so that even a 100% owning spouse could be excluded). It applies only while the marriage exists. When the marriage ends – by death or divorce – it ceases to apply. In that case the parties' rights are catered for by succession law or divorce law, as the case may be.[10]

11.6   If two people own a house in common then, by general property law, each has the right to occupy.[11] Hence, MH(FP)(S)A 1981 does not need to cater for co-owning spouses, as far as conferring a right to occupy is concerned, though, as will be seen,[12] it does have certain provisions which do apply to that case. Nevertheless,

---

[7]   Documents evidencing title to company shares, bonds etc.
[8]   FL(S)A 1985, s 25(3).
[9]   As in *Pyatt v Pyatt* 1966 SLT (Notes) 73.
[10]   On succession law, see **CHAPTERS 26–30** below.
[11]   See **PARA 10.7** above.
[12]   See **PARA 11.10** below.

its main thrust concerns the case where the home is owned only by one spouse. In that case the Act confers 'occupancy rights' on the non-owning spouse.

Occupancy rights

The basic idea

11.7   MH(FP)(S)A 1981 calls the owning spouse the 'entitled spouse' and the other the 'non-entitled spouse'.[13] The latter has 'occupancy rights'. These are '(a) if in occupation, a right to continue to occupy the matrimonial home; (b) if not in occupation, a right to enter into and occupy the matrimonial home'.[14] So, if Jack owns a flat and then he marries Jill, who moves in with him, she acquires occupancy rights, and that means that he cannot require her to leave, even though he remains sole owner.

Third-party effects

11.8   Occupancy rights are not real rights. Nevertheless, they sometimes have effect against third parties, and so might be called 'semi-real'.[15] Section 6 says that no 'dealing' by the entitled spouse can affect the occupancy rights of the other spouse. Suppose that Jack, the sole owner, dispones to his brother, George. Jill's occupancy rights remain unaltered, even though the current owner is not her husband. George acquires ownership, but his ownership is subject to Jill's right to occupy. Nor could he even seek to occupy *with* her.[16] (This state of affairs cannot last forever because it ends when the occupancy rights end, which is when the marriage ends, which is likely to be soon.) Similar protection applies to other 'dealings' such as the grant of a standard security.[17] Since a third party might be unaware of the occupancy rights, there is a complex set of rules – which have caused conveyancers headaches – saying, roughly, that a third party acting in good faith is unaffected by occupancy rights.[18] The third-party effect applies only to 'dealings'. This term is not precisely defined[19] and there are some difficulties with it, but the core idea is that the protection is against third parties who have *voluntarily* acquired rights from Jack. But *other* third parties are unaffected. For example, if he becomes insolvent, his trustee in sequestration is unaffected by Jill's occupancy rights.[20]

---

[13]   MH(FP)(S)A 1981, s 1(1).
[14]   MH(FP)(S)A 1981, s 1(1).
[15]   These third-party effects have been reduced somewhat, by amendment, since MH(FP)(S)A 1981 was originally passed.
[16]   MH(FP)(S)A 1981, s 6(1)(b).
[17]   For standard securities, see **PARAS 21.43–21.56** below.
[18]   MH(FP)(S)A 1981, ss 6(1A) and 8(2A).
[19]   MH(FP)(S)A 1981, s 6(2).
[20]   Subject to Bankruptcy (Scotland) Act 2016, s 113.

Consents, renunciations and dispensations

11.9   The non-entitled spouse is free to consent to a dealing (for example, the grant of a standard security)[21] and can also, though this seldom happens, renounce occupancy rights completely.[22] A consent to a dealing can also be given by the court: this is called a dispensation.[23] Dispensations are rare.

Where the spouses are co-owners

11.10   MH(FP)(S)A 1981 also has two provisions applying where the spouses are co-owners, as opposed to ownership being held by just one of them. First, a dealing by one spouse cannot enable a third party to occupy.[24] For example, Romeo and Juliet are married and co-own the matrimonial home. Juliet dispones her half-share to her Uncle Faustus. He becomes co-owner but may not occupy. Secondly, neither spouse can compel a division and sale unless the court agrees.[25] (If one spouse becomes bankrupt, the other is unprotected.[26])

End of the marriage: (a) death

11.11   A person who dies may be testate or intestate. If the person is married, and dies testate, the will is likely to make reasonable provision for the relict (widow/er). But if not, the relict has a right to a certain minimum share, regardless of what the will says. This is dealt with in **CHAPTER 27**. If there is no will, the relict has defined rights to the estate, discussed in **CHAPTER 29**.

End of the marriage: (b) divorce

11.12   The common-law rule was that in a divorce one party was identified as the innocent spouse and the other as the guilty spouse, and the innocent spouse took from the guilty spouse what he or she would have taken had the latter died. This meant that the property consequences of the ending of marriage were the same regardless of whether the ending was death or divorce. The modern law is different. Section 9 of FL(S)A 1985 gives the court a discretion, with guidelines as to how that discretion is to be exercised. The first guideline is that 'the net value of the matrimonial property should be shared fairly between the parties to the marriage'. Thus, there is a concept of 'matrimonial property', which is defined by s 10 as 'the property belonging to

---

[21]   MH(FP)(S)A 1981, s 6(3).
[22]   MH(FP)(S)A 1981, s 1(5).
[23]   MH(FP)(S)A 1981, s 7.
[24]   MH(FP)(S)A 1981, s 9. This state of affairs cannot last forever because it will end with the marriage.
[25]   MH(FP)(S)A 1981, s 19. For division and sale, see **PARAS 10.12–10.15** above.
[26]   Except Bankruptcy (Scotland) Act 2016, s 113, already mentioned in n 20 above.

the parties or either of them at the relevant date which was acquired … (otherwise than by way of gift or succession.) … during the marriage…' The 'relevant date' means (in the normal case at least) the date of separation. Section 10 says that the matrimonial property is to be 'shared equally or in such other proportions as are justified by special circumstances.' Thus the 'equal sharing' principle is subject not only to the other guidelines in s 9, but also to the 'special circumstances' idea in s 10: a double barrel of discretion. The concept of 'matrimonial property' is of limited importance from a property law standpoint. It exists only in the context of divorce, is subject to judicial discretion, and is about 'value' rather than specific assets. If an asset is owned by Jill then the fact that it is 'matrimonial property' does not give Jack any real right in it – or even any personal right to it. It simply goes towards calculating a figure for the divorce.

11.13 If the court decides that a net transfer should be made by the one to the other, it can, as well as ordering payment of money, make a 'property transfer order'.[27] Suppose that Jack and Jill co-own their house, and are divorced. The court could decide that Jack should dispone his half share to Jill. Such an order creates a personal right: Jill acquires no real right until the transfer is registered. In a divorce the court can also make 'incidental orders', one of which is the order the sale of the house.[28]

CIVIL PARTNERSHIP

11.14 The position of civil partners is generally the same as that of spouses, apart from one or two differences of terminology: for instance, divorce is 'dissolution' and 'family home' means the home of a same-sex couple. In some cases, the Civil Partnership Act 2004 (CPA 2004) amended previous legislation to add references to civil partners. That was done, for example, in the case of the Succession (Scotland) Act 1964 (S(S)A 1964). Elsewhere, the rules were left as free-standing provisions within CPA 2004 itself, for instance the rules (beginning at s 101 of CPA 2004) mirroring MH(FP)(S)A 1981.

COHABITATION

11.15 At common law, cohabitation had no legally recognised status.[29] This fact was, however, of limited importance, because there were a number of ways in which a marriage could be established without the need for a formal ceremony.[30] These were all eventually abolished. The result was that cohabitation became a larger legal

---

[27] FL(S)A 1985, s 8(2). For conditions, see s 15.
[28] FL(S)A 1985, s 14.
[29] 'Les concubines ignorent la loi, donc la loi ignore les concubines' Napoleon is said to have remarked.
[30] See J Thomson, *Family Law in Scotland* (7th edn, 2014) paras 1.11–1.17.

issue and the law had to invent new rules to deal with this. The new law is scattered over different enactments. Particularly important is the Family Law (Scotland) Act 2006 (FL(S)A 2006). Sections 26 and 27 apply to cohabitation the same rules that are in ss 25 and 26 of FL(S)A 1985, discussed above.[31] Section 28 enables the court to order payment of financial provision if the relationship breaks up.[32] Section 29 makes provision for claims on the estate if one party dies intestate.[33] Section 18 of MH(FP)(S)A 1981 enables the court to grant occupancy rights for up to six months. This is not very important, for it needs court intervention and it is only short-term anyway. Finally, cohabitants sometimes sign agreements about their property, to prevent disputes if and when they split up. These are not always well done. For example, in one case the agreement said that the house 'shall be owned by the parties in equal shares.' But in fact the house was owned by just one of them, and a mere agreement cannot transfer a half share of ownership.[34]

11.16   After the end of a relationship, other types of claim may be made. For instance, if X bought the house he lived in with Y and the latter contributed to the price, or to the loan repayments, or the upkeep, it may be that this was a loan. In some cases a claim in unjustified enrichment can be established.[35] In England it is possible to claim the existence of a constructive trust in this type of case, but this is not possible in Scots law. Occasionally an express trust based on oral agreement is alleged.[36]

LITERATURE

11.17   J Thomson, *Family Law in Scotland* (7th edn, 2014) is a helpful account of the law. (See in particular **CHAPTERS 4 and 5**.) For practical details of occupancy rights see Gretton and Reid *Conveyancing* ch 10.

---

[31]   See **PARA 11.4** above.
[32]   See *Gow v Grant* 2012 SLT 829.
[33]   See **PARA 29.20** below.
[34]   *Johnston's Tr v Baird* [2012] CSOH 117, discussed in Reid and Gretton *Conveyancing 2012* (2013) 53.
[35]   *Shilliday v Smith* 1998 SC 725.
[36]   As in *Barbour v Marriott* 2012 GWD 18-358, discussed in Reid and Gretton *Conveyancing 2012* (2013) 51.

Chapter 12

Possession

GENERAL

Definition

12.1   Property is 'possessed' if it is held by a person for his or her own use.[1] This means that the person must have physical control of the thing, together with the intention to possess it. The nature of the control may vary depending on the circumstances of the case. As will be seen, it is possible to possess indirectly, through another person. In principle, because possession requires this control, it is limited to corporeal property.[2]

Fact or right

12.2   Possession may be said to be a fact rather than a right. On this view, it follows that it depends on certain factual criteria being satisfied. These are physical holding, which is generally easy to determine, and the correct state of mind, which is less so. But the fact of possession also gives rise to certain rights, in particular the right not to be dispossessed.[3] Therefore to say that possession is merely a fact is to take too simplistic an approach. There can also be a right to possess held by a non-possessor, such as someone from whom something has been stolen. In summary therefore, a distinction can be made between (i) possession as a fact; (ii) rights that flow from the fact of possession; and (iii) the right to be in possession.

Possession and ownership compared

12.3   The Roman jurist Ulpian said that 'ownership and possession have nothing in common'.[4] Yet, the non-lawyer will often speak of his or her 'possessions' when what are meant is the things that the person actually owns.[5] The reason is that despite clear theoretical differences, ownership and possession regularly coincide. For example, Aoife lives in her house. Therefore, she both possesses and owns that property. She also possesses and owns the contents. If, however, Barry, a burglar, were to steal Aoife's television, he would gain possession of it but not ownership.

12.4   A major difference between possession and ownership is that the former involves a factual relationship to a piece of property. The latter involves a legal relationship. Whether someone is owner depends on whether that person has validly acquired the item. In contrast, a possessor may have no legal right whatsoever to it, as in the case of Barry. Ownership and possession give rise to different rights and

---

[1]   Stair II, 1, 17.
[2]   But see **PARA 12.8** below.
[3]   See **PARA 12.21** below.
[4]   D 41, 2, 12, 1.
[5]   Indeed, A1P1 to the ECHR conflates ownership and possession. See para **32.11** below.

remedies. An owner can, for example, validly transfer ownership of the property or create subordinate real rights over it. In principle, a mere possessor cannot. The remedy to protect ownership of property is vindication, whereas for possession it is spuilzie.[6]

The importance of possession

12.5   Possession is important in a number of areas, such as:

(a) The acquisition of possession is necessary in order to acquire an original title by occupancy.[7]

(b) In the Land Register someone who acquires from a person in possession can in some cases obtain a better title than that other person had.[8]

(c) A person who has possessed land for ten years on the basis of an apparently valid conveyance registered in the Land Register (or Sasine Register) will acquire a good title by positive prescription.[9]

(d) A tenant under a lease of 20 years or less acquires a real right by entering into possession of the property.[10]

(e) Possession is a pre-requisite of certain securities, notably pledge and lien.[11]

(f) There is an evidential presumption that a person in possession of a corporeal moveable is its owner.[12]

(g) A person who is in possession has the remedy of spuilzie if he or she is unlawfully dispossessed.[13]

REQUIREMENTS FOR POSSESSION

General

12.6   Acquisition of possession requires two things. The first is an act of the body (*corpus*). The second is an act of the mind (*animus*). Both are essential. While the distinction is clear in theory, it is less so in practice. The act of mind will often be inferred from the act of the body. For example, if Jean hands her book to Kirsty and Kirsty takes it, Kirsty's intention to take possession may be inferred. The basic rule is that possession can only be held by one person at one time. If, for instance, Bob pickpockets Colin's wallet, then Colin loses possession to Bob. But possession may be shared, as with a couple living together and possessing their flat. And as will be

---

6   See **PARA 12.21** below.
7   See **PARA 9.2** above.
8   See **PARA 7.79** above.
9   See **PARAS 6.7–6.19** above.
10   See **PARA 20.11** below.
11   See **PARAS 21.34 AND 21.58** below.
12   See **PARA 12.19** below.
13   See **PARA 12.21** below.

seen, one party (such as an owner) may be in civil possession while another (such as a tenant) has natural possession of the same property.[14]

Act of body

General

12.7   For possession to be acquired, there must be an act to detain it in the first place. The fish, for example, must be hooked by the angler. Where a piece of moveable property is too large to take hold of, the prospective possessor should enter it. Examples here are cars and tents. For land, it is not necessary to stand on every part of it. Stair states: '[H]e who possesseth a field, needs not go about it all, or touch every turf of it, by himself or his cattle, but by possessing a part, possesseth the whole, unless there were contrary possessory acts.'[15]

12.8   The requirement of an act to detain means that in principle incorporeal property cannot be possessed because one cannot acquire physical control of something which is intangible. By statute, however, it is possible to possess some incorporeal heritable rights, such as servitudes, for the purpose of positive prescription.[16] This is sometimes known as quasi-possession. What is happening is that the right is being exercised. For example, a person asserting a servitude right of way walks over the land in question. Possession of incorporeal property is possible if one is willing to regard exercise as a substitute for detention.

Natural possession and civil possession

12.9   Possession can be acquired through the physical acts of another. For example, Ulrika might purchase a flat as an investment and immediately let it to Verity and Wanda, two students, who move in. This suffices to give Ulrika possession. Her possession here is known as 'civil possession'. An alternative term is 'indirect possession'.[17] In contrast, Verity and Wanda are said to be in 'natural possession', or, alternatively 'direct possession'.[18] Civil possession is common. As well as the foregoing example of a landlord possessing through her tenants, pledgers possess through pledgees,[19] fiars possess through liferenters[20] and owners possess through custodiers such as warehousers and carriers.

---

[14]   See **PARA 12.9** below.
[15]   Stair II, 1, 13.
[16]   In terms of PL(S)A 1973. See **CHAPTER 6** above.
[17]   Cf DCFR Book VIII. – 1:205(3): 'indirect physical control'.
[18]   Cf DCFR Book VIII. – 1:205(2): 'direct physical control'.
[19]   See **PARA 21.35** below.
[20]   See **PARA 22.9** below.

Possession *animo solo*

12.10   While a physical act is necessary to *acquire* possession, it is not necessary to *maintain* it. Possession can be retained by act of mind alone. This is known as possession *animo solo*. For example, students sitting in lectures are still in possession of their flat.[21] Possession *animo solo* is lost if the possessor ceases to intend to possess, for instance by deciding to abandon the property. It also ends if a third party acquires possession without the consent of the *animo solo* possessor, for example where squatters move in to the flat.

Act of mind

12.11   Possession requires the intention, first, to exercise control of the property and, second, to do this for the benefit of oneself. In relation to the former, difficult questions arise in relation to 'container cases'. This is the situation where one piece of property is inside another, for example clothes in a wardrobe. The issue is whether possession of the container is sufficient to possess also the item within. Unusually for Scottish property law, the most influential modern authority is an English case, *Parker v British Airways Board*.[22] Someone found a bracelet in a departure lounge at Heathrow Airport. In English law, the first person to acquire possession of lost or stolen property can retain it unless the true owner vindicates the right. Here, British Airways claimed that it in fact was the first possessor because it possessed the building even although it had no knowledge of the bracelet. It was held possible to possess something without knowing, provided that there is a manifest intention to exercise control of the property it is within. Items within a house are a good example of this. As regards an airport lounge, however, where the general public has through access, there was held to be an insufficient level of control.

12.12   The second part of the act of mind – intention to hold for one's own benefit – means that those who hold solely for another party do not have possession. An example would be a warehouse storing goods. Here, the holder has *custody*. The physical requirement for possession is satisfied, but not the mental element. It is possible to have civil possession of property held by a custodier. The owner of the goods in the warehouse is one case. Equally, it is possible to have civil possession through a natural possessor, such as a landlord's possession of a shop through the tenant. The Latin tag for the relevant mental element is the *animus sibi habendi* (possession for one's own use) rather than the *animus dominii* (possession as owner). The latter, which is found in Roman law, restricts possession to those asserting ownership, as opposed to say a right under a lease.

---

[21]   In contrast to students who were out late the night before and who remain in direct possession of their beds.

[22]   [1982] 1 QB 1004. See Reid *Property* para 124 and *Harris v Abbey National plc* 1997 SCLR 359.

TRANSFER OF POSSESSION

General

12.13   Where possession of a piece of property is transferred from one person to another, this is known as 'delivery'.

Transfer of natural possession: actual delivery

12.14   If a person is in natural possession of property, the possession can be transferred to another by physically handing over the property. This is 'actual delivery'. For example, Rebecca passes a book to Sara.

Transfer of civil possession: constructive delivery

12.15   Where civil possession is held by the transferor, this may be transferred by 'constructive delivery'. Angela is storing her whisky in Bella's warehouse. Angela wants to make a gift of the whisky to Charles. He is willing to accept the gift. To transfer it, she instructs Bella to hold the whisky on his behalf. Charles now has civil possession. It is essential that Bella, the holder of the goods, is told.[23] If Angela merely handed over the warehouse receipt to Charles, that would not be enough.[24] Another instance of constructive delivery is where Alan's property is in Beth's natural possession, say under a contract of loan. If Alan now sells the thing to her, she acquires full possession.[25] A third example is *constitutum possessorium*: delivery by act of mind alone. For instance, Helen might transfer ownership of land to Isabel, but remain in possession as Isabel's tenant. (This is called sale and lease-back.) Helen now possesses on behalf of Isabel as well as in her own right. If *constitutum possessorium* is applied too freely, the publicity principle[26] is undermined, because a third party is unable to see any change of possession. Thus, the courts have limited its application.[27]

12.16   A final case to be mentioned is 'symbolical delivery'. Strictly speaking it is a special type of constructive delivery. It is where a symbol of the property, rather than the property itself is handed over. In practice this type of delivery is confined to the 'bill of lading'. This is the receipt handed over by the shipping company to a person who is having goods shipped. The bill of lading may be regarded in law as symbolising possession of the goods. Hence delivery of the bill amounts to delivery

---

[23]   According to SOGA 1979, s 29(4), where goods are being sold the custodier has to tell the buyer that the goods are now held for him or her.

[24]   *Inglis v Robertson & Baxter* (1898) 25 R (HL) 70.

[25]   Following Roman law, this is known as delivery *brevi manu.*

[26]   See **PARAS 4.19–4.20** above.

[27]   Reid *Property* para 623 (W M Gordon); Carey Miller with Irvine *Corporeal Moveables* para 8.24.

of the goods. Bills of lading are similar to bills of exchange in that they may be classed as either 'bearer' or 'order'. A 'bearer bill' is transferred by mere delivery. An 'order bill' requires to be both delivered and endorsed on the back in favour of the new holder. Hence if an order bill is merely delivered, the new holder may have possession of the bill, but not the goods which it represents.

Transfer of possession by means of a key

12.17   Where goods are stored under lock and key, for example in a warehouse, possession can be transferred by handing over the key.[28] This is not easily categorised as either actual or constructive delivery.

THE RIGHT TO POSSESSION

Possession as of right or without right

12.18   Possessors can be divided into two categories. There are those, such as owners and tenants, who have the right to possess. They are rightful possessors. Then there are those such as thieves and squatters who do not. They are unlawful possessors. A further division can be made as regards rightful possessors. First, there are those whose possession is founded on a real right. The Latin term here is the *ius possidendi*. The right here is not an autonomous right. It depends on holding another right with an entitlement to possession, such as ownership. But it is a right enforceable against the world. Second, there are those who hold a personal right of possession. Thus, if Robert lends a pen to Sally, she is a rightful possessor but she has no real right. A lease of moveable property is another example. By contrast, a lease of heritable property is usually a real right, but sometimes it will, like a lease of moveables, be only a personal right. Therefore, with the exception of spuilzie,[29] such a person must rely on the owner or other party who granted the right to take action against any party who interferes with the possession.

Presumptions

12.19   A possessor of corporeal property is presumed both
(i)   to be in lawful possession; and
(ii)   to be the owner.[30]

---

[28]   Following Roman law, this is known as delivery *longa manu*.
[29]   See **PARAS 12.21–12.22** below.
[30]   Stair IV, 45, 17.

The latter is important because there is no register of ownership of corporeal moveables. Nor, unlike the usual position as regards incorporeal property, where a written assignation is used, corporeal moveable property is often transferred by oral agreement. Accordingly, the presumption can be difficult to rebut. It is not necessary for the possessor to prove good faith.[31]

Possession in good faith

12.20   Someone who possesses property with no right to do so, but while reasonably believing that this right is held, is known as a *bona fide* possessor, or possessor in good faith. Such a person is entitled to harvest the fruits of the property and, on losing possession, is entitled to compensation for improvements made to it.[32] There is a significant body of elderly case law on the subject in relation to land.[33] But with the development of modern land registration it is harder than it used to be to argue lack of knowledge of legal title.

POSSESSORY REMEDIES

Spuilzie

12.21   The mere fact of possession gives rise to the right not to be unlawfully dispossessed. In that event, the remedy of spuilzie (pronounced 'spooley') is available. This is a court action to compel the dispossessor to return the property. The word 'spuilzie' is used to mean the wrongful act of dispossession as well as the remedy resulting from this. In the case of land, spuilzie is also known as ejection.[34] Unlawful dispossession can be referred to as 'vitious' dispossession and happens when the possessor does not consent nor is there judicial warrant for it. The pursuer in an action of spuilzie need only prove two things:

(1) that he or she was in possession and
(2) that he or she was vitiously dispossessed.

Possession may be *animo solo* and in this case the spuilzie is known as 'intrusion'.[35] It is also possible for a civil possessor to use the remedy, but here consent to the dispossession by the natural possessor debars the claim.[36] This point was overlooked in a couple of sheriff court cases where attempts to use spuilzie were made in the

---

[31]   *Chief Constable of Strathclyde Police v Sharp* 2002 SLT (Sh Ct), discussed in D L Carey Miller 'Title to moveables: Mr Sharp's Porsche' (2003) 7 *Edin LR* 221.
[32]   Gordon *Scottish Land Law* paras 14.47–14.59.
[33]   See J Wolffe 'Enrichment by improvements in Scots law' in D Johnston and R Zimmermann (eds) *Unjustified Enrichment: Key Issues in Comparative Perspective* (2002) 384–432.
[34]   See, eg, Stair I, 9, 25–27.
[35]   Stair I, 9, 25.
[36]   Stair I, 9, 20 and IV, 28, 7.

context of goods on hire purchase being delivered to third parties.[37] As spuilzie depends merely on possession, it is possible for a thief to use the remedy. Indeed, a thief could in theory use it against the actual owner of the property if the requirements set out above are satisfied. This, however, would have little point, because the owner, assuming that ownership could be proven, can retort by vindicating the property ie demanding it back because of that ownership.

12.22 Spuilzie is a remedy which is rarely used today. Yet, in fifteenth-century Scotland it was perhaps the commonest type of legal action.[38] There are two main reasons for the change.[39] One is a less lawless society. Second, registration of land ownership commenced in 1617, with the establishment of the Sasine Register. Therefore, those dispossessed of land are now more likely to assert their ownership rather than rely on their prior possession.

Compensation

12.23 A person knowingly in wrongful possession is liable to compensate the rightful possessor for any income derived from the property. There are two levels of compensation. First, 'ordinary profits' may be due. This means the actual income, for example, crops growing on the land in the case of natural possession and rent in the case of civil possession. The second possible claim is for 'violent profits'. In effect these are penal damages and are quantified at the highest level of income which the property could yield. In the case of land, this will probably be double rent.[40] Violent profits are available in the case of vitious dispossession i.e. spuilzie. They are also due where a tenant will not move out at the end of the lease.[41]

Other remedies

12.24 Certain other possessory remedies are available, but they are restricted in principle to parties who can show a real right to possess i.e. the *ius possidendi*.[42] The following are the most important:
   (a) action for delivery, where the real right to possess is being asserted against another in possession of corporeal moveables;

---

[37] *FC Finance Ltd v Brown & Son* 1969 SLT (Sh Ct) 41 and *Mercantile Credit Co Ltd v Townsley* 1971 SLT (Sh Ct) 37. See A F Rodger 'Spuilzie in the Modern World' 1970 *SLT (News)* 33.

[38] J W Cairns 'Historical Introduction' in Reid and Zimmermann *History* vol 1, 14 at 73.

[39] K Reid, 'Property Law: Sources and Doctrine' in Reid and Zimmermann *History* vol 1, 185 at 213–214. See also D Carey Miller 'Spuilzie – dead, dormant or manna from heaven? Issues concerning protection of possessory interests in Scots law' in H Mostert and M de Waal (eds) *Essays in Honour of C G van der Merwe* (2011).

[40] Reid, *Property* para 169.

[41] *Jute Industries Ltd v Wilson & Graham Ltd* 1955 SLT (Sh Ct) 46.

[42] See **PARA 12.18** above.

(b) action for removing or ejection where the real right to possess land is being asserted. In removings the defender will have had a right to possess which has ended, for example under a lease which has expired. In ejections no right will have ever been held;[43]

(c) action for encroachment, where there is a permanent thing preventing possession of land;[44]

(d) action for trespass, where there is temporary interference with the ability to possess land.[45]

LITERATURE

12.25   For detailed general accounts, see Carey Miller with Irvine *Corporeal Moveables* paras 1.18–1.22 and 8.12–8.27, Gordon and Wortley *Scottish Land Law* ch 14, and Reid *Property* paras 114–173 and 619–623. For a historical perspective, see Reid, K, 'Property Law: Sources and Doctrine' in Reid and Zimmermann *History* vol 1, 185 at 210–216. For a comparative perspective, see Van Erp and Akkermans *Property Law* 99–131. Anderson, C *Possession of Corporeal Moveables* (2015) focusses on the physical element. See too Anderson, C *Property: A Guide to Scots Law* (2016) ch 3. There is also much of value in Descheemaeker, E, (ed) *The Consequences of Possession* (2014).

---

[43]   Reid *Property* para 153.
[44]   See **PARAS 18.10–18.16** below.
[45]   See **PARAS 19.30–19.36** below.

Chapter 13

Servitudes

ESSENTIALS

Definition

13.1   A 'servitude' is a real right that allows a landowner to enter or make limited use of neighbouring land. The classic example is a right of access. Servitudes are regulated primarily by the common law, but also by several important provisions in the Title Conditions (Scotland) Act 2003 (TC(S)A 2003), which came into force on 28 November 2004. Roman law has been particularly influential in the development of the law of servitudes in Scotland. Similarly, it has had a tangible effect on the English equivalent – the 'easement'. This is therefore an area where it is worth having regard to English authority. The point, however, should not be pressed too far.[1]

---

[1]   In the important House of Lords decision in *Moncrieff v Jamieson* 2008 SC (HL) 1, the English Law Lords who gave judgments seemed more inclined to use English than Scottish authority, although the case was Scottish. See K G C Reid and G L Gretton *Conveyancing 2007* (2008) 108.

Two properties

13.2   Servitudes require a 'benefited property'[2] and a 'burdened property'. More traditionally, these are called the 'dominant tenement' and the 'servient tenement'.[3] The owner of the benefited property is entitled to enforce the servitude and the owner of the burdened property is obliged to accept this. For example, Neil sells a plot of land to Orla so that she can build a house on it. He grants her a servitude right of access along a path over the retained land so that she can reach the nearest public road. Orla's plot is the benefited property and the land retained by Neil is the burdened property. The right to enforce the servitude attaches to Orla's land as a pertinent[4] and is automatically transferred if she sells her house. The servitude can be said to 'run with the land'. Similarly, if Neil sells the retained land, the new owner continues to be bound, because the servitude is a real right. For this reason too, not only Neil but any tenant of his or occupier of the burdened property, and indeed any member of the public, must respect the servitude.[5]

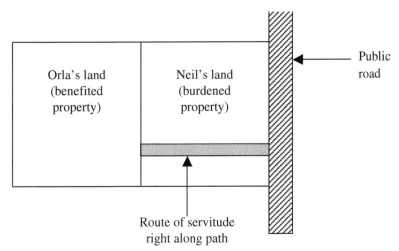

13.3   Normally, the benefited and burdened properties will be contiguous – in other words, adjacent. This is not an absolute requirement. They only require to be in the same neighbourhood 'provided the distance be not so great as to obstruct all benefit from the servitude'.[6] The properties must be reasonably close or the 'praedial requirement'[7] will not be satisfied. In most cases the benefited and burdened

---

2   But the Scottish Government consulted in 2015 on having servitudes without a benefited property in limited cases. See http://www.gov.scot/Topics/Justice/law/17975/ServitudesWithoutA BenefitedProperty.
3   See, eg, Bell *Principles* § 979.
4   For pertinents, see **PARAS 15.9–15.12** below.
5   A contrast can be made here with real burdens. Only negative real burdens are 'real' in this sense. See **PARA 14.41** below.
6   Erskine II, 9, 33.
7   See **PARAS 13.6–13.7** below.

properties will be pieces of land. It is also, however, possible for them to be an incorporeal separate tenement.[8] For example, the holder of a right of salmon fishing may need a servitude of access to get to the river.[9] In contrast, a lease cannot act as a benefited or burdened property.[10] It is rights of ownership which benefit from or are burdened by servitudes. That said, a tenant of the benefited property may exercise a servitude held by that property[11] and, as stated above, a tenant of the burdened property must respect the servitude.

13.4   In principle, the two properties must be in separate ownership. The Latin maxim for this is *res sua nemini servit* (no one can have a servitude over his property). It is, however, possible for a servitude to be registered by an owner of land against the one piece of property, which does not take effect until the land is subdivided.[12] For example, Beverley, a builder, may intend to develop a site for two houses. She can register a deed of conditions giving each house mutual servitude rights, such as of water supply and drainage, exercisable against the other. The servitudes, however, will not be formally created until the houses are sold separately and the title to the site is divided.

A right to enter or make limited use of the burdened property

13.5   The common law recognised two types of servitude. 'Positive' servitudes, such as access, involve a right to enter or make limited use of the burdened property. These exist today. In addition, certain 'negative' servitudes were admitted. These restricted building on the burdened property. Sometimes there was a blanket ban.[13] Sometimes it was only building above a certain height which was prohibited.[14] And sometimes it was only building which interfered with light or view.[15] All of these restrictions could be performed by real burdens,[16] meaning that there was an untidy overlap in the law. Negative servitudes were also open to criticism because, unlike real burdens, registration was not a requirement for creation.[17] This meant that the servitude could be invisible to a purchaser of the land. TC(S)A 2003 addressed these issues by making it incompetent to create new negative servitudes with effect from 28 November 2004.[18] Existing negative servitudes were converted by force of statute into real burdens on that date.[19] Where, however, the right does not appear on the

---

[8]   See **PARA 15.17** below.
[9]   E.g. *Middletweed v Murray* 1989 SLT 11 and *Pullar v Goldie*, 25 August 2004, Arbroath Sheriff Court, discussed in K G C Reid and G L Gretton, *Conveyancing 2010* (2011) 15–16.
[10]   Subject to the deeply obscure Registration of Leases (Scotland) Act 1857, s 3(2).
[11]   See **PARA 13.31** below.
[12]   TC(S)A 2003, s 75(2).
[13]   This was known as a servitude *non aedificandi*.
[14]   This was known as a servitude *altius non tollendi*.
[15]   This was known as a servitude *luminibus non officiendi*.
[16]   See **CHAPTER 14** below.
[17]   *Cowan v Stewart* (1872) 10 M 735.
[18]   TC(S)A 2003, s 79.
[19]   TC(S)A 2003, s 80(1). They are to be known as 'converted servitudes'.

title to the burdened property it was necessary to register a preservation notice before 28 November 2014 failing which it was extinguished on that date.[20]

Praedial benefit

13.6   A servitude must be 'praedial'. This means that it must burden the burdened property for the benefit of the benefited property and not just for the personal benefit of the latter's owner. For example, a purported servitude allowing the benefited proprietor to go on to the burdened property to sing or recite poetry is insufficiently praedial. In *Patrick v Napier*[21] a right allowing a landowner to fish for trout on a nearby river failed the test, since fishing was not to the praedial benefit of his land. Similarly, it has been held that a right of skating or curling on a loch during appropriate cold weather cannot be a servitude.[22]

13.7   Other jurisdictions, such as Louisiana and South Africa, which have been influenced by Roman law, recognise both 'praedial servitudes' and 'personal servitudes'. In a 'personal servitude' there is no benefited property. Rather, a particular person has a right of use or enjoyment of the burdened property. The only personal servitude recognised in Scotland is liferent.[23] In practice, the term 'personal servitude' is seldom used here.[24]

Repugnancy with ownership

13.8   Where a servitude creates a right of use it must be a *limited* one. Use which is too invasive of the burdened proprietor's right of ownership is not permitted.[25] If a comprehensive right of use is desired then a right of lease should be acquired.[26] The rule is not applied absolutely. For example, where a servitude involves laying pipes,[27] this means making exclusive use of the stratum of ground in question.[28] The issue has exercised the courts in relation to car parking. In *Nationwide Building Society v Walter D Allan Ltd*[29] a purported servitude which conferred the right to park two cars on a piece of ground large enough for six was held by Lady Smith to be repugnant with ownership. The case would probably be decided differently now following *Moncrieff v Jamieson*.[30]

[20]   TC(S)A 2003, ss 80(2)–(8) and 115.
[21]   (1867) 5 M 683.
[22]   *Harper v Lindsay* (1853) 15 D 768.
[23]   See **CHAPTER 22** below.
[24]   Rights akin to personal servitudes may be created under certain statutes. See **PARA 13.52** below.
[25]   This is a common-law rule, now enshrined for new express servitudes in TC(S)A 2003, s 76(2).
[26]   See **CHAPTER 20** below.
[27]   See **PARA 13.13** below.
[28]   See *Moncrieff v Jamieson* 2008 SC (HL) 1 at para 76 per Lord Rodger of Earlsferry.
[29]   2004 GWD 25-539.
[30]   2008 SC (HL) 1 discussed in **PARA 13.11** below. See Reid and Gretton *Conveyancing 2007* (2008) 109–110. And see *Holms v Ashford Estates Ltd* [2009] CSIH 28 and *Johnson, Thomas and Thomas v Smith* 2016 GWD 25-456.

Known to the law

13.9   As will be seen,[31] there are several ways in which servitudes can be created. Not all require an express provision to appear on the title of the burdened property and thus may not be obvious to a prospective purchaser. The policy of the courts has therefore been to restrict servitudes to those 'known to the law', in effect to have a fixed list. The idea is that a purchaser can be sure that only a limited number of types of unregistered right could affect the property. Thus in *Mendelssohn v The Wee Pub Co Ltd*,[32] an attempt to establish a servitude of sign-hanging failed, because it was not a recognised servitude in Roman law. In *Neill v Scobbie*[33] the court was unwilling to extend the list to admit a servitude for overhead electricity cables[34] and in *Romano v Standard Commercial Property Securities Ltd*[35] a servitude of 'shop front' was rejected. In contrast, recent years have seen the courts recognising the servitudes of parking and projection.[36] They may also be willing to recognise a new servitude because of economic, social or technological change, for example a servitude of railway[37] or septic tank.[38] The list of known servitudes appears to be the following.

Access

13.10   This is the most important servitude. The owner of land may need to take access over a neighbouring property. Three gradations were recognised in Roman law and still are today:

(1) *iter* (pedestrian);

(2) *actus* (right to lead cattle); and

(3) *via* (vehicular).

In general, the greater right includes the lesser. Therefore, where a vehicular right of access along a road is held, the benefited proprietor may go by foot.[39] A fourth category of 'railway' has been recognised since the nineteenth century, the difference being that the access is taken along rails.[40] But it is rare in practice. Network Rail usually owns the ground on which its rails are laid.

---

[31]   See **PARAS 13.21–13.29** below.

[32]   1991 GWD 26-1518.

[33]   1993 GWD 13-887.

[34]   Of course, the Romans did not have electricity cables. The correctness of the decision may be doubted. See further **PARA 13.19** below.

[35]   2008 SLT 859.

[36]   See **PARAS 13.11 AND 13.14** below.

[37]   See **PARA 13.10** below.

[38]   See eg *Todd v Scoular* 1998 GWD 24-1041.

[39]   Cusine and Paisley *Servitudes and Rights of Way* para 12.194. See, however, *Adams and Son v Cloy* (1998), reported in Paisley and Cusine *Unreported Cases* 365 (express right of vehicular access does not include the right to drive loose cattle).

[40]   *North British Rly Co v Park Yard Co Ltd* (1898) 25 R (HL) 47 at 52 per Lord Watson.

Parking vehicles

13.11   It was only in 2007 that the right to park vehicles was definitively accepted, in *Moncrieff v Jamieson*.[41] Parking can be created as a stand-alone right, or one which is ancillary to a servitude of access.[42] The same probably applies to mooring of boats.

Service media

13.12   Buildings require to be serviced. Three types of service servitude are recognised.
  (1) 'Aqueduct', also called 'watergang'[43] This is the right to lead water through the burdened property. Whether at common law this can be extended to other fluids, to gases and to electricity is unclear.[44] TC(S)A 2003 now does so extend it, and with retrospective effect.[45]
  (2) 'Aquaehaustus', the right to take water from a river, loch or other source on the burdened property. This is more important in rural areas than urban ones where there is the mains water supply.
  (3) 'Sinks', also called 'drainage' or 'outfall'. It permits the benefited proprietor to drain water to the burdened property. It can be for sewage, as where there is a septic tank on the burdened property.[46]

Support

13.13   Two forms are recognised.
  (1) *Oneris ferendi*: the right to be supported by an adjacent building.[47]
  (2) *Tigni immittendi*: the right to insert a beam into a neighbouring building.

Of the two, the first is the more important in practice. Support also commonly exists as a right ancillary to other servitudes, for example, the surface of a road subject to a servitude is supported by the underlying ground and the burdened proprietor cannot dig out the ground and leave a wafer thin of tar upon which the benefited proprietor is expected to drive.

---

[41]   2008 SC (HL) 1. See http://www.moncrieff-v-jamieson.com/.
[42]   *Johnson, Thomas and Thomas v Smith* 2016 GWD 25-456.
[43]   In Latin, *aquaeductus*.
[44]   *Neill v Scobbie* 1993 GWD 13-887; *Ferguson v Tennant* 1978 SC (HL) 19 at 65 per Lord Fraser; *Labinski Ltd v BP Oil Development Ltd* 2002 GWD 1-46 (oil).
[45]   TC(S)A 2003, s 77. On pipeline servitudes generally, see R Paisley 'Aspects of Land Law Relative to the Transportation of Oil and Gas in Scotland' in G Gordon and J Paterson (eds) *Oil and Gas Law – Current Practice and Emerging Trends* (2007) 409. See also *William Rennie & Co Ltd v BP Exploration Operating Co Ltd* [2011] CSIH 10.
[46]   *Todd v Scoular* 1988 GWD 24-1041.
[47]   See **PARAS 18.17–18.20** below. Support by a subjacent building is a statutory right under T(S)A 2004, s 8. See **PARA 16.24** below.

Projection

13.14   The courts have recently accepted the servitude of projection whereby part of a building[48] may overhang into a neighbouring landowner's airspace.[49]

Eavesdrop

13.15   Eavesdrop', also called 'stillicide', is the right to allow water to fall off the eaves of a building on the benefited property onto the burdened property.[50] Nowadays, building regulations prevent properties from being built so close.[51]

Pasturage

13.16   This is the right to graze animals on the burdened property such as cattle[52] and sheep.[53]

Extracting materials

13.17   The right comes in two forms.
  (1) 'Fuel, feal and divot', which allows peat to be taken from the burdened property for fuel, and turf to be taken for fencing and roofing.[54] It is a right of much diminished importance today in an era of central heating and tiled roofs.
  (2) The right to take building materials, such as stone, sand and gravel.[55] Again, this is a relatively dormant area of law.

In both cases, the extracted items can only be used to service the benefited property.[56]

Bleaching and drying clothes

13.18   This right was first recognised by the House of Lords in 1780 in *St Clair v Dysart Magistrates*.[57] Of all the recognised servitudes, it is probably the one which is the most difficult to reconcile with the praedial rule[58] because it is people who benefit from clothes, not land. It remains of some practical importance in tenements where

---

[48]   Or potentially a tree. See K G C Reid and G L Gretton, *Conveyancing 2011* (2012) 97-98.
[49]   *Compugraphics International Ltd v Nikolic* [2009] CSOH 54 affd 2011 SC 744.
[50]   *Stirling v Finlayson* (1752) Mor 14526.
[51]   See generally Cusine and Paisley *Servitudes and Rights of Way* para 3.84.
[52]   See, e.g., *Fearnan Partnership v Grindlay* 1992 SC (HL) 38.
[53]   *Ferguson v Tennant* 1978 SC (HL) 19.
[54]   *Watson v Sinclair* 1966 SLT (Sh Ct) 77.
[55]   *Aikman v Duke of Hamilton and Brandon* (1832) 6 W and Sh 64.
[56]   See **PARA 13.35** below.
[57]   (1780) 2 Pat 554.
[58]   See **PARA 13.6** above.

there is a drying green at the rear of the building but this belongs to the ground floor proprietor, rather than being held in common.[59]

Breaking the fixed list: new expressly created servitudes

13.19   The reason why the courts have been unwilling to recognise an unrestricted list of servitudes is to protect purchasers from unregistered rights.[60] This is not an issue for servitudes created expressly since 28 November 2004 because these have to be registered on both the title of the benefited and the burdened property.[61] Therefore expressly-created servitudes no longer have to be on the recognised list.[62] The general rules of servitudes, in particular lack of repugnancy with ownership,[63] nevertheless must still be obeyed. It is unlikely that there will be many new examples of servitudes without a deed. Importantly, the 'known to the law' requirement remains for servitudes which are not constituted expressly but are created impliedly or by prescription.[64]

Rural and urban servitudes

13.20   The Romans recognised a distinction between 'rural servitudes', which related to land, and 'urban servitudes', which related to buildings.[65] This classification has been used by some of the institutional writers[66] and more recent commentators.[67] There seems, however, no benefit to be had from it now and it is therefore merely noted.[68]

CREATION

Express grant

13.21   A servitude may be *expressly granted* by the owner of the burdened property. As it is a real right in land, formal writing is needed.[69] The benefited property and the burdened property must both be identified.[70] There is, however, no requirement for a detailed description of the *content* of the right because each type of servitude has recognised features. For example, the right to use a pipe for

---

[59]   This is the position unless the titles to the flats say otherwise. See **PARA 16.11** below.
[60]   See **PARA 13.9** above.
[61]   TC(S)A 2003, s 75. There is an exception for cable and pipeline servitudes. See **PARA 13.21** below.
[62]   TC(S)A 2003, s 75(1).
[63]   TC(S)A 2003, s 75(2).
[64]   See **PARAS 13.24–13.27** below.
[65]   See, eg, P du Plessis, *Borkowski's Textbook on Roman Law* (5th edn, 2015) 165–167.
[66]   Eg Bell *Principles* §§ 983 and 1001.
[67]   Eg Gordon *Scottish Land Law* paras 24-21–24-23.
[68]   See further Cusine and Paisley *Servitudes and Rights of Way* paras 1.26–1.27.
[69]   RoW(S)A 1995, s 1(2)(b). See **PARA 31.4** below.
[70]   Cusine and Paisley *Servitudes and Rights of Way* paras 2.15–2.43.

services extends to the full length of the pipe.[71] Suggested wording for a right of way might be 'a servitude right of pedestrian access over the path coloured pink on the plan annexed and executed as relative hereto'.[72] A higher level of description may be required for servitudes which are not on the recognised list. It is not essential to use the word 'servitude',[73] but for the sake of clarity it is wise to do so.[74] The deed creating the servitude must be registered against the title of the benefited and burdened property in order to obtain a real right.[75] This rule, which was mentioned above,[76] came into force on 28 November 2004. Before that, creation could be by mere exercise of the servitude, or by registration against just one property. Cable and pipeline servitudes are exempt from the dual registration requirement because this would be cumbersome in the case of long-distance apparatus.[77]

13.22   Where a servitude is expressly granted, in practice one of two deeds is used. The first is a stand-alone deed, known as a 'deed of servitude'. Imagine that Alice and Benedict are neighbours. He wants to take access through her ground. She is willing to grant him a deed of servitude in return for a one-off payment. The deed is registered. Alice is now the burdened proprietor and Benedict the benefited proprietor. The second type of deed is a conveyance, typically a disposition. Michael is selling part of his large garden to Naomi, so that she may build a house on it. Naomi will need to take access through the land being retained by Michael in order to reach the closest public road. Michael will therefore grant Naomi a right of way in the disposition in her favour. Following registration, Naomi will be the benefited proprietor and Michael the burdened proprietor. It is worth remembering that where a servitude is being created by express grant in a conveyance, it is the benefited property (here, the land being sold to Naomi) which is being conveyed.

Express reservation

13.23   A servitude may be *expressly reserved*. The rules on express grant generally apply,[78] but the factual situation is different. Say that Michael, on selling the land to Naomi, needs to keep the right to have service pipes running through it. In that case, he will expressly reserve a servitude in the conveyance. This time it is Michael who is the benefited proprietor and Naomi who is the burdened proprietor. It is possible to reserve a servitude only in a conveyance. A deed of servitude cannot be used because there the properties are already separate and it is too late to reserve anything. Where

---

[71]   *Axis West Developments Ltd v Chartwell Land Investments Ltd* 1999 SLT 1416 at 1419 per Lord Hope of Craighead.

[72]   For a more detailed example, see Halliday *Conveyancing* vol II, para 35–11.

[73]   This contrasts with the rule for real burdens. See **PARA 14.16** below.

[74]   Cf *Moss Bros Group plc v Scottish Mutual Assurance plc* 2001 SC 779 and *Garden v Arrowsmith* 2013 GWD 4-120.

[75]   TC(S)A 2003, s 75(1). Registration will be in the Sasine or the Land Register depending where the title to the land is registered.

[76]   See **PARA 13.19** above.

[77]   TC(S)A 2003, s 75(3)(b).

[78]   See **PARA 13.21** above. In particular, there must be writing and dual registration.

a servitude is created by express reservation in a conveyance, it is the burdened property (here the land sold to Naomi) which is being conveyed. In practice, 'cross servitudes' are common, that is to say servitudes are both granted and reserved in the same deed.

Implied grant

13.24   Unlike real burdens,[79] servitudes can be created by implication. This can happen only in a conveyance. There is no such thing as an implied stand-alone deed of servitude.[80] The idea is that at the time the benefited and burdened properties were divided a servitude was implied. A servitude may be created by *implied grant* where the *benefited property* is conveyed. But implication is not automatic. A servitude will be impliedly granted only where this is, in the words of Lord Campbell in the leading case of *Cochrane v Ewart*,[81] 'necessary for the reasonable enjoyment of the property'. He continued: 'When I say it was necessary, I do not mean that it was so essentially necessary that the property could have no value whatsoever without this easement, but I mean that it was necessary for the convenient and comfortable enjoyment of the property as it existed before the time of the grant.' The background to the case was that a tanyard[82] and a garden were owned by the same individual. The tanyard drained into a cesspool in the garden. When the tanyard was sold separately, it was held that a servitude right of drainage had been impliedly granted in the conveyance. This demonstrates the point that in cases of implied grant a 'quasi servitude' normally exists at the time the properties are separated. In other words, the right claimed was in effect exercised before the division.[83] As demonstrated by *ASA International Ltd v Kashmiri Properties (Ireland) Ltd*,[84] however, the fact that there has been previous exercise is not conclusive. What matters is whether the servitude Is necessary for the reasonable enjoyment of the property.

Implied reservation

13.25   Implied reservation is the factual converse of implied grant. Here it is the *burdened property* that is conveyed. There exists authority that the test here is stricter than for implied grant, that is to say it is one of 'utter necessity'. Thus, in *Ferguson v Campbell*[85] a servitude of aqueduct was held to have been impliedly reserved in favour of a watermill, because the mill could not function without water.

[79]   See **CHAPTER 14** below.
[80]   Although the uncertain doctrine of constitution *rebus ipsis et factis* (by facts and circumstances) comes close to this. See Cusine and Paisley, *Servitudes and Rights of Way* paras 11.09–11.17.
[81]   (1861) 4 Macq 117 at 123.
[82]   A place where animal skins were tanned into leather. An alternative definition, suggested to one of the authors, is a place where people had their hides tanned.
[83]   See also *Gow's Trs v Mealls* (1875) 2 R 729 and *Harton Homes Ltd v Durk* 2012 SCLR 554.
[84]   [2016] CSIH 70.
[85]   1913 1 SLT 241.

In *Murray v Medley*,[86] however, the sheriff was unwilling to accept that piped water was an utter necessity for a house. The rationale behind the strict test has been stated to be the principle that a granter must not derogate from the grant by impliedly reserving rights. This, however, rests principally on an English case[87] and it is open to question whether it actually represents Scots law. A less stringent test of 'necessary for comfortable enjoyment' appears to have been accepted by the sheriff in a more recent case, *McEwan's Exrs v Arnot*.[88] He also distanced himself from the decision in *Murray v Medley*. It has been argued that the law should apply the same test to both implied grant and implied reservation.[89]

Implied servitudes and landlocked land

13.26   Imagine that Peter sells to Roger an enclave, a piece of land entirely surrounded by land, which he (Peter) is retaining. If the conveyance is silent, a servitude right of access will be impliedly granted over the retained land as this is reasonably necessary to let Roger obtain access. There is, however, an alternative approach. In *Bowers v Kennedy*,[90] the Inner House held that the right to access landlocked land was an inherent part of the ownership of that property. At a practical level, it makes little difference in the beginning whether Roger is exercising his implied right of servitude or his inherent right of property. Later on, however, the importance matters, because while an implied servitude can be lost by negative prescription, the inherent right cannot.[91]

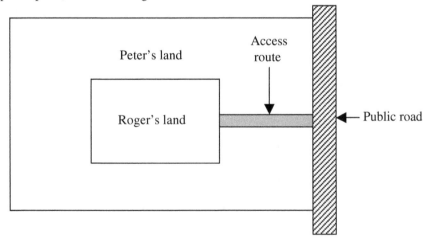

---

86   1973 SLT (Sh Ct) 75.
87   *Wheeldon v Burrows* (1879) 12 Ch D 31.
88   7 September 2004, Perth Sheriff Court, discussed in K G C Reid and G L Gretton *Conveyancing 2005* (2006) 89–92. See also *Inverness Seafield Development Co Ltd v Mackintosh* 2001 SC 46.
89   Reid and Gretton *Conveyancing 2005* at 92.
90   2000 SC 555.
91   See **PARA 13.45** below.

Positive prescription

13.27 A servitude may be acquired by 20 years of 'possession' ie exercise. This may be based on a recorded foundation writ[92] or without any deed at all.[93] In practice, such rights are usually not based on a deed, recorded or not. The possession must be open, peaceable and without judicial interruption, the same requirements as for prescriptive acquisition of ownership.[94] The possession must be 'adverse', that is to say 'as if of right', which is to say, as if the servitude right were actually held.[95] The courts have had difficulty with this requirement.[96] The possession will not be adverse if it is with the tolerance of the landowner. In one case the sheriff held that the party asserting prescription must prove a lack of tolerance.[97] But proving a negative is often impossible and the decision was reversed by the sheriff principal.[98] The correct rule is that a lack of tolerance can be inferred from a high volume of use of the servitude.[99] In terms of a policy adopted for the purposes of the Land Registration (Scotland) Act 1979 the Keeper would only enter servitudes established by prescription in the Land Register where a declarator had been obtained confirming the right.[100] Following the coming into force of the Land Registration etc. (Scotland) Act 2012 this policy has been relaxed.[101]

Special statutory provisions

13.28 A servitude may be created in limited cases under special statutory provisions, for example those conferring compulsory acquisition powers.[102]

---

[92] PL(S)A 1973, s 3(1).

[93] PL(S)A 1973, s 3(2). The Law Commissions have recommended that it should not be possible to acquire a servitude by prescription over a railway line under this provision for safety reasons. See Law Commission and Scottish Law Commission, Report on Level Crossings (Law Com No 339 and Scot Law Com No 234, 2013) paras 5.7–5.12.

[94] See **CHAPTER 6** above.

[95] K G C Reid and G L Gretton *Conveyancing 2006* (2007) 123–124. See also *Livingstone of Bachuil v Paine* [2012] CSOH 161.

[96] See *Aberdeen City Council v Wanchoo* 2007 SLT 289, aff'd [2008] CSIH 6, 2008 SC 278. See also *Webster v Chadburn* 2003 GWD 18-652, where the sheriff principal seemed to say that the pursuer must normally believe that the right of servitude is held. This is not the law. See Reid and Gretton *Conveyancing 2006* 128. And see also A S S Peterson 'Keeping Up Appearances: Prescriptive Possession of Servitudes' (2013) 2 *Edinburgh Student Law Review* 1.

[97] *Neumann v Hutchison* 2006 GWD 28-628.

[98] *Neumann v Hutchison* 2008 GWD 16-297.

[99] Cusine and Paisley *Servitudes and Rights of Way* para 10.19, approved in *Aberdeen City Council v Wanchoo* [2008] CSIH 6 at para 18.

[100] See Scottish Law Commission, Report on Land Registration (Scot Law Com No 222, 2010) vol 1, paras 10.7–10.17. The same policy applied for implied servitudes.

[101] See https://rosdev.atlassian.net/wiki/display/2ARM/Prescriptive+Servitudes.

[102] Eg the Communications Act 2003, Sch 4, para 4(3).

Acquiescence

13.29   According to Bell, 'although it is rightly said that mere acquiescence cannot confer a right of property, it may confer a right of use of property or servitude'.[103] But this is doubtful.[104] Rather, what can happen is that in servitudes which involve an encroachment,[105] such as laying pipes to carry water, a landowner who acquiesces in the work being carried out will be personally barred from objecting later.[106] At least this is the case if significant expenditure has been incurred.[107] Where the encroachment is obvious, successors of the landowner may be bound too.[108] While underground pipes will not generally be obvious, alterations to them may be.[109]

CHECKING FOR SERVITUDES

13.30   A prospective purchaser of the burdened property will want to know of any servitudes that affect it. As has been seen, servitudes created expressly since 28 November 2004 require to be registered on the titles of both properties.[110] So a search of the register will reveal them. But servitudes created in a deed before then might only appear on the title of the *benefited property*[111] or have been made real by possession without registration. Moreover, a servitude may have been created by implication or prescription and therefore not appear on the Land Register.[112] As well as checking the register, the would-be owner can check the state of possession by going and looking at the property. But access taken at dead of night or an underground pipe may not be apparent. This ultimately may mean hoping for the best and if a servitude transpires which is a material encumbrance, pursuing a warrandice claim against the seller.[113]

---

[103]   Bell *Principles* § 947.

[104]   *Moncrieff v Jamieson* 2005 SC 281 (Inner House) at para 27 per Lord Marnoch. In that case, an argument of acquiescence was not pursued in the House of Lords: 2008 SC (HL) 1 at para 19 per Lord Hope of Craighead. For general discussion, see Cusine and Paisley *Servitudes and Rights of Way* paras 11.37–11.46 and E C Reid and J W G Blackie *Personal Bar* (2006) paras 6-56–6-63.

[105]   See **PARAS 18.10–18.16** below.

[106]   *Robson v Chalmers Property Investment Co Ltd* 1965 SLT 381, aff'd 2008 SLT 1068.

[107]   See Reid and Blackie *Personal Bar* paras 6-60–6-61.

[108]   *Macgregor v Balfour* (1899) 2 F 345 at 352 per Lord President Balfour. In addition, the court has a discretion not to order the removal of an encroachment. See **PARA 18.15** below.

[109]   See *Buchan v Hunter* (1993), reported in Paisley and Cusine *Unreported Cases* 311, and *Cheever v Jefferson Properties Ltd* (1995), reported in Paisley and Cusine *Unreported Cases* 439.

[110]   See **PARA 13.21** above. Except for cable and pipeline servitudes.

[111]   *Balfour v Kinsey* 1987 SLT 144.

[112]   While the Keeper is under a duty in terms of LR(S)A 2012 ss 6 and 9 to insert information in a title sheet as to servitudes which benefit and burden the property she cannot do this unless she knows about the servitudes.

[113]   See **PARA 5.10** above.

RIGHTS OF THE BENEFITED PROPRIETOR

General

13.31   The benefited proprietor is entitled to enjoy the servitude to its full extent, subject to any applicable servitude conditions and to the law of nuisance.[114] As a real right, it is enforceable against third parties. The benefited proprietor is entitled to communicate the right to have any party having a direct nexus with the benefited property, such as family members or tenants.[115] In *Grant v Cameron*[116] a right of access provided in the deed to be 'for all purposes' was held exercisable by members of the public visiting a shop on the benefited property. The effect of the wording was therefore to permit a wider than usual class of people to exercise the right. Where the benefited property is divided, in principle the proprietors of each part may continue to use the servitude. But this must not lead to an unwarrantable increase in the burden on the burdened property.[117]

Ancillary rights

13.32   Ancillary rights may be specified in the deed creating the servitude. In the absence of this, these will be implied if:
- (a) the right is necessary for the convenient and comfortable enjoyment of the servitude; and
- (b) it was within the contemplation of the parties at the time the servitude was created.[118]

In *Moncrieff v Jamieson*,[119] on the facts a right of parking was held to be ancillary to the right of access created under a deed. Two common ancillary rights may be mentioned.
- (1) In the case of servitudes such as those of service media, there is the right to carry out work and to leave things such as pipes on the burdened property.
- (2) There is the right to repair and, to a limited extent, improve the burdened property.

Thus in the case of a servitude of access over a road, the benefited proprietor is entitled to carry out repairs and, in some cases, upgrade work. This is provided that its nature is not materially changed and that there is not an unwarrantable increase

---

114   On nuisance, see **PARAS 18.21–18.25** below.
115   Cusine and Paisley *Servitudes and Rights of Way* paras 1.55–1.61.
116   (1991), reported in Paisley and Cusine *Unreported Cases* 264.
117   Cusine and Paisley *Servitudes and Rights of Way* paras 12.195–12.200. See **PARAS 13.36–13.39** below.
118   *Moncrieff v Jamieson* 2008 SC (HL) 1. For discussion, see K G C Reid and G L Gretton *Conveyancing 2007* (2008) 111–117.
119   2008 SC (HL) 1.

in the burden on the burdened property.[120] The road may not be widened beyond the area which is burdened by the servitude.[121] It was held recently that a servitude right of access to reach a cellar did not include the ancillary right to carry out excavation work and create additional steps.[122]

OBLIGATIONS OF THE BENEFITED PROPRIETOR

Express servitude conditions

13.33   Where a servitude has been created expressly the deed may impose express conditions on the benefited proprietor, for example as regards the manner in which the right is to be exercised or the purpose for which it may be used.[123]

To exercise the servitude *civiliter*

13.34   It is implied in a servitude that it must be exercised *civiliter*. This means that the right must be exercised reasonably and the minimum possible burden imposed on the burdened property consistent with full enjoyment of the right.[124] For example, if a servitude right of access is held over a yard, the benefited proprietor may not exercise it along with his dogs with the purpose of letting them defecate.[125] And where a property is gated, a benefited proprietor exercising a right of access over it must shut the gate.[126]

To exercise the servitude for the benefit of the benefited property only

13.35   The second implied obligation is to exercise the servitude for the benefit of the benefited property alone and not for that of neighbouring property which the benefited proprietor also owns. The leading modern case is *Irvine Knitters Ltd v North Ayrshire Co-operative Society Ltd*.[127] The Co-op shop in Irvine was a building that straddled two plots. Plot 1 was the benefited property in a servitude right giving access along a lane to the rear of the building. The front was to the busy High Street. Plot 2 was not part of the benefited property.

---

[120]   Cusine and Paisley *Servitudes and Rights of Way* para 12.126.
[121]   *Lord Burton v Mackay* 1995 SLT 507.
[122]   *SP Distribution Ltd v Rafique* 2010 SLT (Sh Ct) 8.
[123]   Cusine and Paisley *Servitudes and Rights of Way* ch 13.
[124]   Rankine *Landownership* 417.
[125]   *Soriani v Cluckie* 2001 GWD 28-1138.
[126]   *Smith v McLaren* 18 October 2013, Arbroath Sheriff Court.
[127]   1978 SC 109. See R Paisley, 'The Use of Praedial Servitudes to Benefit Land Outside the Dominant Tenement' in F McCarthy, J Chalmers and S Bogle (eds), *Essays in Conveyancing and Property Law in Honour of Professor Robert Rennie* (2015)

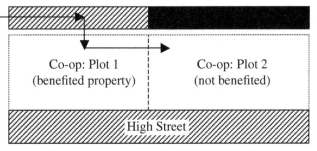

Servitude right of access along lane used by Irvine Knitters to take goods to both plots, with Plot 1 acting as a "bridge" to reach Plot 2

The burdened proprietors sought to interdict the Co-op from using the access to bring in goods to that part of the shop in Plot 2. They succeeded. Lord President Emslie stated:

> '[The benefited proprietors] may not use the way for the purpose of securing access for persons or goods to subjects contiguous to the dominant tenement by using the dominant tenement merely as a bridge between the end of the lane and the non-dominant subjects.'[128]

Not to increase unwarrantably the burden on the burdened property

13.36   The final implied obligation is not to cause an unwarrantable increase in the burden on the burdened property. By 'unwarrantable' is meant not permitted by the servitude in question. The baseline for increase is the extent of the servitude at the time when it is created. In the case of express servitudes the deed may provide for the extent. An example is *Grant v Cameron*[129] where the servitude was stated to be 'for all purposes'. In other cases the deed may not, or there might be no deed. Here, three general rules apply.

13.37   First, a change in the type of use made of the benefited property is not in itself an increase in the burden on the burdened property. The servitude can still be relied upon to support the new use. In *Carstairs v Spence*[130] a servitude right of access had been established by prescription. The benefited property was a market garden which subsequently became a building site. It was held that the benefited proprietor could carry building materials along the access route.

13.38   Second, in passage servitudes such as access or aqueduct, a change in the type of thing passing may be an unwarrantable increase in the burden. Thus, a servitude for pedestrian access cannot be used for vehicular access. In *Kerr v Brown*[131]

---

128   1978 SC 109 at 117.
129   (1991), reported in Paisley and Cusine *Unreported Cases* 264. See **PARA 13.31** above. Cf *Reid v Aberdeen Cafe Co Ltd* 2015 GWD 12-205, a case dating from 1881 and discussed in K G C Reid and G L Gretton, *Conveyancing 2015* (2016) 178-180.
130   1924 SC 380.
131   1939 SC 140.

a servitude to carry waste water from sinks was established by prescription. It was held it could not be extended to cover sewage. This case also demonstrates the rule *tantum praescriptum quantum possessum*: prescription is measured by possession. In other words, a servitude cannot be wider than what prescription established.[132] Nevertheless, modern versions of a previous thing are permitted. For example, cart and carriage roads may now be used for cars.[133]

13.39 Third, whether increased use is an increase in the burden is a question of scale. This is a common issue in practice in relation to access, but the law is rather obscure and each case must be assessed on its own facts.[134] The classic example is where a piece of land is developed for housing. Where, however, there has been an increase in burden for 20 years and this has not been challenged, it will be validated by positive prescription.[135]

RIGHTS OF THE BURDENED PROPRIETOR

13.40 The burdened proprietor has the right to continue to enjoy and make use of the burdened property provided that this does not interfere with the servitude.[136] In addition, the proprietor may enforce any of the express or implied obligations on the benefited proprietor mentioned above.[137]

OBLIGATIONS OF THE BURDENED PROPRIETOR

13.41 The principal obligations of the burdened proprietor are to respect the servitude and not to interfere with its exercise, such as by obstructing the benefited proprietor. Much of the case law, as may be expected, involves access rights. In *Drury v McGarvie*[138] there was a right of way over farmland from a public road to a cottage. The farmer's animals were straying off the land, so he erected stockproof gates at either end of the right of way. The owners of the cottage were elderly and disabled and struggled to open the gates. They objected. It was held that the erection of the gates was reasonable. The criterion was whether the average person could open the gates without difficulty. Where a gate is locked by the burdened proprietor, the benefited proprietor must be provided with a key.[139]

---

[132] See e.g. *Garson v McLeish* 2010 SLT (Sh Ct) 131.
[133] *Smith v Saxton* 1928 SN 59.
[134] For discussion, see Cusine and Paisley *Servitudes and Rights of Way* paras 12.186–12.201.
[135] See **PARA 13.27** above.
[136] Cusine and Paisley *Servitudes and Rights of Way* paras 12.12–12.22.
[137] See **PARAS 13.33–13.39** above.
[138] *Drury v McGarvie* 1993 SC 95.
[139] *Lee v McMurrich* Feb 5 1808, Court of Session, *Hume Session Papers*, vol 97, case 18.

13.42   Unless there is an express servitude condition requiring it, a burdened proprietor is *not* obliged to carry out repairs to an access route.[140] This may be seen as part of a general rule that servitudes must not impose positive obligations.[141] It is possible to oblige the burdened proprietor to repair by means of a real burden.[142]

EXTINCTION

Consensual

13.43   The benefited proprietor may agree to extinguish the servitude. Writing is required to constitute the agreement.[143] The servitude is then actually extinguished by a 'deed of discharge'.[144] This should be registered against the title of the burdened property.[145]

Acquiescence

13.44   Where the benefited proprietor stands by and lets the burdened proprietor carry out works which prevent the exercise of the servitude, the right to object later may be lost.[146] This will be most likely if the work involved substantial expenditure, the value of which would be lost if the objection succeeded.[147] In this situation the servitude is extinguished by *acquiescence*. The acquiescence is to the extent of the breach. For example, in *Millar v Christie*[148] the building work partially blocked an access way. The result was to limit the servitude right which existed to the remaining part. Singular successors will generally be bound by the acquiescence because the building work will be obvious to them at the time of purchase.[149]

Negative prescription

13.45   Where a servitude has not been exercised for 20 years it will be lost through negative prescription.[150] In the case of a pedestrian and vehicular access right, an absence of vehicular use for the prescriptive period will reduce the servitude to foot

---

[140]   *Rodgers v Harvie* (1829) 7 S 287. For the sequel, see (1830) 8 S 611.
[141]   Cusine and Paisley *Servitudes and Rights of Way* para 2.85. But express servitude conditions can override the rule.
[142]   See **CHAPTER 14** below.
[143]   RoW(S)A 1995, s 1(2)(a)(i). See **PARA 31.3** below.
[144]   Again, writing is required, this time under RoW(S)A 1995, s 1(2)(b). See **PARA 31.4** below.
[145]   TC(S)A 2003, s 78.
[146]   Reid and Blackie *Personal Bar* paras 6-46–6-55.
[147]   *Davidson v Thomson* (1880) 17 R 287 at 290 per Lord President Inglis.
[148]   1961 SC 1.
[149]   *Muirhead v Glasgow Highland Society* (1864) 2 M 420 at 426 per Lord President McNeill.
[150]   PL(S)A 1973, s 8.

access only.[151] The inherent right of the proprietor of landlocked land to reach it was held to be a right exercisable as a *res merae facultatis*[152] in *Bowers v Kennedy*[153] and is therefore imprescriptible. Where a deed creating a servitude makes it clear that the right is to subsist even if it is not exercised for an initial period of time, this may also make it as a *res merae facultatis*.[154]

Abandonment

13.46   It is possible for a servitude to be lost in less than 20 years by the benefited proprietor abandoning it. Much will depend on the factual circumstances which can be asserted to prove abandonment.[155]

Destruction

13.47   In general, land is indestructible, so extinction by destruction is rare. Where a servitude is stated to be for the benefit of a particular building and that building is demolished with no intention of rebuilding, the servitude will be lost.[156]

Confusion

13.48   A servitude will normally be extinguished by *confusio* where the benefited and burdened properties come into the same ownership.[157] Hence, if Alex's land has a right of servitude to lay pipes through Beth's land, the right will disappear if he buys her land. Confusion probably does not operate if the two pieces of land are held by the person in different capacities, for example as an individual and as a trustee.[158] It is unlikely that a servitude extinguished by confusion will revive on the land being

---

[151] *Walker's Exrx v Carr* 1973 SLT (Sh Ct) 77.
[152] PL(S)A 1973, Sch 3, para (c). *Res merae facultatis* is 'a property right which cannot be lost by negative prescription either (1) because it is a right whose exercise implies no claim on anyone else or against their rights or (2) because it is a (normal) incident of ownership which can be lost only as a consequence of the fortification in some other person of a right inconsistent with it' (Johnston *Prescription* para 3.16). The subject is obscure. See further D J Cusine (ed), '*Res merae facultatis*: Through a Glass Darkly' in F McCarthy, J Chalmers and S Bogle (eds), *Essays in Conveyancing and Property Law in Honour of Professor Robert Rennie* (2015) 185–202.
[153] 2000 SC 555. See **PARA 13.26** above.
[154] *Peart v Legge* 2007 SLT 982. But this seems similar to contracting out of prescription, which is forbidden by PL(S)A 1973, s 13. For discussion, see K G C Reid and G L Gretton *Conveyancing 2007* (2008) 117–121.
[155] For example, allowing the route to blocked and taking access by an alternative route. See *Thomas v Stephenson's Exr* 4 October 2013, Dunoon Sheriff Court, discussed in Reid and Gretton, *Conveyancing 2013* (2014) 171–172.
[156] Cusine and Paisley *Servitudes and Rights of Way* para 17.21.
[157] Erskine II, 9, 37. Compare the rule for real burdens. See **PARA 14.75** below.
[158] Cusine and Paisley *Servitudes and Rights of Way* para 17.25.

subsequently separated, but new servitudes may be created by implication if the relevant tests are satisfied.[159]

Compulsory purchase

13.49   Where land is compulsorily purchased, servitudes and real burdens encumbering it are normally extinguished.[160] If land is acquired consensually in a situation where compulsory purchase could have been used, these rights can be extinguished by the acquirer giving notice to the benefited proprietor.[161] That proprietor then has the right to apply to the Lands Tribunal to have the servitude or real burden renewed.[162]

Application to the Lands Tribunal

13.50   The burdened proprietor may apply to the Lands Tribunal for the servitude to be varied or discharged.[163] The rules are essentially the same as for real burdens and are discussed in **CHAPTER 14**.[164] But in contrast to the position for most real burdens the application will not be granted as of right if there is no objection.[165] The Tribunal will still have to consider the merits and whether it is reasonable to vary or discharge the servitude.

RIGHTS WHICH ARE SIMILAR TO SERVITUDES

Public rights of way

13.51   Public rights of way are covered elsewhere.[166] Two key distinctions from servitudes are that there is no benefited property and the rights are for access only. As has been seen, servitudes can be for other purposes, such as to lay pipes.

Statutory rights

13.52   Many statutes create rights that are effectively personal servitudes, that is to say there is a burdened property but no benefited property. A common example is

---

[159]   See **PARAS 13.24–13.25** above.
[160]   TC(S)A 2003, s 106. The rights may be saved by express provision in the compulsory purchase order or the conveyance. On compulsory purchase, see **PARAS 8.4–8.9** above.
[161]   TC(S)A 2003, s 107(1) and (4).
[162]   TC(S)A 2003, s 107(5).
[163]   Eg *George Wimpey East Scotland Ltd v Fleming* 2006 SLT (Lands Tr) 2 and 59.
[164]   See **PARAS 14.71–14.73** below.
[165]   TC(S)A 2003, s 97.
[166]   See **PARAS 19.13–19.22** below.

a 'wayleave'. It is like a cable or pipeline servitude and can be created in favour of certain utility companies.[167] Another example is certain private level crossings over railway lines.[168] Access rights exist under various statutes, not least the Land Reform (Scotland) Act 2003.[169]

LITERATURE

13.53   The leading text is Cusine and Paisley *Servitudes and Rights of Way*, but it pre-dates the important changes made by TC(S)A 2003. A second edition is expected shortly. Other important treatments which also pre-date these changes are Gordon *Scottish Land Law* paras 24.01–24.104 and Reid *Property* paras 439–469 (A G M Duncan). For an account focussing on the changes see Paisley, R R M 'The New Law of Servitudes' in R Rennie (ed) *The Promised Land: Property Law Reform* (2008) 91–123. Briefer accounts of the post-TC(S)A 2003 law can be found in Anderson, *Property: A Guide to Scots Law* (2016) ch 11, Gloag and Henderson *The Law of Scotland* paras 34.39–34.50, McDonald *Conveyancing Manual* ch 16 and Rennie *Land Tenure* ch 11.

---

[167]   For example, the Electricity Act 1989, Sch 4, paras 6 and 7. See further Cusine and Paisley *Servitudes and Rights of Way* para 1.04 and chapter 26.
[168]   Railways Clauses Consolidation (Scotland) Act 1845, s 60.
[169]   On LR(S)A 2003, see **PARAS 19.2–19.12** below. More generally, see R R M Paisley 'Personal Real Burdens' 2005 *JR* 377 at 417–420.

Chapter 14

Real burdens

ESSENTIALS

Definition

14.1　A 'real burden' is an obligation affecting land, which normally requires something to be done or not to be done. For example, it may provide for a house to be maintained or insured. In the case of property which benefits more than one owner, such as a tenement roof or a common recreational area, a contribution towards maintenance may be required. Typical examples of burdens which impose restrictions are ones which prevent trading or running a business from a residential property, or prohibit alterations. Usually, real burdens, like servitudes, involve a 'benefited property' and a 'burdened property'.[1] They are normally imposed when a piece of land is sold as a separate unit for the first time. The value of the real burdens is that they 'run with the land'. The owner[2] for the time being of a benefited property can enforce them against the owner[3] for the time being of the burdened property. The types of obligation imposed by real burdens could also be created by simple contract. But a contract would not bind successor owners.

Background

14.2   Unlike servitudes, which come from Roman law, real burdens were developed in conveyancing practice in the nineteenth century. The reason probably lay in the limited scope of servitudes: there was in effect a fixed list and positive obligations could not be imposed.[4] Real burdens were often created in feudal deeds.[5] The superiority acted as the benefited property and the vassal's interest (*dominium utile*) was the burdened property. This was convenient for developers because there was no requirement for the superior to hold neighbouring land. More than anything, this is why the feudal system survived in Scotland until 28 November 2004. Equally, however, it was possible at common law for real burdens to be imposed in non-feudal deeds, such as dispositions. In fact the 1840 House of Lords case of *Tailors of Aberdeen v Coutts*,[6] which provides the foundation of the law of real burdens involved a non-feudal deed.

Title Conditions (Scotland) Act 2003

14.3   When the Scottish Law Commission prepared the report which led to the Abolition of Feudal Tenure etc. (Scotland) Act 2000 (AFT(S)A 2000),[7] it realised that separate legislation would be needed to regulate real burdens in post-feudal land law. This prompted it to issue its *Report on Real Burdens*.[8] This led to the Title Conditions (Scotland) Act 2003 (TC(S)A 2003), most of which, like AFT(S) A 2000, came into force on 28 November 2004. Much of it is a codification of the common law, so the older case law often remains relevant. Particularly important is Pt 1 of TC(S)A 2003, which regulates creation, enforcement and extinction.[9] One might legitimately ask why the legislation is not called the 'Real Burdens (Scotland) Act'. The reason is that while it mainly deals with real burdens, it also deals with

---

[1] There is an exception for personal real burdens. See **PARA 14.50** below.
[2] And certain other parties. See **PARA 14.38** below.
[3] And in the case of negative real burdens, against everyone else too. See **PARA 14.42** below.
[4] See **PARAS 13.9 and 13.42** above.
[5] See **APPENDIX** below.
[6] (1840) 1 Robin 296.
[7] Scottish Law Commission, Report on the Abolition of the Feudal System (Scot Law Com No 168, 1998).
[8] Scottish Law Commission, Report on Real Burdens (Scot Law Com No 181, 2000).
[9] TC(S)A 2003, ss 1–24.

'title conditions' more generally.[10] A 'title condition' is an obligation affecting land which the Lands Tribunal has power to vary or discharge.[11] TC(S)A 2003 gives an exhaustive list, but the most important are:

(a)   real burdens;

(b)   servitudes; and

(c)   conditions in long leases.[12]

Praedial real burdens and personal real burdens

14.4   If a real burden has both a benefited and a burdened property, it is a *praedial* real burden. For example, Yasmin, the owner for the time being of 22 Myles Gardens can enforce the real burdens affecting 24 Myles Gardens. Praedial real burdens are the norm. In very limited circumstances it is possible to have real burdens which do not have a benefited property. Instead, they are enforceable by a particular person. These are *personal* real burdens.[13] For example, Scottish Natural Heritage may have title to enforce a real burden providing for the conservation of a building. Personal real burdens are rare and discussion of them is saved for later.[14] Almost all of this chapter focuses on praedial real burdens.

Subdivisions and common schemes

14.5   It was stated above that real burdens are normally imposed when land is sold as a separate unit for the first time.[15] Two factual situations can be distinguished. The first is where an owner of land sells part of it and imposes burdens on that part. For example, Triin has a large garden. She does not need all of it. Katri offers to buy the part furthest from the house. She wants to build her own house on it. Triin is agreeable to this, but she does not want the land to be used as commercial premises at any time in the future. So in the disposition to Katri she imposes a real burden to that effect. This can be described as a subdivision case. Typically, although not always, the burdens are non-reciprocal. Thus Triin can enforce the trading prohibition against Katri and not vice versa. It is possible for there to be more than one benefited property. For example, in the disposition Triin could have given the right to enforce the burden to the immediate neighbouring properties.

Triin's land	Katri's land
(benefited property)	(burdened property)

Sub-division case

---

[10]   Thus it provides some important rules for servitudes. See **PARAS 13.1, 13.5, 13.19 AND 13.21** above.

[11]   See **PARA 14.72** below.

[12]   TC(S)A 2003, s 122(1).

[13]   The conjunction of the adjectives 'personal' and 'real' sounds odd. The 'real' refers to the burdened property. The 'personal' is because there is no benefited property.

[14]   See **PARAS 14.49–14.57** below.

[15]   See **PARA 14.1** above.

14.6   The second example typically involves a developer or builder. A block of flats or new housing scheme is built. Before the flats or houses are sold, real burdens are imposed on the entire site, regulating matters such as maintenance and use of the properties. These burdens are to be reciprocally enforceable by all the property owners. So Irene, who buys plot 15, has title to enforce against Joanna, who buys plot 16, and vice versa. This is described as a 'common scheme'. Each property within the scheme is both a benefited and a burdened property. Such reciprocal burdens are called 'community burdens'.[16] There are special rules that apply only to this type of burden.[17] It is therefore important when it comes to understanding TC(S)A 2003 to differentiate subdivision cases and common scheme cases.

1	2	3	4
5	6	7	8
9	10	11	12
13	14	15 Irene	16 Joanna

Common scheme case

Affirmative and negative real burdens

14.7   Real burdens requiring something to be done are called 'affirmative burdens'.[18] Those imposing prohibitions are called 'negative burdens'.[19] In general, real burdens cannot give a right to use or enter the burdened property. That is the role of *servitudes*.[20] The distinction can be illustrated by this table.

---

[16]   TC(S)A 2003, s 25.
[17]   See **PARAS 14.61–14.65** below.
[18]   TC(S)A 2003, s 2(1)(a) and (2)(a).
[19]   TC(S)A 2003, s 2(1)(b) and (2)(b).
[20]   See **PARA 13.5** above.

Type of title condition	Servitude	Real burden
Positive obligation	No	Yes
Negative obligation	No	Yes
Obligation to allow use of or entry to the burdened property	Yes	No

14.8   The table is not entirely accurate. It is possible to have real burdens allowing use of or entry to the burdened property for purposes connected with another real burden. This category is known as 'ancillary burdens'.[21] For example, there might be a real burden requiring a property to be maintained and an ancillary burden allowing access onto the property to check that the maintenance obligation is being fulfilled.

14.9   Unlike servitudes,[22] there is no established list of real burdens. But in addition to the requirement that they must normally impose only positive or negative obligations, there are further rules on content. These are discussed in the following paragraphs.

The praedial requirement

14.10   The law here is similar to that on servitudes.[23] A real burden must burden the burdened property to the benefit of the benefited property. The burden must relate to the burdened property and not simply to the person who owns that property.[24] Hence a requirement to sing a song or to support a particular football club or not to wear blue trousers would not be a valid real burden. The burden must benefit the benefited property and not merely fulfil the personal wishes of its owner.[25] Thus the examples given fail the praedial test at the benefited property end too. The benefit protected may be commercial. In *Hill of Rubislaw (Q Seven) Ltd v Rubislaw Quarry Aberdeen Ltd*[26] a real burden which restricted the amount of lettable office space which could be built was upheld by the Inner House. In the case of a *community burden*, it is permissible for the benefit to be to the community as a whole rather than to a particular benefited property.[27] Thus a requirement for a tenement to be factored would meet the test, as it is in the interests of all the owners that the building is well managed.

Restrictions on content

14.11   There are restraints on real burdens which are similar to those found in contract law.[28] They may not be contrary to public policy, such as being an

[21]   TC(S)A 2003, s 2(3) and (4).
[22]   See **PARA 13.9** above.
[23]   See **PARAS 13.6–13.7** above.
[24]   TC(S)A 2003, s 3(1) and (2).
[25]   TC(S)A 2003, s 3(3).
[26]   [2014] CSIH 105, 2015 SC 339.
[27]   TC(S) A 2003, s 3(4).
[28]   See MacQueen and Thomson *Contract* paras 7.1–7.24 and 7.30–7.47.

unreasonable restraint on trade.[29] The real burden in *Hill of Rubislaw (Q Seven) Ltd* (above) was challenged on this basis, but the court concluded that it was in fact in the public interest because its effect was to increase the overall supply of office space in the city.[30] Nor can real burdens be repugnant with the ownership of the burdened property: a burden can go so far but no further.[31] In a nineteenth-century case, Lord Young famously said: 'You cannot make a man proprietor and yet prohibit him from exercising his ownership.'[32] Hence a burden stating that the property cannot be sold or leased is invalid. Nor can a real burden be illegal.[33] Thus a requirement that only women may live in the property would breach sex discrimination legislation.[34] In general, a real burden must not create a monopoly, for example by requiring that a certain company always manages a development.[35] Nor is it possible to allow a person, other than a party with title to enforce the burden,[36] to give permission for the activity prohibited by the burden to take place.[37] Thus if a developer has sold all the properties in a development, a right to vary or extinguish the burdens cannot be reserved as the developer is no longer a benefited proprietor.[38]

Pre-emptions and other options

14.12　It is permissible to have a real burden allowing the owner of a benefited property to have the right to purchase the burdened property if the burdened proprietor decides to sell. This is known as a 'right of pre-emption'.[39] Often the right is to purchase at the same price as that offered by a prospective purchaser. In practice the presence of a pre-emption right may deter such purchasers and therefore it is possible to obtain a pre-sale undertaking from the holder of the pre-emption that the right will not be exercised.[40] In general, a pre-emption right constituted as a real burden will only provide one chance for it to be exercised.[41] Thus if the property is

---

[29]　TC(S)A 2003, s 3(6). See McDonald *Conveyancing Manual* para 15.33.
[30]　[2014] CSIH 105, 2015 SC 339 at para [26].
[31]　TC(S)A 2003, s 3(6). See *Snowie v Museum Hall LLP* 2010 SLT 971.
[32]　*Moir's Trs v McEwan* (1880) 7 R 1141 at 1145.
[33]　TC(S)A 2003, s 3(6).
[34]　Equality Act 2010, s 33.
[35]　TC(S)A 2003, s 3(7). This is subject to other provisions in the Act, notably those on manager burdens (ss 63–67). See **PARA 14.56** below.
[36]　The provision refers to the 'holder' of the burden. This term is defined in TC(S)A 2003, s 122(1) and for praedial rule burdens effectively is restricted to the owner of the benefited property.
[37]　TC(S)A 2003, s 3(8).
[38]　Assuming that the developer does not hold neighbouring land which is provided to be a benefited property in the deed creating the burdens.
[39]　TC(S)A 2003, s 3(5). A challenge to a pre-emption right founded on A1P1 to the ECHR failed on the basis that the existence of the pre-emption was known to the burdened proprietor at the time he acquired the land and that this may have reduced the purchase price. See *MacDonald-Haig v Gerlings,* Inverness Sheriff Court, 3 December 2001 (unreported). See K G C Reid and G L Gretton *Conveyancing 2002* (2003) 63–65.
[40]　TC(S)A 2003, s 83.
[41]　TC(S)A 2003, ss 82 and 84. There is an exception for pre-emptions created in dispositions before 1 September 1974.

offered to the holder of the pre-emption and he or she does not wish to purchase, the right is extinguished. Where there is a pre-emption right and the property is not offered to the holder, the transfer in breach of the pre-emption may be reduced under the 'offside goals' rule.[42]

14.13   Since 28 November 2004, it has no longer been competent to create other types of option as a real burden.[43] TC(S)A 2003 mentions specifically two types, although the prohibition is a general one. A 'right of redemption' allows the granter in a conveyance to repurchase the land, normally at a fixed price and at any time. Under earlier legislation, the lifespan of a right of redemption created as a real burden is limited to 20 years.[44] This means that many such real burdens will cease to exist at latest on 26 November 2024.[45] A right of redemption is an example of a wider class of option known as 'rights of reversion'. These confer the right to re-acquire land, not necessarily in return for payment. The Scottish Law Commission regarded it wrong as a matter of policy that these should be capable of affecting successor landowners.[46]

14.14   It remains possible for options of any type to be created contractually, although of course successor owners of the property affected will not be bound. If, however, someone who knew about the option bought the land in breach of it, the 'offside goals' rule would apply.[47] In practice, solicitors may secure the option by means of a standard security, although the remedies available under the security for default may seem inappropriate.[48] It does mean, however, that a prospective purchaser will be put on notice about the option and allow the 'offside goals' rule to apply if the right is breached.

CREATION

A deed which is dual-registered

14.15   A real burden must be created in a *deed*, which is registered against *both* the title of the benefited property *and* that of the burdened property.[49] This is known as the 'constitutive deed'. The deed must describe both properties or, in the case

---

[42]   *Matheson v Tinney* 1989 SLT 535; *Roebuck v Edmunds* 1992 SLT 1055. On the 'offside goals' rule, see **PARAS 4.47–4.50** above.
[43]   TC(S)A 2003, s 3(5).
[44]   Land Tenure Reform (Scotland) Act 1974, s 12.
[45]   This is because 26 November 2004 was the last date on which a right of redemption could be registered as a valid real burden. (27 November 2004 was a Saturday and the registers were closed for business. The authors remember the day well, as they were at a feudal abolition party.) Redemptions created before 1 September 1974 are unaffected.
[46]   Scottish Law Commission, Report on Real Burdens (Scot Law Com No 181, 2000) para 10.20: 'A person may lose property without his consent and, in some cases, without adequate compensation. This is private compulsory purchase.'
[47]   Scottish Law Commission, Report on Real Burdens (Scot Law Com No 181, 2000) para 10.8.
[48]   Scottish Law Commission, Report on Real Burdens (Scot Law Com No 181, 2000) para 10.9. On standard securities, see **PARAS 21.43–21.56** below.
[49]   TC(S)A 2003, s 4(1) and (5). Previously, the law was that it needed to be registered only against the burdened property. Thus there exist many single-registered burdens.

of community burdens, the community.[50] Before 28 November 2004, it was only possible to create real burdens in two types of deed: conveyances and deeds of conditions. Now, there is no such restriction. Any type of deed may be used. So, for example, a new real burden could be created in a minute of waiver,[51] i.e. a deed that extinguishes a current burden. The *nemo plus* rule[52] applies. Land can be burdened only by the owner,[53] for example, a developer who has constructed houses and is about to sell them. In the example just given of a new real burden being created in a minute of waiver, the burdened property's owner would therefore need to sign the deed, whereas normally only the benefited proprietor signs a waiver. After creation, the burdens cease to have *contractual* effect between the parties.[54]

The term 'real burden'

14.16   It is obligatory to use the term 'real burden' or an equivalent in the deed.[55] An equivalent is permitted where the real burden is of a nameable type,[56] such as a 'community burden'[57] or 'conservation burden'.[58]

The 'four corners of the deed' rule

14.17   In principle, the full terms of the real burden must be set out within the 'four corners' of the constitutive deed. For example, in *Aberdeen Varieties Ltd v James F Donald (Aberdeen Cinemas) Ltd*[59] the owner of two theatres sold one of them and imposed a real burden requiring that the property 'shall not be used in all time coming for the performance of pantomime, melodrama or comic opera or any stage play which requires to be submitted to the Lord Chamberlain under the Act for regulating Theatres 6th & 7th Vict c 68'. It was held that a valid real burden had not been created. To do so, the deed would have had to copy out the full terms of the statute.[60]

14.18   The strict common law rule has been relaxed a little by TC(S)A 2003, s 5. A real burden which requires a contribution towards or the payment of a cost can refer to a public document, without setting out the full terms of that document. By 'public document' is meant 'an enactment or a public register or some record or

---

50   TC(S)A 2003, s 4(2)(c) and (4).
51   On minutes of waiver, see **PARA 14.58** below.
52   See **PARA 4.41** above.
53   TC(S)A 2003, s 4(2)(b).
54   TC(S)A 2003, s 61.
55   TC(S)A 2003, s 4(2)(a). Compare the position for servitudes. See **PARA 13.21** above.
56   TC(S)A 2003, s 4(3).
57   See **PARA 14.6** above.
58   See **PARA 14.50** below.
59   1939 SC 788. See also *Marriott v Greenbelt Group Ltd*, Lands Tribunal, 2 December 2015.
60   Actually, it would have failed even then because of other invalidities, such as restraint of trade.

roll to which the public readily has access'.[61] The provision applies to all burdens, new and old, and is aimed particularly at burdens providing for the maintenance of tenements which apportion liability on the basis of rateable value or feu duty.[62]

Duration

14.19   The constitutive deed may state how long the real burden is to last, but in practice this is rare. Where, as is normally the case, the deed is silent, the real burden is perpetual,[63] subject to the rules of extinction set out at the end of this chapter.[64]

THE BENEFITED PROPERTY

The common law background

14.20   Prior to 28 November 2004 the common law had strict rules that the *burdened property* must be carefully identified[65] and the real burden registered against it.[66] Unlike TC(S)A 2003, which applies these rules to *both* the burdened and the benefited properties, the common law took a lax approach when it came to the identification of the *benefited property*. Sometimes the constitutive deed would nominate this property, but usually it did not. In the latter situation, the courts developed a set of rules under which a benefited property or benefited properties would be *implied*. These rules on implied enforcement rights were complex and barely comprehensible.[67] TC(S)A 2003 for the most part abolished them.[68] In their place it provided another set of rules which are not only complex, but overlap.[69] The result is less than satisfactory.[70] The picture is also complicated by the impact of feudal abolition.

Real burdens created since 28 November 2004

14.21   The rule here is straightforward. As was seen above, the benefited property or properties must be identified in the constitutive deed and the deed registered

---

[61]   TC(S)A 2003, s 5(2).
[62]   'Rateable value' refers to the local government taxation of 'rates', which was replaced for residential properties by the 'community charge' or 'poll tax' in 1989 and then by the 'council tax' in 1993. On feu duty, see the **APPENDIX**. Older real burdens often make flats liable for tenement repairs based on their rateable value or feu duty liability as a proportion of the total liability of the building.
[63]   TC(S)A 2003, s 7.
[64]   See **PARAS 14.59–14.74** below.
[65]   *Anderson v Dickie* 1914 SC 706, aff'd 1915 SC (HL) 79.
[66]   *Tailors of Aberdeen v Coutts* (1840) 1 Robin 296.
[67]   See Reid *Property* paras 397–404 and McDonald *Conveyancing Manual* paras 17.8–17.31.
[68]   TC(S)A 2003, s 49.
[69]   TC(S)A 2003, ss 52–57.
[70]   For discussion, see S Wortley 'Love Thy Neighbour: The Development of the Scottish Law of Implied Third Party Rights of Enforcement of Real Burdens' 2005 *JR* 345 and K G C Reid 'New Enforcers for Old Burdens: Sections 52 and 53 Revisited' in R Rennie (ed) *The Promised Land: Property Law Reform* (2008) 71–90.

against the title to that property.[71] There can be no implied rights of enforcement for such burdens.[72]

Real burdens created before 28 November 2004: seven rules

14.22   For real burdens created before 28 November 2004, it is possible to identify seven rules.[73] These may overlap: more than one rule may apply to the same burden. Most of these rules are in TC(S)A 2003 even though the burdens to which they apply were then already in existence: these rules thus apply retrospectively. (However, to a considerable extent they merely restate what the common law, under which these burdens were set up, actually was.)

Rule 1: express nomination

14.23   The constitutive deed may nominate the benefited property or properties. For example, it is common to find in a deed of conditions granted by a builder over a new development a statement that each house owner has the right to enforce the burden against all the other house owners. This is sometimes stated to be an 'express *jus quaesitum tertio*'. This is an analogy with contract law.[74]

Rule 2: related properties in a common scheme

14.24   TC(S)A 2003, s 53 has caused much difficulty. It provides that where there are 'related properties' forming part of a 'common scheme' of real burdens, the burdens are mutually enforceable by the proprietors.[75] In other words, the burdens are *community burdens*[76] and can be enforced by each member of the community. The legislation does not define 'common scheme' but it seems to mean identical or similar burdens, probably imposed by the same person, for example a builder.[77] Where the same deed applies to a number of houses, for example a deed of conditions, the burdens will usually be identical. If the burdens are imposed in different deeds, for example the individual dispositions for each house, it is more likely that they vary.

---

71   See **PARA 14.15** above. Equally, there must be identification of and registration against the burdened property.
72   There is one exception to this rule, which arises out of TC(S)A 2003, s 53. See **PARA 14.26** below.
73   Gretton and Reid *Conveyancing* para 13-15.
74   Under contract law, successors are not bound. Here, they are.
75   Or tenants etc. See **PARA 14.38** below. The provision does not apply to rights of pre-emption, redemption or reversion or to maintenance obligations, for example as regards roads, which have been taken over by a public authority. See TC(S)A 2003, ss 53(2) and 122(2). A revised version of s 53 applies to sheltered or retirement housing developments by virtue of s 54.
76   See **PARA 14.6** above.
77   Cf *Russel Properties (Europe) Ltd v Dundas Heritable Ltd* [2012] CSOH 175. See also McDonald *Conveyancing Manual* para 17.33; Reid *Feudal Abolition* para 5.2.

14.25 Likewise, 'related properties' is not defined. The matter of whether properties are 'related' requires 'to be inferred from all the circumstances'.[78] In effect it is a subjective decision for the courts. Regard, however, must be had to a non-exhaustive list of factors, namely whether:

(a) it is convenient to manage the properties together because they have a common feature or are obliged to maintain a facility together;

(b) they share common ownership of something;

(c) they are regulated by the same burdens imposed in a deed of conditions; and

(d) they are flats in the same tenement.[79]

The Lands Tribunal has expressed the view that properties subject to the same deed creating real burdens, although this is not a deed of conditions and within (c), may be related.[80] The Minister who introduced the provision, when the legislation was passing through the Scottish Parliament, stated that 'houses on a typical housing estate would be related properties' but not 'scattered properties in rural areas'.[81] Ultimately, each case must be decided on its facts.[82] This is unfortunate, for TC(S) A 2003, s 53 is an important provision which can apply in many cases.[83]

14.26 A final point about this rule is that only one of the properties requires to have been burdened before 28 November 2004. For example, where burdens are imposed in a common scheme on a housing development, TC(S)A 2003, s 53 will apply as long as ownership of one of the houses was transferred to a purchaser before that date. The later houses can still enforce and, reciprocally, have the burdens enforced against them under the rule. This is the one exception mentioned to the rule that implied enforcement rights can only arise for burdens created before 28 November 2004.[84]

Rule 3: unrelated properties in a common scheme

14.27 TC(S)A 2003, s 52 provides for implied enforcement rights for properties in a 'common scheme'. It can apply even if the properties are not 'related' within the meaning of TC(S)A 2003, s 53. In effect it is a statutory restatement of the common law rule established in *Hislop v MacRitchie's Trs*.[85] There are, however, two important pre-requisites for TC(S)A 2003, s 52 to apply.

---

[78] TC(S)A 2003, s 53(2).

[79] TC(S)A 2003, s 53(2).

[80] *Brown v Richardson* 2007 GWD 28-490.

[81] Scottish Parliament *Official Report* Justice 1 Committee, 10 December 2002 col 4372.

[82] See *Thomson's Exr, Applicant* 2016 GWD 27-494 in which shared ownership of and a shared duty to maintain the boundary wall between two properties was held to make them 'related'.

[83] In June 2013 the Justice Committee of the Scottish Parliament recommended that section 53 should be remitted to the Scottish Law Commission for review. See http://www.scottish.parliament.uk/S4_JusticeCommittee/Reports/juR-13-08-w-rev.pdf. This recommendation was accepted by the Scottish Government and the Commission has begun work on the subject.

[84] See **PARA 14.21** above.

[85] (1881) 8 R (HL) 95. However, like TC(S)A 2003, s 53, the rule does not apply to rights of pre-emption, redemption or reversion, or to maintenance obligations taken over by a public authority. See TC(S)A 2003, ss 52(3) and 122(2).

14.28   First, for a property to be subject to implied enforcement rights under the rule, there must be *notice* of the common scheme on the title to that property.[86] Two factual situations are possible. If the deed creating the real burden applies to a wider area, this by itself is sufficient notice of the scheme. For example, the real burden may have been imposed in a disposition of a development site by a farmer in favour of a builder, with the builder subsequently subdividing the site into housing plots. If, in contrast, the deed creating the real burden applies to the burdened property alone, the situation is more complicated. There needs to be something specific in the deed to indicate a common scheme, such as an obligation by the granter to impose the same burdens on subsequently disponed houses.[87]

14.29   Second, there must be nothing in the deed creating the real burdens to negative the creation of mutual enforcement rights.[88] The classic example of this is the granter reserving the right to vary the burdens.[89] Where real burdens have been imposed over an area which is then subdivided, rights of enforcement in favour of the owners of the respective parts cannot arise if there was in fact a prohibition on subdivision.[90]

14.30   This rule is less important than rule 2 above. The reason is that many deeds creating burdens do not give notice of a common scheme or do have a provision allowing the granter to vary the burdens.

Rule 4: facility burdens

14.31   Where a real burden regulates the 'maintenance, management, reinstatement or use of a facility', the benefited properties are the facility itself and any property to which the facility is, and is intended to be, of benefit.[91] Examples of facilities given by the legislation are:
  (a) common parts of a tenement;
  (b) common recreation areas:
  (c) private roads;
  (d) private sewerage systems; and
  (e) boundary walls.[92]

Thus, where a number of properties share a common access road and are subject to real burdens requiring it to be maintained, the burdens are mutually enforceable. The rule does not apply where the obligation to maintain the facility has been taken over by a public authority.[93] In practice, there is often an overlap between this rule

---

[86]   TC(S)A 2003, s 52(1).
[87]   *McGibbon v Rankin* (1871) 9 M 423. See, further, Reid *Feudal Abolition* para 5.15.
[88]   TC(S)A 2003, s 52(2).
[89]   *Turner v Hamilton* (1890) 17 R 494.
[90]   *Girls School Co Ltd v Buchanan* 1958 SLT (Notes) 2.
[91]   TC(S)A 2003, ss 56(1)(a) and 122(1). See *Greenbelt Property Ltd v Riggens* 2010 GWD 28-586.
[92]   TC(S)A 2003, s 122(3).
[93]   TC(S)A 2003, s 122(2).

and rule 2. The reason for this is that rule 2 was only conceived and introduced at a late stage during the passage of the legislation.[94]

Rule 5: service burdens

14.32   Where a real burden regulates the provision of a service, the benefited properties are the properties to which the service is to be provided.[95] For example, a burden may require the provision of water or electricity. In practice, this is rare and the rule is therefore not very important.

Rule 6: reallotted feudal burdens

14.33   Where a feudal real burden was preserved by a notice registered before 28 November 2004, the benefited property is that identified in the notice.[96] Under feudal law, burdens could be enforced by the superior, even although that person did not own any neighbouring land. Where superiors *did* own such land, the legislation that abolished the feudal system gave them a limited chance to 'reallot' burdens so that the benefited property became that land. For this option to be available the neighbouring land normally had to have on it a permanent building in use wholly or mainly as a 'place of human habitation or resort'.[97] Additionally, the building had to be within 100 metres of the burdened property.[98] The policy was that only in such circumstances did the superior have a genuine interest to enforce the burden. About 2,000 notices were registered.[99] This is a small number when set against the total number of separate titles in Scotland.[100]

Rule 7: non-feudal burdens which are not part of a common scheme

14.34   Rule 6 concerned only real burdens imposed in a feudal deed prior to 28 November 2004. In contrast, rule 7 is restricted to burdens imposed in *non-feudal deeds* such as *dispositions*. It applies in cases of subdivision, but *not* where there is a common scheme. The rule is that the benefited property is implied to be the land

---

[94]   See Gretton and Reid *Conveyancing* para 13–15.

[95]   TC(S)A 2003, ss 56(1)(b) and 122(1).

[96]   AFT(S)A 2000, s 18.

[97]   A building was not required in limited cases, for example for rights of pre-emption and redemption or where the nominated benefited property was to be minerals or salmon fishings. See AFT(S) A 2000, s 18(7)(b) and (c). As to whether a toilet block qualified as a building in use as a place of human habitation or resort, see *SQ1 Ltd v Earl of Hopetoun* 2 October 2007, Lands Tribunal, discussed in K G C Reid and G L Gretton *Conveyancing 2007* (2008) 147–150.

[98]   AFT(S)A 2000, s 18(7)(a).

[99]   K G C Reid and G L Gretton *Conveyancing 2004* (2005) 95.

[100]   Approximately 2.3 million.

retained in the neighbourhood at the time that the burdens were imposed.[101] This was established in *J A Mactaggart & Co v Harrower.*[102] For example, Joelle sells a plot of her land to Keith and imposes real burdens. The benefited property is the land which she retains. Say, however, that she sold a second plot to Leah and imposed the same burdens. In principle, Leah's land would be a benefited property as regards Keith's because it was retained at the time of the grant by Joelle to Keith. But because a common scheme is capable of arising in respect of the plots of Keith and Leah, rule 7 does not confer any enforcement rights upon Leah.[103]

14.35   Rule 7 does not apply after 28 November 2014 unless a preservation notice was registered prior to that date nominating the benefited property.[104] The notice had to be registered against both the benefited and the burdened properties.[105]

ENFORCEMENT

General

14.36   For a real burden to be enforced, both title and interest must be proven.[106]

Title to enforce

14.37   Title to enforce is tied to the benefited property and it was seen above how this property is identified.[107] The owner of it has title to enforce.[108] So too does any tenant or proper liferenter holding a real right, or non-entitled spouse or non-entitled civil partner with occupancy rights.[109] In addition, where a real burden imposes an obligation to pay a cost, the benefited property's owner at the time when the cost was occurred has title too.[110] For example, where someone bears a maintenance cost which is to be shared between a number of properties and then that person sells their property (the benefited property) they still have title to enforce.

---

[101]   TC(S)A 2003, ss 49(2) and 50. The rule does not apply to pre-emption rights. See *Braes v Keeper of the Registers of Scotland* 2010 SLT 689.
[102]   (1906) 8 F 1101.
[103]   TC(S)A 2003, s 50(6).
[104]   TC(S)A 2003, s 49(2).
[105]   TC(S)A 2003, s 50(3). Only 159 notices were registered. See K G C Reid and G L Gretton, *Conveyancing 2014* (2015) 124.
[106]   TC(S)A 2003, s 8(1).
[107]   See **PARAS 14.20–14.36** above.
[108]   TC(S)A 2003, s 8(2).
[109]   TC(S)A 2003, s 8(2)(a) and (b). But not as regards pre-emptions or other options to acquire the burdened property. See TC(S)A 2003, s 8(4). On tenants, see **CHAPTER 20** below. On proper liferenters, see **CHAPTER 22** below. On non-entitled spouses and partners, see **CHAPTER 11** above.
[110]   TC(S)A 2003, s 8(2)(c).

Interest to enforce

14.38   Interest to enforce is different from title to enforce: both are necessary for enforcement. There is interest to enforce where the breach of the real burden causes or will cause 'material detriment' to 'the value or enjoyment' of the right held in the benefited property.[111] Two factors particularly relevant are the distance between the properties and the extent of the breach. The greater the distance and the lesser the breach, the less likely it is that there is interest. For example, there is more likely to be interest to enforce a burden preventing building where the burdened proprietor has erected a block of flats as opposed to a shed.

14.39   In *Barker v Lewis*[112] the proprietor of a house in a small rural development began to run a bed-and-breakfast business, which disturbed the neighbouring householders. It breached a real burden prohibiting trading. The neighbours sought interdict, but were unsuccessful before the sheriff, who equated 'material' with 'substantial'.[113] The case was appealed to the sheriff principal. He held that the test was not so strict, but, on the facts, agreed with the sheriff's conclusion that interest had not been shown. In contrast in *Kettlewell v Turning Point Scotland*[114] there was held to be interest to prevent a house being used by a charity as the home for four unrelated disabled adults. The real burden required the house to be used for one family only. There was evidence that the proposed use would reduce the *value*[115] of the neighbouring houses by between 5 and 15% because of noise and parking issues due to carers arriving and departing. More recently, the Lands Tribunal has suggested a lower test from that applied in *Barker*, namely that 'material' should be interpreted as the opposite of 'immaterial'.[116]

14.40   There is a special rule for affirmative burdens requiring the payment of or contribution towards a cost. Here, a person who is seeking performance of the obligation, and who has grounds to do so, has interest.[117] For example, if in a common scheme, a number of proprietors must meet the repair bill for a private road, the proprietor who pays the contractor has interest to recover from the others their share.

---

[111]   TC(S)A 2003, s 8(3)(a). For discussion, see R Rennie 'Interest to Enforce Real Burdens' in R Rennie *The Promised Land: Property Law Reform* (2008) 1–24.
[112]   2007 SLT (Sh Ct) 48, aff'd 2008 SLT (Sh Ct) 17.
[113]   For criticism, see K G C Reid 'Interest to Enforce Real Burdens: How Material is "Material"?' (2007) 11 *Edin LR* 440.
[114]   2011 SLT (Sh Ct) 143.
[115]   In contrast, the focus in *Barker* was on *enjoyment*.
[116]   *Franklin v Lawson* 2013 SLT (Lands Tr) 81 at para [10]. See also *Whitelaw v Acheson,* 28 September 2012, Lands Tribunal.
[117]   TC(S)A 2003, s 8(3)(b).

Liability

14.41   Negative and ancillary burdens are enforceable against the owner of the burdened property and any tenant or other occupier.[118] In effect, they are real rights. The policy is that a prohibition would have little practical value if the owner could circumvent it by, say, granting a lease. In contrast, affirmative burdens, such as obligations to maintain or pay costs, are enforceable only against the owner. All that is required here is that one person performs and the law places that obligation on the party who has ownership.[119]

14.42   Where an owner is liable to perform under a real burden, for example by paying a repair bill, liability persists if the property is sold.[120] The incoming owner is in principle severally liable.[121] Where, however, the obligation is to pay for work already carried out, except where it has been carried out by the local authority, there is only liability if a 'notice of potential liability for costs' has been registered against the title to the property.[122] A similar rule for tenements is found in T(S)A 2004.[123]

Remedies

14.43   At common law it was competent to have an 'irritancy' clause in the constitutive deed.[124] This meant that the benefited proprietor in principle could go to court and have the burdened proprietor's title extinguished if a real burden was breached. The recent legislative reforms sensibly abolished this draconian remedy.[125] This leaves enforcement to be carried out by normal court remedies: action for payment; interdict; specific implement and damages. In the case of interdict, which will be the normal remedy for negative burdens, speed is of the essence. A court is unlikely to order a building which has been completed to be taken down again, even although it breaches a burden.[126] The remedy will become damages and it may be difficult for the benefited proprietor to quantify a loss.

Interpretation

14.44   In the interpretation of real burdens, there is a presumption in favour of freedom. Ambiguous terms are construed *contra proferentem*, that is against the

---

[118]   TC(S)A 2003, s 9(2).
[119]   TC(S)A 2003, s 9(1).
[120]   TC(S)A 2003, s 10(1).
[121]   TC(S)A 2003, s 10(2). In other words, the benefited proprietor(s) may enforce against him or her.
[122]   TC(S)A 2003, s 10(2A) and 10A.
[123]   See **PARA 16.22** below.
[124]   Compare irritancy clauses in leases. See **PARA 20.30** below.
[125]   AFT(S)A 2000, s 53 (feudal burdens); TC(S)A 2003, s 67 (non-feudal burdens). The competency of irritancy in non-feudal cases was in fact doubtful anyway.
[126]   An analogy may be made with encroachments. See **PARA 18.15** below.

benefited party. In one case, a restriction requiring the property to be used as 'a private dwelling house' was held not to be breached when 25 orphan girls were in residence there.[127] Similarly, piano lessons or legal consultations may be offered in properties subject to this type of burden, provided that the business use is ancillary to the residential use.[128] In another case, an obligation to build a house 'which may include a garage' did not prevent a second garage from being erected.[129]

14.45   The approach of the courts in the past to real burdens verged on the hostile.[130] This was probably because before 1970 it was not possible to go to the Lands Tribunal to seek variation or discharge. In recent times the attitude has softened somewhat.[131] Moreover, TC(S)A 2003 now says that 'real burdens shall be construed in the same manner as other provisions of deeds which relate to land and are intended for registration'.[132] The effect is that they should be interpreted reasonably, but objectively. But the presumption in favour of freedom remains, so it is not clear that any of the cases mentioned in **PARA 14.44** would be decided differently today.

DIVISION

Burdened property

14.46   Where a burdened property is divided, each part remains subject to the real burden.[133] This applies whether the division took place before or after 28 November 2004. There is an exception where the burden does not relate to one of the parts. For example, a house with a large garden might be subject to a requirement to maintain the house. If part of the garden is sold, that real burden will not apply to it, because it relates to the house only.

Benefited property

14.47   If a benefited property is divided, the part transferred normally will cease to be able to enforce the real burden.[134] There are three exceptions.

(1)   The rule can be overridden by making contrary provision in the conveyance.[135]

---

[127]   *Brown v Crum Ewing's Trs* 1918 1 SLT 340.
[128]   *Colquhoun's Curator Bonis v Glen's Tr* 1920 SC 737; *Low v Scottish Amicable Building Society* 1940 SLT 295.
[129]   *Carswell v Goldie* 1967 SLT 339.
[130]   Reid *Property* para 415.
[131]   See, for example, *Grampian Joint Police Board v Pearson* 2001 SC 772.
[132]   TC(S)A 2003, s 14.
[133]   TC(S)A 2003, s 13.
[134]   TC(S)A 2003, s 12(1).
[135]   TC(S)A 2003, s 12(1) and (3).

(2) It does not apply to real burdens imposed under a common scheme.[136] Suppose that a house is situated in a development subject to a deed of conditions creating community burdens. If part of the garden is sold, it will continue to be a benefited property in relation to the burdens.

(3) The rule only applies to conveyances since 28 November 2004.

FEUDAL ABOLITION

14.48   Feudal abolition in principle extinguished feudal real burdens.[137] In practice, most continue to exist, non-feudally, because they were imposed as part of a common scheme and thus remain enforceable under the rules outlined above.[138] Moreover, as has been seen, a procedure existed for superiors to reallot feudal burdens if they owned neighbouring land which satisfied certain conditions.[139] In addition, the abolition legislation allowed some feudal burdens to be converted into personal real burdens.[140] This means that essentially the only burdens which were lost were those which were not part of a common scheme and did not have a reallotment or conversion notice registered. If such burdens entered the Land Register, they will continue to be there, because the Keeper could not begin to remove them until 28 November 2014.[141]

PERSONAL REAL BURDENS

General

14.49   As has been seen, feudal real burdens could be enforced even although the superior (the benefited proprietor) did not own any land neighbouring the burdened property.[142] Feudal abolition ended this. It was felt, however, that it was justified in a limited number of cases for there to be real burdens which do not have a benefited property. Accordingly, TC(S)A 2003 introduced the 'personal real burden'.[143] As will be seen, they are generally restricted as to content or holder or both. Apart from the absence of a benefited property, the rules are much the same as for praedial real burdens. Interest to enforce, however, is presumed.[144] Nine types of personal real

---

[136]   TC(S)A 2003, s 12(4).
[137]   AFT(S)A 2000, s 17. On the feudal system generally, see **APPENDIX** below.
[138]   See **PARAS 14.24–14.30** above.
[139]   See **PARA 14.33** above.
[140]   AFT(S)A 2000, ss 18A, 18B, 18C, 27 and 27A. On personal real burdens, see **PARAS 14.50–14.58** below. The numbers of such conversion notices were low: about 1,000 in total. See K G C Reid and G L Gretton *Conveyancing 2004* (2005) 95–96.
[141]   AFT(S)A 2000, s 46 and Abolition of Feudal Tenure etc. (Scotland) (Prescribed Periods) Order 2004 (SSI 2004/478) para 3.
[142]   See **PARA 14.2** above.
[143]   See further Paisley 'Personal Real Burdens' 2005 *JR* 377.
[144]   TC(S)A 2003, s 47.

burden are recognised.[145] They are given in the following paragraphs. In practice, all are unusual.

Conservation burdens

14.50   These can be held only by the Scottish Ministers or by bodies listed by statutory instrument.[146] This list currently includes all local authorities, Scottish Natural Heritage and the Royal Society for the Protection of Birds. Conservation burdens must be for 'preserving or protecting for the benefit of the public the architectural or historical characteristics of land' of its 'other special characteristics' which can include nature conservation.[147] The right to a conservation burden can be assigned to another conservation body or to the Scottish Ministers.[148] If a conservation body is de-listed, the burden is extinguished.[149]

Climate change burdens

14.51   These burdens have the purpose of reducing greenhouse gas emissions and must consist of an obligation for the burdened property to meet specified mitigation and adaptation standards.[150] Climate change burdens can only be held by the Scottish Ministers, any public body entitled to hold a conservation burden, and trusts.[151]

Economic development burdens

14.52   Only the Scottish Ministers or local authorities may hold these burdens.[152] An economic development burden must promote economic development.[153] What is envisaged is a public body selling land, but requiring it to be used for a particular type of industry. An obligation to pay money can be constituted as an economic development burden.[154] For example, the purchaser may be required to make a payment if the land is subsequently sold. The right to an economic development burden cannot be assigned.[155]

---

[145]   TC(S)A 2003, ss 1(3) and 46A.
[146]   TC(S)A 2003, s 38(4).
[147]   TC(S)A 2003, s 38(1).
[148]   TC(S)A 2003, s 39.
[149]   TC(S)A 2003, s 42.
[150]   TC(S)A 2003, s 46A(1) and (2).
[151]   TC(S)A 2003, s 46A(3). See A Steven and R Leslie, 'Cool drafting' 2010 JLSS Nov/54.
[152]   TC(S)A 2003, s 45(1).
[153]   TC(S)A 2003, s 45(1). See *Teague Developments Ltd v City of Edinburgh Council* 27 Feb 2008, Lands Tribunal.
[154]   TC(S)A 2003, s 45(3).
[155]   TC(S)A 2003, s 45(4)(b).

Health care burdens

14.53   Only the Scottish Ministers can hold these burdens, which must promote the provision of health care facilities.[156] For example, land might be sold to a builder on condition that accommodation for nurses is constructed. Like the economic development burden, an obligation to pay a sum of money may be imposed and the right to the burden cannot be assigned.[157]

Maritime burdens

14.54   The Crown on behalf of the public may impose real burdens on the sea bed or foreshore.[158] These cannot be assigned.[159] For example, a section of the sea bed may be sold for the purposes of fish farming, but under certain conditions.

Rural housing burdens

14.55   Only designated 'rural housing bodies' may hold these burdens.[160] Their content is limited to pre-emption rights.[161] The policy is to protect bodies that offer housing at a reduced price. If the purchaser wishes later to sell, a rural housing burden enables the body to buy it back and make it available to others in need of suitable accommodation, as opposed (for example) to it becoming a holiday home. Unlike ordinary pre-emption rights, they are not extinguished on first sale.[162] Like conservation burdens, rural housing burdens are assignable (but only to other rural housing bodies) and will be extinguished if the body is de-listed.[163]

Manager burdens

14.56   These can be imposed by a developer. They give the sole right to appoint a manager for a development until the earlier of (a) 90 days after the last property in the development is sold and (b) the long-stop date.[164] For sheltered or retirement housing developments, the long-stop date is three years after the burden was

---

[156]   TC(S)A 2003, s 46(1).
[157]   TC(S)A 2003, s 46(3) and (4)(b).
[158]   TC(S)A 2003, s 44(1). The right is limited to territorial waters. See TC(S)A 2003, s 44(3) and see **PARA 17.4** below.
[159]   TC(S)A 2003, s 44(2).
[160]   TC(S)A 2003, s 43(1) and (5).
[161]   TC(S)A 2003, s 43(1). On pre-emption rights, see **PARA 13.12** above.
[162]   TC(S)A 2003, s 84(1).
[163]   TC(S)A 2003, s 43(10).
[164]   TC(S)A 2003, s 63(1), (2) and (4).

imposed.[165] For former local authority housing, it is 30 years.[166] In all other cases, it is five years.[167] The policy is to let developers keep a measure of control over incomplete developments. A manager burden is assignable.[168]

Personal pre-emption burdens

14.57   Where a superior registered a conversion notice for a pre-emption burden before 28 November 2004, this became a personal pre-emption burden.[169] The category is thus limited to former feudal burdens which conferred a right of pre-emption. These will normally be extinguished upon the first sale of the property.[170]

Personal redemption burdens

14.58   Like personal pre-emption burdens, these are confined to former feudal burdens for which the superior has registered a conversion notice.[171] Few notices were registered.[172] If created in a post-1974 deed, the burden is limited to a period of 20 years from its constitution.[173]

EXTINCTION

Express discharge

Minutes of waiver

14.59   The form of deed used to extinguish a real burden is variously known as a deed of discharge, or deed or minute of waiver. Obviously, this must be granted by the holder of the burden. The price is a matter for negotiation. (If the burden is one of doubtful validity or one that the Lands Tribunal would be prepared to discharge, the price will be low.) The deed then requires to be registered against the title to the burdened property.[174] Often a minute of waiver varies a burden rather than completely discharging it. For example, a prohibition against building might be waived but only for a new garage.

---

[165]   TC(S)A 2003, s 63(5)(b).
[166]   TC(S)A 2003, s 63(5)(a) and (6).
[167]   TC(S)A 2003, s 63(5)(c).
[168]   TC(S)A 2003, s 63(3).
[169]   AFT(S)A 2000, s 18A.
[170]   Provided that the property is offered to the holder. See TC(S)A 2003, ss 82 and 84(1).
[171]   AFT(S)A 2000, s 18A.
[172]   A total of 642 notices were registered in respect of personal pre-emption and personal redemption burdens. See K G C Reid and G L Gretton *Conveyancing 2004* (2005) 95.
[173]   Land Tenure Reform (Scotland) Act 1974, s 12. See **PARA 14.13** above.
[174]   TC(S)A 2003, ss 15 and 48.

Community burdens

14.60   In the case of community burdens, in principle all benefited proprietors must sign. This is often not practical, as it may involve getting many signatories. The general rule is therefore mitigated by special rules of variation and discharge which allow for minutes of waiver to bind non-signatories.

14.61   TC(S)A 2003, s 33 provides that a simple majority of the owners in the community[175] (or a manager on behalf of the majority of owners in the community) can sign a deed of variation or discharge.[176] Once signed the deed must be intimated to non-signatories. This requires a copy of the deed, and a notice to be sent to non-signatory benefited proprietors.[177] The notice must identify the affected property and the nature of the variation, and intimate that the recipient has at least eight weeks to apply to the Lands Tribunal to preserve the burden.[178]

14.62   An alternative procedure is available under TC(S)A 2003, s 35 which requires the deed to be signed only by the owners of 'adjacent units', that is those properties within 4 metres of the burdened property excluding public roads less than 20 metres wide.[179] This is intended to mirror the neighbour notification rules in planning applications. There are generally two possible options for intimation here: a notice sent to each non-signatory benefited owner;[180] or attaching a notice to the burdened property and to lamp-posts in the vicinity of the burdened property.[181] In practice the latter is more likely because the uncertainty in relation to implied enforcement rights may make the identification of the parameters of a community difficult.[182] If there are no lamp-posts within 100 metres then an advertisement in a local newspaper is competent.[183] The notices identify the burdened property and the burdens in question and intimate to the benefited proprietors that they have eight weeks to apply to the Lands Tribunal to preserve the burden.[184]

14.63   A benefited proprietor who has not assented to the deed may object by applying to the Tribunal within eight weeks of intimation of the proposal to register it.[185] The application is then notified to the burdened proprietor.[186] If he or she does not respond the burden is preserved.[187] If the burdened proprietor objects to the

---

[175]   When calculating what constitutes a majority, the property seeking the waiver is counted. See TC(S) A 2003, s 33(3). It is possible for the deed creating the burden to make special provision, e.g., require a two-thirds majority. See TC(S)A 2003, s 33(1)(a).
[176]   TC(S)A 2003, s 33.
[177]   TC(S)A 2003, s 34(1) and (2).
[178]   TC(S)A 2003, Sch 4.
[179]   TC(S)A 2003, ss 32 and 125. This procedure is not available for facility or service burdens, or in sheltered or retirement housing developments. See s 35(1)(a).
[180]   TC(S)A 2003, s 36(2)(a) and Sch 5.
[181]   TC(S)A 2003, s 36(2)(b) and Sch 6.
[182]   See **PARAS 14.24–14.26** above.
[183]   TC(S)A 2003, s 36(2)(c).
[184]   TC(S)A 2003, s 36(3) and Schs 5 and 6.
[185]   TC(S)A 2003, s 34(3) and 37(1).
[186]   TC(S)A 2003, s 93(1)(c).
[187]   TC(S)A 2003, s 97(1)(c).

application the preservation of the burden is considered by the Tribunal, but it will grant it only if the variation is not in the best interests of the proprietors of all the properties in the community; or is unfairly prejudicial to one or more of them.[188]

14.64   In order to register the deed executed under both TC(S)A 2003, ss 33 and 35, an application must be made to the Tribunal seeking a certificate that either no applications to preserve the burdens were timeously received or that applications were received but withdrawn.[189] An oath must also be sworn or affirmed by the burdened proprietor confirming compliance with the appropriate intimation procedure and the deed endorsed to this effect.[190] It is then registered and the burden is thereby varied or extinguished.

'Sunset rule'

14.65   A special termination procedure was introduced by TC(S)A 2003, known informally as the 'sunset rule'. In principle, any burden created in a deed registered at least 100 years ago may be discharged by the burdened owner.[191] This person is alarmingly called the 'terminator'.[192] The procedure is not available for conservation burdens, maritime burdens, facility burdens and service burdens.[193] A notice is drawn up in the required form[194] and intimated to the benefited proprietors. Those within 4 metres (discounting roads less than 20 metres wide) are sent a copy of the notice.[195] More distant neighbours are notified through posting notices on lamp-posts within the vicinity of the burdened property and by a notice placed at the property itself.[196]

14.66   After receiving notice benefited owners must then decide whether to apply to the Lands Tribunal for renewal of the burden.[197] They have eight weeks to do this.[198] If the application to preserve the burden is successful the burden survives. If unsuccessful the burdens will be varied or discharged. Where no application to preserve is made,[199] the notice of termination can be registered provided it is

---

[188]   For an example of an unsuccessful application, see *Sheltered Housing Management Ltd v Jack* 2007 GWD 32-533.
[189]   TC(S)A 2003, ss 34(4)–(6) and 37(2).
[190]   TC(S)A 2003, s 37(4).
[191]   TC(S)A 2003, s 20. See *Gibson v Anderson* 3 May 2012, Lands Tribunal.
[192]   TC(S)A 2003, s 20(2).
[193]   TC(S)A 2003, s 20(3).
[194]   TC(S)A 2003, s 21 and Schs 2 and 3.
[195]   TC(S)A 2003, s 21(2)(a) and (3)(b).
[196]   TC(S)A 2003, s 21(2)(b). If there are no lamp-posts, advertisement in a local newspaper is competent. See TC(S)A 2003, s 21(2)(c).
[197]   TC(S)A 2003, s 90(i)(b)(i). For an example, where the application was unsuccessful, see *Brown v Richardson* 2007 GWD 28-490.
[198]   TC(S)A 2003, s 20(5).
[199]   Or if it does not extend to all the burdens, or all the benefited properties.

endorsed with a Lands Tribunal certificate confirming the lack of applications.[200] When endorsed and registered the burdens are extinguished.[201]

By breach

Negative prescription

14.67 If a real burden is contravened without challenge for five years, it is extinguished to the extent of the breach.[202] For example, if there was a general obligation not to build and a conservatory was constructed, the passing of five years would mean that this addition could not be challenged but it would not prevent a successful objection to the erection of a new house.

Acquiescence

14.68 The idea of acquiescence is that a benefited proprietor who stands by and watches while a real burden is being breached should not be allowed to object later. The common law here, which is not entirely clear, continues to apply.[203] TC(S) A 2003, however, introduces a parallel rule.[204] The following criteria must be met:

(a) material expenditure is incurred by the burdened proprietor (or other person against whom the burden can be enforced, for example a tenant);

(b) the benefit of the expenditure would be substantially lost if the burden were now to be enforced;

(c) *either* the owner of the benefited property consented to the work, whether formally or informally; *or* (and more typically) *all* those with enforcement rights (including tenants) either consented or did not object within 12 weeks after substantial completion; and

(d) the work is sufficiently obvious that those with the right to enforce knew, or should have known, about it.

If these criteria are satisfied the burden will be extinguished to the extent of the breach. Successors of the benefited proprietor(s) will therefore be bound.

14.69 In fact, TC(S)A 2003 goes further to help a burdened proprietor. If the 12-week period has expired, there is a presumption that no objection was made and

---

[200] TC(S)A 2003, s 23.

[201] TC(S)A 2003, s 24. This is subject to the outcome of any Tribunal application which has been made. For example, only one of the benefited proprietors may have applied. The certificate will then disclose the lack of application from the others.

[202] TC(S)A 2003, s 18.

[203] See Reid *Property* para 427. See also S Wortley 'Real Burdens and Personal Bar' in Rennie *The Promised Land: Property Law Reform* 25–70.

[204] TC(S)A 2003, s 16(1). See E C Reid and J W G Blackie, *Personal Bar* (2006) paras 6-29–6-44.

hence that acquiescence has operated.[205] The presumption is difficult to overcome, particularly where the work was completed some time ago.

No interest to enforce

14.70   A real burden which is breached at a time when there is nobody with an interest to enforce is extinguished to the extent of the breach.[206] Thus it might be the case that there is no longer interest to enforce a burden preventing trading when every other house in the street is now used as business premises.[207]

Lands Tribunal

14.71   The Lands Tribunal[208] was given jurisdiction in 1970 to vary or discharge real burdens.[209] This is now regulated by TC(S)A 2003, Pt 9. Any party who is subject to a real burden, servitude or other title condition is entitled to apply to the Tribunal for its variation or discharge.[210] In the case of community burdens it is competent for the proprietors of at least 25% of the units to apply for variation or discharge as regards the community as a whole.[211] When it receives an application, the Tribunal *must* intimate it to various parties, notably the benefited proprietor(s), or – in the case of a personal real burden – the holder.[212] The Tribunal *may* intimate to other parties, for example, tenants, if it thinks fit.[213] The parties to whom intimation is made are given at least 21 days to make representations.[214]

14.72   Where no benefited owner objects to the application, it is normally granted automatically and without further inquiry.[215] In this event the process is effectively an administrative one. Where, however, objection is made, the Tribunal must consider the application on its merits. It may grant the application if it is reasonable so to do.[216] But regard must be had to ten factors set out in TC(S)A 2003, s 100. Each case is therefore decided on the facts. In most cases, however, the Tribunal has granted

---

[205]   TC(S)A 2003, s 16(2).
[206]   TC(S)A 2003, s 17.
[207]   *Howard de Walden Estates Ltd v Bowmaker Ltd* 1965 SC 163. But compare Reid *Property* para 430.
[208]   See http://www.lands-tribunal-scotland.org.uk/
[209]   CFR(S)A 1970, ss 1 and 2. Application was also possible in respect of other 'land obligations' including servitudes.
[210]   TC(S)A 2003, s 90(1)(a).
[211]   TC(S)A 2003, s 91. See *Patterson v Drouet* 14 November 2012, Lands Tribunal.
[212]   TC(S)A 2003, s 93(1).
[213]   TC(S)A 2003, s 93(3).
[214]   TC(S)A 2003, ss 95 and 96.
[215]   TC(S)A 2003, s 97.
[216]   TC(S)A 2003, s 98.

the application.[217] The discharge or variation then takes effect on registration of the Tribunal order.[218]

14.73 The Tribunal is entitled to award compensation to the benefited proprietor but only in very limited circumstances, or to impose a replacement burden.[219] When determining the question of expenses, the Tribunal must pay particular regard to the extent of the application, or any opposition thereto.[220] Hence, an unsuccessful objector is likely to have to meet the applicant's costs.

Compulsory purchase

14.74 The rules here are the same as for servitudes.[221]

Confusion

14.75 This is not strictly a type of termination but may be dealt with conveniently here. If the benefited proprietor becomes owner of the burdened property, the doctrine of confusion naturally prevents enforcement of the real burden. In this situation, TC(S)A 2003 provides that the burden is not extinguished.[222] In effect, it is 'suspended'. This means that if the properties come into different hands once again then it can be enforced. During the period of confusion, however, the proprietor could register a minute of waiver and this would remove the burden.

LITERATURE

14.76 For further accounts, see Gretton and Reid *Conveyancing* ch 13, McDonald *Conveyancing Manual* chs 15, 17 and 18, Rennie *Land Tenure* chs 5–9 and Reid *Feudal Abolition* chs 2–7. TC(S)A 2003 is based on Scottish Law Commission Report on Real Burdens (Scot Law Com No 181, 2000). For a specialist text on the Lands Tribunal jurisdiction, see Todd, A and Wishart, R *The Lands Tribunal for Scotland: Law and Practice* (2012).

---

[217] See, eg, *Ord v Mashford* 2006 SLT (Lands Tr) 15 and *Church of Scotland General Trs v McLaren* 2006 SLT (Lands Tr) 27. For a review of the initial case law, see Reid and Gretton *Conveyancing 2007* (2008) 83–101. See also A Todd and R Wishart *The Lands Tribunal for Scotland: Law and Practice* (2012).
[218] TC(S)A 2003, s 104(2).
[219] TC(S)A 2003, s 90(6)–(11).
[220] TC(S)A 2003, s 103.
[221] See **PARA 13.48** above.
[222] TC(S)A 2003, s 19. Compare the rule for servitudes: see **PARA 13.47** above.

Chapter 15

Landownership

INTRODUCTION

15.1   This chapter covers three private law aspects of landownership:
(1) determination of horizontal and vertical boundaries;
(2) parts and pertinents; and
(3) separate tenements.

A number of related areas, such as boundary walls and encroachment, are treated in the chapter on neighbour law.[1] At the end of the current chapter we also provide a brief account of recent statutory developments in relation to land reform.

HORIZONTAL BOUNDARIES

Land Register

15.2   As discussed elsewhere,[2] land may be registered either in the Sasine Register or in the Land Register. The latter is superseding the former. Ascertaining the horizontal boundaries of land differs as between the two registers. In the Land Register the title sheet for a property will always identify it by means of a plan based on the Ordnance Map eg 'Cadastral unit ANG12345, 65 Patience Terrace, Forfar, DD88 3VZ', edged red on the cadastral map.[3] In the case of flats, the title plan identifies the site of the building and any surrounding ground owned or co-owned by the flat owner. A verbal description, for example 'Flat 2/1 St Alison's Street, Edinburgh, being the northmost flat on the ground floor of the tenement known as 2 St Alison's Street, Edinburgh', is used to identify the flat itself. It follows in the Land Register that, subject to the limits of scaling on the plans used, it is easy to determine the exact boundaries.

Sasine Register

15.3   In contrast to the Land Register, the Sasine Register is not map-based. Indeed, though this register was established in 1617, it only became competent to record plans attached to deeds in 1924.[4] While plans have been increasingly used, there is no requirement for this and therefore many titles to land are not based on a plan.

15.4   There is a distinction between a 'bounding' description, which states the boundaries, and a 'general' description, which does not. A bounding description can do this in various ways. It might say 'bounded on the north by the southern edge of the High Street'. It can use measurements. It can be a pictorial representation,

---

[1]   See **CHAPTER 18** below.
[2]   See **CHAPTER 7** above.
[3]   LR(S)A 2012, s 6(1)(a)(i). See **PARAS 7.27–7.30** above.
[4]   Conveyancing (Scotland) Act 1924, s 48.

ie a plan. It was common for modern Sasine deeds to use all of these methods. If there is an irreconcilable conflict between them there are rules for resolving this.[5] In particular, the plan will prevail if it is declared to be 'taxative'. It is also possible to have a bounding description by reference to an earlier recorded deed containing such a description.[6] This means that there is no need to have a long verbal description or prepare a fresh plan every time the land is transferred.

15.5 A general description is vaguer than a bounding description. It might be a postal address or the name of a farm. As the boundaries are not given, the dimensions of the title will need to be determined by extrinsic evidence. That evidence is normally the state of possession. Moreover, where there has been possession for ten years which is open, peaceable and without judicial interruption, a title to the land as possessed will be established by positive prescription.[7] This is subject to the deed containing the description being valid on the face of it and being capable of being read as covering the land as possessed.

Sasine Register to Land Register

15.6 A general description will not suffice for the Land Register. So if there is land which, in the Sasine Register, has had only a general description, or indeed a bounding description that is not precise enough, for the land is to be transferred to the Land Register, a plan will be needed so that the Keeper can plot the property on the Ordnance Map.

VERTICAL BOUNDARIES

From the heavens to the centre of the earth

15.7 Ownership of land is *a coelo usque ad centrum* – 'from the heavens to the centre [of the earth]'. Thus, landownership is conical. Above the ground it includes airspace, to a ceiling of 100 kilometres,[8] and anything that has acceded, such as buildings and trees. In England, the position is different. The idea that there is ownership up to the heavens was criticised by a judge as 'leading to the absurdity of a trespass ... being committed by a satellite every time it passes over a suburban garden'.[9] So, south of the border, a landowner only has rights in the airspace 'to

---

[5] Gordon and Wortley *Scottish Land Law* para 4.08.
[6] Conveyancing (Scotland) Act 1874, s 61.
[7] PL(S)A 1973, s 1. See **PARAS 6.17–6.19** above.
[8] Art II of the Outer Space Treaty 1967 provides that 'outer space ... is not subject to national appropriation by claim of sovereignty'. Since national sovereignty ends where space begins, presumably heritable title stops there too. International law has not yet defined the start of space but it is generally regarded as being 100 km above sea level.
[9] *Bernstein v Skyviews and General Ltd* [1978] QB 479 at 487 per Griffiths J.

such height as is necessary for the ordinary use and enjoyment of his land'.[10] The ownership of airspace enables action against trespass into it, as in the situation where the jib of a crane swings across without permission.[11] In the case of aircraft, however, statute provides that there is no trespass if the flight is at a reasonable height, having regard to the wind, the weather and all the circumstances of the case.[12]

The exception of separate tenements

15.8   Ownership from the heavens to the centre of the earth is subject to separate tenements such as minerals and flats. These are discussed below.[13]

PARTS AND PERTINENTS

General

15.9   Ownership of a piece of land carries with it ownership of the 'parts and pertinents'. These are things which are transferred to the new owner automatically, without the need for express written provision. It was nevertheless standard (albeit pointless) practice in a disposition of land in the Sasine Register to have a clause conveying the parts and pertinents. In the Land Register, this is usually omitted. 'Parts' is an obscure and possibly meaningless term. It may mean things that have acceded.[14] 'Pertinents' has a fairly clear meaning: rights exercisable beyond the boundaries of the principal land. Pertinents divide into:
  (1) corporeal pertinents, subdividing into:
       (a) additional land and
       (b) rights of common property, and
  (2) incorporeal pertinents.

Corporeal pertinents

Additional land

15.10   There may be additional heritable property which is regarded as a pertinent of the land. Examples include lock-up garages and parking spaces serving a house or flat. It will become a pertinent in one of two ways. The first is by express grant.

---

[10] *Bernstein* at 488. Professor Paisley is sympathetic to this view: 'since the advent of aviation and the use of space ... any theory asserting infinite nature of the upward boundaries is questionable' (Paisley *Land Law* para 4.22).
[11] *Brown v Lee Constructions Ltd* 1977 SLT (Notes) 61.
[12] Civil Aviation Act 1982, s 76.
[13] See **PARAS 15.13–15.18** below.
[14] Reid *Property* para 200.

For example, when a building company sells a new flat for the first time it conveys it together with a parking space. In the Land Register the pertinent then expressly appears on the title sheet. The second way is by positive prescription in the Sasine Register on the basis of a habile title.[15] However, it is not possible to acquire title to a pertinent this way where a bounding description is used in the would-be foundation writ and the pertinent lies outwith the boundaries of that.[16] In the Land Register, which is map-based, prescription beyond the boundaries on the map is clearly not possible.

Common property

15.11 Rights of common property may be pertinents of the principal land. The most important example is flats. It is possible to make certain parts of the tenement, such as the roof, common property by expressly granting *pro indiviso* shares of these to the flat owners. Moreover, under the Tenements (Scotland) Act 2004, s 3, a number of the parts of the building, notably the close or stair, are deemed to be owned in common and pertinents of the flats which they serve.[17] An example not involving a tenement is a common recreation area owned by the houses surrounding it. In the Land Register such property can be the subject of a shared-plot title sheet.[18]

Incorporeal pertinents

15.12 The only example of any importance of an incorporeal pertinent is the benefit of a title condition,[19] such as a praedial real burden or servitude exercisable over a neighbour's land. As such, it is enforceable by the owner for the time being of the principal land against the owner of the adjacent land.

SEPARATE TENEMENTS

General

15.13 The doctrine of separate tenements is the exception to the rule, discussed above, that ownership of land is from the heavens to the centre of the earth.[20] A 'separate tenement' is a section of the land or a right to do something on the land which is capable of separate ownership. This is a different meaning to 'tenement' in

---

[15]   See **PARAS 6.17–6.19** above.
[16]   Stair II, 3, 73; Erskine II, 6, 3; Bell *Principles* § 739.
[17]   See **PARAS 16.10–16.11** below.
[18]   LR(S)A 2012, s 17. See **PARA 7.36** above.
[19]   See **PARA 14.3** above.
[20]   See **PARAS 15.7–15.8** above.

the sense of a block of flats.[21] A separate tenement is transferred in its own right. It is also possible to create subordinate rights, such as a standard security over it.[22] There are two types of separate tenement: those which are 'conventional' and those which are 'legal'.

Conventional separate tenements

15.14   Where a section of land is separated from the remainder by express conveyance, this is known as a 'conventional separate tenement'. Below ground, it appears that there is no restriction on the creation of conventional separate tenements. The leading example is minerals[23] but tunnels and underground shelters may be other possibilities. Above ground, the position is rather limited. It is, of course, accepted that buildings can be divided into flats. Property such as trees or pipes which have become heritable by accession cannot be made into separate tenements.[24] The position as regards bridges and unoccupied airspace is unclear.

15.15   With one modern exception, all conventional separate tenements must be corporeal. That exception is sporting rights reserved by superiors before 28 November 2004 under the feudal abolition legislation.[25] These are restricted to rights of fishing and game.[26] There were in fact only 65 such preservations.[27] The separate tenement created here is rather peculiar, as it can be non-exclusive.[28] Therefore the right, for example, to fish can be shared with the owner of the principal land. This is contrary to the usual notion of separate tenements.

Legal separate tenements

15.16   As a matter of legal theory all land in Scotland was originally owned by the Crown. Historically, certain rights were considered so important that they were impliedly reserved when land was granted. These rights, known as the *regalia minora*, could be expressly granted to either the new landowner or another person. If they were not, they remained with the Crown. With one exception, all legal separate tenements in so far as not already granted out are Crown property. They can be either corporeal or incorporeal.

---

[21]   But the individual flats are conventional separate tenements. See **PARA 15.14** below.
[22]   CFR(S)A 1970, s 9(2), (8)(b).
[23]   But gold, silver and coal when still in the ground are legal separate tenements. On minerals generally, see R Rennie *Minerals and the Law in Scotland* (2001).
[24]   *Compugraphics International Ltd v Nikolic* 2011 SC 744.
[25]   AFT(S)A 2000, s 65A.
[26]   AFT(S)A 2000, s 65A(9).
[27]   K G C Reid and G L Gretton *Conveyancing 2004* (2005) 96.
[28]   AFT(S)A 2000, s 65A(6).

15.17   The main legal separate tenements are as follows:

(a) The right to fish for salmon. This is the most important legal separate tenement. If, for example, a section of river is sold by the Crown to Audrey, this will include the right to fish for fish other than salmon. The salmon fishing rights do not form part of this title – unless also conveyed – and may be held by someone other than the owner of the river bed or the banks.[29] If Barry owns the salmon rights, both he and Audrey could fish on the same stretch of the river, but for different fish.

(b) The right to gather mussels and oysters.[30]

(c) Mines of gold and silver. Of course, such metals are rare in Scotland. Under the Royal Mines Act 1424, the oldest Scottish statute still in force, mines of these are reserved from grants of land by the Crown. There is, however, a statutory right giving landowners the right to obtain a separate grant of such mines within their land. In return they must pay the Crown one-tenth of all metal mined.[31]

(d) Petroleum and natural gas.[32]

(e) Coal. This is the exception to the rule that the legal separate tenements are part of the *regalia minora*. Coal is vested in the Coal Authority.[33]

No accession across the boundaries

15.18   Accession cannot take place across the boundaries of separate tenements. For example, a chandelier hung by Tom from the ceiling of his ground-floor flat will not accede to the flat above.

LAND REFORM

General

15.19   Recent years have seen a number of statutes being enacted by the Scottish Parliament with the objective of reforming landownership. In particular, there has been a desire to facilitate acquisition of land by community groups.

Land Reform (Scotland) Act 2003

15.20   This legislation has three parts. Part 1, which deals with the so-called 'right to roam', is covered in **CHAPTER 19** below. Part 2, introduced a right to buy for

---

[29]   Stair II, 3, 69.
[30]   Reid *Property* paras 320–330.
[31]   Mines and Metals Act 1592.
[32]   Petroleum Act 1998, Sch 3, para 3.
[33]   Coal Industry Act 1994, s 7(3).

rural community bodies. The right is one of pre-emption, that is to say it depends on the owner deciding to sell. In contrast, the right to buy in Part 3, in favour of crofting community bodies, is not so limited.[34] The owner can be compelled to sell.[35] For both Parts, the consent of the Scottish Ministers is required for the purchase to proceed and market value has to be paid.[36]

Land Reform Review Group

15.21   The Scottish Government established an independent Land Reform Review Group in 2012. It published an interim report in 2013. Its final report, entitled *The Land of Scotland and the Common Good*, was published in 2014.[37] According to its preface, the report seeks to examine 'how the arrangements governing possession and use of land facilitate or inhibit progress towards achieving a Scotland which is economically successful, socially just and environmentally sustainable.' It makes 62 recommendations. A number of these have been taken forward by the Scottish Government following consultation, leading in particular to the Community Empowerment (Scotland) Act 2015 and the Land Reform (Scotland) Act 2016.

Community Empowerment (Scotland) Act 2015 (CE(S)A 2015)

15.22   Under this Act the community right to buy in Part 2 of LR(S)A 2003 is extended from rural Scotland to the entire country.[38] As mentioned above, that right depends on the owner wanting to sell. But CE(S)A 2015 also prospectively amends LR(S)A 2003 to introduce a right of compulsory acquisition by community bodies of specified types of land and buildings.[39] A building which is someone's home is excluded.[40] The right can only be exercised in respect of land which the Scottish Ministers regard as wholly or mainly abandoned or neglected, or where they are satisfied that the use or management of the land is such that it is resulting in or causing harm, directly or indirectly, to the environmental wellbeing of a relevant community.[41] It remains to be seen how widely the criteria will be interpreted by Ministers. They also require to be satisfied among other things that the acquisition is in the public interest and compatible with furthering the achievement of sustainable development, and that the achievement of sustainable development would be unlikely

---

[34]   On crofting, see **PARA 20.50** below.
[35]   In *Pairc Crofters Ltd v Scottish Ministers* [2012] CSIH 96 a challenge to this legislation on the basis of the ECHR failed.
[36]   LR(S)A 2003 ss 51, 59, 73 and 88.
[37]   See www.gov.scot/About/Review/land-reform/events/FinalReport23May2014.
[38]   CE(S)A 2015, s 36.
[39]   LR(S)A 2003, Part 3A as inserted by CE(S)A 2015, s 74.
[40]   LR(S)A 2003, s 97C(5)(a).
[41]   LR(S)A 2003, s 97C(2).

to be furthered by the current owner.[42] The decision by Ministers can be appealed to the sheriff.[43] Where acquisition proceeds market value must be paid.[44]

15.23   CE(S)A 2015 will also allow community bodies to request that certain public bodies, including the Scottish Government, local authorities and Scottish Water, sell or lease land to them.[45] This is to be known as an 'asset transfer request'. The public body must take into account certain factors when considering the request, including whether it would promote economic development and social or environmental wellbeing, and whether it would be likely to reduce inequalities of outcome which result from socio-economic disadvantage.[46] It must agree to the request unless there are reasonable grounds for not doing so.[47] There is a right of appeal to the Scottish Ministers.[48] An obligation is also imposed on the relevant public bodies to have a register of the land which it owns or leases.[49] This will promote transparency of ownership[50] as well as helping community bodies which are considering making a request.

Land Reform (Scotland) Act 2016 (LR(S)A 2016)

15.24   Once brought fully into force, LR(S)A 2016 will make further reforms. Only the most important are mentioned here. Part 1 requires the Scottish Ministers to publish a 'land rights and responsibilities statement', that is to say a statement of principles for land rights and responsibilities in Scotland.[51] In preparing the statement, they must have regard to various matters, including human rights, equal opportunities, community empowerment and sustainable development.[52] Part 2 establishes the Scottish Land Commission, which consists of five ordinary commissioners and a 'Tenant Farming Commissioner'.[53] The commissioners are tasked with advising the Scottish Ministers on land matters.[54]

15.25   Part 3 makes provision for a new register identifying those who have a controlling interest in owners (who of course will be identifiable from the Land

---

[42]   LR(S)A 2003, s 97H(1).
[43]   LR(S)A 2003, s 97V.
[44]   LR(S)A 2003, s 97S.
[45]   CE(S)A 2015, Part 5.
[46]   CE(S)A 2015, s 82(3).
[47]   CE(S)A 2015, s 82(5).
[48]   CE(S)A 2015, s 85. But where the public body is the Scottish Ministers or a local authority there are review procedures instead under ss 86–88.
[49]   CE(S)A 2015, s 94.
[50]   Although such information is in principle available via the Register of Sasines and the Land Register, this will make it more accessible.
[51]   LR(S)A 2016, s 1(2).
[52]   LR(S)A 2016, s 1(3).
[53]   LR(S)A 2016, s 4(4). The Commission was established on 1 April 2017. See http://landcommission. gov.scot/.
[54]   LR(S)A 2016, s 22.

Register or Sasine Register) and tenants of land.[55] The detail is left to regulations. The objective is transparency and the provisions are primarily aimed at companies and trusts.

15.26   Part 4 requires the Scottish Ministers to issue guidance about engaging communities in relation to land which may affect them. The guidance is aimed at those with control over land.[56] Part 5 introduces a further right to buy in favour of community bodies, this time to further sustainable development. This is a right of compulsory acquisition and the rules are similar to those on acquiring abandoned and neglected etc land discussed above.[57] Approval is required from the Scottish Ministers.[58] It remains to be seen, how widely 'sustainable development' is interpreted and more generally how often community bodies will seek to acquire land under the increased number of routes open to them. The Scottish Government's target is to have 1 million acres of land in community ownership by 2020. As of October 2015 the figure was estimated at 480,000 acres, with 52,000 acres having been acquired through the community right to buy.[59]

LITERATURE

15.27   For further accounts of the private law, see Gordon and Wortley *Scottish Land Law* paras 4.01–4.16, Paisley *Land Law* paras 1.11–1.14; 4.16–4.23 and Reid *Property* paras 193–212. For a detailed account of the law on minerals, see Rennie, R *Minerals and the Law in Scotland* (2001). On land reform, see M Combe, 'Digesting the Community Empowerment Act' 2015 JLSS August/40, 'Land reform: back, and here to stay' 2016 JLSS May/18 and 'The Land Reform (Scotland) Act 2016: another answer to the Scottish land question' 2016 JR 291.

---

[55]   LR(S)A 2016, s 39.
[56]   LR(S)A 2016, s 44(5).
[57]   See **PARA 15.22** above.
[58]   LR(S)A 2016, s 56.
[59]   Scottish Government, One Million Acres by 2020 (2015) 17 available at www.gov.scot/Resource/0049/00490614.pdf.

Chapter 16

Tenements and developments

TENEMENTS: GENERAL

The Tenements (Scotland) Act 2004: a default code

16.1   The Tenements (Scotland) Act 2004 (T(S)A 2004) codified the common law of the tenement and filled gaps and clarified uncertainties. It is essential reading. The legislation is based on the Scottish Law Commission Report on the Law of the Tenement[1] to which useful reference may also be made. Like the common law, a fundamental feature of T(S)A 2004 is that it is a 'background' or 'default' law. This means that it is subject to the title of the property in question. An express term in the title, for example a statement as to ownership of a particular part of the building, will prevail over T(S)A 2004.[2] An important part of the legislation is the 'Tenement Management Scheme' which contains a set of model rules governing decision making and liability for costs relating to the building.[3] Again, as a default law, this is normally subject to any real burdens.[4]

Definitions

16.2   All tenements, old and new, are governed by the legislation, provided that they meet the definition of 'tenement'. For the purposes of T(S)A 2004, this is 'a building or a part of a building which comprises two related flats at least two of which (a) are, or are designed to be, in separate ownership; and (b) are divided from each other horizontally'.[5] Horizontal division is crucial. If properties are divided vertically, that is a terrace, not a tenement.[6] The definition is broad and is capable of embracing both a modern multi-storey apartment block and a substantial Victorian dwelling house which has been converted into an upper and a lower flat. A reference to a 'tenement' for the purposes of the legislation includes the *solum*, ie the ground on which the building stands and the land pertaining to the building.[7] In some cases, for example a flatted building on the corner of two roads with a shared roof but different entrances, it may be difficult to ascertain exactly what constitutes the tenement for the purposes of T(S)A 2004. Recourse, however, can be made to the title to the tenement and any real burdens affecting it to determine the matter.[8]

16.3   The word 'tenement' has at least two other usages in Scots law, which are different from the one which is the subject of this chapter. The first is the traditional terms for 'benefited property' and 'burdened property' in relation to a servitude: the

---

[1]   Scottish Law Commission, Report on the Law of the Tenement (Scot Law Com No 162, 1998).
[2]   T(S)A 2004, s 1(1).
[3]   See **PARA 16.12** below.
[4]   T(S)A 2004, s 4.
[5]   T(S)A 2004, s 26(1).
[6]   Although one of the authors has seen the title deeds for a terrace in which it is described as a 'tenement'.
[7]   T(S)A 2004, s 26(1).
[8]   T(S)A 2004, s 26(2).

'dominant tenement' and 'servient tenement'.[9] Here, 'tenement' simply means 'piece of heritable property'. The second is found within the expressions 'conventional separate tenement' and 'legal separate tenement', which were discussed in **CHAPTER 15**.[10] Again, 'tenement' here means 'a piece of property', but specifically one that can be held separately from the ground. A tenement flat is an example of a conventional separate tenement.

16.4 Under T(S)A 2004 the term 'flat' is not limited to residential use or confined to one floor.[11] This confirms that the legislation applies to tenements in which some or all of the units are commercial, for example shops. Moreover, a unit could comprise two storeys, as in the so-called 'double upper flat'.

DEFAULT RULES OF TENEMENT OWNERSHIP

General

16.5 The common law rules are codified and expanded upon by T(S)A 2004, ss 1–3. The legislation uses common ownership very sparingly. There is good reason for this. As has been seen elsewhere, common ownership has a tendency to give rise to disputes and generally requires unanimity for decisions.[12] Where builders have disapplied the common law and used common property expansively, the result may be problematic.[13]

16.6 The starting point is that the individual owners have exclusive ownership of their flats. Rules are then provided to deal with boundaries and pertinents.

Boundaries

16.7 T(S)A 2004 divides the tenement into 'sectors'. A 'sector' is defined to mean '(a) a flat; (b) any close or lift; or (c) any other three dimensional space'[14] in the building. An example of the third category would be a cellar. The boundary between different sectors is normally 'the median of the structure that separates them'[15] – in other words, the centre line or mid-point. For example, the boundary between a flat and the flat above will be the mid-point of the ceiling of the lower flat and the floor of the upper flat. The boundary between a flat and the close (common stair)[16] will be

---

9   See, for example, Cusine and Paisley *Servitudes and Rights of Way* (1998) para 2.05.
10 See **PARAS 16.13–16.17** above.
11 T(S)A 2004, s 29(1). For an example, see *PS Properties (2) Ltd v Callaway Homes Ltd* 2007 GWD 31-526.
12 See **PARA 10.8** above.
13 See *Rafique v Amin* 1997 SLT 1385.
14 T(S)A 2004, s 29(1).
15 T(S)A 2004, s 2(1).
16 See **PARA 16.10** below.

the centre line of the dividing wall. There is an exception to the normal median rule for things which wholly or mainly serve one sector, for example the front door of a flat. Such things are regarded as belonging entirely to the owner of the sector.[17]

16.8　　External walls are owned exclusively by the sector in question.[18] This means, for instance, that the front wall of the building is owned in sections by the owners of the front-facing flats.

16.9　　Ownership of a top flat includes ownership of the roof above it.[19] If there is more than one top flat, the roof will be owned in sections. Similarly, ownership of a bottom flat carries with it the solum under the flat.[20] The 'solum' means 'the ground on which a building is erected'.[21] The close (common stair) includes the roof above it and the solum beneath it.[22] The ownership of the solum (or part of it) includes the ownership of the airspace directly above the building (or relevant part of it).[23] For example, if there is a north basement flat, it includes the north area of airspace. There is a special rule for the triangular sector of airspace above a sloping roof. It belongs to the roof's owner.[24] So a dormer window can be constructed. (Subject to building and planning consent, and assuming that it is not barred by a real burden.)

Pertinents

16.10　　The close (often known as the common stair) is a pertinent of all the flats which take access through it.[25] 'Close' means 'a connected passage, stairs and landings within a tenement building which together constitute a common access to two or more of the flats'.[26] A main-door flat which takes entry directly from the street and not through the close is excluded from ownership of it.[27] There is a similar rule if there is a lift. Once again, it will be co-owned by the flats using it for access, but not, in this case, a ground-floor flat which does not need it.[28]

16.11　　The ground around the building, such as a back green, belongs to the flat adjacent to it.[29] If there is more than one adjacent flat then the ground is owned in sections. There is an exception for paths, outside stairs or other means of access to other sectors of the building. These are covered by a more general rule, namely

---

17　　T(S)A 2004, s 2(2).
18　　T(S)A 2004, s 2(1)(b).
19　　T(S)A 2004, s 2(3).
20　　T(S)A 2004, s 2(4).
21　　T(S)A 2004, s 29(1).
22　　T(S)A 2004, s 2(5).
23　　T(S)A 2004, s 2(6).
24　　T(S)A 2004, s 2(7).
25　　T(S)A 2004, s 3(1).
26　　T(S)A 2004, s 29(1).
27　　T(S)A 2004, s 3(2).
28　　T(S)A 2004, s 3(1) and (2).
29　　T(S)A 2004, s 3(3).

that a part of a building serving a flat is a pertinent of it.[30] Other examples are fire escapes, rhones, pipes, flues, conduits, cables, tanks and chimney stacks. Where such parts serve more than one flat they are the common property of those flats.[31] It does not matter if one section of the thing serves one flat and another section another. For example, an entryphone system is regarded as a single entity even though it has separate wires serving separate flats.[32] Normally the shares in the common property will be equal in size, but there is a special rule for chimney stacks.[33] Here, the share depends on the ratio of the number of flues serving the chimney to the total number of flues in the stack.

DEFAULT RULES OF TENEMENT MANAGEMENT

The Tenement Management Scheme

16.12   Schedule 1 to T(S)A 2004 contains the Tenement Management Scheme (TMS). This is a default set of management rules, which apply unless the Development Management Scheme (discussed below[34]) has been adopted for the building. The rules may also be disapplied by particular real burdens governing the matter in question.[35]

Scheme property

16.13   The Tenement Management Scheme applies only to the parts that fall within the definition of 'scheme property'.[36] This means, first, the strategic parts of the building. These are:

  (a) the ground on which it is built;
  (b) the foundations;
  (c) the external walls;
  (d) the roof (including supporting structures such as rafters);
  (e) any mutual gable wall shared with an adjoining building, to the centre line; and
  (f) any other wall, beam or column that is load-bearing.[37]

These parts do not have to be co-owned (in terms of the title deeds) to be scheme property. For example, if there is one top-floor flat which has sole ownership of the

---

30   T(S)A 2004, s 3(4).
31   T(S)A 2004, s 3(4).
32   This is because T(S)A 2004, s 3(4) confers a right of common property 'in (and in the whole of)' the part.
33   T(S)A 2004, s 3(5).
34   See **PARA 16.32** below.
35   T(S)A 2004, s 4.
36   TMS, r 1.2.
37   TMS, r 1.2(c).

roof, the roof is nonetheless scheme property. Certain things are excluded from the strategic parts mentioned, namely:

(a) an extension forming part of only one flat;

(b) any door, window, skylight, vent or other opening serving only one flat; and

(c) any chimney stack or chimney flue.[38]

16.14   Second, the definition of 'scheme property' includes any part of the building that is owned in common, such as the close.[39] Third, any part of the building which is to be maintained under a real burden by two or more flats is also scheme property.[40]

Scheme decisions

Types

16.15   Some 'scheme decisions' can be made by a simple majority of the flat owners.[41] What constitutes a 'flat' is to be determined at the time the decision is taken, rather than when the building was originally constructed.[42] Of course, real burdens might provide a higher threshold, such as a two-thirds majority, which will then apply.[43] The main type of scheme decision is to carry out maintenance.[44] A decision can also be taken to arrange for an inspection to see whether maintenance is required.[45] 'Maintenance' includes 'repairs and replacement, cleaning, painting and other routine works, gardening, the day to day running of a tenement and the reinstatement of a part (but not most) of the tenement building; but does not include demolition, alteration or improvement unless reasonably incidental to the maintenance'.[46] Thus, a majority of the owners cannot make a scheme decision to demolish the tenement. Where a decision is taken to carry out maintenance, further scheme decisions can be taken to instruct the work or to appoint an owner or a firm to manage it.[47] Importantly, a scheme decision can require all the owners to deposit their estimated share of the cost of the work in advance in an interest-bearing bank or building society account.[48] This means that the owners can be sure that the money is there before the work begins.

---

[38]   TMS, r 1.3. On dormer windows, see *Mehrabadi v Haugh,* 11 January 2010, Aberdeen Sheriff Court, discussed in K G C Reid and G L Gretton, *Conveyancing 2010* (2011) 93-96. But compare *Waelde v Ulloa* 2016 GWD 11-221.

[39]   TMS, r 1.2(a). Except if, oddly, the title deeds provided that this was not common property.

[40]   TMS, r 1.2(b).

[41]   TMS, r 2.5.

[42]   *PS Properties (2) Ltd v Callaway Homes Ltd* 2007 GWD 31-526.

[43]   T(S)A 2004, s 4(4).

[44]   TMS, r 3.1(a).

[45]   TMS, r 3.1(b).

[46]   TMS, r 1.5. On the difference between repairs and alterations, see *Mitchell v Reilly*, 11 July 2006, Glasgow Sheriff Court, discussed in K G C Reid and G L Gretton, *Conveyancing 2015* (2016) 187-189.

[47]   TMS, rr 3.2(a) and (b).

[48]   TMS, r 3.2(c), 3.3 and 3.4.

16.16   Other scheme decisions include appointing a manager (factor) or dismissing a manager; delegating powers to the manager; arranging a common insurance policy; installing an entryphone system; authorising any maintenance that has already been carried out and modifying or revoking any scheme decision.[49] For common property, scheme decisions replace the rule at common law which lets any co-owner carry out necessary repairs and recover the cost from the others.[50]

Procedural requirements and voting

16.17   There is no requirement for a meeting to be held in order for a scheme decision to be made.[51] An owner wishing a repair to be carried out can simply go round the tenement and find out if a majority agree. All the owners must be consulted.[52] Each flat has one vote.[53] If a flat is co-owned and the owners are in agreement, then any one of them can cast that flat's vote.[54] If they disagree, then the vote can be cast by co-owners in agreement who hold more than half of the shares.[55] If this is not the case – for example, there are only two owners and they disagree – no vote is cast. Where a flat is not liable for the maintenance costs in question (for example, a main-door flat would normally have no liability for the upkeep of the close) it does not get a vote about work which would incur these costs.[56]

16.18   Although the vote does not have to be in writing, it would be unwise to instruct major repairs unless the consenting owners confirm their position in writing. Should it be felt that a matter would be best discussed at a meeting, at least 48 hours' notice must be given to the other owners, including notice of the purpose of the meeting.[57] It is worth stressing that what is required to take a scheme decision is the agreement of a majority of the owners and not just a majority of those who attend.[58]

Right of appeal to the sheriff

16.19   Once a scheme decision has been made, all the owners must be notified of it.[59] The decision, unless it is one to carry out urgent work, must wait for 28 days to be implemented, because during this period an owner who opposed the decision, or an incoming owner, may challenge it in the sheriff court.[60] The sheriff can annul the

---

[49]   TMS, rr 3.1(c)–(f) and (h)–(i).
[50]   T(S)A 2004, s 16. See **PARA 10.8** above.
[51]   Unless the titles require one: see *Garvie v Wallace* 2013 GWD 38-734.
[52]   TMS, r 2.7. Unless this is impracticable: for example, where an owner is absent.
[53]   TMS, r 2.2.
[54]   TMS, r 2.4.
[55]   TMS, r 2.4(a) and (b).
[56]   TMS, r 2.3.
[57]   TMS, r 2.6.
[58]   TMS, r 2.5.
[59]   TMS, r 2.9.
[60]   T(S)A 2004, s 5.

decision if satisfied that it is not in the best interests of all the owners or is unfairly prejudicial to one or more of the owners.[61] Where a decision is not successfully challenged it binds the owners and their successors.[62]

Scheme costs

General

16.20   The Tenement Management Scheme sets out the liability of the owners for 'scheme costs'. This means the costs arising out of a scheme decision, for example to carry out maintenance, and any other costs relating to the management of the property.[63] As with the rest of the legislation, this is subject to the titles. Where there is a real burden dealing with a scheme cost it will take precedence provided it deals with the whole bill.[64] For example, say that there are six flats in a building. The titles of four of the flats each impose a one-sixth liability for roof repairs. The titles for the other two are silent on the matter. The real burdens therefore only cover four-sixths of the bill. The result is that they do not apply. The Tenement Management Scheme does instead.

16.21   The normal rule under the scheme is that the flats are liable equally.[65] For maintenance costs, however, there are two other possibilities.
  (1) If the part of the property in question is common, liability is by share of ownership.[66]
  (2) If it is not owned in common but the floor area of the largest flat in the building is more than one and a half times greater than that of the smallest, liability is in proportion to floor area.[67]

There is also a special rule for the section of roof above the close.[68] If the title deeds are silent, then liability is not based on the fact that it is common property under the legislation. Rather, it is either to be equal, or calculated by means of floor area if the second possibility above applies. The idea is that the whole of the roof is to be treated together if the title deeds have nothing to say on the matter. Local authorities have the power to contribute an owner's share if that owner cannot pay or has disappeared.[69] If they do not, the other owners will have to meet that share between them.[70]

---

[61] T(S)A 2004, s 5(5).
[62] TMS, r 8.
[63] TMS, r 4.1.
[64] T(S)A 2004, s 4(6). But it is competent to apply to the Lands Tribunal for discharge of the real burdens so that the default rules will apply. See *Patterson v Drouet*, 14 November 2012, Lands Tribunal. See **PARA 14.71** above.
[65] TMS, r 4.2(b)(ii). Therefore if no flat is owned there can be no liability. Cf *Hunter v Tindale* 2012 SLT (Sh Ct) 2, discussed in K G C Reid and G L Gretton *Conveyancing 2011* (2012) 129-132.
[66] TMS, r 4.2(a).
[67] TMS, r 4.2(a)(i).
[68] TMS, r 4.3.
[69] Housing (Scotland) Act 2006, s 50.
[70] TMS, r 5.

Change of ownership

16.22   Liability for costs such as maintenance arises at the time when the relevant scheme decision is made.[71] If a flat is subsequently transferred, usually because it has been sold, the liability of that owner continues.[72] Where work has been instructed but not carried out, the incoming owner is jointly and severally liable with the outgoing owner for the cost.[73] The former, however, has a right of relief against the latter, in other words a right to be reimbursed.[74] Where work has already been carried out, but not paid for, the incoming owner has no liability unless a 'notice of potential liability for costs' has been registered against the title to the flat.[75] The reason for the distinction is that a purchaser normally obtains a survey report which should flag up the need for repairs. In contrast work which has been completed may be less apparent. The effect of the notice is that the incoming owner becomes jointly and severally liable, in the same way as for work not yet carried out. The notice lasts for three years, but can be re-registered before the end of that period, making it effective for another three years.[76]

Emergency work

16.23   In the case of emergency work, any owner is entitled to instruct or carry this out.[77] 'Emergency work' is defined as 'work which, before a scheme decision can be obtained, requires to be carried out to scheme property (a) to prevent damage to any part of the tenement, or (b) in the interests of health and safety'.[78] Where such work is instructed, the owners all become liable for the cost as if the work had been authorised by a scheme decision.[79]

MANDATORY RULES FOR INSURANCE AND MAINTENANCE IN TENEMENTS

Common interest

16.24   Common law developed certain rules about support, shelter and the protection of natural light, these rules being under the umbrella of the doctrine of 'common interest'.[80] They were replaced by similar statutory obligations in T(S)

---

[71]   T(S)A 2004, s 11.
[72]   T(S)A 2004, s 12(1).
[73]   T(S)A 2004, s 12(2).
[74]   T(S)A 2004, s 12(5).
[75]   T(S)A 2004, ss 12(3) and 13 and Sch 2.
[76]   T(S)A 2004, s 13(3).
[77]   TMS, r 7.1.
[78]   TMS, r 7.3.
[79]   TMS, r 7.2.
[80]   Reid *Property* paras 232–238.

A 2004.[81] The owners of any part of the building providing support or shelter must maintain that part.[82] This obligation is enforceable by the other owners.[83] Such is the importance of these matters that no scheme decision is required. Provided that the part in question is scheme property (or property which must be maintained by virtue of real burdens or the Development Management Scheme[84]), a share of the cost can be recovered from the other owners as if a scheme decision had been taken.[85] The duty to maintain exists only if it is reasonable, having regard to all the circumstances, including the age and condition of the building and cost.[86] In a heavily dilapidated tenement it will not apply.

16.25   The owners or occupiers must not do anything which will, or is reasonably likely to, jeopardise support or shelter, or materially to interfere with the natural light reaching the building.[87] If loss is caused by a failure to provide support or shelter, fault needs to be shown for a damages claim to succeed. The rule is the same whether the action is based on negligence[88] or nuisance.[89]

Insurance

16.26   The flats must be insured for reinstatement value against prescribed risks.[90] These include fire, smoke, lightning, explosion, earthquake, storm, flood, theft, rioting, vandalism, subsidence and damage from certain water or oil leakage.[91] A common policy of insurance must be used if real burdens provide for this or a scheme decision is taken to that effect.[92] If not, separate policies are acceptable. Unlike motor insurance, failure to comply with the statutory requirement is not a criminal offence. Any owner, however, may enforce the obligation against another, if necessary, by going to court.[93] If there is a concern that insurance is not in place, written notice can be given to the owner in question to produce evidence that a policy is held and the premium has been paid.[94]

---

[81]   T(S)A 2004, s 7.
[82]   T(S)A 2004, s 8(1).
[83]   T(S)A 2004, s 8(3).
[84]   See **PARA 16.32** below.
[85]   T(S)A 2004, s 10. See *Humphreys v Crabbe* [2016] CSIH 82.
[86]   T(S)A 2004, s 8(2).
[87]   T(S)A 2004, s 9.
[88]   *Thomson v St Cuthbert's Co-operative Association Ltd* 1958 SC 380. See also *Stewart v Malik* 2009 SC 265.
[89]   *Kennedy v Glenbelle Ltd* 1996 SLT 1186.
[90]   T(S)A 2004, s 18(1).
[91]   Tenements (Scotland) Act 2004 (Prescribed Risks) Order 2007 (SSI 2007/16).
[92]   TMS, r 3.1(e).
[93]   T(S)A 2004, s 18(6).
[94]   T(S)A 2004, s 18(5).

TENEMENT ACCESS RIGHTS

16.27   The owners of the flats are entitled to take access to the other flats for various purposes, including to carry out maintenance in terms of a scheme decision or other management scheme applying to the building; to carry out an inspection as to whether maintenance is required and to ensure that the duties of support and shelter are being fulfilled.[95] Reasonable notice must be given of the desire to take access, except if there is a need to carry out urgent maintenance.[96] The access rights can be delegated, for example to a contractor.[97]

DEMOLITION

16.28   A tenement may have to be demolished, for example if it has been severely damaged by fire. The cost of this in general must be shared equally by the owners.[98] Of course, a real burden may provide otherwise. Additionally, if the largest flat is more than one and a half times the size of the smallest flat then liability is based on floor area.[99] Ownership is unaffected by the demolition. This means that the owner of an upper flat continues to own the airspace where that flat once was.[100] Rebuilding is allowed only if all the owners of the former flats agree, or where there is an obligation to rebuild, normally imposed by a real burden.[101] Any owner can apply to the sheriff court for permission to have the site sold.[102] In this case the proceeds are divided in the same way as the demolition costs: either equally or by floor area, depending on the respective sizes of the former flats.[103] This is subject to any real burden regulating the matter. An application to sell can likewise be made for an abandoned tenement.[104]

STATUTORY NOTICES

16.29   Local authorities have statutory powers to require maintenance and safety work to be carried out. In practice these are used more in relation to tenements than other types of building. The typical case is where an owner cannot persuade others to agree to repairs and so contacts the council. The procedure is that the local authority, if satisfied that work is needed, serves a 'statutory notice' on the owners.

---

[95]   T(S)A 2004, s 17(1) and (2).
[96]   T(S)A 2004, s 17(1) and (4).
[97]   T(S)A 2004, s 17(6).
[98]   T(S)A 2004, s 21(1).
[99]   T(S)A 2004, s 21(2).
[100]   T(S)A 2004, s 20.
[101]   T(S)A 2004, s 22(2).
[102]   T(S)A 2004, s 21(3) and Sch 3.
[103]   T(S)A 2004, s 22(4) and (5).
[104]   T(S)A 2004, s 23.

Examples include defective building notices,[105] dangerous building notices[106] and work notices.[107] These require the owners to carry out remedial work within a certain period. Such a notice will appear on the 'property enquiry certificate' which a prospective buyer always requests from the local authority, and so makes the flat harder to sell unless something is done. If the owners do not carry out the work, the local authority can do it itself and bill them. In the case of tenements, this will be a 'scheme cost', so the rules on determining the respective liability of each flat will apply.[108] The local authority can if necessary secure the cost against the property by means of a charging order.[109]

DEFAULT RULES OF MANAGEMENT AND MAINTENANCE FOR OTHER DEVELOPMENTS

16.30   TC(S)A 2003 contains a set of default rules on management and maintenance. These are for property developments, other than individual tenements, for which there is the Tenement Management Scheme.[110] The legislation applies where two or more properties ('units') are regulated by burdens imposed under a common scheme and are mutually enforceable.[111] In effect it applies to properties governed by the same set of community burdens.[112] It might be a residential development, including one with a mixture of houses and tenements, or an industrial estate. The legislation refers to such properties as a 'community'.

16.31   The default rules are subject to the provisions of the community burdens in place. They are rather like a watered-down version of the Tenement Management Scheme. A majority of the owners in the community may appoint a manager and confer certain powers on that person, such as to carry out maintenance.[113] They may also revoke or vary the powers or dismiss the manager.[114] The owners are liable equally for the manager's remuneration.[115] Where there is a community burden imposing a maintenance obligation, the majority can decide to carry out work.[116] There are similar rules to those in the Tenement Management Scheme on instructing the work and requiring all the owners to deposit their share in advance.[117] All the owners and their successors are bound by such decisions.[118]

---

[105]   Building (Scotland) Act 2003 (B(S)A 2003), s 28.
[106]   B(S)A 2003, ss 29–30.
[107]   Housing (Scotland) Act 2006, s 30.
[108]   TMS, r 4.1(d). See **PARAS 16.20–16.21** above.
[109]   See **PARA 21.66** below.
[110]   TC(S)A 2003, s 31A.
[111]   TC(S)A 2003, ss 25 and 26(2).
[112]   See **PARA 14.6** above.
[113]   TC(S)A 2003, s 28(1)(a), (b) and (2).
[114]   TC(S)A 2003, s 28(1)(c) and (d).
[115]   TC(S)A 2003, s 31.
[116]   TC(S)A 2003, s 29(1) and (2).
[117]   TC(S)A 2003, s 29(2)–(10).
[118]   TC(S)A 2003, s 30.

DEVELOPMENT MANAGEMENT SCHEME

16.32   TC(S)A 2003 provides for a sophisticated management scheme for use in larger developments.[119] This is known as the Development Management Scheme. It is set out in a statutory instrument,[120] based on the draft in Schedule 3 to the draft Bill in the Scottish Law Commission Report on Real Burdens. It is available for any development, for example, a single tenement, group of tenements or group of houses and tenements. Under the scheme the development is run by a manager employed by an owners' association. The association is a body corporate and so has juristic personality. The scheme has detailed rules on budgeting, services charges, meetings, maintenance and other matters. It can be applied (with or without variations) to a development by a deed of application[121] and disapplied by a deed of disapplication.[122] Where it applies to a tenement, the Tenement Management Scheme does not.[123]

LITERATURE

16.33   For more detailed accounts of tenement law, see Gordon and Wortley *Scottish Land Law* paras 15-46–15-178, Reid, D 'The Tenements (Scotland) Act 2004' in R Rennie (ed) *The Promised Land: Property Law Reform* 147–172; Reid and Gretton *Conveyancing 2004* (2005) 121–150 and Rennie *Land Tenure in Scotland* chs 10 and 14. See also Van der Merwe, C G 'The Tenements (Scotland) Act 2004: A Brief Evaluation' 2004 *SLT (News)* 211.

TC(S)A 2003, ss 71–74.
[120]   The Title Conditions (Scotland) Act 2003 (Development Management Scheme) Order 2009, SI 2009/729. See further K G C Reid and G L Gretton, *Conveyancing 2009* (2010) 130–156.
[121]   TC(S)A 2003, s 71.
[122]   TC(S)A 2003, s 73.
[123]   T(S)A 2004, s 4(2).

Chapter 17

Rivers, lochs and the sea

GENERAL

Water

17.1   A distinction exists between running water, such as that in a river, and standing water, ie water in a static state. Running water is ownerless[1] and so it can

---

[1]   Reid *Property* para 274.

be acquired by occupancy,[2] for example by filling a bucket. The law about standing water is less clear but, arguably, it belongs to the person on whose land it stands.[3]

Alveus

17.2   Where water runs or stands in a definite channel, the bed of that channel is known as the *alveus*. The principal examples are lochs and rivers. Ownership of the *alveus* is dependent on whether the water in question is tidal or non-tidal.

TIDAL WATERS

Definition

17.3   As well as the sea itself, the category of tidal waters includes rivers and sea-lochs to the highest point reached by the flow of ordinary spring tides.[4]

Alveus

17.4   The *alveus* of tidal waters belongs to the Crown at common law.[5] This is subject to a limit of 12 nautical miles from the shore.[6] Historically, the view was taken that this ownership was as trustee for the public at large for the purpose of protecting such public rights as navigation.[7] To put it more technically, the Crown's right was regarded as part of the *regalia majora* and so incapable of transfer. This view was departed from at the end of the nineteenth century in *Lord Advocate v Clyde Navigation Trustees*[8] and it is now accepted that the Crown has absolute ownership. This ownership arises from the Royal Prerogative, rather than being an aspect of feudal law.[9] Therefore the sea bed around Orkney and Shetland, parts of Scotland which never received the feudal system, is subject to the same rule. As with other Crown property, the sea bed was, until 2017, managed by the Crown Estate Commissioners,[10] but management has now been devolved to the Scottish Ministers.[11]

---

[2]   See **PARA 9.2** above.
[3]   Reid *Property* para 274.
[4]   J Ferguson *The Law of Water and Water Rights in Scotland* (1907) 107.
[5]   See, eg, *Crown Estate Commissioners, Petitioners* 2010 SLT 741.
[6]   Territorial Sea Act 1987, s 1(1). More accurately, the 12 miles is measured from defined baselines. See the Territorial Sea (Limits) Order, SI 1989/482.
[7]   See, eg, *Agnew v Lord Advocate* (1873) 11 M 309 at 322 per Lord Justice-Clerk Moncreiff.
[8]   (1891) 19 R 174. See N R Whitty 'Water Law Regimes' in Reid and Zimmermann *History* vol 1, 420 at 436–438.
[9]   *Shetland Salmon Farmers Association v Crown Estate Commissioners* 1991 SLT 166.
[10]   Crown Estate Act 1961.
[11]   Scotland Act 2016, s 36.

Foreshore

17.5   The foreshore is that part of the shore (whether mud, sand, shingle or rock) which is covered by the sea at high tide and uncovered at the low tide. Since tides vary, the test is the ordinary spring tide.[12] Under the feudal system which persisted until 2004, the foreshore, like any other land, was originally the property of the Crown. It remains the rule that it belongs to the Crown in so far as the Crown has never granted ownership to any other party, nor has anyone acquired a title to it by positive prescription.[13] The position is different in Orkney and Shetland which have always been subject to udal, rather than feudal, law.[14] There, the foreshore is in private ownership – usually that of the proprietor who owns the land adjacent to it.

Public rights

17.6   A number of public rights, including navigation and recreation, exist in tidal waters and the foreshore. These are discussed elsewhere.[15]

NON-TIDAL WATERS: RIVERS

Alveus

17.7   The *alveus* of non-tidal rivers and burns is owned by the proprietors of the land through which they flow, in sections, corresponding to their ownership of the adjacent dry land. The term 'riparian proprietor' is used to denote such a person.[16] Where a river marks the boundary between two properties it is presumed that the *alveus* is owned by the respective riparian proprietor*s* to the middle line – or, in Latin, *ad medium filum*.[17]

Rights of riparian proprietors

17.8   In general, riparian proprietors are entitled to use their section of water. For example, they may sail upon it. They have the exclusive right to catch fish. Where the river is owned to the middle line, it may be permissible for the proprietors to cast their rods across this.[18] The right to fish excludes salmon, unless the proprietor also

---

[12]   *Fisherrow Harbour Commissioners v Musselburgh Real Estate Co Ltd* (1903) 5 F 387 at 393–394 per Lord Low. A spring tide is when the range between high and low tide is at a maximum. There are two spring tides each lunar month.
[13]   On positive prescription, see **CHAPTER 6** above.
[14]   *Smith v Lerwick Harbour Trs* (1903) 5 F 680.
[15]   See **PARAS 19.25–19.29** below.
[16]   This comes from the Latin *ripa*, meaning river bank. See Whitty 'Water Law Regimes' at 448.
[17]   For an example of the rebuttal of the presumption, see *Safeway Stores plc v Tesco Stores Ltd* 2004 SC 29.
[18]   *Arthur v Aird* 1907 SC 1170.

has the salmon fishing rights, which are a legal separate tenement.[19] Also included is the right to consume the water – but only for domestic purposes.[20]

Obligations on riparian proprietors: common interest

17.9   In private law, the main obligations on riparian proprietors arise from common interest.[21] This doctrine recognises the fact that the *alveus*[22] is owned by several parties and that the actions of one could have adverse consequences for another. Thus it imposes restrictions which arise by operation of law. The principal obligation is not to engage in activities which materially interfere with the water or its natural flow. 'The superior heritor [i.e. a proprietor further up the river] must transmit to the inferior the water of the stream undiminished in quantity and undeteriorated in quality.'[23] Therefore if a proprietor intends to construct a building on the *alveus* which will disrupt the flow of the water, this may be interdicted.[24] Likewise, polluting the river may be a breach of common interest.

17.10   Common interest means that in practice water must not be abstracted except for domestic purposes such as cooking, drinking and washing.[25] Consumption for agricultural or industrial purposes is generally impermissible, unless this can be shown not to interfere materially with the river flow or where a servitude of *aquaehaustus* has been constituted. This might be by 20 years of use, leading to positive prescription.[26] The right to take water is nowadays less important because of the development of the public water supply system.

Other obligations on riparian proprietors

17.11   Proprietors are subject to obligations additional to those arising in common interest. Three will be mentioned here.

(1) All proprietors must ensure that they do not do anything which amounts to a nuisance, such as polluting the water.[27]

(2) Non-tidal rivers may be subject to a common-law public right of navigation and those exercising that right must be tolerated.[28]

---

19   See **PARA 15.17** above.
20   See **PARA 17.10** below.
21   See J Robbie *Private Water Rights* (2015) ch 7. For another case of common interest, see **PARA 17.24** above.
22   The running water itself is ownerless. See **PARA 17.1** above.
23   *Hunter and Aitkenhead v Aitken* (1880) 7 R 510 at 514 per Lord President Inglis.
24   *Morris v Bicket* (1864) 2 M 1082, aff'd (1866) 4 M (HL) 44.
25   Bell, *Principles* § 1105.
26   See **PARA 13.27** above.
27   *Miller v Stein* (1791) Mor 12823; *Montgomerie v Buchanan's Trs* (1853) 15 D 853.
28   See **PARA 19.29** below.

(3) Statute may impose obligations. For example, the public is allowed to canoe along rivers under the Land Reform (Scotland) Act 2003.[29]

Another important piece of legislation is the Water Environment and Water Services (Scotland) Act 2003 which introduced a new licensing regime for the abstraction of water.[30] A final example is the statutory controls on pollution.[31]

NON-TIDAL WATERS: LOCHS

Alveus

17.12 The *alveus* of a freshwater loch is the area ordinarily covered by water all year round. Seasonal variations are not counted.[32] Where the loch is surrounded by land owned by different parties, the presumption is that the *alveus* is owned in sections. An earlier view, that ownership is actually held in common, can no longer be regarded as the law.[33]

Rights of riparian proprietors

17.13 Riparian proprietors naturally have the right to use their section of the loch, for example to fish other than for salmon and to sail. There is also a right in common interest to fish and sail in other parts of the loch.[34] The court in principle may regulate matters, so as to avoid over-fishing, but will intervene only in exceptional cases.[35]

Obligations of riparian proprietors

17.14 Similar obligations exist as with rivers and burns.[36] In addition, each proprietor must permit others to fish or sail in his or her part of the loch.[37] Where a loch forms part of the same water system as a river, the common interest obligations upon the river proprietors also apply to the owners of the loch. In contrast a loch which does not fall into that category (known as a '*stagnum*') is not subject to such restrictions.

---

[29] See **PARA 19.3** below.
[30] For discussion, see B Clark 'Water Law in Scotland: The Water Environment and Water Services (Scotland) Act 2003 and the European Convention on Human Rights' (2006) 10 *Edin LR* 60.
[31] McDonald *Conveyancing Manual* paras 20.33–20.40.
[32] *Dick v Earl of Abercorn* (1769) Mor 12813; *Baird v Robertson* (1839) 1 D 1051.
[33] Reid *Property* para 305.
[34] *Mackenzie v Bankes* (1878) 5 R (HL) 192.
[35] *Menzies v Wentworth* (1901) 3 F 941.
[36] See **PARA 17.11** above.
[37] See **PARA 17.13** above.

LITERATURE

17.15   For more detailed general accounts, see Gordon and Wortley *Scottish Land Law* Ch 7 and Reid *Property* paras 273–343. Robbie, J *Private Water Rights* (2015) is a recent monograph focussing on non-tidal river and lochs. Whitty, N R 'Water Law Regimes' in Reid and Zimmermann *History* vol 1, 420–479 provides a valuable historical perspective.

Chapter 18

Neighbour law

INTRODUCTION

18.1 Neighbour law is the part of property law which regulates the rights and responsibilities of a landowner in a question with neighbouring (not necessarily adjacent) owners. Two important rights – real burdens and servitudes – have their own detailed sets of rules and are treated elsewhere.[1] Moreover, they are normally[2] created expressly. The focus of this chapter is the default set of rules affecting neighbours. These are discussed under the following headings:

  (a) boundary fences and walls;[3]
  (b) encroachment;[4]
  (c) support;[5]
  (d) nuisance;[6]
  (e) *aemulatio vicini* (spiteful acts);[7] and
  (f) use of a neighbour's property.[8]

BOUNDARY FENCES AND WALLS

Construction

18.2 There are two types of boundary fence or wall. Type 1 is wholly on one side of the boundary. Type 2 straddles the boundary, usually with one half on each side. Subject to certain legal restraints such as planning law and real burdens, an owner is entitled to erect a Type 1 fence or wall. The expense must be borne by him or her alone, unless there is a real burden requiring a contribution from the neighbour, or the March Dykes Act 1661 applies. The 1661 Act and the related March Dykes Act 1669 are little used in modern times.[9] It does not apply in towns or cities, nor to plots of land of less than 5 acres.[10] Where it does apply, the court can, on the application of one owner, order that a fence or wall is to be constructed at joint expense.

18.3 A Type 2 fence or wall usually requires the consent of both landowners, failing which it will be an encroachment on the non-consenting owner's land. It is common for real burdens to authorise Type 2 fences or walls to be built. In other words, an owner is given power to build onto his or her neighbour's land. But there is a difficulty here. Since 28 November 2004, real burdens are only capable of imposing

---

[1] See **CHAPTERS 13 AND 14** above.
[2] Real burdens are always created expressly. Servitudes, however, can be created in other ways, for example by prescription. See **PARA 13.27** above.
[3] See **PARAS 18.2–18.9** below.
[4] See **PARAS 18.10–18.16** below.
[5] See **PARAS 18.17–18.20** below.
[6] See **PARAS 18.21–18.25** below.
[7] See **PARAS 18.26–18.27** below.
[8] See **PARAS 18.28–18.30** below.
[9] But see *Corrie v Craig* 2013 GWD 1-55.
[10] *Penman v Douglas and Cochrane* (1739) Mor 10481.

positive (affirmative) or negative obligations[11] and cannot allow use of a neighbour's land. Existing real burdens allowing such use were converted by force of law on that date into servitudes.[12] There is, however, authority to the effect that a reserved right to build on another's land cannot be a servitude.[13] It is, arguably, repugnant with the ownership of the burdened property.[14] In view of this, new real burdens should be drafted to require both neighbours to co-operate in the building of the fence or wall. A time limit should also be imposed for completion or the burden will be invalid.[15]

18.4 There is a special rule for common gables. A 'common gable' is an end wall shared by two buildings, for example terraced houses or adjacent tenements. In towns and cities it is sometimes permissible for a builder to construct a straddling gable.[16] When the adjacent plot is developed, the gable can be used, but only on payment of half the cost of erecting it.[17] This rule was important in nineteenth-century building practice when adjacent plots were normally granted to different builders. Nowadays, the one builder normally builds a whole development. So the rule is now of little importance.

Ownership

18.5 Ownership of a boundary fence or wall is in principle governed by the law of accession.[18] Graeme and Harvey are neighbours and a wall separates their gardens. If the wall is built wholly on Graeme's side of the boundary, it belongs to Graeme. If it is built entirely on Harvey's side, it belongs to Harvey. If it is a straddling wall then each owns it to the middle line.[19] In neither case is the wall common property. (Some older authorities suggesting that it is common property must now be regarded as wrong.[20]) But each party has a right of common interest in the other's part of the wall.

18.6 It is unclear whether the title deeds can alter the rule and make a boundary fence or wall the common property of the neighbours. There is authority that it is impossible to contract out of accession.[21] But the position might be different here because of an express statement in the title deeds. This effectively would treat the wall or fence as a conventional separate tenement.[22]

---

[11]   See **PARA 14.7** above.
[12]   TC(S)A 2003, s 81.
[13]   *Campbell's Trs v Glasgow Corporation* (1902) 4 F 752.
[14]   Compare TC(S)A 2003, s 76(2).
[15]   *Gammell's Trs v The Land Commission* 1970 SLT 254.
[16]   Reid *Property* para 218.
[17]   *Law v Monteith* (1855) 18 D 125; *Sanderson v Geddes* (1874) 1 R 1198; *Robertson v Scott* (1886) 13 R 1127.
[18]   See **PARAS 9.4–9.12** above.
[19]   The Latin expression '*ad medium filum*' is often used to mean 'to the mid-point'.
[20]   Reid *Property* para 223. And see Scottish Law Commission, Report on Boundary Walls (Scot Law Com No 163, 1998).
[21]   See **PARA 9.4** above.
[22]   See **PARA 15.14** above. But the law generally does not admit separate tenements above ground.

Maintenance

18.7   The neighbours are free to agree between themselves as to maintenance and paying for its cost. The position is commonly dealt with by means of a real burden, perhaps stating that each neighbour is liable to pay a half-share of the expense of maintenance. In the case of a Type 2 fence or wall which traverses the boundary, each neighbour is under a duty in common interest to maintain the stability of the structure as a whole. This is a *positive* obligation. If it is not complied with, the other neighbour can carry out the work and recover the cost.[23] In the case of a wall or fence owned in common,[24] either neighbour may carry out necessary repairs and recover a proportion from the other based on the size of the other's share.

18.8   Where the March Dykes Act 1661 applies, it enables an owner to ask the court to require the neighbour to pay half the cost of repairing or rebuilding the fence or wall. The 1661 Act applies where the fence or wall was originally erected by court order under the Act,[25] where it was erected by agreement where a court order could have been so sought; or where it has been always regarded as governed by the legislation.[26] Local authorities also have a battery of powers to deal with defective and dangerous buildings, including to repair the property and to bill the owner(s).[27] The definition of 'building' includes wall and fences.[28]

Alterations

18.9   Subject to any agreement or real burden to the contrary, the owner is free to alter, extend or demolish a Type 1 fence or wall. In the case of a straddling wall, a common interest obligation prevents each neighbour from carrying out any acts which would adversely affect the structure as a whole. The rule here is stated by Lord Jauncey in *Thom v Hetherington*,[29] where one of the neighbours had erected a new fence along the existing wall:

'The presence of the fence up against the wall would only have been actionable if such presence impaired the strength or interfered with the stability of the wall ... Such impairment or interference must in my view be measurable and not merely negligible. It is beyond dispute that the owner of one side of a

---

[23]   *Newton v Godfrey,* Stranraer Sheriff Court, 19 June 2000, Paisley and Cusine, *Unreported Cases* 86.
[24]   If this is possible. See **PARA 18.6** above.
[25]   See **PARA 18.2** above.
[26]   *Strang v Steuart* (1864) 2 M 1015, aff'd (1866) 4 M (HL) 5.
[27]   Building (Scotland) Act 2003 (B(S)A 2003), ss 28–30.
[28]   B(S)A 2003, s 55. Subject to some exceptions, the definition covers 'any structure or erection, whether temporary or permanent'.
[29]   1988 SLT 724.

garden wall would be entitled to insert nails or rose ties into the mortar for the purpose of training roses up it. Theoretically every intrusion into the mortar must weaken the bond which it creates between the bricks, but it is equally clear that the court would not restrain an owner from so acting.'[30]

In principle, the party carrying out the alteration must pay for it.[31]

ENCROACHMENT

General

18.10   Where something permanently or quasi-permanently invades a person's land without consent or lawful authority this is known as 'encroachment'. The effect is to interfere with the right of possession of the owner or other occupier of the land and thereby commit a delict. Encroachment, unlike trespass,[32] is always by things. The typical example is a person building beyond his or her boundaries. An example is the pillars on the front of the Assembly Rooms in George Street in Edinburgh, which were built onto a neighbouring proprietor's land.[33] A number of other cases can be given.

(a) Where a signpost or other object is affixed to a building. The leading modern case involved an Edinburgh chip shop placing a flue on the side of someone else's wall.[34]

(b) Where pipes are laid.[35]

(c) Where a tree's roots spread under or its branches overhang the land.[36]

(d) Where rubbish or other moveable property is left.[37]

Encroachment, even if trivial, is a delict: 'a proprietor is not entitled to encroach upon his neighbour's property even to the extent of driving a nail into it'.[38] Nevertheless, the extent of the encroachment is relevant to the remedies available.[39]

---

[30]   1988 SLT 724 at 728.

[31]   But the parts, of course, are free to agree otherwise; there might be a real burden governing the position or the March Dykes Act 1661, if applicable, might allow the cost to be halved with the neighbour.

[32]   See **PARAS 19.30–19.36** below.

[33]   *Duke of Buccleuch v Magistrates of Edinburgh* (1865) 3 M 528. For more recent examples, see *Young v West,* Elgin Sheriff Court, 3 September 2003, unreported, discussed in K G C Reid and G L Gretton, *Conveyancing 2003* (2004) 83–85 and *Smith v Crombie* [2012] CSOH 52.

[34]   *Anderson v Brattissani's* 1978 SLT (Notes) 42.

[35]   *Cheever v Jefferson Properties Ltd,* Dumfries Sheriff Court, 26 May 1995, Paisley and Cusine, *Unreported Cases* 439.

[36]   *Halkerston v Wedderburn* (1781) Mor 10495; Bell *Principles* § 942.

[37]   Hume, *Lectures* III, 204–205; *Scott v Law,* Cupar Sheriff Court, 20 May 1987, Paisley and Cusine, *Unreported Cases* 21.

[38]   *Leonard v Lindsay & Benzie* (1886) 13 R 958 at 964 per Lord Young.

[39]   See **PARA 18.15** below.

Defences: consent and acquiescence

18.11   There is no encroachment where the owner or lawful possessor of the property expressly agrees to the invasion. The party who has title to the land may also acquiesce in the encroachment. For example, Keith and Leila are neighbours. There is no boundary fence separating their back gardens. Leila builds a summer house, part of which is within Keith's boundaries. Keith makes no objection and lets her complete the work and use the summer house. Only much later does he complain. In these circumstances, he may well be personally barred from having the summer house removed.[40] In the case involving the Assembly Rooms, mentioned in **PARA 18.10**, objection was not made for over 30 years. This was held to be too late.

18.12   In principle, consent and acquiescence do not bind successors. However, where the successor has notice of the encroachment or it is obvious, then that person may be bound.[41] The preferable analysis is that the successor is barred here because of his or her own conduct rather than that the bar itself transmits.[42] Where a predecessor has given consent to the encroachment, the court will take this into account if the successor objects.[43] This may lead to an award of damages rather than removal.[44]

18.13   While consent and acquiescence mean that the encroachment stays in place, in the normal case[45] it will accede to the neighbour's land and fall into his or her ownership. This is likely to cause problems if either piece of land is sold. The way to resolve the matter is a conveyance of the relevant section of land to the encroacher, but this will require the neighbour's agreement.

Other defences

18.14   Only two possible defences will be mentioned. The first is that the encroachment is lawful. The encroacher may actually own the land, so in fact the encroachment is not an encroachment at all. Rather, there is a dispute over the boundary and the neighbour is mistaken. The encroachment might also be permissible under some special statutory rule. For example, in one case it was submitted that the erection of a tent on the foreshore was justified by the White Herring Fisheries Act 1771.[46] Second, the failure to object for a period of 20 years may lead to this right being lost by negative prescription.[47] This is questionable, however, because the right may fall within the definition of a *res merae facultatis*.[48]

---

40   On personal bar more generally, see E C Reid and J W G Blackie *Personal Bar* (2006).
41   Gloag *Contract* 170–171.
42   Reid 'Personal Bar: Case-Law in Search of Principle' (2003) 7 *Edin LR* 340 at 347–348.
43   *Anderson v Brattissani's* 1978 SLT (Notes) 42.
44   See **PARA 18.15** below.
45   There are exceptions. For example, overhanging branches and dumped rubbish.
46   *Montgomerie v Mearns*, Kilmarnock Sheriff Court, 9 January 1976, Paisley and Cusine, *Unreported Cases* 467.
47   PL(S)A 1973, s 7.
48   PL(S)A 1973, Sch 3(c). On the meaning of '*res merae facultatis*', see **PARA 13.45** above.

Judicial remedies

18.15   Three court remedies are available. The first is interdict. Speed is of the essence here, because this is a preventative remedy. If the encroachment is a building and it is complete, or at least substantially complete, it is too late to interdict. The appropriate remedy then becomes an order for removal. However, the court has a discretion not to make such an order. It will do so where 'the encroachment was made in good faith in the belief that it was unobjectionable, that it is inconsiderable and does not materially impair the proprietor in the enjoyment of his property, and that the removal would cause to the encroacher a loss wholly disproportionate to the advantage which it would confer upon the proprietor'.[49] Thus in one case buttresses supporting a gable wall encroached on neighbouring land.[50] The neighbour made no attempt to stop their construction. The level of encroachment was minimal and did not cause the neighbour any cost or inconvenience. It was also in the interests of the neighbour's land that the wall did not collapse. The court accordingly exercised its discretion. In another case, where the building work proceeded even after a warning letter from the owner's solicitor, the court did not exercise its discretion in favour of the encroacher, since good faith had been absent.[51] The third remedy is damages. It is available both in cases where the court has exercised its discretion and those where it has not.[52]

Self-help

18.16   A party whose land is subject to an encroachment can take matters into his or her own hands. However, careful thought should be given to whether to engage in self-help as, in Professor Paisley's words, 'unilateral action may lead to fights on site'.[53] Where the encroachment by accession has become solely the property of the person encroached upon, then that person has power over it and may destroy it. In the case of a building which crosses the boundary the part encroaching can be demolished.[54] With trees, it has been held that if the trunk is on the boundary then the tree is the common property of the neighbours.[55] Therefore it cannot be felled without both agreeing. Where the branches of a neighbour's tree overhang, they may be cut off and returned to the neighbour. The same goes for roots. It is also possible to obtain a court order for removal in such circumstances.[56] Where a building over-

---

[49]   *Anderson v Brattisanni's* 1978 SLT (Notes) 42 at 43.
[50]   *Scott v Law,* Cupar Sheriff Court, 20 May 1987, Paisley and Cusine *Unreported Cases* 21.
[51]   *McLellan v J & D Pierce* [2015] CSIH 80, 2015 GWD 37-594.
[52]   For an example of the way damages are assessed, see *Craig v Powrie,* Perth Sheriff Court, 18 September 1985, Paisley and Cusine, *Unreported Cases* 17.
[53]   Paisley *Land Law* para 4.30.
[54]   This sits uneasily with the fact that if a court order were sought, the court could exercise its discretion to refuse. See Reid *Property* para 179.
[55]   *Hetherington v Galt* (1905) 7 F 706.
[56]   *Halkerston v Wedderburn* (1781) Mor 10495.

hangs, self-help is not available.[57] Finally, rubbish and other moveables may simply be returned to the encroacher with or without the neighbour's compliments.

SUPPORT

Land to land

18.17   There is an obligation upon landowners to support the land above and beside their own land. In other words, there is a duty of both *subjacent* and *adjacent* support. (In practice, subjacent support is more important, particularly where minerals have been worked.) More exactly, the obligation is a negative one: not to withdraw support. Consequently, if Jean owns the minerals under Katie's land, Jean must be careful when working the minerals not to cause subsidence. Otherwise, she will be liable to Katie in damages for the loss suffered. Katie is also entitled to interdict works which endanger support. The extent to which the duty to support includes support for buildings is not clear. On one view, it always does.[58] Others contend that the duty does not apply where there is excessive building on the surface, unless that level of building was contemplated at the time that the strata of land were separated.[59] Where support is withdrawn, there is strict liability. Negligence need not be proven.[60] It is possible for the title deeds to exclude the duty to support, or the right to damages if support is withdrawn. An exclusion of the latter may, depending on the wording, impliedly include the former.[61] Where there has been exclusion, it is possible under statute to make application for restrictions to be imposed on the working of minerals in order to protect support.[62]

Coal specialities

18.18   Formerly, coal was one of the most important industries in Scotland, but no more. Nevertheless, there are many old coal mines which may give rise to support issues. Following privatisation in the 1990s, the Coal Authority has ownership of unworked coal and the power to grant licences to work this.[63] An operator to whom a licence is given can in principle withdraw support in order to work the coal on three months' notice.[64] This, however, leads to a duty to compensate the surface owner or

---

[57]   Bankton II, 7, 8.
[58]   Reid *Property* para 260.
[59]   Gordon and Wortley *Scottish Land Law* paras 6.90–6.92; R Rennie *Minerals and the Law of Scotland* (2001) paras 4.3–4.6.
[60]   *Dryburgh v Fife Coal Co Ltd* (1905) 7 F 1083; *Angus v National Coal Board* 1955 SC 175. Compare **PARA 18.23** below with the rule for nuisance.
[61]   *Buchanan v Andrew* (1873) 11 M (HL) 13.
[62]   Mines (Working Facilities and Support) Act 1966, s 7.
[63]   Coal Industry Act 1994 (CIA 1994), ss 7(3) and 25–36.
[64]   CIA 1994, ss 38 and 39.

to carry out remedial works.[65] There is also liability for damage caused by workings which pre-date the licence.[66] Where there is no licensed operator, liability rests with the Coal Authority.[67]

Buildings to buildings

18.19 Subjacent building-to-building support is regulated by the Tenements (Scotland) Act 2004 (T(S)A 2004) under which the lower part or parts of a building must support the upper part or parts.[68] Adjacently, where two buildings share a common gable, each owning it to the mid-point, there is a duty in common interest to support the other half, just like the position for boundary walls discussed above.[69] There is no such obligation if the wall is wholly within the boundaries of one of the properties, unless there is a servitude of support.[70] Similarly, a servitude is needed for there to be a duty to support the separate wall of an adjacent building.

Servitude of support

18.20 The title to a property may provide for an express servitude of support which goes beyond or limits what the law would imply, for example by being restricted to a certain weight or size of building.[71] A servitude of support may also possibly arise by prescription, but there may be difficulties establishing the requisite 'open' possession required.[72]

NUISANCE

General

18.21 Nuisance[73] is a delict. Owners and other lawful occupiers of land are protected from interference with their use and enjoyment of that land. Members of the public have similar rights in relation to public places.[74] A nuisance will be actionable where what the would-be pursuer is exposed to is *'plus quam tolerabile*[75] when due

---

65 Coal Mining Subsidence Act 1991, ss 2, 7, 8 and 9.
66 CIA 1994, s 43(4)–(6). See *British Coal Corporation v Netherlee Trust Trs* 1995 SLT 1038.
67 CIA 1994, s 43(3)(b).
68 T(S)A 2004, s 11. See **PARAS 16.24–16.25** above.
69 See **PARA 18.7** above.
70 See **PARA 13.13** above.
71 Paisley *Land Law* para 8.9. See **PARA 13.13** above.
72 PL(S)A 1973, s 3. See Cusine and Paisley *Servitudes and Rights of Way* para 3.73.
73 The classic modern treatment is N R Whitty 'Nuisance' in *SME* (Reissue, 2001). See also Gordon and Wortley *Scottish Land Law* paras 26.21–26.35.
74 Whitty 'Nuisance' para 2.
75 'More than tolerable.'

weight has been given to all the surrounding circumstances of the offensive conduct and its effects'.[76] This must be determined objectively. In other words, it is not whether the particular pursuer feels that the interference is more than reasonably tolerable, but whether a reasonable person placed in that situation would be of that view.[77]

Examples

18.22   There is an open-ended list of types of conduct which can be classed as a nuisance, but the case law can be broadly divided into instances of:

(1) physical damage; and

(2) interference with the use and enjoyment of land.[78]

Examples of the former are:

(a) Vibrations which cause structural damage to buildings.[79]

(b) Removing a load-bearing wall, causing damage to a flat above.[80]

(c) Attracting pigeons by frequently putting out feed, the consequence being that the birds' droppings choked pipes and polluted the water in them.[81]

Examples of the latter are:

(a) Noise.[82] In one of the most famous modern cases, an unsuccessful attempt was made to interdict the Edinburgh Military Tattoo on the basis that it was a nuisance.[83]

(b) Disagreeable smells, for example sewage.[84]

(c) Excessive electric light.[85]

(d) Burning plastics and causing smoke that may be carcinogenic.[86]

(e) Releasing contaminating chemicals.[87]

Assessment of nuisance

18.23   In assessing whether conduct is more than reasonably tolerable, the courts take account of various factors including the nature of the harm, the social value of the use or enjoyment invaded, the sensitivity to harm of the persons and property

---

[76]   *Watt v Jamieson* 1954 SC 56 at 58 per Lord President Cooper (Outer House).

[77]   *Maguire v Charles McNeil Ltd* 1922 SC 174 at 191 per Lord Skerrington; Whitty, 'Nuisance' para 41.

[78]   Whitty 'Nuisance' paras 45–46.

[79]   *Lord Advocate v Reo Stakis Organisation Ltd* 1981 SC 104.

[80]   *Kennedy v Glenbelle* 1996 SC 95. This may also be actionable under T(S)A 2004, s 11. See **PARA 16.25** above.

[81]   *Allison v Stevenson* (1908) 24 Sh Ct Rep 214.

[82]   *King v Advocate General for Scotland* [2009] CSOH 169.

[83]   *Webster v Lord Advocate* 1984 SLT 13, aff'd 1985 SLT 361.

[84]   *Houldsworth v Wishaw Magistrates* (1887) 14 R 920.

[85]   *Summers v Crichton* 2000 GWD 40-1495.

[86]   *Green v Chalmers* 2016 SCLR 413.

[87]   *Esso Petroleum Co Ltd v Scottish Ministers* [2015] CSOH 21, 2015 GWD 7-134.

affected.[88] They also consider in relation to the defender the primary purpose of the conduct, the suitability of the conduct to the character of the locality and how practicable it is for the defender to remedy the conduct.[89] Fundamentally, for the defender to be liable, fault (*culpa*) must be proven.[90] For example, referring to one of the cases mentioned above, a party who removes a wall which that party knows to be load-bearing, causing damage to the property above, is at fault and therefore liable.[91]

Defences

18.24   There are a number of available defences. These include:
(1) negative prescription of the right to object (20 years);[92]
(2) acquiescence by the pursuer;[93] and
(3) statutory authorisation.[94]

In an English action against a water company for damage caused by sewers flooding, reliance on the relevant statutory regime was a successful defence to a claim based on both nuisance and ECHR, Art 8 and Protocol 1, Art 1.[95] In contrast, it is no defence that the nuisance was going on before the pursuer arrived at the property, nor that it is in the public interest.[96]

Remedies

18.25   The usual court remedies apply. Interdict is possible. An order *ad factum praestandum* can be sought to make the defender carry out remedial works.[97] Damages are available for the loss suffered.[98]

AEMULATIO VICINI (SPITEFUL ACTS)

General

18.26   Where an owner does something that is in itself lawful but does it merely out of *aemulatio vicini* (spite towards a neighbour), the act is unlawful. (This idea of

---

88   Whitty 'Nuisance' paras 43–66.
89   Whitty 'Nuisance' paras 67–77.
90   *RHM Bakeries (Scotland) Ltd v Strathclyde Regional Council* 1985 SC (HL) 17. See also *Black Loch Angling Club v Tarmac Ltd* 2012 SCLR 501.
91   *Kennedy v Glenbelle* 1996 SC 95.
92   PL(S)A 1973, s 7.
93   Eg *Colville v Middleton*, 27 May 1817 FC.
94   Eg under the Civil Aviation Act 1982, ss 76 and 77.
95   *Marcic v Thames Water Utilities Ltd* [2004] 2 AC 42.
96   *Webster v Lord Advocate* 1984 SLT 13, aff'd 1985 SLT 361.
97   Eg *Adam v Alloa Police Commissioners* (1874) 2 R 143.
98   Eg *Stevenson v Pontifex and Wood* (1887) 15 R 125.

'abuse of right' has been developed in many legal systems, but not much in Scotland, other than in property law.) The doctrine may also be applicable in circumstances where the respective proprietary rights of the parties have not been established, for example where there is a boundary dispute.[99] One example is interference with underground water which would normally percolate to the complainer's property.[100] Another is building fences or growing hedges which block out the complainer's light.[101] But the High Hedges (Scotland) Act 2013 now provides a separate statutory remedy in respect of high hedges with local authorities acting as enforcement bodies. The remedies for *aemulatio vicini*, like nuisance, are the usual court remedies.

USE OF A NEIGHBOUR'S PROPERTY

General

18.27 Clearly, there are many grounds upon which a landowner may make limited use of a neighbour's property. Servitudes and public rights of way are obvious examples.[102] The concern here is merely with two residual rights:
  (a) drainage and
  (b) access for repairs.

Drainage

18.28 A landowner is entitled to let water lying outside a definite channel, such as a river, drain onto lower-lying neighbouring land.[103] The right applies to both surface and underground water. The owner is entitled to carry out works which alter the route of the drainage, but there are certain limitations. Only water naturally arising on the property, for example by rain, may be drained. The drainage must follow the natural lie of the land. Moreover, regard must be had to not damaging the inferior land by overstretching the right,[104] for example by carrying out building works on the superior land which cause an excessive amount of water to come down. In particular, unless there is a servitude of eavesdrop there is no right to collect rainwater on a roof and let it fall onto a neighbouring property.[105]

---

[99] Whitty 'Nuisance' para 34.
[100] *Milton v Glen-Moray Glenlivet Distillery Co Ltd* (1898) 1 F 135. See also *More v Boyle* 1967 SLT (Sh Ct) 38.
[101] *Dunlop v Robertson* (1803) Hume 515; *Glassford v Astley* (1808) Mor 'Property', App, No 7, Hume 516.
[102] See **CHAPTER 13** above and **PARAS 19.13–19.22** below.
[103] *Campbell v Bryson* (1864) 3 M 254.
[104] *Logan v Wang (UK) Ltd* 1991 SLT 580.
[105] On eavesdrop, see **PARA 13.15** above.

Access for repairs

18.29   In an important passage which does not seem to have been founded on in court, Hume states:

'I think it may be maintained with respect to conterminous proprietors in a Burgh, which in many instances, owing to the crowded situation of the building, cannot be repaired without some temporary interference, as by resting ladders on the next area, or suspending a scaffold over the next area, that this slight and temporary inconvenience must be put up with, from the necessity of the case.'[106]

LITERATURE

18.30   On boundary walls, see further Reid *Property* paras 193–226 and Gordon and Wortley *Scottish Land Law* paras 3.37–3.51. On encroachment, see further Reid *Property* paras 175–180 and Gordon and Wortley *Scottish Land Law* paras 13.06–13.09. On support, see further Reid *Property* paras 252–272. On nuisance, see further Whitty, N R 'Nuisance' in *SME* (Reissue, 2001) and Gordon *Scottish Land Law* paras 26.21–26.35. On *aemulatio vicini*, see further Gordon *Scottish Land Law* para 26.20.

---

[106]   Hume *Lectures* III, 207. In tenements there is now a statutory access right to parts owned by others. See **PARA 16.27** above.

Chapter 19

Public access rights

INTRODUCTION

19.1   Private ownership of land is subject to certain rights in favour of the public. At common law the most important is the public right of way. Also significant are rights over water and the foreshore. The common law however, is of less importance given the wide-ranging nature of the Land Reform (Scotland) Act 2003 (LR(S) A 2003) which gives access rights over private land for recreation and other purposes. If there is no right to be on someone else's land whether at common law or under statute, the landowner or other lawful possessor will have the remedy of trespass against those who come onto the land without permission. This is the subject of the final section of this chapter.[1] We begin with statutory access rights.

LAND REFORM (SCOTLAND) ACT 2003

The right to roam

19.2   Part 1 of LR(S)A 2003 was passed to improve access to land. A statutory 'right to roam' (an expression not used in the Act itself) was introduced. The legislation makes it clear that the rights under it are distinct from and do not affect other access rights, for example a servitude or public right of way allowing vehicular traffic.[2] This leads to a rather awkward overlap between LR(S)A 2003 and the common law.

Content of the access rights

19.3   LR(S)A 2003, s 1 confers on everyone statutory *access rights* to land. These rights are:
   (a) the right to be, for specified purposes, on land; and
   (b) the right to cross land.

The specified purposes in relation to (a) are set out in LR(S)A 2003, s 1(3). There are three. The first is 'recreational purposes'. This is not further defined, but the Scottish Outdoor Access Code,[3] introduced under the legislation, gives examples: pastimes such as watching wildlife, sightseeing and photography; family and social

---

[1]   See **PARAS 19.30–19.36** below.
[2]   LR(S)A 2003, s 5(3).
[3]   Scottish Outdoor Access Code para 2.7 (available at www.outdooraccess-scotland.com/).

activities, such as walks, picnics and kite flying; active pursuits, such as canoeing, horse riding,[4] mountaineering, sailing and wild camping; and participation in events such as marathons and mountain biking competitions.[5]

19.4   The second specified purpose for exercising access rights is 'carrying on a relevant educational activity'. This is defined as relating to furthering the understanding of natural or cultural heritage.[6] It allows access rights to be exercised by a leader and his or her students and support staff on a trip to learn about wildlife or landscapes or geological features.[7] The third purpose is 'carrying on, commercially or for profit, an activity which the person exercising the right could carry on otherwise than commercially or for profit'. This is a rather unclear provision, but it would seem to authorise the activities of paid mountain guides and the like. Therefore, John is entitled to charge for a walking tour of hills belonging to Kaira, without Kaira having to be paid. Specific activities are not permitted, in particular hunting, shooting or fishing and using a motorised vehicle or vessel.[8] The right to roam may not be exercised by car or motorbike.

Excluded land

General

19.5   Access rights can be exercised above and below, as well as on, the surface of land,[9] (for example hand-gliding through the air or walking in a cave) with 'land' including bridges, inland waters, canals and the foreshore.[10] But the rights may not be exercised over the land listed in LR(S)A 2003, s 6. The list is a long one but, significantly, includes:

  (a) buildings;
  (b) caravans, tents or other places providing people with privacy or shelter;
  (c) school grounds;
  (d) sports or other playing fields;
  (e) land to which access is prohibited by other legislation;
  (f) land set out for a particular recreational purpose;
  (g) land on which building, civil engineering or demolition works are being carried out; and
  (h) land in which crops have been sown or are growing.[11]

---

[4]   On which see *Tuley v Highland Council* 2009 SC 456. See K G C Reid and G L Gretton *Conveyancing 2009* (2010) 165.
[5]   Scottish Outdoor Access Code para 2.7.
[6]   LR(S)A 2003, s 1(5).
[7]   Scottish Outdoor Access Code para 2.8.
[8]   LR(S)A 2003, s 9.
[9]   LR(S)A 2003, s 1(6).
[10]   LR(S)A 2003, s 32.
[11]   Woodland and orchards are in principle excluded from (h). See LR(S)A 2003, s 7(10)(c)(i).

The list makes no mention of railways, but the Law Commissions have recommended that the legislation should be amended to make it clear that access rights should be excluded at track level.[12]

Three important cases

19.6   Three further types of land on the list require more detailed mention. First, the access rights do not extend to 'sufficient adjacent land' to allow persons living in houses or the places mentioned in (b) above 'to have reasonable measures of privacy in that house or place to ensure that their enjoyment [thereof] is not unreasonably disturbed'.[13] The Scottish Outdoor Access Code attempts to provide some guidance.[14] 'Sufficient adjacent land' is normally to mean an individual's garden. In relation to larger houses with what may be termed 'policies', the Code says that access rights do not apply to those parts 'intensively managed for the domestic enjoyment of the house'. Examples given are lawns, flower beds, paths, seats, sheds, water features and summer houses. But 'less intensively managed' parts such as grasslands and woodlands are to be subject to access rights. The Code's approach was criticised by the sheriff in *Gloag v Perth and Kinross Council*[15] because LR(S)A 2003 does not make the *use* of the land the test. Otherwise, large landowners might be tempted to turn their whole estate into a lawn.[16] More fundamentally, LR(S)A 2003, s 10 says that the Code is about the *how* of access, not the *where*. In the *Gloag* case, well-known businesswoman Ann Gloag obtained declarator that 14.5 acres of her estate at Kinfauns Castle in Perthshire were exempt from access rights under this ground, by reason of the need to protect her privacy. In *Snowie v Stirling Council*[17] the owners of Boquhan House, Kippen sought to have all 70 acres of their estate declared exempt. This failed except for the much smaller area of 12.6 acres.[18]

19.7   Second, land open to the public in return for payment for at least 90 days in the year ending 31 January 2001, and which has continued since then to be open upon payment, is not subject to access rights.[19] The date relates to when the draft Land Reform Bill was first published. It means that an established tourist attraction such as Blair Drummond Safari Park can continue to charge an admission fee but, in principle, someone opening a new safari park cannot restrict access by fee-charging.

---

[12]   But where there is a public level crossing access can be taken by means of the public right of way over that crossing. See Law Commission and Scottish Law Commission, Report on Level Crossings (Law Com No 339 and Scot Law Com No 234, 2013) paras 5.54–5.61.
[13]   LR(S)A 2003, s 6(1)(b)(iv).
[14]   Scottish Outdoor Access Code paras 3.13–3.17.
[15]   2007 SCLR 530 at para 36.
[16]   K G C Reid and G L Gretton *Conveyancing 2007* (2008) 131.
[17]   2008 GWD 13-244.
[18]   Compare also *Creelman v Argyll and Bute Council* 2009 SLT (Sh Ct) 165 and *Forbes v Fife Council* 2009 SLT (Sh Ct) 71.
[19]   LR(S)A 2003, s 6(1)(f).

Such a person should therefore ask the local authority to exempt the land from LR(S) A 2003.

19.8   Land exempted by a local authority is the third type of excepted land referred to above.[20] There are detailed rules on how the authority can make an exemption order.[21] In particular, the order must be confirmed by the Scottish Ministers if it is to last for six or more days. Ministers also have power to exempt land.[22]

Responsible conduct

19.9   Both those exercising access rights and the owner of the land in question must act responsibly.[23] The exercise of access rights is presumed to be responsible if it does not 'cause unreasonable interference' to the rights of others, for example the rights of the landowner or others taking advantage of their access rights.[24] Landowners are prohibited from taking action which has 'the main purpose of preventing or deterring' the exercise of access rights.[25] This expressly includes putting up signs and fences.[26] Local authorities have enforcement powers.[27]

Duty of care of landowners

19.10   The duty of care owed by landowners to individuals present on their land is not altered by LR(S)A 2003.[28] Nevertheless, it is not unreasonable to suppose that more people may exercise access as a result of the legislation. Therefore, the risk in practice of a civil action may increase.[29]

The role of Scottish Natural Heritage

19.11   LR(S)A 2003 imposes certain responsibilities on Scottish Natural Heritage, most notably the creation and issue of the Scottish Outdoor Access Code.[30] The Code

---

[20]   LR(S)A 2003, s 6(1)(j).
[21]   LR(S)A 2003, s 11.
[22]   LR(S)A 2003, s 8.
[23]   LR(S)A 2003, ss 2 and 3.
[24]   LR(S)A 2003, s 2(2).
[25]   LR(S)A 2003, s 14(1).
[26]   Therefore fences, hedges in placed before the 2003 Act came into force are not actionable: *Aviemore Highland Resort Ltd v Cairngorms National Park Authority* 2009 SLT (Sh Ct) 97.
[27]   LR(S)A 2003, ss 13 and 14. See *Caledonian Heritable Ltd v East Lothian Council* 2006 GWD 22-487, *Tuley v Highland Council* 2009 SC 456 and *Forbes v Fife Council* 2009 SLT (Sh Ct) 71.
[28]   LR(S)A 2003, s 5(2).
[29]   For discussion, see D Mackenzie Skene and A M Slater 'Liability and Access to the Countryside: The Impact of Part 1 of the Land Reform (Scotland) Act 2003' 2004 *JR* 353.
[30]   LR(S)A 2003, s 10.

contains much detail about how access rights should be exercised. Its legal status is not entirely clear. A comparison could be made with the Highway Code.

The role of local authorities

19.12 Local authorities are given a wide-ranging regulatory role in relation to the legislation. They have a general duty to uphold access rights.[31] More particularly, they have the power to make byelaws[32] and can install notices and fences, as well as 'means of contributing to the comfort and convenience' of those exercising access rights.[33] Lavatories are expressly mentioned. Local authorities are also tasked with establishing a 'core path' plan, to facilitate the public in gaining reasonable access to land in their area.[34]

PUBLIC RIGHTS OF WAY

General

19.13 At common law, a public right of way can be created giving members of the public a right of access over land in order to travel from one public place to another. There are over 7,000 such rights recorded in the National Catalogue of Rights of Way maintained by the Scottish Rights of Way and Access Society in association with Scottish Natural Heritage.[35] Public rights of way remain important notwithstanding access rights under LR(S)A 2003. For example, they may have a route over land excluded from those rights, or may be vehicular.

19.14 A public right of way is similar to a servitude.[36] But there are some key differences.[37] First, with a servitude there is not only a burdened property but also a benefited property. With a public right of way, there is *only* a burdened property. Second, a public right of way can be exercised by anyone. A servitude can only be exercised by the benefited proprietor.[38] Third, a servitude can facilitate access to private land. A public right of way must connect two public places. Fourth, servitudes allow use of land for various purposes, such as to lay pipes and take building materials. Public rights of way give access rights only. These features are discussed further in the following paragraphs.

---

[31] LR(S)A 2003, s 13.
[32] LR(S)A 2003, s 12.
[33] LR(S)A 2003, s 15.
[34] LR(S)A 2003, ss 17–22.
[35] See www.scotways.com/.
[36] On servitudes, see **CHAPTER 13** above.
[37] See also *Thomson v Murdoch* (1862) 24 D 975 at 982 per Lord Deas; and Cusine and Paisley *Servitudes and Rights of Way* paras 1.12 and 18.11.
[38] And a limited number of other parties such as tenants of the benefited proprietor. See **PARA 13.31** above.

A burdened property

19.15   Land burdened by a public right of way may be in either private or public ownership. The right may be across open ground or through a structure that has acceded, such as a covered walkway over a road.[39] It is an essential requirement, however, that there is a fixed route. A public right of way has the purpose of allowing access from A to B. It cannot permit general wandering.[40] In the words of Lord Sands in one of the leading cases:

> '[T]he right of way claimed must be by a definite path. I do not think that this necessarily requires that under all circumstances that there should be a visible path.'[41]

Where, however, there is not a physical path it may be more difficult to establish the existence of the right.

Two public places

19.16   The requirement that a public right of way requires to connect two public places requires a definition of what is a 'public place'. The courts have approached this question on a case-by-case basis but, in summary, it is a place to which the public has resort for a lawful purpose.[42] The following have been held to be public places:

  (a) a public road;[43]
  (b) Portobello beach, being an example of a beach used by the public regularly for recreation;[44]
  (c) a town;[45] and
  (d) a harbour.[46]

The following have been held not to be public places:

  (a) a market open for four days a week only;[47]
  (b) a sub-post office in a private house;[48]
  (c) a curious natural object such as a large rock;[49] and

---

[39]   *Cumbernauld and Kilsyth District Council v Dollar Land (Cumbernauld) Ltd* 1993 SC (HL) 44.

[40]   *Mackintosh v Moir* (1871) 9 M 574 at 575 per Lord President Inglis and at 579 per Lord Ardmillan.

[41]   *Rhins District Committee of Wigtownshire County Council v Cuninghame* 1917 2 SLT 169 at 171.

[42]   Cusine and Paisley *Servitudes and Rights of Way* paras 20.03–20.22.

[43]   *Jenkins v Murray* (1866) 4 M 1046 at 1052 per Lord Deas.

[44]   *Darrie v Drummond* (1865) 3 M 496 at 501 per Lord Deas. See also *Richardson v Cromarty Petroleum Co Ltd* 1982 SLT 237 and *Lauder v MacColl* 1993 SCLR 753.

[45]   *Duncan v Lees* (1871) 9 M 855 at 856 per Lord President Inglis.

[46]   *Moncreiffe v Lord Provost of Perth* (1842) 5 D 298. But, depending on the facts, a harbour could be private.

[47]   *Ayr Burgh Council v British Transport Commission* 1955 SLT 219.

[48]   *Love-Lee v Cameron* 1991 SCLR 61.

[49]   *Duncan v Lees* (1870) 9 M 274.

(d) Prestwick Airport, on the basis that the public does not have a right to access it at all times.[50]

Access only

19.17   A public right of way permits access across the burdened property only. It does not authorise other rights such as pasturage or the laying of pipes. There is an argument that the public may have certain rights ancillary to that of access, such as the placing of signs to indicate the way.[51] Local authorities have a statutory right to install and maintain facilities 'contributing to the comfort and convenience' of those exercising a public right of way such as gates, stiles, seats and lavatories.[52] The extent of the access, for example, whether it is confined to passage on foot will be determined by what type of right has been created.

Creation

19.18   In principle, a public right of way may be created expressly in a deed granted by a landowner.[53] A grant cannot be made in favour of the public as such; rather, it should be in favour of a representative body such as a local authority or the Scottish Rights of Way and Access Society.[54] The relevant deed may state how the right may be exercised, for example by means of non-commercial vehicles. It is thought that the deed does not have to be registered, but it can be.[55] If it is not, it is unclear whether possession is required to constitute the right. It might be that a right of way does not actually require a deed for it to be voluntarily granted by the landowner. This is discussed below.[56]

19.19   Creation by deed is rare. Constitution by positive prescription is far more common. This requires possession by members of the public for a period of 20 years.[57] No foundation writ or other form of registration is required. The possession must meet a number of requirements.

(1) It must be along the *entire* length of the route.[58]
(2) It must be continuous and uninterrupted.[59]

50   *PIK Facilities Ltd v Watson's Ayr Park Ltd* 2005 SLT 1041.
51   Cusine and Paisley *Servitudes and Rights of Way* para 2.18.
52   LR(S)A 2003, s 15(4) applied by s 31.
53   *Marquis of Bute v McKirdy & McMillan* 1937 SC 93 at 131 per Lord Moncreiff.
54   *Marquis of Bute* at 131 per Lord Moncreiff.
55   Cusine and Paisley *Servitudes and Rights of Way* para 19.11.
56   See **PARA 19.23** below.
57   PL(S)A 1973, s 3(3). The Law Commissions have recommended that it should not be possible to acquire a public right of way over a railway line under this provision for safety reasons. See Law Commission and Scottish Law Commission, Report on Level Crossings (Law Com No 339 and Scot Law Com No 234, 2013) paras 5.45–5.51.
58   *Rhins District Committee of Wigtownshire County Council v Cuninghame* 1917 2 SLT 169.
59   *Mann v Brodie* (1885) 11 R (HL) 52.

(3) The use must be *substantial*. This depends on the facts of the case, in particular whether the route is located in a remote or populous area. Generally, a greater level of use must be made in an urban situation.[60]

(4) Finally, the possession must be 'adverse' and not by tolerance.

This means that if, for example, John, a landowner, explicitly gives permission for a group of local walkers to cross his land then their doing so will not amount to adverse possession. John might, however, not have given permission but not objected either. In that case, 'the law will assume a public right rather than an easy-going proprietor'.[61] Ironically, the introduction of the statutory access rights under LR(S) A 2003 may make it more difficult to establish a public right of way by prescription. This is because a court may attribute the exercise to those rights and this of itself cannot found a prescriptive right of way.[62]

19.20   The extent of a right of way created by prescription is the extent of the possession: *tantum praescriptum tantum possessum*. This means, for example, if access has only been taken on foot, a car may not be used. But the greater right includes the lesser. Hence a right for vehicles will mean that pedestrians and horse riders can use the way.[63] It has been held that bicycles may be ridden where the right was created by pedestrian use, on the ground that 'the pedal cycle is only an aid to pedestrianism'.[64]

Exercise

19.21   Like a servitude, a public right of way must be exercised in a manner which is least burdensome to the landowner.[65] Exercise must not interfere with the rights of other members of the public wishing to take advantage of it either. The landowner is not entitled to obstruct the way.[66] Gates are permissible, if erected for good reason, such as to confine animals.[67] They must not be locked, however, unless a stile or other method of passing the gate is provided.[68] Local authorities have the same powers to deal with obstructions to rights of way as for access rights under LR(S)A 2003.[69] There is similar power available to planning authorities, i.e. local authorities under separate legislation.[70] The landowner is not under a duty to repair the route,[71] but

---

[60]   *Cumbernauld and Kilsyth District Council v Dollar Land (Cumbernauld) Ltd* 1993 SC (HL) 44.

[61]   *Marquis of Bute v McKirdy & McMillan* 1937 SC 93 at 120–121 per Lord President Normand.

[62]   LR(S)A 2003, s 5(5). See R R M Paisley *Access Rights and Rights of Way: A Guide to the Law in Scotland* (2006) 9.

[63]   *Mackenzie v Bankes* (1868) 6 M 936.

[64]   *Aberdeenshire County Council v Lord Glentanar* 1999 SLT 1456. This case was actually decided in 1931.

[65]   *Lord Burton v Mackay* 1995 SLT 507.

[66]   *Lord Donington v Mair* (1894) 21 R 829.

[67]   *Hay v Earl of Morton's Trs* (1861) 24 D 116.

[68]   *Kirkpatrick v Murray* (1856) 19 D 91.

[69]   LR(S)A 2003, s 14, as applied by s 31.

[70]   Countryside (Scotland) Act 1967, s 46(1).

[71]   *Allan v MacLachlan* (1900) 2 F 699.

should consider this matter carefully, given the Occupiers' Liability (Scotland) Act 1960.[72] In principle, members of the public may do so,[73] but in practice this is likely to fall to the local authority under statute.[74]

Extinction

19.22 A public right of way is extinguished by 20 years of non-use.[75] It will also cease to exist if either or both the places at the ends of the way are no longer public places. There are also various statutory powers in favour of public bodies such as local authorities which can be used to bring about the demise of the right.[76] Where a public right of way is extinguished intermediate proprietors may nonetheless take access along the route to reach their properties.[77]

Public roads

19.23 There exists a complex set of common law and statutory rules on public roads. This whole area of law is under-researched and difficult. A local authority may 'adopt' a road.[78] It may do so in relation to roads over which there is a public right of passage.[79] The Inner House has confirmed that a public right of passage means a public right of way.[80] Adoption means that the authority becomes responsible for the maintenance of the road. Ownership is unaffected. How can a public right of passage be created? For roads older than 20 years, positive prescription may have operated.[81] But there is a difficulty with this. Where a developer builds a road for a new development or the Scottish Government constructs a new motorway on land which it has compulsorily acquired, the subsequent use of the road or motorway will be with the consent of the developer or Government. Thus, it will not be 'adverse' possession, as required for positive prescription.[82] It may be that in such circumstances our law permits the creation of a public right of way, or more narrowly, a public road, voluntarily without the need for a deed. This is speculative. The essential point is that our law is obscure. A further argument is that there exists a common law right of highway which may be invoked, although the applicable rules

---

72 *Johnstone v Sweeney* 1985 SLT (Sh Ct) 2. See also J W G Blackie 'Liability as Occupier to User of a Right of Way' 1994 *SLT (News)* 349. But see also *Leonard v The Loch Lomond and the Trossachs National Park Authority* [2014] CSOH 38 (landowner not under a duty to protect against obvious dangers).

73 *Rodgers v Harvie* (1830) 8 S 611.

74 Countryside (Scotland) Act 1967, s 46(2).

75 PL(S)A 1973, s 8.

76 Cusine and Paisley *Servitudes and Rights of Way* paras 24.08–24.13.

77 *Lord Burton v Mackay* 1995 SLT 507.

78 Roads (Scotland) Act 1984, ss 1 and 16.

79 Roads (Scotland) Act 1984, s 15(1).

80 *Hamilton v Dumfries and Galloway Council* 2009 SC 337.

81 See **PARA 19.19** above.

82 See **PARA 19.19** above.

are not certain.[83] Finally, where land is acquired by a public authority in order for a road to be constructed, it can be argued that such a road is irrevocably dedicated to public use.[84] Whether this amounts to the establishment of a public right of way is again uncertain.

19.24   Professor Paisley has identified certain differences between public roads and other public rights of way, some of which may be mentioned.[85] In general, it would seem that a right over a public road is imprescriptible.[86] While public rights of way may be limited to pedestrian use, public roads can always be used by vehicles. Moreover, they may be used to convey services, but this latter right is now under the control of the roads authority.[87] Finally, while limited obstructions such as unlocked gates can be erected on (non-road) public rights of way, there is, subject to statutory exceptions,[88] a prohibition on obstructions across public roads.[89]

RIGHTS OVER WATER AND THE FORESHORE

General

19.25   At common law the public have certain rights over tidal and non-tidal waters, as well as the foreshore.[90] As with public rights of way, there is a rather awkward overlap with the new statutory access rights under LR(S)A 2003. The common-law rights are held in trust by the Crown for the benefit of the public under the doctrine of the *regalia majora*.[91] Thus the Crown is entitled to enforce these rights.[92] But so too are members of the public, by means of an action known as the *actio popularis*.[93] The Scottish Law Commission has recommended that the common-law rights be replaced by a set of statutory rights directly enforceable by the public.[94] If these recommendations are implemented, the Crown's enforcement role would cease. Instead, local authorities would be charged with this.[95]

19.26   With one important exception, the rights arise automatically. That exception is the right to navigate non-tidal waters, which is constituted by 40 years of use.[96] These rights do not require registration for their constitution.

[83]   Cusine and Paisley *Servitudes and Rights of Way* paras 18.03–18.10.
[84]   *Elmford v City of Glasgow Council (No 2)* 2001 SC 267.
[85]   Paisley, *Land Law* para 10.12.
[86]   *Waddell v Earl of Buchan* (1868) 6 M 690.
[87]   Roads (Scotland) Act 1984, ss 61 and 90–93.
[88]   For example, for certain bridge tolls, prior to the Abolition of Bridge Tolls (Scotland) Act 2008.
[89]   *Sutherland v Thomson* (1876) 3 R 485 and Roads (Scotland) Act 1984, s 59.
[90]   For definitions of these terms, see **PARAS 17.3 AND 17.5** above.
[91]   See Gordon *Scottish Land Law* para 27.06.
[92]   *Crown Estate Commissioners v Fairlie Yacht Slip Ltd* 1979 SC 156 at 178 per Lord President Emslie.
[93]   See, eg, *Walford v David* 1989 SLT 876.
[94]   Scottish Law Commission, Report on Law of the Foreshore and Sea Bed (Scot Law Com No 190, 2003) paras 3.1–3.8.
[95]   Report on Law of the Foreshore and Sea Bed paras 3.31–3.35.
[96]   See **PARA 19.29** below.

Tidal waters

19.27   There are two rights over tidal waters. The first is *navigation*. This is confined to waters which are 'navigable', that is waters which in their usual state are capable of navigation.[97] By 'navigation' is meant travelling by boat or equivalent vessel on the water. It does not include propelling a canoe by wading along the sea or river bed.[98] Certain rights ancillary to navigation are permitted, such as dropping anchor. The attaching of fixed moorings to the sea bed is not.[99] The second right is that of *white fishing* and *fishing for shellfish*. By 'white fishing' is meant the right to take all swimming fish other than salmon. By 'shellfish' are meant all shellfish on the sea bed, apart from mussels and oysters. The rights to salmon, mussels and oysters are legal separate tenements and are thus excluded from the public rights.[100]

Foreshore

19.28   Various rights exist over the foreshore. Akin to the rights relating to tidal waters, there are rights ancillary to navigation, such as fishing for white fish and shellfish, embarkation, shooting wildfowl[101] and recreation.[102] The latter does not include selling refreshments.[103] The Scottish Law Commission has recommended the enactment of a non-exhaustive list of recreational activities, including picnicking, sunbathing and making sandcastles.[104]

Non-tidal waters

19.29   At common law there are no public rights in non-tidal waters, except that the right of navigation can be acquired by 40 years of use.[105] In that case the rule *tantum praescriptum quantum possessum*[106] does not apply: the water can be navigated to its full extent.[107] The importance of the common law in this area has been much diminished by LR(S)A 2003, under which non-motorised passage along rivers is

97   *Will's Trs v Cairngorm Canoeing and Sailing School Ltd* 1976 SC (HL) 30 at 165 per Lord Fraser.
98   *Scammell v Scottish Sports Council* 1983 SLT 462.
99   *Crown Estate Commissioners v Fairlie Yacht Slip Ltd* 1979 SC 156; *Crown Estate Commissioners, Petitioners* 2010 SLT 741.
100   See **PARA 15.17** above. But the Scottish Law Commission has recommended that there should be a public right to take mussels and oysters except where the right to these has been specifically granted by the Crown. See Report on Law of the Foreshore and Sea Bed (Scot Law Com No 190, 2003) para 3.19.
101   *Hope v Bennewith* (1904) 6 F 1004.
102   *Nicol v Blaikie* (1859) 22 D 335.
103   *Marquess of Ailsa v Monteforte* 1937 SC 805.
104   Report on Law of the Foreshore and Sea Bed para 3.14.
105   *Will's Trustees v Cairngorm Canoeing and Sailing School Ltd* 1979 SC (HL) 30, about canoeing on the Spey.
106   See **PARA 19.20** above.
107   1979 SC (HL) 30 at 169 per Lord Fraser.

permitted.[108] But the common law right can still apply where the statutory rights cannot, for example where the river is near a house and is excluded by the legislation on the ground of privacy.[109]

TRESPASS

Introduction

19.30   It is sometimes said that there is no law of trespass in Scotland. This, however, is to be 'loose and inaccurate'.[110] Were it to be otherwise, there would be no need for the common law public rights over land and water, nor the new statutory rights under LR(S)A 2003. *Trespass* is the temporary intrusion into the land of another. It is a delict. For example, Ann might take a short-cut through Bob's garden. Someone may trespass by means of an animal (Carol's dog runs about on Donald's lawn) or of a thing (Elspeth's crane swings across Fred's airspace).[111] Trespass is a *transient* interference with someone's right of possession of his or her land exclusively. By contrast, in the case of *encroachment* the interference is more than transient.[112]

Defences

19.31   If a trespass action were to be raised, two main defences are available to the defender.
  (1) That the owner or other lawful possessor has either expressly or impliedly *consented* to the intrusion. For example, a university agrees to the use of its library by its students.[113]
  (2) That the intrusion is permitted by law. For example, Lisa may be entitled to cross Megan's field because of a servitude or a public right of way or the access rights in LR(S)A 2003.[114] The intrusion might also be justified by judicial warrant. An example is where a judicial officer executes diligence.[115]

A further instance is *emergency*. On this basis, escape from a fire, or the chasing of a criminal through the property of another, is justified.[116] The high-profile case of *Scottish Parliament Corporate Body v Sovereign Indigenous Peoples of Scotland*[117] saw an unsuccessful attempt to invoke ECHR articles 10 (freedom of expression)

---

[108]   See **PARA 19.3** above.
[109]   LR(S)A 2003, s 6(1)(b)(iv). See **PARA 19.6** above.
[110]   *Wood v North British Railway* (1899) 2 F 1 at 2 per Lord Trayner.
[111]   *Brown v Lee Constructions Ltd* 1977 SLT (Notes) 61.
[112]   See **PARAS 18.10–18.16** above.
[113]   Reid *Property* para 181.
[114]   See LR(S)A 2003, s 5(1).
[115]   Debtors (Scotland) Act 1987, s 87.
[116]   Hume *Lectures* III, 205–206.
[117]   2016 SLT 761 and 862 affd 2016 SLT 1307.

and 11 (freedom of assembly), as well as numerous other ECHR articles, to resist an action to remove a pro-independence camp from the grounds of the Scottish Parliament.

Criminal liability

19.32   In general, trespass is not a crime. There are, however, a number of statutes making it criminal in particular circumstances. These include the Trespass (Scotland) Act 1865 which makes it an offence to lodge or encamp on private property except where exercising access rights under LR(S)A 2003;[118] the Wildlife and Countryside Act 1981 which is aimed at poachers;[119] and the Criminal Justice and Public Order Act 1994, aimed at New Age travellers.[120]

Civil remedies

19.33   Trespass may be interdicted. In practice, the remedy can be difficult to obtain. The name(s) of the trespasser(s) must be known. It is impossible to interdict the public at large. The courts will not grant interdict unless there is a reasonable likelihood of trespass.[121] Proof of past trespass is the best evidence.[122] The pursuer is expected to have warned the trespasser off before seeking an interdict.[123] Interdict will not be awarded if the trespass is trivial. In *Winans v Macrae*[124] the pursuer sought an interdict preventing the defender 'from putting any lamb, lambs, sheep, cattle, or other bestial' on his 200,000 acres of unfenced rough grazing. The defender, who lived in an adjacent cottage, had only a pet lamb. The action failed.

19.34   A trespasser who causes damage is liable for it. But liability is not strict. There must be *culpa* ie fault.[125] There is an exception for damage caused by certain animals.[126]

Self-help

19.35   Rather than going to court, the landowner or lawful possessor may seek to deal with the trespasser directly. Steps may be taken to stop trespass happening in the first place such as locking gates and erecting high walls. Premises may also be

---

[118]   Trespass (Scotland) Act 1865, s 3.
[119]   Wildlife and Countryside Act 1981, ss 1 and 11G.
[120]   Criminal Justice and Public Order Act 1994, ss 61, 62, 68 and 69.
[121]   *Inverurie Magistrates v Sorrie* 1956 SC 175.
[122]   *Warrand v Watson* (1905) 8 F 253.
[123]   *Paterson v McPherson* (1916) 33 Sh Ct Rep 237.
[124]   (1885) 12 R 1051.
[125]   *Harvie v Turner* (1910) 32 Sh Ct Rep 267.
[126]   See **PARA 19.36** below.

protected by guard dogs, but here there is specific legislation. The dog must be under the control of a person or tied up and there must be notices at the entrances warning of the animal's presence.[127] Where the trespass is taking place, the trespasser may be asked to leave. If he or she does not do so, force may be used but this must be kept to the absolute minimum required in the circumstances. In *Bell v Shand*,[128] a late nineteenth-century case, a landowner was held to be justified in dragging a 15-year-old poacher for some distance by the scruff of the neck. Whether this is good law today is open to question. Force is more justifiable where the trespass is into a private house where the purpose is to commit theft, but it requires to be proportionate. For example, shooting a burglar might lead to criminal charges.[129]

Straying animals

19.36 Trespass by straying animals deserves particular comment. The courts are reluctant to grant interdict here unless the animal is of the type whose movements can be easily restricted, for example chickens. In the case of cattle and sheep and the like, the onus is more likely to be placed on the owner of the land which is being trespassed upon to enclose it by fencing rather than upon the owner of the animal to prevent the intrusion.[130]

19.37 The provisions of the Animals (Scotland) Act 1987 are also relevant. Under that legislation, the occupier of land may detain a straying animal which is not under any person's control in order to prevent injury or damage by it.[131] There is immunity from civil liability where such an animal is killed or injured by the occupier in self-defence or in order to protect another person or livestock.[132] This, however, only applies if the occupier acted in the reasonable belief that there was no other way of preventing or dealing with the attack and where the police are notified within 48 hours.[133] Where damage has been caused, in certain circumstances strict liability is placed upon the 'keeper' of the animal, i.e. its owner or possessor.[134] An example is where the land or its produce is materially damaged by the foraging of particular animals including cattle, goats, horses, pigs and sheep.[135]

---

[127] Guard Dogs Act 1975, s 1.
[128] (1870) 7 SLR 267.
[129] Cf the headline-hitting English case, *R v Martin* [2003] QB 1. For Scots law, see J Chalmers and F Leverick, *Criminal Defences and Pleas in Bar of Trial* (2006) para 3.22.
[130] *Winans v Macrae* (1885) 12 R 1051 at 1064 per Lord Young; *Forest Property Trust v Lindsay* 1998 GWD 31-1581.
[131] Animals (Scotland) Act 1987 (A(S)A 1987), s 3(1).
[132] A(S)A 1987, s 4(1)(a) and (3).
[133] A(S)A 1987, s 4(1)(b) and (4).
[134] A(S)A 1987, ss 1(1)(a), (b), (3) and 5(1)(a). See, for example, *Welsh v Brady* 2008 SLT 363.
[135] A(S)A 1987, s 1(1)(b) and (3)(b).

LITERATURE

19.38   On public rights of way, see further Cusine and Paisley *Servitudes and Rights of Way* chs 18–24, Reid *Property* paras 495–513 and Gordon, *Scottish Land Law* paras 24.105–24.154. Paisley, R R M *Access Rights and Rights of Way: A Guide to the Law in Scotland* (2006) is a concise guide to Part 1 of the 2003 Act and public rights of way. On public rights over water and adjacent land, see further Reid, *Property* paras 514–528. The Scottish Law Commission Report on Law of the Foreshore and Sea Bed (Scot Law Com No 190, 2003) sets out reform recommendations in relation to public rights over the foreshore. On trespass, see further Gordon and Wortley, *Scottish Land Law* paras 13.09–13.14 and Reid, *Property* paras 180–190.

Chapter 20

Leases

INTRODUCTION

20.1   A lease is a contract in which one person (the lessor) grants to another (the lessee) the right to use the property for a fixed time in return for a periodical payment known as rent. Leases are common: many students will lease the flat in which they live. Leases can also be granted over other types of property, such as agricultural and commercial property. It is competent too to lease moveable property. Such a lease is normally referred to as 'hire'. For example, a couple on holiday from abroad might hire a car for a week to drive around Scotland. In the business world, machines are frequently hired. Only leases of land are capable of becoming real rights and for that reason this chapter will be confined to that type of lease. Leases of heritable property divide into three main types:

(1) commercial property;
(2) agricultural property; and
(3) residential property.

The latter two are subject to special statutory regimes – several different ones in each case. This chapter concentrates on the general law of leases, because an account of all the special statutory regimes would be impossible here, though a brief overview of these is given. The special regimes often derogate from the general law, and within the framework of a brief account it is not possible to note all these derogations.

Terminology

20.2 The lessor is commonly called the 'landlord', and the lessee the 'tenant'. 'Tenancy' is often used as an equivalent term for lease, particularly for residential property. 'Tack' is the traditional Scottish word, now seldom encountered. 'Location' is a term which comes from the Roman *locatio*. Its use is now confined to the expression 'tacit relocation' which, as will be seen, means an implied renewal of a lease.[1] 'Mail' is an old Scottish term for rent. As well as having to pay rent, tenants sometimes have to pay a 'grassum', which is a capital payment due at the commencement of the lease, also sometimes called a 'premium'. The duration of a lease is traditionally called the 'term' and the end of the lease the 'ish'.

THE FOUR CARDINAL ELEMENTS

20.3 What are called the 'four cardinal elements' must be present in order for there to be a valid contract of lease. These are:

(a) the parties;
(b) the property;
(c) the rent; and
(d) the duration.

Without these there can be no lease, but even if all four are present no lease may have been created because of a lack of agreement by the parties on other matters.

(a) Parties

20.4 There must be agreement as to who the lessor and the lessee are. It is permissible for either to be joint parties. For example, civil partners might rent out their house or four students might take a lease of a flat. Both natural and juristic persons are capable of being parties to a lease. In the case of (business) partnerships, however, it is common for the partners to act as trustees for the firm and to contract on that basis.[2]

---

[1] See **PARA 20.38** below.
[2] This is also the practice when a partnership buys land, notwithstanding the Abolition of Feudal Tenure etc. (Scotland) Act 2000 (AFT(S)A 2000), s 70.

(b) Property

20.5   The property can be land or buildings. In these cases, the landlord is not entitled to retain natural possession of the land. Fishing rights, mineral rights and shooting rights can also be leased. In these cases, the landlord may continue to use the land over which the lease is granted for purposes other than those which are the subject of the lease. A lease can also include a *pro indiviso* share of neighbouring subjects and this case possession will be shared.[3] Under the general principle of specificity, the subjects of a lease must be identified.[4] If the tenant has already entered into possession it may be possible to refer to that possession to determine the extent of the lease.[5]

(c) Rent

20.6   The rent is usually payable on a monthly basis in residential cases and quarterly in commercial ones. Normally, the rent is monetary, but it is also permissible for rent to be paid in kind, for example by handing over a certain amount of fish or performing certain services.[6] Nowadays non-monetary rent is almost unknown in practice. If the other three cardinal elements are in place and the lessee has already taken possession, then the court may be willing to hold that a lease exists, and to fix a market rent.[7] The requirement for rent is for a periodical payment. A grassum on its own at the start of a lease is insufficient.[8] Older leases often contain provisions whereby a payment to the landlord known as a 'casualty' was triggered on the happening of a specified event. It became incompetent to impose such casualties in 1974[9] and existing ones in leases with a duration of more than 175 years have been abolished.[10]

(d) Duration

20.7   The only requirement about duration at common law is that there is one. A lease for 'as long as the grass groweth up and the water runneth down' is valid.[11] So, too, is a lease for an ultra-long period such as 999 years.[12] There are now statutory restrictions. Leases of dwellinghouses created since 1974 normally cannot

---

[3]   *Gyle Shopping Centre General Partners Ltd v Marks and Spencer plc* [2014] CSOH 59.
[4]   Eg *Conway v Glasgow City Council* 1999 SCLR 248.
[5]   *Andert Ltd v J & J Johnston* 1987 SLT 268.
[6]   Paisley *Land Law* para 7.9.
[7]   *Glen v Roy* (1882) 10 R 239; *Shetland Islands Council v BP Petroleum Development Ltd* 1990 SLT 82.
[8]   *Mann v Houston* 1957 SLT 89.
[9]   Land Tenure Reform (Scotland) Act 1974, s 16.
[10]   Leasehold Casualties (Scotland) Act 2001.
[11]   *Carruthers v Irvine* (1717) Mor 15195.
[12]   *Welwood v Husband* (1874) 1 R 507.

have a duration over 20 years.[13] Leases of other types of property created since 2000 cannot have a duration over 175 years.[14] These rules are not retrospective: for instance, a 999-year lease of a dwellinghouse created in 1821 is still valid. The rules were introduced to prevent leases being used to mimic feudal tenure, which was being dismantled and has now been abolished. Under the Long Leases (Scotland) Act 2012, on 28 November 2015, the day fixed by the Scottish Ministers ('the appointed day'), most existing ultra-long leases were converted into outright ownership. The conversion applied in general to leases with an initial duration of more than 175 years and which, if the lease subjects wholly or mainly comprise a private dwelling-house, had more than 100 years left to run and in other cases had more than 175 years left to run on the appointed day.[15] Finally on duration it must be mentioned that while this is a normal pre-requisite of a lease, if the other cardinal elements are present and the lessee has taken possession, the court will imply a duration of one year.[16]

CONSTITUTION

Leases and other rights of use

20.8   Merely because someone has the right to use the property of another does not mean that there is a contract of lease. It might be some other type of contract. For example, suppose that the possession of land is given for a period in exchange for a grassum but no rent. Lack of *exclusive* possession will again mean that the agreement is not a lease.[17] Thus a season ticket giving a football supporter the right to sit in a particular seat at matches cannot confer a lease as there is only intermittent possession.[18] The possibilities of rights of use not being leases are endless. For example, in *Scottish Residential Estates Development Co v Henderson*[19] the owner of a cottage wrote to a lady, stating that 'you and your sons may have the use of the cottage until we require possession of it'. It was held that there was no intention to create a lease. Co-owners cannot grant a lease to one co-owner.[20]

---

[13]   Land Tenure Reform (Scotland) Act 1974, ss 8–9. But there are exceptions now following the Housing (Scotland) Act 2010, ss 138 and 139 and the Private Rented Housing (Scotland) Act 2011 ss 36 and 37.

[14]   AFT(S)A 2000, s 67.

[15]   Long Leases (Scotland) Act 2012, s 1.

[16]   *Gray v University of Edinburgh* 1962 SC 157.

[17]   *Magistrates of Perth v Assessor for Perth & Kinross* 1937 SC 549.

[18]   *Joint Administrators of Rangers Football Club Plc, Noters* 2012 SLT 599.

[19]   1991 SLT 490.

[20]   *Clydesdale Bank plc v Davidson* 1998 SC(HL) 51.

Lease as a real right?

20.9   If the contractual essentials are satisfied, the tenant will have a valid contract of lease. This, however, is only a personal right. As such, it will not bind a successor owner if the landlord sells the property. For example, Kirsteen owns land and grants to Louise a 25-year lease. A year later, she dispones to Matthew. Unless the lease has been made real, Matthew can require Louise to leave. She may protest: 'But I have a contract allowing me to remain another nine years!' But Matthew can reply: 'You may have a contract, but not with me. Get off my land.' Off Louise must go – though she will have a claim against Kirsteen for breach of contract. Nor would the contract bind the owner's trustee in sequestration. For these parties to be bound, the lease needs to be *also* a real right. At common law this was not possible. A lease was merely a contract and this remains the position for leases of moveables. For land the law was changed by the Leases Act 1449, since when most leases of heritable property have been contracts *with real effect*. How this happens depends on whether the lease is a short lease (20 years or under) or a long lease. (As with all real rights, the *nemo plus* rule[21] applies: the lease must be granted by the right person.) The real right can also extend to a *pro indiviso* share of neighbouring subjects.[22] Although a lease can be a real right, ie a subordinate real right, it is unlike other subordinate real rights. First, it is, unlike these, an ongoing contract, though one that has acquired real effect. A real lease straddles rather awkwardly the law of contract and the law of real rights. Secondly, other subordinate real rights detract from the value of the property: they are pure encumbrances. By contrast, a lease is an encumbrance but it is also a pertinent: it is an asset for the owner. In business terms, it represents an income stream. Indeed, property, especially commercial property, may be more valuable let than unlet, in which case the pertinent aspect of the lease outweighs its encumbrance aspect.[23]

Formalities

20.10   Leases of one year or less do not require writing in order to confer a real right.[24] Those that exceed that period must be subscribed by both parties for the tenant to be able to acquire such a right.[25] But such a lease is still valid contractually without writing.[26] Equivalent rules apply to any prior missives of let (a contract preceding the actual lease[27]), or any transfer, variation or extinction of the lease. If

---

[21]   See **PARA 4.42** above.
[22]   *Gyle Shopping Centre General Partners v Marks and Spencer plc* [2014] CSOH 59.
[23]   See further **PARA 2.4** above.
[24]   RoW(S)A 1995, s 1(7). The rule likewise applies to assignations and renunciations of such leases.
[25]   RoW(S)A 1995, s 1(2)(b).
[26]   *Gray v MacNeil* [2017] SAC (Civ) 9, 2017 GWD 11-149.
[27]   These are sometimes encountered in practice but their status is unclear. A lease is itself a contract, so such missives are contracts to contract – something that is highly problematic in contract law.

the lease or deed relating to it is to be registered in the Land Register or Books of Council and Session, then attestation by a witness or equivalent will be required.[28]

Short leases: possession under the Leases Act 1449

20.11   The Leases Act 1449 (LA 1449) is the second oldest statute still in force.[29] It was passed by the old Scottish Parliament to protect rural tenants from being evicted from the land which they were leasing if the landlord sold. Nevertheless, it is of general application. The property can be any heritable property which is capable of being held as a separate tenement,[30] as well as freshwater fishing rights.[31] Whether LA 1449 applies to shooting rights is uncertain[32] as these cannot normally be a separate tenement.[33] As regards rent, this must not be 'illusory' – in other words, effectively non-existent.[34] In relation to duration, there must be a definite ish. A lease with the duration mentioned above – 'so long as the grass groweth up and the water runneth down' – would not be protected by LA 1449.[35] If these requirements are satisfied, the tenant can obtain a real right by entering into possession. This may be natural possession, by himself or herself, or civil possession by a representative, such as a sub-tenant. In one case, the carrying out of preliminary agricultural operations before the entry date was held not to amount to possession.[36] But even if it did so amount, it would have been irrelevant as it was before the entry date.

Long leases: registration

20.12   Originally LA 1449 applied to leases of any duration, and it was the only way of conferring real effect on a lease. Then the Registration of Leases (Scotland) Act 1857 allowed long leases ie leases of more than 20 years to be recorded in the Sasine Register, thereby acquiring real effect. But this was optional: real effect could still be obtained under LA 1449 without recording. Registration in the Land Register is now the *only* way of obtaining a real right.[37] Hence LA 1449 today applies solely to short leases. If a long lease is not registered it is not a real right. That does not mean it is not a valid lease, but the common law applies, so that it lacks real effect. The requirements for a real right of lease are summarised in the diagram below.

---

28 RoW(S)A 1995, s 6.
29 The oldest is the Royal Mines Act 1424. See **PARA 15.16** above.
30 See **PARAS 15.13–15.18** above.
31 Salmon and Freshwater Fisheries (Consolidation) (Scotland) Act 2003, s 66.
32 *Pollock, Gilmour & Co v Harvey* (1828) 6 S 913; *Palmer's Trs v Brown* 1989 SLT 128. Such rights cannot be separate tenements except under AFT(S)A 2000, s 65A.
33 Except under AFT(S)A 2000, s 65A.
34 For example, a penny a year. See *Alison v Ritchie* (1730) Mor 15196.
35 Such wording points to a period longer than a short lease, in any case.
36 *Millar v McRobbie* 1949 SC 1.
37 Registration of Leases (Scotland) Act 1857 s 20C.

Requirements of lease as a real right

```
              ┌─────────────────┐
              │     Parties     │
              │ Property (land) │
              │      Rent       │
              │    Duration     │
              └─────────────────┘
```

Lease of one year or less	Lease of longer than one year and no more than 20 years	Lease of longer than 20 years
Possession under 1449 Act	Possession under 1449 Act	Writing Registration under 1857 Act

'Offside goals' and leases

20.13   If the owner of land agrees to grant a lease, but then sells the land before the tenant acquires a real right, the tenant may seek to invoke the 'offside goals' rule if the new owner knew about the grant.[38] The balance of authority is against the applicability of the rule here. But the law cannot be regarded as certain.[39] Where the tenant has agreed to assign the lease, but then grants a standard security over it which is made real before the assignation, the assignee may have the security reduced under the 'offside goals' rule if the creditor is in bad faith.[40]

Personal and real conditions

20.14   If the landlord transfers the property, the successor will be bound by the lease, but not by *all* its terms. Only those conditions which can be regarded as real or – to use the standard expression used in this context – *inter naturalia* of the lease are binding. In essence these are the fundamental conditions, such as the duty to let the tenant occupy the property. It is difficult to give a more precise definition as the case law lacks coherence. For example, in a modern case it was held that an 'exclusivity

---

[38]   McDonald *Conveyancing Manual* para 32.60. See also *Rodger v Paton* 2004 GWD 19-425.

[39]   *Jacobs v Anderson* (1898) 6 SLT 234; *Millar v McRobbie* 1949 SC 1. Compare *Greig v Brown & Nicolson* (1829) 7 S 274 (a servitude case). But note *Advice Centre for Mortgages Ltd v McNicoll* 2006 SLT 591 and compare *Gibson v Royal Bank of Scotland Plc* 2009 SLT 444.

[40]   *Trade Development Bank v Crittall Windows* 1983 SLT 510.

clause' providing that the tenant was to be the only optician in a shopping centre was not *inter naturalia*.[41] But earlier case law in relation to similar prohibitions reached the opposite conclusion.[42] So too did a subsequent case, where there was no argument over the matter.[43] A provision for a reduction in rent in return for services performed by the tenant will not bind a successor landlord.[44] Neither, it seems, will an option to purchase.[45] Since the question of what is *inter naturalia* is important in practice, it is unfortunate that the law is so unclear.

Leases and standard securities

20.15   Once a lease becomes a real right, the subsequent grant of a standard security by the landlord cannot affect it. The rule *prior tempore potior jure* applies: the lease is the prior real right.[46] If the creditor has to enforce the security by selling the property, the lease remains in place. The tenant merely has a different landlord. If the landlord grants a lease *after* granting a standard security, then it is the standard security that is the prior real right. It is one of the standard conditions of a standard security that a lease will not be granted without the creditor's consent.[47] If this is not obtained, the creditor can have the lease set aside.[48] Finally, a standard security can be granted over a registered lease itself. If the creditor has to enforce the security by selling the lease, the landlord will have a new tenant. A lease is only of value as a security if it has some capital value, for otherwise a sale would realise little or nothing.[49]

RIGHTS AND OBLIGATIONS OF THE PARTIES

20.16   Most leases will carefully set out the rights and obligations of the landlord and tenant in detail. In the absence of specific terms, the common law implies certain things. Lease is one of the 'nominate contracts' recognised by the law and thus comes with its own set of implied-in-law terms. To exclude the application of the implied terms, there must be clear contrary provision in the lease.[50] In the following

---

[41]   *Optical Express (Gyle) Ltd v Marks and Spencers plc* 2000 SLT 644.

[42]   *Campbell v Watt* (1795) Hume 788; *Davie v Stark* (1876) 3 R 111. See McAllister *Leases* paras 2.43–2.46. The earlier case law was not cited in the later case.

[43]   *Warren James (Jewellers) Ltd v Overgate GP Ltd* 2006 GWD 12–235, aff'd 2007 GWD 6–94.

[44]   *Ross v Duchess of Sutherland* (1838) 16 S 1179.

[45]   *Bisset v Magistrates of Aberdeen* (1898) 1 F 87. In *Davidson v Zani* 1992 SCLR 1001, a successor landlord was held bound on the basis of the 'offside goals' rule. But that case has now been disapproved: *Advice Centre for Mortgages Ltd v McNicoll* 2006 SLT 591. Compare, however, *Gibson v Royal Bank of Scotland Plc* 2009 SLT 444.

[46]   See **PARA 4.45** above.

[47]   CFR(S)A 1970, Sch 3, Standard Condition 6.

[48]   *Trade Development Bank v Warriner & Mason (Scotland) Ltd* 1980 SC 74; *Trade Development Bank v David Haig (Bellshill) Ltd* 1983 SLT 510. See also **PARA 4.51** above.

[49]   See **PARA 20.34** below.

[50]   *Mars Pension Trs Ltd v County Properties & Developments* 2000 SLT 581.

paragraphs, the main implied terms are set out. It must be stressed, however, that in agricultural and residential leases these common-law terms are generally replaced by statutory provisions.

(a) Possession

20.17   The landlord is bound to give the tenant natural possession[51] and not interfere with that possession. In turn, the tenant must enter into possession and use the property. Failure to do so is material breach.[52] Short periods of absence may be permissible. In one case, the absence of the tenant due to detention in Saughton Prison for more than a year meant that the landlord could bring the lease to an end on the ground of material breach.[53]

(b) Plenishing

20.18   If the landlord's hypothec is available to the landlord,[54] the tenant must plenish the property sufficiently to provide security for payment of the rent.[55] Interdict may be obtained to prevent displenishment.[56]

(c) Rent

20.19   The tenant is obliged to pay the rent at the due dates. It is normally paid in advance. Because of inflation, leases for more than about five years usually provide for review of the rent at the end of a certain period, for example, after every five years in a 25-year lease. The lease says that if the parties cannot agree on the new rent, a third party will set it in line with market rates. This is standard practice in commercial leases and there is a constant stream of case law on the interpretation of rent review clauses.[57] But rent review clauses are not implied by law. Such clauses began to be used only in the 1960s. The result is that there are some ultra-long (eg 999-year) leases created before that time (eg in the eighteenth and nineteenth centuries) where the rent has been rendered nominal by inflation.[58]

---

[51]   Unless the lease is an interposed lease. See **PARA 20.32** below.
[52]   *Graham v Black & Stevenson* (1792) Hume 781.
[53]   *Blair Trust Co v Gilbert* 1940 SLT 322.
[54]   See **PARA 20.29** below.
[55]   *Wright v Wightman* (1875) 3 R 68. But the scope of this duty is now unclear because the Bankruptcy and Diligence etc. (Scotland) Act 2007, s 208 allows the hypothec to secure all rent arrears and not just the current year's rent. See A McAllister 'The Landlord's Hypothec: down but is it out?' 2010 *JR 65.*
[56]   *Co-operative Insurance Society Ltd v Halfords Ltd* 1998 SLT 90.
[57]   See McAllister *Leases* ch 12.
[58]   Many of these will be converted into outright ownership by the Long Leases (Scotland) Act 2012. See **PARA 20.7** above.

(d) Purposes of let

20.20   The landlord is obliged to ensure that the property is reasonably fit for the purposes of let. The standard is not one of perfection, but assumes reasonable use by the tenant.[59] For example, in *North British Storage and Transit Co v Steele's Trs*[60] it was held that while a drainage system could have been upgraded to a higher standard, it was adequate as it stood for the purposes of the lease. The tenant must only use the property for the purposes of the let. This is called the 'use clause' or 'permitted user clause'. Breach is known as 'inverting the possession'. Unauthorised alterations also fall under this heading.[61]

(e) State of property

20.21   It is implied in leases of buildings that the landlord must maintain the property in a tenantable condition. For example, in *Gunn v National Coal Board,*[62] a landlord who failed to deal with rising damp was held in breach. In urban leases, where the property is a building, the landlord has a duty to ensure that it is wind and watertight. The obligation is to carry out appropriate repairs once the matter is highlighted by the tenant. It is not a warranty as such, because the landlord is only liable if no action is taken within a reasonable time following notification.[63] The landlord is not required to carry out repairs to damage caused by an act of God (*damnum fatale*) such as lightning.[64] Similarly, where a third party has caused the damage it is that party who is liable and not the landlord. Finally, the landlord is not liable where the damage has been caused by the negligence of the tenant. There the tenant is liable, as well as being in breach of the obligation implied by law to take reasonable care of the property.[65] In rural leases, the common-law position is that the tenant is generally liable for repairs.[66] Of course, most leases have express provisions about repairing obligations, and if so the common law is to that extent excluded.[67]

REMEDIES AVAILABLE TO BOTH PARTIES

20.22   The lease may provide for particular remedies for either party. In addition, general remedies are available.

---

[59]   *Glebe Sugar Refining Co v Paterson* (1902) 2 F 615.
[60]   1920 SC 194.
[61]   Cf *British Linen Bank v Purdie* (1905) 7 F 923.
[62]   1982 SLT 526.
[63]   *Wolfson v Forrester* 1910 SC 675.
[64]   Nor is the tenant: *Little Cumbrae Estates Ltd v Island of Little Cumbrae Ltd* 2007 SC 525.
[65]   *Mickel v McCoard* 1913 SC 896.
[66]   *Little Cumbrae Estates Ltd v Island of Little Cumbrae Ltd* 2007 SC 525.
[67]   But the common-law rules still apply as to any matters not covered: *Little Cumbrae Estates Ltd v Island of Little Cumbrae Ltd* 2007 SC 525.

(a) Specific implement and interdict

20.23   In the case of positive obligations (obligations *ad factum praestandum*) such as the landlord's obligation to carry out repairs, specific implement is the appropriate remedy. The courts, however, only award this is if the obligation is sufficiently clear or precise. There was a stream of cases in the 1990s seeking to enforce so called 'keep open' clauses. These are common in retail unit leases and require the tenant not merely to possess but to trade from the premises on specified days during specified hours. The Scottish courts are willing to enforce such clauses by implement provided that they are clearly drafted.[68] In contrast, their English counterparts have refused to award the equivalent remedy of specific performance, instead awarding damages.[69] Interdict may be used to prevent the other party from doing something, for example unauthorised use.[70]

(b) Damages

20.24   This is a standard remedy. For example, the landlord has failed to carry out repairs, and the tenant has suffered loss as a result.[71] Sometimes quantification is problematic, as in the case of breach of a 'keep open' clause.[72]

(c) Action for payment

20.25   Where one party is obliged to make a monetary payment, the appropriate action is simply one for payment. Typically, it will be used by the landlord to compel payment of rent. Leases often have a clause saying: 'The parties hereto consent to registration of this lease for preservation and execution.' The lease is then registered in the Books of Council and Session.[73] Registration for execution enables a judicial officer to carry out diligence based on an extract copy of the lease. This is known as 'summary diligence' and can take place without a court action.[74]

---

[68]   See, in particular, *Retail Parks Investments Ltd v The Royal Bank of Scotland Plc (No 2)* 1996 SC 227; *Highland and Universal Properties Ltd v Safeway Properties Ltd* 2000 SLT 414 and *Oak Mall Greenock Ltd v McDonald's Restaurants Ltd* 2003 GWD 17-540. See also A Smith 'Keep on Keeping Open: *Highland and Universal Properties Ltd v Safeway Properties Ltd*' (2000) 4 *Edin LR* 336.

[69]   *Co-operative Insurance Society Ltd v Argyll Stores (Holdings) Ltd* [1998] AC 1.

[70]   *Leckie v Merryflats Patent Brick Co* (1868) 5 SLR 619.

[71]   *Gunn v National Coal Board* 1982 SLT 526.

[72]   *Douglas Shelf Seven Ltd v Co-operative Wholesale Society Ltd* [2007] CSOH 53. See M Hogg 'Damages for breach of a keep-open clause' (2007) 11 *Edin LR* 416.

[73]   Leases are often registered in this register. But such registration does not promote the validity of a lease. For example, if a lease is a short lease, and so needs possession to make it real, registration in the Books of Council and Session is no substitute. The same is true if the lease is a long one, in which to become real registration in the Land Register is necessary.

[74]   See, eg, *Cowie v Martalo* 2011 GWD 32-676.

(d) Rescission

20.26   In the case of a material breach by one party, the other party is in principle entitled to rescind the lease. For example, the tenant may do so if the landlord does not provide subjects which are reasonably fit for the purposes of the let.[75] Statute, however, provides that a landlord may not terminate the lease in a case of material breach of a monetary obligation without first serving a written notice giving 14 days to pay.[76] In the case of non-monetary obligations, it must be fair and reasonable to rescind.[77] For breaches which it is possible for the tenant to remedy within a reasonable time, it is a relevant consideration in determining whether the termination is fair and reasonable whether the tenant has been given a reasonable opportunity to remedy the defect.[78]

(e) Retention

20.27   This is a self-help remedy arising out of the doctrine of mutuality of contract. If one party is in breach, the other party may suspend performance of any counter-obligation. Retention of rent is the typical example. For example, the tenant can do this if the landlord is failing to fulfil the obligation to keep the premises wind and watertight. It is competent, however, to contract out of the right to retain.[79] Further, tenants who continue to pay rent during the period in which the landlords are failing in their obligations may be barred from exercising the right of retention later for that breach.[80]

REMEDIES AVAILABLE ONLY TO THE LANDLORD

20.28   In addition to the remedies available to both parties, there are three remedies available only to the landlord.

(a) Landlord's hypothec

20.29   The landlord has a right in security over the goods brought into the property by the tenant – known as the *invecta et illata* – for the rent. This right is discussed in **CHAPTER 21**.[81]

---

[75]   *Kippen v Oppenheim* (1847) 10 D 242.
[76]   Law Reform (Miscellaneous Provisions) (Scotland) Act 1985 (LR(MP)(S)A 1985), s 4(1).
[77]   LR(MP)(S)A 1985, s 5(1).
[78]   LR(MP)(S)A 1985, s 5(3). The Scottish Law Commission has recommended reform: Report on Irritancy in Leases of Land (Scot Law Com No 191, 2003).
[79]   *Skene v Cameron* 1942 SC 393.
[80]   *British Railways Board v Roccio* 1979 SLT (Sh Ct) 11.
[81]   See **PARA 21.65** below.

(b) Irritancy

20.30   Irritancy is the right of the landlord to bring the lease to an end prematurely. The result is to extinguish the lease and any rights in it, such as subleases. The effect is equivalent to the landlord rescinding the lease, but, unlike rescission, which is available in principle for any material breach by the tenant, irritancy has a more defined scope.[82] There is only one type of 'legal irritancy' – in other words, where the right to irritate arises by operation of law. This is where the rent has been unpaid for two years.[83] The tenant is entitled to stop the irritancy – known as 'purging' it – by making payment at any time before decree is extracted. The Scottish Law Commission has recommended that legal irritancy be replaced with an implied option to terminate if rent has not been paid for six months.[84] The lease can also provide *express* grounds upon which the landlord can irritate. This is known as 'conventional irritancy' and most leases have a conventional irritancy clause. Typical examples in commercial leases are the tenant being more than 21 days late paying the rent, or going into receivership or liquidation. If the landlord subsequently accepts payment once irritancy proceedings have begun, this may waive the breach.[85] At common law, it was not possible to purge a conventional irritancy.[86] This was felt to be unfair and the statutory rules described above in relation to rescission were introduced to apply to situations where the landlord was seeking to irritate.[87]

(c) Action for recovery of heritable property

20.31   If the tenant fails to leave the property when bound to do so at the ish,[88] the landlord can raise an action to compel this. The common-law action is one of 'removing', but in modern times the procedure is regulated by statute.[89] If the tenant fails to flit voluntarily, it is unlawful for the landlord to compel, or seek to compel, removal without a court order. To do so is a delict, giving rise to a damages claim, and, in the case of residential tenancies, is also a criminal offence.[90] But a tenant who stays on without agreement after the ish is liable for 'violent profits' – a form of penal damages.[91]

---

[82]   The exact relationship of irritancy and rescission is arguable, but see *Crieff Highland Gathering Ltd v Perth and Kinross Council* 2011 SLT 992.

[83]   In agricultural leases, the period is six months: AH(S)A 1991, s 20.

[84]   Scottish Law Commission, Report on Irritancy in Leases of Land (Scot Law Com No 191, 2003) para 3.15.

[85]   *HMV Fields Properties Ltd v Bracken Self Selection Fabrics Ltd* 1991 SLT 31; *Aubrey Investments Ltd v D S Crawford Ltd* 1998 SLT 628.

[86]   *Dorchester Studios (Glasgow) Ltd v Stone* 1975 SC (HL) 56.

[87]   See **PARA 20.26** above.

[88]   Where tacit relocation has operated, the tenant may stay put. See **PARA 20.38** below.

[89]   Sheriff Courts (Scotland) Act 1971, s 35(1)(c). The statutory action proceeds by way of summary cause, unless a claim is being made for a sum exceeding £5,000.

[90]   Rent (Scotland) Act 1984, s 22.

[91]   *Jute Industries Ltd v Wilson & Graham Ltd* 1955 SLT (Sh Ct) 46.

TRANSFER

Alienation by landlord

20.32   The landlord does not require the tenant's permission to transfer the property. The new owner simply becomes the new landlord. It is also competent for the landlord to create an 'interposed lease' between itself and the tenant.[92] In that event, the original tenant becomes the owner's subtenant.

Alienation by tenant

20.33   It may be possible for the tenant to assign the lease. Say that Rebecca is the landlord and Sara the tenant. If Sara assigns to Tracey, then Sara steps entirely out the picture. Tracey is now the tenant. In deciding whether assignation is permissible, the first thing is to consider the terms of the lease. The lease may expressly authorise assignation, or may expressly forbid it. This is called the 'alienation clause'. A common provision is a half-way house, saying that assignation is forbidden without the landlord's permission, but with a qualification that this permission must not be 'unreasonably withheld in the case of a respectable and responsible assignee of sound financial standing' or words to similar effect. Unsurprisingly, such clauses often give rise to disputes. In one case it was held unreasonable for the landlord to insist on new conditions being written into the lease in return for permission.[93] In another, the landlord was held to have acted reasonably in withholding permission until an outstanding rent review was concluded.[94] If the lease is silent on the question of assignation, then the rule is that permission is required if *delectus personae* exists in the lease. This is the doctrine of whether or not the choice of the other party to the contract was crucial to the contract being concluded.[95] It is presumed in agricultural leases of 'ordinary duration' and furnished house lets. It is not presumed in agricultural leases of 'extraordinary duration' and unfurnished urban lettings, for example shops. The length at which an agricultural lease moves from being ordinary to extraordinary seems to be 21 years.[96]

20.34   An assignation has to be completed by the act which is necessary to create the lease in the first place. For an unregistered lease, this means the assignee taking possession. For a registered lease, this means registration in the Land Register.[97] In practice an assignation will also be formally intimated to the landlord, but the taking of possession or registration may amount to deemed intimation.[98] The effect of an

---

[92]   Land Tenure Reform (Scotland) Act 1974, s 17.
[93]   *Renfrew District Council v AB Leisure (Renfrew) Ltd (In Liquidation)* 1988 SLT 635.
[94]   *Lousada & Co v J E Lesser (Properties) Ltd* 1990 SLT 823.
[95]   See MacQueen and Thomson, *Contract* para 2.87.
[96]   McAllister *Leases* paras 7.20–7.21.
[97]   For long leases, see Registration of Leases (Scotland) Act 1857, s 1(1).
[98]   McAllister *Leases* para 7.30.

assignation has been described judicially as follows: 'The assignation of his lease by a tenant who has power to assign has the effect of making the assignee sole tenant from the time he obtains possession of the subject of the lease, and of discharging the cedent from future liability to the landlord.'[99] The cedent will, however, remain liable for any rent arrears, though the assignee also becomes liable for these.[100] The reasons for the transfer of a lease are as various as the reasons for the transfer of anything else. If a lease has a capital value it may be sold. Whether a lease has a capital value depends on the circumstances. A 999-year lease created in 1720 for a fixed rent of £5 per annum will now have a value virtually the same as that of unencumbered ownership.[101] A 25-year lease created seven years ago at full market rent and with a five-yearly rent review provision has little or no capital value, because the transferee will be taking over liability for the rent, and the rent represents the value. Indeed, if property values (and hence rental values) have fallen,[102] a lease may have a negative capital value and the transferor will have to pay the transferee a lump sum to take the lease off its hands.

Subletting

20.35   If Sara sublets to Tracey, Sara remains the tenant. Tracey becomes the subtenant and is entitled to enter into possession. The Rebecca/Sara lease is the 'head lease' and the Sara/Tracey lease is the 'sublease', also known as an 'under-lease'. If that head lease is terminated, whether prematurely or at the ish, the tenant's right under the sublease to possess will also end. As with assignation, there may be express provision in the lease as to whether subletting is permissible. In the event of silence, the same presumptions in relation to *delectus personae* apply as with assignation and to the same effect. Likewise, a subtenant needs to take the same steps as any lessee to obtain a real right, possession or registration. Whether the sublet can be registered will depend on its length rather than that of the head lease. In a sublet, the liability of the tenant under the original lease remains unaffected. Thus suppose that the rent under the head lease is £100,000 per annum and under the sublease is £105,000, there are two entirely separate payments, one by Sara to Rebecca and one by Tracey to Sara. If Tracey fails to pay Sara that does not affect Sara's continuing obligation to pay Rebecca.

Succession

20.36   In general, the tenant's death does not end the lease. The question of who then takes the lease is complex and the following is a mere outline. Where a lease

99   *Lord Elphinstone v Monkland Iron & Coal Co* (1886) 13 R (HL) 98 at 102 per Lord Watson.
100   McAllister *Leases* para 7.33.
101   *Cf* **PARA 2.4** above. Particularly given the Long Leases (Scotland) Act 2012. See **PARA 20.7** above.
102   Perhaps because of a general turndown. Or it may be that property values fall in a particular location. See, eg, *Burgerking Ltd v Rachel Charitable Trust* 2006 SLT 224.

is freely assignable, the tenant can bequeath it in his or her will. If no such bequest is made, the executor may transfer it to any party who would have been entitled to succeed to the tenant's estate had he or she died intestate, including a spouse or civil partner in respect of their prior rights, or to any party entitled to legal rights. If there is an implied prohibition on alienation, such as if *delectus personae* is presumed, the tenant is entitled to bequeath the lease to any party who could be entitled to succeed to his estate if it was intestate.[103] This could mean any member of the family. Where there is an express prohibition on assignation, the landlord will require to consent before a bequest can take effect. If no bequest is made by the tenant and there is a prohibition on assignation (express or implied), the executor will require the landlord's consent to transfer the lease, unless the transfer is to a person entitled to succeed to the tenant's intestate estate or to claim legal rights or prior rights, in satisfaction of the person's entitlement or claim.[104] There exist special rules on succession to agricultural and residential tenancies.[105]

TERMINATION

Termination at ish

20.37 A lease normally provides a fixed date at which it ends.[106] Nevertheless, if the contracted date arrives without either party having given due notice, the lease will not finish. In other words, a fixed date of termination is regarded as being merely a mutual *option* to terminate at that date. The option is, like any option, exercised by notice. The notice is traditionally called a 'warning to remove' when served by the landlord. But the English term 'notice to quit' is now generally used. When given by the tenant, the notice is called a 'letter of removal'. At common law, notice of not fewer than 40 days before the ish must be given. For example, the lease between Ulrika and Valerie is stated to end on 30 June. If Ulrika gives Valerie notice on 31 May, that is too late.

The common-law period is varied for certain leases by statute. The rules are complex. For agricultural holdings, the period is not less than one year and not more than two years before the ish.[107] The same period applies for leases of land exceeding 2 acres which are not agricultural holdings, but where such a lease is for fewer than

---

[103] S(S)A 1964, s 29(1).
[104] S(S)A 1964, s 16(2).
[105] S(S)A 1964, s 16(2)–(9); AH(S)A 1991, s 11; AH(S)A 2003, ss 21–23; Crofters Holdings (Scotland) Act 1886, s 16; Small Land Holders (Scotland) Act 1911, s 21; Crofters (Scotland) Act 1993, s 10; Rent (Scotland) Act 1984, ss 3 and 3A and Schs 1, 1A and 1B; Housing (Scotland) Act 1988, s 31; and Housing (Scotland) Act 2001, s 22 and Sch 3.
[106] But it is competent for it to provide that it will continue from month to month (or other period) until notice by either party. This might, but does not have to, follow an initial fixed period.
[107] AH(S)A 1991, s 21.

three years, the minimum notice period is six months.[108] For all other leases of four months or fewer, notice of one-third of the length of the lease is required, subject to a minimum period of four weeks.[109] Notices to quit have to be in the right form, and this can vary according to the type of tenancy.[110] Finally, under the Removal Terms (Scotland) Act 1886, if a lease is due to end at Whitsunday or Martinmas and notice of 40 days is required, this period is (confusingly) calculated back from 15 May or 11 November respectively.[111] This legislation applies to a lease of a 'dwelling house, shop or other building and their appurtenances' or a house let with agricultural land. While 15 May and 11 November were recognised as Whitsunday and Martinmas at common law, by statute they have been replaced by 28 May and 28 November.[112] The continued application of the 1886 Act thus leads to a longer notice period.

Tacit relocation

20.38   If proper notice is not given, the lease continues by 'tacit relocation' (Latin *relocatio tacita*), that is to say, by implied re-lease.[113] If the original lease was for a year or more, tacit relocation is for a further year. If it was for less than a year, tacit relocation is for the period of the lease. The doctrine can operate any number of times and it is quite common for a lease to continue long after the agreed length on this basis. The rule applies equally to both parties, but in practice it is more often pled by tenants against landlords than vice versa. But this is not always so. For example, in *Signet Group plc v C & J Clark Retail Properties Ltd*,[114] the tenants served an invalid notice, and also shut down their business and vacated the premises well before the ish. It was held that the lease continued. An example of the doctrine not applying because of the parties' actions is where they enter into a new lease. It is a difficult question whether the parties can contract out of tacit relocation – to contract out of the need to send notice to quit – in the lease itself. According to one sheriff court case, it can.[115] But the position cannot be regarded as settled, except for agricultural holdings where statute prohibits contracting out of the doctrine.[116]

---

[108]   Sheriff Courts (Scotland) Act 1907, s 34. Rather oddly, this Act contains much of the law about the termination of leases.

[109]   Sheriff Courts (Scotland) Act 1907, s 38. For dwellinghouses, see also the Rent (Scotland) Act 1984, s 112.

[110]   See Sheriff Courts (Scotland) Act 1907, Sch 1, para 34.6 and 34.7. For residential tenancies, see also Rent (Scotland) Act 1984, s 112, and Assured Tenancies (Notice to Quit Prescribed Information) (Scotland) Regulations 1988 (SI 1988/2067). There are also special rules for the various types of agricultural tenancy. In practice, notices to quit often fail to comply with the applicable rules and so are invalid.

[111]   Removal Terms (Scotland) Act 1886, s 4.

[112]   Term and Quarter Days (Scotland) Act 1990, s 1(1) and (2)(a).

[113]   For a detailed treatment, see S Halliday 'Tacit Relocation' 2002 *JR* 201.

[114]   1996 SLT 1325.

[115]   *Macdougall v Guidi* 1992 SCLR 167.

[116]   AH(S)A 1991, s 3.

Termination before the ish

20.39   There are various reasons why a lease may not last its full course. Rescission and irritancy have already been considered.[117] At the outset of the lease, the parties may decide that either or both has the right to terminate the lease early. This is known as a 'break clause'. If there is no such clause, it is of course nonetheless open to the parties to agree on premature termination later. In that case, that agreement is given effect to by a 'deed of renunciation'. (The name makes it sound as if it is a unilateral act by the tenant. But a tenant cannot unilaterally renounce a lease.) The lease may also be brought to an early end by frustration, a general doctrine of contract law.[118] Three cases of this can be given.

(1)   The subjects of the lease may be entirely destroyed, for example a shop razed by a fire. This is known as *rei interitus*.[119]

(2)   There may be constructive destruction. This is where there is not total destruction, but the lease can no longer subsist, for example where a house has been damaged to the extent that it is uninhabitable.[120]

(3)   The lease may be unable to continue for other reasons. For example, in *Tay Salmon Fisheries Co v Speedie*[121] a lease of salmon fishings was frustrated by impossibility because the Ministry of Defence designated the area as a firing range.

Finally, the death of the tenant will bring the lease to an end in situations where it cannot be transferred.[122]

TYPES OF LEASE

20.40   Specialities apply to different types of leases. A short overview will be given of these as they apply to commercial, residential and agricultural properties.

Commercial leases

20.41   Many Scottish solicitors specialise in this area.[123] It is little regulated by statute and the terms of the lease are eventually determined by the relative negotiating

---

[117]   See **PARAS 20.26 AND 20.30** above.
[118]   See McBryde *Contract* ch 21; MacQueen and Thomson *Contract* paras 4.91–4.113.
[119]   It is possible to contract out of *rei interitus*: see *Cantors Properties (Scotland) Ltd v Swears and Wells Ltd* 1980 SLT 165. This is standard practice in commercial leases where landlords do not wish to lose the income stream from rent: insurance should pay for reconstruction: see D Cockburn and R Mitchell *Commercial Leases* (2nd edn, 2011) paras 5.10 and 7.13.
[120]   *Duff v Fleming* (1870) 8 M 769.
[121]   1929 SC 593.
[122]   See **PARA 20.36** above.
[123]   The Property Standardisation Group has produced standardised documentation for most commercial lease transactions, apart from the actual lease. See www.psglegal.co.uk/leases_management.php.

strength of the parties. That strength will depend on a number of factors, such as the state of the property market and the demand for the type of premises in question. Heads of terms in commercial leases, such as duration and rent, will normally be agreed by surveyors, before the lawyers draw up the lease. Shopping centres such as the Buchanan Galleries in Glasgow or the Gyle Centre in Edinburgh are usually owned by institutional investors who use the rents from the units as a reliable income stream. Here, the leases will contain a service charge provision, whereby the tenant is liable for a proportion of the cost of cleaning, heating and lighting the common parts of the centre, refuse collection, security provision and the like.[124] Commercial leases are usually entered into on an FRI ('full repairing and insuring') basis. The tenant will be solely liable for all repairs, in contrast to the common-law position. He or she will also be responsible for the payment of insurance premiums. A key feature of commercial leases is detailed rent review clauses, typically providing for the rent to be reassessed on an upward-only basis, every five years.[125] A rare example of statutory intervention in the area of commercial leases is the Tenancy of Shops (Scotland) Act 1949. It enables shop tenants who receive a notice to quit in the run-up to the ish to apply to the sheriff court for renewal of their lease.[126] The sheriff can extend it for a period of a year. The tenant is free to make a repeat application when the extension comes to an end and the lease in theory could continue indefinitely on the basis of annual applications.

Residential leases

Private sector

20.42   Around 13% of homes are privately rented.[127] Detailed regulation of this type of lease began in the early twentieth century, the main original purposes being to keep rental levels below what they would be on a free-market basis and to limit the power of landlords to terminate tenancies. Frequent legislation, reflecting changing political agendas, makes the subject fiendishly complex. The current, but shortly to be replaced, regime is found in the Housing (Scotland) Act 1988 (H(S)A 1988), which introduced 'assured tenancies' and 'short assured tenancies'. Leases created under the prior regime are known as 'regulated tenancies' and although these can still exist, they will not be discussed here.[128] For there to be an assured tenancy, a house must be leased as a separate dwelling and be occupied by the tenant as his or

---

[124]   See *Marfield Properties Ltd v Secretary of State for the Environment* 1996 SLT 1244 and *Mars Pension Trs Ltd v County Properties & Developments Ltd* 2000 SLT 581.

[125]   See McAllister *Leases* ch 11 and M J Ross and D J McKichan *Drafting and Negotiating Commercial Leases in Scotland* (2nd edn, 1993) ch 6.

[126]   Tenancy of Shops (Scotland) Act 1949, s 1(1) and (2). See *Edinburgh Woollen Mill Ltd v Singh* 2013 SLT (Sh Ct) 141. See also McAllister *Leases* ch 14.

[127]   K G C Reid and G L Gretton, *Conveyancing 2015* (2016) 91.

[128]   See McAllister *Leases* paras 17.67–17.102.

her only or principal home.[129] 'House' can mean a flat or, exceptionally, a hotel room occupied by a long-term resident.[130] There is a list of cases where an assured tenancy cannot arise, including leases to students by educational institutions, situations where the landlord is resident and tenancies in favour of asylum seekers.[131]

20.43   The lease starts life as a 'contractual assured tenancy'. It becomes a 'statutory assured tenancy' if the contractual assured tenancy ends by a valid notice to quit – unless, of course, the tenant chooses to remove. A statutory assured tenancy can be ended by the landlord only by persuading the sheriff that one of the specified *statutory grounds* applies. Some of the grounds for recovering natural possession are mandatory. In other words, the sheriff must grant the order if satisfied that the ground exists. Examples include where there has been default on a standard security created before the tenancy and where there are rent arrears of at least three months.[132] The remaining grounds are a matter for the sheriff's discretion. Examples include where the rent is persistently paid late and where the condition of the house has deteriorated because of the tenant's negligence.[133] The landlord can avoid the difficulty of recovering the property by creating the lease at the outset as a 'short assured tenancy'.[134] Such a tenancy must have a minimum length of six months.[135] Advance written notice (Form AT5) must be given to the tenant that this type of lease is being granted. The effect is that when the tenancy comes to an end it comes to an end: there is no security of tenure beyond the ish. Short assured tenancies are popular with landlords.[136] Under the previous regime of 'regulated' tenancies, the tenant was entitled to pay a 'fair' rent, which was in most cases a rent below market rates. The tenant under an assured tenancy (including a short assured tenancy) merely has the right not to pay above market rent. Hence if the landlord proposes a new rent[137] to which the tenant objects, he or she can apply to the local Rent Assessment Committee to fix a market rent.[138]

20.44   The H(S)A 1988 regime is soon to be replaced by a new statutory framework under the Private Housing (Tenancies) (Scotland) Act 2016 (PH(T)(S)A 2016). This will apply to leases entered into after the relevant provisions come into force. All

---

[129]   H(S)A 1988, s 12(1).
[130]   *Uratemp Ventures Ltd v Collins* [2001] 3 WLR 806, a case under the equivalent English legislation.
[131]   H(S)A 1988, Sch 4.
[132]   H(S)A 1988, Sch 5, Pt 1.
[133]   H(S)A 1988, Sch 5, Pt 2.
[134]   H(S)A 1988, ss 32–35.
[135]   See *Calmac Developments Ltd v Murdoch* 2012 GWD 27-565 where the lease was for exactly six months.
[136]   Around 94% of all private sector residential leases are short assured tenancies. See K G C Reid and G L Gretton, *Conveyancing 2015* (2016) 91.
[137]   Of course, a landlord cannot unilaterally increase the rent. One party to a contract cannot unilaterally change its terms. But a landlord can, at common law, decline to renew the tenancy at its ish except at a higher rent. The tenant then must choose to renew or not to renew. The same can work the other way round: a tenant can decide not to renew at the ish unless the landlord agrees a lower rent. At common law all this is simply a matter of bargaining. But once a tenant has a statutory right to ignore the common law ish, the law has to provide a mechanism for determining the rent after the ish.
[138]   H(S)A 1988, s 25.

such leases will be 'private residential tenancies'.[139] It will no longer be possible to enter into assured or short assured tenancies.[140] And unlike in short assured tenancies, the landlord will not have an automatic entitlement to remove the tenant at the contractual ish. There will be security of tenure.[141] The landlord will only be able to recover direct possession if the tenant wishes to leave or by demonstrating to the satisfaction of the First-Tier Tribunal that one of sixteen grounds in Sch 3 to PH(T)(S)A 2016 applies. As with H(S)A 1988 some of the grounds are mandatory and some discretionary. There is also rent control. The landlord may not increase the rent more than once in the same twelve-month period.[142] If the rent is increased, a dissatisfied tenant can apply to a rent officer at Rent Service Scotland for an open market rent to be set, with a right of appeal to the First-Tier Tribunal.[143] PH(T)(S)A 2016 also enables 'rent pressure zones' to be designated by the Scottish Ministers following an application by the local authority. This means that rent increases can be restricted by reference to a formula which includes the consumer prices index.[144]

Deposits

20.45 In private sector residential leases, the tenant is usually required to pay a deposit at the outset, to cover any damage to the property or unauthorised removal of moveable items such as kitchenware. Formerly, the deposit was held by the landlord, If the tenant considered that it was being unjustifiably withheld, ultimately the only remedy was to take court action. The cost of this often made it impractical. The Housing (Scotland) Act (H(S)A 2006) and regulations made under it now require the landlord to pay the deposit to the administrator of an approved tenancy deposit scheme.[145] Landlords who do not comply are liable to be ordered by a sheriff to pay the tenant an amount not exceeding three times of the amount of the deposit.[146] Approved schemes must have a fair and cost-efficient dispute resolution mechanism.[147]

Private landlord licensing

20.46

Though it might not be guessed from the title, the Antisocial Behaviour etc (Scotland) Act 2004 (AB(S)A 2004) introduced a licensing system for private sector

---

[139] PH(T)(S)A 2016, ss 1 and 2.
[140] PH(T)(S)A 2016, sch 5 paras 1 and 2.
[141] PH(T)(S)A 2016, s 44.
[142] PH(T)(S)A 2016, s 19.
[143] PH(T)(S)A 2016, ss 22 to 34.
[144] PH(T)(S)A 2016, ss 35 to 41.
[145] H(S)A 2006 Part 4 and the Tenancy Deposit Schemes (Scotland) Regulations 2011 (SSI 2011/176).
[146] SSI 2011/176 reg 10.
[147] SSI 2011/176 reg 33.

landlords.[148] The licensing body is the local authority and so a landlord with several properties may need several licences. To let out residential property without a licence is a criminal offence.[149] Moreover, in such circumstances the local authority can serve a notice ending the landlord's right to collect rent.[150] Only a person regarded by the local authority as a 'fit and proper person to act as landlord' will be licensed. The legislation also contains provisions enabling local authorities to serve an 'antisocial behaviour notice' on the landlord of a tenant who appears to them to be 'engaging in antisocial behaviour'.[151] The notice requires the landlord to deal with the behaviour. Failure to comply can lead to a number of sanctions being imposed. These include the rent no longer being payable, if the local authority successfully applies to the court to that effect, and criminal liability.[152] It remains to be seen how these rules will operate in practice. There exist other statutory obligations on private sector landlords. For example, they must ensure that any gas pipes and appliances are in a safe condition. Annual safety checks should be made. Failure to comply is an offence.[153] Finally, landlords who intend to lease houses for multiple occupancy, for example to a group of students, must – in addition to the licence mentioned above – obtain a multiple occupancy licence from the local authority.[154]

Public sector

20.47   Public-sector tenancies are regulated by the Housing (Scotland) Act 2001 (H(S)A 2001). The landlord has to be a local authority, water or sewerage authority, or a registered social landlord.[155] The property must be a house let as a separate dwelling and the tenant must be an individual whose only or principal home is that house.[156] There are two types of public-sector tenancy: the 'Scottish secure tenancy' and the 'short Scottish secure tenancy'. These are modelled on the assured and short assured tenancies described above. Once again there is a list of excepted categories, including certain leases of police and fire service accommodation and leases to students where the landlord is the student's educational institution.[157] There is also security of tenure, like the assured tenancy.[158] Repairing obligations are imposed on

---

148   To check if your landlord has registered, see www.landlordregistrationscotland.gov.uk/Pages/ Home.aspx.
149   Antisocial Behaviour etc. (Scotland) Act 2004 (AB(S)A 2004), s 93(1). The offender is the landlord, not the tenant.
150   AB(S)A 2004, s 94.
151   AB(S)A 2004, s 68.
152   AB(S)A 2004, ss 71, 74, 78 and 79.
153   Gas Safety (Installation and Use) Regulations 1998 (SI 1998/2451). See *Mackenzie v Aberdeen City Council* 2002 Hous LR 88.
154   Housing (Scotland) Act 2006 Part 5.
155   H(S)A 2001, s 11(1)(b).
156   H(S)A 2001, s 11(1)(a) and (c). 'House' is defined in s 111 and includes flats and yards, gardens, outhouses and pertinents pertaining to a house.
157   H(S)A 2001, Sch 1. Many of the public bodies who may grant Scottish secure tenancies are clearly not educational institutions.
158   H(S)A 2001, s 14 and Sch 2, Pt 1.

the landlord.[159] An important feature has been the right to buy the property in certain circumstances. This was one of the flagship policies of the Thatcher Government in the 1980s but is now being phased out.[160] There is a discount below market value. The discount is determined by the length of time that the tenant has been in occupation.[161] If the tenant resells the property within three years then the landlord can claw back the discount or part of it.[162] The short Scottish secure tenancy requires a minimum duration of six months and advance notice to the tenant that such a lease is being granted.[163] Its use is limited to a small number of cases, including where the tenant has been guilty of anti-social behaviour or is a homeless person.[164] There is no extended security of tenure, nor right to buy for tenants.[165]

Agricultural leases: general

20.48   Many farms in Scotland have tenant farmers. There are five special statutory regimes. Taking them by the name of the tenant, they are:
- (a) tenants of an agricultural holding;[166]
- (b) crofters;
- (c) cottars;
- (d) small landholders; and
- (e) statutory small tenants.

Of these, the first two are the most important. The law is complex and only the briefest outline is possible here.

Agricultural holdings

20.49   The relevant statutes are the Agricultural Holdings (Scotland) Acts 1991 (AH(S)A 1991) and 2003 (AH(S)A 2003) as prospectively amended by the Land Reform (Scotland) Act 2016 (LR(S)A 2016) Pt 10. Broadly speaking, an 'agricultural holding' is a lease of land used for agriculture as part of a trade or business.[167] The general principle is that the tenant has security of tenure. Usually, where the landlord has served a notice to quit, the tenant can serve a counter-notice.[168] The effect of

---

[159]   H(S)A 2001, Sch 4.
[160]   Housing (Scotland) Act 1987 (H(S)A 1987), ss 61–84.
[161]   H(S)A 1987, s 62.
[162]   H(S)A 1987, s 72. For sales within one year, 100% of the discount is returnable; for sales within two years, 66% and for those within three years, 33%.
[163]   H(S)A 2001, s 34 and the Short Scottish Secure Tenancies (Notices) Regulations 2002 (SSI 2002/315).
[164]   H(S)A 2001, Sch 6.
[165]   H(S)A 2001, s 36; and H(S)A 1987, s 61(2).
[166]   This category itself has subdivisions: see PARA **20.49**.
[167]   AH(S)A 1991, s 1(1); AH(S)A 2003, s 93.
[168]   AH(S)A 1991, s 22. In certain cases, for example, where the tenant is apparently insolvent, a counter-notice may not be served.

the counter-notice is that the landlord can only remove the tenant by applying to the Land Court and proving that one of the limited number of statutory grounds applies.[169] The security of tenure rules were unpopular with most landlords and so avoidance measures developed.[170] AH(S)A 2003 blocked the main avoidance device, which involved the use of a limited partnership. But one of its provisions has been held in part to contravene A1P1.[171] At the same time it introduced two new types of lease, in parallel with the ordinary statutory agricultural holding. These are the 'Short Limited Duration Tenancy' (SLDT) which cannot exceed five years and the 'Limited Duration Tenancy' (LDT) which must be not less than 15 years in length.[172] Tenants under such leases do not have security of tenure after the ish. Under the LR(S)A 2016 amendments new leases cannot be constituted as SLDTs or LDTs. In their place the 'Modern Limited Duration Tenancy' (MLDT) is introduced, which must not be less than 10 years in length.[173] Also provided for is a new form of lease called a 'repairing tenancy', under which there is an initial period (of 5 years or such longer period as is agreed) during the which the tenants can improve the land, rather than farm it.[174] Certain other rights are conferred on tenants of agricultural holdings. Where they have security of tenure, they are entitled to have the rent set by the Land Court and under the LR(S)A 2016 that entitlement is to a 'fair rent' under reference to certain factors.[175] At the termination of the lease there are rights to compensation for improvements and to remove fixtures.[176] In leases which are not SLDTs or LDTs or MDLTs or repairing tenancies, tenants are given a pre-emptive right to purchase the farm.[177]

Crofts

20.50 Crofting tenure has its origins in the Highland Clearances. Resistance led eventually to the Napier Commission (1884) and the first statute to give some protection to the remaining crofters (Crofters Holdings (Scotland) Act 1886). A croft is a piece of leased land with an average size of five hectares.[178] The land will usually be in one of the six crofting counties: Argyll; Caithness; Inverness; Ross and Cromarty; Sutherland; and Orkney and Shetland.[179] Under the Crofting Reform (Scotland) Act 2010 a new Crofting Register was established on 30 November 2012 which is run by the Keeper of the Registers of Scotland and will gradually replace

---

[169]   AH(S)A 1991, s 24.
[170]   See McDonald *Conveyancing Manual* para 26.10.
[171]   *Salveson v Riddell* [2013] UKSC 22. See also **PARA 32.17** below.
[172]   AH(S)A 2003, ss 4 and 5.
[173]   AH(S)A 2003, s 5A.
[174]   AH(S)A 2003, s 5C.
[175]   AH(S)A 1991, s 13 (as amended by LR(S)A 2016) and sch 1A (as added by LR(S)A 2016).
[176]   AH(S)A 1991, ss 33–39 and 18; AH(S)A 2003, ss 43–49 (as amended by LR(S)A 2016).
[177]   AH(S)A 2003, ss 26–38P (as amended or added by LR(S)A 2016).
[178]   See www.crofting.scotland.gov.uk/faq.asp?q=6&catid=1#q6 ('How big is a croft?').
[179]   But under C(S)A 1993, s 3A, the Scottish Ministers have power to designate land outwith these counties as croft land.

the existing Register of Crofts.[180] The Land Court has jurisdiction over crofting matters and there is also the Crofting Commission (Coimisean na Croitearachd), in Inverness,[181] which has significant administrative powers. Crofters have the right to a 'fair' rent,[182] security of tenure[183] and compensation for improvements.[184] In addition, they have the right to buy the land.[185] Recently, crofting communities have been given the right to form a 'crofting community body'. It can seek the approval of the Scottish Ministers to acquire ownership of the land where the community is situated.[186] A challenge to the relevant legislation on the basis of A1P1 failed.[187]

Cottars

20.51   A cottar is a tenant who occupies a house, with or without garden ground, either rent-free or on the basis of an annual lease with a maximum rent of £6 per year.[188] The land must be in one of the crofting counties. Like crofters, cottars have the right to compensation for improvements on their occupation terminating and a statutory right to buy.[189]

Small landholders

20.52   For an agricultural tenant to be a small landholder and be protected by the Small Landholders (Scotland) Act 1911, a number of criteria must be satisfied.[190]

(1)   The holding must have had a rent of not more than £50 a year in April 1912 or be not more than 20 hectares in extent.

(2)   The tenancy must have been in existence when the 1911 legislation was passed or the tenant has been registered with the Land Court since then as a new holder.

(3)   The tenant must cultivate the land by himself or herself, with or without hired labour.

---

[180]   Crofting Reform (Scotland) Act 2010 Part 2. The Register of Crofts is kept by the Crofting Commission. As of September 2016, 3000 of the estimated 18000 crofts have been added to the Crofting Register. See www.crofting.scotland.gov.uk/news/9-sep-2016-crofting-register-reaches-3000-milestone.

[181]   See www.crofting.scotland.gov.uk/. Prior to the Crofting Reform (Scotland) Act 2010 it was called the Crofters Commission.

[182]   C(S)A 1993, s 6.

[183]   C(S)A 1993, s 5.

[184]   C(S)A 1993, ss 30–35.

[185]   C(S)A 1993, ss 12–19.

[186]   LR(S)A 2003, ss 68–97A.

[187]   *Pairc Crofters Ltd v Scottish Ministers* [2012] CSIH 96. 2013 SLT 308.

[188]   C(S)A 1993, s 12(5).

[189]   C(S)A 1993, ss 36 and 12.

[190]   Small Landholders (Scotland) Act 1911, ss 2(1), 7, 10(1) and 26.

(4) Finally, he or she or a predecessor in the same family, must have provided or paid for all or the greater part of the buildings and permanent improvements on the land.

Like a crofter, a small landholder has the right to a fair rent,[191] security of tenure[192] and compensation for improvements.[193] Once again the Land Court has jurisdiction over such holdings.

Statutory small tenants

20.53 This type of tenant in principle would be eligible to be a small landholder. But, because neither he nor she nor a predecessor in the same family provided the greater part of the buildings and permanent improvements on the land, he or she is not.[194] Statutory small tenants have far fewer rights. They may, however, apply to the Land Court for renewal of their lease at the ish, as well as for an *equitable rent*.[195] A process exists whereby statutory small tenants can convert their status to that of small landholder.[196] LR(S)A 2016 provides for the Scottish Ministers to carry out a review of the small landholders and statutory small tenants legislation.[197]

LITERATURE

20.54 For an excellent concise general account, see McAllister *Leases*. Other broad accounts can be found in McDonald *Conveyancing Manual* chs 24–27 and Paisley *Land Law* ch 7. More detailed coverage can be found in Paton, G C H and Cameron, J G S *The Law of Landlord and Tenant in Scotland* (1967), Rankine, J *The Law of Leases in Scotland* (3rd edn 1916, reprinted 1986), Rennie, R et al, *Leases* (2015) and *SME,* vol 13 (landlord and tenant) and vol 14 (location: leasing and hiring of moveables). For specialist books, see Cockburn, D and Mitchell, R *Commercial Leases* (2nd edn, 2011), Gerber, K S *Commercial Leases in Scotland* (3rd edn, 2016), Gill, Rt Hon Lord *Agricultural Tenancies* (4th edn, 2016) and Robson, P *Residential Tenancies: Private and Social Renting in Scotland* (3rd edn, 2012).

---

[191] Crofters Holdings (Scotland) Act 1886, s 6.
[192] Crofters Holdings (Scotland) Act 1886, s 1.
[193] Crofters Holdings (Scotland) Act 1886, s 8.
[194] Small Landholders (Scotland) Act 1911, ss 2 and 32.
[195] Small Landholders (Scotland) Act 1911, s 32.
[196] Small Landholders and Agriculture Holdings (Scotland) Act 1931, s 14.
[197] LR(S)A 2016, s 124.

Chapter 21

Rights in security

GENERAL PRINCIPLES

The purpose of security

21.1   John and Karen wish to buy a house together. Like most couples, they have insufficient savings to meet the purchase price. Their solution is to borrow from a lender, in their case Banff Bank Plc, the loan being secured on the property. This means that if John and Karen do not keep up the repayments then Banff Bank can sell the house. Thus, home loan advertisements state:

'YOUR HOME IS AT RISK IF YOU DO NOT KEEP UP REPAYMENTS ON A MORTGAGE OR OTHER LOANS SECURED ON IT.'[1]

As a matter of law, however, the 'mortgage' is not the loan that the bank gives to John and Karen, but rather the security right which they will give to the bank over the house. (John and Karen may tell their friends that 'the Banff gave us a mortgage'. In fact, it was they who gave the Banff the mortgage.) 'Mortgage' is a term of English law, but is now used commonly north of the border in everyday language. It is even to be found in a statute passed by the Scottish Parliament.[2] The legal name for the security right which John and Karen grant to Banff Bank Plc is a 'standard security'.[3]

21.2   The reason why the bank will insist on a security is to improve its chances of being paid. Before John and Karen receive the money, they will have to enter into a contract of loan with Banff Bank. This might be thought sufficient to protect the bank's interests, because if the couple fail to repay, it can raise an action for payment. In other words, the bank can enforce its *personal right* under the loan contract. A personal right, as we have seen elsewhere,[4] can, however, be a weak right. If John and Karen have become insolvent, that means they cannot pay their creditors in full. In fact this is probably the very reason why they have not been keeping up the repayments. If the bank obtains decree for payment it may seek to carry out diligence against the couple's assets. Once again, however, there may be a shortage and there may be other creditors trying to do exactly the same thing. In contrast, if the bank obtains a standard security, this means that it has a *real right* over the property. That right will prevail over the other creditors and will protect them in the event of John and Karen's insolvency.

Definition

21.3   The accepted definition of a right of security is that of Gloag and Irvine: 'any right which a creditor may hold for ensuring payment or satisfaction of his debt, in distinction from and in addition to his right of action and execution against the debtor'.[5] Thus in our example, the right of action and execution is the right to raise an action of payment and carry out diligence against John and Karen in terms of the

---

[1]   In fact, the debtor's home is at risk if any loan is not repaid because a creditor can carry out diligence against it or have the debtor sequestrated. These may result in the house being sold to pay the debt.

[2]   See the Mortgage Rights (Scotland) Act 2001, most of which has now been repealed by the Home Owner and Debtor Protection (Scotland) Act 2010 discussed at **PARA 21.52** below.

[3]   See **PARA 21.44** below.

[4]   See **PARA 1.17** above.

[5]   Gloag and Irvine *Rights in Security* 2.

contract of loan. The additional right is the standard security which has been granted in favour of the bank.

Benefits of security

21.4   In his sixth-century account of Roman law, Justinian wrote that 'A security is given for the benefit of both parties: of the debtor in that he can borrow money more readily, and of the creditor in that his loan is safer'.[6] We have already seen how the loan is made safer for the creditor. As for debtors, first, it allows them to obtain credit which otherwise would have not been available. Second, a secured loan normally attracts a lower rate of interest than an unsecured loan. Security, however, is not an entirely 'win–win' situation because it means that other creditors who are unsecured lose out if the debtor becomes insolvent. Secured creditors may exhaust the assets leaving nothing for the unsecured creditors. One American scholar has written that 'security is an agreement between A and B that C takes nothing'.[7] It may also be argued that even without security rights banks would have to lend. Otherwise they would not obtain income (from interest charges) and would go out of business. Despite such arguments, security rights have been with us since at least the time of Genesis[8] and their position, for want of another word, is secure.

Personal security and real security

21.5   Rights in security can be divided into 'personal security' (caution) and 'real security' (security over assets). Personal security is a guarantee from another person. For example, Anna, a student, seeks a £7,000 loan from a bank. It agrees but, because Anna has a limited income, it insists that her mother guarantees the repayments. Anna's mother then acts as 'guarantor' (or, to use the correct Scottish legal term, 'cautioner'). If Anna fails to repay, the bank can enforce the guarantee against her mother. No more needs to be said on this subject, as it is not a matter of property law.[9] The rest of this chapter covers real security.

A subordinate real right

21.6   A right in security gives the creditor a subordinate real right in the property in question. To return to the earlier example, the result of John and Karen granting Banff Bank a standard security is that the bank obtains a subordinate real right in the house. This means that there are (at least) two real rights in the house:
  (1) the right of ownership of John and Karen;
  (2) the bank's standard security.

---

[6]   Justinian's *Institutes* 3, 14, 4. Of course, this was not written by the Emperor personally.
[7]   L LoPucki 'The Unsecured Creditor's Bargain' (1994) 80 *Virginia Law Rev* 1887 at 1899.
[8]   Genesis 38:18.
[9]   See further Gloag and Henderson *The Law of Scotland* ch 16.

21.7   The bank's security, being a real right, is good against the world. Most importantly, it is good against *creditors* and *singular successors*.[10] We have already seen how the security is good against creditors. If John and Karen become insolvent, the bank has a right to be paid out of the proceeds of sale of the house, which has priority over the rights of other creditors. Say, however, that the couple, in a bid to escape their creditors, sell the house to Leslie for £300,000 and depart for Penang. This does not affect the bank's right of security. It can still be enforced by selling the house. In practice, Leslie would not buy without the assistance of a solicitor, who would check for any standard securities by means of a search of the register.

Making a security real

21.8   As the law confers an advantage on secured creditors, it usually insists that there is compliance with the *publicity principle*,[11] so that third parties are warned. In general, a security right cannot be created by mere agreement, for agreements are usually private. Thus, an obligation to grant a security is not a good security.[12] In fact, such an obligation has no practical value because if existing obligations are already being performed by the debtor there is no need for a security. It is only where there is default, for example on a loan contract, that a security is beneficial.

21.9   The publicity principle is satisfied for standard securities by the requirement for registration in the Land Register or Sasine Register to make the security real. The appropriate register is determined by where the property is registered.[13] For floating charges there must be registration in the Companies Register. This requirement will be replaced by registration in the new Register of Floating Charges if new legislation is brought into force.[14] For corporeal moveables, the creditor generally has to be placed in possession of the property, but there are some exceptions to this rule.[15]

Registration of securities granted by companies

21.10   There are additional rules to publicise securities granted by companies and limited liability partnerships. Generally, these must be registered at Companies House in the relevant part of the company's file, known as the 'Charges Register'.[16] This must be done within 21 days of the security being created. Failure to do so

---

10   See **PARA 4.4** above.
11   See **PARA 4.19** above.
12   *Bank of Scotland v Liquidators of Hutchison Main & Co Ltd* 1914 SC (HL) 1.
13   See **PARA 21.44** below.
14   See **PARA 21.39** below.
15   See **PARAS 21.35, 21.41 AND 21.65** below.
16   Companies Act 2006, Pt 25. The rules were reformed with effect from 1 April 2013. The terminology is messy: 'Charges Register' sounds as though there is such a register but there is not. It is just a part of a file, so every company's file has its 'Charges Register'.

means effectively that the security cannot be enforced.[17] These rules for registration of company securities apply *only* where the company is the debtor, *not* the creditor. As we have just seen, a standard security becomes real by registration in the Land Register or Sasine Register. It may be questioned what the point is in requiring a separate registration in the Companies Register.[18] This has been recognised by the legislature and the Companies Act 2006, in an important provision, which gives Ministers the power to dispense with the second registration.[19] What will then happen is that the Keeper will transmit the details of the standard security to Companies House. The same procedure may eventually be applied to other registrable security rights.

True securities and functional securities

21.11 It has been mentioned that a right in security gives the creditor a subordinate real right in the property.[20] The debtor retains the real right of ownership. Strictly, however, this is only the position for 'true securities'. In a number of cases, the right of ownership itself acts as the security right. The cases of this are known as 'functional securities'. True securities are sometimes also called 'proper securities' and functional securities 'improper securities'. In a true security, both the debtor and the creditor have real rights. In a functional security, only one of them has a real right and that is ownership. The other has only a personal right. Usually, it is the creditor who has ownership, and the security is sometimes known as a 'right of retention' because it is a right to retain ownership until the debt has been paid. In cases where trusts act as functional securities, it is the debtor who has ownership. Here are some examples of functional securities.

Retention of title in the sale of goods

21.12 As mentioned elsewhere,[21] it is common, especially in commercial cases, for contracts for the sale of goods to have a retention of title clause. The seller retains ownership until the price, or even *all* sums owed by the buyer to the seller, are paid. Here ownership acts in the same way as a security right. But, strictly, it is not a security right: it is ownership.

Hire purchase

21.13 Where a purchaser cannot pay for goods outright, a hire purchase contract might be used. Here ownership of the property is typically transferred by the dealer

---

[17] The actual position is more complex. See G L Gretton 'Registration of Company Charges' (2002) 6 *Edin LR* 146 which pre-dates the reforms which came into force on 1 April 2013.

[18] The counter-argument, for better or worse, is that the Charges Register provides a 'one-stop shop' for checking what securities a company has created. But some securities, in particular pledges, do not require to be registered.

[19] Companies Act 2006, s 893.

[20] See **PARA 21.6** above.

[21] See **PARAS 5.26–5.27** above.

to a financial institution. The price is paid by the institution and the purchaser agrees to repay it in monthly instalments. The purchaser, however, has the immediate use of the goods. Ownership is not acquired until the last instalment is paid. The effect of the contract is that if the purchaser does not keep up the repayments the institution can take back the goods. Its right of ownership functions as a security right.

Transfer in security

21.14   It does not seem to be possible in Scotland to create a subordinate real right over incorporeal moveable property, such as a debt or a life assurance policy or shares in a company.[22] Therefore if the incorporeal is to be used for security, it must be transferred to the creditor by assignation.[23] The holder of the incorporeal (the cedent) assigns to the creditor. The creditor therefore becomes the new holder. For the security to be extinguished there will have to be a retrocession (re-assignation). Statutory prohibitions effectively prevent transfers in security in respect of heritable property and corporeal moveable property.[24]

Trusts

21.15   Trusts are sometimes used as securities.[25] The idea is that the property is placed into a special trust patrimony and therefore becomes unavailable to the debtor's ordinary creditors.[26] For example, in an attempt to protect against the risk of the seller's insolvency, a disposition of land may be drafted to include a clause stating that the seller will hold the land in trust for the buyer pending registration.[27] It may be questioned if such clauses should be enforceable as a matter of policy because they do not satisfy the publicity requirements for the creation of securities. The attitude of the courts has varied and it is impossible to be sure that the trust would be upheld.[28]

Restricted and unrestricted securities

21.16   A security can be for a fixed debt. For example, Banff Bank lends £100,000 to John and Karen. In turn, they grant the bank a standard security to secure that amount. This is the limit of the bank's security. In such circumstances the security can be referred to as 'restricted' or 'special'. If the bank were to make a further

---

[22]   But see below **PARA 21.67** for proposed reform.
[23]   On assignation, see **PARAS 5.38–5.51** above.
[24]   CFR(S)A 1970 s 9(3); SOGA 1979 s 62(4).
[25]   For a recent high profile case, where the trust failed, see *Joint Administrators of Rangers Football Club Plc, Noters* 2012 SLT 599.
[26]   See **PARAS 23.58 AND 23.59** below.
[27]   For discussion, see A J M Steven and S Wortley 'The Perils of a Trusting Disposition' 1996 *SLT (News)* 365 and J Chalmers 'In Defence of the Trusting Conveyancer' 2002 *SLT (News)* 231.
[28]   Compare *Clark Taylor & Co Ltd v Quality Site Development (Edinburgh) Ltd* 1981 SC 111 with *Tay Valley Joinery Ltd v CF Financial Services Ltd* 1987 SLT 207.

advance[29] of £20,000 so that John and Karen could add a conservatory to their house, that amount would be *unsecured*. The bank, however, in practice would want security and that is why standard securities are normally granted for 'all sums due and to become due'. If the security granted by John and Karen were in these terms, then not only would the £100,000 be secured, but also the £20,000 and indeed any sums due to the bank. (Of course, the bank would require to have in mind the value of the house). Such a security is known as 'unrestricted' or 'general' and can cover both existing and future debts.

Accessory nature of security

21.17   As the purpose of security is to ensure payment of a debt (or debts), in principle there can be no security without a debt. The real right of security is *accessory* or parasitic upon the debt. No debt: no security. Thus, if the debt is paid off the security is extinguished.[30] Similarly, if the debt is invalid, so too is the security. In *Nisbet's Creditors v Robertson*[31] a heritable security had been granted by a merchant in Scotland to his supplier in Holland for the price of smuggled goods. The contract was illegal and so the security failed too.

21.18   The accessoriness principle is not absolute because of the competence of securities for future and unrestricted sums. For example, a standard security may be created in security of a future advance. The security will come into effect upon registration but cannot be enforced until the advance is made and the debt is actually due. Similarly, a standard security can secure a bank overdraft. If the bank account goes into credit the security will continue, but cannot be enforced unless and until the account goes back into overdraft. In effect the security is suspended.

Third-party security

21.19   It is competent to grant a security for another person's debt. For example, John sets up a small business. The bank offers him a loan, but on condition that a standard security is granted over the house he owns with Karen. The result is that both the *pro indiviso* shares of the house secure the loan. In doing this, Karen does not become personally liable – though if the debt is not paid, she will lose her share of the house. (Of course, she could alternatively, or additionally, give a personal guarantee for the debt.) In such situations it is important that the bank ensures that Karen is offered independent legal advice on the implications of the security.[32]

---

[29]   Loan. Loans are often called 'advances'.
[30]   *Rankin v Arnot* (1680) Mor 572. See further A J M Steven 'Accessoriness and Security over Land' (2009) 13 *Edin LR* 139.
[31]   (1791) Mor 9554.
[32]   *Smith v Bank of Scotland* 1997 SC (HL) 111. See Gretton and Reid *Conveyancing* para 1-11.

Transfer of securities

21.20   *Accessorium sequitur principale*: the accessory follows the principal.[33] The assignation of a debt carries with it all accessories of the debt, including in principle any security.[34] For real securities, however, further action may be required. A standard security requires to be specifically assigned and that assignation registered.[35] This is part of a more general rule that the same steps required to create a real right are normally needed to transfer it.[36] It is crucial that if a security is to be transferred that the debt is assigned. Otherwise, the security being an accessory right, will be unenforceable.[37]

Transfer of the security subjects

21.21   The existence of the security does not prevent the property being transferred.[38] This is simply an aspect of the wider principle that a subordinate real right does not prevent transfer of the encumbered property. We saw above that John and Karen could transfer their house to Leslie notwithstanding the standard security.[39] The effect of this now needs to be more carefully considered. A distinction can be drawn between 'personal liability' (liability of a person) and 'real liability' (liability of a thing). Neither is affected by the transfer. The personal liability of John and Karen to the bank under the contract of loan remains. The bank cannot sue Leslie directly for payment of the debt as he was not a party to the loan contract. But the real liability, the liability of the house also continues. As the security is a real right, it is not affected by the transfer and therefore the bank can enforce it. The practical result is that Leslie loses the house. As was seen above, in practice this does not happen because his solicitor will have checked the register before the transfer.

Ranking

21.22   It is usually competent for more than one security to be granted over the same property. Thus, one hears of people 'taking out second mortgages'. John and Karen, having granted a standard security to Banff Bank Plc for the £100,000 they needed to buy the house, may then grant a second standard security to Alvah Bank Plc for the £20,000 required to add a conservatory. If the couple default and the securities have to be enforced, then the issue of ranking must be considered. The rule

---

[33]   See *Trayner's Latin Maxims* (4th edn, reprinted with an introduction by A G M Duncan, 1993) 8.
[34]   Stair III, 1, 17; Bankton III, 1, 7; Erskine III, 5, 8.
[35]   CFR(S)A 1970, s 14.
[36]   See **PARA 1.29** above.
[37]   *Watson v Bogue (No 1)* 2000 SLT (Sh Ct) 125.
[38]   The terms of the security may in practice prohibit this. Such a prohibition has, however, contractual, not real, effect. Transfer without consent would be breach of contract, but the transfer would still take effect.
[39]   See **PARA 21.7** above.

is that the earlier the security, the higher the rank: *prior tempore potior jure* (earlier by time, stronger by right). Thus if the house, after the expenses of the sale, is worth £115,000, Banff Bank will receive its £100,000 in full but there will only be £15,000 left for Alvah Bank. It will be an unsecured creditor for the shortfall of £5,000.

21.23   A first-ranked security is known as a security *primo loco* (in the first place). A second-ranked security is known as *secundo loco* and so on and so forth, using Latin. A bottom-ranked security is referred to as *ultimo loco*. Securities ranking equally are referred to as ranking *pari passu*. This will happen if the securities were created at the same time, or (more commonly) because a ranking agreement between the creditors so provides. Clearly the lower the ranking the more the creditor is at risk. This is particularly where house prices fall. If the house is worth less than the value of the security or securities this is known as 'negative equity'. This tends to happen on a substantial scale every time there is a property market downturn.[40]

Enforcement

21.24   Historically, securities were enforced by the property being forfeited to the creditor.[41] This was not fair to the debtor, because the property might be worth several times the debt. Forfeiture was replaced by sale,[42] with any surplus having to be returned to the debtor. If the sale does not meet the debt entirely, then the creditor is left with a personal (unsecured) right against the debtor for the deficit. This right may be worth little if the debtor is insolvent. (And the debtor usually is insolvent, because were it otherwise the enforcement would probably not have happened.) The fact that the debtor is always personally liable is not always understood. For example, some debtors with negative equity think that they can simply 'hand the keys to the bank' and walk away from the loan when they walk away from the property. Not so.

21.25   The creditor is under a duty to sell for the best price which can be reasonably obtained.[43] The reason for this is best explained by an example. Say that a house is worth £300,000 and there is a standard security over it for £100,000. The debtor defaults. All the creditor is interested in obtaining is the £100,000 plus the expenses of the sale. It would be unfair to the debtor if the creditor could sell for this amount. The house is worth almost £200,000 more and the debtor is entitled to that surplus. Hence the law imposes this duty, which also protects any lower-ranked creditors.

---

[40] Of course, it depends on the percentage of value that has been lent. If a property is worth £200,000 and there is a secured loan of £150,000, a market downturn that reduces the property's value to £170,000 does not result in negative equity. But if the bank's loan had been 95% of value, £190,000, there is now negative equity.

[41] See A J M Steven *Pledge and Lien* (2008) para 8-14.

[42] It is doubtful nowadays that even an express forfeiture clause in the contract would be enforceable. See Steven *Pledge and Lien* para 8-17.

[43] This is a common-law duty. For standard securities it is stated expressly in CFR(S)A 1970, s 25.

Extinction

21.26 Securities can be extinguished in a number of ways. These include the following.

Discharge of the debt

21.27 As a security is an accessory right, the discharge of the debt ends the security. No further action is needed, but for registered security rights such as standard securities a discharge will be registered to publicise the extinction.[44] As was seen above,[45] in the case of unrestricted securities, repayment of the present debt suspends rather than discharges the security, because if there is future indebtedness it would be secured. But in this case the owner can require the creditor to sign a discharge, and will in practice do so if there is no intention to borrow in future. In such a case the deed of discharge does not merely *evidence* the fact of a discharge that has already happened (as above), but is itself the discharge.

Property no longer exists

21.28 If the property over which the security exists is destroyed or otherwise ceases to exist, so too does the security. For example, a security over a gold bar will disappear if the bar is melted down and the gold used to make other things. Heritable property is of course generally indestructible. Where a tenement is destroyed and the site is sold the proceeds must be used first to pay the debts due under any standard securities over the former flats.[46]

Renunciation

21.29 The creditor may decide to give up the security voluntarily, even though the debt has not been paid. This of course is rare. However, not so rare is a *partial* renunciation – this is called a restriction[47] – in which the creditor releases part of the property from the security.

Enforcement

21.30 Once enforced and the property sold, the security ceases to affect the property.

---

[44] See **PARA 21.56** below.
[45] See **PARA 21.18** above.
[46] T(S)A 2004, Sch 3, para 5(2)(a).
[47] See **PARA 21.55** below.

Confusion

21.31   If the creditor acquires ownership of the security subjects the security will be extinguished by confusion.[48]

TYPES OF SECURITY

21.32   Real securities can be divided into two main categories: those which are 'voluntary' and those which are 'involuntary'. A voluntary security requires the consent of the owner of the property, normally the debtor. An involuntary security does not.

VOLUNTARY SECURITIES

General

21.33   The main examples of voluntary securities are:
  (1) pledge (for corporeal moveable property);[49]
  (2) floating charge (for the property of companies and limited liability partnerships);[50]
  (3) mortgage (for ships and aircraft);[51]
  (4) securities over intellectual property;[52] and
  (5) standard security (for heritable property).[53]

Pledge

Definition and use

21.34   A pledge is a real right in security over corporeal moveable property, created by the delivery of the property from its owner to another, in terms of an agreement for the property to secure an obligation owed to the other. The agreement normally does not need to be in writing.[54] The granter of the security is the 'pledger' or 'pledgor'. The party receiving the security is the 'pledgee'. Pawnbrokers are professional pledge takers and the website of the National Pawnbrokers Association of the UK reveals that the most commonly pawned items are things made of gold, watches and jewellery.[55]

---

[48]   Cusine and Rennie *Standard Securities* para 10.11.
[49]   See **PARAS 21.34–21.36** below.
[50]   See **PARAS 21.37–21.40** below.
[51]   See **PARA 21.41** below.
[52]   See **PARA 21.42** below.
[53]   See **PARAS 21.43–21.56** below.
[54]   But pledge to a licensed pawnbroker requires writing: Consumer Credit Act 1974, s 115.
[55]   www.thenpa.com/About-Pawnbroking.aspx.

Delivery

21.35 It is essential for the creation of a pledge that the creditor is placed in possession. Moreover, possession must be maintained or the security will be lost. This makes pledge commercially inconvenient because it is not feasible for a company to run its business if it has handed over key assets to a creditor. (Equally, the creditor may not wish to store goods.) There exists authority that pledge can only be constituted by *actual* delivery, that is physically handing over the property.[56] This is probably wrong.[57] Rather, pledge can also be established by constructive delivery where the goods are in the possession of a third party such as a warehouse company by instructing the third party to hold them for the pledgee. In the case of goods being shipped, these can be pledged by delivering the bill of lading to the creditor. This is the special document issued by the shipping company to the person who is having the goods transported. In such cases pledge is perfectly convenient since the debtor is not losing natural possession.

Enforcement

21.36 If the debtor defaults, the creditor's remedy is to apply to the sheriff for authority to sell. But this is not necessary where the contract between the parties authorises sale, and of course in practice contracts do so provide.[58] Moreover, licensed pawnbrokers have a statutory power to sell where the property is not redeemed within six months or such longer period that has been agreed.[59] Where the debt does not exceed £75, there is no sale. Instead, the property is forfeited to the pawnbroker.[60]

Floating charge

General

21.37 The floating charge was not recognised at common law. In the well-known words of Lord President Cooper, 'It is clear in principle and amply supported

---

[56] *Hamilton v Western Bank* (1856) 19 D 152. On delivery more generally, see **PARAS 12.13–12.17** above.
[57] See Steven *Pledge and Lien* paras 6-21–6-34.
[58] *Murray of Philiphauch v Cuninghame* (1668) 1 Br Sup 575.
[59] Consumer Credit Act 1974, ss 116(1)–(3) and 121(1); Consumer Credit (Realisation of Pawn) Regulations 1983 (SI 1983/1568).
[60] Consumer Credit Act 1974, s 120(1)(a), read with SI 1998/997, Sch 1, para 1. This is so even if the thing is worth more than the debt. Tom borrows £70 from Sue, pledging a painting worth £1,000. He fails to redeem within the redemption period. The painting has been forfeited. Does she now owe him £930? That would be fair, but the 1974 Act does not say so. Moreover, it says that forfeiture operates 'notwithstanding anything in s 113'. The meaning of s 113 is obscure but it is probably declaratory of the common-law rule that a creditor cannot obtain a windfall gain from security. Seemingly she gets a windfall profit of £930. Indeed, it has been so held: *Henderson v Wilson* (1834) 12 S 313, construing the similar provisions of the Pawnbrokers Act 1800. (And see *McMillan v Conrad* (1914) 30 Sh Ct Rep 275.) The Scottish Law Commission has proposed reform: see its Discussion Paper on Moveable Transactions (Scot Law Com DP No 151, 2011) paras 6.14-6.17 and 15.8.

by authority that a floating charge is utterly repugnant to the principles of Scots law'.[61] It is in fact a creature of English equity, which was introduced to Scotland by statute in 1961.[62] It was felt then that the common law of security was too restrictive, in particular in relation to the delivery requirement for the pledge of corporeal movables.[63] As a non-possessory security, the floating charge solved this problem. In 1972, receivership, the special procedure by which a floating charge is enforced, was imported too,[64] although the reforms of the Enterprise Act 2002 mean that (with certain exceptions) it only now applies to those charges granted before 15 September 2003.

21.38 The floating charge was introduced with insufficient consideration of how its English equitable features would fit with civilian Scottish property law. This is compounded by the deficient drafting of the legislation, which has led to many difficulties, most notably as regards the relationship between the floating charge and diligence.[65] Some improvements have been made by the new provisions in the Bankruptcy and Diligence etc. (Scotland) Act 2007 (BD(S)A 2007), which are not yet in force.[66]

Creation

21.39 Floating charges may only be granted by companies, limited liability partnerships and a few other commercial entities.[67] Writing is required.[68] The security is created[69] merely by signature of the debtor and delivery of the constitutive deed to the creditor. Registration in the Companies Register must follow within 21 days on pain of nullity.[70] Under BD(S)A 2007, registration in the new Register of Floating Charges will be required to create the security.[71] Usually a floating charge extends to all the company's assets, or, to use the words in the statute, the company's entire

---

[61]   *Carse v Coppen* 1951 SC 233 at 239.
[62]   Companies (Floating Charges) (Scotland) Act 1961.
[63]   *Eighth Report of the Law Reform Committee for Scotland* (1960, Cmnd 1017) para 2.
[64]   Companies (Floating Charges and Receivers) (Scotland) Act 1972. The current legislation is CA 1985, ss 462–487 and the Insolvency Act 1986, ss 50–71. Future regulation may be by the Bankruptcy and Diligence etc. (Scotland) Act 2007, ss 37–49, which provisions are not yet in force. See below at note 65.
[65]   See *Lord Advocate v Royal Bank of Scotland* 1977 SC 155 overruled by *MacMillan v T Leith Developments* [2017] CSIH 17.
[66]   BD(S)A 2007, ss 37–49. These provisions may never be brought into force as there has been strong opposition from the banking sector. The Scottish Government has recently consulted again on the matter but not reached a decision. See www.scotland.gov.uk/Topics/Justice/law/damages/company.
[67]   CA 1985, s 462(1); Limited Liability Partnerships (Scotland) Regulations 2001 (SSI 2001/128), para 3; Co-operative and Community Benefit Societies Act 2014 s 62. See Gordon *Scottish Land Law* para 20-205.
[68]   Not by RoW(S)A 1995, but by the fact that the particulars of the charge must be registered within 21 days of its signature. See CA 2006 s 859A.
[69]   The security is not, however, a real right unless or until it attaches on receivership or liquidation. See **PARA 21.40** below.
[70]   CA 2006, s 859H.
[71]   BD(S)A 2007, s 38.

'property and undertaking'.[72] Therefore, both immoveable and moveable property and corporeal and incorporeal property may be encumbered. The fact that a creditor has a security over the entirety of the company's assets makes the floating charge popular with lending institutions.

Nature and enforcement

21.40 The idea of the security is that it 'floats' over the company's assets in the company's patrimony. When an asset leaves the patrimony, for example as a result of sale, it automatically escapes the charge: no act of discharge by the creditor is needed. When an asset enters the patrimony, for example as a result of purchase, it automatically comes under the charge. Only when (and if) the debtor defaults on the obligation, and the chargeholder enforces the security by appointing an administrator (or in some cases a receiver), or where the company goes into liquidation, does the charge *attach*[73] to the assets.[74] Attachment means that the creditor obtains a limited real right or, in the legislative terminology, the floating charge becomes a 'fixed security'.[75] An attached charge has ceased to float.

Aircraft and ship mortgages

21.41 At common law the captain of a ship had the power to grant a non-possessory security over the ship itself, known as a 'bond of bottomry', and over the cargo, known as a 'bond of respondentia'. Both these securities are *hypothecs*. A hypothec is a security where the creditor does not have possession. Hypothecs can be granted only if funds are needed to continue the journey and the captain is unable to contact the ship's owner. Due to modern global communication technology these securities are now obsolete in practice. What continues to be important is the 'ship mortgage'. This requires registration in the Register of Ships.[76] Much the same applies to aircraft. Aircraft mortgages are registered in the Register of Aircraft.[77] Since 1 November 2015 it has also been possible to create an 'international interest' over aircraft objects as the UK acceded on that date to the Cape Town Convention on International Interests in Mobile Equipment.[78]

---

[72] CA 1985, s 462(1).
[73] The term used in England, 'crystallise', is often used here. (One might think, of course, that a charge that ceases to float should 'sink'.)
[74] CA 1985, s 463(1); Insolvency Act 1986, s 53(7). Enterprise Act 2002, s 250 limits severely the power of a floating charge holder to appoint a receiver, and in most cases an administrator must be appointed.
[75] *National Commercial Bank of Scotland Ltd v Telford, Grier Mackay & Co Ltd* 1969 SC 181.
[76] Merchant Shipping Act 1995, s 16 and Sch 1. For a recent case, see *Air and General Finance Ltd v RYB Marine Ltd* 2007 GWD 35-589.
[77] Civil Aviation Act 1982, s 86.
[78] See the International Interests in Aircraft Equipment (Cape Town Convention) Regulations 2015 (SI 2015/912). Under reg 3, 'aircraft objects' are defined as airframes, aircraft engines and helicopters.

Securities over intellectual property

21.42   Security rights can be granted over intellectual property rights, though the subject is not well developed. A security over a patent can be created by a security registered in the Patents Register.[79] The same rule applies to registered trademarks.[80] There is no special statutory security for copyright, so it if it is used for security it must be assigned to the creditor. There is no requirement for the assignation to be registered.[81] Upon repayment of the debt, the right will be retrocessed to the debtor.

Standard securities

General

21.43   *Standard securities* were introduced by the Conveyancing and Feudal Reform (Scotland) Act 1970 (CFR(S)A 1970), which provided that grants of security over heritable property must be in the form of a standard security.[82] The result is that the types of heritable security which existed before CFR(S)A 1970 can no longer be competently granted.[83] A standard security is a very common type of security. When people talk about 'getting a mortgage from the bank', they are in reality granting a standard security to the bank over the house in security of a loan. (The loan is usually to buy the house in the first place.[84] Here, the security is usually created at once upon the acquisition of the property. Thus in the Land Register the conveyance to the buyer and the security by the buyer to the lender will normally be registered on the same date.)

Creation

21.44   A standard security must be in writing[85] and registered in the Land Register in order to become a real right.[86] The appropriate register depends on where the right over which the security is being granted is itself registered. If the property is on the Land Register then the standard security must be registered there and the Keeper will enter it into Section C of the title sheet.[87] If the property is still in the

---

[79]   Patents Act 1977, ss 31(3) and 33. See further D P Sellar 'Rights in Security over Scottish Patents' (1996) 1 *SLPQ* 137 and T Guthrie and A Orr 'Fixed Security Rights over Intellectual Property Rights in Scotland' (1996) 18 *EIPR* 597. See also *Buchanan v Alba Diagnostics Ltd* 2004 SC (HL) 9.

[80]   Trade Marks Act 1994, ss 24(5) and 25.

[81]   Copyright Designs and Patents Act 1988, s 90.

[82]   CFR(S)A 1970, s 9(3). Terminology: heritable security is security over heritable property. A standard security is thus a species of heritable security – the only species now competent. The creditor in a heritable security is often called the 'heritable creditor'.

[83]   On the older forms of heritable security, see Gordon *Scottish Land Law* paras 20-04–20-102.

[84]   See **PARA 21.1** above.

[85]   RoW(S)A 1995, s 1(2)(b).

[86]   CFR(S)A 1970, s 11(1).

[87]   LR(S)A 2012, s 8(1). See **PARA 7.34** above.

Sasine Register the registration of the standard security now requires a voluntary registration of the property in the Land Register, as the Register of Sasines has been closed since 1 April 2016 to new registrations of standard securities.[88] No security is created by merely handing over the title deeds to the creditor.[89]

Security subjects

21.45   The usual object of a standard security is land itself. For example, John and Karen grant a standard security to the bank over their house. It is also competent, but uncommon, for the right to be granted over a registered lease.[90] A standard security can in principle be granted over a standard security. This mind-boggling arrangement happens, but only very rarely.

Forms

21.46   CFR(S)A 1970 provides two forms of standard security: Form A and Form B.[91] Either can be used. In Form A both the loan contract and the standard security are set out. This is the form commonly used for security over residential property. Unless otherwise stated, the loan is repayable on demand.[92] Form B is a pure grant of security. The loan contract is found in an entirely separate document. Form B is typically used in commercial cases.

Style standard security

21.47   Here is an example of a simple Form A standard security:

'WE, JOHN LITTLE AND KAREN RAE or LITTLE, residing at Twenty Seven Cornwall Road, Aberdeen undertake to pay to BANFF BANK PUBLIC LIMITED COMPANY a company registered under the Companies Acts in Scotland under number SC634637 and having its registered office at 5 Trinity Street, Banff the sum of ONE HUNDRED THOUSAND POUNDS (£100,000) which capital sum shall be repayable on the eleventh day of November in the year two thousand and thirty seven (11 November 2037); With interest on the amount from time to time outstanding from the date hereof at the rate of four and a quarter per centum per annum (4.25%) payable twice yearly on eleventh November and fifteenth May, commencing on fifteenth May two thousand and eighteen; And we agree that should any sum due hereunder not be fully paid timeously

---

[88]   LR(S)A 2012, s 48(2). See **PARA 7.22** above.
[89]   Bell *Commentaries* II, 24.
[90]   CFR(S)A 1970, s 9(2) and (8)(b).
[91]   CFR(S)A 1970, Sch 2. The schedules to the Act are full of over-fussy forms in relation to standard securities and failure to follow them may mean invalidity. See, eg, *Onesavings Bank plc v Burns* [2017] SC BAN 20 but compare *Shear v Clipper Holdings II SARL*, 26 May 2017, OH, unreported.
[92]   CFR(S)A 1970, s 10(1).

as aforesaid the amount unpaid shall be added to and compounded with the outstanding capital as at the missed payment date so that subsequent amounts payable shall be increased accordingly; And we further agree that notwithstanding the foregoing provision should any sum due hereunder remain unpaid in whole or in part more than twenty one days after the due date of payment thereof then in that case the whole moneys hereby secured shall in the option of the said Banff Bank plc (which option must be intimated in writing to us not later than thirty days after the missed payment date) become instantly due and payable; And we also bind ourselves to pay to the said Banff Bank plc all other sums due or to become due by us; For which we GRANT A STANDARD SECURITY in favour of the said Banff Bank plc over ALL AND WHOLE the subjects at Twenty Seven Cornwall Road Aberdeen registered under Title Number ABN 7654321; The Standard Conditions specified in Schedule 3 to the Conveyancing and Feudal Reform (Scotland) Act 1970 and any lawful variation thereof operative for the time being shall apply; And we grant warrandice; And we consent to registration for execution: IN WITNESS WHEREOF we have subscribed these presents at Aberdeen on First November Two thousand and Seventeen in the presence of Jennifer Sharp of Thirty Golf Crescent, Kirkcaldy.

Jennifer Sharp, witness

John Little
Karen Little '

The standard conditions

21.48   Towards the end of this standard security there is a reference to the 'standard conditions'. These are the default terms set out in CFR(S)A 1970, Sch 3.[93] In practice, lending institutions generally have their own set of 'mortgage conditions', and in that case the standard conditions apply only to the extent that they are consistent with the 'mortgage conditions'. The standard conditions can be divided into two categories.

(1) Those that protect the creditor's interests by requiring the debtor, for example, to maintain and insure the property.[94] The creditor's consent is required if the property is leased.[95]

(2) Those that protect the debtor's interests by regulating enforcement and redemption procedures.[96]

[93]   A limited number of the conditions, in particular those relating to enforcement of the security, cannot be varied. See CFR(S)A 1970, s 11(3). And see A J M Steven and D A Massaro 'Standard Securities and Variation to the Standard Conditions' *2008 SLT (News)* 271.

[94]   CFR(S)A 1970, Sch 3, standard conditions 1 and 5.

[95]   CFR(S)A 1970, Sch 3, standard condition 6. In the event of this not being obtained, the creditor may reduce the lease: *Trade Development Bank v Warriner and Mason (Scotland) Ltd* 1980 SC 74.

[96]   CFR(S)A 1970, Sch 3, standard conditions 7–11. 'Redemption' is where the debtor wishes to repay the debt and so get rid of the security.

Assignation

21.49 Standard securities can be assigned by the creditor. The assignation must be registered in the Land Register or the Sasine Register, depending on where the security itself is registered.[97] As was seen above,[98] it is essential to assign the secured debt too.

Ranking

21.50 Standard securities follow the *prior tempore potior jure* principle discussed above, and so rank by order of registration.[99] However, there is a special rule affecting those granted for 'all sums'. It is best explained by an example.

Example

Suppose that John and Karen have granted a standard security to Banff Bank for £100,000 and 'all sums due and to become due'. They wish to add a conservatory. Alvah Bank plc is prepared to lend them £20,000 for this purpose but insists on a standard security. This will rank below Banff Bank's security since it will be registered later. The house is worth £150,000 so there is £50,000 of so-called 'free equity' to reassure Alvah Bank. So far, so good. But suppose that John and Karen subsequently borrow another £50,000 from Banff Bank. As its security is for 'all sums', it prevails. The further advance effectively wipes out the equity on which Alvah Bank was relying. CFR(S)A 1970, s 13 deals with this problem by allowing the postponed creditor (Alvah Bank) to send a notice to the prior creditor (Banff Bank). The effect of the notice is that any further advances made by the prior creditor will not prevail over the postponed creditor. In practice a postponed creditor will always send such a notice. The earlier creditor will still, however, have priority for:

(1) the interest due on the earlier advance(s); and
(2) any subsequent sums lent which have been already contracted.

Thus if Banff Bank had contracted with John and Karen, before the security to Alvah Bank, to make a subsequent advance two years later, then this would have priority over the later security.

Enforcement

21.51 The enforcement rules in CFR(S)A 1970 are complex and require reform.[100] The principal remedy is sale. The first step is normally a 'calling-up notice'.[101] This provides that the entire debt must be repaid within *two months*, failing which the

---

[97]   CFR(S)A 1970, s 14 and Sch 4, Forms A and B.
[98]   See **PARA 21.20** above.
[99]   See **PARAS 21.22–21.23** above.
[100]   See generally M Higgins, *The Enforcement of Heritable Securities* (2nd edn, 2016).
[101]   CFR(S)A 1970, s 19.

creditor may sell. Following the decision of the Supreme Court in *Royal Bank of Scotland Plc v Wilson*[102] it seems that where the debtor has failed to keep up with loan payments a calling-up notice must be used.[103] For non-residential properties nothing more in theory is needed, if the debtor is prepared to yield possession. If the debtor is not willing to do this a court order is needed to get the debtor out of the property.[104] In practice creditors will seek declarator of the right to sell, plus an order for possession.

21.52   Under first the Mortgage Rights (Scotland) Act 2001 and more recently the Home Owner and Debtor Protection (Scotland) Act 2010, the Scottish Parliament has intervened to give the debtor (and certain other parties, such as the debtor's spouse or civil partner)[105] certain protections in the case of standard securities over residential properties. The effect is that a court order is normally required before the security can be enforced. Thus the creditor must obtain an order under CFR(S)A 1970 s 24. The court must be satisfied that the relevant 'pre-action requirements' have been fulfilled.[106] It may only allow enforcement if 'it is reasonable in the circumstances of the case to do so' having regard to certain specified factors.[107] These include the nature and reasons for the default and the ability of the debtor and any other person residing at the property to secure reasonable alternative accommodation.[108]

21.53   The sale of the property is carried out by the creditor rather than the court or a judicial officer, unlike the position in many other countries. There is a specific statutory duty to advertise the sale and to obtain the best price.[109] The distribution of the proceeds is governed by CFR(S)A 1970, s 27. First come the expenses of the sale. Next is any amount owed to a creditor with a higher ranking standard security than the selling creditor. (This is seldom relevant because if there is more than one security it is usually the first-ranked that carries out the sale.) Then comes the amount due to the selling creditor. Next comes the amount due to the holders of any lower-ranked standard security. Finally, if there is anything left, this must be returned to the debtor, or those representing the debtor. (For instance, it is not unlikely in such a case that the debtor has been sequestrated, and in that case payment is made to the trustee.) The real rights of the selling creditor, and of any postponed standard security

---

[102] [2010] UKSC 50; 2010 SLT 1227. See G L Gretton 'Upsetting the Apple-Cart: Standard Securities before the Supreme Court' (2011) 15 *Edin LR* 251.
[103] But see J Barnard, '*RBS v Wilson*: light in the tunnel?' 2012 JLSS May/24.
[104] See the Heritable Securities (Scotland) Act 1894, s 5 for the relevant procedure.
[105] The protections are for natural persons and not companies. See *Westfoot Investments Ltd v European Property Holdings Inc* [2015] SC EDIN 58.
[106] CFR(S)A 1970, s 24A. These include making reasonable efforts to make an agreement with the debtor as to future payments. See *Northern Rock (Asset Management) plc v Millar* 2012 SLT (Sh Ct) 58.
[107] CFR(S)A 1970, s 24(5)(b). See *Accord Mortgages Ltd v Cameron* 2013 Hous LR 22 and *Swift Advances Plc v Martin* [2015] CSIH 65.
[108] CFR(S)A 1970, s 24(7).
[109] CFR(S)A 1970, s 25. See further **PARA 21.25** above. See also *Dick v Clydesdale Bank* 1991 SC 365, *Strickland v Blemain Finance Ltd* 2014 Hous LR 75 and *Peters v Belhaven Finance Ltd* 2016 SLT (Sh Ct) 156.

holders, are extinguished.[110] The result is that the buyer receives an unencumbered title.[111]

Foreclosure

21.54 'Foreclosure' can be used colloquially to mean enforcement of a security. Its legal meaning is narrow: the creditor acquires ownership.[112] The creditor can seek a decree of foreclosure from the court, but only if it has not proved possible to find a buyer for the property. This would be very unusual.

Restriction

21.55 It is possible for the creditor to reduce the physical coverage of the security by granting a deed of restriction, which then must be registered.[113] For example, a developer grants a bank a standard security over a site in order to receive funding to build houses. When each house is built and sold the buyer will require an unencumbered title. The bank will therefore in return for some of the sale proceeds grant a deed of restriction releasing the house from the scope of the security.

Discharge

21.56 CFR(S)A 1970 provides for a form of deed known as a 'discharge', which is granted by the creditor and then registered in the appropriate register.[114] It extinguishes the security. If the security is restricted to a specific sum, the accessoriness principle means that it is automatically extinguished upon repayment, without the need for a deed of discharge.[115] But the discharge is needed for evidential purposes: for example, a prospective purchaser of the land will insist that the register is clear. If the security is for 'all sums' then repayment of the original debt will not extinguish the security, because any subsequent advances will be secured. In this case it is essential to register a discharge to end the security.

INVOLUNTARY SECURITIES

Categories

21.57 Involuntary securities can be subdivided into three groups.

---

[110] CFR(S)A 1970, s 26.
[111] Unless, of course, there is a prior ranked standard security. This is very unlikely.
[112] CFR(S)A 1970, s 28.
[113] CFR(S)A 1970, s 15 and Sch 4, Form C.
[114] CFR(S)A 1970, s 17 and Sch 4, Form F.
[115] See **PARA 21.17** above.

(1) 'Tacit securities' – in other words, those arising by operation of law. The main examples are lien and the landlord's hypothec, discussed below.[116]
(2) 'Judicial securities', comprising rights of security granted by the court – in other words, diligences. The law of diligence is outwith the scope of this book.[117]
(3) Securities which can be constituted by public bodies over the heritable property of a person who owes them money. These are known as 'charging orders' and are discussed below.[118]

Lien

Introduction

21.58   A lien is a real right to retain property until the discharge of an obligation or certain obligations, the property not having been delivered to the retaining party for the purpose of security. A typical example is a jeweller holding on to a watch until the repair bill is paid. Where the property may be lawfully retained until the performance of a single obligation the right is known as 'special lien'. If the law permits retention for more than one obligation the right is known as 'general lien'.

Possession

21.59   A lien depends on the creditor having possession on the property. If that possession is lost, so too normally is the lien.[119] In this way, lien is very similar to pledge.[120]

Types of property

21.60   In modern times lien has been viewed as a security over corporeal moveable property.[121] It is possible to assert a lien over land too,[122] assuming that the requisite possession is held, but such claims seem unknown in current practice.

Lien as an equitable remedy

21.61   The courts can control the exercise of lien and, if the circumstances justify it, order the release of the property. In *Onyvax Ltd v Endpoint Research (UK) Ltd*[123]

---

[116]   See **PARAS 21.58–21.65** below.
[117]   See Gloag and Henderson *The Law of Scotland* ch 48.
[118]   See **PARA 21.66** below.
[119]   For an exception, see *Goudie v Mulholland* 2000 SC 61.
[120]   See **PARA 21.35** above.
[121]   See e.g. *Wilmington Trust Company v Rolls-Royce plc* [2011] CSOH 151.
[122]   *Binning v Brotherstones* (1676) Mor 13401.
[123]   2008 GWD 1-3.

a company asserting a lien over a document containing the results of the trial of a new cancer drug was ordered to hand it over to the company developing the drug on condition of the disputed debt being consigned (paid to the court) until the matter was resolved. It was in the public interest that the information was made available.

Enforcement of lien

21.62   To enforce the lien by sale the authority of the court is necessary, unless of course the debtor consents. Sale is only possible where the property is marketable. This is usually not the case for documents, for example where a law firm, whose fee is unpaid, asserts a lien over the client's papers and deeds held by the firm.

Special lien

21.63   A special lien arises through the doctrine of mutuality of contractual obligations.[124] For example, in a contract for the sale of goods the seller's duty to deliver and the buyer's duty to pay are regarded as reciprocal. The seller therefore has a lien over the goods until paid.[125] Likewise, a warehouse may hold on to goods until the storage charges are met, as can a carrier until the carriage account is settled. Hoteliers (or 'innkeepers', as they are still often called in this context) have a lien over a guest's goods for their bill. In *McKichen v Muir*[126] the Muir family had booked into an inn in order to attend a local ball. On returning from the event, Mr Muir argued about the bill with the innkeeper, who then detained the family's clothes.[127] This meant that they had to walk 8 or 9 miles home on a rainy night, with the ladies wearing only 'thin shoes and light muslin dresses, and without bonnets'.[128] As well as arising in a contractual context, a special lien may be available in situations of unjustified enrichment and – less commonly – delict. For example, where there has been benevolent intervention (*negotiorum gestio*) the intervening party may hold onto the property until compensation is received from the owner.[129]

General lien

21.64   A general lien secures a general balance, for example all the sums owed to a solicitor by the client or to a commercial agent (factor) by that agent's principal. The other main instances of general lien are those of the banker and the broker.

---

[124]   But it is a real right.
[125]   SOGA 1979, ss 39 and 41.
[126]   (1849) J Shaw 223. See McBryde *Contract* para 20-87.
[127]   It is arguable that the right is a hypothec rather than a lien as it depends on the property being brought into the hotel, rather than the hotelier having possession. See Steven *Pledge and Lien* paras 16-86–16-92.
[128]   (1849) J Shaw 223 at 224.
[129]   Steven *Pledge and Lien* paras 11-12–11-34.

A general lien is not an entirely unrestricted security, because it does not secure *all* sums – rather, only those owed to the creditor in the particular capacity of solicitor or banker or agent or broker.[130] Only a limited number of general liens are recognised because of the potential prejudice to other creditors by what is a powerful security.

Landlord's hypothec

21.65   The landlord's hypothec gives the landlord a security over the corporeal moveables in the leased premises – the *invecta et illata* – in respect of the rent. Like so much else in property law its basis is Roman,[131] but it has been curtailed by statute. The Hypothec Abolition (Scotland) Act 1880, as its name suggests, abolished it, but only for agricultural leases of more than two acres.[132] BD(S)A 2007 abolished it for all other agricultural leases as well as for residential ones.[133] The effect is that it is restricted to commercial leases. The hypothec used to be enforceable by a special diligence known as 'sequestration for rent' but BD(S)A 2007 abolished this too.[134] Ordinary diligence has to be used instead. A remarkable feature of the hypothec at common law was its ability to cover goods which were not the tenant's.[135] This rule was removed by BD(S)A 2007, principally because it may have been an unlawful interference with the third party's right to the property in terms of ECHR, A1P1.[136]

Charging orders

21.66   A 'charging order' can be registered by a local authority and certain other public bodies against the title to a heritable property for certain sums owed by the owner.[137] A typical example is where a building is found to be dangerous. The local authority can instruct the owner to repair it or demolish it.[138] If this is not done, the authority can carry out the work itself and bill the owner.[139] If the owner fails to pay, the authority can register a charging order – known in this case as a 'repayment charge' – over the land.[140] The effect is that the land is encumbered by a security. In practice, the owner will be unable to sell the property without paying the debt and having the order discharged.

---

[130]   *McCall & Co v James Black & Co* (1824) 2 Sh App 188; *Largue v Urquhart* (1883) 10 R 1229.
[131]   See A J M Steven 'The Landlord's Hypothec in Comparative Perspective' 2008 *Stell LR* 278.
[132]   Hypothec Abolition (Scotland) Act 1880, s 1.
[133]   BD(S)A 2007, s 208(3). See also **PARA 20.29** above.
[134]   BD(S)A 2007, s 208(1). It is not clear exactly how the security is now to be enforced. See S Skea and A J M Steven 'The Landlord's Hypothec: Difficulties in Practice' 2010 *SLT (News)* 120.
[135]   See, eg, *Scottish and Newcastle Breweries Ltd v Edinburgh District Council* 1979 SLT (Notes) 11.
[136]   BD(S)A 2007, s 208(4).
[137]   See Paisley *Land Law* para 11-32.
[138]   Building (Scotland) Act 2003, ss 28 and 30; Housing (Scotland) Act 2006 (H(S)A 2006), ss 30 and 33.
[139]   H(S)A 2006, s 35.
[140]   H(S)A 2006, ss 172 and 173.

FUTURE REFORM

21.67 There have been periodic proposals to reform the law on security over corporeal moveables.[141] In 2011 the Scottish Law Commission published a Discussion Paper on Moveable Transactions[142] which proposes the introduction of a new true security right over corporeal and incorporeal moveable property which would be created by registration.[143] The Commission is currently working on a final report and draft Bill.

21.68 The Commission will also shortly consider reform of security over land. At European Union level, there have been proposals to harmonise the law and create a 'Euromortgage'/'Eurohypothec'.[144] A compelling case, however, has yet to be made. The different laws in England and Scotland have never been a bar to financial institutions in England lending in Scotland and vice versa.[145]

LITERATURE

21.69 For a general overview see Gloag & Henderson, *The Law of Scotland* ch 36. On standard securities, see D J Cusine and R Rennie, *Standard Securities* (2nd edn, 2002), Gordon, *Scottish Land Law* ch 20, Gretton & Reid, *Conveyancing* chs 21–22, McDonald, *Conveyancing Manual* chs 21–23 and Paisley, *Land Law* ch 11. The leading detailed treatment of security rights in Scotland remains Gloag & Irvine, *Rights in Security*. A modern monograph on two types of security over moveables is A J M Steven, *Pledge and Lien* (2008). The Scottish Law Commission, Discussion Paper on Moveable Transactions (Scot Law Com DP No 151, 2011) surveys the existing law as well as proposing reform.

---

[141] See Scottish Law Commission, Discussion Paper on Moveable Transactions (Scot Law Com DP No 151, 2011) ch 10.

[142] Scot Law Com DP No 151, 2011.

[143] See the symposium of papers at (2012) 16 *Edin LR* 261. See also A J M Steven 'Secured Transactions Reform' (2013) 17 *Edin LR* 133 and A J M Steven and H Patrick, 'Reforming the Law of Secured Transactions in Scotland' in L Gullifer and O Akseli (eds) *Secured Transactions Law Reform: Principles, Policies and Practice* (2016) 253–267.

[144] See O Stöcker 'The Eurohypothec' in S van Erp, A Salomons and B Akkermans (eds) *The Future of European Property Law* (2012) 65 and S van Erp and B Akkermans 'Public or Private Harmonisation of the EU Mortgage Market?' 2013 *ZEuP* 43.

[145] C von Bar and U Drobnig *The Interaction of Contract Law and Tort and Property Law in Europe: A Comparative Study* (2004) 361.

Chapter 22

Liferent

INTRODUCTION

22.1   *Liferent*, also occasionally called 'usufruct' – from the Latin term for this right, *ususfructus* – is the right to use someone else's property for life.[1] It is a subordinate real right, encumbering the other party's ownership. While the word 'liferent' might suggest that rent is paid, that is not so. The holder of the right is called the 'liferenter' or, less often, the 'usufructuary'.[2] The owner is the 'fiar' and

---

[1]   As the Roman jurist Paulus put it, 'usufruct is the right of using and enjoying the things of another person, but without prejudice to the substance of the thing': D 7, 1, 1. (*Ususfructus est ius alienis rebus utendi fruendi salva rerum substantia.*) See also Justinian's *Institutes* 2, 4.

[2]   'Liferentrix' is normally used where the liferenter is a woman. In this chapter 'liferenter' will be used as a gender-neutral term.

the ownership that is encumbered is the 'fee'. The fact that a special term (fee) is used does not mean that this is a special sort of right. It is simply ownership, but subject to this particular subordinate real right. (It can also be called 'bare ownership'.[3]) One may use the terms 'owner' and 'ownership' instead of 'fiar' and 'fee'. Sometimes the English terms 'reversion' or 'reversionary interest' are used instead of 'fee'.

WHY ARE LIFERENTS USED?

22.2 The creation of a liferent can be a commercial arrangement, with money changing hands. For instance, an owner might sell the property, reserving a liferent. Obviously, the buyer would not be prepared to pay the full market value. The amount would depend on the owner's life expectancy. If the owner is 100 years old, the price might be near full market value, whereas if he or she is 25 years old and in excellent health, it would be low. Conversely, an owner might sell a liferent and reserve the fee, although this would be unusual. In fact, most liferents are not created for commercial reasons but as family arrangements. Vera might transfer ownership of her house to her two children, reserving to herself a liferent. Liferents are often testamentary. Thus Tom might bequeath his house in liferent to his widow and to his children in fee.

CREATION

22.3 A liferent is created as a real right by a deed[4] registered in the Land Register.[5] It can be created either by *grant* or by *reservation*. A liferent by grant is where the owner confers a liferent on someone else. For instance, Olivia owns land and grants to Luke a liferent of it. She remains owner. Or she might dispone to Doris and in the same deed grant a liferent to Luke. The alternative is a liferent by reservation. That happens when the owner, Oliver, transfers ownership to Georgina, reserving to himself a liferent. Liferents created *inter vivos* can be either by grant or by reservation. Obviously, testamentary liferents cannot be created by reservation.

22.4 In modern law, liferents come into existence only by the owner's voluntary act. Previously, two sorts of liferent could arise *ex lege*. They were 'terce' and 'courtesy'. These could come into being on the intestate death of the owner, in favour of the widow (terce) or widower (courtesy). They were abolished by the Succession (Scotland) Act 1964.

---

3   Latin *nudum dominium*, French *nue propriété*, German *nacktes Eigentum* etc.
4   Writing is required under the Requirements of Writing (Scotland) Act 1995 (RoW(S)A 1995), s 1(2)
     (b). See PARA **31.4** below.
5   LR(S)A 2012, s 51.

WHO CAN BE A LIFERENTER?

22.5   Since a liferent is a right that lasts for the holder's life, only a natural person can hold a liferent. It is the only real right that cannot be held by a juristic person. Some legal systems, but not Scotland, allow juristic persons to be usufructuaries, with the period of the usufruct defined as a certain number of years.

THE LEGAL NATURE OF LIFERENT

Subordinate real right – or temporary ownership?

22.6

'By the institutional writers a liferent was regarded as a mere burden on the fee ... the more modern view is to treat the rights of liferent and fee as forming two separate and co-existent estates ... the liferenter being no longer regarded as a mere burdener but as interim proprietor.'

wrote Dobie in 1941.[6] This 'more modern' view did not establish itself and the traditional conception of liferent as a subordinate real right remains intact today. A liferenter is not 'interim proprietor' but has a subordinate real right. The fiar is sole owner.

Personal servitudes

22.7   In Roman law liferent was classified as a 'personal servitude'. The contrast was with the praedial servitudes,[7] where the relationship is between two properties (one piece of land 'serves' another), and the benefited party is the owner of one of them, whereas with personal servitudes there is only one property, the encumbered property. The term 'personal servitude' is not now much used. (The same parallel exists with real burdens, which may be either praedial or personal.[8]) In Roman law there were three versions of liferent, namely *ususfructus*, *usus* and *habitatio* but Scots law has just the single category. (*Usus* was liferent minus the right to fruits, and *habitatio* was liferent of a house.)

WHAT SORT OF PROPERTY?

22.8   Liferent is competent for corporeal property, though for moveables it is rare. (About the only example in practice is a liferent of a house *plus contents*.) Whether

---

[6]   W J Dobie *Manual of the Law of Liferent and Fee in Scotland* (1941) 1.
[7]   See **CHAPTER 13** above.
[8]   See **PARA 14.4** above.

there can be a liferent of incorporeal property is not wholly clear, though the answer is probably negative. But this fact does not cause practical problems, because an improper liferent can be used.[9]

POSSESSION AND UPKEEP

22.9 The liferenter has possession. A liferented house can be lived in, a liferented farm can be farmed, and so on. The liferenter's possession may be either natural or civil.[10] For example, a liferent could be granted by Demetrius to Edwina of property tenanted by Fergus. Her possession would then be civil, not natural. Likewise (see below) a liferenter can grant a lease. The lessee would pay the rent to the liferenter rather than to the owner. As for upkeep, the liferenter must not harm what is called the 'substance' of the property. For instance, the liferenter is not free to demolish. Moreover, the property must be maintained by the liferenter in a reasonable condition. But there are complexities and difficulties about how the fiar can enforce this obligation.[11]

DEATH AND RENUNCIATION

22.10 When the *liferenter* dies, the liferent ends. When a liferent ends, no real right *passes* to the fiar. Rather, the liferent is extinguished, vanished like a burst soap bubble. Thus the fiar's ownership, previously encumbered, is no longer encumbered. (A liferent can also terminate by renunciation, also called discharge, in which the liferenter gives up the right.) If the *fiar* dies, there are no special rules: the property is like any other property subject to a subordinate real right. The owner could bequeath the property, for instance. Since liferent is a real right, the liferenter is unaffected by the fiar's death.

INSOLVENCY

22.11 If the *liferenter* becomes insolvent, the creditors can attach the liferent; and likewise if the liferenter is sequestrated the liferent becomes an asset in the sequestration. But it cannot be realised by sale. The way its value is realised is by letting the property out, though any leases will end with the termination of the liferent itself. Alternatively, the trustee in sequestration could seek to do a deal with the fiar whereby the liferent would be renounced in exchange for payment. If the *fiar* becomes insolvent, there are no special rules: the property is like any other property

---

9   See **PARA 22.14** below.
10 See **PARA 12.9** above.
11 *Stronach's Exrs v Robertson* 2002 SC 540. See further P Hellwege, 'Enforcing the Liferenter's Obligation to Repair', 2014 EdinLR 1.

subject to a subordinate real right. The fiar's creditors can attach the property, while, if the fiar is sequestrated the fee will simply become one of the assets in the sequestration. Since liferent is a real right, none of this affects the liferenter.

JURIDICAL ACTS

22.12   A liferenter can use the property, but in general cannot grant real rights over it. Obviously, the liferenter cannot leave a legacy of the liferent. A liferenter can grant a lease but such a lease will end when the liferent ends. A liferent cannot be transferred.[12] It can be sold, in the sense that the liferenter can enter a contract with a buyer whereby the buyer exercises the liferenter's possessory rights: the buyer's right will end with the liferenter's death. Here, the buyer's right is not real, but only personal, being a right against the liferenter.

22.13   The fiar, by contrast, is free to deal with the property in any way, subject only to the liferent. For instance, the property can be sold, or a standard security granted over it. But whatever the fiar does, it cannot affect the liferenter's rights. For example, suppose that the fiar, Fraser, grants a standard security to Selma. Fraser defaults on the loan. Selma enforces the security and sells the property to Bertha. Bertha is the new fiar. None of these events affects the liferenter. A fiar could validly grant a servitude to a neighbour, but the servitude would be unenforceable during the liferent, unless the liferenter consented. (So in practice the neighbour would need to get two signatures on the grant of servitude.)

PROPER LIFERENT AND IMPROPER LIFERENT

22.14   Proper liferent is what has been described above. There is also something else, known interchangeably as 'improper liferent', 'trust liferent' and 'beneficiary liferent'. This is, in functional terms, very similar to the liferent (ie to the proper liferent). The inner legal nature, however, is different[13]. It is a trust[14]. Ownership is vested in Teresa (trustee), while Laura and Fraser have personal rights against her. Laura's personal right is that she is allowed to use the property *as if* she were the proper liferentrix of the property. Fraser's right is that when Laura dies Teresa must transfer ownership to him. Whereas in a true liferent there are two persons involved (owner and liferenter), in a trust liferent there are three (the trustee, the improper liferenter and the improper fiar).[15] And whereas in a true liferent both liferenter and fiar have real rights, in a trust liferent neither the improper liferenter nor the improper

---

[12]   'A liferent right is intransmissible': *Ker's Trs v Justice* (1867) 6 M 627, 631 per Lord Curriehill.
[13]   Most books deal with proper and improper liferents together. This is convenient but can be confusing.
[14]   See **CHAPTER 23** below.
[15]   Of course, there may be more than one trustee and more than one beneficiary with the right to use and more than one beneficiary who is eventually to be given ownership.

fiar has a real right: their rights are only personal. The only person in a trust liferent who has a real right is the trustee, who has ownership.[16]

	Proper	**Improper**
Number of parties	Two (liferenter, fiar)	Three (trustee/s, beneficial liferenter, beneficial fiar)
Number of real rights	Two	One (trustee/s)
Nature of liferenter's right	Real (subordinate)	Personal
Nature of fiar's right	Real (ownership)	Personal

LIFERENTS AND DESTINATIONS

22.15   There exists a legal institution called the 'special destination', which is a little like a liferent.[17] A provision inserted in the title to property, whereby on the owner's death the property passes to a defined person (the 'substitute') rather than to whoever would otherwise inherit it. Here, the similarity between the two institutions ends. In a liferent, the person who 'gets the property next' is already the owner, whereas in a special destination the substitute has (while the previous party is still alive) no real right at all. In other words, the substitute takes by succession, but the fiar does not: strictly the fiar does not 'take' at all, being already owner. Moreover, whereas there is nothing a liferenter can do to prevent the fiar becoming unencumbered owner in due course, a person who is the owner of a property that is subject to a special destination can sometimes divert the succession away from the substitute. This is called 'evacuating' the destination.[18]

22.16   An example is *Cochrane's Exr v Cochrane*.[19] Here, a testament said: 'I William Gilchrist Cochrane ... bequeath all I possess[20] to my sister Mary Jane Slight Cochrane. Anything she may desire to dispose of or realise after my decease ... may be done. On her decease everything of mine to be sold and the proceeds divided' among certain named charities. Did Mr Cochrane intend to give a liferent to Mary (with power to sell) and the fee to the charities? Or did he mean Mary to become the owner but subject to a destination to the charities?[21] Or was Mary to have a right intermediate between ownership and liferent? The court rejected this last argument. A person either has the real right of ownership or some subordinate real

---

[16]   See also **PARAS 23.20 AND 23.30–23.33** below.
[17]   See **PARAS 30.5–30.24** below.
[18]   See **PARAS 30.11–30.18** below.
[19]   1947 SC 134.
[20]   He did not mean 'possess' in its legal sense. He meant everything that belonged to him, all his assets. Obviously, this was a home-made will.
[21]   For destinations, see **CHAPTER 30** below.

right: there is no real right of semi-ownership. The court also held that Mary was meant to receive ownership as opposed to a liferent.[22]

STATUTORY RESTRICTIONS ON LIFERENTS

22.17   By the Law Reform (Miscellaneous Provisions) (Scotland) Act 1968, s 18,[23] a liferent in favour of a person not yet alive will normally give that person a right to the fee, notwithstanding the original grantor's intentions. This policy is to prevent property being tied up for unreasonably long periods.[24] The provisions apply to both proper and improper liferents, but it is doubtful whether a proper liferent could ever trigger the Act's provisions.

LITERATURE

22.18   W J Dobie, *Manual of the Law of Liferent and Fee in Scotland* (1941) remains the standard work: the law has not greatly changed since 1941. A drawback is that the book often takes no notice of the proper/improper distinction. Useful, but shorter, modern accounts are Gloag and Henderson *The Law of Scotland* ch 41, Gordon and Wortley *Scottish Land Law* ch 17 and *SME* vol 13 (S C Styles).

---

[22]   The way the case was pled meant that the court did not have to decide whether or not there was a valid special destination to the charities. However, Lords Cooper and Jamieson said that 'our preference is for the view that the testator intended that the charities should take in succession to the sister as substitutes or quasi-substitutes'.

[23]   Re-enacting earlier statutory provisions which remain in force for older cases. See, eg, *Earl of Balfour, Petitioner* 2002 SC 512, 2003 SC (HL) 1.

[24]   The same policy which led to the abolition of tailzies (entails). See **PARA 24.16** below.

Chapter 23

Trusts: what they are and how they are created

INTRODUCTION

Overview

23.1   Trust law is huge. (As are many other topics in this book.) We sketch it here in three chapters, the first (this one) dealing with what trusts are, the different kinds of trusts, and how they are set up. **CHAPTERS 24** and **25** deal with the way trusts are run, and with their variation and termination.

Sources, and comparative law

23.2   Although the core of the law of trusts remains common law, there are some important statutes, notably the Trusts (Scotland) Act 1921 (T(S)A 1921), the Trusts (Scotland) Act 1961 (T(S)A 1961), and the Charities and Trustee Investment (Scotland) Act 2005 (CTI(S)A 2005). More legislation is likely.[1] The area has been much influenced by English law. Though trust law is often the same, or at least similar, in the two jurisdictions, there are also important differences. (English authorities are often relevant, but are sometimes used uncritically.) In particular, in England trusts form a branch of the law known as 'equity'. There is no such thing

---

[1]   The Scottish Law Commission has published two reports: Variation and Termination of Trusts (Scot Law Com No 206, 2007) and Trust Law (Scot Law Com No 239, 2014). So far neither has been implemented.

in Scots law. English trust law and Scottish trust law achieve fairly similar practical objectives, but using somewhat different underlying conceptions. One might say that what they produce on screen is similar but the software is not the same. Still, the similarities with English law are striking if one compares our law with civilian systems. Few such systems have anything fully equivalent to the trust, though most do have trust-like institutions of one sort or another, such as the French *fiducie* and the German *Treuhand*.

WHAT IS A TRUST? THE BASICS[2]

What is a trust?

23.3   The question of what a trust is cannot be answered in a simple way, and perhaps not even in a complex way. The trust is conceptually problematic. But the basic idea is not difficult. Normally if an asset belongs to someone, that person has the benefit of that asset. If Tom owns a house he can live in it. He can also sell it, and if he does so the price is his to spend or save as he wishes. If he has investments he can spend the income that they produce on whatever he likes. Title and benefit coincide. In a trust, title and benefit are divided. Tom owns the house, but he cannot live there. He has investments, but cannot use the income for himself. He must use his rights (to the house, the shares and so on) not for his own benefit, but for the benefit of someone else, or a set of other persons. Tom is the 'trustee' and the others are the 'beneficiaries'. The person who sets up the trust is the 'truster'. The following diagram gives the general idea, at least for the standard three-cornered trust.

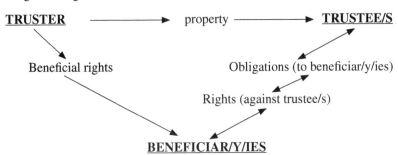

23.4   A trustee is an example of a 'fiduciary', someone who must act in the interests of someone else. Other examples are agents for their principals, company directors for their companies, guardians for their wards and parents for their under-age children. What distinguishes trustees from other fiduciaries is that the assets that they administer actually belong to them. For instance, if Edith and Frieda are trustees of a trust, and the trust owns land, what will be found in the Land Register

---

[2]   The difficult question of the nature of the trust is resumed later in this chapter. See **PARAS 23.59–23.64** below.

will be their names: Edith and Frieda. By contrast, company directors (for example) have no title to the company's assets. These are vested in the company itself, as a juristic person. So, if Edith and Frieda go into business and set up a company, EdiFried Trading (Machrihanish) Ltd, and the company owns land, what will be found in the Land Register will be the name of that company itself, and not the names of Edith and Frieda. Thus company directors are fiduciaries, but they are not trustees.[3] Trustees are fiduciaries *in whom title is vested.*

23.5 Something like a trust can be created simply under the law of contract. Tom is the owner of a house. He contracts with Beatrice to the effect that he will exercise his right of ownership for her benefit. She can live in it. When it is sold she will receive the price, and so on. This comes close to a trust. But trust has additional features that cannot be explained on the basis of contract law. The most important is the 'insolvency effect'. This is the rule that trust property cannot be touched by the trustee's personal creditors. Since Beatrice's right as a beneficiary defeats the rights of Tom's creditors, it looks as if Beatrice has some sort of real right. Indeed, in some countries, such as England, she is considered a sort of owner. She is the owner 'in equity' while Tom is the owner 'in law'. But in Scots law the beneficiary's right is personal, not real.[4]

Real subrogation

23.6 Tom owns some land in trust for Beatrice. He sells it. The money he receives itself becomes trust money. Suppose that he uses this money to buy UK Government stock. The stock is a trust asset, just as the money was. Tom's duties and Beatrice's rights remain the same, but now relate to the stock instead of the land. (And, in the middle, related to the money.) Thus the trust assets form a 'fund' or 'estate' or 'special patrimony' – in this context these terms are interchangeable – the elements of which may change over time, without affecting the fund's identity. The traditional term to describe this replacement, or substitution, of one asset with another, is 'real subrogation'.[5] The word 'real' does not imply that the assets in question are necessarily real rights. They may be personal rights. Indeed, in the example, UK Government stock is simply a personal right against the UK Government. The contrast is with the

---

[3] In England the word 'trustee' is often used not only in the narrow sense but also as a synonym for 'fiduciary'. In Scotland the word is generally used only in its narrow meaning, as explained above, but there are exceptions. For instance, T(S)A 1921, s 2 defines 'trustee', for the purposes of the Act, to include some non-trustee fiduciaries.

[4] See **PARA 23.61** below.

[5] *In universalibus, pretium succedit in locum rei, res in locum pretii.* (In a universality the price stands in the place of the thing [that has been sold] and the thing stands in the place of the price [where something has been bought].) A trust estate is a universality.

doctrine of 'personal subrogation', where, instead of one *asset* being substituted for another, one *person* is substituted for another.[6]

Definitions of 'trust'

23.7   While no one has produced a definition that perfectly captures the essence of the trust In Scotland, the following is good:

'A trust ... is a legal relationship in which property is vested in one person, the trustee, who is under a fiduciary obligation to apply the property to some extent for another person's benefit, the obligation being a qualification of the trustee's proprietary right and preferable to all claims of the trustee or his creditors.'[7]

Here is a longer definition, from an international standpoint:

'(1) In a trust, a person called the "trustee" owns assets segregated from his private patrimony and must deal with those assets (the "trust fund") for the benefit of another person called the "beneficiary" or for the furtherance of a purpose. (2) There can be more than one trustee and more than one beneficiary; a trustee may himself be one of the beneficiaries. (3) The separate existence of the trust fund entails its immunity from claims by the trustee's spouse, heirs and personal creditors. (4) In respect of the separate trust fund a beneficiary has personal rights and may also have proprietary rights against the trustee and against third parties to whom any part of the fund has been wrongfully transferred.'[8]

Finally, the definition in the Hague Trust Convention, given effect to in the UK by the Recognition of Trusts Act 1987, is:

'The term "trust" refers to the legal relationship created – *inter vivos* or on death – by a person, the settlor,[9] when assets have been placed under the control of a trustee for the benefit of a beneficiary or for a specified purpose. A trust has the following characteristics: (a) The assets constitute a separate fund and are not part of the trustee's own estate. (b) Title to the trust assets stands in the name of the trustee or in the name of another person on behalf of the trustee. ... '[10]

---

6   For example, motorist Adam negligently collides with Eve, injuring her. Eve claims on her insurance policy with Z plc. Z pays her. Z can now enforce against Adam Eve's delictual claim against him. One person (Z) stands in the shoes of another (Eve).

7   Wilson and Duncan *Trusts* para 1-63.

8   D J Hayton, S C J J Kortmann and H L E Verhagen, *Principles of European Trust Law* (1999) 13.

9   This is the English term for a truster.

10   Recognition of Trusts Act 1987, Sch 1, Art 2.

Trusts that are not trusts and trustees who are not trustees

23.8   The words 'trust' and 'trustee' are sometimes used where there is no trust. For instance, company directors are sometimes called 'trustees'. What is meant is that they are fiduciaries.[11] The charities legislation uses the term 'charity trustees' to mean 'the persons having the general control and management of the administration of a charity' whether or not the charity is in fact a trust.[12] Perhaps more confusingly, some juristic persons are called trusts, for instance the National Trust for Scotland.[13] Investment trusts are not trusts either. They are ordinary companies, the business of which is investing in other companies. Functionally, they are like unit trusts.[14]

Are trusts part of property law, the law of obligations or the law of persons?

23.9   Trusts can be regarded as part of the law of obligations, or as part of the law of property, or as part of the law of persons. Each viewpoint is valid.[15] First, a trust is to a large extent a set of obligations owed by trustee to beneficiary. Second, trust property can be regarded as a special form of property, and the right of beneficiaries being rights which, though personal, behave rather like real rights. Third, a trust is like a person in its own right, like a juristic person, with the trustees its directors. Indeed, it has sometimes been suggested that trusts should be formally classified as juristic persons.[16] But under current law they are not persons, merely person-ish.

What are trusts used for?

23.10   The French comparative lawyer, Pierre Lepaulle, wrote:

'Si l'on demande à quoi sert le trust, on peut presque répondre "à tout".'[17]

The trust is perhaps private law's strangest institution. It is protean.

---

11   See **PARA 23.4** above.
12   Charities and Trustee Investment (Scotland) Act 2005 (CTI(S)A 2005), s 106.
13   Incorporated by the National Trust for Scotland Order Confirmation Act 1935.
14   See **PARA 23.24** below.
15   Scotland Act 1998, s 126, in defining 'private law', places trusts as part of the law of property.
16   For discussion, see Scottish Law Commission, Discussion Paper on the Nature and Constitution of Trusts (Scot Law Com DP No 133, 2006) paras 2.39–2.45.
17   P Lepaulle *Traité Theorique et Pratique des Trusts* (1932) 12. ('If someone asks what trusts are used for, one could almost answer: "for everything".')

DIFFERENT TYPES OF TRUST

Ways of classifying

23.11   Trusts can be classified in different ways for different purposes. In the following paragraphs some of these are mentioned. The classifications are not necessarily mutually exclusive. For instance, trusts are divided into *inter vivos* trusts and *mortis causa* trusts, and also into private trusts and public trusts, but any given trust might be both *inter vivos* and public, or *inter vivos* and private, and so on.

Inter vivos trusts and *mortis causa* trusts

23.12   An *inter vivos*[18] trust is set up by a living truster. A *mortis causa*[19] trust arises on death and is set up by the truster's testament. It is also called a testamentary trust.[20] In such cases the executor may be the trustee, or may be directed to make over money or property to someone else, who is to be the trustee.

Public trusts and private trusts

23.13   Public trusts are for the benefit of the public or some section of the public. Examples: a trust for helping the long-term unemployed get back into work, or for providing support for elderly people in Fife on low incomes, or for supporting cancer research, or for preserving the historic buildings of Moray, or for providing education for children with special needs. As can be seen, the public benefit may be indirect and selective. The cancer research might never produce useful results. The preservation of the historic buildings of Moray benefits that part of the public, present and future, that has an interest in such buildings. Charitable trusts are a subclass of public trusts. Most public trusts are charitable.[21] Private trusts are for the benefit of particular persons, either named ('my son Dennis McFee') or unnamed but capable of identification either immediately or in due course ('Donna Norman's children'). Sometimes it is difficult to determine whether a trust is public or private. Thus in *Salvesen's Trs v Wye*[22] a truster directed that a part of the trust estate was to be distributed 'among any poor relations, friends or acquaintances of mine'. This could plausibly have been classified as private or public.[23]

---

[18]   'Between the living.'
[19]   'By reason of death.'
[20]   Every intestacy also seems to create a trust, at least in modern law. So, strictly speaking, testamentary trusts are only one kind of *mortis causa* trust.
[21]   See **PARA 23.34** below.
[22]   1954 SC 440.
[23]   In fact, it was held to be private. For another borderline case, see *Lord Glentanar v Scottish Industrial Musical Association Ltd* 1925 SC 226.

Family trusts and commercial trusts

23.14   There is an important distinction, important in practical more than in legal terms, between trusts that are used within commercial or financial arrangements, and trusts that are used within families, often for intergenerational wealth transfer.

Private trusts: examples

23.15   Here are some examples of private trusts.

Example 1

23.16   John is a successful businessman. He wants to benefit his grandchildren. He could give them money now, but they are young and cannot be trusted with capital until they are older, by which time he may no longer be alive. He does not necessarily want them all to take the same amount either by way of income or by way of capital. He sets up a trust. They are the beneficiaries but their beneficial entitlements depend on the discretion of the trustees. Over the years, payments from the trust can be used for their 'education, maintenance and benefit'. Eventually, the capital will be paid out.

Example 2

23.17   Trusts for those unable to manage their own affairs, because they are children, or suffer from mental health problems, are common. In such cases the persons in question will have parents or guardians to manage their affairs so that a trust is not actually necessary. Nevertheless, it can be an attractive way of handling matters, especially from the standpoint of the person giving the money. Moreover, suppose someone wants to make provision for a person who, though not under any legal incapacity, lacks the practical ability to manage substantial assets. Here, a trust can be the sensible solution.

Example 3

23.18   Donald wants to take time out because of illness, or to travel. He appoints his sister, Lucinda, to manage his affairs. He could do this by a power of attorney (ie a general mandate), or he could transfer his assets to her in trust. This is called a 'bare' trust. A bare trust is where there are no trust purposes except to hold for the benefit of one beneficiary, or more than one in common. The beneficiary can at any time insist that the trustee make over the estate to her/him.[24] The trustee's role is passive.

---

[24]   There may be logical difficulties in distinguishing bare trusts from other private trusts since in all private trusts the beneficiaries can jointly insist that the trust be wound up. See **PARAS 25.5–25.10** below.

Example 4

23.19   Shona is a rising politician. She wants to ensure that no one can criticise her for failing to act impartially in cases where political decisions might have an impact – whether positive or negative – on companies she has interests in. So she transfers her investments into a trust for administration, with this speciality: it is a 'blind' trust. In a blind trust the beneficiaries do not know how the fund is invested.

Example 5

23.20   Julia owns a house. It is her wish that after her death it is to go to her only child, Davinia. She expects to die before her second husband, Oliver, who is not Davinia's father, and she wishes to ensure that Oliver has a home in his declining years. She could leave the house to Oliver in liferent and to Davinia in fee.[25] But she decides to leave the house to trustees, to hold for Oliver in liferent and Davinia in fee. This is an 'improper' or 'trust' liferent.[26]

Example 6

23.21   A company wants to set up a pension scheme for its employees, funded by regular contributions partly from the employees and partly from the company. The fund will be vested in trustees. The beneficiaries will be the past and present employees. Only the retired employees will receive pensions, but the pre-retired ones nevertheless count as beneficiaries. One does not have to be in current receipt of money to be a beneficiary.

Example 7

23.22   Olga wants to sell something to Peter but they do not want to have to transfer title, at least for some time, perhaps to save the expenses of transfer, or to keep the sale secret. So she declares that she holds it in trust for him.

Example 8

23.23   Some friends set up a chess club. They subscribe money. There is a bank account into which the subscriptions are paid. Money is spent on chess sets, chess clocks, tea, travel to tournaments and so on. The club is

[25]   See **CHAPTER 22** above.
[26]   See further, **PARA 22.14** above.

an 'unincorporated voluntary association'. The assets, including the bank account, belong to the members jointly.[27] But it would also be possible to vest the assets in the committee as trustees for the members (whose beneficial interests in that case would be joint). Heritable property belonging to unincorporated voluntary associations has to be held through a trust. (Though there are currently recommendations to confer juristic personality on such associations, in which case they could hold property directly.[28])

Example 9

23.24 A group of small investors wish to pool their savings so as to achieve efficiency. They pay their money to a trustee who invests the money on the London Stock Exchange. The legal holder of the investments is the trustee. The investors are beneficiaries. This is a 'unit trust'. The shareholder in the various companies in which the trust invests is the trustee of the unit trust. The companies in which the trust invests pay the dividends to the trustee, which[29] then passes the money on to the beneficiaries. It is the trustee, not the beneficiaries, that votes at annual general meetings. (Functionally similar arrangements can exist without a trust. There is the 'investment trust' which is not a trust, for there is a company that holds the investments, and the investors are shareholders in that company, and there is the open-ended investment company (OEIC) which is similar to the investment trust.)

Example 10

23.25 Iona has become insolvent. A creditor petitions for her sequestration. The petition is successful and James is appointed as her trustee in sequestration. Her assets pass to James, in trust for the creditors: 'The whole estate of the debtor vests for the benefit of the creditors in the trustee in the sequestration.'[30]

Example 11

23.26 Sam has become insolvent. He appoints Tara, a chartered accountant, to be his trustee and he conveys his assets to her, 'for behoof of' his creditors.[31] This is like a sequestration but is extra-judicial.

---

27   See **PARAS 10.17–10.18** above.
28   Scottish Law Commission, Report on Unincorporated Associations (Scot Law Com No 217, 2009).
29   'Which' rather than 'who' because unit trusts have a single corporate trustee.
30   Bankruptcy (Scotland) Act 2016 s 78(1).
31   This expression means 'in trust for'. For discussion, see *Leitch v Leitch* 1927 SLT 575.

23.27 Whether an executor is a trustee in the fullest sense of the term is a point that can be debated.[32] But, for most purposes, at least, an executor is a trustee and those who are to succeed to the deceased are the beneficiaries.

Discretionary trusts

23.28 Discretionary trusts have already been mentioned.[33] Confusingly, this expression has two meanings. It has a meaning in general trust law and it has a second, narrower, meaning in tax law. Under the general law, a trust is a discretionary one if the trustees are given an element of discretion as to the extent to which given beneficiaries will benefit.[34] Suppose that there are three beneficiaries, Mary, Nigel and Olga. The trust deed might authorise the trustees to give more to one and less to the others.[35] A trust may be wholly or partially discretionary. For instance, the trust deed might say that the income is to go for ten years to Mary, Nigel and Olga, in such proportions as the trustees choose, and after ten years the capital is to be paid to Paul. This trust is discretionary as to Mary, Nigel and Olga but not as to Paul. The discretion cannot be too broad. In *Anderson v Smoke*[36] the trustees were directed to 'dispose of the balance in any way they should think proper'. This was invalid. But a discretionary trust is valid if the trust deed sets out a defined class of persons, such as 'my children'.

Taxation and tax-based classifications

23.29 Trust law itself recognises certain different categories of trust: for instance, there are private trusts and public trusts, *inter vivos* trusts and *mortis causa* trusts. But tax law also has its own classifications, the point being that the applicable tax regime depends on which tax slot a given trust is deemed to fit into.[37] A given trust may not fit into any slot very comfortably, but into one or other it must go, even if shoving is necessary. Like most things in tax law, these classifications are devised with English law mainly in mind. (HMRC[38] uses English terminology such as 'settlor' and 'interest in possession.') They are important in practice, and indeed the initial decision whether or not to set up a trust, and, if so, what kind of trust, is often

---

[32] See **PARA 26.48** below.
[33] See **PARA 23.16** above.
[34] 'There is little Scottish authority on the subject of the discretionary trust', comment Wilson and Duncan *Trusts* para 2-22. Despite this, such trusts are common in practice.
[35] This sort of discretion ('distributive' discretion) must be distinguished from 'administrative' discretion. Almost all trusts involve administrative discretion. For instance, trustees almost always have a discretion whether or not to sell the shares in one company and use the money to invest in another. The existence of administrative discretion does not make a trust discretionary: what makes it discretionary is that the rights of the beneficiaries depend on the discretion of the trustees.
[36] (1898) 25 R 493.
[37] For an overview see www.gov.uk/trusts-taxes/types-of-trust.
[38] Her Majesty's Revenue & Customs.

heavily influenced by tax considerations. The classifications are liable to change as tax policy changes. This book does not cover tax law and so nothing more will be said.

Liferent trusts (improper liferents)

23.30   Improper liferents (liferent trusts) were explained briefly above,[39] as one example of why trusts are used. Such liferents are commoner than proper ones, and their importance in practice justifies a few more words.

23.31   One reason why they are more popular than proper liferents is their flexibility. In a proper liferent, if the property is to be sold free of the liferent, that will need the agreement of both parties. But in an improper liferent the trustee can sell, and unless the trust deed says otherwise, the trustee does not need anyone's consent to do this. Suppose that Oliver one day wishes to move to sheltered accommodation. The trustees could sell the house. The money received would be trust money, and so the interests of Oliver and Davinia would be unaltered. The trustees could buy a flat for him in a sheltered accommodation development. Any surplus funds they could invest. The income would be paid over to him, and the capital retained. When Oliver dies, the flat would be sold, and the proceeds, plus the investments, would be made over to Davinia. The trustees in such a case would have the power to sell the house without the consent of the beneficiaries.[40] To achieve a similar result with a proper liferent would need not only Oliver's co-operation but also Davinia's.

23.32   A second reason is that proper liferents of investments are not possible. Yet in practice people often wish to create liferents over investments, or at least, as in the previous paragraph, have the possibility that investments will be part of the liferent. The solution is a trust liferent. The investments are held by the trustees. In the case of company shares, the trustees are the shareholders, with all the rights of shareholders. The same is true, *mutatis mutandis*, for company bonds and public bonds, for bank deposits and so on. The income received (dividends, interest etc.) is received by the trustees and then paid over to the beneficial liferenter. The trustees can change the portfolio, selling some shares and buying others, for example. When the liferent ends, the investments are made over to the fiar.

23.33   Another reason why trust liferents are usually preferred to proper ones is that the trustees can function as neutral intermediaries between liferenter and fiar. If liferenter and fiar have friendly relations, that does not matter. If not, it does.

---

[39]   See **PARA 23.20** above.
[40]   T(S)A 1921, s 4; *Mauchline, Petitioner* 1992 SLT 421.

Charities

23.34 Not all trusts are charities;[41] not all charities are trusts.[42] A charity can take the form of a trust, but it can also take other forms. A common form is that of a non-profit company under the Companies Acts: this is known as a 'company limited by guarantee'. (Not all such companies are charities.) The Scottish universities are all educational charities and are all bodies corporate. An entity which, unlike the other forms, is available only for charities, is the Scottish Charitable Incorporated Organisation (SCIO).[43] This is a juristic person. Each type of charity is governed by the law applicable to the type of organisation in question (trusts, companies limited by guarantee etc.) but in addition they are all subject to the law of charities. 'Charity' is a classification based on an organisation's purpose, not its form.[44] Charities are supervised by the Office of the Scottish Charity Regulator (OSCR).[45] This maintains the Scottish Charity Register.[46]

23.35 Thus, those organising a charity have to decide what form the charity should have. For small charities the trust is the most convenient form. But when a charity grows, has employees and significant assets, the trust is seldom a workable form, and juristic personality is likely to be needed, whether as a company limited by guarantee, or as a SCIO. (As already mentioned, some charities have juristic personality by special legislation, such as universities, and the National Trust for Scotland.)

22.36 Just as a charity may take the form of a trust, so there can also be a trust for the benefit of another charity.[47] Suppose that Tom leaves a legacy of £100,000 to Oxfam. Oxfam is a company limited by guarantee. Tom's executor holds the money on trust for Oxfam, because all executors are trustees. This trust is short-lived. Within a few months of Tom's death, his executor will pay the money to Oxfam. The trust ends. The same analysis would apply if Oxfam had itself been a trust. Then Tom would have created a testamentary trust in which the beneficiary was itself a trust: a trust for a trust. The first trust would, as in the previous case, be short-lived.

---

[41] In fact, most are not.
[42] The traditional technical term for a charity was a 'mortification'. This word has been displaced by the English term 'charity'. Many older charities still have 'mortification' as part of their name.
[43] Under s 49 ff of the Charities and Trustee Investment (Scotland) Act 2005.
[44] See P Ford 'Supervising Charities: A Scottish-Civilian Alternative' (2006) 10 *Edin LR* 352.
[45] CTI(S)A 2005, ss 1–2.
[46] CTI(S)A 2005, ss 3–6.
[47] Eg, *RS Macdonald Charitable Trust Trustees v Scottish Society for the Prevention of Cruelty to Animals* 2009 SC 6.

BIRTH

How trusts are created

General

23.37   A *mortis causa* trust is created on death by the deceased's testament, which will nominate trustees and identify the assets that are to be trust assets. *Inter vivos* trusts are not quite so simple, and indeed some uncertainty exists as to the law about creation, though in practice there are seldom problems.

23.38   The creation of *inter vivos* trusts is usually analysed into two elements:
(a)   the 'declaration of trust'; and
(b)   the vesting of property in the trustee.[48]

In the typical case, the declaration of trust takes the form of a deed of trust signed by the truster and delivered to the trustee. The deed contains details about the beneficiaries and the trust purposes. It will usually be registered in the Books of Council and Session, although this is not a legal requirement. The deed will identify some trust property, but often it is nominal, such as £10. The reason is that it may be convenient to establish the trust before it is possible to transfer the main assets (land, stock market investments etc) to it, but there is authority that a trust cannot exist unless at least *some* assets have vested in the trustees.[49] A truster can add the main assets to the trust after it has been set up with nominal assets. Indeed, other people can also contribute, and in the case of charitable trusts that is normal. Sometimes the truster wishes to be one of the trustees. That makes little difference. Thus if Tom owns land and wants to establish a trust of that land, with himself and Ulrica as trustees, he will sign a deed of trust naming himself and Ulrica, with an initial fund of, say, £1. He then dispones the land to himself and Ulrica 'as trustees acting under the Thomas Tomkins Family Trust established by Deed of Trust by the said Thomas Tomkins dated … and registered in the Books of Council and Session on …'

Truster-as-trustee trusts

23.39   Occasionally it happens that a person wishes to make himself or herself the sole trustee of certain assets that he or she already has. This is sometimes called a 'truster/trustee' or 'truster-as-trustee' or 'self-declared' trust. The rules on how such

---

[48]   Often called 'delivery' to the trustee – but this is a muddle. Delivery is the transfer of possession, and so only physical things can be delivered. (See **PARAS 12.13–12.17** above.) The issue is not one of delivery but of vesting of rights, which may or may not require delivery.
[49]   See further K G C Reid 'Constitution of Trust' 1986 SLT (News) 177; Scottish Law Commission, The Nature and the Constitution of Trusts (Scot Law Com DP No 133, 2006) part 3; *Joint Administrators of Rangers Football Club Plc, Noters* 2012 SLT 599.

a trust is created are 'uncertain and contentious'.[50] In so far as there can be said to be a conventional view it is that such a trust can be created by a written declaration of trust intimated to at least one beneficiary.[51] The assets in question are transferred from the truster/trustee's general patrimony into the trust patrimony, though there could be debate as to whether this is a true 'transfer' since transferor and transferee are the same person.

Magic words?

23.40 'There is no magic in the use of the word "trust".'[52] Normally the word 'trust' is used, but it is not essential. Occasionally, and especially in home-made testaments, the intention is unclear. It sometimes happens, for instance, that the testator says that something is to be done with some asset, but the words are words of request[53] rather than of instruction. If the words of request are directed to the executor, they will normally be regarded as binding, but if they are directed to a legatee they usually will not be.[54] For instance, in *Garden's Exr v More*[55] the testator directed his trustees to convey certain assets to his wife, adding: 'I should like not less than £50 sterling left to the widow of my brother, Alexander Garden, New Elgin, or her family, if she predeceases my wife, and I desire that my wife may make a settlement providing for this.' The wife inherited but herself later died without making any provision for Alexander's widow. It was held that the quoted words created no trust. Cases of this sort turn on their own particular facts.[56]

23.41 Just as the word 'trust' is not necessary, so, conversely, 'Scots law does not recognise the validity of a trust simply on the basis that those responsible for the constituent documents use the language of trust as a matter of drafting'.[57]

23.42 In a *mortis causa* trust writing is necessary, for testaments must be in writing.[58] *Inter vivos* truster/trustee trusts must also be in writing.[59] Other trusts do

---

[50] Scottish Law Commission, Discussion Paper on the Nature and the Constitution of Trusts (Scot Law Com DP No 133, 2006) para 4.16.
[51] This is based on the case which first recognised truster-as-trustee trusts as lawful (*Allan's Trs v Lord Advocate* 1971 SC (HL) 45) but the decision could be criticised. For the need for writing see **PARA 31.8**.
[52] *Macpherson v Macpherson's CB* (1894) 21 R 386 per Lord McLaren.
[53] Such words are known in this context as 'precatory'.
[54] Wilson and Duncan *Trusts* para 2-13.
[55] 1913 SC 285.
[56] For recent cases where vague documentation was alleged, but without success, to establish a trust, see *Johnston's Tr v Baird* [2012] CSOH 117 and *Rangers Football Club Plc, Ptr* 2012 SLT 1156.
[57] *Balfour Beatty Ltd v Britannia Life Ltd* 1997 SLT 10 at 18 per Lord Penrose. For another case on whether the use of the word 'trust' was not enough, see *Clark Taylor & Co Ltd v Quality Site Development (Edinburgh) Ltd* 1981 SC 111.
[58] See **PARA 31.6** below.
[59] RoW(S)A 1995, s 1(2)(a)(iii).

not have to be, though they usually are.[60] The 'no writing required' rule can have odd consequences. John owns a house and Mary claims that he had agreed to transfer it to her on demand. She says that there was an oral agreement. This argument is faced with the problem that an agreement to transfer heritable property must be in writing. But if she says that the oral agreement was one of trust, the problem vanishes. This is all the stranger in that a trust has stronger effects than a simple obligation.[61]

23.43 There is no requirement that the trust deed be registered. If registered property is involved, such as shares or land, the transfer to the trustee will require registration, but the title need not be taken expressly in trust. Thus for instance land may be conveyed to Tom as trustee but that fact may or may not be discoverable from the Land Register. Although trust deeds need not be registered, in practice most are. Testamentary trusts are registered because testaments are registered in the Sheriff Court Books in the sheriffdom where confirmation is granted. *Inter vivos* trusts are usually registered in the Books of Council and Session.

Unusual births

Introduction

23.44 Most trusts are created deliberately, whether *inter vivos* or *mortis causa*. These are voluntary trusts. Occasionally, trusts arise involuntarily. Finally, there are one or two types of trust which arise judicially, and which are hard to classify. One is sequestration. Another is confirmation of executors.[62]

By statute

23.45 An example of a trust imposed by statute is the Conveyancing and Feudal Reform (Scotland) Act 1970 (CFR(S)A 1970), s 27. This says that when a standard security holder sells, the proceeds of sale are held on trust for defined purposes. Another example of a statutory trust occurs in the sale of dematerialised company shares.[63]

Constructive trusts

23.46 When an involuntary trust arises not by statute but by common law it is called a 'constructive' trust. Whereas English law readily recognises constructive

---

[60] RoW(S)A 1995, s 1(1). Before 1995 the rule was that writing was essential, though there were some qualifications to this. See Wilson and Duncan *Trusts* ch 5.
[61] See Reid and Gretton *Conveyancing 2012* (2013) 53.
[62] See **CHAPTER 26** below.
[63] Uncertificated Securities Regulations 2001 (SI 2001/3755), reg 31(4)(b).

trusts, it is uncertain to what extent our law does so. 'I confess an almost instinctive abhorrence of the notion of constructive trusts in the law of Scotland' remarked one judge.[64] Many of the cases commonly cited as examples of constructive trust are doubtful examples, or are not Scottish cases. An obligation by X (eg a seller) to transfer property to Y (eg a buyer) does not make X constructive trustee for Y.[65] The strongest candidate for constructive trust is where a fiduciary, (other than a trustee, for that would be an ordinary trust) holds title to assets. An example is a solicitor holding funds for a client.[66] The same seems to be true of agents.[67]

Implied trusts

23.47　In private law there is a general distinction between the express and the implied. Both arise out of intention, the difference being in the manner in which that intention appears. There is a case for saying that trusts can arise by implied intention. Logically that would be different from the constructive trust, for in the latter the law imposes a trust regardless of the intention of the trustee, whereas in an implied trust the trustee does intend to be a trustee, albeit without expressly saying so: thus the distinction between express and implied trusts would not be a substantive difference. An alternative approach would be to divide implied trusts into implied-in-fact trusts and implied-in-law trusts, the latter being equated with constructive trusts. But the whole subject is very unclear.

Resulting trusts

23.48　It occasionally happens that the trustees carry out all the trust purposes, at least in so far as it is possible to do so, and yet there remain assets. If the trust is a charitable one, the trust will carry on, but there will be an appropriate alteration of its purposes.[68] But otherwise the rule is that the trustees should make the remaining trust estate over to the truster, or, if the truster is dead, to the truster's executor.[69] The term 'resulting trust' is used to describe this situation, but it is misleading, because it is not really a separate type of trust, but rather an implied-in-law longstop trust purpose.

[64]　*Mortgage Corporation v Mitchells Roberton* 1997 SLT 1305 at 1310 per Lord Johnston. See generally G L Gretton 'Constructive Trusts' (1997) 1 *Edin LR* 281 and 408.
[65]　*Bank of Scotland v Liquidators of Hutchison Main & Co Ltd* 1914 SC (HL) 1 is perhaps the classic case. For a more modern illustration see *Ross v Morley* [2013] CSOH 175.
[66]　*Council of the Law Society of Scotland v McKinnie* 1991 SC 355.
[67]　*Ted Jacob Engineering Group Inc v Robert Matthew, Johnson-Marshall and Partners* 2014 SC 579. See further P Hodge, 'Property Law, Fiduciary Obligations and the Constructive Trust' in F McCarthy, J Chalmers and S Bogle (eds) *Essays in Conveyancing and Property Law in Honour of Professor Robert Rennie* (2015).
[68]　See **CHAPTER 25** below.
[69]　An example is *Anderson v Smoke* (1898) 25 R 493.

23.49   Scottish and English trust law differ in a number of respects, not least in the area of constructive, implied and resulting trusts, so English authority needs to be approached with particular caution. For example, in England, if X contributes to the purchase of property by Y (directly, or indirectly e.g. by helping with mortgage payments) the result can be that Y holds the property in trust for both of them. That is not the position in Scots law. X may have a claim in the law of contract (e.g. the contribution may have been a loan) or in unjustified enrichment.[70] If X and Y are spouses or civil partners, the contribution will be taken into account in the divorce that will usually follow. (If the parties are happy, they will resolve financial issues by agreement.) If the parties are cohabitants, the court has certain powers.[71] But trust law is not engaged – unless of course there was an actual, non-constructive, trust.

TRUSTEES AND BENEFICIARIES

Who may be a trustee?

23.50   Both natural and juristic persons can be trustees. There are restrictions on who can be the trustee of a charitable trust: for instance, those with convictions for dishonesty are barred.[72] It is not uncommon for a trustee to be a body corporate (juristic person). For instance, many law firms have a special corporate entity ('Sue Grabbit and Runne Trustee Company Ltd') the sole function of which is to act as a trustee,[73] and which will be at any one time the trustee of numerous different trusts.

Who may be a beneficiary?

23.51   Anyone may be a beneficiary, including juristic persons, though beneficiaries are usually natural persons. Acceptance is unnecessary. Indeed, someone may be a beneficiary without even knowing it. Trusts can exist in favour of persons who are, at the time that the trust is set up, indeterminate and even unborn. (For instance, a trust for the truster's grandchildren, born or to be born.)

The three parties: role-sharing

23.52   At the outset a trust normally involves three parties. There is:

---

[70]   *Shilliday v Smith* 1998 SC 725.
[71]   Family Law (Scotland) Act 2006 s 29; *Gow v Grant* 2012 SLT 829.
[72]   CTI(S)A 2005, s 69.
[73]   In *Ommanney, Petitioner* 1966 SLT (Notes) 13 the court said that 'an impersonal body such as a bank or a trust corporation is not a suitable party to exercise ... a discretion involving personal and family considerations'. But the facts of the case were special. A truster can appoint a corporate trustee even where the trust is discretionary.

(a) the truster[74] who sets up the trust;
(b) the trustee or trustees (for it is common to have more than one trustee); and
(c) the beneficiary or beneficiaries.

Once the trust has been set up, however, the truster drops out of the picture, and the relationship is between the trustees and the beneficiaries, unless the trust deed reserves some ongoing role for the truster. In a private trust the truster has two implied rights. The first is a right to appoint new trustees in the event that the trust becomes a lapsed trust.[75] The second is that if there is a failure of trust purposes, the assets are held in resulting trust for the truster (see above).

23.53   In certain special cases there is no truster. One example is a sequestration. Here, there is a trustee (the trustee in sequestration) and beneficiaries (the creditors) but there is no truster.

23.54   Although in a normal trust there are the three parties – truster, trustees and beneficiaries – some role-sharing is possible. The truster can be a trustee. The truster can be a beneficiary. A beneficiary can be a trustee.

Appointment of trustees

23.55   The first trustees are appointed in the trust deed. There may, however, be a need for future appointments, especially if some trustees have disappeared by death or resignation. The trust deed may make provision about how new trustees can be chosen. But there is a default rule that the trustees in office from time to time can 'assume' (appoint) new trustees.[76] Another default rule is that if the trust is a private one and all the trustees have left office the truster can appoint new ones. Finally, the court can in case of need appoint new trustees.[77]

23.56   On appointment, the new trustee joins the others in the administration of the trust. But appointment does not give a title.[78] To become joint owner of the trust assets, a conveyance is needed to the new trustee. Hence in practice a deed of assumption contains words conveying the whole trust estate, and is thus what is called a 'deed of assumption and conveyance'. The usual way of doing it is for the existing trustees to be not only the granters but also the grantees. Thus suppose that Bella and Carl assume Dugald. The deed would convey the trust estate from Bella and Carla to Bella and Carl and Dugald. For most types of property (for example

---

[74] The English term 'settlor' is also sometimes encountered.
[75] See, eg, *Glentanar v Scottish Industrial Musical Association* 1925 SC 226. For lapsed trusts, see **PARA 24.4** below.
[76] T(S)A 1921, s 3(b). For deeds of assumption, see T(S)A 1921, s 21. Deeds of assumption are usually registered in the Books of Council and Session.
[77] T(S)A 1921, s 22. One of the many striking features of trust law is the extensive role of the court. All trusts are subject to all sorts of intervention by the court.
[78] Is this rule perfectly consistent with the rule that on death or resignation a trustee's title passes to the ongoing trustees without conveyance?

land or shares) the deed in itself will not give a title to the new trustee. Some further step, such as registration, is needed.

23.57 Nobody can be compelled to be a trustee. Acceptance does not have to be in writing, though it commonly is. The mere fact of taking on the administration of the trust constitutes acceptance.[79]

Ex officio trustees

23.58 An *ex officio* trustee is someone who is a trustee of a particular trust simply by virtue of holding a certain 'office'. Thus suppose that someone establishes a trust for the benefit of poor elderly people in a certain area. The deed might nominate the parish minister as a trustee *ex officio*. That would mean that when one minister retired, or died, he or she would automatically cease to be a trustee and the new minister would become one. The subject is full of difficulty.

WHAT IS A TRUST? FURTHER DISCUSSION

The special patrimony

23.59 The patrimony is the totality of a person's assets and liabilities. The general principle is: one person, one patrimony. But in a trust, the trustee has two patrimonies. There is the ordinary, or general, patrimony. And there is the special patrimony of the trust. Each has its own assets and liabilities. A patrimony is like a suitcase, with two compartments, one for assets and the other for liabilities. A trustee has two suitcases. If an asset is sold, the asset leaves the suitcase but the price replaces it. The same happens in reverse if an asset is purchased. Again, if an asset generates income (for example rent from land, or dividends from shares, or interest from a loan) the income forms part of the same patrimony. The trustee is under a duty of segregation, to ensure that the two patrimonies remain distinct, so that there can never be any question to which patrimony an asset belongs. If, as commonly happens, there are two or more trustees, they hold the suitcase together. Figures 23.1, 23.2 and 23.3 give the idea.[80] The first shows the non-trust case of a person with its/her/his ordinary patrimony. The second shows a person who is a trustee, and so with a special patrimony and well as the ordinary patrimony. The third shows the case of joint trustees.

---

[79]   *Ker v City of Glasgow Bank* (1879) 6 R (HL) 52 is an example.
[80]   From G L Gretton 'Trusts without Equity' (2000) 49 *International and Comparative Law Quarterly* 599. For more on the patrimonial analysis of the trust, see K G C Reid, 'Patrimony not Equity: The trust in Scotland' (2000) 8 (3) *ERPL* 427, and *Ted Jacob Engineering Group Inc v Robert Matthew, Johnson-Marshall and Partners* 2014 SC 579.

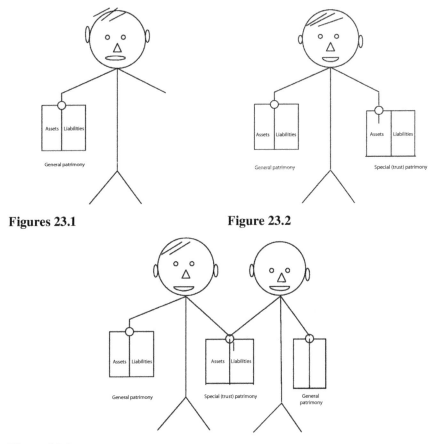

Figures 23.1

Figure 23.2

Figure 23.3

Varying theories of the trust

23.60 'The property of the thing intrusted, be it land or moveables, is in the person of the intrusted, else it is not a proper trust', wrote Stair.[81] This traditional view is also the modern view, but in between there has been some wobbling, especially during the second half of the nineteenth century. According to one theory, the truster remained owner.[82] According to another, ownership was vested in the beneficiary or beneficiaries.[83] Neither theory succeeded in establishing itself, and today Stair's view is almost unquestioned. An important decision in confirming that approach

---

[81]   Stair I, 13, 7.
[82]   For this theory, see G L Gretton 'Radical Rights and Radical Wrongs' 1986 *JR* 51 and 192.
[83]   This was the theory advanced by Lord Watson in *Heritable Reversionary Co v Millar* (1892) 19 R (HL) 43.

was a 1939 case, *Inland Revenue v Clark's Trs*.[84] We quote a couple of passages: 'The beneficiary's right is nothing more than a personal right to sue the trustees and to compel them to administer the trust in accordance with the directions which it contains.'[85] Again: 'The right of property in the estate of the trust is vested in the trustees to the exclusion of any competing right of property, and the right of the beneficiary... is merely a right *in personam* against the trustees to enforce their performance of the trust.'[86] English law divides ownership between beneficiaries and trustees, and this is at the conceptual level perhaps the most important difference between English and Scots trust law.[87]

The nature of the beneficiary's right

23.61 The right of a beneficiary – the 'beneficial interest' as it is often called – is a personal right against the trustee. It is thus part of the beneficiary's patrimony. Like most other rights it can (in most cases) be transferred. This is done by assignation plus intimation.[88] If the beneficiary dies, it will form part of the estate and will be dealt with by the executor according to the law of succession. If the beneficiary becomes insolvent, the beneficial interest is available to the creditors, whether through diligence or an insolvency process.

23.62 This is the normal picture, but there can be exceptions. Everything depends on the trust's terms. For instance, a beneficial interest that ends on death will clearly not pass to the beneficiary's estate. Again, in a discretionary trust the beneficiary's rights depend on the trustees' choices. Such a beneficiary might end up receiving little or even nothing.

The insolvency effect

23.63 One of the most important features of the trust is the 'insolvency effect', the fact that the trustee's ordinary creditors (the liabilities in the general patrimony) cannot attach the assets in the special patrimony.[89] The trust estate is a ring-fenced fund. This principle applies both to diligence and to insolvency processes (sequestration and liquidation). The fact that the beneficiaries' rights survive the trustee's insolvency means that they behave rather like real rights. But they are not. They are personal rights in relation to the special patrimony, while the trustee's

---

[84] 1939 SC 11.
[85] Lord Normand at 22.
[86] Lord Moncreiff at 26.
[87] The European Court of Justice has held that for the purposes of EU private international law the beneficiary's right is personal not real – an approach which fits in with Scots law neatly. See *Webb v Webb* 1984 ECR 1-1717.
[88] See **PARAS 5.38–5.51** above.
[89] See **PARA 23.5** above.

ordinary creditors have personal rights in relation to the general patrimony. Thus in principle the two sorts of claims do not conflict.

Trusts and the publicity principle

23.64 In general, transactions that have third-party effect (for example against creditors) are subject to the publicity principle.[90] Transactions that affect third parties should normally be discoverable by third parties. That is why the law requires, for instance, the registration of standard securities. The law also requires publicity for certain other things. With one exception, juristic persons cannot be created without publicity, such as the registration at Companies House. (The exception is partnership, and the reason why publicity is not required is that there is little effect against third parties.[91] In particular, creditors can hold either the firm itself or any partner liable.[92]) The trust is a virtual juristic person that can be created secretly. Tom owns Blackmains. He signs a deed saying he holds it in bare trust for Barbara. This deed is delivered to Barbara but is otherwise secret. Ten years later Tom becomes insolvent. His creditors find that they cannot touch the land. Had he disponed the land to Barbara, registration would have been needed. Yet by secret deed a similar effect has been achieved. Bare trusts are sometimes used when, for one reason or another, an actual transfer (disposition of land, assignation of a money claim or whatever[93]) is inconvenient to the parties. There is some concern that the policy of the law can thus be circumvented. As well as using trusts as virtual transfers they can also be used as virtual securities, and the same issues arise.[94] There is a case for saying that all such trusts are invalid as being contrary to public policy, but the subject remains undeveloped.[95]

VESTING

Introduction

23.65 Back in 1905, an anonymous writer commented:

---

[90] See **PARAS 4.19–4.20** above.
[91] The governing legislation is the Partnership Act 1890.
[92] This is not so for limited partnerships or for limited liability partnerships. Unsurprisingly, such partnerships need registration: Limited Partnerships Act 1907; Limited Liability Partnerships Act 2000.
[93] See *Tay Valley Joinery Ltd v CF Financial Services Ltd* 1987 SLT 207. The soundness of the decision is open to question.
[94] G L Gretton 'Using Trusts as Commercial Securities' (1988) 33 *JLSS* 53.
[95] *Clark Taylor & Co Ltd v Quality Site Development (Edinburgh) Ltd* 1981 SC 111 is one of the few cases to have raised this issue. In some cases the courts have upheld trusts which were arguably contrary to public policy: a noteworthy example is *Tay Valley Joinery Ltd v CF Financial Services Ltd* 1987 SLT 207, though that case has complicating factors, including cross-border issues.

'The subject of vesting has long been regarded by Scots lawyers with a sort of gloomy despair as a mere chaotic mass of conflicting decisions; one has even heard proposed as the only possible improvement the destruction of all reports dealing with the subject, and the prohibition under severe penalties of reporting any more.'[96]

He was right and matters have not improved – perhaps the opposite – since 1905. The concept of vesting is itself somewhat elusive, while the detailed rules about vesting are complex and perhaps inconsistent.

23.66   Once a beneficial right has 'vested' it is like any other patrimonial right. For instance, Alan dies, leaving his house to Barbara. Barbara dies the next day. Her right to the house is part of her patrimony. The right that she had, when she died, was not ownership, because there would have been no time for ownership to be transferred to her. But it was a right to become owner.[97] Suppose that her testament leaves everything to Carl. Consider the structure of rights at this moment. Barbara had, when she died, a personal right against Alan's executor.[98] Barbara's right passes to her executor, so that Barbara's executor has a personal right against Alan's executor. And Carl has a personal right against Barbara's executor. So Alan's executor will convey to Barbara's executor, who will then convey to Carl. Alternatively and more simply, Alan's executor will convey to Carl at the request of Barbara's executor. Or Barbara, while still alive, could have sold her right to Deirdre. The sale would have been implemented by assignation, completed by intimation to Alan's executor, following which the latter would have been bound to dispone to Deirdre. Or suppose that Barbara were to be sequestrated: her right would pass to her trustee in sequestration, Shona, and Alan's executor would have been bound to dispone to Shona.

23.67   We have just considered a vested legacy. Now an unvested one. Donna leaves her house to Euan, but only if he survives her by thirty clear days.[99] Donna dies on 1 May and Euan dies on 20 May, leaving everything to his children. Will they take the house? That depends on a prior question: is the right to the house part of Euan's estate? No. The legacy was subject to a 'suspensive condition'. That condition was never satisfied. The legacy was not vested and has now lapsed.[100] Who takes the house? That depends. Assuming that the testament had a list of special and pecuniary legacies, and then a legacy of residue, the house would form part of the residue of Donna's estate, and pass to the residuary legatees.

---

[96]   (1905) 21 *Sc Law Rev* 234. This was a review of the first edition of R Candlish Henderson *Principles of Vesting in the Law of Succession*. The second, and last, edition appeared in 1938.
[97]   But a qualified one. For instance, it might have been necessary for Alan's executor to sell the house to pay Alan's debt.
[98]   There are problems here, because the confirmation of an executor takes some weeks. So Barbara has, in the hours between Alan's death and her own, a personal right against … whom?
[99]   Such provisions are common.
[100]   For lapse of legacies, see **PARA 28.41** below.

23.68

'Probably in no other department of law is less influence allowed to precedent. A question of vesting is always decided with reference to the character and phraseology of the particular deed.'[101]

'When the question arises under a *mortis causa* settlement, whether a benefit given is or has become a vested right, the intentions of the testator, in so far as they can be discovered or reasonably inferred from the deed taken as a whole, and from the circumstances, legitimately collected under which the deed was made, should have effect given to them. It is *quaestio voluntatis*.[102] That is the cardinal rule and guide.'[103]

But in reality the task of ascertaining the testator's intention is to a considerable extent artificial, because of the default rules that have developed out of the plentiful case law. Nevertheless, the default rules are complex and probably incoherent and no attempt will be made here to summarise them.

A footnote on the word 'vesting'

23.69   It is sometimes said that when a legacy or other beneficial right vests it becomes the 'property' of the legatee. That is true in the broad sense of 'property' – ie patrimonial rights – but it should not be understood to mean that the beneficiary acquires ownership at that moment. In a trust the beneficiaries do not have *ownership*, for their right is personal, not real. They may have a personal right to acquire ownership.[104]

23.70   A related sense of 'vesting' is that in which the estate is said to 'vest' in the executor on confirmation. An executor has two patrimonies: the ordinary, general, patrimony, and the executry patrimony. Suppose that Alfred owes Beata money. Beata dies, bequeathing the debt to Charles. Donna is confirmed as Beata's executor. The debt owed by Alfred now is apparently vested in two different people: Charles and Donna. In fact, it is not. The debt itself is vested in Donna, as executor. What is vested in Charles is not a right against Alfred, but a right against Donna that she should either (i) collect the debt from Alfred and pay the proceeds to Charles; or (ii) assign the debt to Charles. Likewise, if Beata owned a house and left it to Charles, the house would be vested in Donna,[105] and what would be vested in Charles would be a right to have ownership of the house transferred to him by Donna.

---

101   R Candlish Henderson *Principles of Vesting in the Law of Succession* (2nd edn, 1938) Preface.
102   Latin: 'question of intention'.
103   *Carleton v Thomson* (1867) 5 M (HL) 151 at 153 per Lord Colonsay.
104   For a debate on the concept of vesting see 1986 *JLSS* 148 (Gretton), 1986 *JLSS* 396 (Maher), 1987 *JLSS* 281 (Gordon), 1988 *JLSS* 98 (Patrick) and 1989 *JLSS* 338 (Styles).
105   There are a number of problems in this area. Is Donna's right real? Not unless she completes title in the Land Register or Sasine Register. So is it personal? But against whom?

23.71　The word 'vest' is sometimes used in other senses too. When conveyancers say that 'title to Blackmains is vested in Abracadabra Ltd' they mean that Abracadabra Ltd has the real right of ownership. If they say that title 'was last vested' in Donald Cook, they imply that he has died but that ownership has not, up to now, been transferred to anyone else.[106] The word is also used in this sense about subordinate real rights. Finally, Parliamentary drafters often use the word, but often vaguely, so that the precise meaning has to be guessed.

INTERNATIONAL PRIVATE LAW

23.72　The international private law of trusts is regulated by the Recognition of Trusts Act 1987, giving effect to the 1985 Hague Trust Convention. The salient points are that 'a trust shall be governed by the law chosen by the settlor. Where no applicable law has been chosen, a trust shall be governed by the law with which it is most closely connected.'

LITERATURE

23.73　The standard work on the law of trusts, though now becoming slightly dated, is Wilson and Duncan *Trusts*. Judges and practitioners still make considerable use of an older work, A J P Menzies *The Law of Scotland Affecting Trustees* (2nd edn 1913). A Mackenzie Stuart *The Law of Trusts* (1932) is helpfully readable, though the account in the opening pages about the nature of the trust is unsound. Two valuable more modern texts are K Norrie and E Scobbie *Trusts* (1991) and Chalmers *Trusts*. Gloag and Henderson *The Law of Scotland* ch 41 is a useful overview. A sparkling work for practitioners is J Kessler and W Grant *Drafting Trusts and Will Trusts in Scotland* (2013). For charity law, see J McNeill *A Practical Guide to Charity Law in Scotland* (2016). The Scottish Law Commission, Report on Trust Law (Scot Law Com No 239, 2014), is packed with up-to-date information about, and discussion of, trust law.

23.74　There is a large comparative and historical literature, and what follows is merely a tiny selection. F W Maitland's classic essay 'Trust and Corporation' remains as fascinating as it was when first published. (Printed in H A L Fisher (ed) *The Collected Papers of Frederic William Maitland* (1911). Limiting ourselves to seven modern volumes, we can recommend: R Helmholz and R Zimmermann (eds) *Itinera Fiduciae: Trust and Treuhand in an Historical Perspective* (1998), D Hayton, (ed) *Modern International Developments in Trust Law* (1999), D Hayton S Kortmann

---

[106]　Which raises the question of who *does* own the land. One view is that death ends active personality, but that a dead person still has a passive juridical personality, and thus can still be an owner. On this view, the Land Register does not suddenly become inaccurate when an owner dies. But the precise effect of death remains mired in difficulties. (We speak of the law. Possibly there may also be philosophical and theological issues.)

and H Verhagen (eds) *Principles of European Trust Law* (1999), M Lupoi, *Trusts: A Comparative Study* (2000), P Panico *International Trust Laws* (2010), L Smith (ed) *The Worlds of the Trust* (2013), and R Valsan (ed) *Trusts and Patrimonies* (2015). Trusts have a major role internationally as wealth management vehicles. Those wishing to get a taste of the 'international trust', two journals may be mentioned: *Trusts and Trustees* and *Trust Law International*.

Chapter 24

Trusts: their life in health and in sickness

TRUSTEES: GENERAL

Must the trustees act gratuitously?

24.1   To be a trustee means to accept the onerous responsibility of administering a fund. This is responsible work and may be time-consuming. Trustees are entitled to be reimbursed for reasonable *expenses*, so that they do not end up out of pocket, but the default rule is that they are not entitled to be paid for their *time*. The trust deed may nevertheless provide for payment. In practice it might be supposed that, without payment, nobody would agree to be a trustee. That is sometimes true, but usually not. In public trusts people will usually be happy to act gratuitously, because they are public-spirited and believe in the cause. In family trusts family members will usually agree to act gratuitously out of family solidarity. But if a client wishes to appoint a solicitor as a trustee, the latter will usually insist that the trust deed should provide for remuneration. Likewise, the trustees of a commercial trust will insist on payment, and so on. A special case is the trustee in sequestration, who is entitled to remuneration by statute.[1]

Cessation of office: (1) death, (2) resignation and (3) removal by the court

24.2   A trustee loses office by death, by resignation or by removal by the court. The trust deed can prohibit resignation, but that is rare. The default rule, which usually applies, is that a trustee is free to resign, unless he or she is the sole trustee (in which case the solution is to assume new trustees first, and then resign) or unless he or she is remunerated.[2] Even then the court can authorise resignation. Whether resignation has to be in writing is uncertain. In practice it is assumed that it is. The deed is called a 'minute of resignation'.[3] Unless the trust deed otherwise provides, there is no power for a trustee to be expelled by fellow trustees. But the court can remove a trustee, under a statutory power that covers certain defined circumstances, notably absence

---

[1]   Bankruptcy (Scotland) Act 2016, s 133.
[2]   T(S)A 1921, s 3(a).
[3]   T(S)A 1921, s 19 and Sch A.

and insanity.[4] There is a concurrent common law power which is used where there is 'malversation of office', ie serious breach of trust.[5] The bankruptcy of a trustee, and conviction for an offence, are irrelevant (unless the trust deed so provides) in private trusts. But they disqualify a person from being a trustee of a charity.[6]

24.3   When a trustee demits office, no conveyance to the remaining trustees is necessary. The reason is that the title of trustees is not common but joint, and when a trustee leaves the stage the remaining trustees are automatically the sole owners.[7]

Lapsed trusts

24.4   A trust is said to lapse if no trustee remains in office. This can happen if the sole trustee, or the sole surviving trustee, dies, or, of a body corporate, is dissolved. (The word 'lapsed' might suggest that the trust thereby comes to an end, but that is not so.[8]) It will be necessary for one or more new trustees to be appointed so that the trust administration can be continued. The court can appoint a new trustee.[9]

24.5   The common-law rule is that if a trustee dies in office, no rights pass to his or her executor. In general that is still the law. But if a sole trustee dies, there exists a limited statutory power in favour of the trustee's executor to take up the office.[10]

Deciding and doing

General

24.6   The trust deed is the constitutive document and it can lay down the rules for the trust's administration. The general law applies only in so far as the trust deed is silent. The default rules are as follows. A meeting of trustees must be quorate, and a quorum is a majority of trustees.[11] Decisions can be made by a majority. But the majority must be a majority of the trustees, not merely a majority of those trustees at the meeting. Suppose that there are six trustees. Four turn up to a particular meeting. A decision is taken by a three-to-one majority. The decision is invalid because three is not a majority of six. If a trust has two trustees, they will both have to agree on any decision. Deadlocks are therefore possible, but are uncommon: in most trusts the decisions are not merely majority decisions, but unanimous. Occasionally a

---

[4]   T(S)A 1921, s 23.
[5]   For this power, see *Gilchrist's Trs v Dick* (1883) 11R 22; *MacGilchrist's Trs v MacGilchrist* 1930 SC 635 and *Sharif v Hamid* 2000 SLT 294.
[6]   Charities and Trustee Investment (Scotland) Act 2005, s 69.
[7]   See **PARAS 10.17–10.18** above.
[8]   The word 'lapsed' has a different meaning in succession law: a lapsed *legacy* is void by reason of the legatee's death: see **PARA 27.44** below.
[9]   T(S)A 1921, s 22.
[10]   Executors (Scotland) Act 1900, s 6. This is quite commonly used.
[11]   For the quorum, see T(S)A 1921, s 3(c).

breakdown of relations produces total deadlock: the ultimate remedy is for the court to appoint a judicial factor.

Consultation

24.7   All trustees must be 'consulted': in the absence of consultation any decision reached is invalid. In the leading case, *Wyse v Abbott*,[12] there were three trustees. Two of them appointed additional trustees, but they had not consulted the third. Even though a majority decision was in itself sufficient, the lack of consultation made the appointment invalid. Although the principle is clear, its application in practice is less so. At a minimum it means that every trustee must be notified of forthcoming meetings. But 'consultation' is unnecessary where it would be pointless or impossible, such as where the trustee in question is uncontactable.[13]

Protectors

24.8   In many jurisdictions there is the possibility of having a 'protector' for a trust. A protector is not a trustee but nevertheless has certain powers, including a power of veto for certain matters. Although protectors are not used in current Scottish practice, in the opinion of the Scottish Law Commission 'it is almost certainly competent at present for a Scottish truster to appoint a protector by express provision in a trust deed'[14] and it may be that protectors will in future become an important feature of trust law.

Execution of documents

24.9   Suppose that the trustees vote to sell a plot of land. Must all sign the disposition? This question really has two aspects. (Both are separate from the question of the making of the decision in the first place.) (1) Whether all trustees have a duty, as a matter of trust law, to sign, even if they were minority dissenters when the decision was made. The answer is affirmative. (2) Whether, as a matter of conveyancing law, signature by a majority suffices. The law is unclear. In *Harland Engineering*[15] the Outer House held that it was sufficient if the majority signed. The case was appealed to the Inner House on another point, and there some doubt was expressed as to whether the first-instance decision on signatures had been correct. There is no other authority. The Trusts (Scotland) Act 1921 (T(S)A 1921), s 7 says that in *some* cases majority signature suffices, but the section's exact meaning is obscure. In practice all trustees sign.

[12]   (1881) 8 R 983.
[13]   *Malcolm v Goldie* (1895) 22 R 968.
[14]   Scottish Law Commission, Report on Trust Law (Scot Law Com No 239, 2014) para 15.4.
[15]   1914 2 SLT 292.

TRUST PURPOSES

General

24.10   Every trust has its *purposes*. If these were simply to hold for the beneficiary or beneficiaries, then every trust would be a 'bare' trust.[16] Some trusts are bare, but in most the purposes are rather more complicated, such as to hold for Laura in liferent and for Fiona in fee. It is competent to identify certain beneficiaries and then give the trustees a discretion as to what each is to take. Where that happens, it is common for the truster to give them a non-binding 'letter of wishes' indicating how he or she would like the discretion to be exercised.[17]

Failure

24.11   If the purposes are too indeterminate or too obscure to be interpreted, the trust will be void 'by reason of uncertainty'.[18] A 'secret' trust is a trust where the trust purposes are known only to the trustee. Such trusts are also invalid.[19] There is some tension between that rule and the fact that a discretionary trust is lawful.[20] In a discretionary trust there is an ascertained or ascertainable class of beneficiaries, and the trustees can choose which of them is to benefit and to what extent. If that is the case then the trust is not invalid. The trust is void if its purposes are contrary to public policy. There is also what is sometimes called the 'rule against perpetuities', which places time-limits on private trusts.[21]

24.12   Another way in which a trust may be void is if it confers no substantial human benefit.[22] This is probably a sub-type of the 'contrary to public policy' rule. The cases all deal with testamentary trusts but the principles presumably apply to all

---

[16]   See **PARA 23.18** above.

[17]   See further J Kessler and W Grant, *Drafting Trusts and Will Trusts in Scotland* (2013) para 6.15 ff.

[18]   Eg *Hardie v Morison* (1899) 7 SLT 42, where the trust purpose was the promotion of 'free thought'. In *Grimond v Grimond's Trustees* (1905) 7 F (HL) 90 a trust for 'religious purposes' was likewise held too vague to be valid. But the line is not a sharp one, as is Illustrated by the fact that in this latter case the Inner House had taken the opposite view. In *Chalmers Trustees v Turriff Parish School Board* 1917 SC 676 'charitable purpose or educational scheme for the poor' survived attack. The 'invalid because of uncertainty?' question can arise for both private and public trusts, but most commonly for the latter, for which see Wilson and Duncan *Trusts* ch 14.

[19]   *Sutherland's Trs v Sutherland's Tr* (1893) 20 R 925; *Shaw's Trs v Greenock Medical Aid Society* 1930 SLT 39; Wilson and Duncan *Trusts* para 2-30. What is secret is not the trust but its purposes. There have been one or two decisions to the opposite effect, such as *Warrender v Anderson* (1893) 1 SLT 304 but they seem erroneous.

[20]   *Crichton v Grierson* (1828) 3 W & S 329. For a borderline case where the trust was upheld, see *Smellie's Trs v Glasgow Royal Infirmary* (1905) 13 SLT 450.

[21]   See **PARA 23.15** below.

[22]   What about trusts for animals? The Scottish Society for the Prevention of Cruelty to Animals is a company, not a trust. For the question of private trusts for pets, see K McK Norrie 'Trusts for Animals' (1987) 32 *JLSS* 386.

trusts. In *McCaig v University of Glasgow*[23] John Stuart McCaig left a testamentary trust, which is, alas, too long to quote here, except for a few words:

> 'The purpose of the trust is that my heritable property be not sold, but let to tenants, and the clear revenue or income be used for the purpose of erecting monuments and statues for myself, brothers, and sisters on the tower or circular building called the Stuart McCaig Tower, situated on the Battery Hill above Oban, the making of these statues to be given to Scotch sculptors … '

24.13   The Court of Session declined office but the University ('College') of Glasgow accepted. The truster's sister, Catherine McCaig, sought reduction of the trust. (She would benefit if it were held invalid.) She was successful. It was held that a trust must have beneficiaries, and this trust had none. Actually, that is debatable: it could be argued that there was human benefit in promoting the arts. Many public trusts are regarded as valid even though they confer only remote benefits on living persons. At all events, the case is a leading one. Lord Kyllachy gave the following as examples of purposes contrary to public policy:

> ' … to lay the truster's estate waste, and to keep it so; or to turn the income of the estate into money, and throw the money yearly into the sea; or to expend the income in annual or monthly funeral services in the testator's memory; or to expend it in discharging from prominent points upon the estate, salvoes of artillery upon the birthdays of the testator, and his brothers and sisters …'[24]

Catherine McCaig died soon afterwards, setting up a testamentary trust with – delicious irony – similar purposes. This too was struck down.[25] There have been similar cases, such as *Aitken's Trs v Aitken*.[26] George Aitken set up a testamentary trust:

> 'In respect of the ancient connexion of my family … with the town of Musselburgh, extending over several centuries, and seeing that I am the last of the male line … I wish to be erected on the site of the property at the corner of High Street, Fisherrow, and South Street … a massive equestrian bronze statue of artistic merit, representing me as Champion at the Riding of the Towns Marches; for this purpose the present building will be removed and the site enclosed in an artistic manner and laid out with shrubs or otherwise; the whole work is to be done unsparing of expense … '

24.14   This too was held invalid. Lord Sands commented that 'if the testamentary directions are unreasonable as conferring neither a patrimonial benefit on anybody nor a benefit upon the public or any section thereof, the directions are invalid',[27]

---

[23]   1907 SC 231. On the *McCaig* cases see R Rennie, 'Folly, Guilt and More Folly: The McCaig Cases' in J Grant and E Sutherland (eds) *Scots Law Tales* (2010).

[24]   1907 SC 231 at 242.

[25]   *McCaig's Trs v Kirk Session of United Free Church of Lismore* 1915 SC 426.

[26]   1927 SC 374. And see *Macintosh's JF v Lord Advocate* 1935 SC 406 and *Sutherland's Tr v Verschoyle* 1968 SLT 43.

[27]   1927 SC 374 at 380.

and this is perhaps the best attempt that has been made to state the law succinctly. However, it must be conceded that the authorities in this area are 'confused'.[28] The 'no human benefit' rule is applied in *mortis causa* trusts more readily than in *inter vivos* ones.

24.15   If a trust is invalid then it becomes a resulting trust, which is to say that the trustees hold on bare trust for the truster, or, if dead, for the truster's estate. Battles about the validity of trusts usually arise when the truster is dead, and are between those who would benefit if the trust is upheld and the truster's heirs.

THE RULE AGAINST PERPETUITIES

24.16   The rule against perpetuities[29] is a statutory one rather than a common law one. People have a natural wish to control assets into the future. Some people desire to do so – especially in relation to land – for ever. The law's attitude has varied on whether such desires are socially acceptable or not. The Entail Act 1685 actually assisted such desires. It allowed an owner of land to create a tailzie (entail)[30] whereby the land would pass down the generations in the family until Doomsday. Each successive owner lacked power of sale. This sort of thing is nowadays regarded as unacceptable. The dead should not rule from their graves – or at least only for a reasonable period. The 1685 Act has been repealed.[31] Similar arrangements could, unless prohibited, be achieved by means of trusts. For instance, land could be conveyed to trustees to hold for a successive series of family members until Doomsday. Rules against such devices were first introduced by the Entail Amendment (Scotland) Act 1848 and are now contained in the Law Reform (Miscellaneous Provisions) (Scotland) Act 1968, s 18. As soon as the beneficiary is someone who was unborn when the trust was set up, the trust becomes a bare trust for that beneficiary. Thus, suppose that in 1980 Eustace conveys his land in trust to hold for his heirs-male successively in perpetuity. At this time his eldest son Foster is alive and also Foster's eldest son, Gregor. In 2000 Gregor has a son, Horatio. Eustace dies in 1990, Foster dies in 2010 and Gregor dies in 2030. In 2030 the trust becomes a bare trust for Horatio.[32]

---

[28]   Wilson and Duncan *Trusts* para 14-10.
[29]   See Wilson and Duncan *Trusts* ch 8. For the history, see R Burgess *Perpetuities in Scots Law* (1979). The rule does not apply to public trusts. The rule is in many respects obscure.
[30]   See further **PARA 30.30**. Entails are a blessing for novelists: see, eg, Jane Austen's *Pride and Prejudice*.
[31]   AFT(S)A 2000, s 50. But tailzies had already been virtually destroyed by a series of statutes culminating in the Entail (Scotland) Act 1914.
[32]   An illustration is *Earl of Balfour Petitioner* 2003 SC (HL) 1.

POWERS

General

24.17   *Powers* are different from *purposes*. Purposes are about ends; powers are about means. The distinction is actually somewhat fuzzy but it is a traditional one. Take a trust for Laura in liferent and Fiona in fee. The trust assets are stock market investments. The trustee, Tara, is thinking of selling the shares and using the money to buy, and then let out, heritable property, so that the trust income would be rents rather than dividends. This would be within the purposes of the trust. But it might or might not be within the powers. The trust provisions might not allow investment in land.

24.18   The trustees' powers are determined by the trust deed. In practice trust deeds usually say that the trustees can do virtually anything. The law also has a set of default powers, i.e. powers that exist unless the trust deed excludes them. Some are implied by common law, some by legislation. There is a good deal of overlap between the common-law powers and the statutory powers. The latter are in T(S) A 1921, s 4. Over time it has been much amended,[33] resulting in a higgledy-piggledy list of powers that is almost unreadable. The amendments have been expansions, and the law has now reached the point where trustees have implied powers to do almost anything.[34] T(S)A 1921, s 5 provides that even if the trust deed actually excludes any of the s 4 powers (unlikely in practice) the court may grant such powers. Trustees sometimes wish to employ a professional to manage the investment portfolio, and T(S)A 1921, s 4B empowers them to do this.

Sale by trustees

24.19   A common misconception is that a sale by trustees will be a breach of trust. In fact, trustees presumptively have the right to sell any trust asset.[35] The proceeds will of course themselves be trust property. For example, if a house that is subject to an improper liferent is sold[36] the proceeds of sale would be invested, and the improper liferenter would receive the income. Because the law implies a power to sell, sale would be in breach of trust only if the trust deed were to limit the power, but in practice that seldom happens.

---

[33]   Most recently by the Charities and Trustee Investment (Scotland) Act 2005. As well as extending the implied powers, this Act also made a technical simplification, in that previously trustees' powers were dealt with both by T(S)A 1921 and by the Trustee Investments Act 1961. The latter is now for the most part repealed.

[34]   The list of powers in T(S)A 1921, s 4 is not complete, so one still has to reply on the common law for some powers, e.g. the power to open a bank account.

[35]   T(S)A 1921, s 4(1)(a).

[36]   *Mauchline, Petitioner* 1992 SLT 421.

DUTIES

Investment duties

24.20 Trustees have duties to invest the trust funds in a reasonable manner. The investments must be both 'authorised' (ie within their powers) and 'proper'. This common-law duty is given greater specification by T(S)A 1921, s 4A.[37] One requirement is that the trustee must 'have regard' to the possibility that 'diversification' of investments may be in the best interests of the beneficiaries. In other words, a reasonable trustee will not normally put all the eggs into one basket. Trustees are judged by an abstract objective standard, rather than by the standard of their own personal investment acumen.[38] In England there has been a recent tendency to use as the standard a test of what 'no reasonable trustee' would do: provided that a trustee gets above pass mark, there is no liability.[39] This test is reminiscent of the delictual test of *Hunter v Hanley*[40] and 'Wednesbury unreasonableness' in administrative law.[41]

24.21 An example of an investment that, though authorised, was improper, is *Melville v Noble's Trs.*[42] Here, trustees left money on deposit receipt for 19 years. A deposit receipt[43] was a reasonable way of 'parking' money on a short-term basis, but in the longer term it was likely to prove a poor investment. Although there was no doubt that the trustees had the *power* to put money on deposit receipt, they were held liable for having failed to invest reasonably. In *Clarke v Clarke's Trs*[44] the trustees held certain shares for many years which steadily declined in value, eventually reaching zero. They were held liable to make good the loss. Though this is often regarded as a leading case, the logic is less than clear. They had not reviewed this investment, but there seems to have been no evidence that, if they had done so, they would have acted differently.

24.22 The case perhaps illustrates the economic naïveté common among lawyers: the fact that the value of the shares eventually fell to zero does *not* mean that it was unreasonable to hold on to them. It merely shows that the investment turned out to be a bad one. In principle, it can never be obvious *now* that a share, or other investment asset, *will* lose value, for if it *were* obvious then market forces would mean that that fact would be reflected in its *present* value. Thus it can be reasonable to retain an

---

[37] As inserted by the Charities and Trustee Investment (Scotland) Act 2005 (CTI(S)A 2005), and replacing the now-repealed Trustee Investments Act 1961, s 6.

[38] *Raes v Meek* (1889) 16 R (HL) 31.

[39] See *Daniel v Tee* [2016] 4 WLR 115 and cases cited therein.

[40] 1955 SC 200.

[41] *Associated Provincial Picture Houses Ltd v Wednesbury Corporation* [1948] 1 KB 223.

[42] (1896) 24 R 243.

[43] Deposit receipts were a speciality of the Scottish banking system; with its recent Londonisation they have largely disappeared. A sum was deposited with a bank, on which interest was payable when the money was uplifted. Only the whole amount could be uplifted: unlike a bank account the amount could not be added to or reduced.

[44] 1925 SC 693.

investment asset the value of which in fact declines steadily every year. Equally, it can be unreasonable to retain an investment asset that gains value steadily every year. The rationality of investment decisions can be assessed only on the basis of the information available at the relevant time. It is not clear that the judges in *Clarke's Trs* understood that. The case also opened another elephant trap for trustees. In their administration, the trustees had been very successful, achieving rich profits for the beneficiaries. But none of this was relevant: the ungrateful beneficiaries were entitled not only to those profits but also to help themselves to even more out of the personal resources of the trustees, because one particular investment had proved unlucky. The trustees could not set off the losses against the gains.[45]

24.23   One could express the matter thus: trustees have two types of investment duty. The first is not to invest in a way that is outwith their powers, even if the investment promises to be a good one. The second is to choose wisely between the various possible investments that are within their powers. Trustees actually are faced with a problem. It is a law of economics that the higher the yield, the higher the risk; and the lower the risk, the lower the yield.[46] In *Melville v Noble's Trs* the trustees chose low risk, low yield. They were held personally liable. In *Raes v Meek*[47] the trustees chose high yield, high risk. They were held personally liable. So trustees are between the devil and the deep. In practice they tend to go for a diversified portfolio producing moderate yield and moderate risk, and the courts seem happy with that.

The rule against accumulation

24.24   The rule against accumulation is a rule limiting the powers of trustees to 'accumulate', i.e. to reinvest income so as to build up capital. In 1797 an English banker named Peter Thellusson died.[48] His testament left various large bequests. Even after those bequests the residue was about £600,000.[49] This he left to trustees. They were to re-invest the income until his great-grandchildren had all died, and then they were to distribute the capital to certain defined descendants. The lawfulness of the trust was litigated but upheld. The case attracted much attention, and it was felt that such long-term accumulation was against the public interest. Three years after his death, an Act was passed, limiting the period during which a trust could

---

[45]   But perhaps there is more to be said. See the English case of *Bartlett v Barclays Bank Trust Co Ltd* [1980] 1 Ch 515.

[46]   In principle the two yields should be the same once the risk has been multiplied into the equation. In practice it is not always quite like that: thus, a deposit receipt gives a lower return than certain other investments with an equally low risk. With a deposit receipt the investor is buying the convenience of quick and easy realisation in exchange for a lower return.

[47]   (1889) 16 R (HL) 31.

[48]   For the full story, see P Polden *Peter Thellusson's Will* (2002).

[49]   A fortune in modern money. And there was no inheritance tax.

accumulate income.[50] The rules are now contained in the Trusts (Scotland) Act 1961 (T(S)A 1961), s 5 and the Law Reform (Miscellaneous Provisions) (Scotland) Act 1966, s 6. They are complex and obscure.[51] The basic rule is that income may be accumulated only for the first 21 years of a trust's life. Once the period during which accumulation has elapsed, income has to be distributed to the beneficiaries. Of course, in many trusts there never is any accumulation. An example is a liferent trust. And many trusts do not last long enough for accumulation to be an issue.

Accounting duties and information duties

24.25 Trustees must keep accounts and must retain the 'vouchers': relevant documents such as receipts. Whereas the form of accounts that companies must keep is highly regulated, there is little authority on the form of trust accounts.[52] It is also unclear how long they have to keep records. They must provide information (including the accounts) to the beneficiaries.[53] But, again, it is unclear how much information, and it is unclear to what extent the duty is an active one or whether it is merely that they must produce information if asked. Trust deeds sometimes restrict the rights of beneficiaries to information,[54] and occasionally provide that a beneficiary is not even to be told that he or she is a beneficiary until a certain time has come.[55] The validity of such provisions is untested. But it is generally assumed that such provisions are valid. In the case of charitable trusts information must be given to OSCR (the Office of the Scottish Charity Regulator).

Fiduciary duties of trustees

24.26 To state the obvious: trustees must adhere to the terms of the trust deed and to general trust law. Investment duties have just been mentioned. Trustees, being fiduciaries, are subject to fiduciary duties.[56] A trustee must not, as it is often put, be

---

[50] 39 & 40 Geo III c 98, commonly called the Thellusson Act. The Act was unnecessary for Scotland, where such provisions are invalid at common law: *McCulloch v McCulloch* 28 November 1752, 1 Elchies.

[51] See Wilson and Duncan *Trusts* ch 9. A leading case is *Elder's Trs v Free Church of Scotland* (1892) 20 R 2.

[52] Except for charitable trusts: CTI(S)A 2005, s 44. There are, however, well-established ways of doing things: see, eg, M F Morley *Accounting for Scottish Executries and Trusts* (1984).

[53] Authority is sparse but see *Nouillan v Nouillan's Exrs* 1991 SLT 270. See also the English case of *O'Rourke v Darbishire* [1920] AC 581 and the Manx case of *Schmidt v Rosewood* [2003] 2 AC 709. For discussion see Scottish Law Commission, Report on Trust Law (Scot Law Com No 239, 2014) ch 11.

[54] E.g. the 'blind trust' used by politicians.

[55] Wealthy people often fear that their children or grandchildren will become idlers or spendthrifts if they learn too early that they are to come into money.

[56] This principle has its origin in Roman law: 'a tutor cannot buy a thing belonging to his ward; this rule extends to other persons with similar responsibilities, that is curators, procurators and those who conduct another's affairs': D 18, 1, 34, 7 (Translation A Watson et al).

an *auctor in rem suam*.[57] A trustee must not buy from the trust,[58] or sell to the trust,[59] or borrow from the trust,[60] or lend to the trust[61] or in any other way deal with the trust in his or her personal capacity, except in so far as the trust deed so allows. The justification is this: the trustee's interest as an individual would be in conflict with his or her duty as a trustee. For instance, if the trustee were to buy an asset from the trust, his or her economic interest as a buyer would be to obtain a low price, but the duty as seller would be to obtain a high price. Trustees must not put themselves in such a position where their interest conflicts with their duty. The fact, if it is a fact, that the price was a fair market price is irrelevant. In *University of Aberdeen v Magistrates of Aberdeen*[62] Aberdeen Council owned some land in trust. It then bought the land from itself. The price became part of the trust fund. Many years later some of the beneficiaries sought to reduce the sale. One defence to the action was that the price had been the full market value. This defence was held irrelevant and reduction was granted.[63]

24.27   Trust deeds can derogate from the 'no conflict' principle, and they often do so, especially as to charging for time. The reason is that whilst sometimes trustees are happy to give their time for nothing, sometimes they are not. If a client wishes his or her solicitor to be a trustee, the solicitor will usually agree to do so only if the trust deed allows him or her to charge. Likewise, in unit trusts the trustee will be authorised to charge. The trust deed's authorisation can be implicit as well as express.[64] As with other duties, the duty not to be an *auctor in rem suam* can be waived by the beneficiaries. The same principles apply equally to executors[65] but in practice executors often transact with themselves and their actions are seldom challenged.

24.28   The trustees must (unless the trust deed says otherwise) consider only the beneficiaries' interests. In *Martin v City of Edinburgh*[66] the defenders were trustees who allowed their political outlook to influence their investment decisions. It was held that they were acting in breach of trust: there was a conflict between their duty as trustees and their political agenda. One may suspect that the motivation for the litigation – by a politician of one party against a Council controlled by a different one – was itself primarily political. In the English case of *Cowan v Scargill*[67] where

---

[57]   'Give authority for a transaction in his own interests.'
[58]   Eg *University of Aberdeen v Magistrates of Aberdeen* (1877) 4 R (HL) 48; *Johnston v Macfarlane* 1987 SLT 593.
[59]   Eg *Cherry's Trs v Patrick* (1911) 2 SLT 313.
[60]   Eg *Perston v Perston's Trs* (1863) 1 M 245.
[61]   Eg *Wilson v Smith's Trs* 1939 SLT 120. Here, the rule seems to be applied more strictly than to other sorts of fiduciaries. For instance, while company directors cannot borrow from their company, they can lend to it.
[62]   (1877) 4 R (HL) 48.
[63]   If the land had been sold to a third party at the same price, the sale would have been valid.
[64]   *Sarris v Clark* 1995 SLT 44.
[65]   For examples involving executors, see *Inglis v Inglis* 1983 SC 8; *Johnston v Macfarlane* 1987 SLT 593 and *Sarris v Clark* 1995 SLT 44.
[66]   1988 SLT 329.
[67]   [1985] Ch 270.

the facts were rather similar the same result was reached. The court commented that 'trustees may even have to act dishonourably (though not illegally) if the interests of their beneficiaries require it', citing examples from earlier English case law. It is uncertain whether our law goes as far as that. One hopes not.

BREACH OF TRUST

Types

24.29   'Not every breach of duty by a fiduciary is a breach of fiduciary duty.'[68] Breach of trust can be divided into:

(a)   *ultra vires* breach;

(b)   *intra vires* breach; and

(c)   breach of fiduciary duty.

Ultra vires breach is where the trustees do something that is outwith their powers, such as making an unauthorised investment, or paying the wrong beneficiary. *Intra vires* breach is where they do something that is within their powers but do it badly, such as making an unwise investment decision. Breach of fiduciary duty speaks for itself. The classification is, however, not free from difficulty. One could argue that trustees have no power to act in breach of their fiduciary duties, so that (c) is really an aspect of (a). The distinction between *intra vires* and *ultra vires* breach is said to be important because liability for *ultra vires* breach is strict, whereas liability for *intra vires* breach is fault-based. The authorities are, however, less than clear on this point. A case could be made for the view that there is no liability without fault.

Some consequences of breach of trust

24.30   If trustees are personally liable, they must to restore to the trust the lost value.[69] Breach may not cause loss, and in that case there is no liability. Take the following examples. First, suppose that the trust forbids investment in land. The trustees nevertheless invest £500,000 in land. They sell it three years later and the sale price is £400,000. The trustees are personally liable to make good the loss, ie they must pay £100,000 into the trust. Second, suppose that the land proved a good investment, and that the sale price is £700,000. There is no loss to the trust. Indeed, the trust has made a handsome gain. The trustees have no liability. (These examples actually are oversimplified. Suppose that the trust deed said that the only lawful investment would be in a specific company, whose shares fell in value by 90% during

---

[68]   *Bristol and West Building Society v Mothew* [1998] Ch 1 at 16 per Millett LJ. The same is true in Scots law.

[69]   Trustees can insure against liability, and it is possible for the premiums to be charged to the trust estate, provided the trust deed so provides or the court so permits: *Governors of Dollar Academy v Lord Advocate* 1995 SLT 596.

the three years in question. In the first example, the trustees' liability would be nil. And in the second example, if the value of the shares in that company had risen by 90% in that period, the trustees would be liable. The comparison has to be made with what would have happened if the trustees had acted lawfully. And in practice such counterfactual comparisons can be hard to make.)

24.31 If an unauthorised investment is made, the trustees are bound to realise the investment and reinvest appropriately, and that is so even if the unauthorised investment has proved profitable.

24.32 A transaction with a third party that is in breach of trust will not be void and will not normally be voidable either. At common law such a transaction was voidable, at the instance of the beneficiaries, unless the counterparty gave value and was in good faith. (Which in practice was almost always the case.) The common law was modified by T(S)A 1961, s 2, so that even if the counterparty is in bad faith the transaction is not normally voidable. This provision has raised many eyebrows over the years. Whether a buyer in bad faith might be open to attack in some other way, such as a delictual claim, is unclear. The provision applies only to a sale to a *third party*, and thus not to trustees themselves. As for donations, trustees have no right to give away trust assets (except, of course, to beneficiaries in pursuance of the trust provisions) and if they do it appears that the donation is voidable.

24.33 What has just been said applies to transactions with third parties. If a trustee acts as *auctor in rem suam*, then not only is the trustee personally liable for the loss (if any) so caused, but the transaction is either void or voidable.[70]

24.34 A trustee who is involved in serious breach of trust can be removed by the court on the petition of the beneficiaries or co-trustees.[71] If there are no trustees (for example because the court has removed them all) the court can appoint new ones.[72] Where there has been serious breach of trust this can be particularly useful, for the new trustees can, for instance, sue the former trustees for any losses they have caused.

24.35 The same applies to public trusts, but in addition because public trusts exist in the public interest the Lord Advocate has a common law power to enforce. If the trust is a charitable one, the Office of the Scottish Charity Regulator has extensive statutory powers of supervision, intervention and enforcement.[73]

24.36 The beneficiaries have the usual remedies of civil law, such as actions of declarator and interdict and payment. Another such remedy which can be of particular value is an action of 'count, reckoning and payment'. This is an action for payment which requires the trustees to produce their accounts to the court so as

---

[70] Which of these is applicable is a question of some difficulty.
[71] *Gilchrist's Trs v Dick* (1883) 11 R 22; *MacGilchrist's Trs v MacGilchrist* 1930 SC 635 and *Sharif v Hamid* 2000 SLT 294.
[72] T(S)A 1921, s 22.
[73] CTI(S)A 2005, especially s 34.

to enable the pursuer to determine how much is due.[74] And if trustees overpay one beneficiary, and fail to recover the overpayment (which they can do under the law of unjustified enrichment), the other beneficiaries can step in and sue the overpaid beneficiary direct.[75]

Paying/conveying to the wrong person

24.37   What if trustees distribute property or money wrongly, because they are unaware of someone's status as beneficiary? For instance, Beth, a widow, dies intestate, with three children by her late husband, Carla, Deirdre and Esther. Carla is executor (ie a type of trustee) and divides up the estate between herself and her sisters. Carla does not know that her mother had, before she married, another child, Alana, who had been brought up by her (Alana's) father. Step forward Alana. What happens now? This area of law is not free from difficulty. But there is now a statutory provision saying that a trustee who has acted in good faith and without negligence is not liable for overlooking a beneficiary, ie Carla is not liable to Alana for breach of trust.[76] However, Alana would still have a claim in unjustified enrichment against her three half-sisters.

Judicial relief

24.38   The T(S)A 1921, s 32 provides that if a trustee has incurred personal liability, the court 'may' discharge that liability if the trustee acted 'honestly and reasonably'. This is a strange provision: in what other area of law can a debt that has come into existence be nullified at discretion? Like much trust law, this comes from England, where it is common for rights to be variable by judicial discretion. It would seem more sensible, in the context of Scots law, to say that a trustee who has acted honestly and reasonably has no liability. Indeed, that may well be what the common law is. If so, that would perhaps explain why T(S)A 1921, s 32 has, it seems, never been applied.

Immunity clauses

24.39   Due to the high standards that the law demands of trustees, trust deeds sometimes seek to modify those standards by what is called an 'immunity' or 'exemption' clause. For example: 'My trustees shall not be liable for depreciation in value of the property in my estate, nor for omissions or errors in judgment, nor for

---

74   See, e.g., *Cunningham-Jardine v Cunningham-Jardine's Trs* 1979 SLT 298 and *Nouillan v Nouillan's Executors* 1991 SLT 270.
75   *Armour v Glasgow Royal Infirmary* 1909 SC 916.
76   Succession (Scotland) Act 2016, s 23 inserting a new s 29A into the T(S)A 1921. Whether this changed the law might be arguable. Although it is commonly said that a common law liability for paying the wrong person was strict, was this ever so held where there was no fault?

neglect in management, nor for insolvency of debtors, nor for the acts, omissions, neglects or defaults of each other or of any agent employed by them.'[77] The effect of such clauses has been controversial.[78] A conventional view is that they protect trustees from liability for ordinary negligence, but not from liability for gross negligence or fraud.[79] The distinction between ordinary and gross negligence is not without its problems. Moreover, it might be argued that there is a conceptual difficulty saying, in a trust deed, 'these are your duties, ... but ... only joking, because it doesn't matter whether you carry them out or not!' In other words, it can make sense to set the bar at a middling, rather than a high, level, in which case non-achievement of a high level of success is not negligent in the first place, but it hardly makes sense (or so it might be argued) to set the bar high and then to excuse the trustees for not clearing it. But, however, one conceptualises the issue, defining a middling standard is difficult. Indeed, the whole area is difficult.[80]

Prescription

24.40   Most obligations can be extinguished by negative prescription.[81] The obligations of trustees are an exception.[82] Whether this exception is justifiable is perhaps debatable.

RUNNING FOR COVER

24.41   It sometimes happens that the trustees are uncertain what they should do, for example about the meaning of a provision in the trust deed. There are several ways of bringing the issue before the court. One is a declarator. Another is a special case.[83] Another (though useful only if the issue is about paying or transferring assets to beneficiaries) is multiplepoinding. All those procedures can also be used outwith the field of trust law. Trustees can also 'petition for directions'[84] and seek a 'superintendence order'.[85]

---

[77] Quoted from that valuable work, Alan Barr et al, *Drafting Wills in Scotland* (2nd edn 2009) style 5.11.

[78] And not only in Scotland. The leading English case is *Armitage v Nurse* [1998] Ch 241. For a comparative study, see the Scottish Law Commission, Discussion Paper on Breach of Trust (Scot Law Com DP No 123, 2003), Appendix A.

[79] *Lutea Trs Ltd v Orbis Trs Guernsey Ltd* 1998 SLT 471. In a Guernsey case, *Spread Trustee Co Ltd v Hutcheson* [2012] 2 AC 194 (PC), there were suggestions that in Scots law liability for gross negligence can be excluded. This does not represent the consensus view of Scots lawyers.

[80] For discussion of the current law see Scottish Law Commission, Report on Trust Law (Scot Law Com No 239, 2014) paras 12.23 ff, and J Kessler and W Grant, *Drafting Trusts and Will Trusts in Scotland* (2013) ch 5.

[81] See **CHAPTER 6** above.

[82] PL(S)A 1973, Sch 3. These provisions are not free from obscurity. See, eg, *Hobday v Kirkpatrick's Trs* 1985 SLT 197 and *Ross v Davy* 1996 SCLR 369.

[83] Court of Session Act 1988, s 27.

[84] Court of Session Act 1988, s 6. See *Peel's Trs v Drummond* 1936 SC 786 and *Taylor, Petitioner* 2000 SLT 1223.

[85] T(S)A 1921, s 17.

LIABILITY OF TRUSTEES TO THIRD PARTIES

24.42   If trustees incur liability to third parties (ie parties other than beneficiaries), the question of whether they are *personally* liable is generally of little significance, for even if they are, they are entitled to be reimbursed from the trust estate.[86] The question becomes important in the unusual case where the trust becomes insolvent. In such a case the creditors will wish, if possible, to hold the trustees personally liable. It is commonly said that if trustees enter a contract, they are personally liable on it unless the contract expressly states that they are contracting only as trustees. The alternative view (which we favour) is that no such express declaration is necessary: if they contracted as trustees and the other party knew that, then they are not personally liable.[87]

INSOLVENCY

Four cases

24.43   Four different cases of insolvency must be considered:
(1) that of a beneficiary;
(2) that of a truster;
(3) that of a trustee as an individual; and
(4) that of the trust.

'Insolvency' here is used in a broad sense to cover sequestration, liquidation and also the diligence of creditors.

(1) Beneficiaries

24.44   If a beneficiary becomes insolvent, the beneficial interest is part of his or her patrimony and so is in principle available to the creditors. Suppose, for instance, that John is entitled to £5,000 each quarter from a trust. His creditors could arrest in the hands of the trustees. Or suppose that trustees hold a house in beneficial liferent for Laura and in beneficial fee for Fiona. Fiona is sequestrated. The beneficial fee passes to her trustee in sequestration for the benefit of her creditors. This does not affect Laura's rights.

(2) Truster

24.45   The insolvency of the truster after the trust has been established is normally irrelevant. But there is a qualification. Insolvency law says that those who are

---

[86]   Unless the liability was incurred in the course of breach of trust.
[87]   See R G Anderson 'Contractual Liability of Trustees to Third Parties' 2003 *JR* 45 and Scottish Law Commission, Report on Trust Law (Scot Law Com No 239, 2014) ch 13.

factually insolvent must conserve their assets for the creditors' benefit. If there is such a transfer – what is called a 'gratuitous alienation' – the creditors can insist that the assets be re-transferred. Usually the claim is made after the transferor has been sequestrated, or gone into liquidation, and the claim is made by the trustee in sequestration or the liquidator. This general principle applies as much to transfers to a trust as it does to other transfers.[88]

(3) Trustee as individual

24.46   The insolvency of a trustee as an individual has no effect on the trust. The rule is a common law one, and remains so as far as diligence and liquidation are concerned. For sequestration, the rule has been put on a statutory footing.[89] The common law rule is often traced to the late nineteenth-century case of *Heritable Reversionary Co Ltd v Millar*.[90] In fact, it goes back to the seventeenth century, but at common law there was an exception in relation to heritable property where the fact of the trust was kept secret, i.e. not disclosed on the register. In *Heritable Reversionary Co Ltd v Millar* the House of Lords changed the law so as to remove the exception.

(4) Trust as such

24.47   In the unusual situation where a trust itself becomes insolvent, it can be sequestrated.[91]

LITERATURE

24.48   Much of the literature mentioned in the previous chapter is relevant here too. And see in particular Chalmers *Trusts* chs 6–10, K Norrie and E Scobbie, *Trusts* (1991) chs 7–11, and Wilson and Duncan *Trusts* chs 23–30.

---

[88]   For the law of gratuitous alienations, see W W McBryde *Bankruptcy* (2nd edn, 1995) ch 12.
[89]   Bankruptcy (Scotland) Act 2016, s 98.
[90]   (1891) 19 R (HL) 43.
[91]   Bankruptcy (Scotland) Act 2016, s 6(1)(a).

Chapter 25

Trusts: variation and termination

INTRODUCTION

25.1 'Variation' means the varying of the terms of trust: this is unusual but by no means not rare. 'Termination', or 'extinction', is when a trust comes to an end. The two are connected because a trust may be varied so as to terminate it.

25.2 Most trusts run their course and come to a natural termination without ever having been varied. For instance, in a trust for Letitia in liferent and Fraser in fee, when Letitia dies the trustees will make over the trust estate to Fraser, and the trust will end. When a private trust is finally wound up so that nothing is left in the trustees' hands, the trustees are said to have 'denuded'. Much the same is true of public trusts. For example, there is a natural disaster and a relief fund is set up with generous people giving it money. The money is expended fairly quickly and the trust then comes to an end. (Having said that, some public trusts are long-lasting and may even be permanent.)

25.3   The longer a trust lasts the greater the possibility that its terms may come to be unsatisfactory. Circumstances change. The trust may become richer or poorer than anticipated, the position of the beneficiaries may change, background law, including tax law, may change, and so on. Some trusts are set up with broad powers vested in the trustees, with the result that a need for variation is unlikely to arise, however much circumstances change over time. But that is not always the case. Of course, there is an argument against variation: to vary is to depart from the intentions of the trusters. So in general, in so far as the law allows variation, it does so cautiously.

25.4   How trusts can be varied, or terminated early, depends primarily on whether they are private or public. The common-law position is that (i) private trusts can be varied or terminated early by the agreement of the beneficiaries, but cannot be varied otherwise, eg by the court, and (ii) public trusts cannot be varied or terminated early by the agreement of the beneficiaries, but can, within narrow limits, be varied by the court. Statutory developments beginning in the nineteenth century have to some extent broadened the possibilities of variation, but to understand the law the basic common law position must be kept in mind.

VARIATION AND EARLY TERMINATION OF PRIVATE TRUSTS

The rule in *Miller's Trs v Miller*

25.5   The rule in *Miller's Trs v Miller*,[1] confirmed by the Whole Court in *Yuill's Trs v Thomson*[2] allows the partial or complete termination of a trust at the request of a single beneficiary, where that beneficiary is the only person with an interest.

25.6   The rule is as follows: if a beneficial interest is vested in a given person, and there is no reason for the trustees not to pay or transfer to that person, except for a direction in the trust deed that they must not do so until that person has reached a specified age, then that person, if he or she has reached the age of 16, can demand that the trustees pay, or transfer, to him or her, notwithstanding that the trust deed forbids them to do so.[3] If the beneficiary is the sole beneficiary then the trust is terminated.

25.7   The rule is well illustrated by *Miller's Trs* itself. Sir William Miller set up a trust for his son John. The trust deed provided that the trustees were not to transfer the trust estate to John until he was 25. This was, therefore, a bare trust, with the speciality that a beneficiary could not demand that the trustees denude until a stated

---

[1]   (1890) 18 R 301. The rule is the same in England: *Saunders v Vautier* (1841) 4 Beav 115, 49 ER 282, aff'd (1841) Cr & Ph 240, 41 ER 482. But in some countries the rule is different. Scotland should perhaps be among them: the dissenting opinion of Lord Young is powerful.

[2]   (1902) 4 F 815.

[3]   Actually, a precise statement of the rule is problematic, partly because in both cases the judges explain the rule by the inappropriate use of the word 'fee'. The text is an attempt to state the rule without using that word.

time.[4] Before he was 25, John sued the trustees to have the property made over to him. He was successful.

25.8   If the trust had provided, for example, that if he died before 25 the property would go to someone else then his action would have failed. But there was no reason for the trustees to withhold, apart from the direction to do so. Despite the rule in *Miller's Trs v Miller*, trusters often do provide that assets be withheld from a beneficiary until a certain age – 25 is the typical age chosen – is reached. The reason is obvious: many trusters do not think young adults should be given substantial capital. In practice beneficiaries often do not assert their right under *Miller's Trs v Miller*, and so the truster's wishes prevail.

25.9   What a sole beneficiary can do, can be done collectively by all beneficiaries. That is to say, any private trust can be terminated at any time by the unanimous agreement of the beneficiaries: their wishes override the terms of the trust deed and the views of the trustees. The beneficiaries may also make a unanimous decision for a variation (as opposed to a termination) but in that case it may be (the law seems not quite certain here) that the trustees have to agree. If the trustees do not agree to a variation, the beneficiaries can always terminate the trust and then set up a new one, on the new terms that they want to see, but having a new trust, as opposed to having a varied but existing trust, can cause certain problems.

25.10   The rule that all the beneficiaries can agree to a termination or variation sounds straightforward, but there are two catches. The first is that beneficiaries who are under age[5] cannot consent, and, moreover, it seems that, as far as common law is concerned, nobody can consent for them.[6] The second is that one or more beneficiaries may be as yet non-existent. (An example would be a trust for X in liferent and in fee for those children of Y as are alive when X dies.) The T(S)A 1961 says that the court can consent on behalf of such beneficiaries.[7]

Alimentary trusts

25.11   An alimentary trust is one expressly established for the alimentary support of the beneficiary. Though nowadays unusual, they are not unknown. They have a number of special features, one of which is that the beneficiary's rights are unassignable. A second is that the beneficial interest is, to a limited degree, protected

---

[4]   In fact the trust did not start off as a bare trust. But that complication can be omitted. It had become a bare trust by the time that John sued the trustees.

[5]   Whether this means – for this purpose – 16 or 18 is a complex issue. The Age of Legal Capacity (Scotland) Act 1991 (ALC(S)A 1991) says that the age of capacity for juridical acts in private law is 16, but this rule must be read in the light of T(S)A 1961, s 1(2), as substituted by ALC(S)A 1991, Sch 1. T(S)A 1961, s 1(2) is less than clear. The practical position is that for those aged 16 or 17 the court's consent is needed.

[6]   See A B Wilkinson and K McK Norrie *The Law Relating to Parent and Child in Scotland* (3rd edn, 2013) para 5.37.

[7]   T(S)A 1961 s 1. The leading case is *Phillips, Petr* 1964 SC 141.

from the beneficiary's creditors. The rule in *Miller's Trs*[8] does not apply to alimentary trusts.

Variation of private trusts by the court

25.12 By statute, private trusts can be varied by the court in two respects, namely to enlarge the administrative powers of the trustees[9] and to permit the trustees to make an advance of capital.[10] In practice neither is common.

Termination of a private trust by failure of purposes: resulting trusts

25.13 In a private trust it can occasionally happen that after the purposes have been fulfilled there is still trust property left, or that the trust purposes cannot be fulfilled at all. In these cases the remaining trust property is deemed to be held on a bare trust for the truster. This is a 'resulting trust'.[11]

VARIATION AND EARLY TERMINATION OF PUBLIC TRUSTS

Variation of public trusts

25.14 In a public trust, consent to a variation cannot be given by the beneficiaries because it is the nature of a public trust that there does not exist a finite set of beneficiaries. Variation is nevertheless possible, the original common law rules having been considerably widened by legislation. In some cases it can be done by the trustees themselves. In others the court must be involved, and in some cases the regulatory body for charities, OSCR.[12] There is a distinction, in current law, as to whether the public trust Is charitable or non-charitable. We take the latter first.

Variation of non-charitable public trusts

25.15 Non-charitable public trusts can be varied under the Law Reform (Miscellaneous Provisions) (Scotland) Act 1990 (LR(MP)(S)A 1990), ss 9–11. The main provision is LR(MP)(S)A 1990, s 9. Several grounds exist for variation, such as if the purposes of the trust 'have been fulfilled as far as it is possible to

---

8 (1890) 18 R 301.
9 Trusts (Scotland) Act 1921 (T(S)A 1921), s 5. This provision applies also to public trusts.
10 T(S)A 1921, s 16.
11 See **PARA 23.48** above.
12 For OSCR, see **PARA 23.34** above.

do so'. The court can vary the trust purposes, or provide for the trust assets to be transferred to another trust. Any variation must have regard to the 'spirit' of the trust deed: the new scheme 'must enable the resources of the trust to be applied to better effect consistently with the spirit of the trust's constitutive document, having regard to changes in social and economic conditions since the time when the trust was constituted'.[13] LR(MP)(S)A 1990, ss 10 and 11 provide simplified machinery for the variation of smaller trusts. As well as the statutory rules, the court has a common law power to vary public trusts: this goes by the curious name of the '*cy près* procedure'.[14]

Variation ('reorganisation') of charitable trusts

25.16   The provisions just mentioned used to include charitable trusts. But today LR(MP)(S)A 1990 covers only non-charitable public trusts.[15] Charitable trusts (and indeed charities that are not trusts) are now 'reorganised' under the Charities and Trustee Investment (Scotland) Act 2005 (CTI(S)A 2005).[16] This can be done in two ways. The first is for the trustees to propose a variation to OSCR, which can then if it sees fit approve the proposal. In this case the court does not have to be involved. Alternatively, OSCR can petition the court to approve a variation. Such a petition does not require the trustees' consent. The conditions for such a reorganisation (for example about the 'spirit' of the trust) are similar to those in LR(MP)(S)A 1990.

Cy près

25.17   If a charitable trust is unworkable, the court has power at common law to modify its provisions to make it workable. This is called a '*cy près*'[17] scheme. There are two main types of case. The first is 'initial failure', where the trust cannot be put into operation, and the other is 'supervening failure', where the charitable trust is up and running but later becomes unworkable. In either case the court makes a *cy près* scheme, which is supposed to be as near to the original intention of the truster as possible, consistent with workability. Nowadays the 'supervening failure' cases

---

[13]   Charities and Trustee Investment (Scotland) Act 2005 (CTI(S)A 2005), s 9(2).

[14]   For this procedure, see **PARAS 25.17–25.18** below.

[15]   Law Reform (Miscellaneous Provisions) (Scotland) Act 1990, s 15(9) as amended by CTI(S)A 2005, Sch 4, para 7(e). The terms 'charity' and 'charitable' are rather slippery, and here we use them to mean charities that are registered in the Register of Charities.

[16]   CTI(S)A 2005, ss 39–43. Three minor points: (a) These provisions do not apply to chartered or statutory charities: CTI(S)A 2005, s 42(5). (b) The *cy près* procedure is competent for charitable trusts as it is for other public trusts: CTI(S)A 2005, s 42(4). (c) 'Educational endowments' are governed, in part, by the Education (Scotland) Act 1980, though the scope of this Act has been reduced by CTI(S)A 2005, ss 42(6) and 43. Some educational endowments are centuries old. The local authority is often the trustee.

[17]   Pronounced 'see-pray'. The expression comes from English law but is neither good English nor good French but rather what is called in England 'law French'.

are usually handled through the statutory system already mentioned. For 'initial failure' cases *cy près* remains the only route. But these two main types of case are not exhaustive: a *cy près* scheme is always possible for a charitable trust in the case of 'strong or compelling expediency.'[18]

25.18   There can be many causes of unworkability, such as changes in the law,[19] or changes in social or economic conditions.[20] One type of initial failure is a testamentary trust in favour of a named charity that in fact does not exist – something that happens surprisingly often. In such a case, if it can be established that the testator had a 'general charitable intention' the court will approve a *cy près* scheme.[21] Otherwise the legacy will be void. A *cy près* scheme can take the form of simply directing that the funds be made over to an existing charity.

LITERATURE

25.19   Good accounts can be found in the following: Chalmers *Trusts* (2002) chs 12–13, K Norrie and E Scobbie *Trusts* (1991) chs 12–14; R Paisley *Trusts* (1999) chs 13–14; Wilson and Duncan *Trusts* chs 11–16, though all are now a little out of date.

---

[18]   *RS Macdonald Charitable Trust Trustees v Scottish Society for the Prevention of Cruelty to Animals* 2009 SC 6.
[19]   See, eg, *Burgess's Trs v Crawford* 1912 SC 387.
[20]   See, eg, *Trs of the Domestic Training School etc, Glasgow, Petrs* 1923 SLT 603.
[21]   See, eg, *Pomphrey's Trs v Royal Naval Benevolent Trust* 1967 SLT 61.

Chapter 26

Succession: general issues

INTRODUCTION

Location of succession within private law

26.1   The law of succession regulates what happens to a person's assets and liabilities on death. It can be considered as part of property law, in the sense that it deals with the effect of death on property.[1] It can also be regarded as part of family law.[2] Many legal systems regard it as a separate subject in its own right.

Succession law and trust law

26.2   The relationship of the law of succession and the law of trusts is close. Indeed, the modern position seems to be that every executry is a trust.[3] Whatever the theoretical position, succession law remains a distinct subject.

Sources of the law: past and future

26.3   Our succession law differs from English succession law in many ways: so different are they that English authorities are seldom cited. The law is in part statutory and in part common law, the latter being a mix of Roman law, canon law and customary law. The main statute is the much-amended Succession (Scotland) Act 1964 (S(S)A 1964).[4] The Scottish Law Commission has twice (in 1990 and in 2009) published reports recommending major changes.[5] Some of these recommendations

---

1   The Scotland Act 1998, s 126 assigns succession to property law.
2   Particularly as regards intestate succession. See, eg, K McK Norrie 'Three proposals' 2007 *JLSS* Oct/20 at 21.
3   See **PARA 26.50** below.
4   This implemented, but with significant changes, the Mackintosh Report of 1951 (Cmnd 8144).
5   Scottish Law Commission, Report on Succession (Scot Law Com No 124, 1990); Scottish Law Commission Report on Succession (Scot Law Com No 215, 2009). For discussion see the symposium on succession law (2010 *Edin LR* 308) with papers by D Nichols, A Barr, D Reid and R Kerridge. See also F Burns 'Surviving Spouses' (2013) 33 *Legal Studies* 85.

were implemented by the Succession (Scotland) Act 2016, but others have not. The Scottish Government is considering the possibility of further legislative change.[6]

Different approaches to succession

26.4   When someone dies, what should happen to the estate? The answer depends, in part at least, on basic ideas about the nature of property.

(1) Those who have an individualistic idea of property argue that people should be free to decide what happens to their assets when they die. If Adam wants to disinherit his wife and children, he should be free to do so. People should be guided by conscience, but not coerced by law. This approach is that of 'freedom of testation'.

(2) Those who have a family-based idea of property argue that family members have rights that are indefeasible in conscience and ought to be indefeasible in law. While there may be scope of debate as to how 'family' should be defined, people should be unable to disinherit their families completely.[7]

(3) Those with a socialistic idea of property argue that property ultimately belongs to society. When a member of society dies, the property should revert to society, either in whole or at least in part.[8]

26.5   If there is an intestacy, the first approach is irrelevant. The owner has not expressed any wishes as to what should happen, and so the conflict is only between the second and third approaches. But in a testate case the conflict becomes a three-cornered one.

26.6   Each approach has sub-approaches, and the second has three in particular.

(a) There should be no right of testation at all. Everyone would die intestate, so that the rules of intestacy, which give the estate to the family, would always apply.

(b) There should be a right of testation, but not for the whole estate: a minimum slice should be set aside for the benefit of the family.

(c) Since circumstances vary (one child might be poor and another rich, so why should they receive the same?), the system should be discretionary, with the discretion being vested in a determined person or body, such as a judge.

26.7   The first approach (freedom of testation) has tended to be favoured by the Anglo-American legal systems, while the second, in its (b) version, has tended to be favoured in the civilian tradition.[9] Almost all systems have an element of the

---

[6]   Consultation on the Law of Succession (2015, available at www.gov.scot/Publications/2015/06/7518), published when what is now the Succession (Scotland) Act 2016 had already begun its legislative journey.

[7]   The system of indefeasible inheritance rights for the family is known among comparative lawyers by the rather odd name of 'forced heirship'. The idea behind the phrase is not that heirship is forced on the family but that it is forced on the testator.

[8]   Perhaps this is just a variant of the 'family' philosophy, with the whole of society being the family.

[9]   Eg the French Cc, art 913, and German BGB, § 2303.

third approach by way of death tax – in the UK called inheritance tax.[10] In some Anglo-American legal systems there has been a recent tendency to move towards a mixture of the first approach and the second approach in its (c) version. England is an example, where succession rights are subject to the court's discretion.[11] But such discretion applies only if it is invoked: if no one seeks to invoke it then the estate is distributed according to determinate, default, rules. Moreover, only certain defined persons can seek to invoke the discretion: for instance, suppose that someone dies unmarried and childless and with no dependants, then the court's discretion could not be invoked. The third approach in its pure form (everything to the state) was applied for a few years in the former Soviet Union, but was quickly abandoned.

26.8 Like most legal systems, Scots law is a compromise. Inheritance tax takes away part of the estate, at a rate of 40%, though there are various exemptions, and smaller estates, in particular, are exempt. The second of the three approaches is adopted in its (b) variant – which puts us in the 'civilian' camp. Our law has an institution called (oddly) 'legal rights', whereby the spouse (or civil partner) and children (and sometimes grandchildren) have certain rights that cannot be excluded by the testament of the deceased.[12] But *other* family members have no such protection. Thus those who leave behind them neither spouse (or civil partner) nor issue[13] can write their testaments without concerning themselves about possible rights. As for the first of the three views, people can do what they like with such part of their estates as will be net of taxes and legal rights.

Moral claims

26.9 Succession rights are legal entitlements. Merely moral claims, however strong, have no legal status. Neither need nor merit enter the calculation. The courts have no discretion to depart from the legal rules in favour of a claimant with a strong moral case. Thus suppose that Rosie has two daughters, Shilpa and Tara. Rosie is aged and infirm and is looked after for many years by Shilpa. Tara lives in Australia and never even sends her mother a Christmas card. Shilpa is poor. Tara is rich. If Rosie dies intestate, Shilpa has no greater right than does Tara, and even if Rosie leaves everything to Shilpa, Tara can still claim legal rights. In this approach Scotland is in line with most, but not all, countries. There are strong arguments for the discretionary approach, as the example shows, but there are also strong arguments the other way. There is one exception: in the case of intestacy (only) if there is a cohabitant the court can make a discretionary award to the cohabitant.[14]

---

[10]   Inheritance Tax Act 1984.
[11]   Inheritance (Provision for Family and Dependants) Act 1975, s 2. Both testate *and* intestate succession are subject to the discretionary system.
[12]   See **CHAPTER 27** below.
[13]   'Issue' means children or remoter descendants.
[14]   See **CHAPTER 29** below.

Death

26.10   The Registration of Births, Marriages and Deaths (Scotland) Act 1965 is the governing statute for the registration of deaths.[15] Section 23 provides that

'it shall be the duty of
- (a) any relation of the deceased,[16]
- (b) any person present at the death,
- (c) the deceased's executor or other legal representative,
- (d) the occupier, at the time of death, of the premises where the death took place,
- (e) if there is no such person as is mentioned in the foregoing paragraphs, any other person having knowledge of the particulars to be registered'

to register the death. The person registering the death submits the Medical Certificate of Cause of Death signed by a physician.[17] The Registrar can issue extracts from the Register, and the term 'death certificate' means such an extract, rather than the physician's certificate.[18]

26.11   Sometimes a formal inquiry before the sheriff will be conducted by the procurator fiscal, in order to determine the circumstances of the death: this is regulated by the Fatal Accidents and Sudden Deaths Inquiry (Scotland) Act 2016. Such inquiries happen in three types of case:
- (a) accidents at work;[19]
- (b) deaths in custody;[20] and
- (c) in cases where it is 'expedient in the public interest'.[21]

26.12   If a person disappears, and is thought to have died, but there is no body, a declarator of death can be obtained.[22] The typical example is death at sea. The fact of the shipwreck, aircraft crash etc can be established, plus the fact that the person was on board, and though no body has been recovered the court can be satisfied that death has taken place. Sometimes a person merely disappears: for instance Jade walks out of the house after a quarrel and is not seen or heard of again. Here there is normally no case for saying that she died on the day of disappearance. But if seven years have passed since she was last known to be alive, then the court can deem her

---

[15]   Modifications of the system were introduced by the Certification of Death (Scotland) Act 2011, prompted by the Shipman scandal. See the Government's policy document www.scottish.parliament. uk/S3_Bills/Certification%20of%20Death%20%28Scotland%29%20Bill/b58s3-introd-pm.pdf.

[16]   Since everyone is, ultimately, a relation of everyone else, this means that the duty is imposed on the whole planetary population.

[17]   Registration of Births, Marriages and Deaths (Scotland) Act 1965, s 24.

[18]   Registration of Births, Marriages and Deaths (Scotland) Act 1965, s 27. The official name of a death certificate is an Extract of an Entry in a [sic] Register of Deaths.

[19]   2016 Act, s 2(3).

[20]   2016 Act, s 2(4) ff.

[21]   2016 Act s 4.

[22]   Presumption of Death (Scotland) Act 1977.

to have died at the end of the seven-year period.[23] This opens the way to rights of succession to the estate.[24] Note the difference: in the first case the court declares, on the basis of circumstantial evidence of death, the person to have died at the time of disappearance, but in the second the deemed date of death is seven years after the date of disappearance, and is on the basis of a presumption.

The body

26.13 Bodies are disposed of either by burial or by cremation. Both are regulated by law.[25] One of the questions in the official form asks: 'Did the deceased leave any written directions as to the mode of disposal of his remains?'[26] In practice this means that cremation can be vetoed by the deceased. But not the converse: the family can always choose burial.

26.14 Is a dead body owned? If so, by whom? This has never been absolutely settled but it appears that 'there is no right of property in a dead body'.[27] Presumably, however, it is unlike other ownerless property, for it would be absurd to suggest that ownership could be acquired by occupation. If it has no owner, the question of who is entitled to possession has to be determined without reference to ownership.[28] If no one takes any steps to dispose of a body, the local authority can do so.[29] (This happens quite often: for instance, there are about 200 such burials a year in Edinburgh alone.[30]) The procurator fiscal is entitled at common law to take temporary possession of dead bodies if the public interest so requires: an example would be the body of a murder victim.

WHO MAY INHERIT? THE LIVING AND THE DEAD

General

26.15 There are three principal ways in which one person may inherit from another.

---

[23] Before that period has elapsed, the estate can, if necessary, be administered by a judicial factor.
[24] The Presumption of Death (Scotland) Act 1977 has provisions about what is to happen if the person later turns up.
[25] Burial and Cremation (Scotland) Act 2016, though at the time of writing this was not yet wholly in force. It repeals and replaces the Burial Grounds (Scotland) Act 1855, the Cremation Act 1902 and the Cremation Act 1952. But it leaves in place s 27A of the Registration of Births, Deaths and Marriages (Scotland) Act 1965, whereby the unauthorised disposal of a body is an offence.
[26] Cremation (Scotland) Regulations, SI 1952/1639, Sch 1.
[27] *Robson v Robson* (1898) 5 SLT 351 at 352. See also *McGruer, Petitioner* (1899) 15 Sh Ct Rep 38.
[28] The problems in this area are considerable. See further N R Whitty 'Rights of Personality, Property Rights and the Human Body in Scots Law' (2005) 9 *Edin LR* 194; *C v Advocate General for Scotland* 2012 SLT 103; *C v M* 2014 SLT (Sh Ct) 109, a bitter dispute about funeral arrangements as between the deceased's mother and his widow.
[29] Public Health (Scotland) Act 2008, s 92 and 93.
[30] *The Guardian* 27 August 2016 p 52.

(1) By legacy (also called bequest). This can happen only in a testate case.[31]
(2) By intestate succession.[32]
(3) By legal rights.[33]

Legal rights can operate in both testate and intestate cases. In all three cases there are certain general issues which can arise, and they are discussed below.

26.16   The living can inherit. The dead cannot. These two principles are obvious but it is easy to lose sight of them. Alice's testament gives a legacy of a house to Brian. She dies on Monday and Brian dies on Tuesday. When she dies, Brian is still alive, and the legacy 'vests' in him.[34] That is to say, he acquires a personal right. The fact that from a practical point of view Brian does not live long enough to receive the legacy makes no difference. Personal rights form a part of a person's patrimony just as much as real rights. Suppose that Brian had lived long enough for ownership of the house to be transferred to him. Then when he died the ownership of the house would have been in his estate. Since he died the day after the testator, what was in his estate was a personal right to have ownership of the house conveyed to him. But the financial value of that right is the same as that of ownership itself.[35] What will happen is that Alice's executor will transfer the legacy to Brian's executor. (It is then up to the latter to determine what is to happen to the property as far as Brian's estate is concerned. It is not for Alice's executor to make that determination.)

26.17   Now, reverse the order of deaths. Brian dies on Monday and Alice on Tuesday. The legacy to Brian cannot take effect. The legacy has lapsed.[36] The dead cannot inherit. Thus suppose that Brian's testament left everything to his widow, Clara. All Brian's estate would then pass to Clara[37] but his estate would not include the legacy from Alice.

26.18   Hence small differences in the timing of deaths can make big differences in the effects of the deaths. For example, Deirdre and Ewan are married but have no children. Deirdre's nearest relative is her brother, Fraser. Ewan's nearest relation is his sister, Gina. Deirdre's testament leaves everything to Ewan. Ewan's leaves everything to Deirdre. Deirdre dies on Monday and Ewan dies on Tuesday. The whole of both Deirdre's and Ewan's estates end up with Gina, to the exclusion of Fraser. Why? Because Ewan's testament is without effect, since when he dies, Deirdre, his sole legatee, is already dead – she has predeceased. (The verbs 'to survive' and 'to predecease' are commonly used in succession law. If X 'predeceases' Y that means that X dies before Y. If X 'survives' Y, that means that Y dies before X.) Hence Ewan

---

[31]   See **CHAPTER 28** below.
[32]   See **CHAPTER 29** below.
[33]   See **CHAPTER 27** below.
[34]   It would be otherwise if Alice's testament had made the legacy conditional on Brian's surviving her for a stated period, such as one month. Such conditions are sometimes found. On vesting, see **PARAS 23.65–23.71** above.
[35]   Assuming that Alice's estate is solvent etc.
[36]   For lapse of legacies, see **PARA 28.41** below.
[37]   Subject to debts and legal rights.

dies intestate. So everything of Ewan's, which by now includes a personal right to the whole of Deirdre's estate, passes to his next of kin, his sister Gina. Had the dates of death been reversed, everything would have ended up in the hands of Fraser, for the same reasons.

Common calamity

26.19 'Common calamity' is the name given to the situation where two or more people die in the same incident, such as a road accident or a house fire. If those who die[38] have no potential succession rights to the estates of the others, no issue arises. But what if they have? Sometimes the evidence will show that one died before the other. If it can be shown, on balance of probabilities, that Deirdre died one minute after Ewan, then she survived him, and so would be able to inherit from him. The same is true, the other way round, if he lived for one minute after her. An example from the US, which probably would be decided in the same way here, involved a plane crash in which both husband and wife perished.[39] Each had a will leaving everything to the other. 'The small airplane used 100-octane gasoline, which, in fire, produces carbon monoxide. A small amount of carbon monoxide was found in the wife's blood, and her brain was intact, and therefore the physicians testified that, in their opinion, she had breathed in the carbon monoxide during the fire. On the other hand, the husband had massive injuries of brain and heart and no carbon monoxide. The physicians testified that they concluded that the husband had died instantaneously and that the wife had survived the husband for a very brief interval.'[40] Hence he must have been dead when she drew her last breath, with the result that she had survived him, if only by seconds. Hence she inherited from him.

26.20 If two persons die at the exactly the same moment, then neither survives the other, and so neither inherits from the other. The legislation says that the same is true if 'it is uncertain who survived whom'.[41]

WHO MAY INHERIT? SOME PARTICULAR TYPES OF PERSON

General

26.21 This section deals with particular types of potential claimant, such as adopted children, cohabitants and so on. All such persons may inherit to the extent

---

[38] The Latin term *commorientes* ('those who die together') is sometimes used.
[39] *In the Matter of the Estate of Barbara A. Bucci*, 57 Misc.2d 1001, 293 N.Y.S.2d 994 (1968).
[40] We quote the headnote.
[41] S(S)A 2016, s 9, replacing s 31 of the S(S)A 1964, which had different rules.

that a legacy has been left to them by the deceased.[42] So this section is concerned with whether they have inheritance rights *independently* of any legacy.

Children out of wedlock

26.22 The common-law rule was that children born out of wedlock were not treated, for succession purposes, as the child of either parent. This rule was gradually eroded by legislation, and eventually disappeared.[43] William, a widower, dies intestate at the age of 75. He has one child, Mary, by his late wife, Wendy. At the funeral appears a man, Michael, who can show that Mary's father was his genetic father. Mary and Michael have equal rights to the estate.

Adopted children

26.23 An adopted child is treated, for succession purposes, as a child of the adoptive parent(s), and not as the child of the actual parents.[44] Tom, the child of Ursula and Vernon, is adopted by Wilma and Xerxes, who also have a child of their own, Yolanda. If Ursula dies, Tom receives nothing (unless it happens that she left him a legacy). If Xerxes dies, Tom has the same position as Yolanda. If Tom dies, his birth parents are not treated as being his parents for succession purposes. His adoptive family is treated as being his family.

Stepchildren

26.24 A stepchild is not the child of the stepparent. Iona and James marry and have one child, Kate. James dies and Iona marries Louis. Kate is Louis's stepdaughter. If he dies, she has no succession rights in his estate. (Unless, of course, he left her a legacy.) Were it otherwise, Kate would in effect inherit from *three* parents.

Posthumous children etc

26.25 A baby born after its father's death has the same succession rights as if it had already been born at the time of the death. This rule is usually expressed in Latin as *nasciturus pro jam natus habetur, si de ejus commodo agitur* (an unborn

---

[42] The deceased is sometimes also called the defunct, and also the *de cuius* (also spelled *de cujus*), meaning the 'of whom', ie the person whose estate is to be wound up.

[43] Law Reform (Parent and Child) (Scotland) Act 1986, s 1. And see Family Law (Scotland) Act 2006, s 21.

[44] Adoption and Children (Scotland) Act 2007, s 40.

child is to be considered already born if to do so is in its interests).[45] Whilst the issue commonly arises where the *de cujus* (the deceased) is the child's father, i.e. the posthumous child, it could also arise where the *de cujus* is someone else.[46]

Cohabitants

26.26   Until 2006, cohabitants had no succession rights, unless they left legacies in each other's favour, which, of course, was and is common. The rule now is that in intestate cases the court may, on a discretionary basis, make a cohabitant an award.[47] This is the only case where judicial discretion can be an element in our succession law. In a testate case a cohabitant may receive a legacy, but otherwise has no claim.

Spouses and civil partners: current, former and separated

26.27   Spouses have special succession rights.[48] If Jack and Jill are married, and she dies intestate, he has certain rights to her estate.[49] If she dies testate, she cannot wholly disinherit him.[50] Divorce dissolves marriage and those special succession rights thereby end. (A fair settlement between them should have been achieved at the time of the divorce.) Spouses usually bequeath at least part of their property to the other spouse, and if there is a divorce usually that testament is torn up. But if it is not, the common law was that the legacy takes effect, so that if Jack and Jill are divorced and a few months later she dies, not having changed her will, he takes the legacy. But the law is now that divorce revokes any legacy, so that Jack would now take nothing.[51] Of course, if Jack and Jill had children together, those children will have succession rights in her estate. You can divorce your spouse; blood relationship is indissoluble.[52]

26.28   If a married couple separate but do not divorce, they are, to state the obvious, still married, and so have succession rights in each other's estate. That is true even if they have agreed that they will divorce. What dissolves the marriage is not the decision to divorce, but the divorce itself. There are two qualifications. One is that when spouses part they sometimes sign a separation agreement, and such agreements typically contain a clause of mutual renunciation of all succession rights.[53] The other is that non-cohabitation of spouses can affect intestate succession rights.[54] Formerly,

---

[45]   See R Paisley 'The succession rights of the unborn child' (2006) 10 *Edin LR* 28.
[46]   See Paisley (above) at 39.
[47]   Family Law (Scotland) Act 2006, s 29. See **PARA 29.20** below.
[48]   Civil partners are in the same position. S(S)A 1964, ss 2, 8 and 9; Civil Partnership Act 2004, s 131.
[49]   See **CHAPTER 28**.
[50]   See **CHAPTER 26**.
[51]   S(S)A 2016 s 1.
[52]   Except by adoption.
[53]   But the drafting of such clauses can easily go wrong. See *Price v Baxter* 2009 Fam LR 138.
[54]   See **PARA 29.12** below.

judicial separation barred the husband's rights against the wife's estate but did not bar the wife's rights against the husband's estate.[55] Judicial separation now has no effect on succession rights.[56]

Juristic persons and trusts

26.29 Juristic persons and trusts obviously are not family members and so have no inheritance rights, but it is competent to leave a legacy to them, and indeed it is common to do so, since people often leave legacies to charities, and charities are either juristic persons or trusts.[57]

The unworthy heir

26.30 An 'unworthy heir' (*haeres indignus*) is someone barred from inheriting because he or she unlawfully killed the deceased.[58] (The rule is a common law one, which existed in parallel with a statutory one, the Parricide Act 1594. That Act was ignored in practice and was repealed in 2016.[59]) The typical example is where one spouse kills the other. The result is that the offender is treated as having predeceased the victim, for the purposes of what happens to the latter's estate.[60] Thus all rights are lost, whether by way of legacy, or legal rights, or intestate rights, or rights under special destination.[61] The law was modified by the Forfeiture Act 1982 which provides that the court has a discretionary power to 'modify' the common law rule.[62] The modification may be partial or total.[63] But the power exists only if the killer is convicted of culpable homicide rather than murder.

NO OBLIGATION TO ACCEPT

26.31 No one is obliged to accept anything by way of succession. Succession rights are in fact occasionally refused. Sometimes the family gets together after the

---

[55] Conjugal Rights (Scotland) Amendment Act 1861.

[56] Family Law (Scotland) Act 2006, s 45.

[57] See **PARAS 23.34–23.35** above.

[58] In many jurisdictions the class of unworthy heirs is not limited to killers. In Scots law it is. On this see *Tannock v Tannock* 2013 SLT (Sh Ct) 57, and more generally, J MacLeod and R Zimmermann 'Unworthiness to Inherit, Public Policy and Forfeiture: The Scottish Story' 2013 *Tulane Law Review* 741.

[59] S(S)A 2016 s 17.

[60] This 'as if predeceased' interpretation was enacted by the S(S)A 2016 s 12; the change was aimed at *Hunter's Exrs, Petitioners* 1992 SC 474.

[61] And see *Burns v Secretary of State for Social Services* 1985 SLT 351 (woman who killed husband barred from claiming widow's allowance).

[62] This Act also applies in England and Wales, and its approach is arguably more English than Scottish. For an example of the way the Act works, see *Paterson, Petitioner* 1986 SLT 121.

[63] Forfeiture Act 1982, s 2 as amended by S(S)A 2016, s 15. The change was aimed at *Cross, Petitioner* 1987 SLT 384.

death and agrees a division that is different from what the applicable law (of testate or intestate succession) provides. Such an agreement is usually called a 'deed of variation'. If it is entered into within two years of the death, it is treated, for tax purposes, as if it had effect as from the moment of death.[64] Indeed, deeds of variation are often done purely for reasons of tax planning.

THE ESTATE

Active and passive transmissibility

26.32   The 'estate' is a person's patrimony upon death – the collection of assets and liabilities of the deceased that must be 'wound up' by the executor.[65] 'Winding up' means that the executor pays the debts, pays any tax due, and distributes the balance – in kind or in money – to the beneficiaries. In general, all the deceased's assets form part of the estate: this is sometimes known as the principle of *active transmissibility*. Assets include personal as well as real rights. Suppose that Monica borrows £50 from Lucretius. He dies. The right to repayment forms part of his estate: she must pay his executor. In some special types of case, however, an asset does die with its holder. An example is a liferent.[66] But such exceptions are rare. Solatium claims have proved difficult, and the law has changed more than once. The current position is that such claims are actively transmissible.[67]

26.33   Side by side with the principle of active transmissibility is the principle of *passive transmissibility*.[68] This means that the liabilities of the deceased continue as liabilities of the estate. *Death does not dissolve obligations.* Take the previous example, and vary it, so that it is Monica who dies, not Lucretious. Her debt remains payable: 'It is a general rule that a personal obligation transmits against the personal representatives of the obliger.'[69] (As with active transmissibility, there are one or two exceptions.) It is for the executor to discharge the obligations. This is done by means of the assets. In other words, the executor pays debts by realising assets. It may be that there are sufficient assets in money form (for example, a bank account) to do this without having to sell anything. But the executor has power to sell assets, and must do so if necessary, because debts come first. The rights of the beneficiaries are to be satisfied only out of the *net* estate. The greater the debts, the less the beneficiaries take.[70] If the deceased died with more debts than assets – that is died insolvent – then the beneficiaries take nothing. But that is the worst that can happen. Neither the

---

[64]   Inheritance Tax Act 1984, s 142.
[65]   The word 'estate' is likewise used for the patrimony of a person upon sequestration. This too must be 'wound up', in this case by the trustee in sequestration.
[66]   See **CHAPTER 22** above.
[67]   See the Damages (Scotland) Act 2011.
[68]   The 'active' and 'passive' sides of a patrimony are the assets and liabilities respectively: hence active and passive transmissibility.
[69]   *Morton's Trs v Aged Christian Friend Society* (1899) 2 F 82 at 87 per Lord Kinnear.
[70]   On larger estates inheritance tax is payable. But this book does not cover tax issues.

executor nor the beneficiaries have any *personal* obligation to pay the deceased's debts. If the value of the assets is insufficient to meet the claims of the creditors, then the creditors must grin and bear it.

Heritable and moveable

26.34   Whether an asset is heritable or moveable may make a difference. There are three ways this happens. (1) Legal rights are calculated on the net value of the moveable estate.[71] (2) Whether an asset is heritable or moveable can make a difference where cross-border issues are concerned.[72] (3) It makes a difference to which part of the estate pays off the debts.

Incidence of debts

26.35   As far as the creditors are concerned, it makes no difference which part of the estate is to be realised to meet their claims. No asset is exempt from the possibility that it must be realised to pay creditors. But for the beneficiaries, the issue can be important. Suppose that the estate consists of a house, which is bequeathed to Ivan, and a car, which is bequeathed to Jade. There are debts. Who suffers? Ivan, or Jade, or both? S(S)A 1964 is silent, leaving the topic to the common law.[73] The case law is mostly old and there has not been much academic discussion. The topic is underdeveloped and probably has lurking problems. The account below, taken with the discussion of the sub-topic of abatement in **CHAPTER 28**,[74] is subject to that warning.

26.36   If a debt is secured against a particular asset, for instance a debt secured by standard security over a house, that asset is regarded as the fund out of which that debt is to be paid.[75] In the example just given, suppose that the house is worth £300,000; the car £30,000; and the debts are £290,000, all secured over the house. The house would have to be sold, and Ivan would receive the free proceeds – £10,000. Jade would get the car. (Alternatively, Ivan could choose to pay off the debt, and take the house.) Vary the example by increasing the debts to £310,000, all secured over the house. Both house and car would have to be sold. Jade would receive £20,000 and Ivan nothing. (If the debts amounted to £330,000 or more, neither Ivan or Jade would get a penny.)

26.37   Sometimes a debt is secured over two assets. In that case, both are burdened, in the ratio of their values.[76] Suppose that Alan has a debt of £72,000 which is secured

---

[71]   See **PARA 27.4** below.
[72]   See **PARAS 26.54–26.56** below.
[73]   S(S)A 1964, s 14(3).
[74]   See **PARAS 28.32–28.43** below.
[75]   See, eg, *Stewart v Stewart* (1891) 19 R 310.
[76]   *Graham v Graham* (1898) 5 SLT 319.

both against his house, worth £160,000, and against a life assurance policy, worth £80,000. Then £48,000 of debt is ascribed to the house and £24,000 to the policy.

26.38   In calculating legal rights, all the debts, except those secured against heritable property, are notionally deducted from the moveable part of the estate. For example, Robert dies with moveables worth £200,000 and a house worth £200,000. He owes Sarah £30,000, secured on the house, £30,000 to Tom, secured on certain moveable assets and £40,000 to Una, unsecured. The net moveable estate for the purposes of calculating legal rights is not £170,000 (as one might expect) but £130,000. That is because legal rights are calculated on the basis of the moveable estate minus the 'moveable debts' and the 'moveable debts' are, roughly speaking, all debts except those secured over heritable property. Although this is how the value of legal rights is calculated, legal rights are not necessarily paid out of the moveable estate.[77]

26.39   In a testate case, debts reduce the value of the residuary legacy. Thus Jane leaves her house to Kate and the residue of her estate to Luke. The debts must be paid out of the residue. The only exception to that is if the debts, or part of them, are secured over the house. For example, suppose that the house is worth £300,000 and the residue of the estate is worth £200,000. There are two debts. The first, £100,000, is secured over the house. The second, £50,000 is not. Then Kate could choose to pay off the £100,000 and take the house, or she could choose that the house be sold, in which case she will receive £200,000. The other debt, £50,000, comes out of the residue. By contrast, if neither debt had been secured, both would have been charged against the residue.

26.40   In some cases the debts may be so large, or the residue so small, that other legacies (over and above the legacy of residue) will be affected. In that case the other legacies are 'abated', which is to say scaled down so as to make it possible to pay the debts. The details of abatement are looked at elsewhere.[78]

Executory contracts to buy or sell: 'conversion'

26.41   John owns land. On Monday he contracts to sell it to Kate. On Tuesday he dies. At this stage his estate has two assets and one liability. They are:
  (a) ownership of the land;
  (b) the contractual right to be paid the price by Kate; and
  (c) an obligation to convey the land to Kate, an obligation his executor must perform.[79]

It is usually said that the land is 'converted' into moveable property (i.e. the price). But the land does not become moveable. But the second asset, the right to the money,

---

[77]   See **PARA 27.8** below.
[78]   See **PARA 28.32–28.43** below.
[79]   See, eg, *Chiesley v His Sisters* (1704) Mor 5531.

is moveable, and it is that asset, and not the land, that will be subject to the rights of John's beneficiaries.

26.42   Reverse the facts. John owns land. On Monday he contracts to sell it to Kate. On Tuesday she dies. Her estate has:
 (a) a contractual right to acquire the land; and
 (b) an obligation to pay the price.[80]

(It may also have the money for the purchase.) Her contractual right to the land is itself a heritable right, and will be treated as such for the purposes of her estate. However, since she has died the land is probably now not wanted, so her executor may try to negotiate with John to be released from the contract.

EXECUTRY

Introduction

26.43   The law of succession must deal not only with the question 'Who gets what?' but also with that of 'How do they get it?'. Assets have to move from the patrimony of the person who has died into the patrimonies of the living. The 'how' question is thus in a sense one of conveyancing. This is a large subject and only a brief account is given here.

Executors

26.44   In some legal systems death itself operates as an immediate and complete transfer to the heirs.[81] The 'how' question is thus easy to answer in theory, though in practice there are evidential problems and also complications caused by the need to pay creditors. In some other systems the transfer is direct but not immediate. Historically, Scotland has experimented with both systems, but nowadays we route everything through the executor.[82] Thus whereas in many legal systems an executor is an optional extra, in Scots law the executor is, in most cases at least, essential. We use an executor even in an intestate case.

26.45   There are two sorts of executor.
 (1) An 'executor-nominate', who is appointed by the deceased in the testament.
 (2) An 'executor-dative', who is appointed by the sheriff.

The sheriff has administrative oversight of all executors. Strictly, he or she is acting not as sheriff but as commissary; however, the post of commissary is nowadays

---

[80]   See, eg, *Ramsay v Ramsay* (1887) 15 R 25.
[81]   Eg Germany.
[82]   There are one or two qualifications to this remark. The only important one concerns survivorship special destinations, for which see **PARAS 30.8–30.10** below.

always held by the sheriff, and commissary courts are physically the same as sheriff courts, and the administration of them is almost completed fused. If more than one person seeks appointment as executor-dative, there is an order of priority.[83] An executor-dative is needed if there is no testament, or if there is one but it does not make an effective appointment. As with trustees, a person nominated as executor is free to decline the office. The order of the sheriff appointing someone as executor-dative is called 'decerniture'.

Confirmation

26.46   The executor now prepares an inventory of the estate. All heritable properties, investments and bank accounts will be separately listed but furnishings can normally be lumped together. Each item must be given an estimated value. The executor then petitions the sheriff to be 'confirmed'. The inventory is submitted as part of the petition. The 'confirmation' is a decree authorising the executor to administer the estate: the right of administration does not exist before confirmation.[84]

26.47   The executor's authority only extends to the inventoried assets. An executor who later discovers other assets must petition for the wonderfully named 'eik', whereby the sheriff authorises the executor to administer the additional assets. There can be as many eiks as are necessary. (But in most cases no eik is needed.) The inventory must also be submitted to HM Revenue and Customs for inheritance tax purposes. Once confirmed, the executor can sue for debts owing to the deceased, can convey specific assets to beneficiaries, can pay beneficiaries, and can sell. Sale may be necessary to raise money to pay debts, to pay inheritance tax and to pay legal rights claimants or pecuniary legatees.[85] An executor can also complete title to registered property (land, company shares etc.) in his or her own name, *qua* executor, but this would be unusual.

The executor's position

26.48   The executor's authority includes paying debts and distributing to beneficiaries. But that is not all. The executor has general powers to perform juridical acts on behalf of the estate, such as suing debtors of the deceased who fail to pay up, selling assets and so on. The executor is often said to be *eadem persona cum defuncto* (the same person as the deceased). An executor is in a sense the heir of the whole estate but not for his or her own benefit.[86] In practice, however, the executor may be and usually is, one of the beneficiaries, and sometimes is the sole beneficiary.

---

[83]   See, eg, *Russo v Russo* 1998 SLT (Sh Ct) 32.
[84]   That is at least the basic rule.
[85]   For legal rights and pecuniary legacies, see **CHAPTER 27**.
[86]   The executor has sometimes been called a fideicommissary heir (*haeres fideicommissarius*). The term is accurate.

An executor is thus like a trustee. Whether an executry is in truth a trust is a point of some difficulty. For most purposes it is, both at common law[87] and under the Trusts (Scotland) Acts, which define 'trustee' to include executors.[88]

Insolvency

26.49 Occasionally, the debts are so great that they exceed the value of the estate. There are two ways of handling an insolvent estate. One is for a creditor to be appointed as executor-creditor.[89] This tends to be quick and cheap. The other is for the estate to be sequestrated, and a trustee in sequestration appointed.[90] (And if an executor is confirmed in the ordinary way and later realises that the estate is insolvent, he or she can have the estate sequestrated.[91])

Personal liability of the executor?

26.50 The general principle is that neither the executor nor the beneficiaries have any personal liability for the debts of the deceased. The creditors can sue the executor, but their claims are against the executor only as such. The executor has two patrimonies: his or her own general patrimony, and the executry estate, and it is only against the latter that creditors of the deceased can enforce their claims. The executor can incur personal liability only through fault.

The six-months rule

26.51 Since creditors have priority over beneficiaries, there is a practical problem. It might take years before all creditors came forward, and it would be unfair to the beneficiaries if they had to wait for years before the distribution was made. But equally it would be unfair to the creditors if the executor could wind up the estate more or less immediately, without waiting to see the full extent of the debts.

26.52 So the law sets a period of six months, starting from the day of death.[92] Once the six months are up, the executor is free to wind up the estate on the basis of the debts as known at that time. If the executor distributes the estate within the six-month period, this is done at his or her own risk, in the sense that if new debts come to light the executor may be personally liable for them. Once the six-month period has elapsed, the executor can wind up the estate without having to worry

---

[87] See, eg, Erskine III, 9, 42; Bell *Commentaries* II, 80; *Taylor v Ferguson* 1912 SC 165.
[88] T(S)A 1921, s 2, read with S(S)A 1964, s 20.
[89] *Smith's Trs v Grant* (1862) 24 D 1142 is the leading case.
[90] Bankruptcy (Scotland) Act 2016, s 5.
[91] Bankruptcy (Scotland) Act 2016, s 5.
[92] Act of Sederunt of 28 February 1662 anent Executors-creditors.

about unknown creditors. Suppose that after seven months the estate appears to be solvent, and the executor at that stage distributes the estate. A week afterwards, another creditor turns up. The executor has no personal liability to that creditor. The six-month rule thus means that:

(a) no creditor can insist on payment within the period; and

(b) no beneficiary can force the executor to pay, or convey, within the period.

Personal liability of others?

26.53 Non-lawyers often suppose that a deceased person's family is responsible for ensuring that the debts are paid. That is not the law. If a person dies with debts, no one has any personal liability to pay those debts. The executor is liable, but only as executor, liability being limited to the executry assets. Of course, a family member might be liable for some special reason. For instance, he or she might have been a cautioner for a loan to the deceased. Married couples often take out loans on the basis of solidary (joint and several) liability. But, apart from such special cases, there is no liability. There are two qualifications to the foregoing.

(1) If the executor distributes the estate to the beneficiaries and it later turns out that a creditor has not been paid, the creditor can recover from the beneficiaries, but no beneficiary can be made to pay more than he or she received.

(2) The other is the quaintly named doctrine of vitious intromission. If someone other than the executor 'intromits' with the deceased's property, that person thereby is deemed to become a sort of cautioner for the debts. This can be seen as a penalty, deterring people from unlawful intromission.

INTERNATIONAL PRIVATE LAW

26.54 Often no international issues are involved, as where a Scot dies with assets that are all in Scotland. But quite often there is a cross-border dimension.[93] Scottish international private law says that moveables devolve according to the *lex domicilii* and immoveables according to the *lex situs*. So if Lucy, who is Scottish, dies with (i) a house in France, (ii) its furnishings, (iii) a bank account in Italy, (iv) a house in Scotland, (v) its furnishings, and (vi) investments and moveables in Scotland and England, Scottish international private law would say that (i) devolves according to French law but that everything else devolves according to Scots law.

26.55 This split approach is known as 'scission'. Some other countries have a similar approach, while others adopt the 'unitary' approach, meaning that one

---

[93]   See further A E Anton *Private International Law* (3rd edn, 2011, by P R Beaumont and P E McEleavy) chs 23 and 24 and E B Crawford and J M Carruthers, *International Private Law: A Scots Perspective* (4th edn, 2015) ch 18.

and the same succession law applies to the whole estate. Almost all EU states have the 'unitary' approach, because of the European Succession Regulation.[94] (The exceptions are Denmark, Ireland and the UK.)

26.56 Because different countries have different approaches, conflicts can arise. Hamish is a UK citizen[95] whose domicile and habitual residence[96] are Scottish. He dies. He has some moveables and land in Scotland, and some in sun-kissed Italy. Scots international private law says that the land in Scotland, and all the moveables, are subject to Scots succession law, but that the sun-kissed land is subject to Italian succession law. Italian international private law says that the whole estate, including the land in Italy, is subject to Scots succession law. So for the land in Italy, each system points to the other. Take another case. Francesca is an Italian citizen of Italian domicile and habitual residence. She dies. She has some moveables and land in Italy, and land in Scotland. Scots international private law says that the land in Italy, and all the moveables, are subject to Italian succession law, but that the land in Scotland is subject to Scots succession law. Italian international private law says that the whole estate is subject to Italian succession law. So for the land in Scotland, each system points to itself. All this is of course unsatisfactory.

RELIGIOUS LAW

26.57 It is sometimes asked whether religious law can apply, and, in particular, Islamic law where the deceased was a Muslim. The answer is that Scots succession law takes no notice of a person's religion. (Some countries do so, such as India.) But a Sharia-compliant outcome may sometimes be attainable in practice. Sometimes a testament can be drafted so as to achieve this outcome. Moreover, the result produced by Scots succession law can be varied, after the death, by the agreement of all concerned. But such agreement may not be attainable. For example, since Islamic law[97] requires that in most circumstances males are entitled to inherit twice as much as females, the latter may be reluctant to give up their rights. Again, Islamic law gives indefeasible claims to a broader range of family members than does Scots law, and those family members who would receive less if Islamic law is applied may decline to give up their rights.

---

[94] 650/2012. For the implications from a Scottish standpoint see E Crawford & J Carruthers "'Rome IV: An Unexpected Legacy?" 2016 SLT (News) 51.'

[95] Nationality is not relevant for the succession law of many countries, including Scotland. But many other countries do use it. The European Succession Regulation makes habitual residence the test, but allows testators to choose nationality instead.

[96] Domicile and habitual residence will usually be the same, but not invariably. The reason we mention both is that whilst many countries, including Scotland, use domicile as a test, the European Succession Regulation (and hence Italian law) use habitual residence.

[97] For scholarly work on Islamic succession law, see the references in the chapter by N Yassari, in K G C Reid, M J de Waal and R Zimmermann (eds), *Comparative Succession Law: Volume II: Intestate Succession* (2015).

LITERATURE

26.58 McLaren, J *The Law of Wills and Succession* (3rd edn, 1894), with supplementary volume by D Oswald Dykes (1934), is now very out of date but still carries weight where the law has not changed. It must be said that it is not easy reading. Two useful modern works are Hiram *Succession (see eg* chs 1–2) and Macdonald *Succession (see eg* chs 1–3 and 13–14.) D Bartos *Bartos & Meston on the Succession (Scotland) Act 1964* (6th edn, 2015) and M Meston, *Succession Opinions* (2000) are valuable. J Currie *Confirmation of Executors* (9th edn, by E M Scobbie, 2011) is a practitioner bible. K G C Reid, R Zimmermann and M J de Waal (eds) *Exploring the Law of Succession* (2007) has some valuable essays on Scots law.

26.59 For other legal systems, see L Garb, (ed) *International Succession* (4th edn, 2015). K G C Reid, R Zimmermann and M J de Waal (eds) *Comparative Succession Law* is a series of volumes of which two have so far appeared, subtitled *Testamentary Formalities* (2011) and *Intestate Succession* (2015).

Chapter 27

Legal rights

INTRODUCTION

General

27.1 The relict[1] (if any) and the children (if any) have indefeasible rights, called, rather oddly, legal rights.[2] Civil partners have the same rights as spouses: the term 'relict' is here used to cover them too. Legal rights are common law rights, though

---

[1] A gender-neutral term meaning 'widow or widower'.

[2] For the history see J C Gardner *The Origin and Nature of the Legal Rights of Spouses and Children in the Scottish Law of Succession* (1928), though this work is far from being the last word.

somewhat modified by statute. They are indefeasible in the sense that they cannot be defeated by testament. So if Norma has a husband and three children, and she leaves everything to charity, the charity will not take everything. It will take everything that remains after the legal rights of her husband and children have been satisfied. Other relatives do not have this protection from disinheritance. Had Norma been single and childless, the charity would have received everything, and her relatives nothing. Thus those without spouse (or civil partner) or issue have complete testamentary freedom.

27.2   Legal rights, in one form or another, are common round the world.[3] But in Scots law there is an unusual feature, which is that legal rights are based on the moveable part of the estate only. By contrast almost all other countries that have legal rights make no such distinction.[4] It is difficult to defend the Scottish rule, which makes legal rights depend on the lottery of the respective sizes of the two parts of the estate (ie moveable and immoveable) at death.[5] Xerxes and Yvonne each have money to invest. Xerxes invests on the stock exchange and Yvonne invests by buying a flat to let out. It is hard to see why this choice should affect the rights of their respective families. Indeed, if Yvonne decides to buy the flat via a company she sets up, Yvonne Residential Investments (Lanark) Ltd, a company with one shareholder (her) and one asset (the flat), when she dies the investment is, like Xerxes's, moveable, because company shares are moveable. (As for the flat, she did not own it: her company did.) So her decision to take title through the company has arbitrary effects on succession rights.

Jus relictae, jus relicti and legitim

27.3   The legal right of the relict is called the relict's right or, more commonly, *jus relictae* for a widow or *jus relicti* for a widower. It is a right to the value of a fixed fraction of the moveable part of the estate. If the deceased left issue[6] then the fraction is one-third. If the deceased left no issue, the fraction is one-half. The legal right of the children is called bairns' part or, more commonly, legitim.[7] Legitim is the same in amount as relict's right: one-third of the value of the moveables if there is a relict, or one-half if there is no relict.[8] So if there are both relict and issue, legal rights will take up two-thirds of the value of the moveables.

---

[3]   See, eg, R Zimmermann (ed), *Freedom of Testation/Testierfreiheit* (2011); M Anderson (ed), *The Law of Succession; Testamentary Freedom: European Perspectives* (2011).
[4]   Jersey, like Scotland, applies legal rights only to moveables.
[5]   As noted at **PARA 26.3**, the Scottish Government is contemplating major changes to the law of succession, including legal rights. One possible aspect of the reform would be to eliminate the distinction between heritable and moveable.
[6]   'Issue' means children or remoter descendants.
[7]   From *legitima portio*.
[8]   For some of the details, see N R Allan 'Legal Rights' 1988 *JLSS* 130.

Some examples

27.4   Donald dies, estranged from his second wife, Eva, by whom he had no children, and from his two children, Flora and Gordon, by his divorced first wife. His testament leaves everything to his brother, Harry. Donald's net estate consists of a house worth £200,000, contents worth £50,000 and investments worth £100,000.[9] Despite being disinherited, Eva will receive £50,000 and Flora and Gordon will receive £25,000 each. This is because the value of the moveable estate is £150,000. Eva is entitled to the value of one-third of that. A further third (called the 'legitim fund') goes to the children, i.e. £25,000 each. Harry takes the rest. Donald's first wife has no claim, for divorce, like death, dissolves marriage. Moreover, the fact that the children are not children of Donald's marriage with Eva is irrelevant. The calculation of legal rights is the same whether or not Eva is the mother of Flora and Gordon.

27.5   Suppose that Eva had died shortly before her husband. In that case neither she nor her estate would take anything, for the dead cannot inherit.[10] The legitim fund would have been half the value of the moveable estate, and so Flora and Gordon would have received £37,500 each.[11] Harry would have taken the rest. Thus legal rights are calculated, like other succession rights, on the state of affairs at the moment of death. (For example, suppose that Jill has a husband and a daughter. If she dies when they are alive, they have their legal rights. But if they were to die before her, she would have complete testamentary freedom.) To complete the variations on Donald's estate: if he had had no children, there would have been no legitim, and Eva would have taken half the value of the moveable estate, thus receiving £75,000.

The dead's part

27.6   The expression 'dead's part' is often encountered. This term means that part of the estate that the deceased was free to dispose of by testament. So, the dead's part is the net estate (ie after debts and taxes) minus the legal rights claims, if any. Thus, it is, at a minimum, (i) all the heritable property and (ii) one third of the moveables. Example 1: Farrah dies single and without issue. All her net estate is dead's part. Example 2: she dies married but without issue. The dead's part is all her net estate minus one half of the value of her moveable estate (ie her widower's *jus relicti*). Example 3: She dies with issue but no spouse. The dead's part is the same as in the previous example. Example 4: she dies with both spouse and issue. The dead's part is all her net estate minus two thirds of the value of her moveable estate.

---

[9]   'Net estate' means the estate net of debts and taxes.
[10] See **PARA 26.16** above.
[11] Since Donald would have inherited to at least some extent from Eva, his estate might be different, and larger, than the figures given earlier, but we will leave this complication out of account.

Applicability

27.7   Legal rights operate in both testate and intestate succession. The latter fact is illogical since in intestate succession the estate goes to the family anyway. Put another way: legal rights protect against disinheritance, and so really make sense only in testate succession. This chapter therefore concentrates on legal rights in the context of testate succession.

LEGAL RIGHTS ARE A CLAIM FOR MONEY

27.8   In some countries legal rights give a co-ownership share (a *pars bonorum*). This can be rather awkward in practice. In other countries, including Scotland, legal rights are rights to receive a sum of money based on the value of the estate (a *pars valoris bonorum*).[12] Take the following case. Mary is unmarried. She has one child, Norman. Her estate consists of shares in Royal Bank of Scotland plc (worth £70,000), other moveables (worth £10,000) and some land (worth £200,000). Her testament says: 'I leave my shares to Oliver and the residue of my estate to Paula.' Oliver receives the shares. The legitim fund is £40,000, which goes to Norman. (The moveable estate is worth £80,000, and since there is no relict the legitim fund is half of that figure.) To find the money to pay him, the executor will have to sell the land. Paula will receive a cheque for £170,000. Thus *immoveable* property has been used to pay legal rights. This is because residue is what (if anything) is left over *after* all other claims on the estate have been met.[13] Put another way, residue must abate before special legacies.[14]

PRIORITY

27.9   Legal rights claimants are thus, from one point of view, creditors. Indeed, there is a traditional maxim that 'the relict and the bairns are heirs among creditors, and creditors among heirs'.[15] That means that (a) as between them and actual creditors, they are treated as beneficiaries, so that their claims are postponed to the claims of creditors but (b) as between them and other beneficiaries they are treated as creditors, in that they have claims for money that must be met before other beneficiaries can receive anything.[16]

27.10   This priority operates in an unqualified manner in testate succession, which is the main focus of this chapter. In testate succession the order is:
  (i)   debts (including taxes);
  (ii) legal rights; and
  (iii) legacies.

---

[12]   See, eg, *Cameron's Trs v McLean* 1917 SC 416.
[13]   For legacies of residue, see **PARA 28.27** below.
[14]   For abatement, see **PARAS 28.35–28.40** below.
[15]   *MacGregor's Exrx v MacGregor's Trs* 1935 SC 13 at 18 per Lord President Clyde.
[16]   'Before' here does not refer to time of payment but to priority of right.

In intestate succession the position is more complicated. There, the order of priority is:
- (i) debts (including taxes);
- (ii) prior rights;
- (iii) relict's right;
- (iv) cohabitant's right;
- (v) legitim; and
- (vi) free estate.

It will be seen that in intestate succession legitim is not only postponed to prior rights (which are in favour of the relict), but is even postponed to the cohabitant's right. In intestate succession it is common for the amount available for legitim to be zero. That leads to a paradox. In testate succession the idea of disinheriting one's children is regarded as so shocking that the law forbids it. But in intestate succession such disinheritance is (except in larger estates) not only permitted but indeed compulsory – by force of the law itself.[17]

RENUNCIATION

27.11   Rights of succession can, like most other rights in private law, be renounced. Legal rights are, in fact, often declined. There are two main reasons. The first is altruism; the second is the opposite. First, altruism. Suppose that Jack is married to Jill. They have two children, Dick and Jane. Jack's testament leaves everything to Jill. Indeed, it is common for one spouse to bequeath everything, or almost everything, to the other. It is likely that Jack and Jill both made testaments at the same time, in mirror terms. Jill dies. Dick and Jane could claim legitim. But that would mean claiming against their own mother. In most cases they would not do this, but would, instead, renounce their legitim. But suppose that Jill was not their mother but their stepmother. In that case they might feel differently.

27.12   The other main reason for renunciation is the doctrine of approbate and reprobate, the rule that one cannot take *both* legal rights *and* a legacy. This doctrine is discussed below.[18]

27.13   If a person who is entitled to legal rights renounces them, this does not benefit anyone who does opt to claim. Alan and Beth are married. They have two children, Carla and Donald. Alan dies, his testament leaving everything to Beth. His net moveable estate is £120,000. Beth renounces her relict's right. Carla renounces legitim. Donald claims legitim. How much does he receive? £20,000, that is, one-half of one-third of the value of the net moveable estate. It is the same sum as he would have received if both Beth and Carla had claimed legal rights. Or suppose that

---

[17]   A relict may be better off in intestacy (because of the priority that prior rights have over legitim), so if a spouse can convert a testate estate into an intestate one, he or she may wish to do so. For this odd idea of 'artificial intestacy', see *Kerr* 1968 SLT (Sh Ct) 61 and **PARA 29.28** below.

[18]   See **PARAS 27.15–27.19** below.

Beth and Donald claim legal rights, but Carla does not. Then Beth would receive £40,000 and Donald would receive £20,000.

27.14 What has just been said is true if the renunciation happens *after* the death. It is also competent to renounce legal rights *before* the death, although nowadays this seldom happens. But if it does happen the rule is different. In that case the renunciation *does* benefit those persons who do claim legal rights. Suppose that Carla renounces before Alan's death. Beth and Donald both claim legal rights. Beth receives £40,000 and Donald also receives £40,000. Or suppose that Beth and Donald both renounce before Alan's death, but Carla claims. Carla then receives £60,000.

APPROBATE AND REPROBATE

27.15 People who die testate usually leave much or all of their estate to their family. So it is common to find that those with legal rights are also legatees. For instance, Claire's testament leaves £10,000 to each of her children, David, Eilidh and Frank, and the rest to her husband Greg. Each of those four persons also has legal rights. Can they take both? Or must they take one or the other? Can they perhaps choose? The law is that they can choose; they cannot take both. If David takes the legacy he must renounce legitim. If he decides to take legitim he must reject the legacy. This rule – that they can choose one or the other but not both – is known by the curious name of 'approbate and reprobate'. To accept the legacy is to 'approbate' the testament; to take legal rights instead is to 'reprobate' the testament. The rule is that you can approbate or you can reprobate but you cannot do both. It is a common law one. There existed certain qualifications to the doctrine, but S(S)A 1964, s 13 put the rule into statutory form, without exceptions.

27.16 Usually it will be obvious whether the legacy or legal rights is worth more. However, occasionally it is not so clear. Suppose that the testator, Tom, provides that his second wife, Wendy, is to have a liferent of the house and his daughter Diana the fee. Diana may hesitate between accepting the fee or claiming legitim. If her stepmother, Wendy, is old and in poor health the better bet will be to take the fee. If Wendy is young and healthy the better bet will be to take legitim. The beneficiary is allowed time to decide.[19] Of course, it must not be assumed (except in examination questions) that people will necessarily decide to maximise what they take.

27.17 Sarah's testament gives a trust liferent of her house to her elder daughter, Tara, and the fee to her younger daughter Ursula. Tara claims legal rights, and therefore forfeits the liferent. At common law the question of whether Ursula would take the fee immediately was involved in some complexity: in certain types of case there could be a 'shadow liferent' and Ursula would take nothing until this shadow liferent ended. The rule is now that whenever a liferent ends, whether by death or

---

[19]   *Stewart v Bruce's Trs* (1898) 25 R 965.

otherwise, the fee vests in the fiar, so that the trustees would convey immediately to Ursula.[20]

27.18   Claiming legal rights means forfeiture of any legacy. But it does not mean the loss of other rights. Nicholas's estate is £240,000, all moveable. He has two children, Oliver and Prunella. He is single. His testament leaves a legacy of £80,000 to Oliver, £80,000 to charity and the residue to Quinten, Nicholas's brother. Prunella is not mentioned in the testament. Quinten predeceases Nicholas. Prunella claims legitim. The legitim fund is £120,000. (Half the value of the moveable estate, as there is no relict.) Prunella takes half of this, ie £60,000. (Not the whole, because Oliver's renunciation of legitim does not benefit her – see above.) Oliver accepts the legacy and so gives up legal rights. The residue is worth £20,000. As the residuary legatee (Quinten) predeceased the testator, this legacy fails to take effect, and so the residue falls into intestacy.[21] The heirs in intestacy are the two children. What happens now?

27.19   *Naismith v Boyes*[22] held that if X accepts a legacy, and if the estate is partially intestate, the doctrine of approbate and reprobate does not bar X from claiming legal rights in relation to the intestate estate. How much? Neither *Naismith* nor later cases entirely clarify this issue, but it seems that Oliver takes half (because he is one of two siblings) of a half (because no relict), i.e. £5,000. Prunella does not put her scoop in again at this stage, because she has already taken all her legitim. What is left is £15,000. That goes equally to the two heirs in intestacy, Oliver and Prunella, under S(S)A 1964, s 2.[23]

27.20   Lastly, claiming legal rights does not prevent someone accepting property under a special destination. So if Jack and Jill own a house with a survivorship destination in the title, and Jill dies, Jack could claim legal rights while at the same time taking Jill's half share of the house.

FOUR MISCONCEPTIONS ABOUT LEGAL RIGHTS

27.21   There are four misconceptions about legal rights. The first is that claiming legal rights means a court action. It does not. Of course, any estate could end up in litigation. But it seldom happens, and there is no more reason why claiming legal rights should mean litigation than any other claim on an estate. The second misconception is that claiming legal rights will convert the estate from a testate one

---

[20]   The modern rule is contained in s 7 of the Succession (Scotland) Act 2016.The provision uses the verb 'terminate', which is arguably not right for the case where the liferent fails from the outset, as in the example. Nevertheless, there Is no doubt that the section is intended to cover that case.
[21]   This is called the *lapse* of a legacy. In certain special cases the legatee's predecease does not cause lapse: see **PARAS 28.43–23.48** below.
[22]   (1899) 1 F (HL) 79. And see *Tindall's Trs v Tindall* 1933 SC 419.
[23]   See **PARAS 29.22–29.26** below.

to an intestate one. It does not.[24] The third is that legitim can be claimed only by younger children, such as those under 16, or that it is in some way a dependency-based right. Legitim exists in favour of adult children just as much as young children. If Mark dies at the age of 95, leaving one child, Naomi, aged 70, Naomi is entitled to legitim. Fourthly, decades of marking examination papers have revealed to us a curious fact: that there are always students who do not grasp that legal rights must *come out of the estate*. That means: less for other beneficiaries.

SOME MORE EXAMPLES

27.22   Jane, who is single, dies leaving heritage worth £100,000 and moveables worth £300,000. She is single and has one son, Kevin. Jane's testament leaves the house to Kevin and the residue to Jane's lover, Larry. Kevin claims legitim (£150,000). That means he must renounce the legacy of the house. Larry takes the whole estate, minus £150,000.

27.23   Walter dies. He is single and has two daughters, Alice and Beth. He had heritage worth £100,000, and moveables worth £300,000. His testament leaves the heritage to Alice and Beth equally and also leaves £100,000 to Alice. The residue is left to Walter's brother, Charles. Beth claims legitim, and thus renounces the legacy. Alice claims the legacy, and thus renounces legitim. The legitim fund is £150,000. Beth takes half of this, £75,000. Alice takes half of the heritage plus £100,000. Charles takes the rest.

27.24   Occasionally legal rights can have a dramatic effect. An example that we came across recently involved a successful Edinburgh businessman, a widower, who had three sons. The estate after tax was worth about £12 million. It was all moveable. His testament left everything to the eldest son. The other two claimed legal rights. The legitim fund was thus about £6 million. The eldest son naturally renounced legitim. The other two received about £2 million each. (Not £3 million, because a renunciation does not enhance what claimants receive.[25]) The first son took the rest, ie about £8 million.

REPRESENTATION IN LEGITIM: *PER STIRPES* AND *PER CAPITA* DIVISION

27.25   If a child has predeceased, leaving children (i.e. grandchildren of the *de cujus*), then those children step into their parent's shoes.[26] Suppose that Alice

---

24   In theory it could happen that a residuary legatee claims legal rights, thus throwing the residue into intestacy. But normally this would not happen, for if the residue is worth *more* than the legal rights, the former will be normally claimed, and if worth *less* than the legal rights, the claiming of legal rights reduces the residue to zero.

25   See **PARA 27.13** above.

26   S(S)A 1964, s 11.

has two children, Brenda and Charles. Brenda has two children, David and Ellen. Charles has one, Fraser. Brenda dies on 1 March. Alice dies on 3 March. The legitim fund is £60,000. Charles takes £30,000 and David and Ellen take £15,000 each. (Assuming that all claim legitim.) David and Ellen are said to *represent* their mother. (Representation also applies in intestate succession.[27])

27.26   Why is the legitim fund divided in this way, and not £20,000 to each of the three people entitled? Well, it does not have to be done that way. It depends. The type of division just illustrated is a division *per stirpes*.[28] The opposite method would be a division *per capita*.[29] The rule is this: if all the claimants are of equal propinquity (nearness of kinship) to the deceased then the division is *per capita*, but if of unequal propinquity the division is *per stirpes*. In the example just given, the claimants were of unequal propinquity, because Charles was the child of the deceased, but David and Ellen were the grandchildren. Change the facts a little and suppose that Charles, as well as Brenda, had died before Alice. Then there would have been three legitim claimants: David, Ellen and Fraser. The division would have been *per capita* and so each would have received £20,000. (These rules about representation also apply to intestate succession rights.[30])

27.27   There is representation in legitim but not in the relict's right. Arthur and Guinevere are married. Guinevere dies on Monday, leaving one child, Henry, from a previous relationship. On Tuesday, Arthur dies. Henry cannot claim the relict's right that his mother would have had if the dates of death had been reversed.

REPRESENTATION: WHEN DOES IT APPLY?

27.28   At the risk of repetition, certain points about representation are worth emphasising. Representation is possible for (i) legitim and (ii) intestate succession rights. It is not possible for (i) legacies or (ii) prior rights or (iii) relict's right or (iv) cohabitant's claim. But for legacies, something similar to representation sometimes applies.[31]

COLLATIO INTER LIBEROS

27.29   Sometimes a potential legitim claimant will have been given a substantial gift by the deceased during the latter's life. The law may regard this as a 'collatable advance', a sort of pre-payment of legitim, and if so it must be brought into account, to achieve fairness as between the various legitim claimants. This is the doctrine of

---

27   See **CHAPTER 29** below. See further M Meston 'Representation in Succession' 1995 *SLPQ* 83.
28   The Latin word *stirps* (plural *stirpes*) means a stock, or family.
29   The Latin word *caput* (plural *capita*) means a head.
30   See **PARA 29.26** below.
31   See **PARA 28.46** below.

collatio inter liberos.[32] Suppose that Jack dies, leaving a relict, Rebecca, and three sons, Tom Dick and Harry. There is heritable property of £300,000 and moveable property of £180,000. He leaves the heritable property to Rebecca and everything else to charity. The sons claim legitim. Tom had a collatable advance of £12,000. To claim legitim Tom must notionally add this to the legitim fund. The notional legitim fund is therefore £60,000 + £12,000 = £72,000. Thus, Dick and Harry take £24,000 each, and Tom takes £24,000 less £12,000 = £12,000. The charity receives the rest of Jack's estate.

27.30 One difficulty with applying the doctrine is knowing what counts as a collatable advance. The typical case in the earlier authorities was the 'tocher' – a settlement given on marriage. Only gifts of moveables count[33] and, according to Stair, only money gifts count.[34] Any provision made by virtue of the parent's alimentary obligations is excluded from collation.

27.31 If we change the figures in the example, Tom could end up worse off. For example, suppose that the collatable advance was not £12,000 but £60,000. If that is added to the legitim fund, the result is £120,000. Divided three ways, each brother would be due £40,000. But since Tom would have paid in £60,000, he would suffer a net loss of £20,000. But that does not happen, because there is an additional rule that *a person who opts not to claim legitim does not have to collate.* So Tom would be free to refuse legitim. In that case he would not collate. The legitim fund would remain £60,000. Dick and Harry would each take a third = £20,000 each. (Only a third: as was seen above, if someone rejects legal rights, that does not benefit other legal rights claimants.) Tom will receive nothing from his father's estate – but he will keep the £60,000 that his father gave him.

27.32 If there is only one legitim claimant, there is no collation. Take this case. Maud's estate is £120,000, all moveable. She is single and has two children, Natasha and Olivia. Maud's testament leaves £20,000 to Natasha and £60,000 to Olivia, and the residue to charity. Natasha renounces the legacy and claims legitim. Olivia renounces legitim and claims the legacy. The legitim fund is £60,000, so Natasha takes £30,000. Now, suppose that she had had a collatable advance of £12,000. Does this mean that the legitim fund is £72,000, so that Natasha receives half of that (£36,000) minus the advance = only £24,000? The answer is 'no': being the sole legitim claimant, she does not collate. (She is the sole claimant because it is in Olivia's interests to accept the legacy.) Natasha receives £30,000 legitim and keeps the £12,000 that she received earlier.[35]

---

[32] Latin, meaning 'collation between the children'.
[33] *Duke of Buccleuch v Earl of Tweeddale* (1677) Mor 2369.
[34] Stair III, 8, 45.
[35] *Coat's Trs v Coats* 1914 SC 744.

CIRCUMVENTING LEGAL RIGHTS

27.33   Legal rights cannot be avoided but sometimes their extent can be minimised by forward planning. Sheila has a husband. Tom, and two daughters, Una and Vera. She wishes to disinherit Tom and Vera leaving everything to Una. She cannot do this absolutely. But she can reduce the value of her moveable estate. For instance, she could transfer assets into a trust, with the trustees holding for her in liferent and for Una in fee. Or she could sell investments and use the money to buy an annuity. Or, even more simply, she could give moveable assets to Una. In many legal systems, there is some form of clawback, so that legal rights cannot be defeated. That is not the law here.[36]

27.34   Another possibility would be to maximise her heritable estate. For instance, suppose that she has stock market investments worth £500,000. She could sell those and use the proceeds to buy flats as an investment. The flats, unlike the stock market investments, would not be subject to legal rights. (But if she bought the flats in the name of a company, the trick would not work, because what would be in her patrimony would not be the flats themselves but her shares in her company, and shares are moveable.)

27.35   Yet another method which, however, is possible only in certain types of case, is 'artificial intestacy'.[37]

SOME COMPARATIVE LAW: ENGLAND, FRANCE, GERMANY

27.36   Most legal systems round the world have legal rights on a fixed basis, but the details vary. We mention two: France and Germany. In France, legitim depends on the number of children (if any): one half of the whole estate if there is one child, two-thirds of the whole estate if there are two children, three-quarters of the whole estate if there are three children, and so on.[38] The relict is not protected by legal rights, but may be by the matrimonial property regime, In Germany defined family members (including the relict) are entitled to 50% of what they would have received in an intestacy.[39] Many legal systems (but here Scotland is an exception) allow (depending on the precise circumstances) clawback where there were *inter vivos* gifts that have had a prejudicial effect on the legal rights.[40]

---

[36]   See, eg, Hutton's Trs v Hutton's Trs 1916 SC 860.
[37]   See **PARA 29.28** below.
[38]   'Les libéralités … par testament, ne pourrant excéder la moitié des biens du disposant, s'il ne laisse à son décès qu'un enfant; le tiers, s'il laisse deux enfants; le quart, s'il en laisse trois ou un plus grand nombre….' (Cc art 913.)
[39]   'Ist ein Abkömmling des Erblassers durch Verfügung von Todes wegen von der Erbfolge ausgeschlossen, so kann er von dem Erben den Pflichtteil verlangen. Der Pflichtteil besteht in der Hälfte des Wertes des gesetzlichen Erbteils. Das gleiche Recht steht den Eltern und dem Ehegatten.' (BGB § 2303.) This approach influenced the Scottish Law Commission, Report on Succession (Scot Law Com No 215, 2009).
[40]   See, eg, Cc art 918 ff; BGB, § 2325 ff.

27.37   In the legal systems derived from English law legal rights originally did not exist, but some systems have introduced judicial discretion, so that, for instance, a disinherited child or relict can ask the court for a discretionary award, an idea first introduced in New Zealand. The English rules, too long to quote here, are in the Inheritance (Provision for Family and Dependants) Act 1975. At its best, this enables flexible justice to be done, as opposed to the fixed rules to be found in the civilian systems, and in Scotland. But there are drawbacks too: it encourages family disputes and increases costs.[41] It has never attracted much support in Scotland.

LITERATURE

27.38   Good accounts can be found in Hiram *Succession* ch 3 and Macdonald *Succession* paras 4.34–4.69. For other systems, see eg Anderson, M (ed) *The Law of Succession; Testamentary Freedom*: European Perspectives (2011) and R Zimmermann (ed) *Freedom of Testation/Testierfreiheit* (2012).

---

[41]   See, eg, Lord Wilberforce's comments at HL Deb 20 March 1975 vol 358 c 932 ff: http://hansard. millbanksystems.com/lords/1975/mar/20/inheritance-provision-for-family-and.

Chapter 28

Testate succession

TESTAMENTS

Introduction

28.1 A will or testament[1] is a document saying what is to happen to the granter's estate on death.[2] Many people make their own ('home made wills'). Drafting wills is a standard part of the business of many law firms. Non-lawyer 'will writers' are a modern phenomenon.[3] Here is an example of the sort of thing a solicitor might draft for a client.

'I ALEXANDER ROBERTSON GILLIES, born on third February nineteen hundred and thirty eight,[4] residing at fifty-four Middleton Street Jedburgh, TD8 7YY, being desirous of settling the succession to my means and estate after my decease[5] HEREBY NOMINATE and APPOINT[6] my son THOMAS WOODHEAD GILLIES, residing at 50 Macaulay Place, Berwick-upon-Tweed, and HUGO PONTIFEX SAGAMORE, Writer to the Signet, 88 Scotland Street, Edinburgh, and the survivor and acceptor of them, to be my executors and trustees; and I ASSIGN DISPONE AND CONVEY[7] to them my whole means and estate heritable and moveable real and personal of whatever nature and wherever situated which shall belong to me at the time of my death including without prejudice to the foregoing generality all means and estate held or which may then be held by me under special destinations and all means and estate of which I may have or may

---

[1]   The traditional Scottish term is 'testament' but 'will' is now the word used by all nonlawyers and most lawyers too, though some – especially some judges – are conservative. In English law there is a distinction (not always observed in practice) between testaments and wills: a 'testament' deals with personal property and a 'will' with real property. (In England, 'personal' means, roughly, moveable, and 'real' means, roughly, immoveable.) Hence a document dealing with both is a 'will and testament'. This expression is sometimes copied in Scotland. 'Last will' comes from Latin *ultima voluntas*.

[2]   A 'trust disposition and settlement' is a testament that contains a clause conveying the estate to the executors as trustees for the beneficiaries. There is in modern law no difference between this and an ordinary testament.

[3]   Under the Legal Services (Scotland) Act 2010, ss 101ff there is a regulatory regime, but it has never been brought into force.

[4]   Inclusion of date of birth is in fact unusual.

[5]   The dozen or so preceding words demonstrate 'testamentary intent'. Such intent can be inferred from a document as a whole but it is usual to have express words.

[6]   The nomination of an executor (or joint executors) is normal. But a testament can be valid without such a nomination.

[7]   This conveyance of the estate to the executors is not necessary but it is common, and for certain purposes can be useful.

then have power of disposal or appointment;[8] But these presents are granted for the following purposes only, namely:– (In the first place) for payment of my debts and funeral expenses and the expenses of administering the executry hereby created; (In the second place) for payment or making over of the following legacies, that is to say (primo) to the Scottish Association for Mental Health, Brunswick House, 51 Wilson Street, Glasgow, G1 1UZ, the sum of seven thousand pounds; (secundo) to the Church of Scotland, 121 George Street, Edinburgh, EH2 4YN the sum of six thousand pounds; (tertio) to the National Trust for Scotland, Hermiston Quay, 5 Cultins Road, Edinburgh EH11 4DF the sum of five thousand pounds; (quarto) to my nephew Oliver St John of 1 Hope Street, Durham, all my books;[9] (quinto) to my god-daughter Eleanor Duplessis of 22 Pym Street, Brechin, the sum of ten thousand pounds; (In the third place)[10] to pay and make over the whole residue of my estate to my daughter Janet Mary Gillies or Godwin of 21 St Andrew Square, Peebles, and to my said son Thomas Woodhead Gillies equally between them; DECLARING that should any of the beneficiaries hereunder predecease me leaving lawful issue I direct my executors to pay and make over to such issue *per stirpes*[11] the legacy or share of my estate which his or her parent would have taken; FURTHER DECLARING that in the event of any beneficiary hereunder being under legal incapacity by means of non-age or by law otherwise incapacitated my executors shall pay and make over the legacy or share of my estate to which such beneficiary is entitled to his or her legal representative or guardian or guardians or to any other person who may be willing to act as guardian although not legally appointed, the receipt and discharge of such legal representative or guardian or guardians (legal or otherwise) being a full and sufficient discharge to my executors; WITH POWER to my executors to appoint one of their number to act as solicitors in the executry hereby created at the usual professional remuneration;[12] And I desire that my body may be cremated;[13] And I revoke all former testamentary writings executed by me:[14] IN WITNESS WHEREOF I have subscribed these presents[15] typewritten on this and the preceding page at Edinburgh on the twenty-fourth day of January in the year two thousand and seventeen in the presence of Suzanne Elvenstone of 44 Scotland Street, Edinburgh.

S Elvenstone, witness   *Alex. R. Gillies'*

8	This phrase ('my whole means and estate … power of disposal or appointment') is typical, though of course variations exist. Its length exceeds its substantive content. Part of the phrase is in fact invalid, because destinations cannot be affected by mere general words: see S(S)A 1964 s 30, discussed in **CHAPTER 30** below.
9	This legacy of books is a special legacy, ie a legacy of identifiable assets. The legacies of money are general legacies.
10	Here we come to the legacy of the residue.
11	For the meaning of this term see **CHAPTER 27** above.
12	The default rule is that executors and trustees cannot charge for their services. But they can do so if expressly permitted. A solicitor will be unlikely to accept office unless able to charge.
13	A testator cannot insist on cremation, though, conversely, can veto it.
14	The revocatory clause. It is not essential, but its absence can occasionally cause difficulties.
15	'These presents' = this deed.

Testamentary capacity

28.2   At common law girls attained testamentary capacity at 12 and boys at 14. This was changed to 12 for both.[16] Of course, few young people make wills. A 2006 study gave the percentage of those in each age group who had made a will:[17]

18–24	25–34	35–44	45–54	55–64	65+
4%	14%	30%	40%	52%	69%

28.3   Loss of general capacity, for instance by reason of senility, will mean loss of testamentary capacity. This can be unfortunate. Mary makes a will when she is 70. When she is 80 she becomes senile. She dies when she is 90. By that time the provisions of her testament may have become inappropriate. But they cannot now be changed. That was, at least, the law, and may still be the law. But there have been one or two cases in which the sheriff court has exercised testamentary power on behalf of an incapax.[18] The soundness of these decisions is uncertain.

Execution

28.4   'The rule is inflexible – no subscription, no will'.[19] That has always been the law and remains so. The details of the law on execution are dealt with elsewhere.[20] The one speciality for testaments is that while signature at the end is sufficient for *validity*, for *probativity* not only must there be a witness but the granter (but not the witness) must sign *each sheet*.[21] Forgery is a particular danger because the main potential challenger is dead when the document comes to light. If a testament is improbative, there is a special affidavit procedure for establishing that it was validly executed.[22] In practice courts are lenient towards home-made testaments. Thus 'Connie' and 'Mum' have both been upheld as valid subscriptions.[23] But there are limits to this lenience. In *McLay v Farrell*,[24] Jane McLay left this:

---

[16]   Age of Legal Capacity (Scotland) Act 1991, s 2(2).
[17]   S O'Neill *Wills and Awareness of Inheritance Rights in Scotland* (Scottish Consumer Council, 2006).
[18]   *G Applicant* 2009 SLT (Sh Ct) 122; *T Applicant* 2005 SLT (Sh Ct) 97; *H Applicant* 2011 SLT (Sh Ct) 178.
[19]   *Foley v Costello* (1904) 6 F 365 per Lord Trayner, For the current law see RoW(S)A 1995 s 1(2)(c).
[20]   See **CHAPTER 31** below. For the history, see Kenneth Reid's chapter in K G C Reid, M J de Waal and R Zimmermann (eds), *Comparative Succession Law: Volume I: Testamentary Formalities* (2011).
[21]   RoW(S)A 1995, s 3(2).
[22]   RoW(S)A 1995, s 4. In practice this is simply done as part of the application for confirmation: see RoW(S)A 1995, s 4(4).
[23]   *Draper v Thomason* 1954 SC 136; *Rhodes v Peterson* 1972 SLT 98. These cases pre-date RoW(S) A 1995 but would have been decided the same way under the current law. See RoW(S)A 1995, s 7. See also **PARA 28.10** below.
[24]   1950 SC 149.

'*I leave to*
Lizzie McLay Farrell £50
C Herken £50
Robert Farrell £20
Jane McLay
All to Anne McLay'

28.5 Then, as now, the granter's signature had to be at the end. So the last line (which perhaps meant that the residue[25] was to go to Anne McLay) could not be given effect.

28.6 The international private law is regulated by the Wills Act 1963, which says that 'a will shall be treated as properly executed if its execution conformed to the internal law in force in the territory where it was executed, or in the territory where, at the time of its execution or of the testator's death, he was domiciled or had his habitual residence, or in a state of which, at either of those times, he was a national'.[26]

Codicils, adoption and execution on the testator's behalf

28.7 A 'codicil' is a later document that varies a testament. The rules for execution are the same. In practice it can be difficult working out what the combined effect is supposed to be, and so solicitors usually recommend making a new will rather than using a codicil.[27]

28.8 The concept of the 'adoption' of one document by another is a general one in the law of execution of deeds.[28] A striking example from the law of succession is *Davidson v Convy*,[29] where the deceased left an envelope with 'My will: Agnes Bess Sim' on it. Inside there was a sheet of paper of a testamentary nature but it was unsigned. It was held, perhaps generously, that the envelope was a validly executed testament which adopted the sheet of paper.

28.9 Finally, mention should be made of the testament being executed on behalf of the testator.[30] This is discussed elsewhere[31] but is worth mentioning here because testaments are often made by the dying, and the dying are sometimes unable to use a pen.

---

[25] The residue means the rest of the estate. A legacy of residue may, according to circumstances, be very little, or be the bulk of the estate.
[26] Wills Act 1963, s 1. Sections 27 and 28 of the Administration of Justice Act 1982 are also relevant but have never been brought into force.
[27] In *Burns' Trs v McKenna* 1940 SC 489 the trustee left a testament followed by 49 codicils.
[28] Another example is under the pre-RoW(S)A 1995 law, when documents were 'adopted as holograph'.
[29] 2003 SLT 650.
[30] RoW(S)A 1995, s 9.
[31] See **PARA 31.17** below.

Concluded testamentary intent

28.10   To be valid, a juridical act needs to be based on intention. In most areas of law, juridical acts involve some overt action involving at least one other person, such as the communication of a contractual offer, or getting married, or registering a title in the Land Register. The overt action is powerful (albeit not conclusive) evidence of intention. But a testament is not effected by communication or delivery or registration. It can sit in the testator's desk until death. So, the question of intention is established mainly from the four corners of the document itself. How does one distinguish a true testament from mere musings or provisional thoughts? (Paper musings are very common.) Usually it is obvious.[32] Signature is a strong indicator of intent. But sometimes there can be doubt. The document must exhibit 'concluded testamentary intent' if it is to receive effect, but judging this is not an exact science. In *Draper v Thomason*[33] Constance Tupper wrote a letter to her sister, with the following in it:

> ' ... By the way, while I'm speaking of dying! should anything happen to me (which it will one day) I haven't made a will but everything I have is for Billy, knowing he will do the right thing. Connie.'

It was held that this exhibited concluded testamentary effect, so that the letter was a valid testament. In another case[34] Evelyn Peterson wrote a letter to her daughter:

> 'Dearest Dorothy ... I have been thinking a lot about you recently and I am concerned about your future ... As the boys have their own houses ... I want you to have 63 Merchieston and all the contents ... when I am gone so that I can rest in peace in the knowledge that you are not homeless ... I am not going to say anything to John or Angus about this ... I feel better having at least got this down on paper. Do not lose this letter ... lots of love, Mum.'

It was held that the letter exhibited concluded testamentary intent. Letters to friends or relations are one common type of case. Another is the letter to the solicitor asking that a testament be drawn up in certain terms, with the client dying before this is done. Here is an example, where the client is asking for the existing testament to be changed in certain ways:[35]

> 'I should like if the sum of money left to St Mary's on the Rock was doubled - also that left to Mr David Alexander to be doubled. If the residue of my estate to be divided between my four cousins exceed 5000 pounds I should like that excess amount to be divided between the two charities in my will. I do hope that this can be done. I have been having some pain of late and I just wanted to note this down. E R Jamieson 22.3.80.'

[32]   See, for instance, the formal testament given in **PARA 28.1** above.
[33]   1954 SC 136.
[34]   *Rhodes v Peterson* 1972 SLT 98.
[35]   *Jamieson's Exrs* 1982 SC 1.

It was held that a letter to a solicitor is from its nature provisional: it looks forward to a formal deed. Accordingly, it cannot itself have testamentary effect.[36] In another case the deceased had kept notebooks. On one page was the following:[37]

20/01/12

- Nearly 51?

- Life is s*** [38] *at this time!!!*

*Please remember. If Anne is still alive, I want her to have my wealthy remains - the house, pension, savings and everything else...
I hope my family accept this...

IT IS MY WISH.

Melanie Gibson

At first instance it was held that this did not display concluded testamentary intent, but that decision was reversed on appeal.

Where is the testament?

28.11   If a testament is drafted by a law firm, it is usual for the firm to keep it in its fireproof safe, giving the client a copy. But sometimes testators keep the document themselves, and this is usually the case for 'home-made' wills. The family or friends will – hopefully – find it after the death.[39] But if the will cannot be found that may be because it was deliberately destroyed by the testator. In that case it can never take effect.

Proving the tenor

28.12   If a will cannot be found, and its terms are known – typically because there is a copy – then the deed can be established by an action of 'proving the tenor'. (This action is available to establish any type of lost document, not only testaments. A curious case was *Jollie v Lennie*,[40] where the following fragmentary pencil-written document existed in the possession of one of the deceased's children. Among the missing parts were the date (a crucial point because she had executed another will, and the question was which one was the last) and the surname, because Margaret Watt Dobie had been married twice, first to a Mr Jollie and then to a Mr Lennie, and

---

[36]   There have been a number of such cases. *Munro v Coutts* (1813) 1 Dow 437 is still perhaps the leading one. A decision that went the other way is *Barker's Exrs v Scottish Rights of Way Society Ltd* 1996 SC 396.
[37]   2015 SLT (Sh Ct) 176.
[38]   We quote the SLT report. The deceased in fact wrote the four-letter word in full.
[39]   And if they don't like what they read, there is the possibility that they may quietly destroy it.
[40]   [2014] CSOH 45.

the choice of surname would have been evidence as to date. An action to prove the tenor, including the date asserted by the pursuer, was successful.

> '*To whom it may… I, Margaret Watt… hereby make my… Testimony. To my daughter Les… Anne Jollie + my son Malcolm Alexander Jollie equal shares of any monies which I hold. To my daughter Lesley I bequeath my platinum wedding band … stoned diamond + white gold… also my 3 stoned twist diamond ring. To Malcolm I bequeath my cultured pearl necklace and all gold chain necklaces that I have including a gold St Christopher + horn of plenty+ my grandmother's gold wedding ring. To Malcolm my Heriots Plaque and pen stool + 2 … My share of the house to be passed to my children… ley + Malcolm whosoever doesnt marry shall stay in it until they do or die… the man I was married to for almost… him to care for the two children he gave … + I hope that he can give them all the …. and time he can … he does … any of his relatives to … oved children. He I hope will … to his death remembering that… because of him I have no wish… anymore. I can never forgive him for what he has put me and my children through. I gave him all I had, all my love + now my life and he wasn't worth it. I pray to God my children will be happy, they are too … at present but I feel I have been … + cannot allow myself to destroy my children… mercy and forgive me but I cannot… being loved and wanted each day I am … ldren I love them so… make them happy… to be with my… father + my beloved family who I loved so dea … signed Margaret Watt…*'

How long does a testament last?

28.13 If Silas makes a will when he is 22, and dies aged 102, it is still valid and will take effect, unless he had revoked it. In other words: time does not run against a will. But a will may become 'stale' in the sense that it has ceased, in part or in whole, to be appropriate. Over the years there will be the usual evolutions and vicissitudes of human life, marriages and divorces, births and deaths, friendships gained and lost, money and property gained and lost, not to mention the periodical changes of law, including tax law. Law firms recommend to their clients to review their wills from time to time: the advice is wise.

Revocation

28.14

> 'All is ambulatory during the defunct's life, and may be taken away expressly or implicitly, by posterior or derogatory deeds, unless the defunct by obliged by contract inter vivos, not to alter the same'

as Stair puts it.[41] A testament does not become live until the granter ceases to be so, so that alteration or complete revocation is always competent. (The exception – as Stair says – is if the testator has promised to someone to give them a legacy.[42]) If the testator wishes to alter the will it is usual to revoke it and replace it by a new one. The alternative is a codicil. Or a testator could simply revoke a will without replacing it. If death then happens, the result is intestacy.

28.15 The usual method of revocation is destruction, that is by physically destroying the testament. Suppose that when a person dies no testament can be found, even though it is known that there was one. Does that mean that it was destroyed with the intention of revocation (*animo revocandi*), or might it be that the document has simply been mislaid? This is an evidential question. But if the testament was in the possession of the testator at the time of death, but cannot now be found, the presumption is that it was destroyed deliberately.[43]

28.16 If a testament is drawn up by a solicitor it will in practice always have a clause revoking any previous testament, so that any earlier one will be revoked even if it is not destroyed. Home-made testaments often lack a revocatory clause. If there exists an earlier unrevoked testament, both deeds take effect, but in so far as there is inconsistency the later one prevails, ie the earlier one is revoked to the extent of the inconsistency. For instance, in *Duthie's Trs v Taylor*[44] the first testament contained various pecuniary and special legacies[45] and a legacy of the residue. The later one, which contained no clause of revocation, contained various other pecuniary and special legacies, to some extent inconsistent with the earlier ones, but no legacy of residue. It was held that the later testament had priority, but the earlier remained in force except in so far as there was an inconsistency, so that the legacy of residue in the earlier one was still effective. If the later one deals with the whole estate (as would be normal) the effect is that the earlier, though formally unrevoked, is in effect revoked.

28.17 What if testament 1 is revoked by testament 2 and testament 2 is itself revoked? Does testament 1 revive? Usually the answer to this question does not matter, because the revocation of testament 2 will normally have been done by testament 3 which will typically contain a general revocatory clause (thus killing off everything earlier) and moreover will typically dispose of the whole estate, so that even if any earlier testament was still live, it would be implicitly revoked. But occasionally the answer to the question does matter. At common law, the answer was that testament 1 could revive unless it had been revoked by destruction. The modern law is that testament 1 cannot revive: its revocation by testament 2 is irreversible.[46]

---

41   Stair III, 8, 33.
42   See, eg, *Paterson v Paterson* (1893) 20 R 484. And see D Hutchison 'Succession Agreements in South African and Scots Law' in K Reid, M De Waal and R Zimmermann (eds) *Exploring the Law of Succession* (2007).
43   *Clyde v Clyde* 1958 SC 343.
44   1986 SLT 142.
45   A pecuniary legacy is a legacy of a sum of money and a special legacy is a legacy of a thing, such as a house.
46   S(S)A 2016 s 5.

This rule can apply in a number of types of case. Here is one. Theresa makes a will leaving everything to Ulrich. Later she makes a will leaving everything to Vera, and expressly revoking the first will. Finally she tears up the second will, and thereafter dies. The terms of the second will are known (eg because of a photocopy). At common law the first will would take effect. Under modern law she dies intestate. (The result would have been the same even if the second testament had not contained an express clause of revocation, because by leaving everything to Vera she implicitly revoked the first.)

28.18 Under the doctrine of *conditio si testator sine liberis decesserit*,[47] if a child is born to the testator after the testament has been made, the testament is voidable at the instance of that child.[48] The doctrine is subject to certain qualifications and exceptions.[49] In practice it is often overlooked.

Reduction

28.19 Sometimes suspicion surrounds the making of a testament. If so, it may be challenged by an action of reduction. As with other deeds, the action may be based on the assertion that the testament is an absolute nullity (for instance because of forgery[50] or lack of capacity[51]), or on the assertion that it is valid but voidable, for instance because of facility and circumvention[52] or undue influence. A typical example is where an elderly person, X, has been cared for mainly by Y, and on X's death the testament is found to leave everything or almost everything to Y. Is this a case of simple and reasonable gratitude or has Y taken unfair advantage?

---

47 The Latin means 'the condition that the testator dies without children'. This is hard to connect with the doctrine. (The expression is also used, with equal oddity, in the recently-abolished doctrine of the *conditio si institutus sine liberis decesserit*. See **PARA 28.46** below.) See further W M Gordon 'The *conditiones si sine liberis decesserit*' 1969 *JR* 108, R R M Paisley The Mechanics and Operation of the *Conditio si Testator sine Liberis Decesserit* in Scots law." 2014 JR 187 and R R M Paisley 'The Rationale and Fundamental Structure of the *Conditio Si Testator Sine Liberis Decesserit* in Scots Law' in A R C Simpson, S C Styles, E West and A Wilson (eds) *Continuity, Change and Pragmatism in the Law: Essays in Memory of Professor Angelo Forte* (2016).

48 The *post natus* (the 'after-born').

49 *Stuart Gordon v Stuart Gordon* (1899) 1 F 1005; *Milligan's JF v Milligan* 1910 SC 5; *Stevenson's Trs v Stevenson* 1932 SC 657; *Elder's Trs v Elder* (1894) 21 R 704, (1895) 22 R 505; *Nicolson v Nicolson's Tutrix* 1922 SC 649; *Greenan v Courtney* 2007 SLT 355.

50 Forgery is far from unknown. It was the forgery of a patient's will that led to the downfall of multiple murderer Harold Shipman. See B Whittle *Prescription For Murder* (2000). For a fairly typical forgery case see *Nicol's Legal Representative v Nicol* [2012] CSOH 115. Usually the allegation of forgery relates to just one (alleged) will. But in *Rafique v Ashraf* [2013] CSOH 34 there were two wills and half of the family said that will 1 was a forgery and that will 2 was valid, while the other half said that will 2 was a forgery and that will 1 was valid.

51 See, eg, *Boyle v Boyle's Exr* 1999 SC 479, a classic case where someone had gained influence over an old person and had induced her to sign a will making him her executor and sole beneficiary, the will then being challenged by her children. In some cases mental capacity may not be clear-cut. For a good illustration see an English case, *Burns v Burns* [2016] EWCA Civ 37.

52 See, eg, *McDougal v McDougal's Trs* 1931 SC 102; *West's Trs v West* 1980 SLT 6; *Pascoe-Watson v Brock's Executor* 1998 SLT 40. In *Boyle v Boyle's Exr* (previous footnote) it was held that even if the testator had been capax the will would have been reduced for facility and circumvention.

Solicitor's duty of care to potential legatees?

28.20   In *Holmes v Bank of Scotland*[53] Mary Davidson wrote to her bank to ask them to prepare a new will in favour of her nephew and niece. About two weeks later, she died. The new will was not ready by then. The nephew and niece sued the bank for the amount they would have received if the new will had been prepared and signed, averring that the bank owed them a duty of care which they had breached by their delay. The action was held relevant.[54] It may be wondered whether the law is coherent. Either (a) the letter to the bank disclosed concluded testamentary intent or (b) it did not. If it did, then the letter should have been accorded testamentary effect, so that the whole basis of the claim against the bank would disappear, because the pursuers would have inherited as the letter directed. But if it did not, then the bank could not be charged with having failed to give effect to the deceased's wishes, because the deceased had not finally decided what she wished to happen.

Will substitutes

28.21   There are various alternatives to a testament for ensuring that on X's death Y will have some asset.[55] Julius owns a house and wishes Olivia to have it when he dies. He could dispone it to her with a reservation of a liferent.[56] Of course, the effect is not precisely the same as a legacy to Olivia. In the case of a legacy Julius would still be the owner when he dies, and moreover a legacy is revocable. The same idea could be effected through a trust: Julius dispones to a trustee, who holds for Julius while he lives and then for Olivia. Indeed, in wealthier families assets are often held in trust. Another possibility was formerly the *donatio mortis causa*, in which an asset could be transferred by X to Y, subject to the condition that if at any time X so wished, Y would transfer it back, and that if X died without having demanded it back, Y would keep it. But this has now been abolished.[57] Yet another possibility is the special destination.[58]

SUBSTANTIVE TESTATE SUCCESSION

Introduction

28.22   If there is a valid testament, the estate is distributed according to its provisions,[59] subject always to (a) debts[60] and (b) legal rights.[61] The general idea

---

[53]   2002 SLT 544.
[54]   Following English law: *White v Jones* [1995] 1 AC 207.
[55]   See Macdonald, *Succession* ch 5; D Carr 'Will-substitutes In Scotland' in A Braun and A Röthel (eds) *Passing Wealth on Death* (2016).
[56]   See **CHAPTER 22** above.
[57]   S(S)A 2016, s 25.
[58]   See **CHAPTER 30** below.
[59]   Assuming that the legatees wish to accept. No legatee can be compelled to accept a legacy, and occasionally legacies are indeed rejected.
[60]   See **PARAS 26.35–26.40** above.
[61]   See **CHAPTER 27** above.

of testate succession is thus straightforward. But there are many detailed points of difficulty.

Types of legacy

28.23 A legacy – also called a bequest – is a provision in a testament conferring some benefit on the beneficiary (the legatee). How many kinds of legacy there are depends on how they are classified.

(a) General legacies

28.24 A 'general legacy' is a legacy of a certain quantity[62] of a certain type of thing. For example, a legacy of 'one hundred grammes of pure gold' would be a general legacy. A 'pecuniary legacy' is a sub-type of general legacy. It is a legacy of money, such as a legacy of £10,000. The pecuniary legacy is the only type of general legacy that is ever encountered in practice. A pecuniary legacy's validity does not depend on the testator having liquid funds. Suppose that Tom leaves £15,000 to Ann and everything else to Bob. His estate consists of land worth £100,000 and a bank account with £10,000 in it. Ann will be paid the full £15,000. The executor will have to sell the land. Bob will be paid £95,000 from the sale of the land.

(b) Special legacies

28.25 A 'special legacy' is a legacy of a particular asset, or an identifiable set of assets, such as a house, or a car, or all the testator's books, or the testator's shares in Royal Bank of Scotland plc. A special legacy can be of a share of an asset: thus a special legacy might leave a half-share of a house to one person and the other half to another. A special legacy does not have to be of corporeal property. Suppose that Ant owes Bee £10,000. Bee could leave this as a legacy to Ladybird, so that Ant would have to pay the debt to Ladybird. This is not a pecuniary legacy but a special legacy.

(c) Universal legacies

28.26 A 'universal legacy' is where the testator leaves his or her entire estate in a single legacy, such as 'everything to my daughter Jane'.

(d) Residuary legacies

28.27 A 'residuary legacy' is a legacy of everything that remains (if anything *does* remain) after all other claims on the estate have been met. Any testament, other than

---

[62] A *legatum quantitatis* (see, eg, Erskine 3,9,11).

one with a universal legacy, should have a residuary legacy. Home-made wills often lack one.

28.28   Theodore leaves his house to Ursula, £50,000 to Vernon, and everything else to Wendy and Yvonne equally. The first legacy is a special legacy, the second legacy is a general (and pecuniary) legacy and the third legacy is a residuary legacy. Sometimes the residuary legacy will take the lion's share of the estate, and sometimes little or even nothing. So if Theodore had investments worth £10,000,000, Wendy and Yvonne do well. If his estate, apart from the house, is worth just £75,000, they do badly.

(e)   Demonstrative legacies

28.29   Last, and least important, is the 'demonstrative legacy', which is perhaps best classified as a sub-type of pecuniary legacy. It is a legacy of a certain amount of money to be taken from a particular source, such as '£2,000 to be taken from my account with Bank of Scotland'. If the identified source turns out to be insufficient, the question is then whether it should be topped up from other assets.[63]

Conditions in legacies

28.30   Legacies may be conditional. If a condition is contrary to good morals (*contra bonos mores*) it is void.[64] Only the condition is void, not the legacy.[65] For example, in *Fraser v Rose*[66] a legacy was left on condition that the legatee did not live with her mother. The condition was held to be *pro non scripto*, (as if not written) so the legatee took the legacy free of the condition.

Invalid legacies

28.31   Occasionally a legacy is held invalid because of uncertainty or because it confers no human benefit. This issue is discussed in **CHAPTER 24**.[67] But uncertainty may, depending on the circumstances, be solved through the 'rectification' process described below.[68]

---

[63]   *Reid's Trs v Dawson* 1915 SC (HL) 47.

[64]   See J Chalmers 'Testamentary Conditions and Public Policy' in K G C Reid, M J de Waal and R Zimmermann (eds) *Exploring the Law of Succession* (2007) 99–113.

[65]   See, eg, *Fraser v Rose* (1849) 11 D 1466; *Grant's Trs v Grant* (1898) 25 R 929; *Balfour's Trs v Johnston* 1936 SC 137. The law is the same as for conditions relating to beneficial interests in trusts. See Wilson and Duncan *Trusts* paras 7-22–7-26.

[66]   (1849) 11 D 1466. See also *Grant's Trs v Grant* (1898) 25 R 929 and *Balfour's Trs v Johnston* 1936 SC 137. The law is the same as for conditions relating to beneficial interests in trusts. See Wilson and Duncan *Trusts* paras 7-22–76.

[67]   See **PARAS 24.12–24.14** above.

[68]   See **PARA 27.56**.

Abatement

28.32 It may be impossible to pay, or make over, all legacies in full. Tim leaves a million pounds each to ten different people, but dies with net assets of £100,000. The legacies cannot be paid in full, but must be scaled down. This is known as abatement. (In this case, each legatee would receive £10,000.) When abatement is needed, it is usually not because the gross estate was inadequate, as in Tim's case. Usually it is because, whilst the gross estate is adequate, the net estate is not, ie the debts – which always have priority over legacies or other succession rights – are such that the legacies cannot be met in full.[69] Legal rights can have the same effect.

28.33 There are three rules.[70]
 (1) The residue abates first. In fact, this is not an independent rule because, by definition, 'residue' is what is left after other claims – debts, legal rights and other legacies – have been met.
 (2) General legacies abate before special legacies.
 (3) Legatees in a particular class suffer *pro rata* abatement – i.e. equal suffering.

28.34 For instance, Fiona leaves £100,000 to Gregory, £200,000 to Heather and the rest to Ian. Her estate is a house worth £200,000, a painting worth £100,000 and other moveables worth £100,000. There are £160,000 of debts, all unsecured. The net estate is thus £400,000 minus £160,000 = £240,000. Ian would take nothing, and the £240,000 has to be divided between Gregory and Heather. Gregory would take £80,000 and Heather would take £160,000. (The house and painting would have to be sold by the executor.) What has happened is that the two legacies have abated equally. Gregory's legacy was half of Heather's and so what he receives is also half.

28.35 Suppose that the legacy to Gregory had not been a pecuniary legacy of £100,000, but had been a special legacy of the painting. In that case he would have received the painting, and Heather would have received £140,000. Ian, as before, would have received nothing. The reason is that pecuniary legacies abate before special ones.

28.36 If an asset that is subject to a special legacy has to be sold by the executor, the rights of the legatee are transferred to net proceeds of sale. Suppose that Euan leaves his house to Fraser and everything else to Hilda. The house is worth £200,000 and the rest of the estate is worth £100,000. There are £150,000 of unsecured debts. The house must be sold. Fraser will be paid £150,000. Hilda receives nothing.

28.37 Abatement may also be necessary to make it possible to pay out legal rights claimants.[71] Janette is married to Keith. They have no children. She leaves her house to Luke, £100,000 to Martin and the residue to Norah. The house is worth £200,000, and the rest of the estate, all moveable, is worth £150,000. There are no debts. If it

---

[69] For incidence of debts in general, see **PARAS 26.34–26.40** above.
[70] These are only default rules: the testator could make other provision.
[71] *Tait's Tr v Lees* (1886) 13 R 1104.

were not for legal rights, Luke would take the house, Martin would be paid £100,000 and Norah would receive the balance, worth £50,000. But Keith's *jus relicti* is a claim for £75,000 (half the value of the moveable estate). So Luke takes the house, Keith takes £75,000, Martin takes £75,000 and Norah takes nothing. Martin's legacy suffers rather than Luke's, because pecuniary legacies abate before special ones.

Ademption

28.38 It sometimes happens that the object of a legacy no longer belongs to the testator at the time of death. For instance, Edward leaves his house at 22 Privet Avenue to Finola. Later he sells that house and with the money he buys another, at 11 Acacia Drive. He then dies, without having changed his testament. The legacy is void because it has been 'adeemed'. Sometimes a legacy is so worded as to prevent ademption. For instance: 'I bequeath to Finola Smith my house at 22 Privet Avenue, Turriff, or such other house which I may own at my death as my principal residence.' Finola inherits 11 Acacia Drive.

28.39 Sometimes the asset in question has been converted into some other asset. As in the example just given, the asset is sold and the proceeds are used to buy another, similar, asset. Attempts are sometimes made to argue that the real intention of the testator must have been that the legatee was to receive the substituted asset. But 'it is settled (for better or worse) that ademption is a question of fact, and not of intention'.[72] The test for ademption is simply whether the asset is still in the testator's patrimony or not. If it is not, the legacy is adeemed.[73] For instance, in *Ogilvie-Forbes' Tr v Ogilvie-Forbes' Tr*[74] there was a legacy of some land. When the testator died, it was found that he had transferred title to the land to a company of which he was effectively the sole shareholder. It was held that the legacy had been adeemed. Conversely, if it is still within the patrimony, the legacy is not adeemed. Thus in *Tennant's Tr v Tennant*[75] there was a legacy of some company shares. At the time of the testator's death he had signed and delivered a share transfer document. But the transfer had not been registered with the company. So the legacy had not been adeemed.

Legatum rei alienae

28.40 *Legatum rei alienae* means 'legacy of someone else's property'. Obviously, this seldom happens. An example would be where the testator possesses something and mistakenly believes it to be his/hers. (In a sense, an adeemed legacy is a legacy

---

[72]   *Cobban's Exrs v Cobban* 1915 SC 82 at 89–90 per Lord Dundas.
[73]   For a special case see *Gordon's Exr v Turner* 2012 SLT 877.
[74]   1955 SC 405.
[75]   1946 SC 420.

of someone else's property. In the example above, when Edward dies, 22 Privet Avenue belongs to someone else. But the term *legatum rei alienae* is used to refer to a legacy of property that belonged to someone else at the time of the testament, as well as at the time of death.) The law is succinctly stated by Erskine:

> 'By the Roman law, if one bequeathed a subject which he knew did not belong to himself, the legacy had this effect, that the heir must either have purchased it for the legatee, or paid its value to him if it could not be purchased ... Where the testator ... believed the subject to be his own, which *in dubio* is to be inferred from his act of bequeathing, neither the thing itself, nor its value, could have been claimed from the heir ... These rules... hold also by the usage of Scotland.'[76]

Death of legatee: lapse of legacies

28.41   A legatee who dies before the testator cannot take the legacy. The dead cannot inherit.[77] Nor does the legacy pass to his or her estate. Thus suppose that Fraser leaves his house to Georgiana, and Georgiana leaves everything to Harry. Fraser dies one hour after Georgiana. The house does not go to Georgiana or to Harry. So what does happen to it? Such a legacy is said to have 'lapsed' and the basic rule is that a lapsed legacy is void.[78] Suppose that the testament said 'my house to Georgiana and the residue of my estate to Ian'. Ian would take the house. Suppose, alternatively, that Charlotte's testament says 'my house to David and the residue to Eliza'. David survives her but Eliza does not. The legacy of the residue lapses. Thus Charlotte dies partly testate (as to the house) and partly intestate (as to the residue).

28.42   As mentioned, the basic rule about the effect of predecease is that the legacy lapses. But there are important qualifications. To these we turn.

Express destinations-over[79]

28.43   A 'destination-over' is a provision in a legacy saying that if the legatee predeceases then the legacy is to go to someone else. Thus Fraser leaves his house 'to Gemma whom failing to Jessica'. If, when he dies, both Gemma and Jessica are alive, Gemma takes the house. If Gemma is alive, but not Jessica, then once again Gemma takes the house. But if Gemma is dead while Jessica is alive, Jessica takes the house.

---

[76]   Erskine III, 9, 10. See, generally, *Meeres v Dowell's Exr* 1923 SLT 184.
[77]   See **PARAS 26.15–26.18** above.
[78]   Lapsed legacies should not be confused with lapsed trusts. If a legacy lapses, it is void. If a trust lapses, it is not. For lapsed trusts, see **PARA 24.4** above.
[79]   See further **CHAPTER 30** below.

28.44 A survivorship destination-over (survivorship clause) is of this form: 'I leave my house to Alice and Boris equally between them and to the survivor.' If you unpack that, what it means is: 'I leave a one-half share of my house to Alice, whom failing to Boris, and I leave the other one-half share to Boris, whom failing to Alice.' If both Alice and Boris survive, each takes a half. If Alice survives but Boris predeceases, Alice takes the whole. And if Boris survives but Alice predeceases, Boris takes the whole.

Implied destinations-over: (i) accretion

28.45 As well as the express destination-over, the law in two types of case *implies* a destination-over. The first case is 'accretion'. Suppose that there is a legacy of £20,000 'to Anne and Brian'. If both survive, each receives £10,000. But what if Anne predeceases while Brian survives? Does the legacy lapse to the extent of £10,000, with Brian receiving £10,000? Or does Brian take £20,000? The law presumes that in a joint legacy of this sort the testator meant 'Anne and Brian and the survivor'. This is called 'accretion' and it is said that Anne's share 'accresces' to Brian.[80] But it is only a presumption and so is rebuttable by evidence of contrary intention. The simplest way to avoid accretion is to make the legacies separate, for instance '£10,000 to Anne and £10,000 to Brian'. Alternatively, what are called 'words of severance' can be used. Thus if the legacy is 'to Anne and Brian equally between them', the effect of the words 'equally between them' is to exclude accretion.[81] Conversely, if a testator does want accretion, it is sensible to provides for that expressly ('to Anne and Brian and the survivor'), rather than leave the matter to implication.

Implied destinations-over: (ii) legatee's offspring

28.46 The other implied destination-over covers the case where there is a legacy to a child of the testator, and that child predeceases the testator, leaving one or more grandchildren. There is a presumed destination-over to the grandchild or grandchildren.[82] Mary has a son, Nicholas, who has two children, Olivia and Peter. Her testament leaves her house to Nicholas. He dies. She would probably then make a new will. But if she does not, on her death the legacy goes to Olivia and Peter, so that they would become co-owners of the house. It should be stressed that the rule applies only to offspring[83] of the testator, so that if the legacy had been, say, to Mary's brother Quintus, and he predeceased her, leaving two daughters, Rachael and

---

80   This rule does not apply to special destinations (for which see **CHAPTER 30** below).
81   *Paxton's Trs v Cowie* (1886) 13 R 1191.
82   S(S)A 2016, s 6. This is a revised version of the common-law rule known as the *conditio si institutus sine liberis decesserit*. (This common-law rule was at the same time abolished: 2016 Act s 29.)
83   To be precise, the rule applies to direct descendants. So, a legacy to a grandchild could be carried to a great-grandchild.

Sandra, ie Mary's nieces, the legacy would not go to those nieces. (Unless there were an express provision to that effect).

28.47   The rule is similar to the doctrine of representation. But representation applies to (a) legitim[84] and (b) intestate succession rights,[85] whereas the rule just discussed applies to legacies.

28.48   The rule is an implied-in-law term. As such, it can be overridden by the terms of the legacy, ie if 'it is clear from the terms of the will that the testator intended otherwise.'[86] So if Mary left the house 'to my son Nicholas whom failing to my sister Lorna', then if Nicholas predeceases Mary, the house will pass to Lorna, not to Olivia and Peter. Or suppose that Mary had left her house to 'Nicholas and Tatiana and the survivor of them' (Tatiana being Nicholas's wife) then, in the event of Nicholas predeceasing Mary, the house would pass to Tatiana.[87] But what if the legacy said simply 'to Nicholas and Tatiana'? In that case would Tatiana take the property, because of accretion? Or would she take only half of the property, with the other half passing to Olivia and Peter? The answer is the latter, because the rule is ousted only if 'it is clear from the terms of the will that the testator intended otherwise.'

VESTING

28.49   A succession right is said to 'vest' when the beneficiary acquires a right to it. In almost all cases that is at the moment of the death of the *de cujus*. But occasionally vesting is postponed. Vesting is a subject that belongs to the law of trusts.[88]

Interpretation of testaments

28.50   The interpretation of testaments, like the interpretation of contracts, has a front door, namely the common-law rules, and a back door, whereby 'rectification' may be obtainable. The front door does not allow investigation of subjective intention, but demands that the text be construed objectively according to the words used. The back door allows subjective intention to be considered. For contracts the law about rectification was introduced in 1985.[89] For testaments an equivalent provision was introduced in 2016. It might be thought that in both cases – contracts and testaments – it would be simpler and better to have a single, integrated, system of interpretation,

---

84   See **CHAPTER 27** above.
85   See **CHAPTER 29** below.
86   S(S)A 2016 s 6(2).
87   See S(S)A 2016 s 6(3).
88   See **PARA 23.60** above.
89   Law Reform (Miscellaneous Provisions) (Scotland) Act 1985, s 8.

rather than two separate systems, front and back doors. But that is not the position. Both doors have to be considered separately.

28.51 As with other documents, testaments may be unclear, ambiguous or simply muddled. This is often, but by no means always, true of home-made wills. But sometimes it can also be true of those drawn up by solicitors. Many of the reported cases on the law of succession are cases in which the court has to interpret a testament. In doing so, it may take into account the whole circumstances, but not (as far as the common law goes[90]) direct evidence as to the testator's intention. The following passage sums up the law:

'The difference between saying that the Court does not allow parole evidence to show what the testator intended, but that it does allow, in suitable cases, investigation by parole into what the words used by the testator were intended to mean, although fine, is a very real one … There is no doubt that certain investigations are usually allowable, as to the state of the testator's family and the surrounding circumstances of the making of the will. This is often absolutely necessary for the proper understanding of the will, and it has been for generations accepted that the proper exposition of a testament requires that the interpreting court should be put, as it were, into the testator's chair and given an outlook based on the testator's knowledge.'[91]

28.52 Reported cases on interpretation are countless. They are fact-specific, and quite often more than one interpretation is reasonably possible. Two examples, both involving home-made testaments, may be mentioned not as leading cases, but as typical examples.

'I, Janet Walker Lawson, state the following to be my will after all the expenses are paid incurred by my death. I appoint my brother, Thomas Lawson, 47 Wyke Road, Weymouth, to be Executor, and state that he is to receive all my furniture, belongings, etc. I state that all money I leave has to go to the Edinburgh Royal Infirmary. Signed in my own handwriting. Janet Walker.'

The estate consisted of (i) a house, (ii) its furnishings (iii) cash in house, (iv) bank accounts and (v) investments. How was it to be distributed?[92] The second case:

'I Arthur Underwood residing at 21 South Hermitage St Newcastleton, on the fifteenth day of January nineteen hundred and twenty one year for the settlement of my affairs on my Death do herby give and bequeath my Daughter Grace, Wife of Thomas Armstrong, Chollerton staton My House, No. 6 South Liddle Street Newcastleton To my Grand daughter Charlotte, Wife of Robert Crozier Mason residing their Also all my other

---

[90] Here we consider the common law. For 'rectification' see below.
[91] *Hay v Duthie* 1956 SC 511 at 528–529 per Lord Carmont.
[92] *Lawson's Executor v Lawson* 1958 SLT (Notes) 38.

affect except the clock which I give of my Great Grand daughter Jean Crozier, I alo give to Jams Arthur Crozier my watch and the Bible which I got form my son John in America, and 2 Volums of Christopher Sturm, and all my School copies, also to my Great Grand Daughter Frances Mary Crozier the Life of Christ. All other affects go to Charlotte both in sidside the hous and out side that belongs to me, and all money that I my have at my death. I hereby appoint my Daughter Grace and my granddaughter XX as my Sole excutors to cllect all money that my become due to me and pay all expences. Arthur Underwood.'

Who was to inherit the house that Mr Underwood owned at 21 South Hermitage Street?[93]

28.53   From time to time there may be a difficulty about identifying the legatee. Erskine says:

'A legacy is valid though there should be an error in the name of the legatee … provided his description distinguishes him sufficiently from all others'.[94]

In case of doubt, extrinsic evidence is competent as to which person the testator had in mind. Thus in *Cathcart's Trs v Bruce*[95] there was a legacy to 'the children of General Alexander Fairlie Bruce'. This was claimed by (i) the children of General Alexander James Bruce and (ii) the children of Alexander Fairlie Bruce. Evidence showed that the testator had meant the former. In this case it will be noted that the verbal description did not exactly match either set of claimants. What would happen if it did exactly match, but evidence was available indicating that in reality someone different was intended? This situation arose in *Nasmyth's Trs v NSPCC*.[96] Here, there was a legacy to the 'National Society for the Prevention of Cruelty to Children'. There was an English society of that name, and also a Scottish society called the Scottish National Society for the Prevention of Cruelty to Children. Both claimed the legacy, the Scottish society offering to adduce evidence that it was the intended beneficiary. The Court of Session held that evidence should be heard. The English society appealed to the House of Lords, which held that since the wording of the legacy was unambiguous, evidence as to the testator's real intention could not be adduced.

28.54   Sometimes the description of the legatee may mention some position or relationship, such as 'my daughter-in-law, Jane Black' or 'my gardener, Alan White'. What if, by the time of the testator's death, that relationship, or position, has ceased? That of course depends on intention as expressed or implied in the testament, but, the

---

[93]   *Crozier's Trustee v Underwood* 1963 SLT 69.
[94]   Erskine III, 9, 8.
[95]   1923 SLT 722. A similar case is *Keiller v Thomson's Trs* (1826) 4 S 724.
[96]   1914 SC (HL) 76.

presumption is that the description was not a condition of the legacy.[97] In *Ormiston's Exr v Laws*,[98] Harold Ormiston's testament (January 1962) had a large legacy to 'to my fiancée Mrs Sylvia Martis.' Harold and Sylvia were in fact not engaged, and indeed in September 1963 she married someone else (a friend of Harold's…). Nevertheless, following his death in January 1964 the legacy was held to be effectual.

28.55   A legacy to a 'class' is a legacy to a set of people who are described but not identified, such as a legacy to 'my sister Fiona's children'. Suppose that at the date of the testament Fiona had four children, A, B, C and D. Later, D died. Then the testator died. A year after the death of the testator, Fiona had another child, E. Who receives the legacy? The answer is: A, B and C. A class is normally to be ascertained at the date of the testator's death.

Rectification of testaments

28.56   The Law Reform (Miscellaneous Provisions) (Scotland) Act 1985 allows a court to alter the wording of a document to bring it into line with what was truly intended. But testaments are excluded from the scope of this provision.[99] However, in 2016 parallel provisions were introduced for testaments.[100] The basic idea is that if the testament as worded does not in fact reflect what the testator intended, the court has the power to re-write it to make it reflect the intention. For instance:

'Instead of leaving legacies of £10,000 each to the testator's daughters, G and F, as instructed by the testator, the will, because of a clerical error, leaves two legacies of £10,000 to G and fails to mention F. The will is sent to the testator for signature along with a summary of its provisions. The testator reads the summary, which mentions legacies to G and F but does not read the whole will. He signs it without noticing the error.'[101]

F could apply for the will to be rectified. (Indeed, the application could seemingly be made by *anyone*, for the Act merely says that 'a person' may apply.[102]) Whether the application will succeed depends on the court's assessment of the evidence. A remarkable example of rectification from south of the border was *Marley v Rawlings*.[103] A husband and wife both made wills, but by mistake the husband signed the wife's and the wife signed the husband's. That was in 1999. In 2003 she died and

---

[97]   In *Couper's JF v Valentine* 1976 SC 63. the testament gave a legacy to 'my wife Mrs Dorothy Couper'. Later, the Coupers were divorced. A few months after the divorce, he died, without having changed the testament. It was held that the legacy took effect. (But today this case would have been decided differently because of s 1 of the S(S)A 2016.)
[98]   1966 SC 47.
[99]   Section 8(6).
[100] S(S)A 2016, ss 3 and 4.
[101] Quoted from Scottish Law Commission, *Report on Succession* (Scot Law Com No 215 (2009), para 6.2.
[102] S(S)A 2016, s 3(1)(a).
[103] [2015] AC 129.

in 2006 he died. The error then came to light. The Supreme Court, reversing the Court of Appeal, ordered rectification; the Scottish justice, Lord Hodge, said that the same would be the case in Scotland, at least once the proposed rules for rectification had been introduced, as they now have been.

28.57 Rectification is competent only if 'the will was drafted not by the testator but on the testator's instructions.'[104] Thus wills drafted by a solicitor are rectifiable, but home-made wills are not: in effect the provision is about professional failure to carry out instructions. Two practical points may be added. The first is that rectification application must be made within six months of the death or within six months of the confirmation,[105] but a court has a discretion to accept late applications.[106] The other is that an 'executor is not personally liable for distributing property in good faith in accordance with a will which … is rectified after the distribution.'[107]

LITERATURE

28.58 For drafting, see A Barr et al, *Drafting Wills in Scotland* (2nd edn, 2009). For the substantive law see Hiram *Succession* chs 5–9 and Macdonald *Succession* chs 6–8 and 11.

---

[104] S(S)A 2016, s 3(1)(b).
[105] For confirmation see **PARAS 26.46–26.47**.
[106] S(S)A 2016, s 4(1) and (2). These provisions may not be free from difficulty.
[107] S(S)A 2016, s 8(7).

Chapter 29

Intestate succession

INTRODUCTION

29.1   Although intestacy is common, the larger the estate, the more likely it is that there is a testament. So, testacy tends to be where the money is. But of course, not always. There are always some multi-million pound estates that fall into intestacy.

29.2   Occasionally there can be intestacy even if there is a valid testament. For example, Ursula's testament says 'I leave everything to my husband Vernon'. By the time that Ursula dies, Vernon is already dead. The universal legacy lapses, and as a result there is an intestacy. (There would be no intestacy, however, if her testament had said says 'I leave everything to my husband Vernon whom failing to the National Trust for Scotland.') Even if Vernon were alive, he could renounce the legacy, and then the result would, again, be intestacy. It might seem improbable that he would do that, but, surprisingly, there can be circumstances in which it would be in his interests to do so.[1] Sometimes there can be partial intestacy. For instance, suppose that Henry's testament says 'I leave my house to Iona and everything else to James' and suppose that Henry is survived by Iona but not by James. Iona takes the house, but the bequest of residue lapses. The residue falls into intestacy. It would have been different if it had been the other way round, and Iona had predeceased Henry while James had survived him. Then James would have taken everything, including the house, and there would have been no partial intestacy.

29.3   The law on intestacy is mainly to be found in the Succession (Scotland) Act 1964 (S(S)A 1964), but partly in common law. Over the years there have been some statutory changes, perhaps most notably about cohabitants, but on the whole the law remains much as it was in 1964. The 1964 Act has certain fixed monetary figures, which can be changed from time to time by statutory instrument.[2] The current set of figures is given by the Prior Rights of Surviving Spouse (Scotland) Order 2011 (SSI 2011/436).

POLICY?

29.4   S(S)A 1964 was loosely based on the Mackintosh Report of 1951.[3] This said that 'we have throughout kept in view that when a man dies without a will the law should try to provide as far as possible for the distribution of his estate in the manner he would most likely have given effect to himself if he had made a will'.[4] If this approach were to be taken seriously, it would be necessary to have an enquiry after each intestate death, to find out, as nearly as possible, what the deceased would have wanted to happen. But such an approach would be slow and expensive, and in any case would in most cases be little more than guesswork. The Mackintosh Committee never even contemplated such a possibility. Instead it laid down a single system of fixed rules, with, however, different sub-rules according to whether or not the deceased left a relict or issue.

FIVE STAGES

29.5   In an intestacy one begins, as always, with paying the debts, including taxes. After that, there are up to five stages to go through. These are:

(1) prior rights;

(2) relict's right (including civil partner's right);

---

[1]   See **PARAS 29.28–29.29** below.

[2]   S(S)A 1964 s 8(1), s 8(3) and s 9(1).

[3]   Cmnd 8144. For the relationship of the Act to the Report see K Reid, 'Intestate Succession in Scotland' in K Reid, M De Waal and R Zimmermann (eds), *Comparative Succession Law. Volume II, Intestate Succession* (2015).

[4]   At 8.

(3) cohabitant's right;

(4) legitim; and

(5) free estate.

The prior rights stage itself has three elements. A chart may be useful (see Figure 29.1):

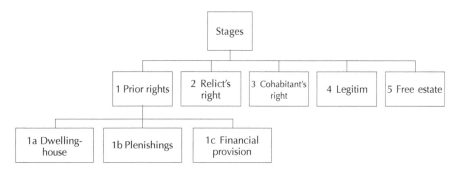

Figure 29.1

29.6   But it must not be supposed that in every intestacy all stages are relevant. If the deceased was single and childless, for example, only the fifth stage would be applicable. Nevertheless, overall the law is complex.

Stage 1: Prior rights[5]

(a)   Dwellinghouse right[6]

29.7   If the deceased had a 'relevant interest'[7] in a dwellinghouse in which the relict was 'ordinarily resident' at the date of death then that 'interest' passes to the relict. Jack and Jill are married. Their home is owned by Jill and is worth £200,000. Jill dies intestate.[8] Jack inherits the house. If the value of the deceased's 'relevant interest' exceeds a set figure (currently £473,000) then the relict does not inherit the property, but is entitled to be paid the sum in question. For instance, suppose that the house is worth £500,000. Jack does not inherit it. Instead he is entitled to be paid £473,000. (But if Jack specifically wants the house, the executor is likely to agree to convey it to him in exchange for £27,000.) The same rules apply if the home is co-owned. Suppose that Moira and Martin co-own their home and it is worth £600,000. Moira dies intestate. Her share is worth £300,000. Martin inherits her share.

---

5   At the risk of stating the obvious, prior rights apply *only* in intestacy, and *only* in favour of a relict.

6   S(S)A 1964, s 8.

7   For almost all practical purposes this means ownership or co-ownership: S(S)A 1964, s 8(6)(d).

8   Jill is said to be 'the intestate' – ie the intestate person. This is an odd usage, because a person who is testate is not called 'the testate'.

29.8   In calculating the value, debt secured on the property is deducted. Suppose that Sophia is the sole owner of a house, worth £600,000. She owes the bank £200,000, secured by standard security. The property's value, for the purposes of prior rights, is £400,000. Her husband Theodore inherits her share (but on condition of accepting liability for the secured loan).

29.9   Often the house is co-owned. One deducts from the value of the deceased's share the amount secured over that share. Bob and Elle co-own a house worth £400,000. Bob borrows £20,000 from Bank X, secured over his share, and Elle borrows £40,000 from Bank Y, secured over her share. Bob dies intestate. The net value of his share is £180,000. That sort of arrangement would be unlikely in practice. Usually If there is a joint loan it is secured over both shares. But the same principles apply.

29.10   Suppose that the house is co-owned by Jack and Jill and is worth £700,000. There is a secured loan of £80,000. The security is over both his share and her share. Assuming that their liability on the loan is equal, the net value of his share is £310,000.

29.11   In the typical case their liability will be solidary (joint and several), so that the whole £80,000 is secured over both shares. One might seek to argue, on the basis of a literal reading of S(S)A 1964, s 8(6)(d), that the whole amount should be deducted, so that the net value of his share is £270,000. But the more commonsense approach, and the one adopted in practice, is to deduct from the gross value of his share the amount that he is liable as between himself and his wife, i.e. £40,000.

29.12   The dwellinghouse right exists only if the relict was ordinarily resident there. Thus, a house owned as an investment and let out would not count. Or suppose that Jack and Jill are co-owners but have separated. Jill lives in the house, and Jack lives elsewhere. If he dies, Jill has the dwellinghouse right. But if she dies, he does not.[9] So the rule can produce arguably arbitrary effects.

(b)   Plenishings right

29.13   The relict has right to 'furniture and plenishings' within the dwellinghouse, up to a set figure (currently £29,000).[10] If the value is less than that figure, the relict takes it all. If the value is higher, the relict chooses items up to the value. (Note that this rule is different from the rule for the dwellinghouse. In that case, if the value is over the limit, the relict takes money in lieu.) In practice most or all of the furniture and plenishings will be co-owned.[11] Thus, suppose that their value is £50,000. The relict will typically take all, because if she co-owns each item, the value of the deceased's share is only £25,000. To have this right the relict must be 'ordinarily

---

[9]   But there may have been a separation agreement: see **PARA 26.28** above.
[10]   S(S)A 1964, s 8(3).
[11]   Co-ownership is presumed by the Family Law (Scotland) Act 1985, s 25.

resident'. Thus, as in the previous example, if Jack and Jill are separated, with Jill living in the house, Jack would not have this prior right if she dies, but she has it if he dies.

(c) Financial provision

29.14 The third prior right is a right to money. The amount depends on whether the deceased left issue. In the absence of issue the figure is (at present) £89,000. Otherwise it is (at present) £50,000. Suppose that Iain dies intestate, survived by his second wife, Jenny, from whom he was separated but not divorced, and by one child from the first marriage, Keira. Jenny is entitled to £50,000. (The marriage of Iain and Jenny was childless, but that is not the point. The deceased had issue.) Naturally, financial provision is payable only if the estate can pay. Thus, suppose that Iain's estate consists of a half-share of a house that he co-owned with Jenny (value of the share being £200,000) and a half-share of the contents (the value of the share being £40,000) and a bank deposit of £10,000. He dies intestate. Jenny takes the whole estate. Jenny receives only £10,000 of the financial provision. She will not receive the rest, since there is no estate out of which it could be paid. In this example there was a handy £10,000 bank deposit. But financial provision does not depend on the existence of a fund of that sort. Suppose that instead of the bank deposit Iain had owned a field worth £10,000. Jenny could still claim her financial provision. Note that Keira takes nothing and that her step-mother takes everything. In smaller intestate estates, the relict (if there is one) tends to take everything. Whether that is fair is arguable. The question tends to be at its starkest where, as here, the issue are excluded not in favour of their own parent, but in favour of a step-parent. It is curious that in testate succession Keira would receive something because in testate succession legal rights come first, but in intestate succession prior rights come before legal rights.

29.15 In calculating legal rights (see below), it is necessary to know how much moveable estate is left after prior rights have been satisfied, because legal rights are calculated on the value of the moveables. Hence there has to be a rule about how the financial provision is to be taken out of the estate, in cases where both heritable and moveable property are available. Actually, in most cases the problem does not arise, because in most cases there is only one piece of heritable property, the dwellinghouse. But sometimes there is other heritable property too. The rule is this: financial provision must be deducted *rateably* from the heritable and the moveable estate.[12] This rule is seen in operation in the case of Paula's estate, below.

29.16 Paula dies intestate survived by her husband, Robert, and their two children, Sandra and Tim. The dwellinghouse is worth £300,000 and is owned in

---

[12]   S(S)A 1964, s 9(3).

common with Robert. The title does not contain a survivorship destination.[13] There is a secured loan of £40,000. The contents are worth £40,000 and are co-owned. There is also a holiday cottage owned by Paula alone, worth £100,000. Paula had stock market investments worth £150,000.

29.17 The first prior right gives Robert the house. The second prior right gives him the contents. After this second prior right there remains free heritage of £100,000 and free moveables of £150,000. The third prior right is financial provision of £50,000. This must come rateably from the remaining heritage (£100,000) and the remaining moveables (£150,000). The ratio is 2:3, so that for every two pennies contributed by the heritage, three pennies must be contributed by the moveables. Hence the heritage must contribute £20,000 and the moveables must contribute £30,000. What is left at the end of the three prior rights is £80,000 of heritage and £120,000 of moveables.

Stage 2: Relict's right

29.18 There are two kinds of legal rights: relict's right (including civil partner's right) and legitim.[14] In testate succession, the two have the same priority: they come first, subject only to the rights of creditors. In intestate succession legal rights also apply, but not in the same way. Both legal rights are postponed to prior rights. And legitim, but not relict's right, is postponed to cohabitant's right.

29.19 The previous example can be continued. Legal rights are calculated on the basis of the net moveable estate. After prior rights, the remaining value of the moveable estate is £120,000. The relict's right is one-third. So Robert takes £40,000.

Stage 3: Cohabitant's right

29.20 Next: cohabitant's right. Paula, we will assume, has no cohabitant, having been faithful to Robert. Nevertheless, we will consider the possibility. In most cases where there is a cohabitant there is no spouse, but there could be both. To speak of the cohabitant's 'right' is misleading. The court has a power to make an award to the cohabitant, but the power is discretionary. The Family Law (Scotland) Act 2006[15] sets out a list of factors which the court should take into account.[16] The award is made out of the 'net intestate estate'. The way that is defined means that the award comes *after* prior rights and relict's right have been satisfied, but *before* legitim or free estate. There is a maximum:

---

[13] The same assumption applies in the other examples in this chapter. A survivorship special destination is a provision in title to heritable property that gives the share of the first to die to the survivor. (See **CHAPTER 30** below.) If that is the case, the share in question does not form part of the estate. Here it would make no real difference, since Robert takes Paula's share anyway.
[14] See **CHAPTER 27** above.
[15] Family Law (Scotland) Act 2006, s 29.
[16] There is little case law. But *Savage v Purches* 2009 SLT (Sh Ct) 36 is interesting.

'An order ... shall not have the effect of awarding to the survivor [= cohabitant] an amount which would exceed the amount to which the survivor would have been entitled had the survivor been the spouse or civil partner of the deceased.'

That maximum does not, however, ensure that the children will receive anything. Suppose that Paula had had a cohabitant, Ulysses. The award to Ulysses might be such as to mean that the two children would receive nothing.

Stage 4: Legitim

29.21 If there is no cohabitant, the legitim is a third of the value of the net moveables. So Sandra and Tim take £40,000 between them, i.e. £20,000 each. As with relict's right, legitim is a right to *money*.

Stage 5: Free estate

29.22 'Free estate' means anything left of an intestate estate after satisfaction of prior rights, legal rights and cohabitant's right. In some cases there may be no free estate. The example above,[17] where Iain died and Jenny took the whole estate by prior rights, shows why this may happen. At the other extreme, if there are no prior rights, legal rights or cohabitant's right, the whole estate is free estate. For example, Natasha dies intestate without spouse, civil partner, cohabitant or issue. Everything is free estate.

29.23 S(S)A 1964, s 2 lists those entitled to inherit the free estate, starting with the children, if any. Confusingly, it says that the persons in question inherit *the whole of the intestate estate*. But in fact s 2 is subject to prior and legal rights.[18] The s 2 list is a modern statutory form of the common law conception of 'next of kin'. Thus at common law if Mary dies survived by her three children, Norman, Olivia and Perpetua, those three children are the next of kin. ('Next of kin' means 'nearest by blood'.) At common law the spouse is never the next of kin. (Unless cousins marry and have no nearer relatives.) The s 2 list departs somewhat from the common-law conception, one of the departures being that the spouse does appear in the s 2 list, though only a long way down. It is unusual for a relict to inherit under s 2. So while relicts do well under prior rights and legal rights, they do less well at this third stage. Suppose that Aileen has a civil partner and two children. If she dies intestate with an estate worth £40,000, the civil partner takes everything and the children nothing. If she dies intestate with heritage worth £2,000,000 and investments worth £1,000,000, the children take the lion's share.

---

[17] See **PARA 29.14** above.
[18] The explanation is to be found in S(S)A 1964, s 1(2) which says that 'nothing in this part of this Act shall affect legal rights or the prior rights of a surviving spouse'.

29.24 What is left of Paula's estate after (i) prior rights and (ii) legal rights? Answer: £40,000 of moveables and £80,000 of heritage. All this goes to Sandra and Tim, equally.

29.25 All the possibilities inherent in S(S)A 1964, s 2 will not be discussed here. Only a few examples will be given.
  (1) Brian has no issue. He is an only child. Both his parents survive him. His estate goes to them, equally.
  (2) The same, but only one parent is alive. That parent takes all.
  (3) Carla has no issue. She has two brothers. Her parents are dead. Her two brothers take her estate, equally.
  (4) Deirdre has no issue. Her parents, Ewan and Faye, are dead. Deirdre has one sibling, Genevieve. Genevieve is from Faye's first marriage, and thus Deirdre's half-sister. Genevieve takes all.
  (5) The same, but with one difference, namely that Ewan and Faye had another child, Hilda. Thus Hilda, unlike Genevieve, is Deirdre's sister of the full blood. Hilda takes everything.[19]

In these examples it would make no difference, as far as the free estate (if any) is concerned, if the deceased (Brian or Carla or Deirdre) had been married. Their spouses would have the benefit of prior rights and legal rights, but they would not be the section 2 heirs.

29.26 The rules about representation are substantially the same as for legitim.[20] Kate and John have three children, Laura, Marie and Nigel. Kate and Nigel died some years ago. Nigel was married to Ottalie. They had two children, Paula and Rosi. Marie now dies, childless, single and intestate. Prior rights and legal rights are inapplicable. So everything is free estate. Under the S(S)A 1964, s 2 rules, a half goes to her father, John, a quarter to her sister Laura and an eighth each to her nieces Paula and Rosi. (The division as between Laura on the one hand and the two nieces on the other is a division *per stirpes*, since the heirs are of unequal propinquity. Had Laura predeceased leaving one child, Robert, then Robert, Paula and Rosi would have taken one-sixth each.)

ULTIMUS HAERES

29.27 In some legal systems only relatives within a certain degree can be intestate heirs. Thus if someone dies and the nearest relative is a fifth cousin, that cousin does not inherit. In our law there is no limit. Someone could inherit who had never even heard to the deceased (The American term 'laughing heir' is sometimes used.) Since

---

[19] S(S)A 1964, s 2(2) admits siblings of the half blood, but s 3 gives priority to siblings of the whole blood.
[20] For which see **CHAPTER 27** above. But whereas the representation rules for legitim are in S(S)A 1964, s 11, the representation rules for s 2 rights are in S(S)A 1964, ss 5 and 6.

everyone is related to everyone else, it follows that nobody can die heirless. But in practice it occasionally happens that someone dies intestate and no relative can be traced. The Crown is the *ultimus haeres*.[21] Hence if nobody else can be traced, the Crown takes. The splendidly named Queen's and Lord Treasurer's Remembrancer (QLTR) administers such inheritances for the Crown.[22] The beneficiary is not the UK Treasury but the Scottish Consolidated Fund.

ARTIFICIAL INTESTACY

29.28   David and Evelina are married. David had one child, Fraser, by a previous relationship. David dies. His testament leaves everything to Evelina. The estate is worth £60,000. It is all moveable. Fraser can claim legitim, receiving £20,000. Evelina takes the rest, ie £40,000. Suppose that Evelina rejects her legacy. The estate is now intestate. She claims prior rights. There is no house. There are no plenishings. She takes financial provision of £50,000, leaving £10,000. She takes one-third of this under her relict's right = £3,333. Fraser takes £3,333 by way of legitim, and he then takes the remaining £3,333 under S(S)A 1964, s 2. Thus, by renouncing her legacy Evelina is better off than she would have been had she accepted it: £53,333 as opposed to £40,000. This curious result, known as 'artificial intestacy', follows from the logic of S(S)A 1964.[23]

28.29   Artificial intestacy makes sense for the relict only if she would get more in that way than by accepting the legacy. If the estate is a large one, artificial intestacy would not make sense for her. Nor would artificial intestacy make sense if the legacy says, for example, 'all to Evelina whom failing to Oxfam'.

PARTIAL INTESTACY

29.30   Partial intestacy happens when the testament (combined with legal rights and cohabitant's right, if applicable) fails to dispose of the whole estate. An example was given at the beginning of this Chapter: Henry's testament says 'I leave my house to Iona and everything else to James'. He is survived by Iona but not by James. Iona takes the house, but the bequest of residue lapses. It falls into intestacy, and is distributed under S(S)A 1964, s 2.

29.31   Partial intestacy becomes difficult where there is a relict. This is because (i) prior rights rank before legal rights, and (ii) legal rights rank before legacies and (iii) legacies rank before prior rights. Thus, there is a circle of priority. The problems seem to be insoluble.[24]

---

[21]   Latin, meaning 'last heir'.
[22]   www.qltr.gov.uk/.
[23]   For an example, see *Kerr* 1968 SLT (Sh Ct) 61
[24]   G L Gretton 'Partial intestacy' 1986 *SLT (News)* 201.

EVALUATION

29.32 Succession law policy is inevitably an area where different people have different views: it is no accident that succession laws vary greatly across the world, even as between countries that are culturally similar. Three particular criticisms are commonly heard of the current system of intestate succession, in relation to the case where there are both relict and issue. (i) The system is complex. (ii) It is to some extent arbitrary in that the relict's position varies greatly according to whether or not the deceased's assets included a house where the relict lived. And (iii) if there are also children, some (but not others) consider the law to be too favourable to the relict. As noted earlier,[25] the Scottish Government is considering the possibility of major changes to the law of intestate succession.

LITERATURE

29.33 Useful accounts can be found in Hiram *Succession* ch 4, Macdonald *Succession* ch 4 and D Bartos and M Meston *Bartos & Meston on the Succession (Scotland) Act 1964* (6th edn, 2015). A valuable study, including the history, can be found in K Reid, 'Intestate Succession in Scotland' in K Reid, M De Waal and R Zimmermann (eds) *Comparative Succession Law. Volume II, Intestate Succession* (2015).

---

[25]   See **PARA 26.3**.

Chapter 30

Destinations

INTRODUCTION

30.1   In **CHAPTER 28** above something was said about destinations-over.[1] Here, a more detailed treatment of destinations is given. There are two kinds:

(a) destinations-over; and

(b) special destinations.

---

[1]   See **PARAS 28.43–28.48** above.

A destination-over is found in a testament, or trust, as part of the terms of a legacy or beneficial right. Any type of property may be involved. A special destination is found in a disposition, and enters the Land Register, or the Sasine Register.[2]

30.2   In both types of destination, a transferor (testator, truster, disponer) is saying that property is to go to X but when X dies, the property is then to pass to Y. Sometimes a destination-over can convert itself into a special destination. While some special destinations are thus born out of destinations-over, most are not. The law of destinations stands on the cusp between succession law and property law.

DESTINATIONS-OVER: THE BASICS

30.3   If in a testament there is a legacy to Jack, and Jack predeceases the testator, the legacy normally lapses.[3] But if the testament says 'to Jack *whom failing to Jill*', then the result is different. If Jack predeceases the testator, then Jill, if she is alive, takes the legacy. An important sub-type of destination-over is the survivorship destination-over. Here, Tara leaves a legacy to 'Jack and Jill and the survivor'. That is really two legacies: (1) half to Jack whom failing to Jill; and (2) half to Jill whom failing to Jack. Thus suppose that when Tara dies, Jill is alive but Jack is not. Then Jill takes both halves.

30.4   In a destination-over the primary legatee (Jack) is the 'institute'. The secondary legatee (Jill) is either (1) the 'conditional institute' or (2) the 'substitute'. Those latter two terms do not mean quite the same thing. How they differ, and how to determine which Jill is, will be discussed below.

SPECIAL DESTINATIONS

The basics

30.5   Alan owns a house. He dispones it to 'Beth whom failing to Clara'. The disposition is registered. The owner is Beth. Clara is not a co-owner and indeed has no real right. Beth is the institute and Clara is the substitute.

Effect

30.6   If both (a) when Beth dies Clara is still alive and (b) the property is then still owned by Beth, Clara takes the property.[4] In other words, the property does not

---

[2]   It is also possible to have special destinations of moveable property but they are rare, and nothing will be said about them here.
[3]   See **PARA 28.41** above.
[4]   Normally. For the exception, see **PARA 30.13** below.

form part of Beth's estate for succession purposes. For example, suppose that Beth was married to Duncan. She dies intestate. Duncan claims prior rights, including the dwellinghouse right.[5] He will fail. The house goes to Clara. The destination thus prevails if Beth dies *intestate*. But what if she dies *testate*? What if her testament says 'I leave my house to my darling husband Duncan'? The answer is: usually the destination defeats the legacy. Occasionally the legacy can defeat the destination. The rules are given below.[6]

30.7   While the destination may work in favour of Clara on Beth's death, it does *not* prevent Beth from transferring the property while she (Beth) is still alive.[7] If Beth does that, Clara takes nothing. Or suppose that Beth dies still owning the property, but having granted subordinate real rights. Such rights are valid and Clara takes subject to them.

Survivorship

30.8   The sort of special destination mentioned above (to Beth whom failing to Clara) is nowadays rare. Special destinations are indeed common, but almost all of them are survivorship special destinations. Archie and Barbara are married, or perhaps just living together. They buy a house. They are likely to want to be co-owners. So the disposition will, in the typical case, be to both of them, as common property. This can be done in two ways: first, 'to Archie and Barbara' and second 'to Archie and Barbara and the survivor'.

30.9   In both cases they become co-owners. Nevertheless, the effect of the two is different. In the first, if Archie dies, his half share will form part of his estate. It may then go to Barbara. But it may not. The second is equivalent to: 'half to Archie whom failing to Barbara and half to Barbara whom failing to Archie'. If Archie dies, his share will normally go to Barbara, even if Archie's will leaves it to someone else. Although one speaks of a 'survivorship destination' in the singular, the reality is plural, for there are two destinations – one for one half-share and another for the other.[8]

29.10   Most people who buy a property together opt for one of these survivorship special destinations. It is the seller who signs the disposition but the terms of the disposition in such matters are chosen by the buyers.

---

5   For prior rights, see **PARAS 29.7–29.17** above.
6   See **PARAS 30.13–30.15** below.
7   *Steele v Caldwell* 1979 SLT 228; *Smith v Mackintosh* 1989 SLT 148.
8   So the evacuation of the one leaves the other intact, with consequences that can be unexpected: see *Gardner's Exrs v Raeburn* 1996 SLT 745.

Evacuation

30.11   To remove the effect of a destination is called 'evacuating' the destination. That is what Beth sought to do by leaving the house to Duncan. Can this be done, and if so, how?[9]

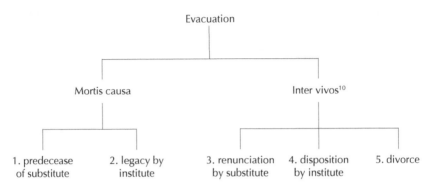

30.12   First, a destination is evacuated by the death of the substitute. Suppose that there is a disposition 'to Charlotte whom failing Fergus'. Fergus dies on Monday and Charlotte dies on Tuesday. Neither Fergus nor his estate takes the property. Fergus was the substitute, and he prececeased the institute (Charlotte). The destination died with him. Or suppose that Beth and Duncan are co-owners with a survivorship destination. Beth dies on Monday and Duncan dies on Tuesday. When she dies, her share passes to him. But when he dies, his initial half-share does not pass to her estate.

30.13   Second, a destination is *sometimes* validly evacuated by a legacy by the institute. For such a legacy to succeed, two conditions must *both* be satisfied:
- (a) a power to evacuate[10] must exist; and
- (b) the evacuating legacy must conform to the requirements of the law, currently contained in S(S)A 1964, s 30.

30.14   To ascertain if there is a power to evacuate, the first step is to look at the title. This may say expressly that there is, or is not, power to evacuate. If so, well and good. Usually it is silent. In that case certain presumptions apply. The most important is that laid down in *Perrett's Trs v Perrett*.[11] This is that if the destination is a survivorship destination, and if both parties contributed to the price, as is almost always the case, then there is no power of evacuation by either co-owner. Since most married and co-habiting homeowners are co-owners, and since most of them opt for

---

9   For a fuller account, see Reid and Gretton *Conveyancing 2005* (2006) 72 ff.

10   Sometimes the term 'evacuation' is used only for *mortis causa* evacuation. Here we use the term in its broader sense.

11   1909 SC 522. See further M Morton 'Special Destinations as Testamentary Instructions' 1984 *SLT (News)* 133.

a survivorship destination in the title, and since in practice both will have contributed to the price, it will be seen that survivorship destinations are both common and usually non-evacuable.

30.15   The issue of power to evacuate arises only in a testate case. In an intestate case there is no testament, and so obviously no attempt at evacuation has been made.

30.16   In the third place, the substitute can renounce the benefit of the destination.

30.17   In the fourth place, a special destination takes effect only if the institute still owns the property at death. An institute is free to dispone. For example, go back to Beth and Duncan. While they are both alive, she dispones her half-share to Ethel. If Beth dies the next day, Duncan does not take her share, for Ethel has it. But had it been Duncan who had died, Beth would still have taken his share. Parties who co-own with a survivorship destination can thus cheat.

30.18   The four ways of evacuation are all common-law ways. A fifth – statutory – way also exists. If a married couple are co-owners with a survivorship destination, divorce will automatically evacuate the destination.[12] The same applies to civil partners.

Practical significance of special destinations

30.19   Often, a special destination transfers the property to the person who would have received it anyway. Suppose that in the case of Archie and Barbara there had been no special destination. Then (a) if he had died *testate* he would probably have bequeathed his half-share to her anyway, and (b) if he had died *intestate* then it is likely that she would have taken his half share anyway by virtue of the first prior right – assuming that they were married. But sometimes special destinations do work to take property off in a different direction from the direction that it would otherwise have taken.

30.20   Special destinations are rather weak. They can be defeated by an *inter vivos* transfer or, to say the same thing, they operate only if the person who dies still owned the property at that time. Additionally, a special destination only operates if the substitute is still alive.

Special destinations: transferring to the substitute

30.21   If the institute dies, the *method* of transfer of ownership to the substitute depends on whether it is a *survivorship* destination. In a survivorship special destination, the share of the institute passes to the substitute without any act of

---

[12]   Succession (Scotland) Act 2016, s 2, replacing Family Law (Scotland) Act 2006, s 19.

conveyance and without any entry in the Land Register. For other destinations, it is necessary to have a conveyance from the institute's executor.[13]

Special destinations and insolvency

30.22 If the institute dies insolvent, does the substitute take free of the creditors' rights? For example, title is held by Archie and Barbara and the survivor. Barbara dies insolvent. Archie can be required to pay the value of the half-share that he took from Barbara.[14]

Special destinations, joint property and liferents

30.23 Common ownership of X and Y with a survivorship destination is like joint property, in that if X dies, Y will normally then be the sole owner, and *vice versa*.[15] In fact, one decision held that they were the same.[16] But the two are in fact different.[17] For example a joint owner, unlike an owner in common, cannot grant a disposition of his or her share, and cannot raise an action of division and sale.

30.24 Common ownership of X and Y with a survivorship destination is also slightly like a proper liferent.[18] If property is conveyed to X whom failing Y, that is a bit like a liferent to X and fee to Y. Nevertheless liferent is very different. In a proper liferent Y is the owner. By contrast, in the destination, Y is not only not the owner, but in fact has no real right at all. X is the owner, and is free to sell the property (thereby ending Y's hope of succession), or to grant subordinate real rights in it.

BACK TO DESTINATIONS-OVER

30.25 Tom bequeaths a house to Dick whom failing Harry. Take the following possibilities. When Tom dies:
   (a) Dick is alive but Harry is not. In that case Dick takes the house. End of story.
   (b) Harry is alive but Dick is not. In that case Harry takes the house. End of story.
   (c) Both are alive. Then Dick takes the house. *But the story may not end here.*

30.26 If the destination-over was a *conditional institution* then the story *does* end here. Dick takes the house and that is that. But if the destination-over was a *substitution* then the story does *not* end here. The destination-over is converted into

---

13   S(S)A 1964, s 18. The distinction was introduced by a mistaken decision, *Bisset v Walker* 26 Nov 1799, FC. But mistakes can become law.
14   *Fleming's Tr v Fleming* 2000 SC 206.
15   See **CHAPTER 10** above.
16   *Munro v Munro* 1972 SLT (Sh Ct) 6.
17   *Steele v Caldwell* 1979 SLT 228; *Smith v Mackintosh* 1989 SLT 148.
18   See **PARA 22.15** above.

a special destination. In other words, Tom's executor dispones 'to Dick whom failing to Harry'.

30.27 How does one know whether there is a conditional institution or a substitution? First, look at the wording of the testament. This may make it clear. (The traditional method is this: if the testator leaves the property to 'to B, whom failing before or after me, to C' that is a substitution, and 'to B whom failing before me to C' is a conditional institution.) If it does not make it clear, the legal presumption applies, which is that it is a conditional institution.[19]

30.28 Suppose that William leaves his house to 'Beth and Nicola and the survivor'. Beth and Nicola survive William. Should his executor dispone the house to 'Beth and Nicola' or to 'Beth and Nicola and the survivor'? That depends on the question just discussed. If the legacy was a conditional institution (which it is presumed to be) then the former is correct. If it is a substitution then the latter is correct.

JUS AND *SPES*

30.29 The substitute is said to have a *spes successionis* (hope of succession) rather than a *jus* (right). If the substitute dies before the institute then the *spes* vanishes. It does not form part of the substitute's estate. It is said to 'fly off'.

TAILZIES (ENTAILS)

30.30 Scots law used to have a type of special destination called the 'tailzie' (also called the 'entail'). Here, the destination (a) operated perpetually and (b) prevented alienation *inter vivos*. It was thus much stronger than the ordinary special destination. For example, land could be tailzied to 'X and the heirs-male of his body'. That would mean that the land would descend to a chain of heirs until Doomsday. Each current owner's ownership would be so limited that it was, functionally speaking, rather like a liferent, for he could not alienate, so on his death the land would pass to the next heir as defined in the original deed of tailzie. Tailzies had to be registered in the Register of Tailzies.[20] The Entail Amendment Act 1848 made disentailment possible. After the Entail (Scotland) Act 1914 no new tailzies could be created. The Abolition of Feudal Tenure etc. (Scotland) Act 2000 abolished the few remaining tailzies.[21] What was once an important aspect of property law has thus now disappeared.

---

[19] Succession (Scotland) Act 2016, s 8, replacing the common-law rule, which was the same, except where the property was heritable, in which case substitution was presumed.
[20] Entail Act 1685.
[21] AFT(S)A 2000, s 50.

NON-DESTINATIONS: BANK ACCOUNTS

30.31   Lastly, it is common for two people to have a joint bank account. Such accounts can take various forms, depending on the terms of the contract. But a common one is the 'either and survivor' account. Here, the bank pays out on the signature of either party. That continues to be so if one dies. Suppose that Darby and Joan have such an account. Darby dies. Joan can draw out from the account on her sole signature, just as she could when her husband was still alive. This looks like a survivorship destination. But it is not. The rule is that when he dies, she can withdraw all the money, but she cannot necessarily keep it. That depends on to what extent, as between her and her husband, the money was his or hers. To the extent it was not hers, she must pay it to her husband's executor. On that issue the law is, unfortunately, not wholly clear, but it is probably (a) that if there was an agreement, that has effect; (b) if there was no agreement, then the money is divided accordingly to which party was the source;[22] (c) if neither (a) nor (b) can be established, the division is equal. (In practice she may end up getting the money anyway, as beneficiary of the estate.)

LITERATURE

30.32   Gretton and Reid *Conveyancing* ch 26 has a detailed account. See also Hiram *Succession* paras 9.13–9.16 and 11.12–11.15, and Macdonald *Succession* paras 5.02–5.27 and 11.26–11.37. Some comparative and historical material can be found in G Gretton 'Fideicommissary Substitutions: Scots Law in Historical and Comparative Perspective' in K Reid, R Zimmermann and M J de Waal (eds), *Exploring the Law of Succession: Studies National, Historical and Comparative* (2007).

---

[22]   *Cuthill v Burns* (1862) 24 D 849; *Dinwoodie's Exr v Carruther's Exr* (1895) 23 R 234; *Forrest-Hamilton's Tr v Forrest-Hamilton* 1970 SLT 338.

Chapter 31

Execution of documents

THE NEED FOR WRITING

Requirements of Writing (Scotland) Act 1995

31.1   In general, the law does not insist that transactions are set out in writing. For example, Penelope can buy groceries without entering into a written agreement for the transfer of the goods. Roger can hire Simona to mow his lawn without drawing up a contract of employment. Tamsyn can pledge her watch to Ulrika in security of a loan, once again without writing anything down.[1] In a limited number of cases, however, the law regards the transaction as significant enough to insist on writing. This has always been so. The current rules are in the Requirements of Writing (Scotland) Act 1995 (RoW(S)A 1995). (Although this changed the law in many ways, much of it is similar to or the same as the pre-1995 law.) As well as setting out the categories where a written document is mandatory, it also provides how parties are

[1]   See **PARA 21.34** above.

to sign and, importantly, what is required for a document to be *presumed* to be valid. RoW(S)A 1995 has been amended by the Land Registration etc. (Scotland) Act 2012 to facilitate the use of all-electronic documents i.e. documents which are signed digitally. These are regulated by Part 3 of RoW(S)A 1995 as amended. In contrast Part 2 sets out the rules for 'traditional documents', which are defined as 'documents written on paper, parchment or some similar tangible surface'.[2] But first of all Part 1 sets out where writing is required.

The six categories where writing is required

31.2   RoW(S)A 1995 Act lists six categories where writing is mandatory. In all other situations, it is not.[3] But, of course, even in such cases the parties may *choose* to use writing, and usually will do so in important transactions. A £1m machine can be sold without writing, just as much as a £1 screwdriver. But in practice the contract would be in writing. The six categories are:

(a)   A contract or unilateral obligation for the creation, transfer, variation or extinction of a real right in land[4]

31.3   This deals with documents which create personal rights, either under a contract or a promise (unilateral obligation), relating to real rights in land. The commonest example is a contract for the sale of land, i.e. 'missives'.[5] Missives are an agreement for the transfer of the real right of ownership in land in return for payment. A second example is an option. Bob Ltd grants Colin plc the option of buying a development site at any time within the next ten years. A third example is an agreement by a landowner to lease land to a prospective tenant. But writing is not needed if the real right to which the personal right relates is a lease of a year or less.[6]

(b)   The creation, transfer, variation or extinction of a real right in land[7]

31.4   This provision deals with documents relating directly to the real right in question. A document that *creates* a real right is a 'deed of constitution'. Examples include a lease[8] and a standard security.[9] A document that *transfers* a real right is a

---

2   RoW(S)A 1995 s 1A.
3   RoW(S)A 1995 s 1(1). But other legislation may require writing in specific cases.
4   RoW(S)A 1995, s 1(2)(a)(i).
5   See **PARA 5.2** above.
6   RoW(S)A 1995, s 1(7). See **PARA 20.8** above.
7   RoW(S)A 1995, s 1(2)(b).
8   See **CHAPTER 20** above.
9   See **PARAS 21.43–21.56** above.

'deed of transmission'. Examples include a disposition,[10] which transfers ownership of land, and an assignation,[11] which transfers incorporeal property. Then there are deeds of 'variation', which neither transfer nor create a real right, but alter one, such as a minute of waiver,[12] under which a benefited proprietor varies the terms of a real burden. Finally there are 'deeds of extinction' such as a renunciation[13] of a lease or a discharge[14] of a standard security.

31.5   All the deeds just mentioned are *inter vivos*. This Latin term means 'between living persons'. Most of the deeds are unilateral, in the sense that *only* the granter has to sign. For example, in a disposition the seller signs, but the buyer does not have to and normally does not. The reason is that the deed places obligations on the granter not the grantee. This, however, is not entirely accurate. Unilateral deeds can place obligations on the grantee, for example a standard security places obligations on the creditor although he or she does not sign it.[15] In such cases, the grantee becomes bound by the obligations by accepting delivery of the deed.[16] Deeds which are signed by both parties are known as 'bilateral'. The most common example is a lease, which will be signed by both the landlord and the tenant.

(c)   Wills, testamentary trust dispositions and settlements, and codicils[17]

31.6   These documents provide how a person's estate is to be distributed on death. A 'testamentary trust disposition and settlement' is a sophisticated version of a will, requiring some or all of the estate to be held in trust for a certain period.[18] A 'codicil' is a document amending an existing will or testamentary trust disposition and settlement.[19] All of these can be described as *mortis causa* (on the occasion of death) deeds. This means that they take effect on the granter's death.

(d)   Gratuitous unilateral obligations, except in the course of a business[20]

31.7   Gratuitous unilateral obligations must be in writing. There is an exception where the promise is made in the course of a business. Thus if a bank's customer owes an obligation to a third party and the bank gives to that third party a guarantee that the obligation will be performed, no writing is required by RoW(S)A 1995.

---

10   See **PARA 5.8** above.
11   See **PARA 5.42** above.
12   See **PARA 14.59** above.
13   See **PARA 20.39** above.
14   See **PARA 21.56** above.
15   In particular in relation to enforcement of the security. See **PARAS 21.51–21.53** above.
16   See **PARA 31.57** below.
17   RoW(S)A 1995, s 1(2)(c).
18   See **PARA 28.1** above.
19   See **PARA 28.7** above.
20   RoW(S)A 1995, s 1(2)(a)(ii).

In practice, however, banks never grant guarantees gratuitously. The customer pays them a premium to do so. But as Professor MacQueen has said, 'a voluntary obligation is gratuitous when its beneficiary comes under no counterpart obligation'.[21] So if customer A asks bank B to give a guarantee to A's creditor C, the guarantee is gratuitous *in relation to* C. Writing is therefore still not needed. (In practice, however, writing would be used.) In contrast, if a wife guarantees her husband's business debts a document *is* required, because *she* is not acting in the course of a business.

(e) Truster-as-trustee trusts[22]

31.8   Where persons declare themselves to be sole trustee of their own property or property to be subsequently acquired, the declaration must be in writing.[23] The policy is to protect third parties, in particular the person's creditors. In practice, almost all trusts are constituted in writing by means of a trust deed.[24]

(f) Agreement under section 66(1) of the Land Registration etc. (Scotland) Act 2012

31.9   This concerns an agreement in relation to alluvion and is relatively unimportant.[25]

Failure to use writing

31.10   Where writing is required but is not used, the basic rule is that the purported transaction is void. For example, an oral agreement to buy land is unenforceable. There is an exception, which applies to contracts, promises and trusts but not to deeds dealing with real rights, such as leases[26] The person who wants to deny that the obligation in question has been created may be *personally barred* from doing so as a result of the actings of the other party.[27] For the provisions to apply the other party must as a result of these actings have been affected to a material extent and if the obligation were not now to be enforced would be adversely affected, once again

---

[21]   H L MacQueen 'Constitution and Proof of Gratuitous Obligations' 1986 *SLT (News)* 1 at 2.
[22]   RoW(S)A 1995, s 1(2)(a)(iii).
[23]   See **PARA 23.39** above.
[24]   See **PARA 23.39** above.
[25]   On alluvion, see para 9.15 above.
[26]   For the exception see *Advice Centre for Mortgages Ltd v McNicoll* 2006 SLT 591, discussed by E Reid 'Personal Bar: Three Cases' (2006) 10 *Edin LR* 437 at 437–440. See also *Gray v McNeil's Exr* 2016 SLT (Sh Ct) 250 rev'd [2017] SAC (Civ) 9.
[27]   RoW(S)A 1995, s 1(3)–(6). See generally, E C Reid and J W G Blackie *Personal Bar* (2006) ch 7.

to a material extent.[28] The idea is that it would be unfair for the obligation not to be enforceable.[29]

Reasons for requiring writing

31.11   Why does the law insist on writing for certain significant transactions?

(1) The first reason is to provide evidence. The parties to the transfer of a piece of land which imposed real burdens in 1890 are no longer alive but the disposition which gave effect to it can still be examined. This leads to the second reason.

(2) Writing facilitates registration. The reason that the 1890 disposition can be inspected is that it is in the Sasine Register.

(3) The requirement for writing communicates to the parties the seriousness of the transaction being carried out. This is important for juridical acts such as creating or transferring real rights in land.

(4) Writing reduces the risk of fraud.

The role of notaries

31.12   In Scotland, the role of notaries public is more limited than in most other European countries. A notary acts as a state official[30] who supervises the execution of a deed and keeps a copy of it. In most European countries the conveyancing deeds require a notary. Here, few deeds require to be notarised.[31] The Scottish rules about execution of deeds are undemanding; some would say not demanding enough.[32]

The Books of Council and Session

31.13   In practice deeds that are not registered in the Land Register or Sasine Register are often registered in the Books of Council and Session or the sheriff court books. As with the notarial system, that ensures that an official copy can always be obtained, so accidental loss is not a concern, and like the notarial system, registration makes possible proof that a document existed by a certain date. Any probative deed can be registered, whether or not it contains a clause consenting to registration,[33] but such clauses are commonly found, and are necessary if the registration is not only for

---

28   RoW(S)A 1995, s 1(4). See *Caterline Ltd v Glasgow International Prestwick Airport Ltd* 2005 SLT 1083.

29   Reid and Blackie *Personal Bar* paras 7-21–7-33.

30   In Scotland, only solicitors may be notaries. The system is administered by the Law Society of Scotland, and notaries must holding a practising certificate. See the Legal Profession and Legal Aid (Scotland) Act 2007, s 62.

31   An example is a notice to preserve a real burden under TC(S)A 2003, s 50 and Sch 7. See **PARA 14.35** above.

32   See Gretton and Reid *Conveyancing* para 17-25.

33   RoW(S)A 1995, s 6(4).

'preservation' – which is what has just been described – but also for 'execution'. For example, at the end of most commercial leases the tenant consents to 'registration for preservation and execution'. If a deed is registered for execution that means that summary diligence can be carried out, for example for unpaid rent, in other words diligence without the need for a court order.[34] It is good practice to register a will in the Books of Council and Session after the testator's death.

TRADITIONAL DOCUMENTS: FORMAL VALIDITY

Formal validity: the one requirement

31.14   There is only one requirement for formal validity. The granter must subscribe the document.[35] In the case of contracts constituted by separate offer and acceptance documents, both must be subscribed.[36] Documents can also be subscribed in counterpart ie duplicate copies can be signed separately by the parties.[37]

Meaning of 'subscription'

31.15   RoW(S)A 1995 defines 'subscription' in relation to traditional documents as signing at the end of the last page of the document, excluding any annexations.[38] There is an exception for Her Majesty the Queen. She is entitled to 'superscribe' documents, that is to say, sign at the top.[39] Where there is more than one granter, only one of them needs to sign at the foot of the final page. The other or others may sign on an additional blank sheet of paper.[40] The signature does not have to be legible.[41] But legibility will be needed for the document to be probative.[42]

Execution on behalf of someone else

31.16   A document can be signed on behalf of the granter by a mandatory or agent. In principle, the mandate or agency does not need to be constituted in writing. In practice, it is normally created by a probative deed called a 'power of attorney'.[43]

---

[34]   See Gloag and Henderson *The Law of Scotland* para 48.01.
[35]   RoW(S)A 1995, s 2(1).
[36]   RoW(S)A 1995, s 2(2).
[37]   See **PARAS 31.55–31.56** below.
[38]   RoW(S)A 1995, s 7(1). For annexations, see **PARA 31.47** below.
[39]   RoW(S)A 1995, s 13(1)(a)(i). Her Majesty's formal signature is 'Elizabeth R'. The 'R' stands for '*Regina*', the Latin for 'Queen'.
[40]   RoW(S)A 1995, s 7(3).
[41]   *Stirling Stuart v Stirling Crawfurd's Trs* (1885) 12 R 660.
[42]   On probativity, see **PARAS 31.26–31.45** below.
[43]   RoW(S)A 1995, s 12(2).

For example, John, who works abroad, might appoint Kirsten, his solicitor, as his 'attorney'.

31.17 There is a special procedure for execution of documents where a person is blind or unable to write. It is sometimes called 'notarial execution'. This is misleading because there is no requirement for a notary. The document may be signed on the person's behalf by a solicitor who holds a practising certificate, an advocate, a justice of the peace or a sheriff clerk.[44] The granter must declare orally that he or she is blind or unable to write and the signatory must read out the document before signature, unless the granter states that this need not be done.[45] The document must be signed in the granter's presence.[46] Blind people are not obliged to use the procedure and can sign the document themselves.[47]

31.18 Where a granter is mentally incapable, an application will have to be made to the sheriff court for an intervention order or guardianship order under the Adults with Incapacity (Scotland) Act 2000.[48] The guardian or intervener may be given power to execute. Where, however, a continuing power of attorney was executed by the granter under this legislation – that is a power of attorney which continues to have effect despite the granter's subsequent mental incapacity – the attorney may execute, assuming of course that this power has been given.[49]

Methods of signing

Natural persons

31.19 There are three ways in which natural persons can subscribe traditional documents.
(1) The first is to sign their last name and a forename (or initial or abbreviation or familiar form of forename).[50] This can be described as the 'standard method'. Examples are 'Thomas N Johnston', 'T N Johnston', 'T Johnston' and 'Tom Johnston'. The flexibility applies only to the forename.
(2) The second possibility is to sign the full name by which the granter is identified in the document.[51] This can be described as the 'longstop method'. An example would be 'Thomas Nelson Johnston'.

---

[44] RoW(S)A 1995, s 9(1) and (6) and Sch 3.
[45] RoW(S)A 1995, s 9(1).
[46] RoW(S)A 1995, s 9(2).
[47] RoW(S)A 1995, s 9(7).
[48] Adults with Incapacity (Scotland) Act 2000, ss 53–79. Note also the Adult Support and Protection (Scotland) Act 2007. See A Ward *Adult Incapacity* (2003) ch 10 and Reid and Gretton *Conveyancing 2002* (2003) 100–111 (A J M Steven and A Barr).
[49] For continuing powers of attorney, see the Adults with Incapacity (Scotland) Act 2000 ss 15–24.
[50] RoW(S)A 1995, s 7(2)(b).
[51] RoW(S)A 1995, s 7(2)(a).

(3) The third and final possibility is to sign by means of any other name or description or initial or mark.[52] This can be described as the 'informal method'. Examples are 'Thomas', 'Tom', 'Johnston', 'T' or 'Dad'. In this case, however, the signature must either be the granter's normal method of signing the type of document in question, or be intended by the granter to be his or her signature.[53] Importantly, a deed *cannot* be probative if this method is used.[54]

Juristic persons

31.20   Juristic persons, of course, cannot write. Someone has to sign on their behalf. RoW(S)A 1995 sets out special rules in Schedule 2.

(a)   Partnerships

31.21   A signature of a partner or a person authorised to sign on behalf of the partnership is required.[55] Signatories can use their own name or that of the partnership itself.[56]

(b)   Companies

31.22   Either a director or the secretary or an authorised person may sign on behalf of the company.[57]

(c)   Limited liability partnerships

31.23   Documents must be signed by a member of the LLP.[58] There is no provision for authorised persons, but there would nothing to stop the partnership granting a power of attorney in favour of such a person.

(d)   Local authorities

31.24   The signature of the proper officer of the authority is needed.[59] This will be a person designated to carry out this function.

---

[52]   RoW(S)A 1995, s 7(2)(c).
[53]   RoW(S)A 1995, s 7(2)(c)(i) and (ii).
[54]   On probativity, see **PARAS 31.26–31.45** below.
[55]   RoW(S)A 1995, Sch 2, para 2(1).
[56]   RoW(S)A 1995, Sch 2, para 2(2).
[57]   RoW(S)A 1995, Sch 2, para 3(1).
[58]   RoW(S)A 1995, Sch 2, para 3A(1).
[59]   RoW(S)A 1995, Sch 2, para 4(1).

(e) Other bodies corporate

31.25 This is a residuary category and includes building societies, industrial and provident societies, trade unions, universities and foreign companies. The signature of a member of the governing board of the body (or a member of the body itself if there is no board), or the secretary, or an authorised person is required.[60]

TRADITIONAL DOCUMENTS: PROBATIVITY

Definition

31.26 'Probative' is a word which has been given different meanings over the years and is in fact not used by RoW(S)A 1995. It is, nevertheless, a useful term to describe a document which complies with s 3 of the legislation. In other words, a 'probative' document is one which is *presumed to be validly executed.*

Probative versus improbative

31.27 The presumption of validity is one conferred by the law of evidence. It is particularly important where the document is the subject of litigation. Suppose that Cathy sues David on the basis of a probative document. She does not have to prove that the document was validly executed. The law presumes this. The onus is on David if he claims that it is not validly executed. In contrast, if Martin sues Nicola on the basis of an improbative document, and she denies that the deed was validly executed, the onus falls on him. This may be an uphill or impossible task, particularly where the document is old. If Martin is unable to prove the matter, his case will fail.

Achieving probativity

31.28 A traditional document that is subscribed under RoW(S)A 1995, s 2 is valid but not necessarily probative. To achieve probativity, more is required. Normally, the document must be witnessed. This is 'probativity by attestation'.[61] For certain juristic persons, there are other possibilities, involving additional signatures.[62]

Probativity by attestation

31.29 Under this rule, a traditional document is made probative by obtaining a witness to the granter's subscription. There are three requirements. The first is

---

[60] RoW(S)A 1995, Sch 2, paras 5(1) and (2).
[61] See **PARAS 31.29–31.32** below.
[62] See **PARAS 31.36–31.40** below.

that the document bears to have been subscribed by the granter.[63] However, only the standard or the longstop methods of signature may be used.[64] And because the document must *bear* to have been subscribed by the individual in question an illegible signature will not do either.

31.30   The second requirement is that the traditional document bears to have been signed by a witness to the granter's signature and the name and address of the witness are given.[65] The legislation requires the witness to 'sign' rather than 'subscribe' but in practice the witness's signature is always added at the end of the document, beside that of the granter. The witness must sign using either the standard or longstop methods, just like the granter.[66] The same person may witness the signatures of more than one granter and if that is the case requires only to sign once.[67] It is crucial that the witness is designed by name and address. RoW(S)A 1995 allows this to be done in the deed itself or in the testing clause.[68] Until recently a 'testing clause' has been a standard addition to most deeds following signing. It will usually give the date and place of execution, although this is not mandatory.[69] Indeed the testing clause itself is not compulsory, because the witness details could be given in the deed.

31.31   Here is an example of a testing clause:

'IN WITNESS WHEREOF these presents typewritten on this and the preceding page are subscribed by me, the said Sydney John Legge at Aberdeen on Fifth July Two Thousand and Seventeen before this witness, Margaret Dutch of Two High Street, Elgin.'

The expression 'these presents' simply means 'this document'. The testing clause is added after execution using a typewriter. A space is left for it, normally marked out in pencil. This means that, strictly speaking, the testing clause is not part of the deed itself. As typewriters have fallen into disuse it has become practice to replace testing clauses with 'signing blocks' i.e. designated spaces at the end of the document for the granter and witness details.

31.32   The third requirement is a negative one. There must be nothing in the traditional document or the testing clause which indicates that the document was not subscribed in the way which it bears to have been, nor anything to indicate that it was not validly witnessed.[70] RoW(S)A 1995 gives a list of requirements for the witnessing to be valid.

(1) The witness's signature must not be forged.[71]

---

[63]   RoW(S)A 1995, s 3(1)(a).
[64]   See **PARA 31.19** above and RoW(S)A 1995, s 7(2)(c).
[65]   RoW(S)A 1995, s 3(1)(b).
[66]   RoW(S)A 1995, s 7(5).
[67]   RoW(S)A 1995, s 7(5).
[68]   RoW(S)A 1995, s 3(1)(b) and (4)(f).
[69]   However, if given, this information will be presumed to be correct. See **PARA 30.41** below.
[70]   RoW(S)A 1995, s 3(1)(c).
[71]   RoW(S)A 1995, s 3(4)(a).

(2) A granter of the deed cannot be a witness.[72] So, if there are two granters they cannot each witness the other's signature.

(3) The witness must know the granter, be 16 years old or over and be mentally capable of acting as a witness.[73] The legislation defines 'know' for these purposes as having 'credible information' as to the identity of the granter.[74] The granter and the witness can be acquaintances rather than close friends.

(4) The person who signed as witness must actually have witnessed the granter's subscription.[75] The legislation permits the witness either to be there as the granter subscribes or to have the subscription acknowledged to him or her at a later time.[76]

(5) The witness must sign after the granter has signed, or after the granter has acknowledged his or her signature and this must be 'one continuous process'.[77] RoW(S)A 1995 does not define 'one continuous process' but, in a case under earlier legislation, the court reluctantly said that a gap of 45 minutes was not too long.[78] The witness therefore should sign straight away. In acknowledgement cases, however, the witness could sign months or years after the granter's subscription provided that this was immediately after the acknowledgment of that subscription.

(6) The designation of the witness must be added before the document is founded on in court, or registered, and must not in any material respect have errors in it.[79]

Probativity is all about appearance

31.33 Probativity may be compared to the WAGs (wives and girlfriends) of some of our famous footballers – it is all about appearance. Whether a document is probative is determined by visual inspection. Either it looks valid or does not. For probativity, looks are everything. Recourse to extrinsic evidence is not permitted.[80] The judgment must be made by looking at the deed alone. And the judgment must be made. No sitting on the fence is permissible. There is no such thing as (as is often suggested in exam answers) a document which is presumed to be probative. Either it is probative or not. Of course if it is probative, it is presumed to be valid.

31.34 This means that if a fault in executing or witnessing cannot be determined by visual inspection, the document is still probative. A forged deed will be probative,

---

[72]   RoW(S)A 1995, s 3(4)(b).
[73]   RoW(S)A 1995, s 3(4)(c).
[74]   RoW(S)A 1995, s 3(5).
[75]   RoW(S)A 1995, s 3(4)(d).
[76]   Acknowledgement in principle should be by the granter saying 'this is my signature' or words to this effect but something less express may do. See *Lindsay v Milne* 1995 SLT 487 and *McLure v McLure's Exr* 1997 SLT 127.
[77]   RoW(S)A 1995, s 3(1)(e).
[78]   *Thomson v Clarkson's Trs* (1892) 20 R 59.
[79]   RoW(S)A 1995, s 3(4)(f).
[80]   Extrinsic evidence can be used to challenge probativity but not to support it.

unless the forgery is apparent, which is unlikely. A document that has been witnessed by a four-year-old is probative, unless the child's signature reveals that he or she is underage. This will be more likely the younger the child is. If the subscription and witnessing are not one continuous process, the document will still be probative, unless the gap in time is revealed on the face of the deed. This follows from the wording of RoW(S)A 1995, s 3(1): the document is probative if it *bears* to have been validly subscribed and witnessed.

Special rule for wills

31.35   There is an additional requirement to make traditional testamentary documents such as wills probative. They must be signed on every sheet of paper comprising the document.[81] While what is strictly required is *signature* on *each sheet* rather than subscription, in practice the granter will sign at the bottom of *each page*. Therefore if both sides of the paper are used the granter will subscribe twice.

Probativity by other methods: juristic persons

31.36   Attestation is the only method of achieving probativity where the granter is a natural person or partnership.[82] In other cases, there is an alternative method.

(a)   Companies

31.37   The document may be subscribed by a second signatory. The three permitted combinations are:
   (1)   two directors;
   (2)   a director and the company secretary; or
   (3)   two authorised signatories.[83]

'Mixed doubles' – such as a director and an authorised signatory – are not allowed. This means that in total there are six ways in which a company can execute a document in a probative manner: the three mentioned already, as well as (4) a director plus a witness; (5) the secretary plus a witness; and (6) an authorised signatory plus a witness.

(b)   Limited liability partnerships

31.38   The document may be subscribed by two members of the LLP.[84]

(c) Local authorities and other bodies corporate

31.39   Once the document is subscribed in accordance with the relevant requirements of RoW(S)A 1995,[85] it is sealed with the body's *common seal*.[86] This must be done by a person with authority on the same day as subscription.[87]

(d) Appearance again

31.40   Once again, with these alternative methods it is appearance that matters. Thus, for example, if it cannot be seen from the face of the document that the common seal was not attached by an authorised person then, even if this was the case, the document is probative.

Three presumptions

31.41   The probativity of a document generates three presumptions. The first and most important is that it is presumed to have been validly executed.[88] The idea is to give some protection against forgery. The point of requiring a witness etc is to make it harder for a fraudster to impersonate the granter. Compared with other countries which insist on notarial execution,[89] the level of protection is low, because the witness can be complicit in the fraud, and indeed the fraudster can simply forge the signature of the 'witness' as well. Happily, such criminality is uncommon but certainly not unknown.[90] The second presumption is that the document was subscribed on the *date* stated in the document or testing clause.[91] It is not compulsory to give the date, but if this is done then this presumption applies. The third presumption is that it was subscribed at the *place* stated in the document or testing clause.[92] Again, it is not mandatory to state the place, but the presumption applies where this is done.

31.42   As evidential presumptions, they may be rebutted by evidence to the contrary. A probative document can be challenged in two ways.[93] The first ('direct attack') is to prove that the granter did not subscribe. A successful challenge will result in the document being declared void. The second way ('indirect attack') is to show that the attestation or equivalent was not properly carried out, for example because the witness was under age or the granter and witness did not subscribe in one continuous process.[94] A successful result is that the document is declared to

---

85   See **PARAS 31.24** and **31.25** above.
86   RoW(S)A 1995, Sch 2, paras 4(5) and 5(5).
87   RoW(S)A 1995, Sch 2, paras 4(6) and 5(6).
88   RoW(S)A 1995, s 3(1).
89   See **PARA 31.12** above.
90   For an example, see *Kaur v Singh* 1999 SC 180.
91   RoW(S)A 1995, s 3(8).
92   RoW(S)A 1995, s 3(8).
93   See Gretton and Reid *Conveyancing* para 17–13.
94   See **PARA 31.32** above.

be improbative and then the onus of proving valid execution is now on the person seeking to rely on it. That person may or may not be able to do so.

31.43 Probativity *only* concerns execution. The document may be invalid for other reasons, for example, it may be void from uncertainty or because the granter lacks legal capacity, or lacks title to grant it. Thus if John grants a deed transferring Jane's property it will be void because of the *nemo plus* rule.[95] Just because a deed is probative does not mean it is valid.

The benefits of probativity

31.44 A traditional document may be subscribed under RoW(S)A 1995, s 2 or made probative by attestation (or the equivalents for juristic persons) under s 3. Making a document probative has the obvious benefit of presumed validity, which as mentioned previously, is particularly important for older documents.[96] Documents prepared by solicitors will normally be in probative form. There are two further benefits to probativity. The first is that, subject to minor exceptions, only probative documents can be recorded in the Sasine Register or Land Register or in the Books of Council and Session or sheriff court books.[97] The second benefit relates solely to testamentary documents. An executor is only able to obtain confirmation under a will or other testamentary document if it is probative.[98]

Converting improbative documents into probative documents

31.45 It may be wished, or indeed required, for a document to be made probative some time after subscription. For example, registration or confirmation is sought. Here there are two possibilities.

(1) The granter is alive and available. In that case the granter may be asked to acknowledge his or her signature to a witness who then signs, thus achieving probativity by attestation.

(2) The granter is dead or otherwise unavailable, for example no longer has mental capacity. Here, an application can be made to the sheriff court to have the document endorsed by a certificate stating that it was subscribed by the granter.[99] It is necessary to provide evidence of valid subscription, but this may be done by means of an uncorroborated affidavit by someone who knows the granter's handwriting.[100]

---

[95] See **PARA 4.41** above. Of course, there are qualifications: for instance, John might be Jane's agent.
[96] See **PARA 31.11** above.
[97] RoW(S)A 1995, s 6.
[98] S(S)A 1964, s 21A. See **PARA 28.4** above.
[99] RoW(S)A 1995, s 4(1). For procedure, see Act of Sederunt (Requirements of Writing) 1996 (SI 1996/1534).
[100] RoW(S)A 1995, s 4(3).

ADDING TO TRADITIONAL DOCUMENTS

Incorporation of earlier documents

31.46   Under the common law a document can incorporate by reference some or all of an earlier document. This is done to save repeating the terms of the earlier document in full. For example, in dispositions recorded in the Sasine Register the practice is to refer to the detailed description of the land in the break-off disposition.[101] There is in fact a statutory procedure for descriptions by reference.[102] The general common law procedure for incorporation has two requirements.

(1) The document must contain words of incorporation, for example 'but always with and under the burdens set out in [reference to deed imposing real burdens]'.

(2) The earlier document must be described in such a way that it can be identified. Therefore, if it has been registered the registration details should be given. The earlier document does not need to be signed or marked.

Annexations

31.47   It is common in practice to incorporate an annexation into a document, for example a plan describing land, or a schedule setting out a service charge provision in a lease.[103] Usually such annexations are physically attached, typically by a staple in the case of relatively brief documents. This, however, is not mandatory. It is competent to incorporate annexations at common law, but in practice the provisions in RoW(S)A 1995, s 8 are relied upon for traditional documents. The first requirement is that the document contain words of incorporation,[104] for example 'which subjects are shaded pink in the plan annexed and executed as relative hereto'. The second is that the annexation is identified on its face as being the annexation referred to in the document,[105] for example 'This is the plan referred to in the foregoing Disposition by Isabel Cook in favour of Alice Hay dated 22 June 2017'. The third and final requirement only applies where the annexation describes land. Here, if it is pictorial, that is to say 'a plan, drawing, photograph or other representation',[106] it must be signed on each page. If it merely describes the land in writing, it only needs to be signed on the last page.[107]

Alterations

31.48   After the document is completed, a mistake may be noticed that needs correction. This is less common nowadays with word processing, but still possible.

---

[101] That is the first disposition of the land as a separate unit.
[102] See the Conveyancing (Scotland) Act 1874, s 61.
[103] See **PARA 20.41** above.
[104] RoW(S)A 1995, s 8(1)(a).
[105] RoW(S)A 1995, s 8(1)(b).
[106] RoW(S)A 1995, s 8(1)(c)(i).
[107] RoW(S)A 1995, s 8(1)(c)(ii).

RoW(S)A 1995, s 5 regulates alterations to traditional documents. An 'alteration' is defined as including 'interlineations, marginal addition, deletion, substitution, erasure or anything written on erasure'.[108] It is necessary to distinguish 'pre-subscription' and 'post-subscription' alterations. A pre-subscription alteration, that is one made before subscription, does form part of the document.[109] A post-subscription alteration, that is one made after subscription, does not unless the granter signs it.[110] Of course, it is usually impossible to tell when the alteration was made simply by looking at the document. Evidence may have to be led. But if the document is probative and there is a statement in the testing clause or the document itself that the alteration was added before subscription, that statement is *presumed* to be correct.[111] The onus then falls on the person asserting that the alteration was added later to prove this.

ELECTRONIC DOCUMENTS

Validity

31.49　An electronic document under RoW(S)A 1995 is document which 'rather than being written on paper, parchment or some similar tangible surface [is] created in electronic form'.[112] There are two requirements for such a document to be validly executed. First, it must be *authenticated* by the granter.[113] 'Authenticated' means that the electronic signature of that person must be incorporated into or logically associated with the electronic document and that signature must be created by the person by whom it purports to have been created.[114] Thus if the signature is applied by someone else the document will not be validly executed. The electronic signature itself must also be of a type that satisfies any requirements prescribed by the Scottish Ministers. Under the Electronic Documents (Scotland) Regulations 2014 an 'advanced electronic signature' is required.[115] This type of signature is defined by reference to the Electronic Signatures Regulations 2002 and requires sophisticated technology.[116] As most granters do not have direct access to this, the signature has to be applied by an agent, usually a solicitor. Solicitors can sign documents electronically by means of their Law Society of Scotland smartcard in association with a reader which is connected to their computer.

108　RoW(S)A 1995, s 12(1).
109　RoW(S)A 1995, s 5(1)(a).
110　RoW(S)A 1995, s 5(1)(b).
111　RoW(S)A 1995, s 5(4) and (5).
112　RoW(S)A 1995, s 9A.
113　RoW(S)A 1995, s 9B(1)(a).
114　RoW(S)A 1995, s 9B(2). For the definition of 'electronic signature', see RoW(S)A 1995, s 12(1).
115　Electronic Documents (Scotland) Regulations 2014 (SSI 2014/83), reg 2.
116　Electronic Signatures Regulations 2002 (SI 2002/41).

31.50   Secondly, the document itself must meet any requirements prescribed by the Scottish Ministers.[117] As with traditional documents, where the granter is signing in more than one capacity he or she only has to sign the once.[118]

Probativity

31.51   There are three requirements for probativity in the case of electronic documents. First, the document must bear to have been authenticated by the granter.[119] Secondly, there must be nothing in the document or in the authentication to indicate that it was not so authenticated.[120] Thirdly, the electronic signature incorporated into, or logically associated with, the document has to satisfy certain pre-requisites.[121] It must be of a type, as well as satisfying such requirements, as may be prescribed by the Scottish Ministers. It must also be used (i) in such circumstances as may be prescribed[122] and/or (ii) bear to be *certified*. If only (ii) is satisfied the certification has to be of a type and satisfy such requirements as may be prescribed. 'Certification' is defined as meaning confirmation in a statement that (a) the electronic signature, (b) a means of producing, communicating or verifying that signature or (c) a procedure applied to that signature is either on its own or combined with other factors, a valid means of establishing the authenticity of the document, its integrity or both its authenticity and its integrity.[123] It does not matter whether the statement is made before or after authentication.

31.52   Under the Electronic Documents (Scotland) Regulations the electronic signature must be an 'advanced electronic signature'[124] and be certified by a 'qualified certificate'.[125] Once again this term is defined by reference to the Electronic Signatures Regulations 2002. The certification must be carried out by a 'certification-service-provider'. Currently, the Law Society of Scotland is the only such provider in Scotland. The chip in its smartcard contains the required certificate and therefore any document authenticated by such a card is both formally valid and probative.

31.53   As with traditional documents it is possible to achieve probativity by application to the court. This is possible where the electronic document bears to have been authenticated by the granter but the other requirements set out in the previous

---

[117]   RoW(S)A 1995, s 9B(1)(b).
[118]   RoW(S)A 1995, s 9B(4).
[119]   RoW(S)A 1995, s 9C(1)(a).
[120]   RoW(S)A 1995, s 9C(1)(b).
[121]   RoW(S)A 1995, s 9C(1)(c).
[122]   Such circumstances have yet to be prescribed. For the background to this provision, see Scottish Law Commission, Report on Land Registration (Scot Law Com No 222, 2010) para 34.49.
[123]   RoW(S)A 1995, s 12(1).
[124]   As for validity. See **PARA 31.49** above.
[125]   Electronic Documents (Scotland) Regulations 2014 (SSI 2014/83), reg 3.

paragraph have not been satisfied.[126] Again, as for traditional documents, electronic documents normally require to be probative before they can be registered.[127]

Alterations, annexations, authentication and execution by or on behalf of individuals with a disability

31.54 The Scottish Ministers have the power under RoW(S)A 1995 to make regulations as regards formal validity or probativity of (a) any alterations made to an electronic document (whether before or after authentication); (b) the authentication of electronic documents; (c) the authentication by or on behalf of a person with a disability of an electronic document and (d) annexations to electronic documents.[128] The Electronic Documents (Scotland) Regulations 2014 made under this power provide that for an annexation to be incorporated into an electronic document it must be (a) referred to in the document; (b) identified on its face as the annexation referred to in the document and (c) annexed to the document before the electronic signature is incorporated into or logically associated with the document and the annexation.[129]

EXECUTION IN COUNTERPART

31.55 Sometimes the parties who are to execute a document are geographically remote. For example, a company in Edinburgh might be entering into a contract with a company based in Bristol or Brussels or Buenos Aires. Indeed, the Edinburgh company might be entering into a single contract with companies from all three of these places. For the parties to execute the same document it would have to be sent round them for signature or their representatives would have to travel to a 'signing ceremony'. This costs time and money. It was unclear at common law whether the parties could instead 'execute in counterpart', that is to say sign their own versions ('counterparts of the same document').[130] But this is now possible under the Legal Writings (Counterparts and Delivery) (Scotland) Act 2015 (LW(CD)(S)A 2015).[131]

31.56 The parties have two options. The first is to execute a number of counterparts equal to the number of parties to the document and then send one of the counterparts to each of the other parties.[132] The second and simpler option is to send the counterparts

---

[126] RoW(S)A 1995, s 9D(1).
[127] RoW(S)A 1995, s 9G.
[128] RoW(S)A 1995, s 9E(1).
[129] Electronic Documents (Scotland) Regulations 2014, reg 4.
[130] See *Smith v Duke of Gordon* (1701) Mor 16987 and *Wilson v Fenton Bros (Glasgow) Ltd* 1957 SLT (Sh Ct) 3.
[131] The legislation is based on the draft Bill appended to Scottish Law Commission, Review of Contract Law: Report on Formation of Contract: Execution in Counterpart (Scot Law Com No 231, 2013). For an overview, see H MacQueen, C Garland and L Smith, 'The Legal Writings (Counterparts and Delivery) (Scotland) Act 2015' 2015 *SLT (News)* 111.
[132] LW(CD)(S)A 2015, s 1(1), (2), (5) and (6).

to a person nominated to take delivery of the counterparts and collate them.[133] This will normally be a solicitor to one of the parties. The counterparts together are deemed to be a single document.[134] That document can comprise either of all the counterparts in their entirety, or one of the counterparts in its entirety collated with the signed pages from the other counterparts.[135] Execution in counterpart under LW(CD)(S)A 2015 is available for both traditional and electronic documents,[136] but in practice is likely to be used more for the former given that electronic documents can be sent quickly and inexpensively between the parties.

DELIVERY OF DOCUMENTS

31.57   In general, a unilateral document is not effective unless it is delivered to the grantee. In *Creditors of Sir James Stamfield v The Children of James Scot of Bristo*,[137] Sir James had signed an assignation of his share of a business. He left the document in his house, before travelling to his country estate to spend the night. His body was found the next morning in a river. The assignation was held to be ineffective as it had not been delivered to the assignee. There may be some exceptions to the requirement for delivery, such as deeds granted by parents in favour of their children, but they are open to question.[138] The rules on delivery of traditional documents are mainly common law, but LW(CD)(S)A 2015, s 4 enables electronic delivery by sending a copy. For electronic documents RoW(S)A 1995 provides that these must be delivered electronically or by such other means as are reasonably practicable.[139] Further, the document must be in a form and the delivery be by a means either which the intended recipient has agreed to accept or which it is reasonable in all the circumstances for that person to accept.[140]

LITERATURE

31.58   For alternative accounts see Gretton and Reid *Conveyancing* ch 17 and McDonald *Conveyancing Manual* ch 2. The most detailed and up-to-date commentary on the 1995 Act is Reid, K G C, *Requirements of Writing (Scotland) Act 1995* (2nd edn, 2015). The 1995 Act was based on Scottish Law Commission Report on Requirements of Writing (Scot Law Com No 112, 1988).

---

[133] LW(CD)(S)A 2015, ss 1(1), (2), (5), (7) and 2.
[134] LW(CD)(S)A 2015, s 1(3).
[135] LW(CD)(S)A 2015, s 1(4).
[136] LW(CD)(S)A 2015, s 3.
[137] (1696) 4 Brown's Supplement 344.
[138] See McBryde *Contract* paras 4-44–4-69.
[139] RoW(S)A 1995, s 9F(1).
[140] RoW(S)A 1995, s 9F(2).

Chapter 32

Human rights

THE LEGISLATION

European Convention on Human Rights

32.1   In the aftermath of the Second World War, the Council of Europe was founded in 1949 by ten of the continent's nations as a means of preserving peace. Upholding human rights was a high priority for the new organisation. The European Convention for the Protection of Human Rights and Fundamental Freedoms (ECHR) was drawn up by the Council and entered into force in September 1953. It sets out a number of specific guaranteed rights. At the same time the European Court of Human Rights (ECtHR) in Strasbourg was established to hear and determine disputes about the application of the ECHR. A number of 'protocols' (add-on provisions) have since been attached to the ECHR, adding further guaranteed rights. Since 1949, many countries have acceded to the ECHR.[1] Originally, the ECHR was binding on the United Kingdom simply as an international treaty. Indeed, it still is. Later, those who considered that their Convention rights had been breached could take a case against the United Kingdom to the ECtHR.[2] Such a case was not an appeal from the decisions of the domestic courts, but an entirely distinct action. And such cases are still competent.

Human Rights Act 1998

32.2 In 1998 the position changed: the ECHR was incorporated into domestic law by the Human Rights Act 1998 (HRA 1998), in force from 2000.[3] Convention rights can now be enforced in domestic courts, without the delay and expense of an application to Strasbourg. A court or tribunal is obliged to 'take into account' any relevant case law of the ECtHR when determining questions involving Convention rights.[4] Primary and subordinate Westminster legislation must be read and given effect to in a way which is compatible with Convention rights, but only 'so far as it is possible to do so'.[5] Where a court determines that such legislation is not capable of such interpretation, a 'declaration of incompatibility' may be made.[6] Public authorities, such as the Scottish Government, local authorities, courts and tribunals, must not act in a way which is incompatible with Convention rights.[7] Where there is a breach of Convention rights, the court 'may grant such relief or remedy, or make such order, within its powers as it considers just and appropriate'[8] including damages.

32.3 It is clear that Convention rights may be invoked against the state and other public authorities. This is known as 'vertical effect'. It is less certain whether they can be invoked in cases between private individuals, or other non-public persons, such as companies, in other words, whether there is 'horizontal effect'. This is important for property lawyers because many property disputes are between non-public parties.

---

[1] See, generally, Lord Reed and J Murdoch *Human Rights Law in Scotland* (4th edn, 2017) ch 2. As of 2017, the ECHR applies in 47 states.

[2] See *James v UK* (1986) 8 EHRR 123 for an example of a pre HRA 1998 case.

[3] And also, in another way, by the Scotland Act 1998 (in force from 1999) See **PARA 32.4** below.

[4] HRA 1998, s 2. Case law includes any judgments, decisions, declarations or advisory opinions of the ECtHR, as well as advisory opinions and decisions of the former European Commission on Human Rights and decisions of the Committee of Ministers of the Council of Europe.

[5] HRA 1998, s 3(1).

[6] HRA 1998, s 4.

[7] HRA 1998, s 6. The effect of the Convention on the Scottish Government is also channelled through s 57 of the Scotland Act 1998.

[8] HRA 1998, s 8.

It appears that certain provisions of HRA 1998 have some horizontal effect. The requirement on the courts to interpret legislation in a Convention-compliant manner, as far as it is possible to do so, applies irrespective of whether a party to the case is a public body. Further, because a court is a 'public body' in terms of HRA 1998 it must act in a way which is Convention-compliant. This opens up the possibility for parties to argue that a court failing to uphold a claim for a breach of a Convention right by one party against another would itself be acting in a manner incompatible with the Convention.[9]

Scotland Act 1998

32.4

'An Act of the Scottish Parliament is not law so far as any provision of the Act is outside the legislative competence of the Parliament. A provision is outside that competence so far as ... it is incompatible with any of the Convention rights.'[10]

If successfully challenged, it is void.[11] The consequences of breaching Convention rights are thus more radical for legislation of the Scottish Parliament than they are for that of the UK Parliament. The Scotland Act 1998 also applies the ECHR to the actions of the Scottish Government including statutory instruments.[12]

THE ECHR AND PROPERTY RIGHTS: A1P1

General

32.5   The ECHR as originally drafted did not protect property rights. This was added later as Article 1 of Protocol 1 to the Convention (commonly called 'A1P1'), which provides:

'Every natural or legal person is entitled to the peaceful enjoyment of his possessions. No one shall be deprived of his possessions except in the public interest and subject to the conditions provided for by law and by the general principles of international law.

---

[9]   See Lord Reed and J Murdoch *Human Rights Law in Scotland* paras 1.81–1.82 and A J M Steven 'Property Law and Human Rights' 2005 *JR* 293 at 295–297.

[10]   Scotland Act 1998, s 29(1) & (2). For an example of a judgment in which the legislative provision at issue was deemed to be incompatible with the ECHR see *Salvesen v Riddell* [2013] UKSC 22 discussed at **PARA 31.17** below. For an example of a judgment deeming a legislative provision to be within the Scottish Parliament's competence, see *AXA General Insurance Ltd, Petitioners* 2012 SC (UKSC) 122.

[11]   Subject to s 102. For an example of an unsuccessful challenge, see *Adams v Advocate General* 2003 SC 171.

[12]   Scotland Act 1998, ss 54 and 57.

The preceding provisions shall not, however, in any way impair the right of a State to enforce such laws as it deems necessary to control the use of property in accordance with the general interest or to secure the payment of taxes or other contributions or penalties.'[13]

32.6 It is generally accepted that the article comprises three distinct rules.[14] The second sentence, on *deprivation,* and the third, on *control,* represent particular examples of state interference with the right enunciated in the first sentence. Thus if state action does not constitute deprivation or control, it may nevertheless violate the right to the peaceful enjoyment of possessions.[15]

State deprivation of property

32.7 The second sentence of A1P1 strikes principally at actions which result in extinction of a person's title to property.[16] Only formal and permanent deprivation by the state is therefore likely to be considered a violation. However, *de facto* appropriation is also within the ambit of A1P1. This occurs where ownership remains with the affected party although the practical reality is that the retained title is rendered worthless.[17]

32.8 The protection afforded is not absolute. Deprivations are permissible in the 'public interest' but any state action must be in accordance with law.[18] States are also granted a 'margin of appreciation', i.e. a degree of flexibility, thus allowing divergence on issues where national authorities are deemed better placed to assess the requirements of their societies.[19] Although not expressed in A1P1, proportionality has been added as an additional criterion, requiring a fair balance between the means employed and the result sought by any state action.[20] Finally, there is a presumption of a right to compensation for deprivation in all but exceptional circumstances.[21] In other words, if compensation is not paid there is likely to be a breach of Convention rights.

---

[13] The convention is authentic in two versions, English and French. The French text of A1P1 is very different. See G Gretton 'Property Rights' in A Boyle, C Himsworth, H MacQueen and A Loux (eds) *Human Rights and Scots Law* (2002) 275.

[14] *Sporrong and Lönnroth v Sweden* (1983) 5 EHRR 35 at para 61.

[15] See, eg, *Loizidou v Turkey* (1996) 23 EHRR 513.

[16] See, eg, *James v UK* (1986) 8 EHRR 123 and *Lithgow v UK* (1986) 8 EHRR 329.

[17] See *Papamichalopoulos v Greece* (1993) 16 EHRR 440, where the inability of the applicants to sell, bequeath, grant security over, make a gift of, make use of or even obtain access to their properties was held to be a *de facto* expropriation.

[18] See Reed and Murdoch *Human Rights Law in Scotland* paras 8.18–8.20.

[19] See Reed and Murdoch *Human Rights Law in Scotland* paras 3.139–3.145.

[20] *James v UK* (1986) 8 EHRR 123 at para 50.

[21] See, eg, *Pinnacle Meat Processors v UK* (Application 33298/96), 21 October 1998.

State control of property

32.9   The third sentence of A1P1 deals with the situation where there is state interference with a person's right to property but no expropriation. Examples of state control include restricting the purposes for which land may be used,[22] imposing positive obligations on land owners[23] and restricting who may live in a particular property.[24]

32.10   As with deprivation, control is permissible only if certain requirements are met. There will be no violation of A1P1 where the control is deemed necessary in accordance with the general interest or is required to secure the payment of taxes or other contributions, or penalties.[25] States rarely have trouble convincing the Strasbourg Court that measures are in the general interest. It is considered not for European judges to determine the best solutions to national problems.[26] Again, there is a requirement that any state control must be in accordance with law. Greater leeway is given for margins of appreciation in control cases than for deprivations.[27] Proportionality is a factor that will be considered in determining the legitimacy of state control, though, in contrast to state deprivation, there is no presumption of compensation for control of property.[28]

What sort of property?

32.11   A1P1 speaks vaguely of 'possessions' and 'property'. The ECtHR has construed the provisions broadly, to include, for example, monetary claims,[29] leases,[30] intellectual property rights,[31] liquor licences[32] and social security benefits.[33]

---

[22]   *Pine Valley Developments v Ireland* (1991) 14 EHRR 319.
[23]   *Denev v Sweden* (Application 12570/86) (1989) 59 DR 127.
[24]   *Gillow v UK* (1989) 11 EHRR 335.
[25]   'General interest' for state control has been interpreted as akin to 'public interest' for state deprivation. See *James v UK* (1986) 8 EHRR 123 at para 43.
[26]   Wide-ranging general interest justifications have been accepted: eg environmental protection in *Pine Valley Developments v Ireland* (1991) 14 EHRR 319 and combating alcohol abuse in *Tre Traktörer Aktiebolag v Sweden* (1989) 13 EHRR 309.
[27]   *Handyside v UK* (1976) 1 EHRR 737.
[28]   See D Anderson 'Compensation for Interference with Property' [1999] EHRLR 543 at 550.
[29]   *Stran Greek Refiners v Greece* (1994) 19 EHRR 293; *Pressos Campania Navra v Belgium* (1995) 21 EHRR 301.
[30]   *Mellacher v Austria* (1989) 12 EHRR 391.
[31]   *Lenzing v UK* (1999) EHRLR 132.
[32]   *Tre Traktörer Aktiebolag v Sweden* (1989) 13 EHRR 483.
[33]   *Gaygusuz v Austria* (1996) 23 EHRR 365; *Szrabjer v UK* (1998) EHRLR 230.

IMPACT OF A1P1 ON SCOTTISH PROPERTY LAW

General

32.12 The incorporation of the ECHR into national law under HRA 1998 has had a noticeable effect upon Scottish property law and will continue to do so.[34] Some areas where Convention rights have been considered are:

(1) real burdens;
(2) positive prescription;
(3) diligence on the dependence;
(4) agricultural tenancies; and
(5) wayleaves.

(1) Real burdens

32.13 *Strathclyde Joint Police Board v The Elderslie Estates Ltd*[35] concerned the Lands Tribunal's powers of variation and extinction of real burdens.[36] The applicants in the case claimed that the right to extract a fee for a minute of waiver was a 'possession' in terms of A1P1 and refusal by the Lands Tribunal to allow compensation[37] was therefore a 'deprivation' of that possession.[38] While the Lands Tribunal was willing to accept that the right to extract a fee for waiver was indeed a possession,[39] there was found to be no violation of the Convention. The statutory provisions at issue were deemed to pursue a legitimate aim in the public interest, namely removing the ability of a benefited proprietor to demand unreasonable sums from a burdened proprietor in exchange for discharging a burden.

(2) Positive prescription

32.14 *J A Pye (Oxford) Ltd v UK*[40] involved a challenge to the English law on adverse possession.[41] This is the broad equivalent of positive prescription under the

---

[34] See generally A J M Steven 'Property Law and Human Rights' 2005 *JR* 293; F McCarthy 'Human Rights and the Law of Leases' (2013) 17 *Edin LR* 184 and T Tabori, "Growth industry: article 1 of the First Protocol to the ECHR" 2013 *JR* 194. See further A J M Steven 'Rights in Security' and D Carey Miller 'The Human Rights of Property in Land Law: Comparing South Africa and Scotland' in E Reid and D Visser (eds) *Private Law and Human Rights: Bringing Rights Home in Scotland and South Africa* (2013).

[35] 2002 SLT (Lands Tr) 2.

[36] Now governed by TC(S)A 2003, ss 90–104. See **PARAS 14.71–14.73** above.

[37] CFR(S)A 1970, s 1(4)(i).

[38] Before feudal abolition, the jurisdiction of the Lands Tribunal was governed by CFR(S)A 1970, ss 1 and 2.

[39] This decision is itself questionable in the light of *S v UK* (Application 10741/84) (1984) 41 DR 226.

[40] (2006) 43 EHRR 3. See also *Beaulane Properties Ltd v Palmer* [2006] Ch 79.

[41] The law has now been reformed by the Land Registration Act 2002, Sch 6, para 2. See Law Commission, Report on the Limitation of Actions (Law Com No 270, 2001) paras 4.126–4.135.

Prescription and Limitation (Scotland) Act 1973 (PL(S)A 1973).[42] The European Court found the rules on adverse possession to contravene A1P1. Parallels between the Scottish and English rules cast doubt upon whether positive prescription would stand up to similar challenge. The legislation both north and south of the border effectively extinguished the owner's title to the property, without compensation.

32.15 The case was subsequently heard by the Grand Chamber and the decision overturned.[43] The Grand Chamber considered that limitation periods pursue a legitimate aim in the general interest. Extinction of the owner's title following expiry of a relatively lengthy limitation period was deemed to be a proportionate measure and one that fell within the United Kingdom's margin of appreciation.[44]

(3) Diligence on the dependence

32.16 *Karl Construction Ltd v Palisade Properties plc*[45] concerned a challenge to the ECHR-compatibility of inhibition on the dependence. The law permitted this diligence to be carried out more or less automatically in favour of a creditor upon raising an action for payment of a debt. The effect was to prevent the debtor disposing of land. Lord Drummond Young found that the automatic entitlement to this remedy violated A1P1. The requirement for a judicial hearing before diligence on the dependence was introduced.[46] The later case of *Advocate General for Scotland v Taylor*[47] restricted the impact of *Karl Construction* by removing the need for an actual hearing. Since these cases, the law has undergone statutory reform, with the new provisions ensuring, among other things, that the procedure should be ECHR-compatible.[48] It has been suggested recently, however, that summary diligence carried out by landlords may raise comparable A1P1 issues.[49]

(4) Agricultural tenancies

32.17 One of the principal purposes of agricultural lease legislation is to give tenants security of tenure.[50] Various methods to circumvent this protection have been devised over the years, leading to anti-avoidance provisions being enacted. In

---

[42] See **PARAS 6.7–6.20** above.

[43] (2008) 46 EHRR 45. For further discussion see Scottish Law Commission, Report on Prescription and Title to Moveable Property (Scot Law Com No 228, 2012) para 1.5.

[44] Due to the absence of compensation, the Grand Chamber also reclassified the case as one of state control rather than state deprivation. See G L Gretton 'Private Law and Human Rights' (2008) 12 *Edin LR* 109.

[45] 2002 SC 270.

[46] *Karl Construction* dealt with inhibition on the dependence. It was applied to arrestment on the dependence by *Fab-Tek Engineering Ltd v Carillion Construction Ltd* 2002 SLT (Sh Ct) 113.

[47] 2003 SLT 1340.

[48] Bankruptcy and Diligence etc. (Scotland) Act 2007, Pt 6.

[49] F McCarthy 'Human Rights and the Law of Leases' (2013) 17 *Edin LR* 184 at 200.

[50] See **PARA 21.49** above.

Salvesen v Riddell[51] the Supreme Court ruled that one of these provisions[52] led to a disproportionate interference with the rights of landlords under A1P1. Legislation aimed at correcting the issue came into force in 2014.[53]

(5) Wayleaves

32.18   In *William Tracey Ltd v Scottish Ministers,*[54] the court found that there had been no breach of A1P1 regarding an absence of statutory compensation for encroachment on land by electricity lines in the period prior to the grant of a necessary wayleave. It was held that the statute clearly made provision for compensation only in the situation where a wayleave had been granted.[55] The court considered the aim of the statute to be legitimate and observed that it would necessarily involve some interference with the enjoyment of land over which power lines would be run.

THE ECHR AND PROPERTY RIGHTS: OTHER RELEVANT ARTICLES

32.19   While A1P1 deals specifically with property law, a number of other ECHR articles are relevant. Three are worth mentioning.
   (1) Art 6, on the right to a fair trial in the determination of civil rights and obligations.[56]
   (2) Art 8 ensures respect for family and private life. The access rights regime under the Land Reform (Scotland) Act 2003 was a possible candidate for Art 8 disputes but specific protection for the privacy of householders has helped to avert a challenge thus far.[57] Attempts have been made to use this article as a defence against eviction from residential property, but thus far without success.[58]
   (3) Art 10 provides the right to freedom of expression. In a case in which campaigners for a second independence referendum sought to challenge their eviction from their makeshift camp outside the Scottish Parliament,[59]

---

51   [2013] UKSC 22, 2013 SC (UKSC) 236. See D J Carr 'Not law but not yet effectively not law' (2013) 17 *EdinLR* 370.
52   Agricultural Holdings (Scotland) Act 2003, s 72(10).
53   Agricultural Holdings (Scotland) Act 2003 Remedial Order 2014 (SSI 2014/98). And for the compensation claim in respect of the breach, see *McMaster v Scottish Ministers* [2017] CSOH 46, 2017 SLT 586.
54   [2016] CSOH 131, 2016 SLT 1049.
55   Electricity Act 1989, Sch 4 para 7.
56   There existed uncertainty as to whether the system under the Land Registration (Scotland) Act 1979 was acceptable in this respect, but any problems seem to have been removed by the Land Registration etc. (Scotland) Act 2012.
57   Land Reform (Scotland) Act 2003, s 6(1)(b)(iv). See *Gloag v Perth and Kinross Council* 2007 SCLR 530 at paras 61–65. See **PARA 19.6** above.
58   *South Lanarkshire Council v McKenna* 2013 SLT 22.
59   *Scottish Parliamentary Corporate Body, Petitioner* [2016] CSOH 113, 2016 SLT 862.

Lord Turnbull considered whether their Art 10 rights had been violated. Acknowledging that restrictions can be placed on the exercise of this right, he found the interference with Art 10 rights to be proportionate.[60] His decision was upheld by the Inner House.[61]

(4) Art 11, concerning the right to freedom of assembly and association, was also invoked in the above case, with no violation found for comparable reasons.

(5) Art 14, which ensures that Convention rights are enjoyed without discrimination, is relevant to all Convention rights.[62]

TRUSTS AND SUCCESSION

32.20   Little consideration appears to have been given to the issue of human rights within trusts and succession law. A couple of English cases concerning succession rights under the Housing Act 1980 have made their way to Strasbourg.[63] An unsuccessful challenge was made under A1P1 and Art 14 of the ECHR to the rules on inheritance tax which provide tax exemptions for spouses and civil partners, but not to cohabiting family members.[64] The ECtHR has ruled that national laws may not distinguish for inheritance purposes between legitimate and illegitimate children.[65] Human rights have been a concern in the reform of Scottish trust law, with certain proposals being dismissed due to their potential for challenge under A1P1.[66] As yet, however, there appears to have been no Scottish case law on trusts or succession in which Convention rights have been invoked.

LITERATURE

32.21   For a general account of human rights law from a Scottish perspective, see Reed, Lord and Murdoch, J *Human Rights Law in Scotland* (4th edn, 2017). Specialist accounts in relation to property law include Rennie *Land Tenure* ch 16, Rook, D *Property Law and Human Rights* (2001), Springham, K 'Property Law' in Lord Reed (ed) *A Practical Guide to Human Rights Law in Scotland* (2001) 235–276 and Steven, A J M 'Property Law and Human Rights' 2005 *JR* 293.

---

[60]   *Scottish Parliamentary Corporate Body, Petitioner* [2016] CSOH 113 at para [63], 2016 SLT 862.

[61]   *Scottish Parliamentary Corporate Body v 'The Sovereign Indigenous Peoples of Scotland'* [2016] CSIH 81, 2016 SLT 1307. See M Combe 'The Indycamp: Demonstrating Access to Land and Access to Justice' (2017) 21 *EdinLR* 228.

[62]   For discussion of Art 14 in the context of property law, see D Rook *Property Law and Human Rights* (2001) ch 6.

[63]   See *S v UK* (Application 11716/85) (1986) 47 DR 274 and *Fitzpatrick v Sterling Housing Association Ltd* [1999] 4 All ER 705.

[64]   *Burden v UK* (Application 13378/05), 29 April 2008.

[65]   *Marckx v Belgium* (1979/1980) 2 EHRR 330; *Mazurek v France* (2006) 42 EHRR 9; *Merger v France* (2006) 43 EHRR 51; *Pla v Andorra* (2006) 42 EHRR 25.

[66]   For example, Scottish Law Commission, Report on Variation and Termination of Trusts (Scot Law Com No 206, 2007) paras 5.12–5.15.

Appendix

The feudal system

FULL CIRCLE

A.1   There has been a full circle: from civilian ideas to feudal ideas, and from feudal ideas back to civilian ones. The Roman law distinguished private law from public law. Roman property law recognised no fundamental difference between moveables and immoveables. Where Roman lawyers saw distinction, medieval lawyers saw unity, and where Roman lawyers saw unity, medieval lawyers saw distinction. In the medieval worldview, public law and private law were merged. And immoveables were utterly different from moveables. Not only this, but the law of immoveable property was itself public law. In modern law we distinguish ownership (*dominium*) from sovereignty (*imperium*). So did Roman law. But in the medieval worldview, to have land was to have sovereignty, and to have sovereignty was to have land. This was the feudal vision.

HISTORY OF FEUDALISM: A ONE-MINUTE SUMMARY

A.2   Feudalism, in its earliest forms, originated in the Frankish empire and eventually spread over most of western Europe. (But not Scandinavia. This is why feudal law never fully extended to Orkney and Shetland, which until 1468/9 belonged to Norway.) Land was not owned. It was held by one person 'of' another person. Land law was relationship law. The 'vassal' held land of the 'superior' or 'lord'. They owed each other reciprocal duties. In some ways (not in all ways) it was like a mafia boss and his followers. Each owed the other loyalty, including a duty to fight. In giving land to his vassal, the lord increased his own power. The relationship just described could be more than dyadic. The superior had an over-superior. There could be many links in the chain. At the top was the king, or, in the Holy Roman Empire, the Emperor. But the top was not the top. For king and Emperor were alike vassals of God. Everyone in the upper links of the chain was, to that extent, sovereign. He could and did hold courts in both civil and criminal matters. Indeed, the feudal superior's right to hold courts was not fully abolished until feudalism itself was abolished in 2004. For *dominium* and *imperium* were one, and land meant relationships: those on the land were the lord's subjects.

A.3   The decline of feudalism happened in different ways and at different speeds in different countries. Much had already faded by the end of the eighteenth century, when the hurricane of the French Revolution blew down the remains of feudal law over much of Europe. It survived in several parts of Germany till the 1850s, and in one or two until 1919. In England the decline began the earliest but dragged on the longest. There feudalism went into sharp decline as a result of the statute Quia Emptores (1290), which prohibited subinfeudation. Cromwell abolished most of what remained. A fragment called copyhold survived until 1925. Since then English law has no feudal characteristics left. But the Crown superiority, though now empty of content, has never been abolished there.

A.4   In Scotland too feudalism's decline was prolonged. It was cut back little by little by a series of statutes beginning in the 15th century and continuing until recent times. By the late 20th century little was left, but the concept was by no means vacuous, as it was in England. The final abolition of feudalism on 28 November 2004, by the Abolition of Feudal Tenure etc. (Scotland) Act 2000, was thus by no means a mere gesture. It genuinely changed the law.[1]

---

[1]   For instance, no fewer than 46 entire statutes were repealed.

THE FEUDAL CHAIN

A.5   The feudal system was, at least in its latter days, like a system of leases, sub-leases and sub-subleases. At the top was the Crown. Below the Crown were the Crown vassals, those holding directly of the Crown. Typically, these were peers. Then there were those at the next stage down, and so on. As one went down the chain, the units tended to become smaller. Thus the Earl of Cumbernauld might hold 10,000 hectares of the Crown. Under him might be three sub-vassals each holding 2,000 hectares. (The remaining 4,000 hectares here being held by the Earl without any sub-vassal.) These sub-vassals might have sub-sub-vassals for all or parts of their land, and so on. One might easily have a chain of half a dozen or even more. Figure A.1 gives the idea of the holding for a single plot of land of, say, a hectare.

Crown

Alan
(Crown vassal)

Beth

Ciaran

Ciaran is the Crown's sub-sub-vassal. But he is also Alan's sub-vassal and Beth's vassal. It is rather like child, grandchild, great-grandchild. Conversely, Beth is Ciaran's superior. Alan is Beth's superior, and is also Ciaran's over-superior. Ciaran's over-over-superior is the Crown. Each superior may have more than one vassal, rather as any parent may have more than one child. Thus while Ciaran holds one hectare of Beth, Donald might hold a neighbouring plot from her as well. In that case they are co-vassals.

THE TYPES OF TENURE

General

A.6   In a lease periodical payments are due to the landlord. Likewise the vassal had obligations to the superior: the 'reddendo'. It varied according to the type of 'tenure'. The following kinds existed.

(1) Wardholding

A.7   Wardholding was the pure ancient feudal tenure, because what the vassal had to give was, literally, military service. Since it was thought that women should not fight, a woman could not hold land on this tenure. It was abolished (and converted into feufarm) by the legislation passed following the 1745 Jacobite Rebellion.

(2) Mortification

A.8   In the tenure of mortification, the vassal was the church and the service due was prayer, and especially prayer for the superior's soul. It disappeared as a result of the Reformation. (But the word lived on, with the meaning of 'charitable trust or foundation'.)

(3) Burgage tenure

A.9   Burgage tenure was the tenure in burghs. It was feudal in name only. The land was held of the Crown, and only two links in the chain were possible: the Crown and the vassal. It was eventually merged into feufarm.

(4) Blench

A.10   In blench tenure, the reddendo was nominal, typically 'one penny Scots but only if asked for'.

(5) Feufarm

A.11   By the time that feudalism was finally abolished, feufarm was the main tenure. Originally the reddendo could be money or goods, typically agricultural produce. This was the 'feuduty', for 'reddendo' was a general word and the reddendo for each tenure had its own terminology. Over time non-money feuduty was 'commuted' into money. Feuduty was payable twice a year, at the term-days of Whitsunday and Martinmas. Each reddendo was separate. Thus the reddendo due by Ciaran to Beth was independent of the reddendo due by Beth to Alan. Feuduty was sometimes regarded as an imposition by evil superiors. In reality it was a way that people could buy land even if they could not afford the full price. Nowadays such a buyer will typically borrow the amount needed from a financial institution. In the past such loans were harder to come by. Instead, the buyer and seller would agree that only part of the value of the property would be paid, and the balance would be represented by feuduty. For example, land worth £1,000 might be sold for £700 plus £15 per annum feuduty. The sale would be done by way of feu, making the seller the buyer's superior. The seller could then turn the feuduty into a lump sum by selling the superiority to someone else for a price of around £300.

DOMINIUM DIRECTUM, DOMINIUM UTILE, DOMINIUM EMINENS

A.12   Once upon a time, the words 'ownership' and 'feudal' could hardly occur in the same sentence. The system of real rights, revolving round the real right of ownership, applied to moveable property, but not to land. In the second half of the eleventh century, the study of Roman law began to revive, first of all in Italy. Lawyers were unhappy that feudal tenure did not fit in with civilian law. So they began to civilianise it. (Since feudalism did not arrive in Scotland until rather late, namely the twelfth century, this process was in fact already just beginning by the time that feudalism arrived here.) These new thinkers decided that there had to be ownership of land as well as of moveables, and they decided that ownership was shared between the various people in the feudal chain. The Latin word for ownership is *dominium*.[2] The new lawyers decided to call the ownership at the foot of the feudal chain (Ciaran) *dominium utile*. Each superiority was called, without distinction, a *dominium directum*.[3] Thus the Crown, Alan and Beth all have a *dominium directum* – but not the same *dominium directum*. The highest one was also called the *dominium eminens*.

A.13   This idea of shared ownership did not work well at the conceptual level: it was simply not possible for feudalism and civilian property law to be happy bedfellows. Some theorists argued that the system should be made coherent (i.e. coherent in civilian terms) by saying that only the person at the top had ownership, while everyone else had some sort of subordinate real right. But this view did not make much progress anywhere and was not accepted in Scotland. From a purely practical point of view, it would have been nearer the truth to say that the person at

---

[2]   There is also another Latin word with the same meaning: *proprietas*.
[3]   Literally, these expressions mean 'useful ownership' and 'direct ownership' but that does not help much. Actually, the *utile/directum* distinction had its origins in procedural law, not in substantive property law.

the foot of the chain – Ciaran – had ownership and that all the superiorities were mere subordinate real rights of some sort. Certainly, as time went on, superiorities dwindled into rights of only slight significance, and in practice the person at the foot of the chain was simply called 'the owner'. But in theory shared ownership remained.

A.14   As feudalism declined and fell, no alternative system had to be created, because the bedrock of civilian property law already existed, Feudalism was a surface layer, that grew thinner over time and vanished altogether in 2004.

CASUALTIES AND IRRITANCIES

A.15   A casualty was a payment due to the superior on either the death of the vassal or on a transfer by the vassal. The abolition of casualties was begun by the Conveyancing (Scotland) Act 1874 and completed by the Feudal Casualties (Scotland) Act 1914. An irritancy was the forfeiture of a feu because of breach of the feudal terms, such as failure to pay feuduty. The idea is similar to the irritancy of a lease. Irritancy cut the chain. Suppose that Alan irritated because of Beth's breach. That would not only terminate Beth's right but Ciaran's too. Since the *dominium utile* is definitionally the foot of the chain, Alan would now have held the *dominium utile*. No compensation was due, so irritancy could mean a windfall gain.

A ME AND *DE ME*

A.16   Suppose that Ciaran wanted to transfer his right to Fiona. He could do this in either of two ways.

(1) In the first place he could simply have disponed it to her. The result would be that Fiona would then be substituted for Ciaran as Beth's vassal. Ciaran would disappear from the feudal chain.

(2) The alternative was that he could feu the land to her. He would remain Beth's vassal, and he would now be Fiona's superior. Fiona would be Beth's sub-vassal. This was called subinfeudation.

In the first case the deed used was the disposition. In the second case it was a feu disposition.[4] In a disposition the magic words were, then as now, 'do hereby dispone'. In the case of a feu disposition (etc.) the magic words were 'do hereby dispone in feufarm fee and heritage forever'.[5] Feu dispositions were much less common than dispositions. They were used only for special reasons. In particular, if the parties had agreed that real burdens were to be imposed, in general a feu disposition was used. More terminology: a feu disposition was a conveyance *de me*, meaning 'of me'

---

[4]   Or feu charter, or feu contract: the three terms were, in substance, interchangeable.

[5]   It is being assumed that the tenure was feufarm. For other tenures, details would differ.

because Fiona would hold 'of' Ciaran, he would be her superior. A disposition, by contrast, was a conveyance *a me*, meaning 'from me' or 'away from me'. That meant that Ciaran was divesting himself wholly.

A.17   Just as Ciaran could dispone, or grant a security, so could Beth or Alan. Thus if Beth disponed her superiority to Peter, Peter would be Alan's vassal, and also the superior of Ciaran. This conveyance would necessarily be an *a me* conveyance, for only the person at the foot of the chain had the option of conveying either *a me* or *de me*.

At common law a conveyance *a me* required the superior's consent. Before 1500, means had been developed whereby the superior could be, so to speak, compelled to consent. But a deed from the superior remained necessary until 1874.

REAL BURDENS

A.18   Real burdens were perhaps the main reason why feudalism lasted so long. Although real burdens could be created non-feudally, over one property in favour of a neighbouring property, as in modern law, that fact was not well known and in any case there were technical drawbacks in doing it that way. If one wished to create a real burden the normal method was to feu. After the creation of feuduties was prohibited in 1974 (see below), the creation of real burdens was really the only reason for a seller to feu rather than to dispone. Moreover, the vast mass of existing feudal real burdens presented a hurdle for the final abolition of feudalism: if all superiorities were to be abolished, what would happen to all the existing feudal burdens? For the way in which the formidable technical problems were eventually overcome, see **CHAPTER 14**.

'THE FEUDAL SYSTEM OF LAND TENURE ... IS... ABOLISHED'

A.19   By the 1960s, feudalism was a mere shadow. A consensus emerged that what remained should be done away with. One obstacle was feuduty. In 1974 a statute was passed prohibiting the creation of new feuduties and providing a mechanism for the gradual redemption of existing ones.[6] But redemption did not extinguish the superiority. Moreover, land could still be feued, albeit without feuduty, and this continued to happen. It was not until 30 years later that the final step was taken. 'The feudal system of land tenure, that is to say the entire system whereby land is held by a vassal on perpetual tenure from a superior is, on the appointed day, abolished.'[7] The appointed day was 28 November 2004. All superiorities, including the ultimate superiority of the Crown, were extinguished, and so every *dominium*

---

[6]   Land Tenure Reform (Scotland) Act 1974.
[7]   AFT(S)A 2000, s 1.

utile became simple ownership. Ownership of land is now like the ownership of moveables: ownership in the Roman sense.

POSTSCRIPT (1): ULTRA-LONG LEASES

A.20 Ultra-long leases, such as 1000-year leases, are formally not feudal, but functionally they are. The owner is a quasi-superior, the tenant a quasi-vassal, the rent a quasi-feuduty and so on. Even before AFT(S)A 2000, work had begun towards their abolition. For practical reasons, the issue was left out of that Act, but eventually the Long Leases (Scotland) Act 2012 was passed. Its structure is similar to that of AFT(S)A 2000, with ultra-long leases being converted into ownership.[8]

POSTSCRIPT (2): 'FEUDALISM' IS A POLYSEMIC TERM

A.21 In this **APPENDIX** 'feudalism' is taken in its legal sense. The student should be aware that the term is often used in related, but different, senses, in particular (i) sociological, to describe a state of society, and (ii) condemnatory, to describe a state of affairs that the speaker regards as involving unacceptable economic dominance.

LITERATURE

A. 22 For an account of feudal tenure and feudal conveyancing see Reid *Property* paras 41–113 (Gretton). For the final abolition see Reid *Feudal Abolition* ch 1. Taking the broader perspective, there Is the classic work by FL Ganshof *Qu'est-ce que la féodalité?* (1944), published in English translation as *Feudalism*. A work that challenges standard concepts of feudalism is Reynolds S *Fiefs and Vassals* (1994).

---

[8]   See **PARA 20.7** above.

Index

[all references are to paragraph number]

A me
feudal system, and, A.16–A.17
Abandoned property
ownership, and, 3.8–3.10
Abandonment
servitudes, and, 13.46
Abatement
testate succession, and, 28.32–28.37
Access
repairs, and
generally, 18.28
introduction, 18.27
servitudes, and, 13.10
tenements, and, 16.27
Accession
compensation, 9.18
conversion, 9.6
effects, 9.6–9.7
elements, 9.5
extinguishment, 9.6
fixtures and fittings, 9.8
fruits, 9.16
functional subordination, 9.9
general, 9.4
generally, 3.11
land to land, 9.15
moveables to land, 9.8–9.12
moveables to moveables, 9.13–9.14
permanency, 9.10–9.12
physical union, 9.8
severance, 9.7
Accounts
trustees, and, 24.25

Accretion
generally, 4.52
testate succession, and, 28.45
Acquaehaustus
servitudes, and, 13.12
Acqueduct
servitudes, and, 13.12
Acquiescence
neighbour law, and
encroachment, 18.11–18.13
nuisance, 18.24
real burdens, and, 14.68–14.69
servitudes, and
creation, 13.29
extinction, 13.44
Acquisition
derivative acquisition, 3.11
involuntary transfer
compulsory purchase, 8.4–8.10
death, 8.17–8.18
diligence, 8.12–8.14
forfeiture, 8.19
generally, 3.12
insolvency, 8.15–8.16
introduction, 8.1–8.3
sale by secured creditor, 8.11
special statutory rules, 8.20
original acquisition
accession, 9.4–9.18
bills of exchange, 9.23
commixtion, 9.19
confusion, 9.19
generally, 3.11